Heath
WORLD GEOGRAPHY

by Charles F. Gritzner

TEXAS
TEACHER'S ANNOTATED EDITION
Correlated to the Texas Essential
Elements

Teaching Guide by Linda Scher
Curriculum Developer, Raleigh, North Carolina

 D.C. HEATH AND COMPANY
Lexington, Massachusetts / Toronto, Ontario

Published simultaneously in Canada

Printed in the United States of America

International Standard Book Code Number 0-669-17288-X

2   3   4   5   6   7   8   9   0

HEATH WORLD GEOGRAPHY

Everything you need in Texas and more . . .

Pupil Text

HEATH WORLD GEOGRAPHY addresses the five major themes in geography: relative and absolute location, physical and cultural characteristics of place, relationships within places, human interaction, and regions. These five themes are also the focus of the guidelines for geographic education outlined by the National Council for Geographic Education and the Association of American Geographers. In addition, those themes are reflected in the Texas Essential Elements for World Geography.

HEATH WORLD GEOGRAPHY introduces students to the study of geography as a discipline. Students explore not only the physical and human characteristics of environments but also the ways people have modified those environments. They study the great variety of ways people interact with one another as they travel, communicate, and trade both products and ideas. Students consider too how regions form and change as they compare and contrast the major regions of the world.

The text is organized to facilitate learning. Key geographic concepts are introduced in Chapters 1–6. Those concepts are then consistently maintained, reinforced, and extended in Chapters 7–18. The skill development strand, built right into the program, supports the Essential Elements and provides your students with ample opportunities to develop and apply geographic skills.

Teacher's Annotated Edition

The **Teacher's Annotated Edition** provides solid support for building a course in geography around the Essential Elements. On-page annotations correlate each lesson to the Essential Elements. Correlation charts give you added confidence that each Element is not only covered in the pupil text but also reinforced and extended in the various components found in the Teacher's Resource Binder.

D.C. Heath shows you how you can perform at your best in the classroom. The Teaching Guide bound into the front of the Teacher's Annotated Edition provides help in planning, evaluating student progress, reteaching, and extending each lesson—just what you need to fit the Texas Teacher Appraisal System (TTAS) instrument.

Teacher's Resource Binder

Additional support materials are found as copymasters in a three-ring binder for your convenience. These materials include

- Independent Practice Worksheets for every lesson, every Skill Workshop, and every Map Workshop.
- Building Basics Worksheets that provide reteaching activities for every lesson.
- Tests for every chapter.
- The Teaching Guide that accompanies the Computer Test Bank contains extra questions that can be used to create quizzes, alternate chapter tests, midterm exams, or finals.
- Outline Maps of the world and major regions of the world.
- Map Tests
- The Geography Laboratory Manual with enrichment activities that extend and enrich key chapter concepts and build critical thinking skills.

Computer Test Bank

The Computer Test Bank is designed to help you in evaluating student mastery of the Essential Elements. With the Test Bank, you have the flexibility of testing the Essential Elements by lesson as well as constructing chapter, unit, midterm, and final exams.

Extra Support for Teaching World Geography

Maps are an essential part of a course in geography. HEATH WORLD GEOGRAPHY provides you and your students with ancillaries that reinforce and maintain important map skills. Those ancillaries also build critical thinking skills.

Heath Student Atlas

The Atlas contains 121 pages of physical, climate, population density, and land use maps, a complete Map and Globe Skills review section, Data Banks for all major cultural regions, a special United States information section, a gazetteer, and a glossary of geographic terms.

Heath Atlas Transparencies

The 64 full-color overhead transparencies provide reinforcement and extension of important concepts and skills. The teaching suggestions and accompanying worksheets will help your students master key Essential Elements. The activities are carefully correlated to the **Heath Student Atlas.**

MAPS

MAPS, the **Map Ancillary Program Support,** contains in transmaster form 26 Outline Maps and 27 Map Tests. Transmasters are overhead transparencies that can also be used as duplicating masters. Each map test comes with an answer overlay.
With HEATH WORLD GEOGRPAHY, you will be sure you are teaching your students all they need to know about each Essential Element.

Correlation of Social Studies
Essential Elements to *Heath World Geography*

In the charts that follow, you can see how closely HEATH WORLD GEOGRAPHY matches the Texas Essential Elements. The first chart shows where in the pupil text and in the Teacher's Resource Binder each element is covered as shown by lesson number, feature, or worksheet number. In addition, on pages ixT-xvT, you will find a second correlation showing how each lesson in the student text and each worksheet in the Teacher's Resource Binder matches the Texas Essential Elements. On-page annotations in the Teacher's Annotated Edition also key each lesson to one or more Essential Elements.

Key	MG	Map and Globe Review (Pupil's Text)
	SW	Skills Workshop (Pupil's Text)
	MW	Map Workshop (Pupil's Text)
	BB	Building Basics Worksheet (Reteaching)
	WB	Workbook (Independent Practice Worksheet)
	Inv	Investigation provided in the Geography Laboratory Manual (Enrichment)

1. Nature of geography. The textbooks for World Geography Studies shall include content on:

A. specialized fields of geography (e.g., physical, cultural, political, economic, historical);

Pupil Text   1.1, 1.3, 5.1, 5.2, 5.3, 6.1, 6.2, 11.1

B. geographic terminology; and

Pupil Text   MG1, MG2, MG3, MG4, MG5, MG6, MG7, MG8, MG9, 1.1, SW1, 1.2, 1.3, 2.1, 2.2, 2.3, 2.4, 3.1, 3.2, 3.3, 4.1, 4.2, 4.3, 4.4, 5.1, 6.1, 6.3, 7.1, 8.1, 15.1, 16.1, 17.1, 18.1
Teacher's Resource Binder   **BB** 1.1, 1.2, 1.3, 2.1, 2.3, 3.2, 3.3, 4.1, 4.2, 4.3, 4.4, 5.1, 5.3, 6.1, 6.3, 7.1, 15.1, 16.1   **WB** 1, 2, 3, 4, 5, 6, 7, 8, 9, 10, 11, 15, 17, 18, 19, 20, 21, 24, 25, 26, 30, 31, 32, 33, 34, 35, 38, 47   **Inv.** 2

C. geographical tools and methodologies.

Pupil Text   MG1, MG2, MG3, MG4, MG5, MG6, MG7, MG8, MG9, SW1, 1.2, MW1, 1.3, 2.1, MW2, SW2, 2.3, 2.4, 3.1, MW3, SW3, 4.2, MW4, SW4, MW5, 6.1, SW6, 7.1, MW7, 8.1, MW8, SW8, 9.1, MW9, SW9, 10.1, SW10, MW10, 11.1, MW11, SW11, 12.1, MW12, SW12, 13.1, MW13, SW13, 14.1, SW14, MW14, 15.1, MW15, SW15, 16.1, MW16, 17.1, MW17, SW 17, 18.1, MW18, SW18
Teacher's Resource Binder   **BB** 17.1   **WB** 1, 2, 3, 4, 5, 6, 7, 8, 9, 14, 16, 19, 20, 21, 22, 23, 28, 29, 30, 36, 37, 44, 45, 51, 60, 66, 67, 74, 75, 79, 83, 85, 86, 90, 91, 92, 97, 98, 103, 104, 105, 106, 110, 111, 112, 113, 115, 116, 117, 118, 119, 124, 125, 127, 129, 130, 131, 132, 133, 137, 138, 139   **Inv.** 1, 2, 3, 4, 5, 6, 7, 8, 9, 10, 11, 12, 13, 14, 15, 16, 17, 18

2. Physical setting of the earth. The textbooks for World Geography Studies shall include content on:

A. Earth-sun relationship;

Pupil Text   2.1, MW13
Teacher's Resource Binder   **BB** 2.1, 2.2, 2.3, 2.4, 3.1, 3.3   **WB** 17, 19, 20, 21, 103, 124   **Inv.** 2, 3, 5, 18

B. major landforms, regions, and features of the earth; and

Pupil Text MG4, 1.1, SW1, 1.2, 1.3, 2.2, 2.3, 3.2, 3.3, 7.1, SW7, 8.1, 8.3, 9.1, 10.1, 11.1, 12.1, 13.1, 14.1, 15.1, 16.1, 17.1
Teacher's Resource Binder   **BB** 1.1, 1.2, 1.3, 2.2, 2.3, 3.2, 3.3, 7.1, 8.3, 9.1, 10.1, 11.1, 12.1, 13.1, 14.1, 15.1, 16.1, 17.1, 18.1   **WB** 11, 13, 14, 15, 19, 20, 25, 26, 30, 61, 65, 77   **Inv.** 1, 3

C. physical and human forces that alter the earth's features.

Pupil Text   1.2, 1.3, 2.2, 2.3, 3.4, 4.5, 5.2, 8.1, 9.1, 10.1, 11.1
Teacher's Resource Binder   **BB** 1.2, 1.3, 2.2, 2.3, 3.4, 5.2, 9.1, 10.1, 11.1   **WB** 12, 13, 16, 18, 19, 20, 32, 33, 35, 69, 76, 77

3. Interaction of physical and cultural environments. The textbooks for World Geography Studies shall include content on:

A. interrelationships of people and their environments;

Pupil Text   3.1, 3.2, 3.3, 3.4, 4.1, 4.2, 4.5, 5.1, 5.2, 5.3, 6.3, 7.3, 7.4, 7.6, 9.3, 10.2, 10.5, 10.6, 14.2, 15.2, 16.2, 16.3, 16.4, 17.4, 18.3
Teacher's Resource Binder   **BB** 3.2, 3.3, 3.4, 4.1, 4.2, 4.5, 5.1, 5.2, 5.3, 6.3, 7.3, 7.4, 7.6, 9.3, 10.2, 10.5, 10.6, 14.2, 15.2, 16.2, 16.3, 16.4, 17.4, 18.3   **WB** 24, 25, 26, 27, 28, 29, 31, 32, 39, 40, 41, 49, 56, 57, 59, 71, 78, 92, 93, 136   **Inv.** 3, 15

B. economic importance of water, energy sources, and other productive resources to regions;

Pupil Text   3.4, 4.4, 4.5, 5.4, 5.5, 6.3, 6.4, 7.2, 7.3, 7.4, 7.5, 7.6, 8.1, 8.2, 8.3, 9.2, 9.3, 9.4, 9.5, 10.3, 10.4, 11.2, 11.3, 11.4, 12.3, 13.2, 13.3, 14.4, 15.3, 15.4, 16.2, 16.3, 16.4, 17.2, 17.3, 18.2, 18.3, 18.4
Teacher's Resource Binder   **BB** 3.4, 4.4, 4.5, 5.4, 5.5, 6.3, 6.4, 7.2, 7.4, 7.5, 7.6, 8.1, 8.2, 8.3, 9.2, 9.4, 9.5, 10.3, 10.4, 11.2,11.3, 11.4, 12.3, 13.3, 14.4, 15.3, 15.4, 16.2, 16.3, 16.4, 17.2, 17.3, 18.2, 18.3, 18.4,   **WB** 27, 35, 36, 43, 49, 50, 58, 59, 65, 70, 71, 72, 73, 79, 101, 136   **Inv.** 4

C. agricultural base of regions; and

Pupil Text   3.3, 5.3, 7.4, 7.6, 9.2, 9.3, 9.4, 9.5, 10.2, 10.5, 10.6, 11.2, 11.3, 11.4, 11.5, 12.3, 13.2, 13.3, 14.2, 14.3, 14.4, 15.3, 15.4, 16.2, 16.3, 16.4, 17.2, 17.3, 17.4, 18.2, 18.3, 18.4
Teacher's Resource Binder   **BB** 3.3, 5.3, 7.3, 7.6, 9.2, 9.3, 9.4, 9.5, 10.2, 10.5, 10.6, 11.2, 11.3, 11.4, 11.5, 12.3, 13.3, 14.2, 14.3, 14.4, 15.3, 15.4, 16.2, 16.3, 16.4, 17.2, 17.3, 17.4, 18.2, 18.3, 18.4   **WB** 70, 72, 73, 78, 101, 121   **Inv.** 4

D. uses, abuses, and preservation of natural resources and the physical environment.

Pupil Text   3.2, 3.4, 4.1, 4.2, 4.3, 4.5, SW4, 5.2, 5.3, 5.4, 5.5, 6.2, 6.3, 7.2, 7.3, 7.4, 7.6, 8.2, 9.3, 9.5, 10.2, 10.3, 10.4, 10.6, 11.2, 11.3, 11.4, 11.5, 12.3, 13.2, 13.3, 14.2, 14.3, 15.2, 15.3, 16.4, 17.3, 17.4, 18.2, 18.3, 18.4
Teacher's Resource Binder   **BB** 3.2, 3.4, 4.1, 4.2, 4.3, 4.4, 4.5, 5.2, 5.4, 5.5, 6.2, 7.2, 7.3, 7.4, 7.6, 8.2, 9.3, 9.5, 10.3, 10.4, 10.6, 11.2, 11.3, 11.4, 11.5, 12.3, 13.3, 14.2, 14.3, 15.2, 15.3, 17.3, 17.4, 18.2, 18.3, 18.4   **WB** 31, 32, 33, 34, 35, 37, 38, 40, 43, 56, 57, 71, 79, 101   **Inv.** 4

4. World Regions. The textbooks for World Geography Studies shall include content on:

A. criteria for determining regions;

Pupil Text   2.4, 3.2, 3.3, 5.1, MW5, 7.1
Teacher's Resource Binder   **BB** 2.4, 3.1, 3.2, 5.1, 10.5, 13.1, 16.1, 16.3, 18.1   **WB** 26, 27, 39, 44, 59, 61, 62, 63, 64, 73, 77, 78, 81, 82, 88, 90, 93, 94, 102, 104, 109, 116, 120, 137   **Inv.** 2, 8, 9, 10, 11, 12

B. physical setting of world regions;

Pupil Text 2.4, MW3, 3.2, 3.3, 6.1, 7.1, 8.1, 9.1, 10.1, 12.1, 13.1, 14.1, 15.1, 16.1, 17.1, 18.1
Teacher's Resource Binder **BB** 2.4, 3.1, 3.2, 6.1, 7.1, 8.1, 9.1, 10.1, 11.1, 12.1, 13.1, 14.1, 15.1, 16.1, 17.1, 18.1 **WB** 24, 25, 26, 28, 47, 54, 59, 61, 62, 63, 68, 69, 77, 82, 86, 87, 88, 90, 94, 99, 100, 106, 113, 115, 116, 120, 123, 127, 134, 140 **Inv.** 8, 10, 11, 13, 15, 17

C. population distribution, growth, and movements;

Pupil Text 5.4, 6.1, 7.2, 7.3, 7.4, MW7, 7.5, 7.6, 8.2, 8.3, 9.2, 9.4, 10.2, 10.3, 10.5, 10.6, 11.2, 11.3, 11.5, 12.2, 13.2, 13.3, 14.2, MW14, 14.3, 14.4, 15.1, 15.2, SW15, 15.3, 15.4, 17.2, 17.3, 18.4
Teacher's Resource Binder **BB** 5.4, 6.1, 7.2, 7.3, 7.4, 7.5, 7.6, 8.2, 8.3, 9.2, 9.4, 10.2, 10.3, 10.5, 10.6, 11.2, 11.3, 11.5, 12.2, 13.2, 13.3, 14.2, 14.3, 14.4, 15.1, 15.2, 15.3, 15.4, 17.2, 17.3, 18.4 **WB** 42, 47, 51, 55, 56, 57, 58, 60, 61, 62, 64, 65, 70, 72, 78, 79, 82, 87, 88, 95, 99, 101, 102, 108, 109, 110, 114, 115, 118, 122, 126, 128, 129, 130, 131, 137, 140 **Inv.** 6, 7, 10

D. major cultural, political, and economic activities within and among major world regions;

Pupil Text 5.3, 5.4, SW6, 6.2, 6.3, 6.4, 7.2, 8.2, 8.3, 9.2, 9.3, 9.4, 9.5, 10.2, 10.3, 10.4, 10.5, 10.6, 11.2, MW11, 11.3, 11.4, 11.5, 12.2, MW12, 12.3, 13.2, 13.3, 14.2, 14.3, 14.4, 15.2, 15.3, 15.4, 16.2, MW16, 16.3, 16.4, SW16, 17.2, 17.3, 17.4, SW17, 18.2, 18.3, 18.4
Teacher's Resource Binder **BB** 5.3, 5.4, 6.2, 6.3, 6.4, 7.2, 7.5, 8.2, 8.3, 9.2, 9.3, 9.4, 9.5, 10.2, 10.3, 10.4, 10.5, 10.6, 11.2, 11.3, 11.4, 11.5, 12.2, 12.3, 13.2, 13.3, 14.2, 14.3, 14.4, 15.2, 15.3, 15.4, 16.2, 16.3, 16.4, 17.2, 17.3, 17.4, 18.2, 18.3, 18.4 **WB** 41, 42, 45, 46, 48, 49, 50, 52, 53, 55, 62, 64, 65, 70, 71, 72, 73, 78, 79, 80, 81, 82, 83, 87, 88, 89, 90, 91, 95, 96, 97, 98, 101, 102, 107, 108, 110, 114, 116, 121, 122, 123, 124, 125, 126, 128, 129, 130, 132, 135, 137, 140 **Inv.** 6, 7, 8, 9, 10, 11, 12, 13, 14, 16, 17

E. settlement patterns in terms of rural/urban location, structure, and function; and

Pupil Text 5.3, 5.5, 6.1, 7.3, 9.2, 10.4, 10.5, 11.5, 14.3, 15.4, 16.2, 16.3, 17.2, 17.4, 18.2

Teacher's Resource Binder **BB** 5.3, 5.5, 6.1, 7.3, 7.4, 9.2, 10.4, 11.4, 11.5, 14.3, 15.4, 16.2, 17.2, 17.4, 18.2 **WB** 29, 41, 43, 47, 56, 70, 80, 81, 89, 96, 112, 117, 122, 128, 135, 140 **Inv.** 7, 10

F. geographic influences on various issues (e.g., environmental, political, cultural, economic).

Pupil's Edition 5.1, 5.4, 5.5, 6.2, 7.1, 8.2, 8.3, 9.2, 9.4, 9.5, 10.5, 10.6, 11.4, 12.3, 13.1, 14.2, 14.4, 15.2, 16.1, SW16
Teacher's Resource Binder **BB** 5.1, 5.4, 5.5, 6.2, 8.3, 9.4, 9.5, 10.6, 12.3, 14.2, 14.4, 15.2 **WB** 39, 42, 43, 46, 48, 53, 64, 65, 72, 81, 82, 89, 91, 98, 109, 111, 120, 121, 125 **Inv.** 5, 16, 18

Content, where appropriate, shall be included to provide a basis for:

1. developing attitudes and values appropriate to democratic beliefs

   Pupil Text 6.2, 7.2, 8.2, 9.2, 10.2, 11.2, 12.2, 13.2, 14.2, 15.2, 16.2, 17.2
   Teacher's Resource Binder **WB** 48, 55, 64, 95

2. supporting the United States free enterprise system

   Pupil Text 5.5, 6.3, 7.2, 13.2
   Teacher's Resource Binder **WB** 43, 84, 104

3. developing and applying social studies skills including those related to critical thinking, decision making, and problem solving

   Pupil Text See Skill Workshop, Chapters 1–18; Geography Laboratory, Chapters 1–18
   Teacher's Resource Binder The Building Basics Worksheets build vocabulary and reading comprehension skills. The Workbook promotes a variety of other important social studies skills, including those related to critical thinking, decision making, and problem solving. Note in particular WB pages 16, 27, 40, 41, 42, 43, 52, 61, 67, 75, 84, 92, 93, 98, 104, 105, 118, 124, 125, 128, 139. The Geography Laboratory Manual develops critical thinking skills as well as those related to problem solving and decision making.

Lesson-by-Lesson Correlation to the Essential Elements

Pupil Text	Texas Essential Elements	Teacher's Resource Binder	Texas Essential Elements
Reviewing Map and Globe Skills			
1. Using Globes	1B, 1C	WB, 1	1B, 1C
2. Understanding Map Projections	1B, 1C	WB, 2	1B, 1C
3. Interpreting Map Symbols and Legends	1B, 1C	WB, 3	1B, 1C
4. Reading a Physical Map	1B, 1C, 2B	WB, 4	1B, 1C
5. Telling Directions	1B, 1C	WB, 5	1B, 1C
6. Using Scale	1B, 1C	WB, 6	1B, 1C
7. Using a Grid	1B, 1C	WB, 7	1B, 1C
8. Using Latitude and Longitude	1B, 1C	WB, 8	1B, 1C
9. Following Circle Routes	1B, 1C, 2A	WB, 9 WB, 10	1B, 1C 1B
Chapter 1 The Face of Earth		Inv. 1	1C, 2B
1.1 Land and Water	1A, 1B, 2B	BB 1.1 WB, 11	1B, 2B 1B, 2B
Skill Workshop: Interpreting a Diagram of Landforms and Bodies of Water	1B, 1C, 2B	WB, 15	1B, 2B
1.2 The changing Earth: Forces from Within	1B, 1C, 2B, 2C	BB 1.2 WB, 12	1B, 2B, 2C 2C
Map Workshop: Reading a Contour Map	1C	WB, 14	1C, 2B
1.3 The Changing Earth: Forces from Without	1A, 1B, 1C, 2B, 2C	BB 1.3 WB, 13 WB, 16	1B, 2B, 2C 2B, 2C 1C, 2C
Chapter 2 A World of Climates		Inv. 2	1B, 1C, 2A, 4A, 4B
2.1 The Sun and Climate	1B, 1C, 2A	BB 2.1 WB, 17	1B, 2A 1B, 2A
Map Workshop: Reading a Weather Map	1C	WB, 21	1B, 1C, 2A
2.2 Water and Climate	1B, 2B, 2C	BB 2.2 WB, 18	2A, 2B, 2C 1B, 2C
Skill Workshop: Interpreting a Diagram	1C	WB, 23	1C

Pupil Text	Texas Essential Elements	Teacher's Resource Binder	Texas Essential Elements
2.3 Other Factors Affecting Climate	1B, 1C, 2B, 2C	BB 2.3 WB, 19	1B, 2A, 2B, 2C 1B, 1C, 2A, 2B, 2C
Skill Workshop: Reading a Climate Graph	1C	WB, 22	1C
2.4 Climates of the World	1B, 1C, 2A, 4A, 4B	BB 2.4 WB, 20	2A, 4A, 4B 1B, 1C, 2A, 2B, 2C

Chapter 3 Ecosystems: A Living Network

		Inv. 3	1C, 2A, 2B, 3A
3.1 One Environment: A Network of Ecosystems	1B, 1C, 3A	BB 3.1 WB, 24	1B, 2A, 4A, 4B 1B, 3A, 4B
Map Workshop: Reading an Annual Rainfall Map	1C, 4B	WB, 28	1C, 3A, 4B
3.2 Forest and Grassland Environments	1B, 2B, 3A, 3D, 4A, 4B	BB 3.2 WB, 25	1B, 2B, 3A, 3D, 4A, 4B 1B, 2B, 3A, 4B
Skill Workshop: Interpreting Landsat Images	1C	WB, 29	1C, 3A, 4E
3.3 Polar, Desert, Mountain, and Oceanic Environments	1B, 2B, 3A, 3C, 4A, 4B	BB 3.3 WB, 26	1B, 2A, 2B, 3A, 3C 1B, 2B, 3A, 4A, 4B
3.4 Changes in Ecosystems	2C, 3A, 3B, 3D	BB 3.4 WB, 27 WB, 30	2C, 3A, 3B, 3D 3A, 3B, 3D 1B, 1C, 2B

Chapter 4 Earth's Resources

		Inv. 4	1C, 3B, 3C, 3D
4.1 Resources: An Overview	1B, 3A, 3D	BB 4.1 WB, 31	1B, 3A, 3D 1B, 3A, 3D
4.2 Water and Soil Resources	1B, 1C, 3A, 3D	BB 4.2 WB, 32	1B, 3A, 3D 1B, 2C, 3A, 3D
4.3 Biotic Resources	1B, 3D	BB 4.3 WB, 33	1B, 3D 1B, 2C, 3D
4.4 Mineral Resources	1B, 3B, 3D	BB 4.4 WB, 34	1B, 3B, 3D 1B, 3D
4.5 Managing Resources	2C, 3A, 3B, 3D	BB 4.5 WB, 35 WB, 38	3A, 3B, 3D 1B, 2C, 3B, 3D 1B, 3D
Map Workshop: Comparing Information on Fuel Deposit Maps	1C	WB, 36	1C, 3B
Skill Workshop: Reading Energy Graphs	1C, 3D	WB, 37	1C, 3D

Chapter 5 Human Imprints of the Past

		Inv. 5	1C, 2A, 4F
5.1 Culture: The Human Difference	1A, 1B, 3A, 4A, 4F	BB 5.1 WB, 39	1B, 3A, 4A, 4F 3A, 4A, 4F
5.2 Early Technologies and Cultural Patterns	1A, 2C, 3A, 3D	BB 5.2 WB, 40	2C, 3A, 3D 3A, 3D

Pupil Text	Texas Essential Elements	Teacher's Resource Binder	Texas Essential Elements
5.3 Fields and Cities	1A, 3A, 3C, 3D, 4D, 4E	BB 5.3 WB, 41	1B, 3A, 3C, 4D, 4E 3A, 4D, 4E
Skill Workshop: Reading a Time Line	1C	WB, 45	1C, 4D
5.4 An Age of Trade and Expansion	3B, 3D, 4C, 4D, 4F	BB 5.4 WB, 42	3B, 3D, 4C, 4D, 4F 4C, 4D, 4F
Map Workshop: Reading a Map of Culture Regions	1C, 4A	WB, 44	1C, 4A
5.5 The Industrial Revolution	3B, 3D, 4E, 4F	BB 5.5 WB, 43 WB, 46	3B, 3D, 4E, 4F 3B, 3D, 4E, 4F 4D, 4F
Chapter 6 The Human Imprint in the Modern World		Inv. 6	1C, 4C, 4D
6.1 Population and Settlement	1A, 1B, 1C, 4B, 4C, 4E	BB 6.1 WB, 47	1B, 4B, 4C, 4E 1B, 4B, 4C, 4E
Map Workshop: Reading a Road Map	1C	WB, 51	1C, 4C
Skill Workshop: Interpreting a Cartoon	4D	WB, 52	4D
6.2 Political Patterns	1A, 3D, 4D, 4F	BB 6.2 WB, 48	3D, 4D, 4F 4D, 4F
6.3 Using the Land and Its Resources	1B, 3A, 3B, 3D, 4D	BB 6.3 WB, 49	1B, 3A, 3B, 4D 3A, 3B, 4D
6.4 Many Nations in One World	3B, 4D	BB 6.4 WB, 50 WB, 53	3B, 4D 3B, 4D 4D, 4F
Chapter 7 The United States		Inv. 7	1C, 4C, 4D, 4E
7.1 The Physical Environment	1B, 1C, 2B, 4A, 4B, 4F	BB 7.1 WB, 54	1B, 2B, 4B 4B
7.2 The Human Imprint	3B, 3D, 4C, 4D	BB 7.2 WB, 55	3B, 3D, 4C, 4D 4C, 4D
7.3 The Northeast	3A, 3B, 3D, 4C, 4E	BB 7.3 WB, 56	3A, 3C, 3D, 4C, 4E 3A, 3D, 4C, 4E
7.4 The Midwest	3A, 3B, 3C, 3D, 4C	BB 7.4 WB, 57	3A, 3B, 3D, 4C, 4E 3A, 3D, 4C
Skill Workshop: Mastering What You Read	2B	WB, 61	2B, 4A, 4B, 4C
Map Workshop: Using a Baseball Map to Interpret Population Trends	1C, 4C	WB, 60	1C, 4C
7.5 The South	3B, 4C	BB 7.5 WB, 58	3B, 4C, 4D 3B, 4C

Pupil Text	Texas Essential Elements	Teacher's Resource Binder	Texas Essential Elements
7.6 The West	3A, 3B, 3C, 3D, 4C	BB 7.6 WB, 59 WB, 62	3A, 3B, 3C, 3D, 4C 3A, 3B, 4A, 4B 4A, 4B, 4C, 4D
Chapter 8 Canada		Inv. 8	1C, 4A, 4B, 4D
8.1 The Physical Environment	1B, 1C, 2B, 2C, 3B, 4B	BB 8.1 WB, 63	3B, 4B 4A, 4B
8.2 The Human Imprint	3B, 3D, 4C, 4D, 4F	BB 8.2 WB, 64	3B, 3D, 4C, 4D 4A, 4C, 4D, 4F
Map Workshop: Reading a Subway Map	1C	WB, 66	1C
Skill Workshop: Using the Library	1C	WB, 67	1C
8.3 The Regions of Canada	2B, 3B, 4C, 4D, 4F	BB 8.3 WB, 65 WB, 68	2B, 3B, 4C, 4D, 4F 2B, 3B, 4C, 4D, 4F 4B
Chapter 9 Middle America		Inv. 9	1C, 4A, 4D
9.1 The Physical Environment	1C, 2B, 2C, 4B	BB 9.1 WB, 69	2B, 2C, 4B 2C, 4B
9.2 The Human Imprint	3B, 3C, 4C, 4D, 4E	BB 9.2 WB, 70	3B, 3C, 4C, 4D, 4E 3B, 3C, 4C, 4D, 4E
Map Workshop: Using Latitude and Longitude	1C	WB, 74	1C
9.3 Mexico	3A, 3B, 3C, 3D, 4D	BB 9.3 WB, 71	3A, 3B, 3C, 3D, 4D 3A, 3B, 3D, 4D
9.4 Central America	3B, 3C, 4C, 4D, 4F	BB 9.4 WB, 72	3B, 3C, 4C, 4D, 4F 3B, 3C, 4C, 4D, 4F
9.5 The Caribbean Islands	3B, 3C, 3D, 4D, 4F	BB 9.5 WB, 73 WB, 76	3B, 3C, 3D, 4D, 4F 3B, 3C, 4A, 4D 2C
Skill Workshop: Using a Gazetteer	1C	WB, 75	1C
Chapter 10 South America		Inv. 10	1C, 4A, 4B, 4C, 4D, 4E
10.1 The Physical Environment	1C, 2B, 2C, 4B	BB 10.1 WB, 77	2B, 2C, 4B 2B, 2C, 4A, 4B
10.2 The Human Imprint	3A, 3C, 3D, 4C, 4D	BB 10.2 WB, 78	3A, 3C, 4C, 4D 3A, 3C, 4A, 4C, 4D
Skill Workshop: Comparing Employment Graphs	1C	WB, 79	1C, 4D
10.3 Brazil	3B, 3D, 4C, 4D	BB 10.3 WB, 79	3B, 3D, 4C, 4D 1C, 3B, 3D, 4D

Pupil Text	Texas Essential Elements	Teacher's Resource Binder	Texas Essential Elements
10.4 Colombia, Venezuela, and the Guianas	3B, 3D, 4D, 4E	BB 10.4 WB, 80	3B, 3D, 4D, 4E 4D, 4E
10.5 Andean South America	3A, 3C, 4C, 4D, 4E, 4F	BB 10.5 WB, 81	3A, 3C, 4A, 4C, 4D 4A, 4D, 4E, 4F
10.6 Southern South America	3A, 3C, 3D, 4C, 4D, 4F	BB 10.6 WB, 82 WB, 85	3A, 3C, 3D, 4C, 4D, 4F 4A, 4B, 4C, 4D, 4F 1C
Map Workshop: Interpreting a Transportation Map	1C	WB, 83	1C, 4D
Chapter 11 Western Europe		Inv. 11	1C, 4A, 4B, 4D
11.1 The Physical Environment	1A, 1C, 2B, 2C	BB 11.1 WB, 86	2B, 2C, 4B 1C, 4B
11.2 The Human Imprint	3B, 3C, 3D, 4C, 4D	BB 11.2 WB, 87	3B, 3C, 3D, 4C, 4D 4B, 4C, 4D
Map Workshop: Interpreting a Language Map	1C, 4D	WB, 91	1C, 4D, 4F
11.3 The British Isles and Northern Europe	3B, 3C, 3D, 4C, 4D	BB 11.3 WB, 88	3B, 3C, 3D, 4C, 4D 4A, 4B, 4C, 4D
Skill Workshop: Analyzing a Photograph	1C	WB, 92	1C, 3A
11.4 The European Heartland	3B, 3C, 3D, 4D, 4F	BB 11.4 WB, 89	3B, 3C, 3D, 4D, 4F 4D, 4E, 4F
11.5 Southern Europe	3C, 3D, 4C, 4D, 4E	BB 11.5 WB, 90 WB, 93	3C, 3D, 4C, 4D, 4E 1C, 4A, 4B, 4D 3A, 4A
Chapter 12 Eastern Europe		Inv. 12	1C, 4A, 4D
12.1 The Physical Environment	1C, 2B, 4B	BB 12.1 WB, 94	2B, 4B 4A, 4B
12.2 The Human Imprint	4C, 4D	BB 12.2 WB, 95	4C, 4D 4C, 4D
Map Workshop: Using Maps for History	1C, 4D	WB, 97	1C, 4D
Skill Workshop: Using Graphs to Interpret Economic Trade Patterns	1C	WB, 98	1C, 4D, 4F
12.3 Nations of Eastern Europe	3B, 3C, 3D, 4D, 4F	BB 12.3 WB, 96 WB, 99	3B, 3C, 3D, 4D, 4F 4D, 4F 4B, 4C
Chapter 13 The Union of Soviet Socialist Republics		Inv. 13	1C, 4B, 4D
13.1 The Physical Environment	1C, 2B, 4B, 4F	BB 13.1 WB, 100	2B, 4A, 4B 4B

Pupil Text	Texas Essential Elements	Teacher's Resource Binder	Texas Essential Elements
Map Workshop: Understanding World Time Zones	1C, 2A	WB, 103	1C, 2A
13.2 The Human Imprint	3B, 3C, 3D, 4C, 4D	BB 13.2 WB, 101	4C, 4D 3B, 3C, 3D, 4C, 4D
Skill Workshop: Analyzing Statistics	1C	WB, 104	1C, 4A
13.3 Regions of the Soviet Union	3B, 3C, 3D, 4C, 4D	BB 13.3 WB, 102 WB, 105	3B, 3C, 3D, 4C, 4D 4A, 4C, 4D 1C
Chapter 14 East Asia		Inv. 14	1C, 4D
14.1 The Physical Environment	1C, 2B, 4B	BB 14.1 WB, 106	2B, 4B 1C, 4B
14.2 The Human Imprint	3A, 3C, 3D, 4C, 4D, 4F	BB 14.2 WB, 107	3A, 3C, 3D, 4C, 4D, 4F 4D
Skill Workshop: Using a Graph to Make Comparisons	1C	WB, 111	1C, 4F
Map Workshop: Reading a Cartogram	1C, 4C	WB, 110	1C, 4C, 4D
14.3 The East Asian Mainland	3C, 3D, 4C, 4D, 4E	BB 14.3 WB, 108	3C, 3D, 4C, 4D, 4E 4C, 4D
14.4 The Pacific Islands of East Asia	3B, 3C, 4C, 4D, 4F	BB 14.4 WB, 109 WB, 112	3B, 3C, 4C, 4D, 4F 4A, 4C, 4F 1C, 4E
Chapter 15 South Asia		Inv. 15	1C, 3A, 4B
15.1 The Physical Environment	1B, 1C, 2B, 4B, 4C	BB 15.1 WB, 113	1B, 2B, 4B, 4C 1C, 4B
Map Workshop: Using Scale	1C	WB, 117	1C, 4E
15.2 The Human Imprint	3A, 3D, 4C, 4D, 4F	BB 15.2 WB, 114	3A, 3D, 4C, 4D, 4F 4C, 4D
Skill Workshop: Reading a Population Pyramid	1C, 4C	WB, 118	1C, 4C
15.3 India and Its Neighbors	3B, 3C, 3D, 4C, 4D	BB 15.3 WB, 115	3B, 3C, 3D, 4C, 4D 1C, 4B, 4C
15.4 Southeast Asia	3B, 3C, 4C, 4D, 4E	BB 15.4 WB, 116 WB, 119	3B, 3C, 4C, 4D, 4E 1C, 4A, 4B, 4D 1C
Chapter 16 North Africa and the Middle East		Inv. 16	1C, 4D, 4F
16.1 The Physical Environment	1B, 1C, 2B, 4B, 4F	BB 16.1 WB, 120	1B, 2B, 4A, 4B 4A, 4B, 4F

Pupil Text	Texas Essential Elements	Teacher's Resource Binder	Texas Essential Elements
16.2 The Human Imprint	3A, 3B, 3C, 4D, 4E	BB 16.2 WB, 121	3A, 3B, 3C, 4D, 4E 3C, 4D, 4F
Map Workshop: Reading Maps and Tables of Oil Economies	1C, 4D	WB, 124	1C, 2A, 4D
16.3 North Africa	3A, 3B, 3C, 4D, 4E	BB 16.3 WB, 122	3A, 3B, 3C, 4A, 4D 4C, 4D, 4E
16.4 The Middle East	3A, 3B, 3C, 3D, 4D	BB 16.4 WB, 123 WB, 126	3A, 3B, 3C, 4D 4B, 4D 4C, 4D
Skill Workshop: Distinguishing Between Fact and Opinion	4D, 4F	WB, 125	1C, 4D, 4F
Chapter 17 Africa South of the Sahara		Inv. 17	1C, 4B, 4D
17.1 The Physical Environment	1B, 1C, 2B, 4B	BB 17.1 WB, 127	1C, 2B, 4B 1C, 4B
17.2 The Human Imprint	3B, 3C, 4C, 4D, 4E	BB 17.2 WB, 128	3B, 3C, 4C, 4D, 4E 4C, 4D, 4E
Map Workshop: Interpreting a Map of Colonial Territories	1C	WB, 131	1C, 4C
17.3 West and Central Africa	3B, 3C, 3D, 4C, 4D	BB 17.3 WB, 129	3B, 3C, 3D, 4C, 4D 1C, 4C, 4D
17.4 East and Southern Africa	3A, 3C, 3D, 4D, 4E	BB 17.4 WB, 130 WB, 133	3A, 3C, 3D, 4D, 4E 1C, 4C, 4D 1C
Skill Workshop: Using Graphs to Trace Literacy Rates	1C, 4D	WB, 132	1C, 4D
Chapter 18 The South Pacific		Inv. 18	1C, 2A, 4F
18.1 The Physical Environment	1B, 1C, 2B, 4B	BB 18.1 WB, 134	2B, 4A, 4B 4B
Map Workshop: Using a Polar Projection	1C	WB, 138	1C
18.2 The Human Imprint	3B, 3C, 3D, 4D, 4E	BB 18.2 WB, 135	3B, 3C, 3D, 4D, 4E 4D, 4E
18.3 Australia	3A, 3B, 3C, 3D, 4D	BB 18.3 WB, 136	3A, 3B, 3C, 3D, 4D 3A, 3B
18.4 The Islands	3B, 3C, 3D, 4C, 4D	BB 18.4 WB, 137 WB, 140	3B, 3C, 3D, 4C, 4D 1C, 4A, 4C, 4D 4B, 4C, 4D, 4E
Skill Workshop: Using an Almanac	1C	WB, 139	1C

Heath

WORLD GEOGRAPHY

by Charles F. Gritzner

ANNOTATED TEACHER'S EDITION

Annotations by Linda K. Hillestad
Social Studies Teacher, Brookings Middle School, Brookings, South Dakota

Teacher's Guide by Linda Scher
Curriculum Developer, Raleigh, North Carolina

D.C. HEATH AND COMPANY
Lexington, Massachusetts / Toronto, Ontario

HEATH

CONTENTS

Copyright © 1989 by D.C. Heath and Company

All rights reserved. No part of this publication may be reproduced or transmitted in any form by any means, electronic or mechanical, including photocopy, recording, or any information storage or retrieval system, without permission in writing from the publisher.

Published simultaneously in Canada
Printed in the United States of America

International Standard Book Number: 0-669-17287-1

2 3 4 5 6 7 8 9 0

Checklist for HEATH World Geography

In examining HEATH WORLD GEOGRAPHY, be sure to notice the following features:

HEATH WORLD GEOGRAPHY is organized for comprehension.
It puts first things first. In Unit 1, students learn about Earth's landforms, bodies of water, climates and ecosystems, and resources. In Unit 2, students read about the development of cultures and the impact of culture on settlement patterns, political systems, and economic activities. Unit 3 applies the concepts learned in Units 1 and 2 to Earth's culture regions. Each chapter in Unit 3 gives complete coverage of a region, including descriptions of its physical features, its peoples, and its cultures.

HEATH WORLD GEOGRAPHY is flexible in its approach to regional studies. You can tailor assignments to the way you teach the course. Once students have been introduced to key geographic concepts and skills, culture regions can be taught in any order. With 18 chapters, HEATH WORLD GEOGRAPHY is ideal for either half or full courses.

HEATH WORLD GEOGRAPHY is designed to teach map skills. There are more than 150 colorful maps. A handbook of map and globe skills precedes Unit 1. With this handbook, you can review basic map and globe skills right at the start. In addition, 18 Map Workshops—one in each chapter—build and extend those skills. End-of-section and chapter-end questions also emphasize map skills. The text concludes with an Atlas and Gazetteer. (Outline Maps and Map Tests are available. The *Heath Student Atlas* and *Heath Atlas Transparencies* also accompany HEATH WORLD GEOGRAPHY.)

HEATH WORLD GEOGRAPHY has extra supports built right into the text. Each chapter has a Skill Workshop that reviews a social studies skill. A World Data Bank appears in each regional chapter, enabling students to compare countries in terms of area, population, population growth rate, and per capita GNP. Important new terms are defined in a Glossary. A World Reference Section provides a handy source of interesting facts about the world's landforms and peoples.

How **HEATH World Geography** Works in the Classroom

HEATH WORLD GEOGRAPHY builds confidence in working with maps.

"Reviewing Map and Globe Skills" is a handbook of 9 two-page, skills-building lessons.

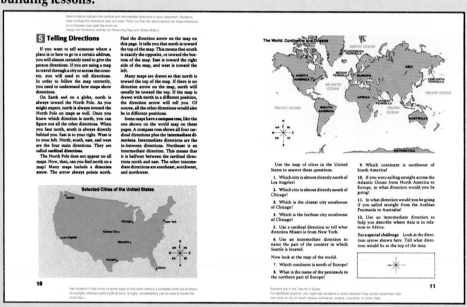

□ Each lesson fully explains a map skill.

□ Each lesson includes maps for illustration and practice.

□ Questions labeled "For a special challenge" develop interpretive and analytical skills.

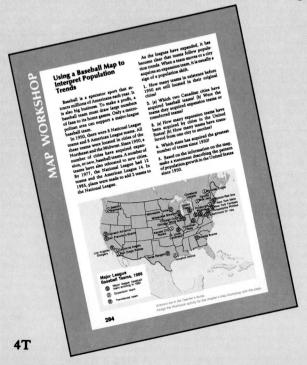

Map skills lessons are found in every chapter.

□ Each chapter has a Map Workshop, focusing on a particular map skill.

Special maps clarify and enrich content.

□ HEATH WORLD GEOGRAPHY has a variety of special maps. These maps enable students to learn about life within a region, to compare regions, or to understand the unique features of a region.

HEATH WORLD GEOGRAPHY shows students where places are.

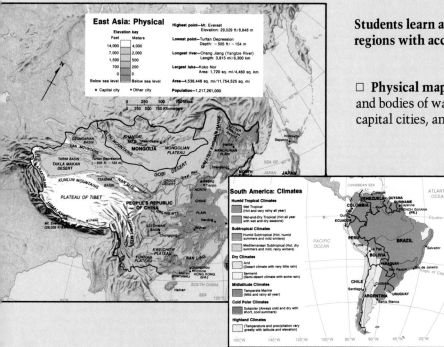

Students learn about each of Earth's regions with accurate, up-to-date maps.

☐ **Physical maps** show landforms, rivers and bodies of water, political boundaries, capital cities, and other major cities.

☐ **Climate maps** show a region's major climate areas. An easy-to-read key makes these maps easy to use and interpret.

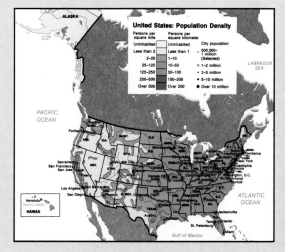

☐ **Population maps** show settlement patterns and major urban areas.

☐ **Land-use maps** show resources and patterns of economic activity for each region.

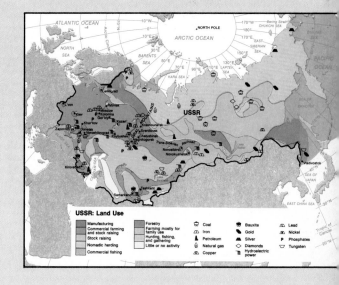

HEATH WORLD GEOGRAPHY has frequent location checks.

☐ Each section review has place-location exercises that make use of nearby maps.

☐ Map Study questions make sure that students can find places on each map.

☐ In each chapter review, there is an outline map and a location exercise based on it.

HEATH WORLD GEOGRAPHY promotes good study skills.

CHAPTER 7

In this chapter, students will study the physical environment of the United States, which has been divided into four major landform regions. The section on the human imprint will reveal the importance of immigration and economic development to the nation's growth. The United States is then broken into four cultural regions. Students will learn where people live, what they do, and what trends are currently affecting each of the four regions.

Texas Essential Elements 1B. Geographic terminology. 1C. Geographical tools and methodologies. 2B. Major landforms, regions, and features of the earth. 4A. Criteria for determining regions. 4B. Physical setting of world regions. 4F. Geographic influences on various issues.

The United States

The United States stretches across the middle of North America. About 500 years ago this area was sparsely settled. Groups of Indians were scattered across the land. These groups lived differently from one another, in the vast wilderness. Along the Pacific coast, for example, Chinook took salmon and other fish from the ocean. Iroquois of the eastern woodlands hunted deer in vast forests and raised crops in small fields nestled in the woodlands.

By 1650, the face of the continent had changed little. European newcomers had built a few settlements on the eastern coast and in the southwestern desert. At first, the Europeans lived in small areas within the great wilderness. Gradually, however, in search of wealth or trade or better land, they expanded their settlements. Over the next few centuries, continued expansion and the growing use of resources would change the face of North America on a scale never equaled in human history.

Today neither the Indians nor the European settlers of the 1600's would recognize the land they lived in. Where there were once millions of bison roaming wild, there are now but a few thousand, herded largely onto government lands. Their home—the plains area—is now a place for the grazing of domesticated cattle and the farming of grain. City skyscrapers and factories rise where forests and prairies once covered the land.

The photo shows Houston, Texas.

184

Answers are in the Teacher's Guide.
Assign the Workbook activity for this chapter's Skill Workshop with this page.

1 The Physical Environment

In no part of North America have the changes been as rapid and as great as in the part that became the United States. There are a number of reasons for the unparalleled changes in this region. Industrious and daring people came from all over the world to settle in the United States. These people brought the skills and knowledge needed to farm, to trade, and to make many kinds of goods. America's economic and political systems gave them great freedom.

The people who came to North America found a large land, rich in resources. Before learning about the American people, you should consider the country's environments and ecosystems.

Landforms

In terms of area, the United States is the fourth largest country in the world. The landforms in this vast area offer remarkable contrasts. To take just one example, the peak of Alaska's Mount McKinley, with an elevation of 20,320 feet (6,194 meters), is the highest point in the United States. The lowest spot is Death Valley, California, where the surface of the land is 282 feet (89 meters) below sea level.

The Coastal Plains The eastern coast of the United States is a long, gently rolling lowland area. These coastal plains reach from Maine to Texas. The lowlands along the Atlantic Ocean are known as the Atlantic Coastal Plain. Those that border the Gulf of Mexico are called the Gulf Coastal Plain. The southern part of the coastal plains reaches many miles inland. This inland area has fertile soil, which makes the plain well suited to farming. In the northern portion, the plain is narrower and less suited to farming.

A ranger makes her rounds in a valley in Yellowstone National Park, Wyoming.

The Appalachian Mountains At the western edge of the Atlantic Coastal Plain, the land rises to form the hills of the Piedmont (pēd'mont'). The Appalachian (ap'ə lā'chən) Mountains lie to the west of the Piedmont. The Appalachians run from the northern part of Maine southwest into Alabama. They have different names in different parts of the country. The mountains hold an abundance of minerals, especially coal.

The Appalachians form a natural barrier between the coastal plains and the interior part of the United States. But the Appalachians have been worn down by erosion and are not very high. Rivers have carved out a number of narrow valleys, called gaps. These gaps create east-west openings in the mountains.

185

I refer to the physical map on pages 186–187 as they read Section 1. Have a states located on the Atlantic Coastal Plain and the Gulf Coastal Plain.

Each chapter is divided into manageable sections.

☐ Terms new to students appear in boldface type. Each is defined in context as well as in the text's Glossary.

☐ Abundant tables provide the facts and figures on the world's nations.

☐ Section reviews check mastery of vocabulary and comprehension of content.

☐ Every chapter has built-in checks on students' ability to locate places.

Have students refer to the information in this chart as they read and study more about the individual countries in Western Europe.

WORLD DATA BANK

Country	Area in Square Kilometers	Population/Growth Rate		Per Capita GNP/GDP
Andorra	466	47,000	(5.4%)	NA
Austria	83,835	7,540,000	(0.0%)	$ 8,904 (GNP)
Belgium	30,540	9,856,000	(0.0%)	8,243 (GNP)
Denmark	43,076	5,109,000	(0.1%)	11,026 (GNP)
Finland	337,113	4,894,000	(0.4%)	10,186 (GNP)
France	547,026	55,094,000	(0.4%)	9,478 (GDP)
Greece	131,944	9,966,000	(0.6%)	3,544 (GNP)
Iceland	102,845	241,000	(1.0%)	8,898 (GNP)
Ireland	70,282	3,590,000	(1.0%)	4,263 (GNP)
Italy	301,233	57,149,000	(0.3%)	6,308 (GNP)
Liechtenstein	160	28,000	(1.8%)	16,900 (GNP)
Luxembourg	2,586	367,000	(0.0%)	13,988 (GNP)
Malta	313	355,000	(0.5%)	3,145 (GDP)
Monaco	1.9	28,000	(1.2%)	NA
Netherlands	40,844	14,467,000	(0.4%)	9,120 (GNP)
Norway	324,219	4,160,000	(0.4%)	13,300 (GNP)
Portugal	92,082	10,045,000	(0.5%)	2,137 (GNP)
San Marino	62	23,000	(1.6%)	NA
Spain	504,782	38,629,000	(0.5%)	5,276 (GNP)
Sweden	449,964	8,338,000	(0.0%)	10,434 (GDP)
Switzerland	41,228	6,512,000	(0.2%)	15,890 (GNP)
United Kingdom	243,977	56,437,000	(0.1%)	8,124 (GNP)
Vatican City	.438	1,000	(0.1%)	NA
West Germany	248,577	61,132,000	(0.2%)	10,673 (GNP)

REVIEWING THE FACTS

Define

1. Indo-European
2. literate
3. Protestant
4. Holocaust
5. welfare state
6. constitutional monarchy
7. neutral
8. European Economic Community
9. Common Market

Answer

1. Describe settlement patterns in Western Europe.

2. What are some of the cultural divisions in Western Europe?

3. What forms of government are most common in Western Europe?

4. What are Western Europe's main economic activities?

Locate

Refer to the map on page 284.

(a) Name the sea between Iceland and Norway. (b) Between England and Norway. (c) East of Greece. (d) South of Europe.

292

Answers are in the Teacher's Guide.

Here students locate the countries in the British Isles and Northern Europe on the physical map on page 284 and on the population density map on page 286. These two parts of Western Europe offer a wide contrast in population density.

3 The British Isles and Northern Europe

The British Isles and much of Northern Europe are separated from the rest of Europe by water. The United Kingdom—made up of England, Wales, Scotland, and Northern Ireland—and Ireland occupy the British Isles. England, Wales, and Scotland are located on a single island, Great Britain. This entire area has a mild climate because of the influence of the Gulf Stream.

Iceland, Finland, and the countries of Scandinavia—Sweden, Norway, and Denmark—lie to the north of most of the British Isles. Known as Norden, these countries are isolated from the parts of Europe lying to the south. Generally their coastal lowlands are warmed by ocean currents and breezes. But inland the climate is bitterly cold.

The People

With more than 55 million people, the United Kingdom is one of the most densely populated countries in the world. The countries of Norden, on the other hand, have small, sparse populations. There, people live mainly along the coastal lowlands. The frigid interior highlands of these countries have very few residents.

People living in Norden and the British Isles have a generally high standard of living. For example, the per capita income in Norway, Sweden, and Denmark is higher than that in the United States. Norway, Sweden, and Denmark were among the first countries in the world to have large-scale social-welfare programs. Government services are paid for by taxes that are far higher than those paid by residents of the United States and Canada.

The Regions of Western Europe

British Isles and Northern Europe / Southern Europe / European Heartland

Map Study What bodies of water border the British Isles and Northern Europe? The European Heartland? Southern Europe?

Economic Development

Most countries of northern Europe and the British Isles have a great deal of manufacturing. Fishing, farming, mining, and forestry are also important. As in other industrial regions, many people work in service industries. In the United Kingdom, Sweden, and Norway, more than 50 percent of the workers are employed by the government and other services.

Ocean Resources All northern Europe is located on islands or peninsulas. As a result, the people of the region have learned

293

Finland means "land of fens and marshes."
Answers to Map Study questions: Atlantic Ocean, North Sea, Mediterranean Sea
Assign the Workbook activity for Chapter 11, Section 3, with pages 293–297.

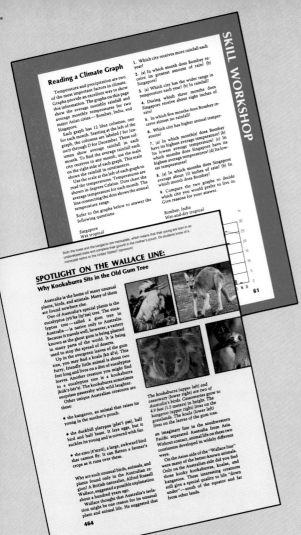

Social studies skills are taught in every chapter.

☐ Students learn to interpret graphs, understand diagrams, analyze cartoons and photographs, find information in encyclopedias and almanacs, and use the library.

High-interest features make reading each chapter like visiting a new place.

☐ "Spotlights" describe daily life or present the story behind a significant fact or trend.

Chapter reviews highlight the main points and check student comprehension.

☐ Every Geography Laboratory has a map exercise.

☐ Students can read a quick summary of the material covered in the chapter.

☐ The Geography Laboratory gives students a variety of ways to apply what they have learned.

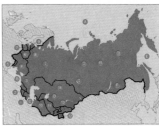

HEATH WORLD GEOGRAPHY provides the ancillaries you and your students need.

■ The **Teacher's Annotated Edition** helps you make the most of your time.

A Teaching Guide is bound into the front of the Teacher's Annotated Edition. It provides an assignment guide for every chapter, lesson objectives with activity ideas that develop those objectives, and suggestions for evaluation, reteaching, and enrichment. The guide also includes answers to all questions in the student text.

On-page annotations provide additional aids in adapting the text to your curriculum and to the needs of your students.

■ The **Teacher's Resource Binder** offers a variety of teaching options.

- Outline Maps of the world and each region covered in the text.

- Map Tests that measure mastery of key map and globe skills as well as knowledge of the location of key places in the world.

- The Workbook—in copymaster form—with 140 independent practice activity sheets, one for each section of the student text, every Map Workshop, and every Skill Workshop.

- The Teacher's Annotated Edition of the Workbook.

- Building Basics Worksheets—reteaching activities keyed to each section of text. The worksheets strengthen vocabulary and reading comprehension skills.

- The Geography Laboratory Manual— enrichment activities keyed to every chapter. The high-interest activities allow students to deepen their knowledge of geography and build research and critical-thinking skills.

- Tests—a two-page test for each chapter.

- The Teacher's Guide for The Computer Test Bank, providing a variety of questions for each section of the text. All questions are keyed to level of difficulty.

- A copy of the Heath Student Atlas

■ The **Computer Test Bank** allows you to individualize testing.

You can edit existing questions or add new ones. You can quickly assemble computer-generated quizzes as well as chapter, unit, midterm, and final examinations.

■ **Heath Atlas Transparencies** and **Heath Student Atlas** enhance the teaching of key geography concepts and skills.

Sixty-four full-color overhead transparencies with teaching suggestions and correlated worksheets provide a unique way of focusing on important ideas and building critical thinking skills. The Heath Atlas Transparencies are correlated to maps in Heath Student Atlas.

■ **MAPS**—the **Map Ancillary Program Support**—with 26 Outline Maps and 27 Map Tests in transmaster form.

Transmasters are overhead transparencies that can also be used as duplicating masters. Each map test comes with an answer overlay. The outline maps and maps are available in copymaster form in the Teacher's Resource Binder.

■ The **Workbook** contains the same independent practice activities that appear in copymaster form in the Teacher's Resource Binder. Answers may be found in a Teacher's Annotated Edition.

Reviewing Map and Globe Skills *(pages 1–19)*

ASSIGNMENT GUIDE

■ *Teacher's Resource Binder*

Assign after

pp. 2–3   Independent Practice Worksheet:
          Practicing Using Globes WB p. 1
          Map Test: Reviewing Map and Globe Skills 1

pp. 4–5   Independent Practice Worksheet:
          Practicing Using Projections WB p. 2
          Map Test: Reviewing Map and Globe Skills 2

pp. 6–7   Independent Practice Worksheet:
          Practicing Using Maps and Legends WB p. 3
          Map Test: Reviewing Map and Globe Skills 3

pp. 8–9   Independent Practice Worksheet:
          Practicing Reading a Physical Map WB p. 4
          Map Test: Reviewing Map and Globe Skills 4

pp. 10–11 Independent Practice Worksheet:
          Practicing Telling Directions WB p. 5
          Map Test: Reviewing Map and Globe Skills 5

pp. 12–13 Independent Practice Worksheet:
          Practicing Using Scale WB p. 6
          Map Test: Reviewing Map and Globe Skills 6

pp. 14–15 Independent Practice Worksheet:
          Practicing Using a Grid WB p. 7
          Map Test: Reviewing Map and Globe Skills 7

pp. 16–17 Independent Practice Worksheet:
          Practicing Using Latitude and Longitude WB p. 8
          Map Test: Reviewing Map and Globe Skills 8

pp. 18–19 Independent Practice Worksheet:
          Practicing Following Circle Routes WB p. 9
          Map Test: Reviewing Map and Globe Skills 9

■ *Outline Map 1*   Use with pages 2–3
■ *Outline Map 2*   Use with pages 16–17
■ *Outline Map 7*   Use with pages 6–7

REVIEWING MAP AND GLOBE SKILLS 1:

Using Globes (pages 2–3)

VOCABULARY

globe, p. 2; hemisphere, p. 2; equator, p. 2

TEACHING STRATEGIES

After students have read pages 2–3, have them study the drawings of Earth on these two pages. Ask them to name the continents that lie in each hemisphere.

If possible, bring an actual globe into class and have students use masking tape or colored string to mark the hemisphere divisions.

CHECK FOR UNDERSTANDING

Show students a globe on which you have marked some parallel of latitude other than the equator with tape or colored string. Ask them if this line divides the globe into hemispheres. Students should be able to explain that only a line at the globe's widest point divides the globe into hemispheres.

CORRECTIONS/EXTENSIONS

Reteaching Give students copies of **Outline Map 1.** Ask them to mark the line that divides the Northern and Southern hemispheres in one color. Then have them use another color to mark the line that divides the Eastern and Western hemispheres.

Enrichment Ask students to use an encyclopedia to learn about the difference between Earth's geographic poles and its magnetic poles.

Answers

1. (a) Northern Hemisphere (b) Eastern Hemisphere 2. Northern, Western Hemispheres 3. north; east 4. north

For a special challenge: Africa; Both the equator and the line (Prime Meridian) that divides Earth into the Eastern and Western Hemisphere pass through it.

REVIEWING MAP AND GLOBE SKILLS 2:

Understanding Map Projections (pages 4–5)

VOCABULARY

map, p. 4; projection, p. 4

TEACHING STRATEGIES

Have students read pages 4–5 and identify the different projections shown there. Ask the class why mapmakers have experimented with such varied ways of showing the world. (to overcome the problem of showing a round object with a flat drawing)

CHECK FOR UNDERSTANDING

Ask students which projections would be most useful for each of the following tasks: planning a voyage across the Atlantic (Mercator or Mollweide); comparing the distances across North America and Australia (Mollweide or interrupted); planning a trek across Antarctica (polar).

CORRECTIONS/EXTENSIONS

Reteaching List the four projections on the chalkboard. Next to the list, make two columns, one headed *Advantages* and the other *Dis-*

advantages. Ask students to complete the chart by filling out those columns.

Enrichment Tell students to watch for examples of world maps on nightly news broadcasts and in newspapers and magazines. Discuss which projection is most widely used and what impression of the world it creates. (The Mercator projection, for example, makes the Northern Hemisphere appear much larger—and therefore more important—than the Southern Hemisphere.)

Answers

1. Mercator 2. Mollweide 3. Mercator
4. It is wider and looks more like a square on the Mercator projection.
5. (a) South Pole (b) Antarctica

REVIEWING MAP AND GLOBE SKILLS 3:

Interpreting Map Symbols and Legends (pages 6–7)

VOCABULARY

political map, p. 6; symbol, p. 6; legend, p. 6; key, p. 6

TEACHING STRATEGIES

Ask students to look at the maps on pages 6 and 7. For each map, ask them to list the symbols used. Point out that color is used as a symbol on page 6, helping to highlight the political divisions. Ask the class what symbols for the map on page 7 do *not* appear in the key. (boundaries, blue for water)

CHECK FOR UNDERSTANDING

Have the class turn to one of the atlas maps (pages 486–500) and identify the symbols used on it.

CORRECTIONS/EXTENSIONS

Reteaching Give the class copies of **Outline Map 7** and ask them to look at the atlas map on page 494, which shows North America as a whole. Ask students to label each country on their outline maps with its name and put the boundary symbol in the key box. Then ask them to choose a symbol for a capital city and put it in the key box on their map. Tell them to put the capital city for each country in the correct location, using the map on page 494 as a guide.

Enrichment Encourage students to bring in a variety of maps from other sources. Compare the symbols used for special-purpose maps such as highway maps and subway maps. Discuss how a good choice of symbols can make a map easy to read, while a poor choice makes it difficult.

Answers

1. (a) People's Republic of China, Mongolia, North Korea, South Korea, Taiwan, Japan (b) Mongolia, North Korea
2. Tokyo 3. Shanghai
4. (a) forests (b) fish
5. (a) All consist of letters within a block. (b) The letter varies according to the first letter of the resource.
6. forests, iron, Zinc, stone/sand, fish
7. (a) Maine (b) Delaware
8. (a) Pennsylvania, Maryland (b) Pennsylvania; This is the state with the most symbols for coal placed in it.
9. Iron ore 10. Pennsylvania

REVIEWING MAP AND GLOBE SKILLS 4:

Reading a Physical Map (pages 8–9)

VOCABULARY

physical map, p. 8; elevation, p. 8; sea level, p. 8; highlands, p. 8; lowlands, p. 8; high relief, p. 8; low relief, p. 8

TEACHING STRATEGIES

After students have read page 8, ask them to describe the kinds of information that a physical map provides. Ask for an example of each type of information from the map on page 8.

CHECK FOR UNDERSTANDING

Ask students to explain the difference between a political map and a physical map.

CORRECTIONS/EXTENSIONS

Reteaching Have students write sentences on the board that include each of the vocabulary words. Ask students to leave a blank space where the defined word should go. Students can take turns filling in the blanks.

Enrichment Have students design the symbols they would use for a map of their own community.

Answers

1. Andes Mountains
2. Amazon Basin
3. (a) between 1,500 and 7,000 feet (500 and 2,000 meters) (b) moderate
4. (a) between 7,000 and 14,000 feet (2,000 and 4,000 meters) (b) between 1,500 and 7,000 feet (500 and 2,000 meters)
5. Most of Uruguay lies at 0 to 700 feet (0 to 200 meters) above sea level, except for a tiny portion of slightly higher elevation in the northwest. The relief is low.

For a special challenge: The elevation varies from 0 feet above sea level to over 14,000 feet (4,000 meters) above sea level. The southwest is the highest part of Bolivia. The relief is high.

REVIEWING MAP AND GLOBE SKILLS 5:

Telling Directions (pages 10–11)

VOCABULARY

cardinal directions, p. 10; direction arrow, p. 10; compass rose, p. 10; intermediate directions, p. 10

TEACHING STRATEGIES

Ask students to name the cardinal and intermediate directions. If possible, bring a compass to class and find out how your classroom is oriented.

CHECK FOR UNDERSTANDING

Have students locate the direction arrow on one of the atlas maps (pages 494–499) and quiz each other on directions between pairs of cities from that map.

CORRECTIONS/EXTENSIONS

Reteaching Have each student draw a compass rose like the one on page 11. Then help students use a compass to align the compass roses correctly on their desks. Identify the cardinal and intermediate directions for objects in the room.

Enrichment Some students may wish to make their own compasses. They will need a magnet, a needle, a cork, tape, and a dish of water. Tell them to magnetize the needle by pulling it lengthwise along the magnet ten times or more, always in the same direction.

Then they can tape the needle to the cork and float the cork in the dish of water. The needle will point north/south.

Answers

1. Seattle 2. Memphis 3. Kansas City 4. Los Angeles 5. north 6. northwest 7. Africa 8. Scandinavian Peninsula 9. North America 10. east 11. southeast 12. northeast

For a special challenge: east

REVIEWING MAP AND GLOBE SKILLS 6:

Using Scale (pages 12–13)

VOCABULARY

scale, p. 12

TEACHING STRATEGIES

To help the class understand the idea of scale, discuss the idea of a scale model. Be sure students understand that the proportions of a scale model must be the same as those of the full-size object. Ask students to identify the map on which an inch stands for *more* miles. (the map on page 12)

CHECK FOR UNDERSTANDING

Ask students to compare the atlas map on pages 492–493 with the one on page 494. On which map does an inch stand for *fewer* miles? (the one on pages 492–493)

CORRECTIONS/EXTENSIONS

Reteaching Show students how to estimate distances. Have them mark the distance between two places on the edge of a piece of paper. Then help them measure the distance between the marks against the scale.

Enrichment For examples of very detailed (large-scale) maps, students can obtain maps of their own community from the U.S. Geological Survey. Discuss uses for which such maps are valuable.

Answers

1. 4,900 miles 2. 1,100 miles 3. less than 600 miles 4. about 500 miles 5. The distance between Khartoum and Tripoli is greater.

REVIEWING MAP AND GLOBE SKILLS 7:

Using a Grid (pages 14–15)

VOCABULARY

grid, p. 14

TEACHING STRATEGIES

After students have read page 14, ask them to identify the grid coordinates for several sites on the map on page 15. They can check their answers by looking at the index below the map.

CHECK FOR UNDERSTANDING

Ask students to identify the grid coordinates through which Highway 45 passes, starting from the north (A2).

CORRECTIONS/EXTENSIONS

Reteaching Ask students to define a grid. Use letters and numbers to make a grid based on the desks in the classroom, and have students identify various seats.

Enrichment Give students a state road map with an index of towns. Have them locate various towns using the index. Pairs of students can challenge each other to find places within a certain time, such as 30 seconds.

Answers

1. D2 2. (a) C2, C3 (b) I10, I45 3. Texas Southern University, University of Houston; both are in D3 4. (a) C4, D4, D5 (b) C7 5. C4 6. W.P. Hobby Airport

REVIEWING MAP AND GLOBE SKILLS 8:

Using Latitude and Longitude (pages 16–17)

VOCABULARY

global grid, p. 16; parallels of latitude, p. 16; meridians of longitude, p. 16; degrees, p. 16; prime meridian, p. 16

TEACHING STRATEGIES

Review the concept of hemispheres with the class. Point out that the latitudes south of the equator are equivalent to the Southern Hemisphere, and so on. Help students relate the grid of parallels and meridians to the letter-number grid they have already studied.

CHECK FOR UNDERSTANDING

Using the map on page 17, write a list of co-ordinates on the chalkboard. Ask students to identify the correct continent or ocean for each pair of coordinates.

CORRECTIONS/EXTENSIONS

Reteaching Give students a copy of **Outline Map 2.** Ask them to use one color to mark the equator and another to mark the prime meridian. Give them several pairs of coordinates. For each pair, have them mark the location on the map. They may find it helpful to extend the relevant lines through the land areas.

Enrichment Point out to students that *any* meridian could have been chosen as the prime meridian, the starting point for measuring longitude. Ask some students to research the history of longitude and report on why the line through Greenwich, England, became the prime meridian.

Answers

1. (a) Equator, Prime Meridian
   (b) Atlantic Ocean
2. (a) North America
   (b) Pacific Ocean
3. (a) Atlantic Ocean
   (b) Pacific Ocean
4. (a) Asia
   (b) Africa
5. (a) Europe, Africa
   (b) Africa, Europe, Asia, Australia
   (c) North America, South America

REVIEWING MAP AND GLOBE SKILLS 9:

Following Circle Routes (pages 18–19)

VOCABULARY

great circle route, p. 18; great circle, p. 18

TEACHING STRATEGIES

Ask students to define a great circle, based on the information on pages 18–19. If possible,

use a globe to demonstrate the concept of great circles as described on page 19.

CHECK FOR UNDERSTANDING

Ask students to use a globe and a string to show a great circle. Tell them that the circle they show should be neither the equator nor a meridian of longitude.

CORRECTIONS/EXTENSIONS

Reteaching Let students work with a globe and string comparing circle routes with non-circle routes.

Enrichment Students can look in atlases or write to airline companies for examples of airline route maps. Have them compare these maps to the polar map on page 19. Note that such a projection can be drawn for any point on Earth as well as for the poles.

Answers

1. A, B, C are all great circle routes. A and C are because they lie on meridians. B lies on the equator, which divides the world into halves.
2. Every meridian is a great circle, which is the shortest distance between two points on Earth.

SUPPLEMENTARY MATERIALS

Books
Dicks, Brian (ed.), *The Children's World Atlas*, Celestial Arts, 1981
Goode's World Atlas, 17th edition, Rand McNally, 1985
Hovinen, Elizabeth, *Teaching Map and Globe Skills*, Rand McNally, 1982

Other Media
Fisher, William M., *Geo-Cepts* (D-G: 30 booklets, teacher's guide, chart, tests)
Geography (EDNA: cassette/diskette for Apple or PET)
How to Use Maps and Globes (Troll: filmstrip)
Latitude and Longitude (EB: film/video)
The Language of Maps (EB: film/video)
Slated Outline Map (R-McN: world and U.S. outline maps for chalk marking)
Using Maps: Measuring Distance (EB: film/ video, Spanish version available)

ASSIGNMENT GUIDE

■ Text Features

Skill Workshop, p. 26   Spotlight, p.39
Spotlight, p. 31   Chapter Review, pp. 44–45
Map Workshop, p. 33

■ Teacher's Resource Binder

Assign after

p. 25 Building Basics Worksheet 1.1
       Independent Practice Worksheet 1.1 WB p. 11
p. 26 Skill Workshop: Interpreting a Diagram of Landforms and
       Bodies of Water WB p. 15
p. 32 Building Basics Worksheet 1.2
       Independent Practice Worksheet 1.2 WB p. 12
p. 33 Map Workshop: Reading a Contour Map WB p. 14
p. 43 Building Basics Worksheet 1.3
       Independent Practice Worksheet 1.3 WB p. 13
p. 45 Map Test 1
       Chapter Test 1
       Enrichment Chapter 1 WB p. 16

■ Geography Laboratory Manual: Investigating Chapter 1

Use with pages 22–45

■ Outline Map 2   Use with pages 22–45

OVERVIEW

This chapter discusses Earth's physical makeup. It begins by introducing students to Earth's water and land areas and concludes by discussing the natural forces—such as, continental drift, tectonic activity, mountain building, volcanic action, running water, moving ice, waves and currents, and wind—that change Earth's surface.

INTRODUCING THE CHAPTER

Read the chapter title to the class: "The Face of Earth." Ask students what they think of when they hear this title. Do they think of cities and towns or of oceans and mountains? Now have students turn to the picture of Earth on page 22. Ask them what information can be obtained from studying this photograph of the face of Earth. What might the white areas be? (clouds) The gray-blue areas? (water) The reddish brown areas? (land) After students have made some guesses, have them read the chapter introduction and find out whether or not they guessed correctly. Then tell the class that in this chapter, they will learn about the land and water that make up Earth's surface and about the internal and external forces that change the face of Earth.

1.1 Land and Water
(pages 23–25)

MAIN IDEAS

■ Land and water make up the surface of Earth.
■ The two types of water on Earth are salt water—in oceans and seas—and fresh water—in lakes, streams, and rivers.
■ Land areas—such as continents, isthmuses, islands, and archipelagos—differ in size and shape.
■ Landforms—such as mountains, hills, plains, and plateaus—differ in elevation and shape.

VOCABULARY

sea, p. 23; gulf, p. 23; bay, p. 23; strait, p. 23; tributary, p. 24; river system, p. 24; continent, p. 24; isthmus, p. 24; island, p. 24; archipelago, p. 24; peninsula, p. 24; cape, p. 25; elevation, p. 25; sea level, p. 25; mountain, p. 25; hill, p. 25; plain, p. 25; plateau, p. 25

OBJECTIVES

Students should be able to:
- distinguish freshwater and saltwater areas.
- identify different types of land areas and discuss how they differ from each other.
- relate elevation to landforms.

TEACHING STRATEGIES

Distinguishing between Freshwater and Saltwater Areas Have the class turn to the map on pages 492–493. Then divide the class into small groups. Assign each group one area on the map. Ask each group to identify all the bodies of water in their assigned area, indicating whether these bodies of water are fresh or salt water. Groups can make up questions about the bodies of water and present them to the class, such as: "What body of fresh water is southeast of the state capital?"

Using Outline Map 2 to Identify Land Areas Distribute Outline Map 2. Ask the class to name the largest kind of land area (continent) and to say how many of these land areas there are (7). Have students name them. (Europe, Asia, Africa, North America, South America, Australia, Antarctica) Now ask students to find and label each of the following. Refer them to the maps in the book for help: (1) an isthmus (such as the Isthmus of Panama, which connects North and South America), (2) an island (such as Cuba, Haiti, or Puerto Rico), (3) an archipelago (such as the Aleutian Islands, off the coast of Alaska), and (4) a peninsula (such as Florida).

Relating Elevation to Landforms Ask the class to name the four kinds of landforms and define them. (*mountains*—high rugged landforms; *hills*—a low raised area of land; *plains*—large area of level or rolling land; and *plateaus*—like plains but higher in elevation and surrounded by cliffs) Ask the class where people are most likely to plant crops or build homes (plains and plateaus). Have students look at the physical map of Latin America on page 9. Which areas of South America are most likely to be plains or plateaus (Great Plains, Pampas, Llanos), hills (Guiana Highlands, Brazilian

Highlands), or mountains (Andes Mountains)? Students should give reasons for their answers.

CHECK FOR UNDERSTANDING

Ask the class to invent a continent. Have students come to the board to draw and describe what the surface of that continent might look like. Encourage them to use words from "Reviewing the Facts," on page 25.

CORRECTIONS/EXTENSIONS

Reteaching Have students write sentences on the board that include each of the words from "Reviewing the Facts" on page 25. Ask students to leave a blank space where the defined word should go. Students should take turns filling in the blanks.

Enrichment Have students select an island or island group and research how these islands were formed. Small groups of students might also be asked to create relief maps showing the various types of landforms, land areas, and bodies of water discussed in this section.

1.2 The Changing Earth: Forces from Within
(pages 27–32)

MAIN IDEAS

- The theory of continental drift explains why continents have matching coastlines.
- The drifting of continents is caused by tectonic activity—the shifting of plates that make up the Earth's crust.
- Mountain formation—formed by folding, faulting, and volcanic action—is evidence of tectonic activity.

VOCABULARY

theory, p. 27; continental drift, p. 27; crust, p. 28; mantle, p. 28; core, p. 28; tectonic plates, p. 28; tectonic activity, p. 28; rift, p. 29; fold, p. 29; faulting, p. 30; fault, p. 30; lava, p. 32; eruption, p. 32

OBJECTIVES

Students should be able to:
- explain the theory of continental drift.
- understand that tectonic activity affects continental drift.
- describe the ways mountains are formed.

TEACHING STRATEGIES

Explaining the Theory of Continental Drift
Direct students to the three maps at the bottom of page 27. Point out that the first map shows how Earth might have looked as a single land-mass 200 million years ago, that the center map shows Earth as it looks today, and that the last map shows what Earth may look like in 10 million years. Ask students to describe the theory of continental drift as it applies to these maps. What evidence do scientists use to support this theory? (matching coastlines, similar fossils, and rock formations)

Understanding Tectonic Activity Ask students to look at the diagram of Earth's interior on page 28. Remind the class that what happens inside Earth affects what happens on the surface of Earth. Have them describe tectonic activity. Ask them the ways plates can move and what the results are (apart, creating steep cliffs, or colliding, causing mountain ranges to be made)

Describing Mountain Formation Divide the class into three groups. Ask each group to prepare a short oral report on one of the following processes of mountain building: folding, faulting, or volcanic action. Encourage students to draw diagrams for their presentations. Each group should give at least one example of a mountain range formed in this way.

CHECK FOR UNDERSTANDING

Have students write a paragraph explaining how tectonic activity results in mountain building and in continental drift. (Continents sit on tectonic plates and move as the plates move. This motion causes plates to separate or collide resulting in land formations.)

CORRECTIONS/EXTENSIONS

Reteaching Ask students to imagine that they are traveling in parts of the Appalachian Mountains, the Sierra Nevada Mountains, or in the Hawaiian Islands. Have class members write letters to friends back home explaining how the mountains were formed.

Enrichment Have the class read "Spotlight on Earthquakes" on page 31. Ask students to write short reports on the methods used today to predict earthquakes or the way in which the Richter Scale is used to measure the strength of earthquakes. Other class members can report on how volcanoes help scientists understand Earth's interior.

1.3 The Changing Earth: Forces from Without
(pages 36–43)

MAIN IDEA

■ Erosion by running water, glacial ice, wind, and waves reshapes the surface of Earth.

VOCABULARY

erosion, p. 36; silt, p. 36; delta, p. 36; glacier, p. 38; moraine, p. 40; fjord, p. 40; Ice Age, p. 40; loess, p. 40; continental shelf, p. 41; tsunami, p. 42

OBJECTIVE

Students should be able to:
■ describe the four causes of erosion and identify their effects.

TEACHING STRATEGIES

Describing the Causes of Erosion Make a three-column chart on the chalkboard. Label the columns: *Type of Erosion, How Caused, Effects.* In the first column, list *running water, glacial activity, wind,* and *waves and currents.* Have students complete the chart by briefly describing the process each of these forces cause and their effects. Ask which among these causes the most erosion. (water) Why do trees and grasses help slow erosion? (Their roots hold soil and absorb some water.)

CHECK FOR UNDERSTANDING

Remind students that in an earlier section of this chapter they looked at the four major land-forms found on Earth—mountains, hills, plains, and plateaus. Have students identify the forces that have helped create these landforms.

CORRECTIONS/EXTENSIONS

Reteaching Tell students that the forms of erosion balance out each other. Glaciers, for example, might erode land in one area, but wind might carry leftover silt elsewhere. Ask students to choose one example of this rear-ranging process and make a diagram showing it.

Enrichment Have students choose one of the following activities:
(a) Identify areas in the local community where signs of erosion of land or shoreline are evident.

For every example, have students identify its probable source. (b) Report on the factors that led to the Dust Bowl. Discuss how soil erosion could create another Dust Bowl in the future.

Answers

1.1 REVIEWING THE FACTS (p. 25)

Define

1. *sea:* a body of salt water or area in an ocean
2. *gulf:* a part of a sea or ocean, partially surrounded by land, usually larger than a bay
3. *bay:* a body of salt water, partly enclosed by land, having an opening to the sea
4. *strait:* a narrow channel of water connecting two larger areas of water
5. *tributary:* a stream feeding a larger river or lake
6. *river system:* a river and all of its tributaries
7. *landform:* a natural feature of Earth's surface measured by elevation
8. *continent:* any of the seven largest of Earth's landmasses
9. *isthmus:* a narrow strip of land connecting two larger landmasses
10. *island:* a landmass smaller than a continent and surrounded by water
11. *archipelago:* a chain of islands
12. *peninsula:* a finger of land jutting out from a landmass
13. *cape:* a narrow piece of land reaching into the sea
14. *elevation:* the height of land above sea level
15. *sea level:* the level of the surface of the ocean
16. *mountain:* a high, rugged landform
17. *hill:* a raised area lower than a mountain
18. *plain:* a broad, flat land area
19. *plateau:* a broad, flat land area that is usually higher in elevation than a plain and is bordered by an escarpment

Answer

1. salt water, fresh water
2. (a) one of the seven largest landmasses on Earth (b) by volcanoes, by coral, and by sandbars 3. Answers will vary.

Locate

1. Andes Mountains in South America; Himalaya Mountains in Asia
2. Mediterranean Sea

SKILL WORKSHOP (p. 26)

1. Both are bodies of water that are partly surrounded by a landmass.

2. Both are land areas that reach into a body of water.
3. The source is the inland place the river begins; the mouth is the place the river empties into a body of water.
4. A tributary is a stream that flows into a river. A river and its tributaries are a river system.
5. An isthmus joins two larger land areas, while a peninsula juts into a body of water without connecting to another land area.

For a special challenge: The human-made body of water is the reservoir. It was formed by the building of a dam.

1.2 REVIEWING THE FACTS (p. 32)

Define

1. *theory:* an idea that seeks to explain how certain facts came to be
2. *continental drift:* the theory that holds that the continents broke off from a single landmass and began moving apart 200 million years ago
3. *crust:* the thin layer of rock just below Earth's surface
4. *mantle:* the thick layer of rock and metal below Earth's crust
5. *core:* the center part of Earth, made up of an outer layer of liquid metal and an inner layer of solid rock
6. *tectonic plate:* moving part of Earth's crust
7. *tectonic activity:* the movement and collision of tectonic plates
8. *rift:* a separation in Earth's crust caused when tectonic plates pull apart
9. *fold:* the buckling of Earth's crust when two sections push together
10. *faulting:* the breaking of Earth's crust due to tectonic activity
11. *fault:* a break in Earth's surface caused by faulting
12. *lava:* the melted rock that escapes from Earth's crust when a volcano erupts

Answer

1. Scientists have found that rock samples in Africa match samples in South America, that fossils of ancient plants from the two continents match despite climate differences, and that the ocean floor is spreading in some places.
2. Mountains are formed by folding, faulting, and volcanic action. *Examples:* by folding, the Appalachians; by faulting, the Sierra Nevada range; by volcanic action, the Hawaiian islands

Locate

1. North Carolina, Virginia, West Virginia, Pennsylvania 2. (a) Hawaii, Maui, Kauai, Molokai, Oahu (b) Hawaii

1. (a) northern (b) eastern 2. Mt. Whitney
3. Kern River

1.3 REVIEWING THE FACTS (p. 43)

Define

1. *erosion:* the process by which rock and soil are stripped away and moved
2. *silt:* tiny bits of earth carried and deposited by water
3. *delta:* an area near the mouth of a river, built up by deposits of silt
4. *glacier:* a body of moving ice
5. *moraine:* a ridge of soil and rock deposited by a retreating glacier
6. *fjord:* a steep valley formed by a glacier that has retreated and filled with sea water
7. *Ice Age:* a time in Earth's past when glacial activity was widespread
8. *loess:* wind-deposited silt
9. *continental shelf:* a coastal plain that extends under the ocean
10. *tsunami:* a giant ocean wave caused by an earthquake

Answer

1. (a) running water, glacial ice, wind, ocean waves (b) Running water breaks down rocks, carves valleys, and moves silt toward the ocean. Glaciers scour valleys, move rocks and soil, and form fjords and lakes. Wind moves soil and sand, smooths jagged rock surfaces, and builds dunes. Waves change shorelines, carrying away sand and rock from some places and depositing them elsewhere.
2. Rapidly flowing waters erode Earth's surface to carve valleys. Plains are built up when rivers deposit silt during floods. Near the ocean, rivers widen and lose speed; they deposit silt, building up deltas at their mouths.
3. Like land surfaces, the ocean floor has mountains, valleys, and canyons called trenches. Both earthquakes and volcanoes shape the floor of the ocean and land surfaces.

Locate

1. Kentucky, Tennessee, Mississippi
2. (a) Egypt, Sudan, Ethiopia, Uganda
   (b) Mediterranean Sea

GEOGRAPHY LABORATORY (pp. 44–45)

Speaking Geographically

1. Island does not belong, because unlike a cape and a peninsula it is completely surrounded by water.

2. Tributary does not belong; unlike a bay and a gulf it is not part of an ocean or sea.
3. Glacier does not belong, because it creates moraines and fjords.
4. Delta does not belong, because unlike loess and silt it is a landform.
5. Erosion does not belong; unlike faulting and folding it does not build mountains.
6. Tsunami does not belong, because unlike volcanoes and eruptions it is related to the size of ocean waves.
7. Plateau does not belong, because unlike hill and mountain it is a broad, flat land area.
8. Isthmus does not belong; unlike river and strait it is a land area, not a body of water.

Testing Yourself

1. oceans 2. continents 3. elevation
4. plains 5. hills 6. mountains 7. plateaus
8. continental drift 9. tectonic activity
10. folding 11. faulting 12. volcanic action
13. erosion

Building Map Skills

1. Arctic Ocean 2. Atlantic Ocean
3. Pacific Ocean 4. Indian Ocean
5. North America 6. South America
7. Europe 8. Asia 9. Africa
10. Australia 11. Antarctica

Applying Map Skills

1. north 2. southwest 3. north
4. south 5. east

SUPPLEMENTARY MATERIALS

Books

Asimov, Isaac, *How Did We Find Out About Volcanoes?*, Walker, 1981
Beiser, Arthur, *The Earth* (Life Nature Library), Time-Life, 1970
Goldner, Kathryn, and Carole G. Vogel, *Why Mount St. Henens Blew Its Top*, Dillon, 1981
Lampton, Christopher, *Planet Earth*, Franklin Watts, 1982
Smith, Sandra, *Discovering the Sea*, Rand McNally (Trewin Cobblestone Books), 1981

Other Media

Geology: *Our Dynamic Earth* (NG: filmstrips, including "The Face of the Earth," "The Changing Land," "The Restless Earth," "Geology and You"; cassettes)
The Fractured Look (NASA: film, shows how Landsat monitors fracturing of crust)
Recognizing Physical Features (CIM:film
The Rock Cycle (EB: film/video, Spanish version available)
Understanding Our Earth: Glaciers (CIM; film)

ASSIGNMENT GUIDE

■ **Text Features**

Map Workshop, p. 49   Spotlight, p. 57
Skill Workshop, p. 54   Chapter Review, pp. 74–75

■ **Teacher's Resource Binder**

Assign after
p. 49 Map Workshop: Reading a Weather Map WB p. 21
p. 52 Building Basics Worksheet 2.1
      Independent Practice Worksheet 2.1 WB p. 17
p. 54 Skill Workshop: Interpreting a Diagram WB p. 22
p. 56 Building Basics Worksheet 2.2
      Independent Practice Worksheet 2.2 WB p. 18
p. 60 Building Basics Worksheet 2.3
      Independent Practice Worksheet 2.3 WB p. 19
p. 73 Building Basics Worksheet 2.4
      Independent Practice Worksheet 2.4 WB p. 20
p. 75 Map Test 2
      Chapter Test 2
      Enrichment Chapter 2 WB p. 23

■ **Geography Laboratory Manual: Investigating Chapter 2**

Use with pages 46–75

OVERVIEW

This chapter examines the factors that influence climate and weather : the sun; the Earth's rotation on its axis and its movement around the sun; latitude; water and its changes through the hydrologic cycle; wind; ocean currents; elevation; and an area's nearness to water. The final section examines the differences in temperature, yearly precipitation, humidity, and season length between the six major climate types—humid tropical, subtropical, dry, mid-latitude, cold polar, and highland.

INTRODUCING THE CHAPTER

Ask the class what they think of when they hear the words *weather* and *climate*. Point out that the two terms do not mean the same thing. Have students read the first paragraph of Section 1 on page 47 to understand these differences. Ask students to think about when people in a community might likely be concerned about weather, about climate: Which

are students themselves more likely to be interested in—weather or climate? Why? Then tell the class that in this chapter, they will be looking closely at the facets that influence both weather and climate and at the kinds of climates found around the world.

2.1 The Sun and Climate (pages 47–52)

MAIN IDEAS

■ The sun has great influence on Earth's climate and weather.
■ The amount of the sun's energy a place receives varies because of the way Earth moves in space.
■ The amount of energy Earth receives from the sun changes with latitude.

19T

VOCABULARY

weather, p. 47; climate, p. 47; radiation, p. 47; rotation, p. 48; axis, p. 48; revolution, p. 48; orbit, p. 48; equinox, p. 51; solstice, p. 51; latitude, p. 51; Tropic of Cancer, p. 51; Tropic of Capricorn, p. 51; tropics, p. 51; polar region, p. 51; temperate zone, p. 52

OBJECTIVES

Students should be able to:
- discuss the impact the sun's energy has on Earth's climate and weather.
- understand Earth's rotation on its axis and its revolution around the sun.
- explain the relationship between latitude and climate.

TEACHING STRATEGIES

Discussing the Sun's Impact on Climate and Weather Remind students that weather is the condition of the air at any one time, and climate is the pattern of weather over a period of time. Draw two circles on the board, labeling one "Earth," the other "sun." Have students come to the board to diagram the relationship between the sun and Earth and to discuss the process. (The diagram would show rays from the sun reaching Earth. Arrows would show that some of the sun's energy is reflected back into space, and some is absorbed into the atmosphere.) Ask how this energy affects temperature. (The more heat retained on Earth, the warmer the temperature.) Ask how day and night affect temperature. (Nights are cooler because they are not receiving the sun's heat.)

Understanding the Earth's Movement and the Sun Divide the class into three groups. Ask two members from each group to play the roles of sun and Earth. The first group should present to the class how Earth's rotation on its axis causes day and night. The second group should show how Earth's revolution around the sun causes seasons and why it is fall and winter in the Northern Hemisphere when it is spring and summer in the southern Hemisphere. Finally, the third group should explain the differences between the equinox and the solstice and why the shortest day of the year—the winter solstice—in the Northern Hemisphere, is the longest day of the year—the summer solstice—in the Southern Hemisphere.

Explaining Relationships between Latitude and Climate Tell students that the amount of energy received from the sun changes with latitude. Have students discuss why each of the following statements is true: (a) Most places in the tropics or low latitudes have a warm climate. (The tropics always receive the sun's most direct rays.) (b) Places in the polar regions or high latitudes have a cold climate with short summers. (These areas receive no sun some of the year and during the rest, only slanting or indirect rays.) (c) Most places in the middle latitudes have a temperate climate, warmer than the polar regions and cooler than the tropics. (The sun's rays reach Earth at a high angle for part of the year and at a slant for the rest of the year.)

CHECK FOR UNDERSTANDING

Have students write a few sentences explaining how Earth's movements—rotation and revolution—affect temperature and climate and how latitude affects climate.

CORRECTIONS/EXTENSIONS

Reteaching Make a two-column chart on the chalkboard. Label the columns *Cause* and *Effect*. Have class members complete the chart by indicating what effect each of the following factors has on the temperature and climate of Earth. (a) radiation of the sun's energy (provides heat to Earth), (b) rotation of Earth on its axis (creates days and nights), (c) revolution of Earth around the sun (results in seasons), (d) latitude (a place's distance north or south of the equator affects how much sun it receives).

Enrichment After the class has read the Map Workshop feature on page 49, ask students to bring to class a current national weather map. Have each student find an example of a cold front, a warm front, or a stationary front on the weather map and indicate the direction in which the front is moving. After viewing the map, the class can make predictions about the type of weather their area can expect for the next two or three days. Write predictions on the chalkboard and have the class check their accuracy by listening to or reading newspaper weather reports for the time period.

2.2 Water and Climate
(pages 53–56)

MAIN IDEAS

- The hydrologic cycle—the constant movement of water from ocean to air to land and back to ocean—is one way water influences Earth's climate.

- The steps in the hydrologic cycle work to balance one another and vary from region to region.

VOCABULARY

hydrologic cycle, p. 53; water vapor, p. 53; evaporation, p. 53; transpiration, p. 53; condensation, p. 55; precipitation, p. 55; groundwater, p. 55

OBJECTIVES

Students should be able to:
- describe the hydrologic cycle and how it affects Earth's climate.
- analyze changes in the water balance.

TEACHING STRATEGIES

Describing the Hydrologic Cycle Ask students to turn to the diagram on page 54. Remind the class that a cycle is a series of events that happen one after another over and over again. Have students define the following terms in the diagram: evaporation (the process by which water becomes water vapor), transpiration (the process by which water from plant pores becomes water vapor), condensation (water vapor becomes droplets of water), precipitation (water that falls to the ground as rain, snow, sleet, or hail), groundwater (water deep in the earth that supplies springs and wells). Then discuss the interplay of each term in the process.

Analyzing Changes in the Water Balance State that the water cycle is like a natural checks and balance system. Each part keeps the others in balance. Tell students to remember that the balancing systems vary from place to place depending on the conditions there. Discuss this delicate balance in terms of a rain forest (where precipitation is so heavy that water cannot be stored) and a desert (where heat causes water to evaporate before it reaches the ground).

CHECK FOR UNDERSTANDING

Have students use the seven terms listed in "Reviewing the Facts" on page 56 to write a paragraph describing the hydrologic cycle.

CORRECTIONS/EXTENSIONS

Reteaching Divide the class into small groups. Assign each group a different geographic region. Have each group create a diagram showing the steps in the hydrologic cycle for their particular region, giving attention to the

way the water balance can be disrupted. (freezing, flooding, drought) Have groups present their diagrams to the class.

Enrichment Have students look in newspapers for examples of the effects of unexpected or seasonal changes in the water balance, such as torrential rains or spring thaws that cause landslides and flooding or droughts that cause crop failure and famines. As students find articles, they can indicate whether the imbalance is the result of an increase or decrease in precipitation and whether it is the result of a seasonal change.

2.3 Other Factors Affecting Climate
(pages 56–60)

MAIN IDEAS

- Winds affect climate by moving warm or cold air and moisture.
- Ocean currents affect climate by distributing heat or cold and moisture in certain patterns throughout the world.
- Large bodies of water moderate the climate of the land nearby them.
- Temperatures change with elevation.

VOCABULARY

prevailing wind, p. 56; monsoon, p. 56; current, p. 58; marine, p. 59; continental, p. 59; windward, p. 60; leeward, p. 60

OBJECTIVES

Students should be able to:
- describe how winds affect climate.
- describe how ocean currents affect climate.
- explain the moderating effects by bodies of water on climate.
- discuss how elevation affects climate.

TEACHING STRATEGIES

Describing How Winds Affect Climate Ask class members to explain the difference between prevailing winds and monsoons. (Prevailing winds blow constantly from one direction. Monsoons change their direction seasonally.) Direct students' attention to the map on page 56. Ask: What type of wind patterns does the map show? (prevailing winds) How do they affect the climate? (They bring the temperatures from their place of origin. They also bring moisture from the sea.)

Describing How Ocean Currents Affect Climate Ask students how ocean currents are like prevailing winds. (They follow certain patterns of motion, carrying with them heat and cold.) Direct students to the map of world ocean currents on page 58. Have class members use the map to describe how currents affect land temperatures.

Explaining the Moderating Effects of Bodies of Water on Climate Ask a student to explain the moderating effects of bodies of water on climate. Write key points on the chalkboard. Make sure students understand the relationship between water temperature and air temperature. (Large bodies of water do not gain or lose heat as quickly as nearby land does. The water's temperature affects the air above it, which also remains moderate. As the air circulates, it spreads its effect throughout the area.)

Discussing How Elevation Affects Climate Ask a student to describe how elevation affects climate temperature. (The higher you go, the colder it gets.) Ask the class to give an example of where they might be surprised to find a cold climate. (in highland regions near the equator) Ask the class how mountains and bodies of water together make certain kinds of climate. (Mountains block the moderating winds coming off the ocean from reaching an area.)

CHECK FOR UNDERSTANDING

Have students use the maps on pages 56 and 58 to explain how an area's weather and climate would be affected by each of the following: (a) North Polar Easterly prevailing winds, (b) the Gulf Stream, (c) nearness to the Atlantic Ocean, (d) location in a valley on the leeward side of the Sierra Nevada Mountains, (e) location on the windward slope of the Sierra Nevada Mountains.

CORRECTIONS/EXTENSIONS

Reteaching Have students write one or two sentences explaining how each of the following affect climate: wind patterns, ocean currents, an area's nearness to water, and an area's elevation. Pair students so that they can exchange and check answers.

Enrichment Have the class read the special feature "Spotlight on Monsoons" on page 56. Students can then find out more about monsoons and how they affect people and landforms. Encourage students to look in newspapers for reports of monsoons.

2.4 Climates of the World *(pages 62–73)*

MAIN IDEAS

■ The six climate groups of the world—humid tropical, subtropical, dry, mid-latitude, cold polar, and highland—differ in average temperature, length of seasons, yearly precipitation, and humidity.

VOCABULARY

humid, p. 62; arid, p. 67; semiarid, p. 67; subarctic, p. 70; permafrost, p. 71; tree line, p. 73

OBJECTIVE

Students should be able to:
■ identify climate groups by investigating temperature, length of season, amount of precipitation, temperature, and humidity.

TEACHING STRATEGIES

Identifying Climate Groups Have the class begin by comparing the graphs on page 61. Next ask students to turn to the climate map on pages 64–65. Compare the major climate groups within each major climate group. Ask: Where would the following be most likely to happen? Hottest daytime temperatures in the world? (arid climates) Climates that are warmer than their latitude suggests because their temperatures are moderated by ocean currents? (temperate marine) during one season, streams overflow; during another, the soil is parched? (wet-and-dry tropical)

CHECK FOR UNDERSTANDING

Ask students to select one climate group discussed in this section and write a paragraph explaining how a variety of the following factors affect it: latitude, nearness to a large water body, degree of precipitation, and elevation.

CORRECTIONS/EXTENSIONS

Reteaching Make a five-column chart on the chalkboard. Across the top write: *Climate, Types of Climate within Climate Group, Average Temperature* (i.e., high, moderate, low), *Seasons* (a brief description), and *Example* (select a city from the map on pages 64–65). In the first column, list the following: Humid Tropical, Subtropical, Dry, Mid-Latitude, Cold

Polar, Highland. Have students take turns at the board filling in the columns.

Enrichment Ask students to think about a climate they might like to visit. Have each student prepare a climate graph for a city in that area. The completed graphs can become part of a bulletin board display.

Answers

MAP WORKSHOP (p. 49)

1. (a) October 15, 1987 (b) autumn
2. (a) red (b) blue 3. (a) Denver, Fargo, Minneapolis (b) Oklahoma City, Memphis, Atlanta, New Orleans 4. no 5. (a) colder (b) The map indicates a warm front moving southeast toward Salt Lake City. 6. stay the same

2.1 REVIEWING THE FACTS (p. 52)

Define

1. *weather:* the condition of the air at any given time
2. *climate:* the pattern of weather in a given place over many years
3. *radiation:* the sun's rays
4. *rotation:* the spinning of Earth on its axis
5. *axis:* an imaginary line through the center of Earth from pole to pole
6. *revolution:* the movement of Earth around the sun
7. *orbit:* the nearly circular path of a planet or other body
8. *equinox:* the times of year at which the number of daylight hours and the number of nighttime hours are exactly the same all around the world
9. *solstice:* the times of year at which the difference between the length of the day and the length of the night are at a maximum
10. *latitude:* the distance north or south of the equator
11. *Tropic of Cancer:* the line of latitude 23½° north of the equator
12. *Tropic of Capricorn:* the line of latitude 23½° south of the equator
13. *tropics:* the latitudes that are between the Tropic of Cancer and the Tropic of Capricorn
14. *polar region:* an area north of 66½° N or south of 66½° S
15. *temperate zone:* the area between the tropics and the polar regions

Answer

1. (a) rotation (b) revolution
2. (a) spring or summer (b) fall or winter
3. in the tropics, because they receive the most direct sunlight year-round

Locate

1. Mexico
2. Brazil, Paraguay, Argentina, Chile

SKILL WORKSHOP (p. 54)

1. precipitation, evaporation, transpiration, condensation 2. (a) lakes, streams, plants, oceans (b) It holds .005 percent of all water. 3. rain, sleet, hail, snow 4. Groundwater seeps into a body of water and eventually evaporates. 5. evaporation, transpiration

2.2 REVIEWING THE FACTS (p. 56)

Define

1. *hydrologic cycle:* the process by which water constantly changes form, moving from ocean to air to land and back to ocean
2. *water vapor:* water in gaseous form
3. *evaporation:* the process by which bodies of water give off water vapor
4. *transpiration:* the process by which plants give off water vapor
5. *condensation:* the process by which water vapor changes into water
6. *precipitation:* water that falls to the ground as rain, sleet, hail, or snow
7. *groundwater:* underground water

Answer

1. (a) As temperatures increase, both transpiration and evaporation increase. Both processes slow down as temperature decreases. (b) Some falls directly into bodies of water; some falls on land and runs off into streams and rivers; some seeps underground.
2. (a) The amount of precipitation is balanced by evaporation, storage, and runoff. (b) In wet regions, most precipitation becomes runoff because the ground is already holding its maximum groundwater. In dry regions, more water evaporates than falls.

Locate

1. Arctic, Atlantic, Pacific, Indian
2. (a) Atlantic (b) Pacific

2.3 REVIEWING THE FACTS (p. 60)

Define

1. *prevailing wind:* a wind that blows from a constant direction
2. *monsoon:* a wind that brings a wet season and a dry season to parts of Asia
3. *current:* the motion of water
4. *marine:* having to do with the ocean; a climate moderated by a nearby ocean

5. *continental:* a climate not moderated by nearness to an ocean
6. *windward:* the side of a mountain or other place that faces the wind
7. *leeward:* the side of a mountain or other place that faces away from the wind

Answer

1. Winds and ocean currents distribute hot or cold air and moisture.
2. (a) Bodies of water moderate climate. (b) Water is slow to gain heat during the day, so it cools nearby areas during hot times. It is slow to lose heat at night, so it keeps nearby areas warm during cold periods.
3. (a) Temperatures cool at higher elevations. Mountains may also block wind and rain; leeward areas thus get less moisture than windward areas. (b) The mountain will be cooler.

Locate

1. (a) South America (b) cold
2. North America

SKILL WORKSHOP (p. 61)

1. Singapore
2. (a) July (b) January, November, December
3. (a) Bombay (b) Bombay
4. March, August, October
5. January–April, December
6. The two cities have nearly equal annual temperatures.
7. (a) April (b) January (c) April–October (d) December–January
8. (a) January, November, December (b) September
9. Answers will vary.

2.4 REVIEWING THE FACTS (p. 73)

Define

1. *humid:* a wet or damp climate
2. *arid:* a dry climate
3. *semiarid:* a dry climate with a wet season and a dry season
4. *subarctic:* a climate that, because of its nearness to the poles, is cold
5. *permafrost:* a layer of soil frozen all year round
6. *tree line:* an imaginary line at an elevation above which trees cannot grow

Answer

1. (a) Both are warm all year round. (b) Humid subtropical climates have more frequent and heavier rains than Mediterranean subtropical.
2. arid, in which there is little rain all year, and semiarid, in which there is a wet season.
3. *Temperate marine* climates are moderated by the ocean, which brings rain and extra warmth. *Humid continental* climates have precipitation that occurs evenly throughout the year, cool winters, and warm summers. *Subarctic* climates are found near the Arctic Circle; winters are long and very cold; summers are short and cool.
(a) subpolar and polar (b) highland climates vary with elevation. At very high elevations, the climate resembles polar climates.

Locate

1. Los Angeles, California
2. Dakar, Kinshasa, Lagos, Nairobi

GEOGRAPHY LABORATORY (pp. 74–75)

Speaking Geographically

1. weather 2. climate 3. rotation 4. axis
5. revolution 6. orbit 7. equinox
8. solstices 9. latitude 10. Humid, arid

Testing Yourself

1. rotation 2. tilt 3. solstices 4. fall
5. tropics 6. condensation 7. tropical

Building Map Skills

10—India	9—Singapore
8—Brazil	7—China
6—France	5—Sudan
3—Canada	2—Soviet Union
1—United States	4—Australia

Applying Map Skills

1. (a) India: New Delhi, 29°N; Brazil: Brasília, 16°S; France: Paris, 49°N; Canada: Ottawa, 45°N; United States: Washington, D.C. 39°N; Singapore: Singapore, 2°N; China: Beijing, 40°N; Sudan: Khartoum, 16°N; Soviet Union: Moscow, 55°N; Australia: Canberra, 35°S (b) Singapore (c) Moscow
2. humid subtropical

SUPPLEMENTARY MATERIALS

Books

Besier, Arthur, *The Earth*, Time-Life, 1970
Branley, Franklin M., *Water for the World*, Thomas Y. Crowell, 1982
National Geographic, *An Introduction to Weather*, 1981
Sattler, Helen R., *Nature's Weather Forecasters*, Nelson, 1978

Other Media

Understanding Weather and Climate (SVE, #404-SR-set: 6 filmstrips and 3 records)
Water: A Precious Resource (NG: film/video, includes sequence on hydrologic cycle)
The Water Cycle (EB; film/video)
Weather (SSSS: transparencies)
Weather and Climate (TERF: filmstrip)

3 Ecosystems: A Living Network *(pages 76–101)*

ASSIGNMENT GUIDE

■ *Text Features*

Map Workshop, p. 80   Spotlight, p. 92
Skill Workshop, p. 88   Chapter Review, pp. 100–101

■ *Teacher's Resource Binder*

Assign after
p. 79   Building Basics Worksheet 3.1
         Independent Practice Worksheet 3.1 WB p. 24
p. 80   Map Workshop: Reading an Annual Rainfall Map WB p. 28
p. 87   Building Basics Worksheet 3.2
         Independent Practice Worksheet 3.2 WB p. 25
p. 88   Skill Workshop: Interpreting Landsat Images WB p. 29
p. 96   Building Basics Worksheet 3.3
         Independent Practice Worksheet 3.3 WB p. 26
p. 99   Building Basics Worksheet 3.4
         Independent Practice Worksheet 3.4 WB p. 27
p. 101   Map Test 3
         Chapter Test 3
         Enrichment Chapter 3 WB p. 30

■ *Geography Laboratory Manual: Investigating Chapter 3*

Use with pages 76–101

■ *Overhead Transparency 3 and Worksheet*

Use with pages 76–101

OVERVIEW

Chapter 3 explores Earth's physical environments—or ecosystems—and how they interconnect. Students will learn about the forest and grassland ecosystems where most of Earth's people live. They will also learn about the more harsh polar, desert, mountain, and oceanic ecosystems. The chapter concludes by exploring the ways ecological balances within these ecosystems are endangered by nature and humans.

INTRODUCING THE CHAPTER

Direct students to the photographs on page 76. Point out the differences in the colors on the surface of the three planets, focusing particularly on the photograph of Earth. Have the class read the chapter introduction. Then remind the class of the chapter title. Have students speculate on why Earth seen from space might have been chosen to introduce a chapter that talks about Earth as a "Living Network." Ask: What is a network? (a system of lines that cross or are related to each other) Suggest that Earth seen from space shows how closely land, water, and atmosphere are tied to each other.

3.1 Our Environment: A Network of Ecosystems
(pages 77–80)

MAIN IDEAS

- Earth's surface is a vast network of different interconnected environmental systems called ecosystems.
- Plant life, or vegetation, is an important living element in ecosystems.

VOCABULARY

physical environment, p. 77; ecosystem, p. 78; vegetation, p. 78; soil, p. 78; succession, p. 78; climax, p. 78; climax vegetation, p. 78

OBJECTIVES

Students should be able to:
- understand the concept of ecosystems.
- trace the development of vegetation.

TEACHING STRATEGIES

Understanding Ecosystems   Write the words *climate, soil,* and *vegetation* on the chalkboard. Have class members explain how each of these factors affect an ecosystem's development. (Climate affects what type of plant and animal life live in a certain place. Soil affects the type of plants that can grow in a certain place. Plants protect and nourish the soil and provide food for some animals.)

Tracing the Development of Vegetation Divide the class into small groups. Have each group make a diagram illustrating the stages of succession and climax that can be seen after a fire has destroyed a forest. (See pages 78–79.) Students should label the parts of their diagrams and give them titles.

CHECK FOR UNDERSTANDING

Have students write a paragraph defining an ecosystem. They should explain why climate, soil, and plant life are the three most important factors in an ecosystem.

CORRECTIONS/EXTENSIONS

Reteaching   Divide the class into small groups. Have each group write a few sentences explaining the main ideas from each subsection. Have groups compare papers for accuracy.

Enrichment   Have the class write short research papers on how forest fires affect vegetation growth in forests. Students should be encouraged to use newspapers to document actual forest fires.

3.2 Forest and Grassland Environments
(pages 81–87)

MAIN IDEAS

- The forest and grassland ecosystems are the richest in plant and animal life.
- The main forms of vegetation in a forest ecosystem are trees, including needleleaf, broadleaf, and rain forests.
- Vegetation in grassland ecosystems—prairies, savannas, and steppes—is a variety of tall, medium, or short grasses.

VOCABULARY

needleleaf, p. 81; broadleaf, p. 81; rain forest, p. 84; nutrient, p. 85; pampas, p. 85; savanna, p. 85; prairie, p. 86; steppe, p. 87; irrigation, p. 87

OBJECTIVES

Students should be able to:
- identify needleleaf, broadleaf, and rain forest trees.
- distinguish between grassland ecosystems.

TEACHING STRATEGIES

Identifying Needleleaf, Broadleaf, and Rain Forest Trees   Divide the class into three groups. Ask each group to find or draw pictures of the three different types of forest—broadleaf, needleleaf, rain. Ask the class whether rain forest leaves more closely resemble broadleaf or needleleaf trees. (broadleaf) Ask students to explain how rain forest leaves differ from other broadleaf leaves. (They keep their leaves all year round.) Which kind of forest is most common? (needleleaf)

Distinguishing between Grassland Ecosystems   Have several class members explain how the grasses found in prairie, savanna, and steppe ecosystems differ. (The main difference is height and thickness.) Ask students to identify the main reason for these differences. (precipitation) Then have the class turn to the ecosystem map on pages 82–83 and locate a prairie, savanna, and steppe area. Work with students in seeing that the rainfall map on page 80 confirms what they have learned about the link between precipitation and vegetation.

CHECK FOR UNDERSTANDING

Ask each student to write one paragraph explaining how climate and rainfall affect the vegetation in the three types of forest ecosystems discussed in this section. Then have class members write a second paragraph explaining how climate and rainfall affect the vegetation in grassland ecosystems.

CORRECTIONS/EXTENSIONS

Reteaching   Make a five-column chart on the chalkboard. Label the columns *Forest Ecosystem, Types of Trees, Most Common Climate*

Region, Precipitation Needs (amount needed for plants to grow), Uses of Forest Products. In the first column, list needleleaf forest, broadleaf forest, and rain forest. Have students complete the remaining columns. Ask students to make a similar chart for grassland environments labeling the columns Grassland Ecosystem, Height of Grass, Most Common Climate, and Precipitation Needs.

Enrichment   Ask students to do short research reports on the changes taking place in the rain forest ecosystems of the Amazon Basin. These can then be presented to the class.

3.3 Polar, Desert, Mountain, and Oceanic Environments (pages 89–96)

MAIN IDEAS

- Polar region, desert, and mountain environments experience more extreme conditions than forests and grasslands.
- Oceans have ecosystems as land areas do.

VOCABULARY

polar ice cap, p. 90; adaptation, p. 90; tundra, p. 90; desert, p. 91; oasis, p. 93; hibernate, p. 95

OBJECTIVE

Students should be able to:
- understand how adaptation helps plants and animals survive in a harsh environment.

TEACHING STRATEGIES

Understanding Adaptation   Have the class read "Spotlight on Deserts" on page 92. Next have a class member define the term "adaptation." Ask the class for examples of how plants and animals adapt to their environments. Encourage class members to cite examples of human adaptations to extreme environments.

CHECK FOR UNDERSTANDING

Have students identify the factors that make the climate in each of the following ecosystems harsh: (a) polar (extreme cold), (b) desert (dryness or lack of water), (c) mountain (great variations in rainfall and temperature within a short period of time), (d) ocean (fish are constantly prey for other fish).

CORRECTIONS/EXTENSIONS

Reteaching   Have students write a few sentences describing each of the words in "Reviewing the Facts" on page 96.

Enrichment   Divide the class into four groups. Have each group prepare a poster or collage showing one of the ecosystems discussed in this section. The poster should indicate the climate, the types of plant and animal life found in the ecosystem, and the adaptations humans must make to live in this type of environment. Have each group present and explain its poster to the class. The poster can then be used as a bulletin board display.

3.4 Changes in Ecosystems (pages 96–99)

MAIN IDEA

- The balance in an ecosystem can be upset by natural disasters or by human activity.

VOCABULARY

acid rain, p. 98

OBJECTIVE

Students should be able to:
- identify activities that upset the balance in ecosystems.

TEACHING STRATEGIES

Identifying Activities That Upset the Balance in Ecosystems   Make a three-column chart on the chalkboard. Label columns Activity, Purpose, Costs to the Environment. In the first column, list the following activities: (a) making steppe lands into farmlands, (b) cutting or burning forests, (c) building dams, (d) irrigation. Have class members complete the chart.

CHECK FOR UNDERSTANDING

Ask each class member to write the following words on a sheet of paper: land, water, and atmosphere. Tell students to leave several lines of space between each word. Then have students write examples of ways pollution or misuse of land, water, or air can affect ecosystems.

CORRECTIONS/EXTENSIONS

Reteaching   Write the chapter title on the chalkboard: "Ecosystems: A Living Network."

Have class members point out ways that the environmental problems discussed in this section show that Earth's ecosystems are closely tied to each other. Through discussion, students should recognize that upsetting the balance in one ecosystem such as a rain forest or an ocean ecosystem can have long-term effects on other ecosystems as well.

Enrichment Ask students to bring a newspaper article to class on one of the following: problems in land use, problems in water use, or atmospheric or ocean pollution. Students should indicate where the problem exists, the causes of the problem, what its affects on the environment are, and what efforts, if any, are being made to correct the problem. Students should also consider whether they think the problem is likely to be corrected or get worse in the future.

Answers

3.1 REVIEWING THE FACTS (p. 79)
Define
1. *physical environment:* the nonliving elements and living things on Earth
2. *ecosystem:* an environment including its living and nonliving elements and the ways they work together
3. *vegetation:* plant life
4. *soil:* a mixture of rock particles and decayed plant matter
5. *succession:* a gradual change in an ecosystem as old plants are replaced
6. *climax:* the final stage of succession in an ecosystem
7. *climax vegetation:* the permanent plant life of an ecosystem, which—left undisturbed—keeps renewing itself

Answer
1. (a) climate, soil, plant life (b) Climate helps determine which plants and animals can survive in an area. The kind of soil in an area affects plant growth. Plants help soil by holding it in place and depositing dead leaves and nutrients in it. 2. soil and climate

Locate
1. (a) tundra, evergreen, mid-latitude broadleaf, tropical rain forest, savanna, prairie, steppe, desert, ice cap, mountain (b) gray 2. tundra

MAP WORKSHOP (p. 80)

1. Europe (Students may realize that, despite its low precipitation, Antarctica also has no deserts.) 2. (a) southeastern (b) western

3. equator 4. Rainfall grows heavier.
5. southwestern

For a special challenge: North America—evergreen forest; South America—savanna; Europe—evergreen or temperate climate broadleaf; Asia—tropical rain forest or evergreen forest; Africa—savanna; Australia—savanna; Antarctica—no areas receive this precipitation

3.2 REVIEWING THE FACTS (p. 87)
Define
1. *needleleaf:* having needle-shaped leaves; such trees usually keep their leaves year round
2. *broadleaf:* having wide leaves; such trees usually lose their leaves in the fall
3. *rain forest:* a dense tropical forest that receives heavy rainfall
4. *nutrient:* a substance in the soil that nourishes plants
5. *savanna:* a medium-length grassland
6. *prairie:* a grassland with tall grasses
7. *pampa:* a prairie in southern South America
8. *steppe:* a grassland with short grasses and almost no trees
9. *irrigation:* the bringing of water to fields

Answer
1. (a) They cut trees for lumber for building and for wood pulp to make paper. (b) Broadleaf forests exist in moderate climate areas, where people have cut trees for farms and cities and to provide lumber and pulp. (c) The heavy rains wash away the soil's nutrients.
2. (a) prairie, because it gets adequate rainfall and has a moderate climate (b) steppe, because it gets little rainfall and is subject to droughts
3. large areas of prairie and steppe; a small area of savanna

Locate
1. (a) west and central (b) north central
2. Africa

SKILL WORKSHOP (p. 88)

1. (a) snow, ice (b) high elevation
2. rocks and soil, rangeland
3. muddy, silted, or polluted water that is shallow; probably a river
4. an area of vegetation
5. This is an area of high elevation, with many valleys (shown by the white, brown, and yellow colors on the Landsat image). There are few towns, cities, or highways (because there is no bluish-gray or bluish-black on the image). Because of the little pink or brown, there is little harvested cropland.

3.3 REVIEWING THE FACTS (p. 96)

Define

1. *polar ice cap:* the parts of the Arctic and Antarctica that are always covered with ice
2. *adaptation:* the adjustment of plants and animals to environment
3. *tundra:* the area south of the Arctic ice cap that has a permanently frozen layer of ground, short summers, and small, hardy plants
4. *desert:* a region with a very dry climate and little vegetation
5. *oasis:* a place in the desert that is supplied with fresh water
6. *hibernate:* to pass the winter in a sleepy, inactive condition

Answer

1. (a) People live in polar regions by hunting and fishing. Nomadic herders, depending on oases, live in deserts. Some people irrigate desert areas to farm. Very few people live high in the mountains. (b) Tundra plants have short root systems that do not reach the permafrost; they also have strong stems. Desert plants have tough skin and few leaves, enabling them to keep what water they absorb. Mountain plants grow quickly during the warm months and lie dormant in winter.
2. Any change can upset these ecosystems. Vehicle tracks remain in tundra for years. Lack of vegetation means that erosion occurs easily.
3. (a) microscopic fish and plants, fish, fish-eating birds, coral reefs; cold and warm currents (b) Fish are an important food resource.

Locate

1. Australia (Students may also answer Antarctica.) 2. Africa, Asia

3.4 REVIEWING THE FACTS (p. 99)

Define

acid rain: rainwater that has chemically changed into an acid through contact with air pollution

Answer

1. Farming of steppe lands has contributed to erosion. Overgrazing has destroyed some African grasslands, contributing to drought and erosion. Slash-and-burn farming has destroyed wildlife. Improper disposal of wastes has polluted air and water.
2. Dams hold back silt, reducing the deposits made by rivers. Downstream plains may become less fertile and dry out as a result. Irrigation can also reduce the supply of groundwater and cause harmful mineral salts to build up on soils.

Locate

1. North America, Europe, Asia
2. Antarctica

GEOGRAPHY LABORATORY (pp. 100–101)

Speaking Geographically

1. An ecosystem is a specific physical environment.
2. Vegetation grows in soil. Soil nourishes vegetation; vegetation protects soil and adds to its nutrients.
3. Climax vegetation is the final stage of succession.
4. Needleleaf and broadleaf are two kinds of forest ecosystems.
5. Prairie and savanna are two kinds of grassland ecosystems.
6. An oasis is an area with fresh water in a desert.

Testing Yourself

1. keep their leaves all year long 2. broadleaf 3. low 4. savannas 5. no trees 6. irrigation 7. acid rain

Building Map Skills

1. Himalayas in Asia
2. Appalachians in N. America
3. Alps in Europe 4. Rockies in N. America
5. Andes in S. America
6. Atlas in Africa

Applying Map Skills

1. tropical rain forest, savanna
2. evergreen and mid-latitude broadleaf forest
3. savanna, mid-latitude broadleaf forest, desert, rain forest, mountain, steppe, prairie
4. northern Europe, Asia, and N. America

SUPPLEMENTARY MATERIALS

Books

Lerner, Carol, *Seasons of the Tallgrass Prairie,* Morrow, 1980

National Geographic, *The Desert Realm: Lands of Majesty and Mystery,* 1982

Perry, Richard, *Life in Forest and Jungle,* Taplinger, 1975

Other Media

A Desert's Living Sands (NG: film/video)

Exploring Ecology (NG: 5 sound filmstrips, including "The Mountain," "The River," "The Woodland," "The Prairie," "The Swamp")

The Grasslands (EB: film/video, Spanish version available)

The Sea: Mysteries of the Deep (EB: film/video, Spanish version available)

Water Pollution (WS: filmstrips and cassettes)

4 Earth's Resources *(pages 102–121)*

OVERVIEW

The chapter begins by defining the term *natural resource* and identifying ways resource needs and uses change. Students learn that the resource base humans rely on is divided into three groups—water and soil, plants and animals, and minerals. The next three sections of the chapter examine each of these resource groups in detail. The final section explores the methods people have developed to wisely manage soil, water, and mineral use.

INTRODUCING THE CHAPTER

Introduce the chapter by asking the class what they think of when they hear the term "natural resources." Write responses on the chalkboard. Then tell the class that in this chapter they will be looking at Earth's three main groups of resources—water and soil, plants and animals,

and minerals—and at the problems caused by the misuse of these resources.

4.1 Resources: An Overview *(pages 103–104)*

MAIN IDEAS

■ People rely on the natural resources of water and soil, plants and animals, and minerals.
■ The supply of natural resources varies in quantity and from place to place.

VOCABULARY

natural resource, p. 103; raw material, p. 103; recyclable resource, p. 104; renewable resource, p. 104; nonrenewable resource, p. 104

OBJECTIVES

Students should be able to:
- identify various uses of raw materials.
- explain the concept of resource distribution.

TEACHING STRATEGIES

Identifying Uses of Raw Materials Remind students that, with the exception of water, few resources are used in their original form. Now ask students to name ten or twelve items commonly found in the classroom or in a home. List these on the chalkboard. Finally, next to each item, have students name the natural resources or raw materials from which each of these goods is made. Ask students to think about how, over time, one resource replaces another resource. Ask students to think of examples.

Explaining Resource Distribution Have students identify ecosystems that are most likely to provide the greatest resources for living. Then have students list the types of natural resources each of the ecosystems they studied in Chapter 3 is likely to provide. Point out that answers to this question are not always obvious. Desert ecosystems, for example, might seem to be resource poor. However, the Arabian Peninsula, which is almost entirely desert and steppe ecosystems, is rich in energy resources but limited in water resources.

CHECK FOR UNDERSTANDING

On a sheet of paper, have students write the names of the three main groups of resources (water and soil, plants and animals, minerals), giving examples of each one.

CORRECTIONS/EXTENSIONS

Reteaching Ask students to write a definition of a natural resource (any material or element from the environment that is used by humans) and give one example of how our need for a resource may change (such as a decrease in the use of whale oil or an increase in the need for petroleum).

Enrichment Have students prepare a bulletin board display showing examples of renewable, recyclable, and nonrenewable resources. The display might provide a definition of each type of resource and then use illustrations from magazines and newspapers to show examples of each type of resource.

4.2 Water and Soil Resources *(pages 105–108)*

MAIN IDEAS

- Water is essential to human life.
- Soil is an essential natural resource to humans.

VOCABULARY

topsoil, p. 107; parent material, p. 107; mechanical weathering, p. 107; chemical weathering, p. 107; humus, p. 107; leach, p. 108

OBJECTIVES

Students should be able to:
- identify water resource distribution patterns.
- understand soil content.

TEACHING STRATEGIES

Identifying Water Resource Distribution Patterns Have students explain why water is considered a recyclable resource. (It is neither created nor destroyed by natural forces.) Why have farmers found living in river valleys desirable? (Rivers supply fresh water and provide rich soil.) Then direct students to the map on pages 64–65. Have class members draw on their knowledge of climate differences to identify regions that are rich or poor in water resources. Next have the class explain how too much water can be as much of a problem as too little water and how the water resources of an area can vary greatly, depending upon seasonal changes or changes in weather patterns.

Understanding Soil Content Ask the class to describe what soils are made of. (mineral particles and humus) Ask: What is humus and why is it good for soil? (decayed plant life contains rich nutrients) What are two processes that create the mineral particles that form soil? (mechanical and chemical weathering) Then ask students to identify the various ways that heat and moisture influence soil development. What is leaching and how does this process affect soil composition? (drains soil of nutrients) How does light rainfall affect soil composition? (Plant growth will be light, and little humus will be added to the soil. However, soil will retain mineral nutrients.) Have students explain why desert soils are often poor in humus but rich in minerals. (Plant growth is minimal, but there is little leaching.)

CHECK FOR UNDERSTANDING

Have students explain why both water and soil are considered recyclable resources. Then ask each student to write one or two sentences explaining why water resources are important and a second set of sentences explaining why soil resources are important.

CORRECTIONS/EXTENSIONS

Reteaching Divide the class into five or six groups. Assign each group a different region or area of the United States. Ask each group to use the maps on pages 64–65 and page 80 to write a paragraph describing the water and soil resources in the area assigned. Students should indicate whether a region is rich or poor in water resources and what types of soil students might find there. Have students provide reasons for their answers. Have each group present its paragraph to the class. Groups should be prepared to give reasons for their answers.

Enrichment Tell the class that water resources can vary in quality or purity. Both developing countries—where supplies of fresh water are scarce or inaccessible—and industrial nations, like the United States, face water quality problems. Tell students that impure water can be a carrier of a wide variety of diseases. Have students do short reports on factors that affect the quality of drinking water either here or abroad.

4.3 Biotic Resources
(pages 109–110)

MAIN IDEA

■ Plants and animals or biotic resources are the living materials people use for food, clothing, and shelter.

VOCABULARY

biotic resources, p. 109

OBJECTIVE

Students should be able to:
■ identify biotic resources.

TEACHING STRATEGIES

Identifying Biotic Resources Have each student bring to class a magazine advertisement

showing a product made from a biotic resource. Have students identify the resource in presentations to the class.

CHECK FOR UNDERSTANDING

Ask the class why biotic resources are considered renewable resources. (Plants and animals renew themselves.) Have students identify the kinds of biotic resources. (plants used for food, animals used for food, plants and animals used as raw materials) Then have students give an example found in their community of each type of resource.

CORRECTIONS/EXTENSIONS

Reteaching Ask each student to make an outline of Section 3. Remind the class that the topic sentence in a paragraph often states the main idea of the paragraph. The main ideas can become the Roman numerals or major headings for their outlines.

Enrichment Point out that like other types of natural resources, biotic resources are not evenly distributed. They are also not the same from one ecosystem to another. Have students write short papers identifying the factors that influence the distribution of biotic resources. Among the factors that students might mention are harshness of climate, temperature and rainfall, quality of soil, and availability of water resources.

4.4 Mineral Resources
(pages 110–112)

MAIN IDEAS

■ Minerals are nonliving resources.
■ The three main groups of minerals are metals or metallic resources, nonmetallic minerals, and energy fuels.

VOCABULARY

metallic resource, p. 110; nonmetallic mineral, p. 110; energy fuel, p. 110; ore, p. 110; fossil fuel, p. 111; petroleum, p. 111

OBJECTIVE

Students should be able to:
■ classify mineral resources as metals, nonmetallic minerals, or fossil fuels.

TEACHING STRATEGIES

Classifying Mineral Resources Ask each student to make a three-column chart on a sheet of paper. Have students label the columns *Type of Mineral Resource, Examples,* and *Uses.* In the first column, have students list Metals, Nonmetallic Minerals, and Fossil Fuels. Class members can complete the chart by naming different minerals that belong in each category and describing briefly the industrial or agricultural uses of each.

CHECK FOR UNDERSTANDING

Ask students to name one way in which metals, nonmetallic minerals, and fossil fuels are alike (i. e., they are all minerals). Then ask students to give an example of each one, explaining how fossil fuels differ from the other two.

CORRECTIONS/EXTENSIONS

Reteaching Divide the class into three groups. Assign each group one of the subsections of Section 4. Have each group prepare a short report for the class in which they explain how the mineral resource group assigned to them differs from the others. Have students give examples of minerals within their group and describe their uses.

Enrichment Tell the class that trade in mineral resources and particularly fossil fuels such as oil has greatly influenced international relations in recent decades. Have students write short research papers based on recent history or current events to support this statement.

4.5 Managing Resources
(pages 112–119)

MAIN IDEAS

- Conservation of water and soil is essential to human life.
- Finding alternative sources to replace fossil fuels is important in conserving energy resources.

VOCABULARY

conservation, p. 112; terracing, p. 114; contour farming, p. 114; crop rotation, p. 114; strip-mining, p. 116; nuclear energy, p. 119; solar energy, p. 119

OBJECTIVES

Students should be able to:
- identify strategies used to manage natural resources.
- analyze current strategies for managing specific resource problems.

TEACHING STRATEGIES

Identifying Resource Management Strategies Divide the class into three groups. Assign each group one of the following topics: (a) Managing water resources, (b) Managing soil resources, (c) Managing energy resources. Have each group prepare a three-part oral report. The report should identify the problems facing people in the management of this resource. The report should also list ways that people have attempted to meet this problem or conserve the resource. The report should conclude by giving the group's opinion about how successfully people appear to be meeting the challenge of conserving this resource based on what group members have read.

Analyzing Current Strategies for Resource Management Have students bring to class newspaper or newsmagazine articles showing efforts to manage resources. Ask class members to look for articles showing both renewable and nonrenewable resources. Have class members bring their articles to class indicating (a) the resource that is being managed, (b) the problem that has created a need for resource management, (c) how this resource is being redistributed or conserved, (d) how successful the management effort is to date.

CHECK FOR UNDERSTANDING

Ask each class member to select one of the conservation techniques discussed in this section (i.e., irrigation, dams, terracing, contour farming, crop rotation, use of fertilizers, conservation of fuels, nuclear energy, solar energy) and write a paragraph explaining how it is used, why it helps conserve the resource, and any drawbacks of the use of this method.

CORRECTIONS/EXTENSIONS

Reteaching Make a four-column chart on the chalkboard. Label the columns *Natural Resource, Problem, Solution, Limitations of Solution.* In the first column, list the following: water, soil, fossil fuels. Have students complete the chart by giving examples of problems that arise in the management of each resource, various solutions to the problems, and the un-intended consequences or drawbacks of the solutions, if any.

Enrichment   Tell the class that recycling is also a way of conserving both mineral and energy resources. Ask students to write short reports on the way a recycling process works. If there is a recycling plant in the community, a worker at the plant might be asked to speak about the recycling process and the types of resources recovered during that process.

Answers

4.1 REVIEWING THE FACTS (p. 104)

Define
1. *natural resource:* any material or element from the environment used by humans
2. *raw material:* any resource that can be made into a product
3. *recyclable resource:* a resource that can be used over and over without destroying it
4. *renewable resource:* a resource that can be replaced after use
5. *nonrenewable resource*: a resource that cannot be replaced after use

Answer
1. (a) petroleum, uranium
(b) Petroleum is used to heat buildings, to produce electricity, to make chemicals, and to power vehicles. Uranium is used to produce nuclear energy.
2. (a) water and soil, plants and animals, minerals (b) Resources are distributed unevenly. Amounts differ from ecosystem to ecosystem.

Locate
1. Lake Michigan 2. Lake Erie
3. Lake Superior

4.2 REVIEWING THE FACTS (p. 108)

Define
1. *topsoil:* the thin, upper layer of soil
2. *parent material:* bits of rock that make up the soil
3. *mechanical weathering:* the process by which heat and cold break down rocks
4. *chemical weathering:* the process by which chemicals break down rocks
5. *humus:* decayed animal and plant matter found in the soil
6. *leach:* to drain nutrients from soil

Answer
1. It is needed by all forms of life.
2. (a) Soils differ in their mineral content, humus content, and, thus, in their nutrients. (b) Heavy rains can leach soils.

Locate
1. Rio Grande 2. Missouri River
3. Colorado River 4. Mississippi River

4.3 REVIEWING THE FACTS (p. 110)

Define
biotic resources: plants or animals used as food or raw materials

Answer
1. (a) plants used for food, animals used for food, plants or animals used in manufacturing. (b) Answers will vary.
2. because plants renew themselves by producing seeds and animals renew themselves by producing offspring

Locate
1. Japan 2. Soviet Union 3. China
4. Peru 5. United States

4.4 REVIEWING THE FACTS (p. 112)

Define
1. *metallic resource:* a metal found in nature, such as iron or copper
2. *nonmetallic resource:* a mineral, such as sand or salt
3. *energy fuel:* a mineral that can be used to produce energy
4. *ore:* a rock that contains large amounts of metal
5. *fossil fuel:* a mineral, such as coal or oil, formed from the remains of plants and animals that died many millions of years ago
6. *petroleum*: a liquid fossil fuel

Answer
1. (a) *iron*—mixed with other minerals to make steel; *copper*—used to make wire and pipes; *lead*—used to make pipes, paints, dyes, and pottery glazes; *tin*—mixed with other minerals to make lightweight metal objects; *aluminum*—made from bauxite for a variety of products like cans (b) salt (c) to season and preserve food; needed for human life
2. Through pressure by layers of rock on plant and animal remains; The process took millions of years.
3. (a) Recycling allows people to reuse minerals that cannot be replaced from the natural en-

vironment. (b) Students may cite coal, petroleum, or natural gas.

Locate
1. Soviet Union 2. Saudi Arabia
3. United States 4. Mexico
5. Venezuela 6. China 7. United Kingdom
8. Indonesia 9. Iran 10. Nigeria

MAP WORKSHOP (p. 117)

1. coal 2. (a) Kansas, Oklahoma, Texas, Louisiana (b) Texas 3. coal, natural gas, petroleum 4. coal 5. Petroleum and natural gas are found in roughly the same places. 6. Answers will vary.

For a special challenge: Appalachians

SKILL WORKSHOP (p. 118)

1. household/commercial uses
2. coal 3. waterpower (hydro)
4. hydro, gas 5. Texas
6. about three times as much
7. about three times as much

4.5 REVIEWING THE FACTS (p. 119)

Define
1. *conservation:* the careful use of natural resources
2. *terracing:* the cutting of flat areas into hillsides for farming
3. *contour farming:* the planting of crops across slopes to prevent erosion
4. *crop rotation:* the growing of different crops in different years to keep an area's soil fertile
5. *strip-mining:* the removal of the top layers of soil to mine coal
6. *nuclear energy:* the energy produced by the splitting of atoms
7. *solar energy:* the energy produced by the use of the sun's radiation

Answer
1. leaching of nutrients from soil, the buildup of mineral salts in soil
2. Farmers use terracing and contour farming to control erosion. They also build up grasslands and forests to reduce erosion. They rotate crops and spread fertilizer to improve soil.
3. (a) population growth, increased desires for goods and services, energy-using inventions (b) nuclear energy, wind power, tidal and ocean wave energy, solar energy

Locate
1. Alabama 2. California
3. Illinois 4. New York

GEOGRAPHY LABORATORY (pp. 120–121)

Speaking Geographically
Column 1—*Natural Resources:*
recyclable resources, nonrenewable resources, renewable resources
Column 2—*Nonliving Resources:*
fossil fuels, nonmetallic resources, metallic resources
Column 3—*Soil Conservation:*
terracing, crop rotation, contour farming
Column 4—*Alternative Energy Resources:*
wind power, solar energy, nuclear energy

Testing Yourself
1. petroleum 2. fresh water
3. rain 4. nutrients 5. natural resource
6. raw materials 7. radioactive water
8. metals 9. conservation 10. floods
11. fertilizers 12. strip-mining 13. scarcity

Building Map Skills
1. Mississippi River 2. Great Lakes
3. Columbia River 4. Missouri River
5. Ohio River 6. Colorado River

Applying Geography Skills
1. Students should make bar graphs using the data provided.
2. Between 1925 and 1975, the share supplied by coal decreased and the share supplied by oil increased. After 1975, however, the trend appears to be reversing with coal holding its own and oil decreasing.

SUPPLEMENTARY MATERIALS

Books
Branley, Franklyn M., *Feast or Famine? The Energy Future,* T.Y. Crowell, 1980
Halacy, D.S., *Earth, Water, Wind, and Sun: Our Energy Alternatives,* Harper & Row, 1977
Hyde, Margaret Oldroyd, *Energy: The New Look,* McGraw-Hill, 1981

Other Media
The House of Man I: Our Changing Environment (EB: film/video)
Landforms and Human Use (CIM: film)
Problems of Conservation: Our Natural Resources (EB: film/video, Spanish version available)
Riches from the Earth (NG: film/video)
Riches from the Sea (NG: film/video)
Water: A Precious Resource (NG: film/video)

5 Human Imprints of the Past *(pages 124–153)*

ASSIGNMENT GUIDE

- ### Text Features

  Skill Workshop, p. 134   Map Workshop, p. 146
  Spotlight, p. 138   Chapter Review, pp. 152–153

- ### Teacher's Resource Binder

  Assign after
  p. 128 Building Basics Worksheet 5.1
          Independent Practice Worksheet 5.1 WB p. 39
  p. 131 Building Basics Worksheet 5.2
          Independent Practice Worksheet 5.2 WB p. 40
  p. 134 Skill Workshop: Reading a Time Line WB p. 45
  p. 141 Building Basics Worksheet 5.3
          Independent Practice Worksheet 5.3 WB p. 41
  p. 146 Map Workshop: Reading a Map of Culture Regions WB p. 44
  p. 148 Building Basics Worksheet 5.4
          Independent Practice Worksheet 5.4 WB p. 42
  p. 151 Building Basics Worksheet 5.5
          Independent Practice Worksheet 5.5 WB p. 43
  p. 151 Map Test 5
          Chapter Test 5
          Enrichment Chapter 5 WB p. 46

- ### Geography Laboratory Manual: Investigating Chapter 5

  Use with pages 124–153

- ### Outline Map 1

  Use with pages 124–153

OVERVIEW

Chapter 5 explores the concept of culture by tracing the technological advances from prehistoric times through to the Industrial Revolution. Students will learn how farming lead to the rise of cities and how trade during the Age of Exploration caused cultures to borrow ideas from one another and further advance technology. Finally, the effects of rapid industrialization are explored.

INTRODUCING THE CHAPTER

Direct students to the Unit Opener photograph on page 122. Put the chapter title on the chalkboard: "Human Imprints of the Past." Ask the class what they think human imprints might mean. Have the class look closely at the picture of New York City at night and identify the objects in the picture that have been put there by humans. Next have the class read the introduction to the chapter on page 124. According to the introduction, what does the term human imprints mean?

5.1 Culture: The Human Difference *(pages 125–128)*

MAIN IDEAS

- Culture is the total way of life followed by a group of people.
- All cultures share elemental similarities, such as family, religious beliefs, communication through language, economic systems, and government.

VOCABULARY

habitat, p. 125; culture, p. 125; economic system, p. 126; technology, p. 126; culture region, p. 126; cultural borrowing, p. 127

OBJECTIVES

Students should be able to:
- understand the concept of culture.
- identify common elements in all cultures.
- examine the effects of cultural changes.

TEACHING STRATEGIES

Understanding the Concept of Culture
Have a class member define the word *culture*. (the total way of life that are followed by a group of people) Ask students to give examples of cultural differences from their own experience. Point out that culture affects everything people do from the type of foods they eat to their attitudes about religious practices or their desire for a particular form of government.

Identifying Common Elements in Cultures
Ask students what general cultural elements they have in common with all other cultures. List these on the board. (desire for family, type of government, belief in religion, education of children, law and enforcement of rules, economic systems, technology) Explain that cultures differ in ways people apply these elements.

Examining the Effects of Cultural Changes
Remind the class that the invention of the computer has had a major impact on culture. Point out that changes in technology often lead to social change. Have students cite other examples of effects of changes in technology.

CHECK FOR UNDERSTANDING

Ask each class member to use the vocabulary words in "Reviewing the Facts" on page 128 in a paragraph that explains the concept of culture.

CORRECTIONS/EXTENSIONS

Reteaching Divide the class into small groups. Ask each group to bring to class photographs from newspapers or magazines showing activities taking place in cultures other than their own. Have each group identify elements common to all cultures. Students should also cite the way these elements are unique to the culture being presented.

Enrichment Have students think about the cultures their ancestors came from and the differences between those cultures and that of the United States. Ask students to report orally on how their ancestral culture may have influenced American culture.

5.2 Early Technologies and Cultural Patterns
(pages 128–131)

MAIN IDEA

- The earliest technologies were developed by people who were hunters and gatherers.

VOCABULARY

hunters and gatherers, p. 128; archaeologist, p. 128

OBJECTIVE

Students should be able to:
- understand the relationship between technology and cultural development.

TEACHING STRATEGIES

Understanding the Relationship between Technology and Cultural Development
Write the word *technology* on the chalkboard and have students provide its definition. (all the tools and methods people use in developing their resources and producing goods and services) Then ask: What was the physical environment of the Ice Age? (harsh, cold climate) What was the technology of early humans? (spears, stone blades, fire) How did these tools help early humans adapt their physical environment? Discuss with the class how the technology of early people changed when the end of the Ice Age brought warmer temperatures. (For example, with the growth of forests, early people invented bows and arrows to capture swift forest animals.)

CHECK FOR UNDERSTANDING

Write the term *hunters and gatherers* on the chalkboard. Have students define this term and describe the lifestyle of hunters and gatherers both during and after the Ice Age.

CORRECTIONS/EXTENSIONS

Reteaching Make a two-column chart on the chalkboard. Label the columns *During Ice Age* and *After Ice Age*. In the first column, have class members list technological advances made during the Ice Age. In the second column, have students list technological changes that occurred shortly after the Ice Age ended. Have class members explain how each of the tools or processes listed helped early peoples adapt their physical environment.

Enrichment   Archaeologists have discovered many remarkable examples of the art of early peoples. Among the most famous are the cave paintings of Altamira in Spain and Lascaux in France. Have students go to the library and find books that contain examples of this art. What do the cave paintings show? What do they tell us about early people?

5.3 Fields and Cities
(pages 131–141)

MAIN IDEAS

- Domestication of plants and animals led to the development of farming.
- Ancient farming practices varied from place to place.
- Changes in farming produced food surpluses that led to the growth of cities.
- Ancient cultures that developed following the Ice Age made remarkable achievements in many areas including the development of writing, iron working, and written law.

VOCABULARY

domesticate, p. 132; agriculture, p. 133; nomad, p. 135; urban, p. 137; scribe, p. 137; artisan, p. 137; bronze, p. 137

OBJECTIVES

Students should be able to:
- analyze why different types of farming practices developed in different regions of the world.
- explain the relationship between farming and the rise of cities.
- discuss the kinds of accomplishments made by ancient cultures.

TEACHING STRATEGIES

Analyzing Farming Cultures in Different Regions of the World   Have students name the technological advances that made the development of farming possible. (domestication of

animals and plants) Divide the class into five groups. Assign each group one of the following areas: Southwest Asia, North Africa, East Asia, Middle America, South America. Have each group prepare a short oral report for the class, describing the climate in the area assigned, the types of crops grown or livestock raised, and a description on how the kind of physical environment influenced the kind of agricultural practices used. Have students use the chart on page 132 and the climate map on 64–65.

Explaining the Relationship between Farming and the Rise of Cities   Tell students that the shift to farming had far-reaching effects. It led to many other changes in the culture of early peoples. Have class members describe how the shift to farming affected social and economic structures. (building of permanent rather than temporary shelters, changes in diet and in division of labor, creation of cities) Have class members identify the features of the physical environment that encouraged the development of cities. Ask: Where did the first cities develop in North Africa, South Asia, and East Asia? (along rivers in river valleys) Why? (Rich soil attracted farmers. As farming grew, so did food surpluses. As surpluses grew, cities grew.)

Discussing Accomplishments by Ancient Cultures   Have class members call out accomplishments by ancient cultures that have affected our lives. List them on the board. (domestication of plants and animals for food and clothing; the use of brick, stone, wood for house-building; the invention of paper and glass; boat building; iron for tools and building; systems of government and written law; creation of alphabets; the beginning of today's religions; forms of art and literature; the idea of roads and bridges)

CHECK FOR UNDERSTANDING

Have students describe one way that each of the following changed the way of life of early peoples: (a) domestication of plants and animals, (b) creation of food surpluses, (c) irrigation of dry lands, (d) writing, (e) iron working.

CORRECTIONS/EXTENSIONS

Reteaching   Have class members name the technological advances discussed in this section. List student responses on the chalkboard. Have students rank these achievements in order of importance and then give reasons for their opinions.

Enrichment Have students report on some societies that still earn a living by hunting and gathering (for example, the King of Africa's Kalahari Desert and the Aborigines of Australia). What conclusions about hunting and gathering do scientists make by studying these societies? Students might also use **Outline Map 1** to locate the regions of the world where farming and cities first arose. Have students label present-day countries that exist in these areas.

5.4 An Age of Trade and Expansion
(pages 142–148)

MAIN IDEAS

- Early cultures were nearly self-sufficient.
- During the Age of Exploration, new possibilities for trade became available.
- European expansion accelerated the pace of cultural borrowing and the spread of ideas and inventions.

VOCABULARY

colonies, p. 145; Indians, p. 145

OBJECTIVES

Students should be able to:
- identify factors that led to the revival of trade in Europe.
- assess the impact of European expansion on various cultures.

TEACHING STRATEGIES

Identifying Factors That Led to European Trade Revival Write the following phrases on the chalkboard: (a) fewer wars, (b) return of people to cities, (c) voyages of Marco Polo to Asia. Have students explain how each of these developments led to a revival of trade in Europe beginning in the 1100's. Then have class members explain how the control of trade with Asia by Italian merchants encouraged European exploration. (Because Italy controlled the overland routes to Asia, other European nations wanted a share of this lucrative trade and sought a faster water route to Asia.)

Assessing the Impact of European Expansion Have each student list the following groups of people on a sheet of paper, leaving several lines of space between each item on the list: Aztec and Inca Indians, Africans, Chinese, Europeans, Native American Indians. Next to the name of each group on the list, have students write one or two sentences describing some way in which the culture of this group changed or its way of life was affected by the European Age of Exploration. Have several class members read their responses aloud. Then as a class, discuss which groups on the list benefited the most or were the most harmed as a result of European expansion.

CHECK FOR UNDERSTANDING

Have students explain how the revival of trade led to the Age of Exploration. Then have students identify two positive and two negative effects of European exploration and colonization.

CORRECTIONS/EXTENSIONS

Reteaching Have students use the photographs in this section to discuss the importance of each of the following: the growth of cities (page 143), the impact of the printing press (page 144), Columbus's voyages (page 145), and the exchange of goods that resulted from trade (page 147).

Enrichment Have students find out more about one of the following early explorers: Prince Henry, Bartholomeu Dias, Vasco da Gama, Ferdinand Magellan. What routes did they take? Why are their voyages significant?

5.5 The Industrial Revolution (pages 148–151)

MAIN IDEAS

- The Industrial Revolution was the change from manufacturing goods made by hand to producing goods by power-driven machines.
- The Industrial Revolution left a more long-lasting human imprint on Earth than earlier cultural changes.

VOCABULARY

capital, p. 149; Industrial Revolution, p. 149; steel, p. 149

OBJECTIVES

Students should be able to:
- identify factors that contributed to the Industrial Revolution.
- assess the impact of the Industrial Revolution on various cultural groups.

TEACHING STRATEGIES

Identifying Contributing Factors of the Industrial Revolution Write the following phrases on the chalkboard: (a) improvements in farming, (b) population growth, (c) improvements in transportation, (d) overseas trade and colonization by England, (e) movement of displaced farmers to cities. Have class members explain how each of these developments laid the foundation for industrialization in England.

Assessing the Impact of the Industrial Revolution Make a two-column chart on the chalkboard. Label the columns *Benefits* and *Effects.* Have students complete the chart by listing both the benefits that the spread of industrialization brought and the negative effects or costs of industrialization. When the chart is completed, students should recognize that the industrialized nations of Western Europe, Asia, and the United States received the greatest benefits from industrialization. What were some drawbacks of rapid industrial growth? (poor working and living conditions for factory workers)

CHECK FOR UNDERSTANDING

Ask each class member to write two or three sentences describing one cause or factor that led to the Industrial Revolution and one effect of this revolution on people and the environment.

CORRECTIONS/EXTENSIONS

Reteaching Divide the class into four groups. Assign each group one of the subsections in Section 5. Ask each group to find the main idea or ideas in the subsection assigned to it. Each group should also pick out two or three supporting statements for each main idea they have identified. Have each group write its main idea and supporting statements on the chalkboard for presentation to the class.

Enrichment Have students prepare short research papers on one invention developed during the industrial revolution that still affects our lives today.

Answers

5.1 REVIEWING THE FACTS (p. 128)

Define

1. *habitat:* the particular physical environment of certain plants or animals
2. *culture:* the total way of life followed by a group of people
3. *economic system:* an organized way of meeting people's needs and wants and of exchanging goods and services
4. *culture region:* a place where people's ways of life are similar
5. *technology:* the tools and methods people use to develop their resources and produce goods and services
6. *cultural borrowing:* the process of adopting goods and practices from other cultures

Answer

1. People can consciously change their physical environment to suit their needs and wants.
2. *Differences* include clothing, ways of making and moving goods, kinds of buildings people live in, music, food, and beliefs and values; *Similarities* include the family as the basic unit of living, some form of religion, the existence of some set of ideas about beauty and how to enjoy life, instruction of young people, a government, an economic system, and some form of technology.
3. Cultures change because young people do not always carry out customs exactly as their parents did, because of new inventions and ideas, and because of contacts with other cultures.

Locate

1. western part 2. pink

5.2 REVIEWING THE FACTS (p. 131)

Define

1. *hunters and gatherers:* people who live by killing wild animals and collecting wild plants
2. *archaeologist:* a scientist who studies the human past by examining tools, bones, and other ancient remains

Answer

1. Archaeologists have found evidence of early technologies—weapons, cooking utensils, and other tools. They have found cave art and some evidence of trade among peoples.

2. Early peoples were skilled hunters and tool makers. They learned to start fire, to adjust to various environments, and to make use of many kinds of plants for food. Cave art suggests that early peoples had ceremonies to ensure good hunting. Evidence of trade suggests contact between different groups of people.

3. To hunt, people fashioned stones into sharp weapons, attaching them to long sticks. Stone blades were used to clean animals and scrape away skins used for clothes. Fires were made by rubbing sticks or with flintstones. Cave art was painted with mixtures of clay, minerals, charcoal, and animal fat; it usually depicted animals and sometimes hunters. Obsidian, a mineral used in tool making, was frequently traded.

4. the availability of plant and animal resources in an area

5. paintings on cave walls, burning of some forests

Locate

1. Asia, North America, South America, Antarctica, Europe 2. north from central Asia, across a bridge of land joining present-day Alaska and the Soviet Union

SKILL WORKSHOP (p. 134)

1. 7,000 years 2. 1,000 years
3. 5000 B.C. 4. 1492
5. before the beginning of democracy in Greece
6. about 2,500 years ago
7. in 1492, or about 500 years ago

5.3 REVIEWING THE FACTS (p. 141)

Define

1. *domesticate:* to care for plants and animals so that they become dependent on humans for life
2. *agriculture:* the herding of animals and the farming of land
3. *nomad:* a person who wanders from place to place without any permanent dwelling
4. *urban:* having to do with cities
5. *artisan:* a skilled worker who makes objects by hand
6. *bronze:* a metal made from a mixture of tin and copper
7. *scribe:* a person who wrote letters and business contracts for merchants and others in urban places

Answer

1. Farmers cultivate a particular area, while hunters and gatherers tend to move from place to place in search of wild animals and plants.
2. at the eastern end of the Mediterranean and along the Tigris-Euphrates River in Southwest Asia; along the Nile River in North Africa; along the Indus River in South Asia; along the Huang He in East Asia; in present-day Mexico and the Andes in the Americas
3. Farming produced food surpluses that led to city growth.
4. the domestication of many plants and animals; the making of cloth; the building of dwellings and large structures; such inventions as paper, glass, the sail, and iron; forms of government and systems of law

Locate

1. Italy
2. Mediterranean Sea

MAP WORKSHOP (p. 146)

1. (a) ten (b) two
2. North Africa and the Middle East
3. (a) South Asia (b) East Asia (c) East Asia (d) Western Europe (e) Latin America (f) North America (g) North Africa and the Middle East (h) South Pacific (i) Africa South of the Sahara

For a special challenge: These countries were once part of the Roman Empire. Thus, they share a history.

5.4 REVIEWING THE FACTS (p. 148)

Define

1. *colonies:* areas or countries governed by another country
2. *Indians:* name used by Europeans to refer to inhabitants of the Americas

Answer

1. (a) distances between cultures, poor transportation and communication systems, limited needs and wants (b) long periods of peace, curiosity about other ways of life stimulated by contacts between cultures
2. *Portugal:* sponsored early explorations of Africa and Indian Ocean, responsible for navigation inventions; *The Netherlands:* established trading ports in many parts of the world by late 1500's, later founded colonies; *England:* established many overseas trading posts and colonies (in India, North America, and the Caribbean) in 1600's
3. the destruction of Indian cultures in the Americas, the bringing of slaves from Africa to the Americas, introduction of American food

crops to many parts of the world, stimulation for new inventions and technologies

Locate
1. (a) Antioch (b) London
2. Tangier, Rome, Pompeii, Carthage, Brundisium, Athens, Alexandria

5.5 REVIEWING THE FACTS (p. 151)

Define
1. *capital:* money used to start or expand a business
2. *Industrial Revolution:* the change from making goods by hand to producing goods by means of power-driven machines
3. *steel:* a hard metal made from iron and carbon

Answer
1. (a) improvements in farming and transportation, wealth gained from colonies, increased interest in new goods, improved ways of making goods (b) During the 1600's and 1700's, English businesses gained fortunes in foreign trade. Making use of England's ample resources, businesses began investing in new processes and products. At the same time, improvements in farming meant that farms employed fewer people; more workers were thus available for a larger manufacturing effort.
2. the countries of Western Europe, the United States
3. Africa, India, Southeast Asia

Locate
1. Gabon, Congo, Zaire, Uganda, Kenya, Somalia
2. Tunisia, Lesotho, and Swaziland are totally in middle latitudes. Morocco, Algeria, Libya, Egypt, Namibia, Bostwana, South Africa, Mozambique, Mali, Mauritania, and Madagascar are partly in middle latitudes.

GEOGRAPHY LABORATORY (pp. 152–153)

Speaking Geographically
1.–10. Answers will vary.

Testing Yourself
A. 7, 2, 6, 1, 9, 4, 10, 5, 3, 8
B. 1. b 2. d 3. a 4. e 5. c

Building Map Skills
1. Spain 2. Mali 3. Italy 4. Pakistan
5. India 6. Thailand 7. Japan 8. China
9. United Kingdom (England) 10. Mexico

Applying Map Skills
1. southeast; Turkey, Iraq, Syria; Persian Gulf
2. north; Sudan, Egypt, Uganda, Ethiopia; the Mediterranean Sea
3. south; China, India, Pakistan; Arabian Sea
4. northeast; China; East China Sea

SUPPLEMENTARY MATERIALS

Books
Chapman, Keith, *People, Patterns, and Processes: An Introduction to Human Geography,* Halsted, 1980

Giedeon, Siegfried, *Mechanization Takes Command,* Norton, 1969

Hamblin, Dora Jane, *The First Cities,* Time-Life, 1973

Higham, Charles, *The Earliest Farmers and the First Cities,* Lerner Publications, 1977

The Last Two Million Years, Reader's Digest, 1979

Macaulay, David, *Pyramid,* Houghton Mifflin, 1975

Unstead, R.J., *How They Lived in Cities Long Ago,* Arco Publishing, 1981

Vialls, Christine, *The Industrial Revolution Begins,* Lerner Publications, 1982

Other Media
The Age of Iron (LF: film/video; covers 2000 B.C.–A.D. 200)

The Agricultural Revolution (LF: film/video; covers 8000 B.C.–5000 B.C.)

Ancient Civilizations (NG: five filmstrips, five cassettes, guide)

Ancient Civilizations (ROP: disk/cassette for Apple or PET)

The Birth of Civilization (LF: film/video; covers 6000 B.C.–2000 B.C.)

Cave Dwellers of the Old Stone Age (EB: film/video)

The Human Imprint in the Modern World
(pages 154–181)

ASSIGNMENT GUIDE

■ *Text Features*

Spotlight, p. 158   Skill Workshop, p. 162
Map Workshop, p. 160   Chapter Review, pp. 180–181

■ *Teacher's Resource Binder*

Assign after
p. 160 Map Workshop: Reading a Road Map WB p. 51
p. 162 Skill Workshop: Interpreting a Cartoon WB p. 52
p. 164 Building Basics Worksheet 6.1
      Independent Practice Worksheet 6.1 WB p. 47
p. 169 Building Basics Worksheet 6.2
      Independent Practice Worksheet 6.2 WB p. 48
p. 176 Building Basics Worksheet 6.3
      Independent Practice Worksheet 6.3 WB p. 49
p. 179 Building Basics Worksheet 6.4
      Independent Practice Worksheet 6.4 WB p. 50
p. 181 Map Test 6
      Chapter Test 6
      Enrichment Chapter 6 WB p. 53

■ *Geography Laboratory Manual: Investigating Chapter 6*

Use with pages 154–181

■ *Outline Map 1*

Use with pages 154–181

■ *Overhead Transparencies 4–6 and Worksheets*

Use with pages 154–181

OVERVIEW

Chapter 6 begins by examining patterns of population growth and urban expansion since the industrial age began. Students learn about the various forms of government in the modern world and consider the economic organization of each. The chapter concludes by outlining the trade links and the cultural, scientific, and political ties that draw together the nations of the world.

INTRODUCING THE CHAPTER

Ask students to skim Chapter 6, looking at the section titles and captions. Remind the class of the chapter's title—"The Human Imprint in the Modern World." Ask students what kinds of human imprints they think Chapter 6 might discuss. Then have the class read the chapter introduction. Tell the class that in this chapter they will see the far-reaching consequences of changes that began with the Industrial Revolution—such as advances in transportation and medicine—that not only affect where and how people live but also the ways the nations of the world interact with each other.

6.1 Population and Settlement *(pages 47–52)*

MAIN IDEAS

■ The world population is greater today than ever before due to medical advances, improved public health, and increased food supplies.
■ Knowledge of population changes and pop-

43T

ulation distribution helps leaders plan for the future.

■ Since the Industrial Revolution, the world's population has become increasingly urban.

VOCABULARY

death rate, p. 155; famine, p. 155; infant death rate, p. 155; birth rate, p. 155; life expectancy, p. 156; migration, p. 157; immigrant, p. 159; rural, p. 159; suburb, p. 159; population density, p. 161; developing country, p. 163; metropolitan area, p. 164; megalopolis, p. 164

OBJECTIVES

Students should be able to:
■ explain the relationship between population growth and industrialization.
■ analyze population distribution.

TEACHING STRATEGIES

Explaining the Relationship between Population Growth and Industrialization Tell the class that reasons for the burst of growth in world population can be found in the changing technology of the industrial age. Have class members explain how each of the following was an outgrowth of the Industrial Revolution and how each contributed to the population explosion: (a) medical advances (vaccines halt spread of diseases, thus lowering death rates), (b) improved public health (modern water treatment and waste disposal reduce threats of disease), (c) increased food supplies (large-scale food production, airtight food packaging, refrigeration).

Analyzing Population Distribution Have students turn to the map of population density on pages 490–491 of the Atlas. Discuss the meaning of population distribution. (the way people are spread out over the areas in which they live) Then, as students study the map, ask if population distribution is spread evenly throughout the world. (no) Which parts of the world have the largest areas of high population density? (East Asia, South Asia, and Europe) Have students compare this map with the map of world ecosystems on pages 82–83. In what ecosystems do the fewest number of people live? (tundra, deserts, ice cap, mountains)

CHECK FOR UNDERSTANDING

Have students describe one trend in population growth since 1900 (population increasing more rapidly), one trend in population distribution since 1900 (more people living in urban areas), and one trend in size of cities since 1900 (becoming more spread out or less compact).

CORRECTIONS/EXTENSIONS

Reteaching Make a two-column chart on the chalkboard. Label the first column *Effect* and the second column *Cause.* In the first column, list the following developments: rapid population growth, increased urban growth, outward spread of cities. Have students complete the chart by describing the causes of each of these population trends.

Enrichment Have students write research reports on population statistics. By using census information, students might report on whether their community has increased or decreased in size since the last census, its current population density, and whether or not it is a part of a larger metropolitan area. The class can then speculate on the reasons for changes in population patterns since the last census. Ask students to think about the following when preparing their reports: internal migration patterns, transportation improvements, employment opportunities.

6.2 Political Patterns
(pages 165–169)

MAIN IDEAS

■ Nations established recognized borders to prevent disputes with other nations competing for resources.
■ Forms of government differ.
■ The people of a nation not only share land and government but also similar values and beliefs.

VOCABULARY

frontier, p. 165; border, p. 165; unitary government, p. 166; federal government, p. 166; authoritarian government, p. 167; dictator, p. 167; totalitarian government, p. 167; democratic government, p. 167; representative democracy, p. 167; nation, p. 168; nationalism, p. 169

OBJECTIVES

Students should be able to:
■ understand the purpose of borders.
■ distinguish different political systems.
■ analyze nationalism in world affairs.

TEACHING STRATEGIES

Using Outline Map 1 to Understand Frontiers and Borders   Have students define *border*. (a real or imaginary dividing line between countries or states) What function do borders perform? (They prevent conflicts over resources by clearly defining areas of ownership of resources.) Have students fill in the names of countries in the Western Hemisphere on Outline Map 1, using the maps in the book as a model. Ask students to name countries that share borders (such as the United States and Canada or the United States and Mexico).

Distinguishing between Political Systems Write the following pairs of terms on the chalkboard: (a) *unitary government* (central decision-making body), *federal government* (central decision-making body shares power with smaller political units, like states or provinces) (b) *authoritarian government* (one person or small body governs many), *democratic government* (citizens take part in politics). Have class members explain the differences and similarities between each set of terms.

Analyzing the Role of Nationalism   Write the word *nation* on the board. Ask the class to list elements that the people of the United States share because they belong to the same nation. Lists should include cultural elements, such as language, technology, common history, government, foods, holidays, customs.

CHECK FOR UNDERSTANDING

Check student comprehension by asking class members to explain what political purpose borders serve. (reduce conflict) The class can also identify ways in which unitary and federal forms of government differ and the ways in which authoritarian and democratic governments differ.

CORRECTIONS/EXTENSIONS

Reteaching   Use the photographs on pages 167 and 168 to discuss the differences between authoritarian and democratic governments.

Enrichment   In 3100 B.C., an Egyptian ruler names Menes united Lower Egypt and Upper Egypt to form the world's first nation. Have students research the nation of ancient Egypt, especially the cultural factors that united its people. Egypt was a farming nation whose people relied on the waters of the Nile and worked together to control those waters. For ancient Egyptians, this formed a strong bond that kept them unified. Ask what kind of government ancient Egypt had. (authoritarian)

6.3 Using the Land and Its Resources
(pages 170–176)

MAIN IDEAS

■ The processes involved in developing resources can be divided into primary, secondary, and tertiary economic activities.
■ Economic systems differ in terms of who owns and controls resources, technology, and businesses.
■ The most common measures of economic activity are gross national product—or GNP—and per capita GNP.

VOCABULARY

primary economic activity, p. 170; secondary economic activity, p. 170; tertiary economic activity, p. 170; service, p. 170; linkage, p. 171; free enterprise, p. 171; socialism, p. 171; communism, p. 172; commercial activity, p. 172; consumer, p. 172; standard of living, p. 173; subsistence activity, p. 174; gross national product, p. 175; per capita GNP, p. 175

OBJECTIVES

Students should be able to:
■ classify economic activities as primary, secondary, or tertiary activities.
■ compare ownership and control of resources in free enterprise, socialist, and communist economic systems.
■ compare economic levels in industrialized and developing nations.

TEACHING STRATEGIES

Classifying Economic Activities   Have students name various occupations they are familiar with. List responses on the chalkboard. Then have students classify the activities involved in each job as primary, secondary, or tertiary/service . Next have students identify the primary economic activities that might have preceded each of the secondary economic activities. (Primary economic activities involve the land, its plants, animals, and mineral resources. Secondary economic activities involve the manufacture of resources and raw materials. Tertiary economic activities are services provided for people by others.)

Comparing Ownership and Control of Resources in Economic Systems   Divide the class into three groups. Assign each group either

45T

free enterprise, socialism, or *communism.* Have each group prepare a short oral report explaining who owns and controls the resources, technology, and business under this system. The groups should give one or two examples of countries that have this type of system.

Comparing Economic Levels in Industrialized and Developing Nations   Make a three-column chart on the chalkboard. Label the columns *Areas of Differences, Industrialized Countries,* and *Developing Countries.* In the first column, list types of economic activity (commercial or subsistence), degree of economic choice, presence of transportation linkages, presence of service industries, standard of living. Have students complete the chart by indicating the differences between industrialized and developing nations.

CHECK FOR UNDERSTANDING

Have students give one example of each of the following types of economic activities: primary, secondary, and tertiary. Then have class members explain who owns and controls resources in free enterprise, socialist, and communist economic systems.

CORRECTIONS/EXTENSIONS

Reteaching   Have students write definitions for the vocabulary terms in Reviewing the Facts on page 176. Then have them take turns giving their definitions to the class and asking for the word being defined.

Enrichment   Divide the class into small groups. Ask each group to prepare a table and a bar graph like the ones on page 176 for a selected group of six countries. Have groups choose both industrialized and developing countries for their graph and table. The data for the table and graph are available in most world almanacs or in the *World Bank Atlas* published yearly by the World Bank, 1818 H Street, NW; Washington, DC 20433.

6.4 Many Nations in One World *(pages 177–179)*

MAIN IDEAS

- Patterns of trade today create interdependencies between nations.
- A nation's balance of trade is a record of its imports and exports.

- Trade among nations has led to cultural exchanges and cultural borrowing.

VOCABULARY

interdependent, p. 177; export, p. 177; import, p. 177; balance of trade, p. 178; tariffs, p. 178; free trade, p. 178; common market, p. 178; alliance, p. 179

OBJECTIVES

Students should be able to:
- identify patterns in international trade.
- understand the concept of balance of trade.
- identify examples of economic, cultural, scientific, and political ties among nations.

TEACHING STRATEGIES

Identifying Patterns of Trade   Have class members state the two main patterns in international trade. (Trade has made the nations of the world more interdependent. Industrial nations and developing nations play different roles in world trade.) Have students explain each of these statements and give examples from the text to support each.

Understanding the Balance of Trade   Write the terms *export, import,* and *balance of trade* on the chalkboard and have students define these terms and explain the relationships among them. Ask: Why do countries that export finished goods tend to make more money than those that export raw materials? (Manufacturing adds value to raw materials.) What is an example of favorable balance of trade? (A nation exports more than it imports.) What are two reasons why the United States has an unfavorable balance of trade? (Americans buy more consumer goods in other countries. Goods made in the United States often cost more than those made in other countries.)

Analyzing Ties between Nations   Have students bring to class newspaper articles showing cultural, scientific, or political ties between nations. Have each class member then describe to the class the type of cooperation the article shows.

CHECK FOR UNDERSTANDING

Have students explain why today's trade patterns can be described as interdependent. Then have the class distinguish between an import and an export and indicate the relationship between exports and imports in calculating a nation's balance of trade.

CORRECTIONS/EXTENSIONS

Reteaching   Have students create an outline of Section 4, using these three main headings.
I. Trade Ties
II. Cultural and Scientific Ties
III. Political Ties

Enrichment   Working in pairs, have groups of students select one developing and one industrialized nation to compare the types of goods produced in each country. Students can use the information they find as the basis for a bulletin board display showing trading patterns among the countries of the world.

Answers

MAP WORKSHOP (p. 160)

1. (a) U.S. 131 (b) 55 miles
2. (a) southwest (b) 60 miles
3. Kentwood 4. Albion

SKILL WORKSHOP (p. 162)

1. urban problems
2. to show that cities face many difficult problems
3. (a) A small human figure represents cities; tall buildings represent problems. (b) that the problems are overwhelming
4. The cartoonist seems to be saying that urban problems have become too large for cities to deal with unless they get help.
5. Answers will vary.

6.1 REVIEWING THE FACTS (p. 164)

Define

1. *death rate:* the yearly number of deaths for every 1,000 people
2. *famine:* severe food shortage
3. *infant death rate:* the number of infants out of every 1,000 born each year who die in their first year
4. *birth rate:* the number of live births each year for every 1,000 people
5. *life expectancy:* number of years a person born in a given year is expected to live
6. *migration:* the movement of people from one country to another, or from one region within a country to another
7. *immigrant:* a person who leaves one country to settle in another
8. *rural:* having to do with areas in the countryside

9. *suburb:* a residential community on the outskirts of a city
10. *population density:* the average number of people living within each square mile
11. *developing country:* a country that is just beginning to industrialize and in which most people live by farming or craftwork
12. *metropolitan area:* a city and its surrounding suburbs
13. *megalopolis:* a large area made up of a number of uninterrupted cities

Answer

1. (a) has increased 9 times, from about 600 million to about 5 billion (b) medical advances, better public health practices, and increased food supplies
2. North America, South America, Africa, Australia
3. (a) East Asia, South Asia, and a small portion of Europe (b) most of Europe, about half of Asia, about a third of North America, and smaller parts of South America and Africa (c) northern North America, the central part of South America, northern Africa, central and northern Asia, and most of Australia
4. In the early 1900's, people's residences were built close to shops and workplaces. Improved transportation has led to the growth of residential communities farther and farther from downtown sections of cities, where business and shopping activities still take place.

Locate

1. Baltimore 2. California

6.2 REVIEWING THE FACTS (p. 169)

Define

1. *frontier:* a stretch of unsettled land
2. *border:* a boundary, or imaginary line, between countries
3. *unitary government:* a form of government in which the central government holds power and governments of states or departments carry out its decisions
4. *federal government:* a form of government in which the central government shares power with states or provinces
5. *authoritarian government:* a government in which one person or a small group of people has complete authority for making and carrying out the laws
6. *dictator:* a ruler with total decision-making power
7. *totalitarian government:* a government in which almost all activities of citizens are subject to government control

8. *democratic government:* a form of government in which the people rule either directly or through representatives

9. *representative democracy:* a form of government in which people rule themselves through elected leaders

10. *nation:* a group of people who live in a common area, believe they belong together, and share common beliefs and values

11. *nationalism:* the belief that people who consider themselves a nation ought to have their own land and government

Answer

1. As population increased, countries took a new interest in lands once thought unusable. New technology enables farmers to turn wasteland into farmland, and the search for resources that accompanied industrialization led to exploitation of rain forests, deserts, and mountain ranges.

2. (a) With a unitary government, most power rests with the central government; states or departments do little more than see that decisions made by the central government are carried out. With a federal government, the central government and the states or provinces share power. (b) With an authoritarian government, one person or a small group of people has complete authority for making and carrying out the laws. With a representative democracy, decision-making authority is broader: the people have authority to govern through elected leaders. In addition, individual rights are protected.

3. Longstanding similarities in language, customs, and religion led people to feel that they had a shared history and that they belonged together.

Locate

1. Answers will include three of the following: Japan, Philippines, Indonesia, Malaysia, Solomon Islands, Australia, New Zealand, Papua New Guinea, Bahamas, Equatorial Guinea, Cape Verde, United States.

2. (a) Brazil (b) Spain, Italy, Switzerland, West Germany, Luxembourg, Belgium

6.3 REVIEWING THE FACTS (p. 176)

Define

1. *primary economic activity:* the most basic step in resource and land development; results in the production of food, raw materials, and mineral resources

2. *secondary economic activity:* the processing of raw materials into manufactured goods

3. *tertiary economic activity:* the distribution of manufactured goods to people; also called services

4. *service:* work done to help people get or use products rather than produce them

5. *linkage:* transportation and communication systems that help get products to people and bring people together

6. *free enterprise:* an economic system in which private citizens own most of the resources, technology, and businesses and are free to use what they own, largely as they see fit

7. *socialism:* an economic system in which the government owns such basic resources as coal and iron and may also own many businesses. Private individuals own and operate smaller businesses, which may be subject to many government controls

8. *communism:* an economic system in which the government owns nearly all resources and businesses and plans and directs the use of resources and business operations

9. *commercial activity:* the producing of food, raw materials, or manufactured goods for sale

10. *consumer:* a person who buys goods and services

11. *standard of living:* a measure of how well off a group of people is

12. *subsistence activity:* the producing of just enough food and raw materials for a person's own use, with no surplus

13. *gross national product:* the total value of all goods and services produced by a country in a year

14. *per capita GNP:* a country's gross national product divided by its total population

Answer

1. People in industrialized countries engage largely in commercial activity and have stable populations, good transportation and communication linkages, increasing amounts of services, and a high standard of living. Developing countries are just beginning to industrialize, engage largely in subsistence activity, have rapidly growing populations, little modern technology, poorly developed transportation and communication linkages, and a generally lower standard of living than do industrialized countries.

2. by GNP, which measures the total performance of the economy, and by per capita GNP, which measures the amount of goods and services an economy produces for each person living in a country

Locate

(a) Europe, North America

(b) Asia, Africa (c) North America, Europe

6.4 REVIEWING THE FACTS
(p. 179)

Define

1. *interdependent:* the dependence of nations upon one another in meeting economic needs
2. *export:* to sell goods to another country
3. *import:* to buy goods from another country
4. *balance of trade:* the relationship in terms of dollar value between a country's exports and imports
5. *tariff:* a tax on imports
6. *free trade:* a government policy of seeking agreements with other governments to keep tariffs low
7. *common market:* a group of nations that agree to remove tariffs on goods sold to one another and to take other actions that expand trade
8. *alliance:* an agreement among nations to assist one another if threatened or attacked

Answer

1. (a) export of raw materials, minerals, and food; import of manufactured goods (b) export of manufactured goods and large amounts of food; import of raw materials and minerals
2. (a) by imposing tariffs to raise the price of imported goods; by refusing to sell more than a certain amount of particular resources each year to conserve resources and drive up the price of the resource on the world market (b) by reaching agreements with other governments to keep tariffs low and by creating common markets in which tariffs are removed and other actions are taken to expand trade
3. (a) to expand trade. (b) The European Economic Community
4. *Cultural and scientific ties:* an agreed-upon system of symbols on signs in public places, measurement of time in a standard way, use of the metric system for weights and measures; *Political ties:* alliances, such as NATO and the Warsaw Pact and international organizations, such as the United Nations

Locate

1. Caribbean Sea, Atlantic Ocean, Rio de la Plata 2. Caribbean Sea and Atlantic Ocean to the east, Pacific Ocean to the west

GEOGRAPHY LABORATORY
(pp. 180–181)

Speaking Geographically

1. birth rate 2. suburb 3. tertiary economic activity 4. free enterprise 5. developing country 6. GNP 7. per capita GNP 8. balance of trade

Testing Yourself

1. b 2. a 3. c 4. a 5. c
6. b 7. a 8. a 9. b 10. b 11. b

Building Map Skills

1. Belgium 2. Denmark 3. France
4. Iceland 5. Italy 6. Luxembourg
7. The Netherlands 8. Norway
9. Portugal 10. United Kingdom
11. Greece 12. Turkey 13. West Germany
14. Spain

Applying Map Skills

Answers will vary. Students should note that sparsely populated areas are typically found in climate zones with dry or polar climates and in polar, tundra, desert, mountain, and rainforest ecosystems. These are areas where lack of adequate rainfall, extremely hot or cold temperatures, or soils unsuitable for plant life greatly limit the population that can be supported.

SUPPLEMENTARY MATERIALS

Books

Ardley, Neil, *Transport on Earth*, Watts, 1981

Hills, C.A., *World Trade*, David and Charles, 1981

Metropolitan America: Geographic Perspectives and Teaching Strategies, National Council for Geographic Education, 111 West Washington Blvd., Chicago, IL 60602

Status of the World's Nations, U.S. Government Printing Office (published annually)

Stavrianos, L.S., *Global Society: The Third World Comes of Age*, Quill, 1981

Switzer, Ellen, *Our Urban Planet*, Atheneum, 1980

Other Media

The Development of Transportation (2nd edition) (EB: film/video)

Enough Food for Everyone (IER: 6 film- strips, 6 cassettes, duplicating masters)

The Modern World (LF: film; covers 1945 to present)

Industrialization and Economic Interdependency: Latin America as a Case Study (EVE: filmstrip)

U.S. Cities (Growth and Development) (EB: film/video)

7 The United States *(pages 184–213)*

ASSIGNMENT GUIDE

■ *Text Features*

Skill Workshop, p. 202   Spotlight, p. 208
Map Workshop, p. 204   Chapter Review, pp. 212–213

■ *Teacher's Resource Binder*

Assign after
p. 189 Building Basics Worksheet 7.1
        Independent Practice Worksheet 7.1 WB p. 54
p. 197 Building Basics Worksheet 7.2
        Independent Practice Worksheet 7.2 WB p. 55
p. 200 Building Basics Worksheet 7.3
        Independent Practice Worksheet 7.3 WB p. 56
p. 202 Skill Workshop: Mastering What You Read WB p. 61
p. 203 Building Basics Worksheet 7.4
        Independent Practice Worksheet 7.4 WB p. 57
p. 204 Map Workshop: Using a Baseball Map to
            Interpret Population Trends WB p. 60
p. 207 Building Basics Worksheet 7.5
        Independent Practice Worksheet 7.5 WB p. 58
p. 211 Building Basics Worksheet 7.6
        Independent Practice Worksheet 7.6 WB p. 59
p. 213 Map Test 7
        Chapter Test 7
        Enrichment Chapter 7 WB p. 62

■ *Geography Laboratory Manual: Investigating Chapter 7*

Use with pages 184–213

■ *Outline Maps 3 and 4*

Use with pages 184–213

■ *Overhead Transparencies 7, 14, 15, 16, 17, 18, and Worksheets*

Use with pages 184–213

OVERVIEW

The chapter begins by introducing students to the landforms, climates, and ecosystems of the United States. Next the chapter provides an overview of settlement and population patterns and of economic and political organization of the United States. The remaining sections of the chapter consider population and land-use patterns as well as recent trends and future challenges for the four subregions of the United States—the Northeast, the Midwest, the South, and the West.

INTRODUCING THE CHAPTER

Direct students to the small map of the world at the top of page 184. Note that the country or region of the world discussed in each of the remaining chapters of the book will be shown in blue on a map like this on the first page of each chapter. Have students locate the United States on the map, noting its neighbors to the north and south (Canada and Mexico) and the water bodies that form its borders to the east and west (Atlantic Ocean and Pacific Ocean). Point out that Units 1 and 2 prepared students for ways to examine countries in greater detail. Point out that each chapter in the remainder of the book examines a specific country or region of the world. Ask students to skim this chapter looking for familiar headings, such as "The Physical Environment" and "The Human Imprint." Next have students read the introduction to the United States on page 184.

7.1 The Physical Environment *(pages 185–189)*

MAIN IDEAS

- The United States is divided into five major landform areas—coastal plains, Appalachian Mountains, interior plains, Rocky Mountains and western plateau, and Pacific West.
- Most of the United States has a moderate climate, but because of the country's vast size, climates vary greatly.

VOCABULARY

coastal plains, p. 185; Central Plains, p. 188; Great Plains, p. 188; basin, p. 189

OBJECTIVES

Students should be able to:
- locate the five major landform regions of the United States.
- analyze climate areas of the United States.

TEACHING STRATEGIES

Using Outline Map 4 to Locate Landform Regions of the United States Using the map on pages 186–187 as a model, students can label the major landforms of the United States on Outline Map 4. Ask various class members to identify the landform feature that distinguishes each region and to name the states that are within each area.

Analyzing Climate Areas of the United States Direct students to the climate map on page 188. Ask: What two climate zones cover most of the eastern half of the United States? (temperate marine and humid continental) Locate the areas of the United States with highland climates. What landforms have helped create these climate zones? (Rocky Mountains, Sierra Nevada Mountains, Cascade Mountains) What part of the United States has the harshest and coldest climates? (Alaska)

CHECK FOR UNDERSTANDING

Write the following statements from the text on the board: (a) The landforms of the United States offer remarkable contrasts. (b) There is great variety in the climates of the United States. (c) Nearly every kind of ecosystem is found in the United States. Have students explain why each statement is true, giving examples from the text to support each.

CORRECTIONS/EXTENSIONS

Reteaching Write the following terms on the chalkboard: *coastal plains, Appalachian Mountains, interior plains, Rocky Mountains and western plateaus, Pacific West.* Ask students to turn to the map of the United States on pages 186–187. Have students locate the approximate area each of these landforms occupy and describe each landform's distinctive character.

Enrichment Divide the class into five groups. Assign each group one of the regions of the United States and have group members gather materials for a collage of resources and economic activities specific to their region. The collage can use illustrations and advertisements from magazines.

7.2 The Human Imprint *(pages 190–197)*

MAIN IDEAS

- Many different nationalities and racial groups make up the population of the United States.
- The United States is a representative democracy with a free enterprise economy.

VOCABULARY

Hispanic, p. 190; mobile, p. 192; legislative branch, p. 193; bicameral, p. 193; executive branch, p. 193; judicial branch, p. 193

OBJECTIVES

Students should be able to:
- identify populations in the United States.
- analyze the political patterns in the United States.

TEACHING STRATEGIES

Identifying Populations in the United States Write the following headings on the board: *The First Americans, Early European Settlers, The Arrival of Africans, Recent Immigrations.* Work with the students in filling in this chart with information from the section. When the chart has been completed, ask students to find evidence in their community of the influence of other cultures. (such as place names and ethnic restaurants)

Analyzing the Political Patterns Have the class study the diagram of the government of the United States on page 193. Then have students close their books and answer questions about the diagram, such as "What branch of government enacts the laws?" (Congress) Students can check the diagrams from time to time. Point out that this form of government is a federal government (page 166), that is, the federal government shares power with the states. Tell students each state also has a constitution with three branches of government. What powers do states have? (establish public schools, issue drivers' licenses, regulate traffic rules and write rules of business conduct)

CHECK FOR UNDERSTANDING

On a sheet of paper, ask each student to write the following phrases: settlement, population, political activities, economic activities. Tell class members to leave two or three lines of space between each phrase. Under each heading, have students write one or two sentences describing a pattern or trend in each of the areas.

CORRECTIONS/EXTENSIONS

Reteaching   Divide the class into two or three groups. Tell each group to imagine it is being interviewed by a correspondent for a foreign television network. The reporter wants to know about patterns of settlement, population, political organization, and economic activity in the United States today. Have each group select a representative to interview the other members of the group on these topics.

Enrichment   Have students write reports for presentation to the class on one of the following topics: (a) the population shift from the snowbelt to the sunbelt area of the United States, (b) how an unfavorable balance of trade is affecting the economic health of the United States, (c) the shift from an industrial to a service economy as the United States enters the post-industrial age.

7.3 The Northeast
(pages 197–200)

MAIN IDEAS

■ The Northeast is densely populated and highly urbanized.
■ Economic activities are varied with service industries employing a great many workers.

VOCABULARY

New England, p. 197; Middle Atlantic states, p. 197; dairy farming, p. 199; truck farming, p. 199

OBJECTIVES

Students should be able to:
■ understand where people live in the Northeast.
■ analyze economic activities in the Northeast.

TEACHING STRATEGIES

Using Outline Map 3 to Understand Where People Live in the Northeast   Have students locate the Northeast on the map on page 198. Then ask class members to label the states of the Northeast on Outline Map 3. Have the class distinguish between New England and Middle Atlantic states. (New England: Maine, New Hampshire, Massachusetts, Vermont, Rhode Island, and Connecticut. The remaining states belong to the Middle Atlantic group.) Then ask the class to examine the population density map on page 192. Where is the population the densest in the Northeast? (along the coast)

Analyzing Economic Activities in the Northeast   Have students explain why farming is a more important economic activity in the Middle Atlantic States than in New England. (New England has poor soil, long winters, and hilly land. Middle Atlantic states have longer growing seasons and better soil.) What resources have helped the people of New England develop economic activities other than farming? (forests and oceans)

CHECK FOR UNDERSTANDING

On the map of the United States on page 192, have students identify the Northeast region and point out the areas of heaviest settlement. Then have class members rank each of the following economic activities in order of their importance to the economic life of the region: farming, fishing, forestry, mining and manufacturing, providing services. Have students give reasons for their rankings.

CORRECTIONS/EXTENSIONS

Reteaching   Divide the class into an even number of small groups. Have each group compose a set of questions that can be used to test the class's understanding of the information in this section. Have groups write their questions and present them to the class, prepared with correct answers.

Enrichment The subsection "Recent Changes" on pages 199–200 identifies the decline in manufacturing and the loss of population in the 1960's and 1970's as two major changes that have taken place in the Northeast in recent decades. Ask students to find newspaper articles identifying ways in which communities in the Northeast have worked to combat migration from the area and to revive dying economies.

7.4 The Midwest
(pages 201–203)

MAIN IDEAS

- The Great Lakes region of the Midwest is highly urbanized and industrialized.
- The Midwest is an important farming area producing large quantities of corn, wheat, and dairy products.

VOCABULARY

agribusiness, p. 200

OBJECTIVES

Students should be able to:
- understand where people live in the Midwest.
- analyze economic activities in the Midwest.

TEACHING STRATEGIES

Using Outline Map 3 to Understand Where People Live in the Midwest Have students locate the Midwest on the map on page 198. Next ask class members to name the states that make up the region and label these states on Outline Map 3. Point out that the Midwest occupies the northern part of the interior plain. Then have the class examine the population density map on page 192 and the land use map on page 195. Ask: What areas of the Midwest region are most heavily settled? (near the Great Lakes, southern Ohio)

Analyzing Economic Activities in the Midwest Have students identify the agricultural crops that are most important in the Midwest. (corn, wheat, meat, and dairy products) What is the result of agribusiness farming? (Farms produce almost twice as much as Americans can consume.) What are some of the factors that have helped make the Midwest part of the nation's industrial heartland? (mineral resources, such as iron ore, limestone, and coal) What role does transportation play in the Midwest's manufacturing success? (Detroit is considered the world capital of auto making. Other midwestern factories produce farm equipment.)

CHECK FOR UNDERSTANDING

Ask students to turn to the map of the United States on page's 186 and 187. Have students identify the Midwest region and point out the areas of heaviest settlement. Ask class members to describe the features of the physical environment that helped make manufacturing important in some parts of the Midwest. (waterways, canals, rivers) Then have students give reasons why farming is important in other areas of the region. (good soils, flat plains, adequate rainfall for corn, wheat, and grazing land)

CORRECTIONS/EXTENSIONS

Reteaching Write the following statement from the text on the chalkboard: "The Midwest has level fields, excellent waterways, abundant minerals and other resources which make it one of the most varied and productive regions in the world." Have students support this statement with information from the text.

Enrichment Ask students to report to the class on one of the following: (a) the problems facing the farmers of the Midwest today, indicating both the causes and consequences of these problems for the individual small farmer and for agribusinesses, (b) why the region is sometimes referred to as the "Rust Belt."

7.5 The South
(pages 205–207)

MAIN IDEAS

- Although less urbanized than other parts of the country, the South has many fast-growing urban areas.
- The Southern economy, once dependent on agriculture, is now more diversified, with manufacturing increasing in importance.

VOCABULARY

fall line, p. 205; plantation, p. 205

OBJECTIVES

Students should be able to:
- understand where people live in the South.
- analyze economic activities in the South.

TEACHING STRATEGIES

Using Outline Map 3 to Understand Where People Live in the South   Have students locate the South on the map on page 198. Ask class members to name the states that make up the region and label these states on Outline Map 3. Then direct students to the population density map on page 192. Point out that population shifts that have created economic problems for the Northeast and Midwest have brought economic opportunities and benefits to the South. Have students list the reasons many businesses have chosen to relocate in the South. (low wages, low land prices, low taxes, educated and skilled work force, warm climate, low energy costs)

Analyzing Economic Activities in the South   Make a two-column chart on the chalkboard. Label the columns *Economic Activities* and *Crops/Products*. In the first column, list the following economic activities: *farming, forestry, fishing, mining, manufacturing,* and *services.* Have students complete the chart by indicating the types of crops or products produced in the South in each area of economic activity. (Cotton, peanuts, and poultry are important farm crops, and tourism is an important service.)

CHECK FOR UNDERSTANDING

Ask class members to name one way in which the South has changed since the early 1900's in terms of where people live and the type of work they do. (More people live in or near cities, and more work in manufacturing or service industries than in the past.)

CORRECTIONS/EXTENSIONS

Reteaching   Divide the class into small groups representing different regions in the South. Ask each group to imagine it belongs to a regional business organization. The job of this organization is to attract foreign businesses and tourists to the South. Have each group prepare a short presentation for the class describing its population distribution and economic activities and why business would thrive in their particular region.

Enrichment   Have students report to the class on how the migration to the sunbelt is affecting one of the following Southern cities: Birmingham, Alabama; Atlanta, Georgia; Memphis, and Nashville, Tennessee; Greenville, South Carolina; Raleigh, North Carolina; and Norfolk, Virginia. Reports can focus on both positive and negative changes.

7.6 The West
(pages 207–211)

MAIN IDEAS

- The West is less heavily populated than other parts of the United States.
- Economic activities in the region are varied, including manufacturing, farming, mining, ranching, and oil related industries.

OBJECTIVES

Students should be able to:
- understand where people live in the West.
- analyze the major economic activities in the West.

TEACHING STRATEGIES

Using Outline Map 3 to Understand Where People Live in the West   Have students locate the West on the map on page 198. Ask students to name the states that make up the region and label these states on Outline Map 3. Then ask the class to examine the population density map on page 192 and the climate map on page 188. Ask: What areas of the West are most sparsely settled? Most heavily settled? (Coastal areas are more heavily settled than interior regions.) What physical features or climatic conditions might account for the uneven distribution of population within the area? (mountains and deserts or arid and semiarid conditions in low density areas)

Analyzing Economic Activities in the West   Have the class locate the three major farming areas in the West on the land use map on page 195. (Great Plains, Pacific Coast states, Hawaiian Islands) Have students identify the types of crops grown in each of the three areas. Then have class members describe briefly the types of forest, fishing, and mineral resources that are important to the region's economy. (evergreen forests in northwest, fishing for salmon and tuna along coast, large deposits of oil in Texas and Oklahoma, coal in the Rockies, copper in Arizona, etc.)

CHECK FOR UNDERSTANDING

Have students identify the West on the map on pages 186–187. Have them point out the areas of heaviest settlement. Then have other class members locate the three major farming areas, the areas where fishing and forestry are important, and the areas where petroleum and copper are found.

CORRECTIONS/EXTENSIONS

Reteaching Divide the class into small groups. Ask each group to imagine its members are travel agents. Their job is to plan a tour through the West for students from east coast states. The purpose of the tour is to teach the others about the main economic activities of the West and the challenges or changes the region is facing.

Enrichment Ask several students to report to the class on either of the following: (a) the efforts California and other southwestern states are making to ensure an adequate water supply, (b) the effects of oil price declines in the 1980's on the economies of western states dependent on this resource.

Answers

7.1 REVIEWING THE FACTS (p. 189)

Define

1. *coastal plains:* the long, gently rolling lowland area along a seacoast
2. *Central Plains:* the moist, eastern portion of the interior plains of the United States
3. *Great Plains:* the dry, western portion of the interior plains of the United States
4. *basin:* a low-lying area into which rivers drain

Answer

1. (a) Directly along the coast, there is a strip of plains. To the west of these plains is a hilly area called the Piedmont. West of the Piedmont, the Appalachians—low mountains with many gaps—rise.
(b) The interior plains are a vast lowland area, broken only by a few highlands. They are divided into a wet, eastern section and a dry, western section. (c) The Rocky Mountain area is made up of a series of rugged mountain ranges extending north-south from Alaska through New Mexico. Just west of these ranges

is an area of plateaus, basins, and isolated peaks. (d) Along the Pacific are high mountains, among which are broad, fertile valleys; Alaska is mountainous; so is Hawaii, which has many active volcanoes.
2. (a) broadleaf forests, mixed broadleaf and needleleaf forests (b) grasslands (c) mountain and desert (d) thick needleleaf forests along the coast; mosses, grasses, and short bushes, as well as mountain forests in Alaska; tropical forests and semidesert in Hawaii

Locate

1. Answers will include: Bitterroot Range, Lewis Range, Bighorn Mountains, Absaroka Range, Wasatch Range, Uinta Mountains, Front Range, San Juan Mountains, Sangre de Cristo Mountains, Sacramento Mountains.
2. (a) Nevada (b) Arizona (c) Utah

7.2 REVIEWING THE FACTS (p. 197)

Define

1. *Hispanic:* of Spanish ancestry
2. *mobile:* given to frequent or constant movement
3. *legislative branch:* the branch of a government that makes laws
4. *bicameral:* having two parts, or chambers
5. *executive branch:* the branch of a government that carries out laws
6. *judicial branch:* the branch of a government, made up of courts, that judges whether people's actions are in accord with the laws

Answer

1. (a) people known as Indians, whose ancestors were Asian hunters who migrated from Asia (b) English, Scottish, Irish, French, Dutch, German, Hispanic, and African newcomers
2. *1840–1860:* Irish, English, German, and Scandinavian immigrants were most numerous. *1880–1930:* Immigrants from southern and eastern Europe (Italy, Russia, Poland, Hungary) dominated; many Chinese came as well. *1950–present:* Large numbers of immigrants have come from Mexico and other Latin American countries, Asia (the Philippines, Korea), and the West Indies.
3. The United States has a representative democracy and a federal system. A bicameral Congress is the legislative branch. The President heads the executive branch. There is also a national system of courts making up the judicial branch. The powers of the national government are described in the Constitution, which also guarantees people's rights and protects powers of the states.

4. abundant resources, adequate supplies of energy, good linkages, skilled managers and workers, the incentives of the free-enterprise system

Locate

1. (a) Appalachians, Rockies (b) the southwestern part of the interior plains, on the Gulf of Mexico, in Alaska (c) near the Great Lakes, the southwestern part of the interior plains, the south (d) the northern Great Lakes area, Rockies, Appalachians
2. (a) Pacific coast, northern Rockies, area around Great Lakes, Appalachians (b) Midwest and West

7.3 REVIEWING THE FACTS (p. 200)

Define

1. *New England:* the northern part of the northeastern United States
2. *Middle Atlantic states:* the southern and western part of the northeastern United States
3. *dairy farming:* production of milk and cheese from cows
4. *truck farming:* production of poultry and fruits and vegetables for sale

Answer

1. along the Atlantic coast from Boston, Massachusetts, to Washington, D.C.; around the Great Lakes
2. (a) poor soil, long winters, hilly terrain (b) dairy and truck farming
3. (a) electrical and transportation equipment, consumer goods, metals, processed foods, paper, chemicals, petroleum products, electronics goods, medical equipment, computers (b) banking, shipping, insurance, education, development of computer software, medical research, entertainment, tourism and recreation
4. because their factories and equipment were older and less efficient than those elsewhere

Locate

1. Maine, New Hampshire, Vermont, New York, Rhode Island, Massachusetts, Connecticut, Pennsylvania, New Jersey, Delaware, Maryland
2. all except Vermont, Pennsylvania

SKILL WORKSHOP (p. 202)

Sample Answer:
1. *Question:* Where are the Appalachian Mountains? *Answer:* west of the Piedmont; run from northern part of Maine southwest into Alabama

2. *Question:* Where are the Interior Plains? *Answer:* extend westward from Appalachians to Rockies
3. *Question:* What are the Rockies? *Answer:* a series of ranges that lie to the west of the Great Plains
4. *Question:* What does the western plateau look like? *Answer:* steep cliffs and canyons, isolated mountains, and basins
5. *Question:* What is the Pacific West? *Answer:* made up of the states that lie along western coast plus Alaska and Hawaii
6. *Question:* What is the climate of the United States like? *Answer:* mainly moderate
7. *Question:* What ecosystems are found in the United States? *Answer:* needleleaf and broadleaf forests in east, tall grasses farther west, deserts in southwest, thick needleleaf forests along coast; tundra in Alaska; dense rain forests and dry desert regions in Hawaii

7.4 REVIEWING THE FACTS (p. 203)

Define

agribusness: large-scale farming conducted by corporations

Answer

1. (a) in cities around the Great Lakes, stretching from Chicago, Illinois, eastward through Ohio
(b) the western and southern parts
2. such farm products as corn, wheat, soybeans, meat, milk, and cheese; such manufactured goods as steel, cars and other transportation equipment, machine parts, appliances
3. Businesses have lost out to foreign competitors, forcing them to lay off workers and close factories. Farmers have had trouble selling grain and other products, causing incomes to decline.

Locate

1. Ohio, Indiana, Michigan, Wisconsin, Illinois, Missouri, Iowa, Minnesota, North Dakota, South Dakota, Nebraska, Kansas
2. Minnesota, Wisconsin, Michigan, Illinois, Indiana, Ohio

MAP WORKSHOP (p. 204)

1. ten 2. (a) Toronto, Montreal
(b) expansion teams 3. (a) six
(b) eight 4. California
5. Since 1950, the areas of the country that gained the most in population were the Pacific Coast and the South.

7.5 REVIEWING THE FACTS
(p. 207)

Define
1. *fall line:* the point at which the Atlantic Coastal Plain and the Piedmont meet; rivers flowing toward the ocean break into waterfalls and rapids at this point
2. *plantation:* a large farm worked by slave laborers in the southern United States before the Civil War

Answer
1. The South is less urbanized than other regions.
2. (a) cotton (b) cotton, peanuts, peaches, apples, oranges, grapefruit, soybeans, corn, winter vegetables
3. textiles, steel, automobiles, dyes, insect sprays, chemical products, processed foods
4. *businesses:* for skilled workers and wages, taxes, and low energy costs; *people:* warm climate, low energy costs

Locate
1. West Virginia, Virginia, North Carolina, Kentucky, Tennessee, Arkansas, Louisiana, Mississippi, Alabama, Georgia, South Carolina, Florida 2. (a) Virginia, North Carolina, South Carolina, Georgia, Florida (b) Florida, Alabama, Mississippi, Louisiana

7.6 REVIEWING THE FACTS
(p. 211)

Answer
1. *Great Plains:* wheat growing, cattle ranching; *Pacific Coast:* growing of vegetables, fruits, nuts; *Hawaiian islands:* growing of sugarcane, tropical fruits
2. petroleum, coal, copper, zinc, manganese, silver, molybdenum, gold, sulphur, lead
3. finding adequate water supplies for a growing population

Locate
1. Montana, Idaho, Washington, Oregon, California, Nevada, Utah, Wyoming, Colorado, Arizona, New Mexico, Oklahoma, Texas, Hawaii, Alaska 2. (a) Washington, Oregon, California, Hawaii, Alaska (b) Texas

GEOGRAPHY LABORATORY
(pp. 212–213)

Speaking Geographically
1. Great Plains 2. plantations 3. New England
4. truck farming 5. agribusinesses
6. fall line 7. executive 8. legislative

Testing Yourself
1. Northeast, West, and Midwest 2. South
3. West 4. Midwest 5. West 6. West
7. West 8. Northeast 9. Midwest
10. South and Northeast

Building Map Skills
1. New York 2. Boston 3. Pittsburgh
4. Memphis 5. Miami 6. New Orleans
7. Detroit 8. Chicago 9. Minneapolis 10. St. Louis 11. Dallas 12. Denver 13. Phoenix
14. Los Angeles 15. Seattle 16. Honolulu
17. Anchorage 18. San Francisco

Applying Map Skills
1. New York 2. Texas 3. New Hampshire
4. Wyoming 5. Indiana 6. Hawaii 7. South Dakota 8. Alabama 9. Georgia 10. Oklahoma   The city is Washington, D.C.

SUPPLEMENTARY MATERIALS

Books
Gilfond, Henry, *The Northeast States*, Franklin Watts, 1984

Jacobson, Daniel, *The North Central States*, Franklin Watts, 1984

Lawson, Don, *The Pacific States*, Franklin Watts, 1984

National Geographic, *Our Continent: A Natural History of North America*, 1976

National Geographic, *Picture Atlas of Our Fifty States*, 1980

Thomson, Betty F., *The Shaping of America's Heartland: The Landscape of the Middle West*, Houghton Mifflin, 1977

Other Media
Branches of Government Series (NG: 3 films/videos, covering judicial, legislative, executive branches)

Building a Nation: The Story of Immigration (NG: 2 filmstrips, 2 cassettes)

Climates of the United States (CIM: film)

The Game of States (PLP: software for Apple)

The Great Lakes: North America's Inland Seas. 2nd edition (EB: film/video)

The Mississippi System: Waterways of Commerce (EB: film/video)

Regions of the U.S.A. (UL: 6 filmstrips, 6 cassettes, duplicating masters)

Roadsearch Plus (PLP: software for Apple, Commodore 64)

States and Capitals (M-Ed: software for Commodore 64)

United States Government and How It Works (EGM: 4 filmstrips, 2 cassettes)

U.S. Geography Adventure (PLP: software for Apple, IBM, MAC)

Canada *(pages 214–233)*

ASSIGNMENT GUIDE

- ***Text Features***

  Map Workshop, p. 220 — Spotlight, p. 230
  Skill Workshop, p. 227 — Chapter Review, pp. 232–233

- ***Teacher's Resource Binder***

  Assign after
  p. 218 Building Basics Worksheet 8.1
  Independent Practice Worksheet 8.1 WB p. 63
  p. 220 Map Workshop: Reading a Subway Map WB p. 66
  p. 226 Building Basics Worksheet 8.2
  Independent Practice Worksheet 8.2 WB p. 64
  p. 227 Skill Workshop: Using the Library WB p. 67
  p. 231 Building Basics Worksheet 8.3
  Independent Practice Worksheet 8.3 WB p. 65
  p. 233 Map Test 8
  Chapter Test 8
  Enrichment Chapter 8 WB p. 68

- ***Geography Laboratory Manual: Investigating Chapter 8***

  Use with pages 214–233

- ***Outline Maps 5 and 6*** Use with pages 214–233

- ***Overhead Transparencies 7, 19, 20, 21, 22 and Worksheets***

  Use with pages 214–233

OVERVIEW

The chapter begins with an examination of the five land regions of Canada: the Appalachian Highlands, the St. Lawrence-Great Lakes Lowlands, the Canadian Shield, the Western Interior Plains, and the Western Mountains. Students also learn about the climates and ecosystems within the country. Next the chapter outlines the major population groups that have settled Canada and introduces students to the parliamentary system of Canadian government. Students also learn about the nation's major economic activities. In the final section of the chapter, each of Canada's five subregions are examined in greater detail with economic changes and challenges highlighted.

INTRODUCING THE CHAPTER

Tell the class that although Canada is the second largest country in the world and the nearest northern neighbor to the United States, many Americans know relatively little about this country. To emphasize this point, give the class a not-for-credit quiz. Ask class members to number a sheet of paper from 1 to 5 and answer the following questions: (1) Which nation is larger—the United States or Canada? (Canada) (2) What type of government does Canada have? (representative democracy) (3) What is the title of Canada's head of government? (prime minister) (4) What city is the national capital of Canada? (Ottawa) (5) Why does the British monarch have an official part in the Canadian government? (Canada is part of the British Commonwealth.) Provide answers to the quiz and have students check their own papers. Then tell the class that in this chapter they will learn about many aspects of Canadian life.

8.1 The Physical Environment *(pages 215–218)*

MAIN IDEAS

- Canada is divided into five major landform areas—the Appalachian Highlands, the St.

Lawrence-Great Lakes Lowlands, the Canadian Shield, the Western Interior Plains, and the Western Mountains.

■ Because it lies so far north, most of Canada is cold with harsh winters and short summers.

VOCABULARY

Canadian Shield, p. 215; hydroelectric power, p. 215; alpine, p. 217; taiga, p. 217

OBJECTIVES

Students should be able to:
■ identify the five major landform regions of Canada.
■ understand settlement patterns in Canada based on knowledge of landforms and climate.

TEACHING STRATEGIES

Using Outline Map 6 to Identify Landform Regions of Canada Using the map on page 216 as a model, students can label the regions of Canada on Outline Map 6. Judging by the map, in which landform regions would students expect farming to be an important land use? (Great Lakes Lowlands, Western Interior Plains) Which landform regions do not appear to be well suited to farming based on their physical features? (all mountain regions)

Understanding Settlement Patterns in Canada Direct students to the climate map on page 217. Within what climate area does most of Canada fall? (midlatitude climates) What type of midlatitude climate is found there? (subarctic) What parts of Canada have a midlatitude climate most like that of the United States? (southern Canada and the northwestern coastal area) Next have students turn to the population density map on page 221. Ask students where highest population densities are located. Then ask: What conclusions may be drawn from students' knowledge of climate and population density?

CHECK FOR UNDERSTANDING

Write the names of the five major land regions of Canada on the chalkboard. Have students indicate the landform associated with each region. Then have students explain why most of Canada has a cold climate with harsh winters (located in northern latitudes) and indicate the parts of Canada that have a milder climate (southern and southwestern coast).

CORRECTIONS/EXTENSIONS

Reteaching Divide the class into five groups. Ask each group to prepare an oral report on one of the land regions of Canada. Have them use the maps on pages 216 and 217 to identify the landforms, climate areas, and ecosystems characteristic of their region.

Enrichment Have students do short research reports on how glaciers are formed and their effects on landforms in Canada. If possible, the report should be accompanied by pictures of Canadian glaciers.

8.2 The Human Imprint
(pages 218–226)

MAIN IDEAS

■ The population of Canada is predominantly English and French with descendants of Inuit Eskimo's.
■ While Canada has more land than the United States, its population is far smaller.
■ Canada is a parliamentary democracy.
■ Canada's economy relies on the existing wealth of natural resources.

VOCABULARY

Inuit, p. 218; bilingual, p. 219; confederation, p. 222; province, p. 222; head of state, p. 222; parliamentary democracy, p. 222; parliament, p. 222; prime minister, p. 223; head of government, p. 223; cabinet, p. 223; governor general, p. 223; pulp, p. 225

OBJECTIVES

Students should be able to:
■ identify the groups that settled Canada.
■ understand the population density of Canada.
■ understand Canada's government.
■ analyze economic patterns in Canada.

TEACHING STRATEGIES

Identifying Groups That Settled Canada Write the names of the following groups on the chalkboard in this order: *British, Asian, Inuit, French*. Have students arrange these groups in the order in which they settled Canada. Then ask class members to identify the two groups that originally came as colonists from a European country. (French and English)

Using Outline Map 5 to Understand the Population Density of Canada Direct students to the population density map of Canada on page 221. Have class members identify the parts of Canada that are most heavily and most sparsely settled. Encourage the class to look for relationships between climate and settlement to explain these patterns. Then have students create their own population density map of Canada using Outline Map 5.

Understanding Canada's Government Have the class note similarities between the forms of government in the United States and Canada. (Both are representative democracies with a federal system of government.) Have students compare the charts on pages 193 and 223 to note the differences between the governments. (Canada has a parliamentary democracy; the legislative and executive powers are not divided between separate branches.)

Analyzing Economic Patterns in Canada Ask the class what Canada's main export is. (natural resources) With the class's help, list these resources and their uses on the chalkboard. (vast forests for lumber and pulp; fish for food; farmland for growing crops; raising of cattle for food; minerals for manufacturing purposes) What is Canada's main import? (manufactured goods)

CHECK FOR UNDERSTANDING

Have students describe one way in which each of the following aspects of life in Canada is different from that in the United States: (a) composition of the population (Eskimo, French, English) (b) population patterns (due to harsh climate, most Canadians live in the southern region) (c) form of government (parliamentary) (d) the free-enterprise system (government owns many more businesses than in the United States).

CORRECTIONS/EXTENSIONS

Reteaching Write the following statements on the chalkboard: (a) There are both similarities and differences in the groups that settled Canada and the United States. (b) A major difference between the economy of Canada and that of the United States is the extent of government ownership of business. (c) Manufacturing is the most important part of Canada's economy. Divide the class into three groups. Have each group select a spokesperson to explain one of the statements to the class, providing supportive evidence from the text.

Enrichment Point out to the class that relationships between the English-and French-speaking groups in Canada have not always been friendly. At various times in Canada's recent history, French-speaking people, particularly in the province of Quebec, have called for independence from Canada. Divide the class into an English group and a French group. Have students research the Separatist movement through the perspective of their assigned group.

8.3 The Regions of Canada *(pages 228–231)*

MAIN IDEA

■ Climate, terrain, soil, and mineral resources in the five regions of Canada create differences in economic activities.

VOCABULARY

Atlantic provinces, p. 228; Grand Banks, p. 228

OBJECTIVE

Students should be able to:
■ analyze the differences in the regions of Canada.

TEACHING STRATEGIES

Analyzing Differences in the Regions of Canada Make a three-column chart on the chalkboard. Label the columns *Regions of Canada, Major Economic Activities, Reasons for Differences.* In the first column, list the five regions discussed in Section 3. Have students complete the second column by indicating the major economic activities in each region. Have students complete the chart by identifying land and water factors that have contributed to the marked differences between regions.

CHECK FOR UNDERSTANDING

Have students identify the types of economic activities associated with the five landform regions of Canada and explain how the physical environment has influenced activities that have become important in each region.

CORRECTIONS/EXTENSIONS

Reteaching Divide the class into small groups. Ask each group to prepare five statements about one of the regions of Canada. Each set should describe one of the regions but not mention its name. Allow five points if the name of the region is guessed after the first statement, four points after the second statement is read and so on.

Enrichment The Canadian cities of Toronto, Montreal, Quebec, and Vancouver have attracted visitors from all over the world. Many of these cities still show the influence of the French or British settlers who founded them. Have students choose one of the cities mentioned above to report to the class on its history and unique architectural features.

Answers

8.1 REVIEWING THE FACTS (p. 218)

Define
1. *Canadian Shield:* the horseshoe-shaped area of hills and plateaus covering about half of Canada
2. *hydroelectric power:* electricity created by water-driven turbines
3. *alpine:* relating to mountains
4. *taiga:* an extensive needleleaf forest

Answer
1. (a) This region has low hills and mountains that are the northern part of the Appalachian Mountains. (b) It has lowlands with lakes, among which are the Great Lakes. The St. Lawrence River empties into the Gulf of St. Lawrence. (c) The Shield is an area of hills and plateaus; it is heavily forested and dotted with glacial lakes. The rivers flowing into these lakes have many waterfalls and rapids. (d) This is a plains region, with broad, gently rolling prairie. (e) In the West, there are narrow mountain ranges of the Rockies and Coastal Mountains, separated by a rugged strip of valleys, basins, and plateaus.
2. In northern Canada, the climate is subarctic. The far north has a tundra ecosystem. South of this region is the taiga. Large areas have permafrost. Southeastern Canada has a humid continental climate moderated by the Atlantic Ocean. The natural vegetation of southeastern Canada is forest. Central Canada has a drier climate than the southeastern region. On the plains, winters are very cold and dry, and summers are short. In southwestern Canada, there is a temperate marine climate. This part of Canada is covered by evergreen forests.

Locate
1. Laurentian Highlands 2. Lakes Winnipeg, Great Slave, Great Bear, and Athabasca

MAP WORKSHOP (p. 220)

1. University, Bloor, Yonge 2. St. Patrick, Queen's Park 3. Bloor-Yonge
4. (a) Osgoode (b) University
(c) St. Andrew or Union

8.2 REVIEWING THE FACTS (p. 226)

Define
1. *Inuit:* hunting and fishing peoples of the coastal areas of northern Canada; also known as Eskimos
2. *bilingual:* speaking two languages
3. *confederation:* a loose association under a common government
4. *province:* a political subdivision of Canada
5. *head of state:* symbolic leader of a nation
6. *parliamentary democracy:* a democratic government in which the legislative body both makes laws and sees that they are carried out
7. *parliament:* the lawmaking body to which the executive is responsible in most parliamentary democracies
8. *prime minister:* the top executive official in a parliamentary democracy
9. *head of government:* the official responsible for directing a government; in a parliamentary democracy, the prime minister
10. *cabinet:* a group of advisers who assist the head of government on such matters as defense, justice, industrial development, and the environment
11. *governor general:* the British monarch's official representative; appears at official ceremonies and has other symbolic duties
12. *pulp:* the soft fiber of wood products that is ground and mixed with water to make paper

Answer
1. (a) Like the United States, the earliest immigrants came from Europe; but unlike the United States, most settlers in the 1600's and 1700's were French. By the 1800's, most immigrants to Canada were from Great Britain, while immigrants to the United States during the same years came from all parts of Europe. Unlike the United States, Canada did not again experience large waves of immigration until 1945, when immigrants started coming from Caribbean, Asian, and European nations. (b) French and English
2. (a) lowlands of the St. Lawrence-Great Lakes region (b) the far north
3. (a) In 1867, with British approval, four British colonies formed the confederation of Canada, with a government for all of Canada. The Canadian government continued to recognize the

authority of the British monarch. In 1918, Canada gained control of its relations with foreign nations. (b) member of the British Commonwealth, with a government equal in standing and powers to that of Great Britain; enjoys certain trade advantages with other Commonwealth countries and assistance with defense; considers British monarch as head of state

4. Canada is a parliamentary democracy with two branches of government, parliament and the national court system. The national court system decides cases arising under the nation's laws. Parliament makes the laws and sees that they are carried out. The head of government, the prime minister, is elected by the majority in parliament and is the leading official. The prime minister is assisted by a cabinet composed of the members of parliament.

5. *Primary:* harvesting and exporting wood products, fishing, farming and stock raising, mining; *Secondary:* food processing, manufacturing of cars and car parts, the processing of logs for lumber and wood pulp.

Locate

1. The capital is Ottawa, in the province of Ontario. 2. (a) Ontario (b) British Columbia (c) Manitoba (d) Ontario (e) Quebec

SKILL WORKSHOP (p. 227)

1. Carolyn Meyer 2. (a) Yes. (b) The notation *illus.* indicates the book has photos or drawings. 3. Eskimos—Canada; Eskimos—history 4. (a) The Independent Inuit (b) Macleans (c) 94:8 (d) June 14, 1986 5. (a) It discusses the descendants of Henson and Peary. (b) The notations *il* and *pors* indicate there are illustrations and portraits.

8.3 REVIEWING THE FACTS (p. 231)

Define

1. *Atlantic provinces:* the four provinces located in the Appalachian Highlands region of Canada: New Brunswick, Nova Scotia, Prince Edward Island, and Newfoundland
2. *Grand Banks:* a fishing area just off the coast of Newfoundland

Answer

1. (a) Fishing is the main activity; there is little industry or farming. (b) drilling for natural gas and petroleum, mining of coal, livestock ranching, wheat growing (c) lumbering; forestry; mining; making of wood and paper products; refining of crude oil; assembly of automobiles and ships
2. beginning development of mineral resources, such as iron, silver, zinc, copper, gold

3. as a source of hydroelectric power and as a major shipping route

Locate

1–2. *Newfoundland:* St. John's; *Prince Edward Island:* Charlottetown; *New Brunswick:* Fredericton; *Nova Scotia:* Halifax; *Quebec:* Quebec; *Ontario:* Toronto; *Manitoba:* Winnipeg; *Saskatchewan:* Regina; *Alberta:* Edmonton; *British Columbia:* Victoria; *Yukon Territories:* Whitehorse; *Northwest Territories:* Yellowknife

GEOGRAPHY LABORATORY (pp. 232–233)

Speaking Geographically
Answers will vary.

Testing Yourself
1. second 2. territories 3. four 4. French 5. Quebec 6. Ottawa 7. prime minister 8. Alberta 9. western 10. southeastern 11. St. Lawrence-Great Lakes lowlands

Building Map Skills
1. Newfoundland 2. Nova Scotia 3. New Brunswick 4. Quebec 5. Ontario 6. Manitoba 7. Saskatchewan 8. Alberta 9. British Columbia 10. Yukon 11. Northwest Territories 12. Prince Edward Island
A. Atlantic Ocean B. Great Lakes C. Hudson Bay D. Arctic Ocean E. Pacific Ocean

Applying Map Skills
A. Newfoundland Island, Laurentian Highlands, Montreal, Lake Ontario, Hudson Bay, Winnipeg, Regina, Great Slave Lake, Rocky Mountains, Vancouver
B. Ellesmere Island, Baffin Bay, Baffin Island, Labrador, St. Lawrence River, Lake Erie

SUPPLEMENTARY MATERIALS

Books
Blades, Ann, *A Boy of Tache,* Tundra Books, 1973 National Geographic, *Canada's Wilderness Lands,* 1982
National Geographic, *Our Continent: A Natural History of North America,* 1978
Sabin, Louis, *Canada,* Troll Associates, 1985

Other Media
Canada: Land of New Wealth (EB: 5 filmstrips, 5 cassettes or phonodiscs)
Canada: Our Northern Neighbor (BFA: film)
Canadians (EB: 5 filmstrips, 5 cassettes)
The Canadians: Their Cities (EB: film/video)
The Canadians: Their Land (EB: film/video)

CHAPTER 9

Middle America *(pages 234–255)*

ASSIGNMENT GUIDE

- **Text Features**

  Map Workshop, p. 242   Skill Workshop, p. 252
  Spotlight, p. 246   Chapter Review, pp. 254–255

- **Teacher's Resource Binder**

  Assign after
  p. 238 Building Basics Worksheet 9.1
  Independent Practice Worksheet 9.1 WB p. 69
  p. 242 Map Workshop: Using Latitude and Longitude WB p. 74
  p. 245 Building Basics Worksheet 9.2
  Independent Practice Worksheet 9.2 WB p. 70
  p. 249 Building Basics Worksheet 9.3
  Independent Practice Worksheet 9.3 WB p. 71
  p. 250 Building Basics Worksheet 9.4
  Independent Practice Worksheet 9.4 WB p. 72
  p. 252 Skill Workshop: Using a Gazetteer WB p. 75
  p. 253 Building Basics Worksheet 9.5
  Independent Practice Worksheet 9.5 WB p. 73
  p. 255 Map Test 9
  Chapter Test 9
  Enrichment Chapter 9 WB p. 76

- **Geography Laboratory Manual: Investigating Chapter 9**

  Use with pages 234–255

- **Outline Maps 7 and 8**

  Use with pages 234–255

- **Overhead Transparencies 7, 23, 24, 25, 26, and Worksheets**

  Use with pages 234–255

OVERVIEW

Chapter 9 examines the three subregions of Middle America: Mexico, Central America, and the Caribbean Islands. Students first learn about the landforms of the mainland and the physical features of the islands. Then the chapter outlines the ecosystems and climates of the region. Next students learn about the effects of Spanish colonization on the mainland and the influences of British, Dutch, French, and African cultures on the peoples of the Caribbean. In the remaining sections, the chapter explores the political and economic patterns of the three subregions.

INTRODUCING THE CHAPTER

Discuss associations students have with the term "Middle America." Where is "Middle America"? How many countries in the region can students name? Have the class locate the region on the small map at the top of page 234. What nation forms the northern border of the region? (United States) What continent forms the southern border? (South America) Point out that part of the region is an island chain. From looking at the map, can students explain why the region is called "Middle America"? Now have students read the introduction on page 234.

9.1 The Physical Environment *(pages 235–238)*

MAIN IDEAS

- The landforms in Middle America are predominantly mountainous.

- Elevation, wind, and rainfall patterns create variations in the region's mainly tropical climate.

VOCABULARY

trade winds, p. 238

OBJECTIVES

Students should be able to:
- identify landforms of Middle America on a map of the region.
- analyze climate areas of Middle America.

TEACHING STRATEGIES

Using Outline Map 8 to Identify Landforms of Middle America   Look up the term "isthmus" in the text's glossary and define it together. (a narrow strip of land joining two larger land areas) Ask students to turn to the map on page 236. Then ask: What isthmus is found in Middle America? (Isthmus of Panama) What larger land areas does it connect? (North and South America) Trace the mountains of this region that the text calls "Y-shaped." What mountain ranges form the upper part of the Y? (Western Sierra Madre and Eastern Sierra Madre) Where are these ranges located? (Mexico) What land form characterizes the area between these ranges? (plateau) Where does the mountain range begin that makes up the lower part of the Y? (just south of Mexico City) What range do these mountains join farther south? (Andes Mountains in South America) Label these landforms on Outline Map 8.

Analyzing Climate Areas of Middle America   Direct students to the climate map on page 237. Ask: Which part of this region has dry climates? (northern Mexico) What two climate areas are found throughout the rest of the region? (wet tropical and wet-and-dry tropical) Remind students that latitude, wind and rainfall patterns, and elevation all play a part in the climate of the region. Have students explain why most of the area has a tropical climate. (Most of the area is between the Tropic of Capricorn and the Equator within the tropics or low latitudes.)

CHECK FOR UNDERSTANDING

Have students identify the areas in which each of the following landforms are found in Middle America: mountains, plateau, plains, isthmus, island. Then have students describe two ways mountains influence the climate of the region.

(Higher elevations create highland or temperate climates. Mountains stop precipitation from reaching west coast of mainland.)

CORRECTIONS/EXTENSIONS

Reteaching   Divide the class into small groups. Ask each group to prepare a two-part oral report for the class. The first part should focus on landforms, the second on factors that affect that region's climate. (latitude, elevation, wind and rainfall patterns)

Enrichment   Have students choose between one of the following to report to the class: (a) the catastrophic effects of recent earthquakes on the region, (b) how Mexico City and other places in the region are attempting to make their cities safer from future earthquakes.

9.2 The Human Imprint
(pages 238–245)

MAIN IDEAS

- The people of Middle America are descendants of Indians, Spanish settlers, and Africans.
- Political instability has characterized the region since Spanish colonies became independent in the 1800's.
- Farming is the primary economic activity in the region.

VOCABULARY

mestizo, p. 239; Creole, p. 240

OBJECTIVES

Students should be able to:
- identify the population groups in Middle America.
- understand political trends in Middle America.
- identify economic patterns in Middle America and recognize their effects on the economic life of the region.
- explain the effects of colonization on current political patterns in Middle America.

TEACHING STRATEGIES

Identifying Population Groups in the Region   Have students explain why many of the people on the mainland of Middle America are of Spanish, Indian, or mestizo descent. Then ask the class why population patterns on the Caribbean Islands is different from the pattern on the mainland. (Plantation agriculture practiced by Europeans on the islands influenced settlement patterns: colonial rulers brought African slaves to their plantations as workers.) Have students describe the effects on the population of colonial settlement patterns. (sharp decline in Indian population, concentration of wealth in hands of European families)

Understanding Political Trends in Middle America   Have students explain why developments of the colonial period have made it difficult to create stable governments after independence. (Wealthy landowners retained control of governments after independence, while the majority of people were poor and were given no voice.)

Identifying Economic Patterns in Middle America   Have students turn to the land use map on page 244. Have students identify economic activities that are most important to the region. (agriculture, oil production, and mining) Next ask students to locate areas of manufacturing on the map. (Mexico City) Ask students how the sparcity of manufacturing has impacted Middle America's economy. (The region must rely on industrialized nations for its finished goods.) Tell the class that Middle America must export its raw materials in order to purchase finished goods from industrialized nations. What factors create obstacles to trade in Middle America? (Natural barriers such as mountains, valleys, tropical forests, and wide rivers create poor linkages with other nations.)

CHECK FOR UNDERSTANDING

Have students decide whether the following sentences are true or false. If a statement is false, ask students to correct it.
1. The lands of Middle America were at one time colonies of *European* powers. (T)
2. The earliest people to live in Middle America were of *Spanish* origin. (F; Indian)
3. In recent years, great numbers of Middle Americans have moved to *cities*. (T)
4. Middle America has had a pattern of *democratic* rule. (F; dictatorial rule and rebellion)
5. Except in Mexico, there is little *farming* in Middle America. (F; manufacturing)

CORRECTIONS/EXTENSIONS

Reteaching   Divide the class into small groups. Ask each group to imagine it has been asked to write a one-page article for an American newsmagazine. The topic of the article is Middle

America today. The article should describe briefly the racial makeup of the population, the political organization, and major economic activities in the region. Each group should also list items exported and those they believe would have to be imported. Students can use any additional pictures or charts to help illustrate their articles. Have each group select a representative to read its article aloud to the class.

Enrichment   Have students choose one country in Middle America to report on the following: (a) the country's relationship with the United States over the last 20 years, (b) its relationship with the other nations of the region for the past 20 years, (c) the role of political elections in that nation.

9.3 Mexico   *(pages 247–249)*

MAIN IDEA

■ Mexico is the most powerful nation in the region with an economic system that combines free enterprise and socialism.

VOCABULARY

peon, p. 247; ejido, p. 247

OBJECTIVE

Students should be able to:
■ analyze economic patterns in Mexico.

TEACHING STRATEGIES

Analyzing Economic Patterns in Mexico
Remind students that Mexico is the largest country in the region with the highest population and GNP. Have students refer to the land use map for the region on page 244. Ask students what form of economic system Mexico has. (free enterprise and socialist) Ask: In what ways is Mexico a free enterprise economy? (Many businesses are owned and operated by private citizens.) How is it like a socialist economy? (Government owns much of the manufacturing and industry, such as auto and steel plants, the nation's oil company; the government also owns the television and radio stations and has established the ejido farming system.) Point out that the ejido system is an example of land reform efforts in the region to reduce the gap separating rich and poor. Aside from industry, what is another source of Mexico's GNP? (tourism)

CHECK FOR UNDERSTANDING

Have students give specific examples of how farming, ranching, mining, manufacturing, and services affect Mexico's economy.

CORRECTIONS/EXTENSIONS

Reteaching   Have students locate the areas on the map on page 236 where commercial agriculture, mining, and industry are the major land uses. Then have class members rank the following in order of their impact on Mexico's economy: farming, mining, manufacturing, tourism. Have students give reasons for their choices.

Enrichment   Ask students to imagine that they are government officials working for the Mexican government. Their job is to attract foreign investors. Have them write a speech to present to visiting executives and bankers explaining why Mexico is a good place to build factories and commercial farms.

9.4 Central America
(pages 249–250)

MAIN IDEA

- Central America is a largely agricultural region.

OBJECTIVE

Students should be able to:
- identify barriers to economic development in Central America.

TEACHING STRATEGIES

Identifying Barriers to Economic Development in Central America   Remind students that Middle America must rely on industrialized nations for its finished goods. Ask students how this might create economic problems for the region. (With limited capital, nations must purchase expensive finished goods from other nations.) Have students identify the primary economic activities important to this subregion. (subsistence and commercial farming) What are chief crops grown in the region? (bananas, sugarcane, cacao, citrus fruits, chicle, cotton, and coffee) Ask students to describe the effects on Central American economies if world market prices for sugar and coffee fall. (When prices for these exports decline, incomes drop and

nations have to borrow money from foreign banks to purchase necessary imports.) Tell students that this pattern eventually saddles nations with heavy foreign debts. Ask students to speculate on how this affects nations. (Nations must repay debts with capital that might otherwise be used to develop secondary activities or provide basic services.)

CHECK FOR UNDERSTANDING

Have students use **Outline Map 7** to label the seven countries that make up Central America. Ask class members to describe the major economic activities in the subregion and explain why economic growth has been slow.

CORRECTIONS/EXTENSIONS

Reteaching   Divide the class into small groups. Have each group use **Outline Map 7** to create a product map of Central America. The map should show the areas where various agricultural products are grown. When groups have completed their maps, identify relationships between the physical environment and the types of crops grown in the region.

Enrichment   Have students research and report to the class on the reasons for the revolution in Nicaragua. Students should describe the country before and after the revolution and the status of the Nicaraguan economy today.

9.5 The Caribbean Islands   *(pages 251–253)*

MAIN IDEAS

- The diversity of cultural influences in the Caribbean reflect past economic patterns of colonial settlement.
- Agriculture is the most important economic activity on the Caribbean Islands.

OBJECTIVES

Students should be able to:
- identify population groups in the Caribbean.
- analyze economic activities on the Caribbean Islands.

TEACHING STRATEGIES

Identifying Population Groups of the Caribbean   Have the class refer to the map on page 245 to answer the following: What are the three major island groups that make up the Caribbean Islands? (Bahamas, Greater Antilles, Lesser Antilles) In which island group are United States territories located? (Greater Antilles) Who were the first people to live on the Caribbean Islands? (Indians) Why do so few Indians live there today? (killed by diseases spread by Europeans following colonization) Why do many islands have large black populations today? (The ancestors of these people were brought from Africa as slaves to work the plantations colonized by Europeans.) What European nations established colonies in the Caribbean Islands? (France, England, Spain, The Netherlands) Which islands are still colonies of a European country? (Aruba, Bonaire, and Curacao are controlled by the Dutch.)

Analyzing Economic Activities in the Caribbean Islands   Direct students to the Data Bank on page 243. Ask class members to locate the eleven Caribbean Island countries on the chart. Have students determine which is the smallest and the largest of these islands. Which has the most people? The least people? The fastest natural increase and the slowest natural increase? Point out that the Caribbean Island subregion contains the nation with the highest (Bahamas) and the lowest (Haiti) per capita GNP. The text refers to the region as having one-sided economic development. What is one-sided about the area's economic development? (primarily agricultural) How does this dependence on agriculture contribute to the poverty of the area?

CHECK FOR UNDERSTANDING

Have the class label the major Caribbean Islands on **Outline Map 7,** using the map on page 245 as a model. Next, have students give examples of ways European or African cultures have influenced the Caribbean Islands. (language, population makeup, dress, food, music, architecture) Indicate whether primary or secondary economic activities are more important to the economic life of the area. (primary)

CORRECTIONS/EXTENSIONS

Reteaching   Make a three-column chart on the chalkboard. Label the columns *Type of Economic Activities, Specific Activities, Where Found.* In the first column, list the terms *Primary Activities, Secondary Activities, Services.* Have students complete the chart.

Enrichment   Divide the class into five groups. Assign each group one of the following countries: Cuba, the Bahamas, Dominican Republic,

Trinidad and Tobago, Haiti. Ask each group to prepare a short report on the country assigned. The report should describe the political and economic organization of the country, its major economic activities, the basis of the country's prosperity or the reasons for its poverty, and its major imports, exports, and trading partners.

Answers

9.1 REVIEWING THE FACTS (p. 238)

Define
trade winds: winds that blow almost constantly southwestward across the Atlantic Ocean and the Caribbean

Answer
1. The mountains extend through the center of Mexico in a Y shape. The northern part of the Y is made up of the Western Sierra Madre and the Eastern Sierra Madre. South of Mexico City, the Western and Eastern Sierra Madre join to form a single mountain range, making up the lower part of the Y and extending southward to join the Andes in South America. Together with the Andes, these mountains are part of the Rim of Fire that encircles the Pacific Ocean. Within this zone, earthquakes and volcanic eruptions are common.
2. These islands are part of a chain of undersea mountains. Volcanic activity has pushed the tops of some of these mountains above sea level; in other cases, other geologic forces have lifted limestone ridges above sea level.
3. (a) Humid Tropical (b) Most of the region gets a great deal of rainfall. Northern Mexico, however, is a semiarid and arid desert area. The east coast, across which the trade winds blow, gets heavier rains than the west coast. (c) The high mountains of the mainland cut off the trade winds from the west coast; as a result, the west coast does not have nearly as much precipitation as the east coast.

Locate
1. Pacific Ocean 2. Gulf of Mexico
3. Atlantic Ocean

MAP WORKSHOP (p. 242)

1. (a) Redonda (b) Anguilla (c) St. Barthelemy (d) Saba
2. Look for answers that approximate these coordinates:
   (a) Charlestown: latitude 17°08′N, longitude 62°37′W

(b) Plymouth: latitude 16°42′W, longitude 62°13′W

(c) Basseterre: latitude 17°18′N, longitude 62°43′W

(d) Sandy Point: latitude 17°22′N, longitude 62°50′W

9.2 REVIEWING THE FACTS (p. 245)

Define

1. *mestizo:* a person of mixed European and Indian ancestry
2. *Creole:* a person of Spanish ancestry born in the Spanish colonies of the Americas

Answer

1. The Maya lived in parts of present-day Mexico and Guatemala. Most Maya lived in farming villages, but there were also large cities that served as religious centers. Maya priests had an advanced system of mathematics and an accurate calendar. The Aztec lived in present-day Mexico. They established their capital city on an island in Lake Texcoco. Crops were grown in the capital city by building islands from mud at bottom of the lake. The Aztec ruled Indian groups throughout Mexico. Conquered peoples paid tribute in farm goods or luxury items, such as gold.
2. (a) Spain (b) Spanish, Portuguese, Dutch, French, English, and African cultures
3. Military rule and other forms of authoritarian government such as dictatorial rule by a single leader, as is the case in Communist Cuba, are common. A few countries—Costa Rica is one —have democratic governments.
4. Middle America has mostly primary economic activities; agriculture, the production of oil, and mining are all important. There is little manufacturing, except in Mexico. Commercial farming is done on sugar, rubber, banana, and coffee plantations. There is some cattle ranching along the west coast of the mainland. Most agriculture is subsistence farming, with farmers growing such crops as corn, beans, and citrus fruits.
5. United States businesses have millions of dollars invested in Middle America. The United States government gives financial and military assistance to many Middle American countries. Historically, through the Monroe Doctrine, the United States has protected Latin American nations from interference by European nations. Since the 1820's, the United States has sent troops to help Middle American governments stop rebellions and has given aid to rebel groups, particularly those that are resisting efforts by Cuban or Soviet-backed groups to gain influence in the region.

Locate
1. Cuba 2. El Salvador 3. Jamaica

9.3 REVIEWING THE FACTS (p. 249)

Define

1. *peon:* a poor farm worker who lives on and works the land of a landowner
2. *ejido:* a rural farm settlement in which the land belongs to the whole community, each family being able to use the land as long as it lives in the community

Answer

1. Mexico has both large commercial farms and smaller-scale farming. On some farms, called ejidos, each family works an individual plot on communally owned land. The government provides financial assistance to small farmers and helps them in such areas as education, irrigation, and some transportation services. Commercial agriculture takes several forms. In semiarid northern Mexico, there are large cattle ranches. The northern end of Baja California has irrigated fields where intensive farming is practiced. Plantations on the Yucatan Peninsula produce agave, from which cord and rope are made. 2. Mexico has become one of the world's leading exporters of oil, although an oil glut in the 1980's has caused a sharp drop in income from this source.
3. population growth; foreign debt

Locate
1. Durango 2. Mexico City 3. Puebla

9.4 REVIEWING THE FACTS (p. 250)

Answer

1. Most Central Americans are mestizos, except in Guatemala (where most residents are Indians), in Costa Rica (where most residents are of Spanish descent), and in Belize (where half the population is of African descent).
2. few energy or mineral resources, poor inland transportation, and a lack of capital
3. agriculture, especially subsistence farming, along with the raising of such cash crops as sugarcane and coffee, usually on plantations
4. (a) sugarcane, cacao, citrus fruits, chicle, and cotton (b) coffee

Locate
1. Belize: Belmopan

2. Guatemala: Guatemala
3. Honduras: Tegucigalpa
4. El Salvador: San Salvador
5. Nicaragua: Managua
6. Costa Rica: San Jose
7. Panama: Panama City

SKILL WORKSHOP (p. 252)

1. page 492
2. page 498
3. latitude 41°56′N, longitude 120°35′W
4. (a) a strait (b) latitude 35°55′N, longitude 5°45′W
5. Great Bear Lake, California
6. Wyoming and Utah

9.5 REVIEWING THE FACTS (p. 253)

Answer
1. the Bahamas, the Greater Antilles, the Lesser Antilles
2. English, French, Dutch, Spanish, and African cultures
3. (a) *Farming:* sugar, tobacco, bananas, coconuts, fruits, spices, coffee; *Mining:* bauxite, nickel, manganese, petroleum, natural gas; *Manufacturing:* refined sugar, oil products, alcoholic beverages, clothing, textiles, chemicals, fertilizer, machinery (b) These nations lack the capital they would need to develop industry; they have heavy debts that they cannot repay; their economies have little diversification.

Locate
1. Cuba 2. Jamaica
3. Dominican Republic 4. Haiti

GEOGRAPHY LABORATORY (pp. 254–255)

Speaking Geographically
1. peon 2. ejido 3. mestizo
4. trade winds 5. Creole

Testing Yourself
1. Mesa Central 2. volcanoes 3. Cuba
4. Costa Rica 5. Panama Canal
6. Spain 7. United States 8. coffee
9. Pan American Highway

Building Map Skills
1. Pacific Ocean 2. Mexico
3. Gulf of Mexico 4. Guatemala
5. Belize 6. El Salvador 7. Honduras
8. Nicaragua 9. Costa Rica 10. Panama
11. Cuba 12. Jamaica 13. Haiti
14. Dominican Republic 15. Puerto Rico
16. Caribbean Sea 17. Atlantic Ocean

Applying Map Skills
1. Baja California
2. El Salvador
3. Belize
4. Eastern Sierra Madre
5. Belize, Guatemala, Mexico
6. Belize
7. Cuba
8. Lake Nicaragua
9. the Bahamas, Mexico
10. Panama

SUPPLEMENTARY MATERIALS

Books
Beck, Barbara L., *The Aztecs*, Franklin Watts, 1983
The Ancient Maya, Franklin Watts, 1983
Fincher, E.B., *Mexico and the United States: Their Linked Destinies*, Thomas Y. Crowell, 1983
Williams, Margot, and Josephine McSweeney, *Cuba from Columbus to Castro*, Julian Messner, 1982

Other Media
Central America: Finding New Ways, 2nd edition (EB: film/video)
Central America: A Human Geography (CIM: film)
Crescent of Crisis (UL: 8 filmstrips covering Mexico, Central America, and Cuba)
Mexico—Facing Tomorrow's Challenges (SVE: 4 filmstrips, 4 cassettes, teacher's guide)
Mexico: Our Dynamic Neighbor (NYT: filmstrip)
Story of the Aztecs (FI: film)

10 South America *(pages 256–281)*

ASSIGNMENT GUIDE

■ *Text Features*

Skill Workshop, p. 266   Map Workshop, p. 278
Spotlight, p. 269   Chapter Review, pp. 280–281

■ *Teacher's Resource Binder*

Assign after
p. 260 Building Basics Worksheet 10.1
        Independent Practice Worksheet 10.1 WB p. 77
p. 266 Skill Workshop: Comparing Employment Graphs
           WB p. 84
p. 267 Building Basics Worksheet 10.2
        Independent Practice Worksheet 10.2 WB p. 78
p. 271 Building Basics Worksheet 10.3
        Independent Practice Worksheet 10.3 WB p. 79
p. 273 Building Basics Worksheet 10.4
        Independent Practice Worksheet 10.4 WB p. 80
p. 276 Building Basics Worksheet 10.5
        Independent Practice Worksheet 10.5 WB p. 81
p. 278 Map Workshop: Interpreting a Transportation Map WB p. 83
p. 279 Building Basics Worksheet 10.6
        Independent Practice Worksheet 10.6
           WB p. 82
p. 281 Map Test 10
        Chapter Test 10
        Enrichment Chapter 10 WB p. 85

■ *Geography Laboratory Manual: Investigating Chapter 10*

Use with pages 256–281

■ *Outline Maps 9 and 10*

Use with pages 256–281

■ *Overhead Transparencies 8, 27, 28, 29, 30, and Worksheets*

Use with pages 256–281

OVERVIEW

The chapter begins with an examination of South America's landforms and varied eco-systems and climate areas. The chapter then explores the Indian, European, and African populations whose influences remain central to the cultures of the region. Students will learn about factors contributing to political instability in the region and are introduced to an overview of economic patterns. The re-maining four sections of the chapter—Brazil, Colombia, Venezuela and the Guianas, the Andes, and Southern South America—focus on challenges facing the particular nations of the region.

INTRODUCING THE CHAPTER

Have students locate South America on the map at the top of page 256. Remind the class that South America and Middle America to-gether make up the Latin American culture region. How might these two regions be similar? (languages, religious practices, the arts, political and economic patterns) Next, have students read the introduction on page 256.

10.1 The Physical Environment (pages 257–260)

MAIN IDEAS

■ South America's landform areas include highland and plains areas.
■ South America has a great variety of climates.

OBJECTIVES

Students should be able to:
■ identify the landform areas of South America.
■ identify climate areas of South America.

TEACHING STRATEGIES

Using Outline Map 10 to Identify Landform Areas Distribute Outline Map 10, South America: Physical. Have students draw in the following landform areas on their maps: (1) Andes Mountains, (2) Brazilian Highlands, (3) Guiana Highlands, (4) Patagonia, (5) Llanos Plains, (6) Amazon Basin, (7) South-Central Lowlands. Have students use the map on page 258 to label the countries these landform areas pass through.

Identifying Climate Areas of South America Ask students what accounts for the wide variety of climates and ecosystems in South America. (its extension through 67 degrees of latitude) Next, have students use the climate map of South America on page 259 to locate the part of South America that has a climate similar to that of the southeastern United States. (subtropical climate area in Brazil, Paraguay, and Argentina)

CHECK FOR UNDERSTANDING

On the map of South America on page 258, have students locate the four highland areas and the three plains areas. Also ask students to locate the major areas of tropical, subtropical, highland, and desert climates.

CORRECTIONS/EXTENSIONS

Reteaching Divide the class into small groups. Ask each group to plan a tour of South America that will give visitors an understanding of the seven landform and the major climate areas on the continent.

Enrichment Have students research and report to the class on the plant, animal, or human life found within the Amazon's tropical rain forest. Students should consider how the modern world challenges life in the rain forest.

10.2 The Human Imprint (pages 260–267)

MAIN IDEAS

■ The population of South America is Indian, European, and African.
■ Most nations in South America are ruled by dictators.
■ Most South American countries have government-owned, free-enterprise economic systems.

VOCABULARY

Guianas, p. 262; coup, p. 263; nationalize, p. 264

OBJECTIVES

Students should be able to:
■ examine how the legacy of colonial rule has affected South American political life.
■ understand South America's economy.

TEACHING STRATEGIES

Examining the Impact of Colonial Rule on Political Life Discuss ways the colonial legacy in South America is similar to that in Middle America. (social inequalities; concentration of land, wealth, and political power in the hands of a few wealthy families; strong influence of the military in political affairs; and political instability and rebellions arising from dissatisfactions of the landless and the poor)

Understanding South America's Economy Ask students what type of economy most South American countries have. (free enterprise) How do these systems differ from free-enterprise systems in other parts of the world? (Strong dictatorships in South America have nationalized major industries.) Have students rank the following activities in order of their importance to South America: mining, farming, manufacturing.

CHECK FOR UNDERSTANDING

Ask students who are the major population groups in South America today. (Indian, European, and African) Then ask class members to explain how most governments in South America differ from representative democracies. (dictatorships or military governments, without elected leaders) Have students name one way that free-enterprise economies in South America are different from free enterprise systems in other parts of the world. (many industries are nationalized and government-owned)

CORRECTIONS/EXTENSIONS

Reteaching Have students find evidence in the section to support one of the following main ideas: (a) Despite the fact that the South American continent is sparsely settled, the region faces population pressures. (b) Independence came more easily to Brazil than to neighboring countries. (c) Although most new South American nations modeled their governments on the United States, today most are not representative democracies.

Enrichment Have students report on the history and cultural legacy of the Inca people. Reports can focus on the language, food, clothing, religious practices, and economic activities of the Incas and should indicate where there influence is still felt today.

10.3 Brazil *(pages 268–271)*

MAIN IDEAS

- Over half of all South Americans live in Brazil.
- Development of energy resources has aided Brazilian manufacturing.

VOCABULARY

gasohol, p. 270

OBJECTIVES

Students should be able to:
- identify challenges to Brazil's economic development.

TEACHING STRATEGIES

Identifying Challenges to Brazil's Economic Development Have students explain ways that dependence on a single crop or product has hurt the Brazilian economy in the past. (foreign competition, falling price on international market) Have class members name

the major strains on Brazil's economy. (foreign debt, rapid population growth) Have students explain why foreign debt and rapid population growth put strains on the economy. (If the population growth rate exceeds the economic growth rate, overall standard of living declines.)

CHECK FOR UNDERSTANDING

Have students identify areas of heavy and sparse settlement in Brazil. Ask class members to explain why the government moved the capital of Brazil from Rio de Janeiro to Brasilia.

CORRECTIONS/EXTENSIONS

Reteaching Divide the class into three groups, corresponding to the subsections in this chapter: *People and Settlement Patterns, Brazil's Economy, Resource Development.* Each group should make an outline on the chalkboard highlighting the subsection's main ideas. Questions should be asked of each group by other class members and answers given by citing examples from the text.

Enrichment Divide the class into small groups. Ask groups to imagine that its members belong to a government agency whose job it is to encourage resettlement in the Amazon Basin or the central highland area. Students should write a plan indicating (a) incentives to be used to encourage settlement in the area, (b) benefits to the country, (c) the ways news of this plan can be passed on to the public. Tell the class that one fourth of the people in Brazil cannot read, and people in many areas do not have televisions or radios.

10.4 Colombia, Venezuela, and the Guianas *(pages 272–273)*

MAIN IDEAS

- Poor transportation linkages affect small villages in Colombia while Venezuela has one of the highest standards of living in Latin America.
- Guyana, Suriname, and French Guiana make up the region known as the Guianas.

OBJECTIVES

Students should be able to:
- identify the countries of the region.

- compare political and social patterns in the region.

TEACHING STRATEGIES

Using Outline Map 9 to Identify the Countries of the Region   Distribute Outline Map 9, South America: Political. Using the map on page 267 as a model, students can label the three bodies of water surrounding this region as well as the countries of the region.

Comparing Political and Social Patterns in the Region   Ask students to describe one way that the political organization of Colombia and Venezuela are similar. (Wealth is concentrated in the hands of a few families.) What are differences in social class organization between the two countries. (Class lines are more fixed in Colombia than in Venezuela.) What is one reason for political instability in Guyana and Suriname? (cultural differences)

CHECK FOR UNDERSTANDING

Have students describe the major economic activities in each of the countries of the region. Then have them give reasons for the political instability that has plagued Guyana and Suriname since independence.

CORRECTIONS/EXTENSIONS

Reteaching   Divide the class into five groups. Ask each group to prepare an oral report on one of the countries of the subregion. The presentation should include: (a) a hand-drawn map of the country and its capital city, (b) identification of the country's landforms, (c) a description of the country's climates, (d) a list of the most important economic activities in the country.

Enrichment   Have students research how one of the following has affected Venezuela's high standard of living: (a) concentrated wealth in the hands of a few, (b) oil deposits along the Caribbean coast, (c) commercial ranching, (d) government subsidy to the poor.

10.5 Andean South America *(pages 274–276)*

MAIN IDEAS

- Unlike other regions of South America, centers of population in the Andean region

of Peru, Ecuador, and Bolivia are in the highland areas.
- Economic development in the region is primarily limited to farming.

VOCABULARY

altiplano, p. 274

OBJECTIVES

Students should be able to:
- compare levels of economic development in Peru, Ecuador, and Bolivia.

TEACHING STRATEGIES

Comparing Levels of Economic Development   Have students identify the factors that have been barriers to economic development in the region. (poor climate and soil, lack of modern farming methods, poor transportation linkages, reliance on a single crop) Have students turn to the World Data Bank on page 264. What is the largest country in the region? (Peru) What accounts for Peru's economic success in the region? (diversification of economic activities) What has hurt Bolivia's economy? (reliance on only tin to sustain Bolivia's economy)

CHECK FOR UNDERSTANDING

Have students describe current patterns of population distribution in Andean South America and explain why these patterns are starting to change. Have class members also list the economic activities important to each of the countries of the region.

CORRECTIONS/EXTENSIONS

Reteaching   Divide the class into three groups. Ask each group to prepare an oral report on one of the countries of the subregion. Students should: (a) locate the country and its capital on a map of South America, (b) identify the landforms characteristic of the country, (c) describe the country's climates, (d) indicate the areas of heaviest and sparsest settlement. Groups should then indicate the resources or economic activities that have either helped or been a barrier to the country's economic development.

Enrichment   Ask students to imagine themselves as tourists visiting Peru. Have students write home describing their visit to the ancient Incan ruins of Machu Picchu.

10.6 Southern South America *(pages 276–279)*

MAIN IDEAS

■ Despite political unrest, Southern South America is one of the more prosperous areas of Latin America.

VOCABULARY

estancia, p. 277; gaucho, p. 277; junta, p. 277

OBJECTIVES

Students should be able to:
■ assess economic development in Southern South America.

TEACHING STRATEGIES

Assessing Economic Development Have students identify the major economic activities in each country. Ask students how the physical environment in Argentina has affected its economy. (fertile land, level ground, long growing season) What conditions prevent Chile from producing enough food for its people? (poor soil, unproductive farms) Ask students to describe the difference between the types of farming found in Paraguay and Uruguay. (Paraguay has subsistence farming; Uruguay has a thriving commercial farming sector.) How have good linkages helped Uruguay achieve one of the higher standard of living in Southern South America? (goods are easily moved within the country)

CHECK FOR UNDERSTANDING

Have students locate the subregion on the map on page 258 and point out the areas of heaviest and sparsest settlement. Have students name the countries where the largest portions of the population are of European ancestry (Argentina and Uruguay) and the country where most people are mestizo (Paraguay). Then ask class members to describe the major economic activities in Argentina, Chile, Paraguay, and Uruguay.

CORRECTIONS/EXTENSIONS

Reteaching Make a three-column chart on the board. Label the columns *Country, Economic Activities, Assets/Barriers to Economic Growth.* Write the names of the following countries in first column: Argentina, Chile, Paraguay, Uruguay. Have class members come to the board to complete the chart.

Enrichment Ask students to imagine themselves as journalists writing articles for the local newspaper. Have students report on the disappearance of more than 9,000 Argentine citizens, many of them teen-agers, during the rule of the military junta from 1976 to 1978. Reports should also include what relatives of the missing have done to investigate their family members' fates.

Answers

10.1 REVIEWING THE FACTS (p. 260)

Answer

1. There are four highland areas: the Andes Mountains, the Eastern Highlands, the Brazilian Highlands, and the Guiana Highlands. There are three areas of plains: the llanos in the north, the Amazon Basin in Brazil, and the plains drained by the Paraná and Paraguay rivers (including the pampas of Argentina).

2. Earthquakes, volcanoes, and folding continue in the Andes. This indicates that the continental plate on which the Andes rise is still moving west, continuing its collision with the Nazca plate under the Pacific Ocean.

3. The continent has mainly a tropical climate. The Amazon Basin is hot and rainy all year round. The rest of the tropical area is hot all year, with a rainy season and a dry season. The Amazon Basin is the world's largest area of tropical forest. The climate of the Andes changes from hot to cold as the elevation increases. The southern Andes have a moist and cool climate, with forests like those of the Pacific Northwest in the United States. The Atacama Desert along the western slopes of the Andes is the driest desert in the world. The northern and southern plains are grasslands with savanna ecosystems.

4. because it extends through 67° of latitude

Locate

1. Venezuela, Guyana, Suriname, French Guiana

2. large parts of Brazil, Peru, Equador, Colombia, Suriname, Guyana, French Guiana; small parts of Bolivia, Uruguay, Venezuela

3. large areas in Peru, Chile, Argentina; small areas in Venezuela, Colombia, Equador, Brazil, Bolivia, Paraguay

4. Wet Tropical

SKILL WORKSHOP (p. 266)

1. (a) 19 percent (b) 36 percent (c) 20 percent
2. (a) Chile (b) Ecuador 3. (a) Venezuela
(b) Ecuador 4. Venezuela
5. (a) Each has about a third of its workers in industry. (b) Chile has only 9 percent of its work force in agriculture, while Paraguay has 44 percent. Chile has nearly twice as high a percentage in services—31 percent to Paraguay's 18 percent. Also, a large part of Chile's work-force is in the "other" category (27 percent), while only a small part of Paraguay's is.

For a special challenge: While both Argentina and Chile have low percentages in farming and high percentages in industry and services, Venezuela's economy seems even more developed. Over 80 percent of its workers are in services and industry.

10.2 REVIEWING THE FACTS (p. 267)

Define

1. *Guianas:* two countries along the northeast coast of South America (including Guyana and Suriname) and a department of France (French Guiana)
2. *coup:* a sudden, and sometimes violent, overthrow of an existing government by a small group, usually of military officers
3. *nationalize:* to place a business under government control

Answer

1. (a) Spain, Portugal (b) Portugal
2. (a) in the first part of the 1800's (b) Dictatorships usually ignore the constitution and courts, end elections, and abolish the legislature. They help to keep wealth in the hands of the few. The landless and poor are given little chance to improve their lives or take part in government. People who speak out against these conditions may be jailed, kidnapped, or killed.
3. mining, production of oil, subsistence farming, growing of some cash crops (coffee and wheat in particular), ranching, food processing, textile making, steelmaking, metal production, chemical refining

Locate

1. Brazil, Chile 2. Bolivia, Paraguay

10.3 REVIEWING THE FACTS (p. 271)

Define

gasohol: a fuel made from agricultural crops, prepared by mixing gasoline and alcohol

Answer

1. Ninety percent live within 200 miles of the Atlantic Ocean, on the coastal plain and bordering uplands.
2. high foreign debt, rapidly increasing population, high unemployment and widespread poverty, particularly in rural areas
3. coffee and sugar

Locate

1. Brasília 2. Chile, Ecuador

10.4 REVIEWING THE FACTS (p. 273)

Answer

1. (a) Mestizos and people of European ancestry (b) Many blacks and people of European ancestry oppose East Indians.
2. (a) It is more varied than in the past. At one time, the country's economy was based mainly on the export of coffee. Colombia now mines coal, iron ore, and limestone and has several oil fields. These resources supply textile mills, steel plants, shoe factories, and chemical refineries. (b) Much of Venezuela's wealth is based on oil obtained from large deposits along the Caribbean coast. The government has nationalized the oil industry, encouraged farm production by giving farmland to landless farmers and supporting irrigation projects. Venezuela has a democratic government, no rigid class differences, and a middle class; the poor receive help with housing, health care, and jobs.

Locate

1. *Colombia:* Bogota; *Venezuela:* Caracas; *Guyana:* Georgetown; *French Guiana:* department of France; *Suriname:* Paramaribo
2. Pacific Ocean, Caribbean Sea

10.5 REVIEWING THE FACTS (p. 276)

Define

altiplano: a high plateau in Bolivia

Answer

1. in the mountains and upland valleys
2. *Peru:* finding new sources of income from oil and timber production, building plants to process agricultural products and refine metals and oil, developing tourism *Ecuador:* attempting to diversify through increased mining and oil production
3. Because of the rugged and steep terrain of the Andes Mountains and the dense rain forests of the eastern lowlands, there are few good roads or railroads.

Locate
1. *Peru:* Lima;
Ecuador: Quito;
Bolivia: La Paz and Sucre
2. Ecuador

MAP WORKSHOP (p. 278)

1. (a) auto and truck (roads), trains (railroads), airplanes (airports) (b) Montevideo
2. (a) Trinidad (b) Montevideo (c) most likely by railroad to Montevideo, then by ship to Europe
3. (a) railroad (b) Tacuarembo, Paso de los Toros, Durazno, Florida, Canelones
4. (a) Melo (b) about 300 miles
5. The most likely route would be by rail. First, the goods would be shipped north to Canelones. Then they would go on the northeast rail line, taking the east-northeast spur to Treinta y Tres. From Treinta y Tres, they would travel northeast again, reaching Rio Branco after going a total of about 375 miles.

10.6 REVIEWING THE FACTS (p. 279)

Define
1. *gaucho:* a cowhand on an Argentine cattle ranch
2. *estancia:* an Argentine cattle ranch
3. *junta:* a military council that controls a government

Answer
1. Paraguay has the highest rate of population growth in South America. Population growth in Chile, Argentina, and Uruguay is the lowest in Latin America.
2. (a) wheat, corn, flax, wool, and mutton (b) packed meats and textiles
3. copper
4. (a) Paraguay is building dams on the Paraná River to harness waterpower. When the dams are completed, Paraguay is likely to become the world's largest exporter of hydroelectric power. (b) Uruguay's income from exports of wool, hides, grain, meat, and leather exceeds the costs of imports of manufactured goods and energy.

Locate
1. *Argentina:* Buenos Aires;
Chile: Santiago;
Paraguay: Asunción;
Uruguay: Montevideo.
2. Uruguay

GEOGRAPHY LABORATORY (pp. 280–281)

Speaking Geographically
1. altiplano 2. pampas 3. gauchos
4. estancias 5. llanos

Testing Yourself
1. Brazil 2. oil 3. in the interior
4. Spain 5. Bolivia 6. Bolivia 7. Chile

Building Map Skills
1. *French Guiana:* a department of France which has no capital
2. *Suriname:* Paramaribo
3. *Guyana:* Georgetown
4. *Venezuela:* Caracas
5. Colombia: Bogotá
6. Ecuador: Quito 7. Peru: Lima
8. Bolivia: La Paz, Sucre
9. Chile: Santiago
10. Argentina: Buenos Aires
11. Uruguay: Montevideo
12. Paraguay: Asunción
13. Brazil: Brasília

Applying Map Skills
from Valparaiso: through the Pacific Ocean, the Panama Canal, the Caribbean Sea, and the Gulf of Mexico.
from Buenos Aires: through the Rio de la Plata, the Atlantic Ocean, the Caribbean Sea, and the Gulf of Mexico

SUPPLEMENTARY MATERIALS

Books
Baker, Nina B., *He Wouldn't Be King: The Story of Simon Bolivar,* Vanguard, 1941
Clark, Ann Nolan, *Secret of the Andes,* Viking, 1952
The Incredible Incas and Their Timeless Land, National Geographic, 1975
Mangurian, David, *Children of the Incas,* Four Winds, 1979
Price, Willard, *Amazon Adventure,* Merrimack, 1983

Other Media
The Amazon: People and Resources of Northern Brazil (EB: film/video, available in Spanish)
Brazil: South America's Giant (BFA: film)
Industrialization and Economic Interdependence: Latin America as a Case Study (EVE; filmstrip)
Latin America (ED: 4 filmstrips, 2 cassettes, teacher's guide)
South America: History and Heritage (BFA: film)

CHAPTER 11 Western Europe *(pages 282–307)*

ASSIGNMENT GUIDE

■ ***Text Features***

Map Workshop, p. 288	Spotlight, p. 301
Skill Workshop, p. 294	Chapter Review, pp. 306–307

■ ***Teacher's Resource Binder***

Assign after

p. 285	Building Basics Worksheet 11.1 Independent Practice Worksheet 11.1 WB p. 86
p. 288	Map Workshop: Interpreting a Language Map WB p. 91
p. 292	Building Basics Worksheet 11.2 Independent Practice Worksheet 11.2 WB p. 87
p. 294	Skill Workshop: Analyzing a Photograph WB p. 92
p. 297	Building Basics Worksheet 11.3 Independent Practice Worksheet 11.3 WB p. 88
p. 302	Building Basics Worksheet 11.4 Independent Practice Worksheet 11.4 WB p. 89
p. 305	Building Basics Worksheet 11.5 Independent Practice Worksheet 11.5 WB p. 90
p. 307	Map Test 11 Chapter Test 11 Enrichment Chapter 11 WB p. 93

■ ***Geography Laboratory Manual: Investigating Chapter 11***

Use with pages 282–307

■ ***Outline Maps 11 and 12***

Use with pages 282–307

■ ***Overhead Transparencies 9, 31, 32, 33, 34, and Worksheets***

Use with pages 282–307

OVERVIEW

Chapter 11 begins by examining the major landforms of Western Europe—the Great European Plain, the Central Uplands, the Alpine Mountains, and Northwest Mountains. The chapter then discusses how the climates and ecosystems of much of the region are moderated by nearness to water. Next, the cultural differences of language, religion, and education between regions are explored. Students will also learn that most Western European nations are parliamentary democracies with mixed free-enterprise economies. The remainder of the chapter looks at the three subregions of Western Europe—the British Isles and Northern Europe, the European Heartland, and Southern Europe.

INTRODUCING THE CHAPTER

Have students read the chapter introduction on page 282. Then ask the class to name the three areas of Europe that will be studied in this chapter. (Western Europe, Eastern Europe, and the Soviet Union) Have students locate Greece on the map on page 284. Tell students that from its location, Greece would appear to be a part of the Eastern Europe region. Ask class members to explain why Greece is included in the study of Western Europe. (It has political ties to Western Europe.) What traits do the countries of Eastern Europe share? (These countries share democratic governments, free enterprise or socialist economic systems.)

11.1 The Physical Environment *(pages 283–285)*

MAIN IDEAS

- Western Europe has four major landform areas—the Great European Plain, the Central Uplands, the Alpine Mountains, and the Northwest Mountains.
- Despite level of latitude, many parts of Western Europe have moderate climates due to the moderating influence of the Gulf Stream.

OBJECTIVES

Students should be able to:
- locate the major landforms of Western Europe on a map.
- identify climate areas of Western Europe.

TEACHING STRATEGIES

Using Outline Map 12 to Locate Major Landforms   Divide the class into small groups. Provide each group with a copy of Outline Map 12, Western Europe: Physical. Ask students to use the map on page 284 to identify the countries of Western Europe. Next, have groups label the following landform regions: Great European Plain, Central Uplands, Alpine Mountain System, Northwest Mountains. Groups should also label the following rivers: Rhone, Seine, Po, Rhine, Loire, Thames, and Tiber rivers and the following larger bodies of water: Mediterranean, Atlantic Ocean, North Sea, Baltic Sea. Have groups construct keys for their maps.

Identifying Climate Areas of Western Europe   Direct students to the climate map on page 285. Ask the class in which areas they think each of the following has the greatest influence on climate patterns: nearness to water and ocean currents (temperate marine areas), prevailing winds (carry warm air across Europe), latitude (warmer in lower latitudes), elevation (cooler as elevation rises).

CHECK FOR UNDERSTANDING

Ask students to name the major landforms of Western Europe. (Great European Plain, Central Uplands, Alpine Mountains, Northwest Mountains) Have students discuss the factors that have given much of Western Europe a milder climate than Canada despite the fact that both are at the same latitude.

CORRECTIONS/EXTENSIONS

Reteaching   Write the following terms on the chalkboard: *Great European Plain, Central Uplands, Alpine Mountains, Northwest Mountains.* Have students locate the approximate area each of these regions occupies on the map on page 284. Then ask them to describe the landforms that give each region its distinctive character. Next, have students point out the areas of temperate marine and humid continental climate, the areas of subarctic and subpolar climate, the area of highland climate, and the areas of Mediterranean subtropical and semiarid climates. As each is located on the map, have students indicate the factors that have influenced climate patterns in the area.

Enrichment   Have students research the effects of acid rain on West Germany's Black Forest. Students should consider what steps the government is taking to protect that ecosystem.

11.2 The Human Imprint *(pages 286–292)*

MAIN IDEAS

- Nations of Western Europe differ from one another in language, level of education, and religion.
- Some governments in Western Europe are constitutional monarchies while the majority are parliamentary democracies.
- Most Western European countries have mixed free enterprise systems.

VOCABULARY

Indo-European, p. 287; literate, p. 287; Protestant, p. 287; Holocaust, p. 289; welfare state, p. 289; constitutional monarchy, p. 289; neutral, p. 290; European Economic Community, p. 291; Common Market, p. 291

OBJECTIVES

Students should be able to:
- identify cultural differences among Western European countries.
- describe political patterns in Western Europe.
- analyze economic activities in the region.

TEACHING STRATEGIES

Identifying Cultural Differences   Write the words *Language, Education,* and *Religion* on the chalkboard. Ask students to choose two countries in the region and compare them in terms of these cultural elements.

Describing Political Patterns   Write the following terms on the chalkboard: *presidential system, parliamentary system, constitutional monarchy, welfare state,* and *multiparty political system.* Have class members explain each term and tell how it applies to political patterns in Western Europe. (Students should understand that a country can be both a parliamentary democracy and a constitutional monarchy—a king or queen is head of state, while a prime minister is head of government.)

Analyzing Economic Activities   Direct students to the land use map of Western Europe on page 291. Ask: How does the type of farming done throughout most of Western Europe differ from the farming done in much of Latin America? (commercial farming rather than subsistence) In what countries is logging or forestry an important activity? (Norway, Sweden, Finland) What mineral resources might have helped the north-northwest area to industrialize? (coal, iron, natural gas) Have the class compare the land use map with the population density map on page 266. Ask students what relationships they see between population densities and industrial areas. (The most heavily settled areas are also the most highly industrialized.)

CHECK FOR UNDERSTANDING

Ask students to describe the population density and growth rate in Western Europe. (heavily populated and low growth rate) Have students supply the key terms that describe the political and economic systems in Western Europe. (representative democracy and constitutional monarchies; mixed free-enterprise system)

CORRECTIONS/EXTENSIONS

Reteaching   Divide the class into small groups, each representing a country in Western Europe. Have each group prepare six interview questions for the other groups. Questions should focus on aspects of culture, politics, and economics.

Enrichment   Have students report on the steps that led to formation of the Common Market and its impact on the economies of the region.

Students should consider its setbacks, challenges, and goals for the future.

11.3 The British Isles and Northern Europe
(pages 293–297)

MAIN IDEA

■ The people of the British Isles and Norden have a generally high standard of living.

VOCABULARY

Norden, p. 293

OBJECTIVE

Students should be able to:
■ analyze economic activities and the standard of living in the region.

TEACHING STRATEGIES

Analyzing Economic Activities and Standard of Living   Have students locate the region on the map on page 293. Tell students that the area is made up of countries that are either islands or peninsulas. Ask: How has nearness to the sea influenced agricultural activities? (Sea moderates climate and allows people to grow crops farther north than would otherwise be possible; winds from the sea ensure adequate rainfall for farming.) Have students identify some of the factors that have lowered Great Britain's position as the leading industrial power. (building of new, more efficient factories by other nations and failure of British factories to modernize, exhaustion of iron and coal resources, and increased reliance on imports of raw materials) Have students explain why Norway was slower to industrialize than most other countries of Western Europe. (lack of energy and mineral resources) How did Norway overcome these limitations? (developed hydroelectric power and imported coal)

CHECK FOR UNDERSTANDING

Have students locate the British Isles and the countries that make up Norden on the map on page 284. Ask class members to point out the areas of heaviest settlement. Ask students how the region has made use of the sea. Have students turn to the map on page 291 to identify land use in the region.

CORRECTIONS/EXTENSIONS

Reteaching   Make a two-column chart on the chalkboard. Label the columns *British Isles* and *Norden*. Then have the class rank each of the following economic activities in order of their importance to the economic life of the British Isles and Norden: farming, fishing, forestry, mining, services that include government workers, and manufacturing.

Enrichment   Tell students that Western Europe exports many of its products to the United States. Evidence of this can be found in grocery stores, car dealerships, and department stores. Have students create symbols of items they find—from sardines and cheeses to wool sweaters and watches—that represent Western European imports. Pin these symbols to a large outline map of Western Europe. Have students be prepared to tell the raw materials that went into each product and where those might have come from in the region.

11.4 The European Heartland *(pages 297–302)*

MAIN IDEAS

- The European heartland is densely settled.
- Both France and West Germany have well-balanced economies with strong manufacturing and agricultural sectors.
- Service industries such as banking and shipping are important in the Low Countries.

VOCABULARY

heavy industry, p. 298; light industry, p. 298; Low Countries, p. 300; Benelux, p. 300

OBJECTIVES

Students should be able to:
- understand population density in land areas of the heartland.
- identify economic activities in the region.

TEACHING STRATEGIES

Understanding Population Density   Have students locate the European heartland on the map on page 293 and name the countries of the region. (France, West Germany, Belgium, the Netherlands, Luxembourg, Switzerland, Austria, Liechtenstein) Ask: Which country of the European heartland is largest in land area? (France) What country in the subregion has the largest population? (West Germany) Two countries in this subregion have the highest per capita GNPs in Western Europe. Which countries are they? (Liechtenstein, Switzerland) Which country in the heartland subregion has the lowest per capita GNP? (Austria)

Identifying Economic Activities in the Region   Divide the class into four groups—France, West Germany, the Low Countries, the countries of the Alps. Have each group prepare a short oral report on each of the following topics: (a) type of crops grown in the area, (b) the major products of the area, (c) any economic activities that are unique or particularly important to the area.

CHECK FOR UNDERSTANDING

Have students label the countries of the European heartland on **Outline Map 11.** Ask class members to point out the areas of heaviest settlement. What are some physical features in the environment that have helped make agriculture and manufacturing important to parts of the subregion? (rich soils of the plains, mineral resources, such as iron ore and coal) How have a central location and good transportation helped the area industrialize?

CORRECTIONS/EXTENSIONS

Reteaching   Ask class members to explain why the following are true or false: (a) The European heartland is an area of dense settlement. (b) Few countries of the heartland have a high standard of living. (c) Despite poor transportation linkages, the countries of the region are beginning to industrialize. (d) In most countries of the subregion, both primary and secondary economic activities are important. (e) Austria's greater natural resources has enabled it to industrialize more rapidly than Switzerland.

Enrichment   Austria and Switzerland are members of the European Free Trade Association. Ask students to research this group, identifying how this group differs from the Common Market and naming the association's other members.

11.5 Southern Europe *(pages 303–305)*

MAIN IDEAS

- Portugal is among the least industrialized nations of Europe.

- Under a constitutional monarchy, industry and commerce have become important to Spain's economy.
- Italy has the most developed economy of southern Europe.
- Shipping is the leading industry in the country of Greece.

OBJECTIVES

Students should be able to:
- understand the population density of southern Europe.
- assess economic development in southern Europe.

TEACHING STRATEGIES

Understanding Population Density Have students locate southern Europe on the map on page 293 and name the countries of the region. Tell the class that the countries of Andorra, Monaco, Malta, San Marino, and Vatican City are not found on the map. Have students note the size and population of these countries on the World Data Bank chart on page 191 and then on the physical map on page 284. According to the chart, is the population in this region higher or lower than other parts of Europe? (higher)

Assessing Economic Development in Southern Europe Have students find evidence on the World Data chart on page 191 to support the fact that southern Europe lags behind the rest of Europe economically. (The per capita GNPs of most of these countries are well below those of the other nations in the region.) Based on per capita GNP, ask students which of the larger countries of southern Europe appears to be the least developed? (Portugal) The most developed? (Italy) What accounts for the lower level of economic development in southern Europe? (lack of energy and mineral resources, many areas with land poorly suited to farming, poor transportation linkages in some areas)

CHECK FOR UNDERSTANDING

Have students label the countries of southern Europe on **Outline Map 11.** Which are the four largest countries in the region? (Spain, Portugal, Italy, Greece) Have students identify the major economic activities in each of these four countries and explain how the area differs from other parts of Western Europe in terms of economic development. (less industrialized, lower standard of living)

CORRECTIONS/EXTENSIONS

Reteaching Distribute **Outline Map 11** to the class. Have students turn to page 288, Interpreting a Language Map. Have class members ask each other questions about languages spoken in Western Europe, such as "Where is English spoken?" Have students identify the country of the spoken language and fill it in on their outline map.

Enrichment Have students research one of the smaller countries of southern Europe—Monaco, Andorra, or Vatican City. Students should report on the form of government and economic activities found there and how political and economic activities in these countries differ from the larger countries in the region.

Answers

11.1 REVIEWING THE FACTS (p. 285)

Answer
1. Western Europe has four major land areas—the Great European Plain (a vast lowland across the northern mainland), the Central Uplands (in the interior of the mainland), the Alpine Mountains (south of the Central Uplands), and the northwest highlands (dominating Great Britain and Scandinavia).
2. because of the moderating influence of the Gulf Stream

Locate
1. (a) the Appennines (b) the Pyrenees (c) the Alps 2. Norway, Sweden, Finland

MAP WORKSHOP (p. 288)

1. (a) three (b) twenty-five (c) one
2. (a) Indo-European (b) Germanic
3. France, Spain, Romania, Portugal, Italy
4. *Family:* Indo-European; *Branch:* Slavic

11.2 REVIEWING THE FACTS (p. 292)

Define
1. *Indo-European:* the family of languages from which come most of the languages spoken in Western Europe
2. *literate:* able to read and write
3. *Protestant:* a member of a branch of Christianity formed in the 1500's as a protest against certain practices of the Roman Catholic Church

4. *The Holocaust:* the systematic murder of six million European Jews by the Nazis during World War II

5. *welfare state:* a government that provides such services to its citizens as medical care and old-age insurance

6. *constitutional monarchy:* a form of government under which the government is operated according to a constitution, and the head of state is a monarch with few powers, real power belonging to elected officials

7. *neutral:* not taking sides in international conflicts

8. *European Economic Community:* an organization of 12 Western European countries whose main purpose is furthering trade among its members

9. *Common Market:* another name for the European Economic Community

Answer

1. Western Europe is highly urbanized. The highest density is found in the southern British Isles, the Netherlands, and the Ruhr Valley. The north, the Alps, and parts of the south are less populous than the central areas.

2. People in Western Europe are divided by language (more than 50 are spoken in the region), education (northern countries have higher literacy and better educated citizens than do southern countries), and religion (the two major groups are the Protestants, concentrated in the north, and the Roman Catholics, concentrated in the south).

3. Most of the region's countries are parliamentary democracies; a number of these are constitutional monarchies.

4. manufacturing, mining, extraction of oil, intensive farming, raising of livestock

Locate

(a) Norwegian Sea (b) North Sea
(c) Aegean Sea (d) Mediterranean Sea

SKILL WORKSHOP (p. 294)

1. Bergen is sandwiched between the sea and mountains.

2. selling flowers; activities associated with a seaport—boating, fishing, etc.

3. summer

4. Students should include some of the following information in their answers:
(a) well-dressed, cheerful people, evidence of industry in the form of boats, flower market, cars
(b) boats and sea in background
(c) climate appears mild; lots of outdoor activity

5. cheerful, colorful place

11.3 REVIEWING THE FACTS (p. 297)

Define

Norden: the northern subregion of Western Europe, made up of the countries of Scandinavia along with Iceland and Finland

Answer

1. United Kingdom

2. It is very high; per capita income exceeds that of the United States.

3. protection from invaders, development of fishing industry, production of North Sea oil, moderate climate and long growing season for farmers

4. fishing; farming; forestry and making of pulp products; textile making; manufacturing of machinery, steel, cars, precision equipment

Locate

1. (a) United Kingdom (b) Ireland (c) Norway (d) Sweden (e) Finland (f) Denmark (g) Iceland

2. Kjolen Mountains

11.4 REVIEWING THE FACTS (p. 302)

Define

1. *Low Countries:* Belgium, the Netherlands, and Luxembourg; so-called because most of the plain on which these three countries lie is near sea level

2. *Benelux:* another name for Belgium, the Netherlands, and Luxembourg; created by combining the first letters of each country's name

3. *heavy industry:* manufacturing that uses large amounts of raw materials and large machines

4. *light industry:* manufacturing that uses small quantities of raw materials and small tools

Answer

1. French farmers live in towns or villages and travel to and from their fields each day; in the United States, farmers live on the land they farm.

2. (a) Germany was divided at the end of World War II. The eastern part of the country—then occupied by the Soviet army—became a Communist country. The western part—controlled by the United States, the United Kingdom, and France—became the country of West Germany.
(b) the Ruhr Valley

3. farming (production of cheese and other dairy goods, raising of livestock and a variety of crops), banking, shipping, making of textiles, steel-

making, and production of chemicals

4. to overcome the lack of major energy resources and the poor linkages of the Alpine area

Locate

1. (a) France (b) West Germany (c) Belgium (d) the Netherlands (e) Switzerland (f) Austria 2. (a) Seine River (b) Rhine River

11.5 REVIEWING THE FACTS (p. 305)

Answer

1. Its standard of living is lower than that of the European heartland; per capita GNP is about half that of the rest of Western Europe.
2. Spain's dictatorship was replaced by a constitutional monarchy; industry, commerce, and cities have all grown.
3. the Po River
4. shipping, tourism

Locate

1. (a) Portugal (b) Spain (c) Italy (d) Greece
2. (a) Sicily (b) Crete (c) Corsica

GEOGRAPHY LABORATORY (pp. 306–307)

Speaking Geographically

1. literate
2. Norden
3. welfare state
4. constitutional monarchy
5. Benelux
6. neutral
7. Common Market
8. The Holocaust
9. Indo-European

Testing Yourself

Low Countries: reclaimed land, busiest ports in the world
Scandinavia: North Sea oil, subarctic climate
West Germany: Ruhr Valley, Saar Valley
Southern Europe: Po Valley, Appennines, olive oil, Mediterranean climate, Iberian Peninsula

Building Map Skills

1. Iceland
2. Norway
3. Sweden
4. Finland
5. Denmark
6. United Kingdom
7. Ireland
8. the Netherlands
9. Belgium
10. Luxembourg
11. West Germany
12. France
13. Spain
14. Portugal
15. Italy
16. Switzerland
17. Austria
18. Greece

Applying Map Skills

Stockholm, Copenhagen, Amsterdam, London, Bonn, Paris, Bern, Rome, Madrid, Athens

SUPPLEMENTARY MATERIALS

Books

Di Franco, Anthony, *Italy: Balanced on the Edge of Time*, Dillon, 1983

Ferrara, Peter L., *NATO: An Entangled Alliance*, Franklin Watts, 1984

Fradin, Dennis, *The Republic of Ireland*, Children's Press, 1984

Jones, Madeline, *Finding Out about Industrial Britain*, David & Charles, 1984

Rutland, Jonathan, *Take a Trip to Spain*, Franklin Watts, 1981

Scandinavia, Time-Life, 1985

Shirer, William L., *The Rise and Fall of Adolf Hitler*, Random/Landmark, 1984

Tomlins, James, *We Live in France*, Franklin Watts, 1984

West Germany, Time-Life, 1985

Other Media

British Isles (SVE: 6 filmstrips and 6 cassettes)

Central Europe (NG: 3 filmstrips, 3 cassettes, teacher's guide)

European Cities: Rome, Madrid, Stockholm, Vienna (EB: 4 filmstrips and 4 cassettes)

Geography of Europe Series (NG: filmstrips)

Germany: A Regional Geography (IFB: film)

Italy: The Land and the People (CIM: film)

Life in Mediterranean Lands (CIM: film)

Netherlands: Past and Present (CIM: film)

Northern Europe: The Nordic Countries (NG: filmstrip, cassette)

Southern Europe (NG: 3 filmstrips and 3 cassettes)

Western Europe (M-Ed: software for Commodore 64)

Western Europe (NG: 3 filmstrips, 3 cassettes, teacher's guide)

12 Eastern Europe *(pages 308–327)*

ASSIGNMENT GUIDE

■ **Text Features**

Spotlight, p. 312   Skill Workshop, p. 318
Map Workshop, p. 316   Chapter Review, pp. 326–327

■ **Teacher's Resource Binder**

Assign after
p. 310 Building Basics Worksheet 12.1
     Independent Practice Worksheet 12.1 WB p. 94
p. 316 Map Workshop: Using Maps for History WB p. 97
p. 318 Skill Workshop: Using Graphs to Interpret
        Economic Trade Patterns WB p. 98
p. 320 Building Basics Worksheet 12.2
     Independent Practice Worksheet 12.2 WB p. 95
p. 325 Building Basics Worksheet 12.3
     Independent Practice Worksheet 12.3 WB p. 96
p. 327 Map Test 12
     Chapter Test 12
     Enrichment Chapter 12 WB p. 99

■ **Geography Laboratory Manual: Investigating Chapter 12**

Use with pages 308–327

■ **Outline Maps 13 and 14**

Use with pages 308–327

■ **Overhead Transparencies 9, 35, 36, 37, 38, and Worksheets**

Use with pages 308–327

OVERVIEW

The chapter begins by discussing Eastern Europe's landforms—an area of unbroken plains and plains broken up by mountain ranges—and its climate. Students look at the region's population diversity, its languages and religions, the impact of nationalism, and events in the region that led to political and economic control by the Soviet Union. The final section of the chapter considers the major economic activities in each of the countries of Eastern Europe.

INTRODUCING THE CHAPTER

Tell the class that Eastern European nations are linked by similarities in their economic and political systems. Have the class read the chapter introduction on page 308. Next, ask the class to locate the region on the world map at the top of page 308. Point out that the introduction refers to Eastern Europe as caught between a "rock and a hard place." Have class members explain how this expression applies to this region. The introduction also calls the region a "shatter belt." Explain this term (an area of conflict and political instability) and have students note possible reasons for the region's position as a center of conflict. (Central location made it a crossroads for migrating peoples whose cultures then clashed, or territorial conflicts ensued.)

12.1 The Physical Environment *(pages 309–310)*

MAIN IDEAS

■ Eastern Europe is made up of plains—the Great European, the Great Hungarian, and the Walachian; and mountain ranges—Erzgebirge, Sudeten, Carpathian, Transylvanian Alps, Dinaric Alps, the Balkan and Rhodope Mountains.

■ Eastern Europe has two main types of climates—a humid continental climate and a mild marine climate.

OBJECTIVES

Students should be able to:
■ identify Eastern Europe's landforms.
■ describe climate areas in Eastern Europe.

TEACHING STRATEGIES

Using Outline Map 14 to Identify Landforms of Eastern Europe Distribute Outline Map 14: Eastern Europe: Physical. Direct students to the map on page 309. Have students take turns asking each other questions about the landform areas and bodies of water in the region. As students answer questions correctly, have them mark the landform or body of water on their maps.

Describing Climate Areas of Eastern Europe Have students turn to the climate map on page 310. Ask: What are the two major climate areas in Eastern Europe? (midlatitude and subtropical) What Eastern European countries have a humid continental climate? (Poland, Hungary, Romania, Yugoslavia, and part of Czechoslovakia) Why does most of Eastern Europe have a colder climate than Western Europe? (farther from the Atlantic Ocean and the moderating influence of the Gulf Stream) What factors have helped create a Mediterranean climate in parts of this region? (nearness to the Black and Adriatic Seas, lower latitude or closer to the equator)

CHECK FOR UNDERSTANDING

Have students name the two types of landforms found in Eastern Europe (mountains, plains). Ask students to identify the factors that have given much of the region a colder and drier climate than Western Europe. (distance from the Atlantic Ocean and Gulf Stream)

CORRECTIONS/EXTENSIONS

Reteaching Distribute **Outline Map 13** to the class. Using the maps on pages 309 and 310, students can fill in the countries of Eastern Europe on their outline maps. Next, ask them to label major landform areas. Students should also list the climate found in each country.

Enrichment Have students draw maps of the Danube River and the course it travels. Ask students to also report on ways the river has

been important to Eastern Europeans through recent and past history.

12.2 The Human Imprint *(pages 311–320)*

MAIN IDEAS

■ Eastern Europe is densely settled, with highest population density in the cities.
■ Since the end of World War II, Eastern Europe has been dominated politically by the Soviet Union.
■ The major goal in Eastern Europe is to develop heavy industry and modernize agriculture.

VOCABULARY

ethnic group, p. 311; Ural-Altaic, p. 313; minority, p. 313; satellite, p. 315; martial law, p. 315; capital goods, p. 317; consumer goods, p. 317; COMECON, p. 319

OBJECTIVES

Students should be able to:
■ describe population diversity in the region.
■ analyze political patterns in Eastern Europe.
■ assess economic development in Eastern Europe.

TEACHING STRATEGIES

Describing Population Diversity Write the terms *ethnic group* and *minority* on the chalkboard. Have students define each term and distinguish between them. (*ethnic group:* a group sharing similar customs, language, religion, and tradition; *minority:* a group within a country that differs from the majority of the population) Which country in Eastern Europe has the greatest ethnic mix? (Yugoslavia) How has the presence of ethnic groups affected Eastern European boundaries? (Disputes have arisen over which country a minority group belongs to, and where that country's border lies.)

Analyzing Political Patterns in Eastern Europe Ask students in what way Eastern Europe is a political region. (Communist governments and domination by the Soviet Union) Ask: What are the factors that have helped Yugoslavia maintain some independence from the Soviet Union? (no border with Soviet Union, long seacoast making it accessible to western Europe)

Assessing Economic Development Ask students to describe the difference between consumer goods and capital goods and to give examples of each. (Consumer goods are products used by individuals, like Televisions, radios, refrigerators, etc.; capital goods are products used by industries or are forms of transportation, like trucks, heavy machinery, ships, etc.) What is a major economic goal of most Eastern European nations? (to build industry) How has the emphasis on capital goods affected Eastern Europe's trade with other nations? (hurt it, because the region has few consumer goods to sell abroad)

CHECK FOR UNDERSTANDING

Have students describe one way in which settlement patterns in Eastern Europe have changed since 1950. (Population is more urbanized and is growing very slowly or declining.) Ask class members to name the kinds of differences among the peoples of the region. (language, religion, cultural traditions) and indicate ways these differences have affected the history of the region. (led to political instability and conflict) Then have students discuss the political and economic patterns in Eastern Europe. How have different nations responded to the Soviet presence?

CORRECTIONS/EXTENSIONS

Reteaching Divide the class into small groups. Ask each group to make a three-column chart. Have groups label the columns *Areas of Comparison, Eastern Europe, Western Europe.* In the first column, have groups list the following items, leaving several lines of space after each phrase: *Population Density, Population Growth, Impact of Ethnic Differences, Political Patterns, Economic Patterns.* Have groups complete their charts by comparing the two regions according to the categories listed in Column 1.

Enrichment Tell students that the Warsaw Pact is a Communist security alliance that parallels NATO. COMECON is the economic alliance that resembles Western Europe's Common Market. Assign students to report to the class on the goals and operations of each of these organizations. Other students should report to the class on the reasons that Yugoslavia and Albania do not belong to either organization and the ways the governments of these nations have achieved political independence from the Soviet Union.

12.3 Nations of Eastern Europe *(pages 320–325)*

MAIN IDEAS

- East Germany and Czechoslovakia have the strongest economies in Eastern Europe due to industrialization.
- Hungary, Poland, and East Germany have large, productive agricultural areas.
- Albania, Romania, Bulgaria, and Yugoslavia are among the least industrialized nations in Europe.

VOCABULARY

collective farm, p. 321; state farm, p. 321

OBJECTIVES

Students should be able to:
- identify the nations of Eastern Europe.
- analyze economic differences among Eastern European nations.

TEACHING STRATEGIES

Identifying the Nations of Eastern Europe Divide the class into eight groups. Assign each group one of the countries of the region. Have each group write a paragraph describing its country's location, major landforms and bodies of water, the important economic activities, its standard of living or level of economic development, and any unique or unusual features of its political or economic system. Paragraphs should then be presented to the class.

Analyzing Economic Differences Have the class turn to the World Data Bank on page 319. Have students use the per capita GNPs to rank the countries of the region in order of standard of living. What factors have contributed to East Germany's ability to develop a strong economy? (more heavy industry than other Eastern European countries, good transportation linkages, good farmland and strong agricultural sector) What has helped Czechoslovakia achieve a strong economy compared to other Eastern European nations? (mineral resources for industrialization; Historically close ties with Western Europe enabled country to share in early technological and industrial advances.) What factors contribute to the low standard of living in Albania? (subsistence farming, poor linkages, rugged mountain terrain, and little industry)

CHECK FOR UNDERSTANDING

Have students identify the major economic activities in each of the nations of Eastern Europe and how these activities impact the standard of living in the region.

CORRECTIONS/EXTENSIONS

Reteaching   Make a list of the nations of Eastern Europe on the chalkboard. Have students list the level of industrialization and the importance of agriculture in each. Point out that countries with higher industrialization tend to have higher per capita GNPs than countries with economies based primarily in agriculture.

Enrichment   Divide the class into small groups. Ask each to plan a two-week vacation in Eastern Europe. Groups can consult guide books or tourist agencies to find names of places that are popular tourist attractions. Class members can also be asked to report on the restrictions or rules governing travel by Westerners in Soviet-bloc countries.

Answers

12.1 REVIEWING THE FACTS (p. 310)

Answer

1. because the welter of different peoples living in the area has made it hard to form strong, stable countries
2. (a) The eastern portion of the Great European Plain extends through this area. (b) In this area, there is a tangle of small mountain ranges and plains.
3. (a) Eastern Europe has two main types of climates—a humid, continental climate that is colder and drier than that of Western Europe and a mild, marine climate. (b) The humid, continental climate is found in most of the region; the marine climate is found in the south, along the Adriatic and Black seas.

Locate

1. (a) East Germany (b) Poland (c) Czechoslovakia (d) Hungary (e) Romania (f) Yugoslavia (g) Bulgaria (h) Albania 2. (a) Baltic Sea (b) Black Sea (c) Adriatic Sea

MAP WORKSHOP (p. 316)

1. Greece 2. Ottoman empire
3. (a) Bulgarians, Romanians, Albanians
(b) Czechs, Serbo-Croatians, Austrians, Hungarians

4. Austria-Hungary, Russia, and Germany
5. Warsaw 6. Belgrade
7. (a) Italy, Austria-Hungary, Montenegro, Ottoman empire, Greece
(b) Italy, Yugoslavia, Albania
8. Lithuania, Poland, Czechoslovakia, Hungary, Romania, Bulgaria, Greece
9. (a) Ottoman empire (b) Turkey
10. Poland has gained territory in the north and west and lost territory in the east.

For a special challenge: Macedonians, Serbo-Croatians

SKILL WORKSHOP (p. 318)

1. (a) fuels and raw materials (b) agricultural and forestry products (c) largest share—fuels and raw materials; smallest share—manufactured consumer goods
2. (a) machinery and heavy equipment (b) fuels and raw materials, plus machinery and heavy equipment
3. Hungary 4. Poland
5. Both have a large share of trade with the Soviet Union (32 percent for Hungary and 65 percent for Poland); for Hungary, the COMECON nations are also important trading partners. 6. Poland

12.2 REVIEWING THE FACTS (p. 320)

Define

1. *ethnic group:* a group of people who have in common many customs and traditions that give its individuals a feeling of identity and belonging
2. *Ural-Altaic:* the family of languages to which Hungarian belongs
3. *minority:* any group of people within a country that differs in some way from most of the population
4. *satellite:* a country that is dominated politically and economically by another, more powerful country
5. *martial law:* rules under which the military takes control of a country's government
6. *capital goods:* products used mainly by industry in the making or shipping of other goods
7. *consumer goods:* products used mainly by individuals
8. *COMECON:* the Council for Mutual Economic Assistance, which is an organization to which the Soviet Union and all Eastern European countries except Albania and Yugoslavia belong; its main purpose is furthering mutual trade

Answer

1. Population in rural areas has declined, while the population in industrial cities has grown.
2. (a) Most Eastern Europeans speak a Slavic language, but German, Romance languages, and Ural-Altaic languages are also spoken in the region. (b) Roman Catholics, followers of the Eastern Orthodox church, Muslims, and Jews
3. Because many ethnic groups with strong nationalistic feelings live in the area, competition among groups has undermined stability.
4. a defense treaty that joins the Soviet Union and most Eastern European countries
5. The Soviet Union is the real power behind most Eastern European governments. The Soviet Union forced Poland to declare martial law to defeat Solidarity. The Soviet Union is a major trading partner; Comecon is dominated by the Soviet Union.

Locate

1. Hungary, Czechoslovakia
2. Budapest, Bucharest, Belgrade
3. the Great European Plain, which stretches across the northern part of the region

12.3 REVIEWING THE FACTS (p. 325)

Define

1. *collective farm:* a farm run by a group of farmers under government direction, with members of the collective each earning a share of the collective's income
2. *state farm:* a farm run by the government, with workers receiving a wage from the government for their work

Answer

1. East Germany, Czechoslovakia, and Poland
2. (a) Romania has refused to support Soviet foreign policy toward China and has strengthened its trade ties with Western Europe.
(b) Yugoslavia does not belong to COMECON or the Warsaw Pact and has ties with Western European countries.
(c) Albania is a member of neither COMECON nor the Warsaw Pact and maintains strict isolation from the Soviet Union and other countries.
3. (a) higher wages, more food and consumer goods, lower prices, and more personal freedom
(b) It has granted some freedoms, allowed small-scale free enterprise, and improved living standards.

Locate

1. East Germany, Czechoslovakia, Hungary, Yugoslavia, Albania, Bulgaria
2. (a) Poland (b) Albania

GEOGRAPHY LABORATORY (pp. 326–327)

Speaking Geographically

1–12. Answers will vary.

Testing Yourself

1. East Germany 2. Albania
3. Czechoslovakia 4. Hungary
5. Bulgaria 6. Romania 7. Poland
8. Yugoslavia 9. Poland
10. Czechoslovakia 11. Yugoslavia

Building Map Skills

1. East Germany 2. Poland 3. Czechoslovakia 4. Hungary 5. Romania 6. Bulgaria 7. Yugoslavia 8. Albania

Applying Geography Skills

Population:
Largest—Poland	37,800,000
Smallest—Albania	3,100,000

Population Density:
Highest—East Germany	154 people/sq km
Lowest—Bulgaria	80 people/sq km

Land Area:
Largest—Poland	120,726 sq mi
Smallest—Albania	11,100 sq mi

Natural Increase:
Fastest—Albania	2.0 percent
Slowest—East Germany	0.0 percent

SUPPLEMENTARY MATERIALS

Books

Dornberg, John, *Eastern Europe: A Communist Kaleidoscope,* Dial, 1980
MacShane, Dennis, *Solidarity: Poland's Independent Trade Union,* Dufor, 1982

Other Media

An Introduction to Capitalism, Socialism, and Communism (NG: 4 film strips, 4 cassettes, including "Capitalism," "Socialism," "Communism," "Comparative Systems Today")
Czechoslovakia (GA: 3 filmstrips and 3 cassettes)
Eastern Europe: Unity and Diversity (CF: film)
Germany: Divided Berlin (EVE: 2 film strips, 2 cassettes, teacher's guide)
Poland (CF: film)

13 The Union of Soviet Socialist Republics
(pp. 328–351)

ASSIGNMENT GUIDE

■ **Text Features**

Spotlight, p. 332   Skill Workshop, p. 344
Map Workshop, p. 341   Chapter Review, pp. 350–351

■ **Teacher's Resource Binder**

Assign after
p. 332 Map Workshop: Understanding World Time Zones
      WB p. 103
p. 333 Building Basics Worksheet 13.1
      Independent Practice Worksheet 13.1 WB p. 100
p. 341 Skill Workshop: Analyzing Statistics WB p. 104
p. 343 Building Basics Worksheet 13.2
      Independent Practice Worksheet 13.2 WB p. 101
p. 349 Building Basics Worksheet 13.3
      Independent Practice Worksheet 13.3 WB p. 102
p. 351 Map Test 13
      Chapter Test 13
      Enrichment Chapter 13 WB p. 105

■ **Geography Laboratory Manual: Investigating Chapter 13**

Use with pages 328–351

■ **Outline Maps 15 and 16**

Use with pages 328–351

■ **Overhead Transparencies 9, 39, 40, 41, 42, 43, and Worksheets**

Use with pages 328–351

OVERVIEW

The chapter begins with an examination of the six landform regions of the Soviet Union —the Great European Plain, Ural Mountains, West Siberian Plain, Central Siberian Plateau, East Siberia Uplands, and the Central Asian Ranges—and discusses the region's climates and ecosystems. Students next learn about the diverse ethnic groups that make up the nation's population, the 1917 revolution that put Communist rulers in power, and the way the Communist party exercises power today. The chapter concludes with a look at economic activities and prospects for future development in the Soviet Union's five subregions. These subregions are the western Soviet Union, Transcaucasia, Soviet Central Asia, Western Siberia, and Eastern Siberia.

INTRODUCING THE CHAPTER

Give the class the following quick quiz to gauge their knowledge of the Soviet Union: (1) On what continent(s) is the Soviet Union located? (Europe, Asia) (2) Name three countries that share a border with the Soviet Union. (China, Afghanistan, Iran, Poland, Czechoslovakia, Romania, Finland) (3) What do the initials U.S.S.R. stand for? (The Union of Soviet Socialist Republics) (4) Which country is larger in area—the Soviet Union or the United States? (Soviet Union) (5) Which country has more people—the Soviet Union or the United States? (Soviet Union) (6) How many time zones does the Soviet Union have? (11) (7) What city is the national capital of the Soviet Union? (Moscow) Tell the class that in this chapter, they will learn more about the Soviet Union.

13.1 The Physical Environment (pages 329–333)

MAIN IDEAS

- The Soviet Union has six major landform regions—the Great European Plain, Ural Mountains, West Siberian Plain, Central Siberian Plateau, East Siberia Uplands, Central Asian Ranges.
- Although large parts of the Soviet Union are no farther north than Western Europe, the Soviet Union has a far colder climate.
- Ecosystems in the Soviet Union include tundra, taiga, mixed needleleaf and broadleaf forests, steppe, prairie, and desert.

VOCABULARY

Siberia, p. 330

OBJECTIVES

Students should be able to:
- make a map of the six major landform regions of the Soviet Union.
- analyze climate patterns in the Soviet Union.

TEACHING STRATEGIES

Using Outline Map 16 to Create a Landform Map   Divide the class into small groups. Give each group a copy of Outline Map 16. Have students label the following bodies of water on the map: Black Sea, Caspian Sea, Aral Sea, Lake Balkhash, Lake Baikal, Atlantic Ocean, Pacific Ocean, Bering Sea, Arctic Ocean, Baltic Sea. Next, have groups label the following rivers: Lena, Don, Ob, Dnieper, Volga, Irtysh, Yenisey. Then have students show the areas of the country that are plains, mountains, and plateaus. The class can use the information on landforms on pages 329–330 and the map on page 329 as references. Remind groups to make keys for their maps.

Analyzing Climate Patterns in the Soviet Union   Have the class compare the climates of the Soviet Union with other countries at the same latitudes on the world climate map on pages 64–65. Ask: How is the climate in most of the European part of the Soviet Union different from the climate in Western Europe? (Western Europe has a mild temperate marine climate, while the European part of the Soviet Union has a humid continental climate with greater extremes in temperature between winter and summer.) What factors help to explain the colder climate in the Soviet Union? (The Soviet Union is too far inland to benefit from the warming effect of the Gulf Stream.) What two types of climates are found in most of the Asian part of the Soviet Union? (subarctic and subpolar) What country in North America has a climate similar to that of Siberia? (Canada) What part of the Soviet Union has a very dry climate? (southwest)

CHECK FOR UNDERSTANDING

Have students explain why most of the Soviet Union has a colder climate than Western Europe. (Western Europe blocks the Soviet Union from the warming effect of the Gulf Stream.) Ask class members to distinguish between tundra, taiga, and steppe and indicate which type of ecosystem is best for agriculture. (steppe)

CORRECTIONS/EXTENSIONS

Reteaching   Divide the class into small groups. Have each group prepare maps showing the landforms, climate areas, and ecosystems of the Soviet Union. The landform presentation should indicate which parts of the country are plains, mountains, and plateaus. The climate presentation should include an explanation of the reasons for the coldness of the climate. The ecosystem presentation should indicate relationships between climate and the type of vegetation found in each ecosystem. The world ecosystem map on pages 82–83 can serve as a reference for the ecosystem map. The USSR physical and climate maps on pages 329 and 331 can be used as resources for the other maps.

Enrichment   Have students make climate graphs for three cities in the USSR like the one for Moscow on page 69. The *Reader's Digest Almanac and Yearbook* and the *Weather Almanac* are useful resources for this activity.

13.2 The Human Imprint (pages 333–343)

MAIN IDEAS

- The Soviet Union is made up of many different ethnic groups.
- The Communist party dominates Soviet politics.
- The Soviet Union is the leading economic power among Communist countries.

VOCABULARY

tsar, p. 333; Russ, p. 333; Soviet Central Asia, p. 334; Bolsheviks, p. 336; premier, p. 337; general secretary, p. 338; kolkhoz, p. 340; sovkhoz, p. 340; nonaligned, p. 343

OBJECTIVES

Students should be able to:
- analyze a population density map of the USSR.
- analyze political patterns in the Soviet Union.
- describe economic patterns in the USSR.

TEACHING STRATEGIES

Analyzing the Population Density of the USSR Have students locate the cone-shaped area of densest settlement on the population density map on page 335. Ask: What type of climate does the area of heaviest population density have? (humid continental) What types of climates do the areas that are most sparsely settled have? (subpolar and subarctic) Which ethnic group is the largest? (Russian) How many cities with major population centers shown on the map on page 329 are located on the Trans-Siberian Railroad? (6)

Analyzing Political Patterns in the Soviet Union Write the following statement from the text on the chalkboard: *The Communist party is the real power in the Soviet government.* Have class members explain this statement drawing on the information on pages 336–338. Discussion should focus on the powers of the Communist party in Soviet political life. (Only members of the Communist party can run for political office. No other political parties are permitted to exist. Party members choose candidates for the Supreme Soviet, propose laws, and select top leaders for the government. Tight control of the media by party and government officials and harsh punishment of dissenters severely limits the ability of people outside the party to influence the political system.)

Describing Economic Patterns in the USSR Ask students what kinds of farming can be found in the USSR. (collective and state farms—the kolkhozes and sovkhozes, and commercial farming) What evidence is there that collective farming has not been entirely successful? (Although 3 percent of all Soviet farmland is given to private plots, these plots produce nearly half of all eggs and about one third of the milk, fruit, and vegetables consumed in the country.) Why hasn't collective farming been more productive? (lack of incentives for farmers on collective and state farms; uncertainty of rainfall) Have students identify the incentives farmers on privately owned farms have been given to increase production.

CHECK FOR UNDERSTANDING

Have students locate on the map on page 329 the most densely settled area of the USSR and explain why so much of the population lives in this area. Students should also describe the role of the Communist party in the Soviet political system and identify the major economic activities in the nation.

CORRECTIONS/EXTENSIONS

Reteaching Group students into pairs. One member of each pair should be an American student and the other a Soviet student. Each Soviet student should state the region of the country he or she represents. Have American students interview the Soviet students asking about the region's population, and its economic and political life. The questions should be ones that can be answered using the information in Section 2.

Enrichment Have students report on one of the following: (a) the various ethnic groups living in the Soviet republics, (b) the Soviet Union's treatment of religious minorities or political dissidents, (c) the changes in economic and political policy that have taken place under Mikhail Gorbachev.

13.3 Regions of the Soviet Union
(pages 345–349)

MAIN IDEAS

- The Soviet Union can be divided into five regions: western Soviet Union, Transcaucasia, Soviet Central Asia, Western Siberia, and Eastern Siberia.
- The regions of the Soviet Union differ in their economic development.

OBJECTIVES

Students should be able to:
- identify the regions of the Soviet Union.

- compare economic patterns and level of development among the regions of the Soviet Union.

TEACHING STRATEGIES

Using Outline Map 15 to Identify the Regions of the Soviet Union   Distribute Outline Map 15. Direct students to the map on page 345. Have students mark the region's areas on their maps when they answer the following questions correctly. Ask: Which region is the smallest? (Transcaucasia) Which region is the largest? (Eastern Siberia) Which regions are in Europe? (western Soviet Union, Transcaucasia) What two regions have the Yenisey River as a border? (Eastern and Western Siberia) What region has the Caspian Sea as part of its western border? (Soviet Central Asia)

Comparing the Regions of the Soviet Union   Divide the class into small groups. Ask each group to make a six-column chart. Have groups label the columns *Region, Republics within Region, Climate Patterns, Primary Economic Activities, Secondary Economic Activities, Mineral Resources.* In the first column, have groups list the following regions of the Soviet Union: *western Soviet Union, Transcaucasia, Soviet Central Asia, Western Siberia, Eastern Siberia.* Have groups leave several lines of space between the names of regions. Groups should then complete the chart.

CHECK FOR UNDERSTANDING

Write on the chalkboard the names of the five regions of the Soviet Union found on page 345. Have students locate each region on a map of the Soviet Union and identify the major economic activities associated with it.

CORRECTIONS/EXTENSIONS

Reteaching   Make a list of the regions of the Soviet Union on the chalkboard. Have students rank these regions in order of their economic development. Ask class members to explain and give evidence to support their rankings. Then have students identify the resources of the less developed regions that make the government eager to settle and develop these areas.

Enrichment   Tell the class that in order to encourage settlement in Siberia, workers there are paid an average of 40 percent more than workers elsewhere and can double their salary by staying five years. They also have a yearly six-week holiday and get a round-trip ticket to anywhere in the USSR every other year. Ask students to report on the unique conditions faced by people living in Siberia, including the hardships due to severe cold; on the construction problems workers have faced building there; and on how successful the government's industrialization and resettlement program for Siberia has been.

Answers

MAP WORKSHOP (p. 332)

1. (a) 4:00 A.M. (b) 8:00 P.M.
2. 11 time zones
3. 6:00 P.M.
4. 10 hours
5. 2:00 P.M.
6. Boundaries have been adjusted to reflect settlement patterns. The reason for these adjustments is that a city or a small country can be kept within a single time zone.

13.1 REVIEWING THE FACTS (p. 333)

Define
Siberia: the part of the Soviet Union that lies east of the Ural Mountains

Answer
1. (a–b) *Great European Plain*: extends from Eastern Europe into the Soviet Union and as far east as the Ural Mountains, has few highland areas; *Ural Mountains*: extends northward from the Aral Sea to the Arctic Ocean, are low and easy to cross; *West Siberian Plain*: lies immediately east of the Urals, drained by the Ob River, is largely swamp and marsh; *Central Siberian Plain*: lies between the Yenisey and Lena rivers, has highlands rising to about 500 feet; *East Siberian Uplands*: make up a mountainous region along the Pacific coast, ringed by a giant horseshoe of mountains around the Central Siberian Plateau; *Central Asian Ranges*: are a mountainous area along the southern border of the Soviet Union, include several tall mountain ranges
2. far colder, because Western Europe blocks the Soviet Union from the warming effect of the Gulf Stream
3. tundra, taiga, mixed needleleaf and broadleaf forests, steppe, prairie, and desert

Locate
1. Arctic Ocean, Pacific Ocean
2. Ural Mountains, Ural River

SKILL WORKSHOP (p. 341)

1. 20–59 years old
2. 35.2 percent
3. (a) 10.2 percent (b) 16.8 percent
4. Moscow, Leningrad, Kiev
5. (a) Russia, the Ukraine
(b) Russia, Kazakhstan
6. (a) Estonia (b) Armenia, Moldavia

13.2 REVIEWING THE FACTS (p. 343)

Define

1. *tsar:* absolute ruler of Russia until 1917
2. *Russ:* Scandinavian people who dominated the Slavs in the Ukraine in the 800's; during this time, the Slavs became known as the Russians
3. *Soviet Central Asia:* the area of the Soviet Union lying between the Caspian Sea and China
4. *Bolsheviks:* the group of Russian revolutionaries who overthrew Russia's new republican government in 1917; later became the Communist party
5. *premier:* as the head of the Council of Ministers, the highest official in the Soviet government
6. *general secretary:* the most powerful official in the Communist party and the Soviet Union
7. *kolkhoz:* a collective farm in the Soviet Union, owned by the people who work on it
8. *sovkhoz:* a state farm in the Soviet Union, owned by the Soviet government
9. *nonaligned:* not wishing to side with either superpower in world affairs

Answer

1. Russians
2. (a) Population is densest in a coneshaped area whose base is in the western, European part of the country and whose tip extends across the Urals and the city of Omsk. (b) Siberia
3. Real power in Soviet government is held by the Communist party. Only party members may run for office; no other political parties are permitted to exist. Once in office, party members carry out party policies.
4. (a) the lack of incentives for farmers on collective and state farms; uncertain rainfall (b) Historically, capital goods have been emphasized. However, recently such consumer goods as radios, television sets, appliances, and clothing have been given greater emphasis.
5. *Relations with the United States:* The United States has opposed Soviet domination of Eastern Europe and what it believes is the Soviet effort to dominate certain African, Latin American, and Asian countries. *Relations with China:* The Soviet Union and China have clashed over the territory along their shared border and over policies for carrying out Communist ideas. Like the United States, China has opposed what it believes are efforts by the Soviet Union to gain control over less powerful countries.

Locate

(a) Dnieper (b) Volga (c) Irtysh
(d) Ob (e) Yenisey (f) Lena

13.3 REVIEWING THE FACTS (p. 349)

Answer

1. It is the center of politics, population, and production.
2. Farmers in Georgia and Azerbaidzhan produce cotton, tobacco, olives, and almonds. Farmers in Georgia grow citrus fruits, tea, and grapes for wine. Mining of manganese takes place in Georgia. In Azerbaidzhan, oil production is important. Industrial production centers on Armenia's capital, Yerevan, where synthetic rubber, textiles, tobacco products, and machinery are produced. Mining, crop growing, and livestock production take place in outlying areas.
3. Large parts of the Kazakhstan steppe have been opened to cultivation, mostly by farmers on kolkhozes. Through irrigation, Turkmenistan and Uzbekistan are now growing cotton, fruit, and vegetables; goats and sheep are also being raised. Farming is now taking place in Tadzhikistan and Kirghizia, where cotton, rice and other grains, fruits, and vegetables are grown. Coal, lead, zinc, tungsten, and uranium mined in Kazakhstan are used by factories within the republic. Other industrial gains include the manufacture of iron, steel, and chemicals.
4. Western Siberia is rich in natural resources. It has half the world's known coal reserves and great deposits of natural gas. The government hopes to develop industry in the region. Eastern Siberia has coal, natural gas, and waterpower resources. Wood, fish, gold, and tin are plentiful. To promote development of this area, the government is building a railroad to link up with the Trans-Siberian Railroad. In this way, the area's resources can be shipped by rail to industrialized parts of the country.

Locate

(a) Finland (b) Afghanistan
(c) China (d) Japan

GEOGRAPHY LABORATORY
(pp. 350–351)

Speaking Geographically
1. d 2. e 3. c 4. g 5. a
6. f 7. b

Testing Yourself
1. Ural 2. Communist 3. Russian
4. the Ukraine 5. Kuznetsk Basin

Building Map Skills
1. Azerbaidzhan
2. Armenia
3. Georgia
4. Moldavia
5. Ukraine
6. Belorussia
7. Lithuania
8. Latvia
9. Estonia
10. Turkmenistan
11. Uzbekistan
12. Tadzhikistan
13. Kirghizia
14. Kazakhstan
15. Russia

A. Arctic Ocean
B. Black Sea
C. Caspian Sea
D. Aral Sea
E. Sea of Okhotsk
F. Lake Baikal

I. Volga River
II. Ob River
III. Yenisey River
IV. Lena River

Applying Map Skills
Odessa, Volgograd, Moscow, Leningrad, Archangel'sk, Murmansk, Tashkent, Sverdlovsk, Novosibirsk, Vladivostok

SUPPLEMENTARY MATERIALS
Books
Hewitt, Philip, *Looking at Russia*, Lippincott, 1977

Journey across Russia: The Soviet Union Today, National Geographic, 1977

Resnick, Abraham, *Russia: A History of 1917*, Children's Press, 1983

The Soviet Union, Time-Life Books, 1984

Topalian, Elyse, *V.I. Lenin*, Franklin Watts, 1983

Other Media
Inside the USSR (EEM: 8 filmstrips)

Journey across Russia (NG: 2 filmstrips)

The Making of Russia (LF: film/video, covers the years 1480 to 1860)

The Soviet Union (SVE: 4 filmstrips, 4 cassettes, teacher's guide)

The Soviet Union: A Changing Nation (PLP: software for Apple)

The Soviet Union: Epic Land (EB: film/video)

The Soviet Union: Faces of Today (EB: film/video)

USSR: A Regional Study (EGH: 6 filmstrips, 6 cassettes)

14 East Asia *(pages 352–375)*

ASSIGNMENT GUIDE

■ *Text Features*

Skill Workshop, p. 358   Spotlight, p. 372

Map Workshop, p. 364   Chapter Review, pp. 374–375

■ *Teacher's Resource Binder*

Assign after

p. 355 Building Basics Worksheet 14.1
        Independent Practice Worksheet 14.1 WB p. 106

p. 358 Skill Workshop: Using A Graph to Make
            Comparisons WB p. 111

p. 364 Map Workshop: Reading a Cartogram WB p. 110

p. 365 Building Basics Worksheet 14.2
        Independent Practice Worksheet 14.2 WB p. 107

p. 370 Building Basics Worksheet 14.3
        Independent Practice Worksheet 14.3 WB p. 108

p. 373 Building Basics Worksheet 14.4
        Independent Practice Worksheet 14.4 WB p. 109

p. 375 Map Test 14
        Chapter Test 14
        Enrichment Chapter 14 WB p. 112

■ *Geography Laboratory Manual: Investigating Chapter 14*

Use with pages 352–375

■ *Outline Maps 17 and 18*

Use with pages 352–375

■ *Overhead Transparencies 10, 44, 45, 46, 47, and Worksheets*

Use with pages 352–375

OVERVIEW

Chapter 14 begins with a study of the landforms and ecosystems of East Asia's mainland and islands. Then the chapter examines East Asia's various ethnic groups and religions and traces the political history of the region, highlighting changes that have taken place in China, Japan, and Korea since World War II. The chapter also considers economic trends in the region, including changes in the Chinese economy and a discussion of Japan's remarkable economic growth.

INTRODUCING THE CHAPTER

Write the chapter title—East Asia—on the chalkboard. Ask students to name the countries they think belong to the East Asian region. Have students locate the region on the world map at the top of page 352. Note the large islands that belong to this region. Ask students what countries they think these islands are. (Japan, Taiwan) What ocean borders this region? (Pacific) Tell the class that one very large country dominates this region. What country might this be? (China) Next, have the class read the chapter introduction and name the countries of the region. According to the introduction, what is the most striking feature of East Asia? (its huge population) Have the class speculate on how a large population might affect the economic life of a nation. After a brief discussion, tell the class that in this chapter, they will look more closely at these questions and at the history and people of the region.

14.1 The Physical Environment *(pages 353–355)*

MAIN IDEAS

- East Asia is divided into two areas—a vast mainland area and three groups of islands.
- East Asia has mountains that are among the highest in the world.
- The climate patterns of East Asia are similar to those in the United States.

OBJECTIVES

Students should be able to:
- identify the landforms of East Asia.
- analyze climate patterns in East Asia.

TEACHING STRATEGIES

Using Outline Map 18 to Identify Landforms of East Asia Distribute Outline Map 18 to the class. Have students use the physical map on page 353 to help label the following areas on their Outline Maps: (a) the countries that occupy East Asia's mainland (China, Mongolia, North Korea, South Korea), (b) the three island areas of East Asia (Japan, Taiwan, Ryukyu Islands), (c) the plateau area with the highest elevation (Plateau of Tibet), (d) the mountain range that forms the western boundary of the region (Himalayas), (e) the two plains areas on the mainland (North China Plain, Manchurian Plain), (f) the four large plateaus in the region (Mongolian Plateau, Yunnan Plateau, Kweichow Plateau, Plateau of Tibet), (g) the mountain range that forms the northwest border between China and the Soviet Union (Tian Mountains), (h) the river that forms the border between North Korea and China (Yalu), (i) the three desert areas in East Asia (Takla Makan, Gobi, Ordos deserts), (j) the mountain range forming the northern boundary between China and the Soviet Union (Altai Mountains).

Analyzing Climates of East Asia Direct students to the climate map on page 355. Have students locate the area with the highland climate. What causes the highland climate in this area? (Himalayas) What causes the highland climate on the western border of Mongolia? (Altai Mountains) Then have the class identify the zones with the driest climate. Ask class members to explain how landforms contribute to the dryness of the area. (The Himalayas and the Plateau of Tibet block the moist, warm air moving north from the Indian Ocean and

prevent it from reaching this area.) What part of the region has the mildest climate? (east, southeast) What two climate zones are found on most of the islands of the region? (humid subtropical, humid continental) Based on climate, which region would appear to have the least suitable climate for farming? (Mongolia)

CHECK FOR UNDERSTANDING

Have students name the two distinct areas in East Asia. (island and mainland) Next, ask the class to identify the parts of the region with plains, deserts, and the world's highest mountain range. Students can also explain how the climate of the northern and western part of the mainland differs from the climate of the southwest and the east. (Northern and western parts are arid and semiarid due to the blocking affect of Himalayas. East has a midlatitude climate. Southeast is humid continental.)

CORRECTIONS/EXTENSIONS

Reteaching Using **Outline Map 18,** students can label the climate regions or major landforms of East Asia. Refer students to the maps on pages 353 and 355 for help.

Enrichment Ask students to write short research reports on how people have adapted to living in the Himalaya Mountains. Ask students to describe who these people are and what their lives are like.

14.2 The Human Imprint *(pages 356–365)*

MAIN IDEAS

- Most of East Asia's people live on less than one fifth of the region's land.
- Each country of East Asia is dominated by a single ethnic group.
- Three major religions—Confucianism, Taoism, and Shintoism—began in the region.
- The countries in East Asia all have authoritarian governments except Japan, which has a representative democracy.
- Economic activities vary greatly from country to country in East Asia.

VOCABULARY

dialect, p. 356; character, p. 356; Cultural Revolution, p. 361; paddy, p. 362; Pacific Rim, p. 365

OBJECTIVES

Students should be able to:

■ understand the population density in East Asia.

■ identify the cultures of the area.

■ discuss political patterns in East Asia.

■ identify major economic activities in the region.

TEACHING STRATEGIES

Understanding the Population Density in East Asia   Divide the class into small groups. Have each group study the map on page 357, picking out areas that are most heavily and most sparsely settled. Ask each group to compare this map with the physical map of the region on page 351 and the climate map on page 355. Using the information gained from these maps, students should write a paragraph describing ways in which the physical environment has contributed to population patterns in specific areas. (the sparse settlement in the west and northwest can be explained in part by the dry climate and the high mountains and plateaus) Emphasize that most of East Asia's people live on less than one fifth of the region's land.

Identifying Cultures   Ask a class member to define the word *dialect*. (a form of language that differs from other forms of the same language in vocabulary, pronunciation, and grammar) Tell the class that like Eastern Europe, East Asia has a great cultural diversity. Ask students why East Asia, then, is not a shatter belt like Eastern Europe. (Each East Asian country has one dominant ethnic group; there is one common written language for the region despite different dialects, and China has had a powerful influence in the region as a unifying cultural force.) Who played an important role in a major religion of China? (Confucius, a philosopher) What is the emphasis of the Taoist religion? (that people should live in harmony with nature) Shintoism, in ancient Japan, was influenced by what religion? (Buddhism)

Discussing Political Patterns in East Asia
List the following countries on the chalkboard: *Japan, China, North Korea, South Korea, Taiwan.* Tell the class that these countries adopted their present form of government after World War II. Ask class members to explain how that is true for each country listed on the chalkboard and to describe the current form of government.

Identifying Major Economic Activities   Direct students to the land use map of East Asia on page 363. Ask: What is the dominant land use in the western and northwestern parts of the region? (nomadic herding) Which country has no major manufacturing areas? (Mongolia) Which country has the only major commercial farming area? (Japan) What type of farming takes place in China? (farming mostly for family use) Where are the major industrial areas in China located? (along the east coast and in the south central area) What types of energy resources are found in China? (coal and petroleum) What other country of the region has some coal? (Japan) In which countries of the region is fishing important? (all but Mongolia, because it is landlocked)

CHECK FOR UNDERSTANDING

On a sheet of paper, ask each student to write the following phrases: *population distribution, ethnic groups, religions, political patterns, economic changes.* Tell class members to leave space between each phrase. Under each heading, have students write one or two sentences describing a pattern or trend in East Asia.

CORRECTIONS/EXTENSIONS

Reteaching   Write the following statements on the chalkboard:
(1) The physical features of East Asia tend to isolate its people from other regions of the world. (2) Most of East Asia's people live on less than one fifth of the region's land. (3) Each country of East Asia is dominated by a single ethnic group. (4) Japan is the only East Asian nation with a truly representative government. (5) East Asia's growing trade is part of a remarkable change in the world's economy. Have each student select one of the statements and write a paragraph explaining it. Have class members read their paragraphs aloud.

Enrichment   Have students write research reports on the impact of China's Cultural Revolution. Reports should indicate what the goals of this movement were, its impact on the economic and political life of the nation, and how China's current leaders view this period of turmoil in China's history.

14.3 The East Asian Mainland *(pages 365–370)*

MAIN IDEAS

■ China dominates East Asia's mainland in size and population.

- Since the late 1970's, greater economic freedoms have been taking place in China.
- Mongolia is the least industrialized country in the region.
- North Korea has many mineral resources and has an economy based on heavy industry.
- South Korea has few natural resources but is a successful exporter of consumer goods.
- Hong Kong is a successful exporter of consumer goods and a major banking center in the Far East.

VOCABULARY

commune, p. 366; buffer state, p. 368

OBJECTIVES

Students should be able to:
- analyze economic changes taking place in China.
- compare the economies of North and South Korea and of Macau and Hong Kong.

TEACHING STRATEGIES

Analyzing Economic Changes in China
Have students describe some of the changes that have taken place in Chinese economic life since Deng Xiao-ping came to power in the late 1970's. (Greater economic freedom for individuals who may now own small businesses exists; China seeks investments from foreign countries; the government is making large investments in industry and in educational programs to train scientists, managers, and technicians; the commune system has broken down; peasants may now plant and harvest their own crops on assigned plots, buy their own equipment, and hire workers.) List responses on the chalkboard.

Comparing Countries of the East Asian Mainland Have students compare first the countries of North and South Korea and then the island colonies of Hong Kong and Macau in short papers. Comparisons of North and South Korea should focus on their differences and on how political patterns have influenced economic policies. The comparison of Hong Kong and Macau should focus on differences in economic activities and ways the physical setting has helped or hindered the economic development of each island.

CHECK FOR UNDERSTANDING

List the countries and colonies of mainland East Asia on the chalkboard. Have students identify the recent changes in the economic policies of the Chinese government and explain how these policies have affected agriculture and industry. Then have class members describe the major economic activities associated with each of the other countries of the subregion.

CORRECTIONS/EXTENSIONS

Reteaching Divide the class into an even number of small groups. Have each group compose a set of questions that can be used to test the class's understanding of the information in this section. Have groups write their questions on a notecard and their answers to the questions on a separate notecard. Groups can then exchange question notecards, write answers to the set they have been given, and return answers for checking to the group who wrote the questions. Set a time limit for answering the questions. The first group to answer all of its questions accurately wins.

Enrichment Tell the class that China's population will double in 72 years at its current rate of growth. The population of China presently increases by over 10 million people per year. Have students research the government's population control program and what the results of such a program would mean. Students may also want to investigate how the Chinese themselves feel about the program.

14.4 The Pacific Islands of East Asia
(pages 370–373)

MAIN IDEAS

- Japan is the most developed country in Asia.
- Throughout much of its history, Taiwan's economy was based on agriculture but is now successfully industrializing.

OBJECTIVES

Students should be able to:
- describe Japan's economic development.
- assess Taiwan's economic development.
- make a map of East Asia, showing major landforms, cities, and subregions.

TEACHING STRATEGIES

Describing Economic Development in Japan
Tell the class that Japan has been called the

"miracle of Asia" because of its rapid economic development in the postwar period. Japan's economic success seems particularly impressive when it is compared in size and population with the United States and the Soviet Union, the only two countries that rank above it as industrial powers. Examine with the class the reasons for Japan's economic miracle. Have students note the many obstacles to its economic progress. (Four fifths of the land is mountainous; scarce flatland is taken up by towns and cities; it is a small country with few resources, located within the Ring of Fire; it has an isolated location surrounded by water and far from major export markets.) Have students identify the ways the Japanese have overcome these obstacles. (built a network of air and water linkages between islands, created one of the world's largest fleets of merchant ships to carry goods worldwide, compensated for lack of resources by importing raw materials and energy fuels, adapted techniques and technologies of developed countries to the needs of Japanese business) How did the destruction of Japanese industry during World War II help the nation's economy in the postwar period? (Japanese factories rebuilt with the most modern equipment available, making Japanese industry very efficient and highly competitive with other industrialized nations.)

Assessing Taiwan's Economic Development
Taiwan is called "one of the four new Japans." Ask a class member to explain this statement. (It refers to the industrialization and strong economic growth these countries are experiencing.) Then focus discussion on the changes that have enabled Taiwan to fit this description.

Using Outline Map 17 to Make a Map of East Asia
Distribute copies of Outline Map 17, East Asia: Political to all class members. Have students create map puzzles for their classmates by numbering on their maps the locations of major cities or islands; important mountain ranges, rivers, or other physical features; or distinctive subregions within a country—such as China's rice bowl. On a separate sheet of paper, students should write a series of numbered clues corresponding to their map puzzles. Have students exchange map puzzles and try naming the places on each other's puzzles.

CHECK FOR UNDERSTANDING

Have students make a list of the obstacles to Japan's economic development and note the ways Japan overcame these obstacles. Then ask class members to describe the ways Taiwan's economy has changed in recent years.

CORRECTIONS/EXTENSIONS

Reteaching Have students explain why Japan's economic success surprised the world and identify the factors that have contributed to this success. Then have students compare the economic development of Taiwan and Japan, noting ways the economic changes taking place in Taiwan are similar to the steps that led to Japan's industrial growth.

Enrichment Have students research Japan's business management techniques and how these have been used in the United States. Students should then report to the class on whether the techniques that have been so successful in Japan have done equally well in the United States.

Answers

14.1 REVIEWING THE FACTS (p. 355)

Answer
1. China's main lowlands region is the North China Plain, which extends southward from the Beijing region almost to the Chang Jiang River; lowlands also are found in Manchuria and in the southeast along the Xi River.
2. (a) They block moist, warm air moving north from the Indian Ocean, keeping it from reaching central China. As a result, west-central China gets little rainfall and has several deserts. (b) During the summer months, the monsoon comes from the Pacific Ocean, bringing heavy rains and hot temperatures to the region. During the winter months, the monsoon shifts direction. It brings cold, dry air from inland areas.

Locate
1. (a) Huang He (b) Chang-jiang
2. South China Sea

SKILL WORKSHOP (p. 358)

1. Costa Rica
2. 1962, 1975
3. declined
4. (a) China's birth rate rose sharply between 1962 and 1964, after which it fell with only a few interruptions until beginning a slight rise in 1980. (b) Costa Rica's pattern was similar to China's except the birth rate rose between 1964 and 1966. Costa Rica's birth rate was higher than that of China throughout the period.

MAP WORKSHOP (p. 364)

1. Canada is far smaller on the population cartogram.
2. (a) the Soviet Union (b) China
3. Japan appears far larger on the population cartogram; it is one of the ten largest countries in the world in terms of population.

14.2 REVIEWING THE FACTS (p. 365)

Define

1. *dialect:* a form of a language that differs from other forms of the same language in vocabulary, pronunciation, and grammar
2. *character:* a series of pen or brush strokes representing a word or syllable in Chinese languages
3. *Cultural Revolution:* an unsuccessful effort by radical leaders to speed up change in China by violently attacking traditional ways of life and keeping out foreign ideas
4. *paddy:* flooded fields where rice is grown
5. *Pacific Rim:* the countries that border or lie in the Pacific Ocean, including the United States, Canada, New Zealand, Australia, the countries of East and Southeast Asia, and the countries of Latin America

Answer

1. the Han
2. Confucianism, Taoism, Shintoism, and Buddhism
3. Mongolia, North Korea, China
4. East Asia is now tied to the rest of the world by its extensive trade. Its manufacturers sell consumer goods all over the world.

Locate

Mongolia

14.3 REVIEWING THE FACTS (p. 370)

Define

1. *commune:* a farm owned by the people who work on it
2. *buffer state:* a country that lies between rival countries

Answer

1. China's GNP has become one of the fastest growing in the world.
2. the lowlands of eastern China, particularly the valleys of the Xi, Chang Jiang, and Huang He rivers
3. (a) the export of meat, wool, hides, and furs; less developed are coal and copper mining, food processing and the manufacture of textiles and chemicals (b) the manufacture of textiles, food products, and electronic items (c) the making of iron and steel; the manufacture of farm machinery and textiles (d) the manufacture and export of textiles, clothing, toys, plastics, watches, and clocks; banking (e) tourism and textile production

Locate

1. (a) Beijing (b) Ulaanbaator (c) Seoul (d) P'yongang (e) British colony; no capital (f) Portuguese colony; no capital
2. Amur River

14.4 REVIEWING THE FACTS (p. 373)

Answer

1. limited resources, large mountainous areas, difficult linkages between many separate islands, active volcanoes and earthquakes, long distances to markets in other countries
2. Japan specializes in making high-value, lightweight manufactured goods. The Japanese learned to make such goods by studying methods that were already in use in developed countries and altering these methods for improved efficiency and quality.
3. Taiwan's economy was traditionally based on agriculture. The emphasis has shifted to industry. Taiwan produces textiles, clothing, electronic products, and processed foods.

Locate

1. (a) Tokyo (b) Taipei
2. Honshu, Hokkaido, Shikoku, and Kyushu

GEOGRAPHY LABORATORY (pp. 374–375)

Speaking Geographically

1.–7. Answers will vary.

Testing Yourself

1. Himalaya Mountains, Karakoram Mountains, Tian Mountains, Altai Mountains, and Khingan ranges
2. Huang He, Chang Jiang, Xi, Amur, Han, Yuan, Yalu, Mekong, Salween, Brahmaputra, Sungari, and Kerulen rivers
3. Xi, Yangzi (Chang Jiang), and Huang He river valleys
4. Mongolia, North Korea, and China
5. Taiwan, North Korea, South Korea, Japan, and China (plus Canada, the United States, and countries of Southeast Asia, the South Pacific, and Latin America)
6. rice, wheat, cotton, millet, sorghum, and tobacco
7. oil, iron ore, and coal

8. Japan, Taiwan, North Korea, and South Korea

9. Confucianism, Taoism, and Shintoism

10. arid, semiarid, humid subtropical, humid continental, highland, subarctic, and wet tropical

11. the Takla Makan, Gobi, and Ordos deserts

12. Japan, Ryuku Islands, Taiwan

13. allowing individuals to own businesses, seeking foreign investment, investing in education and modern industry, permitting peasants to farm some land for themselves, and improving living standards for peasants

14. adoption of a new constitution, establishment of a parliamentary government, reduction in the role of the emperor to symbolic head of state, modernization of industry, rapid economic growth, economic competition with the United States, and a strong political alliance with the United States

Building Map Skills

1. Mongolia 2. China 3. North Korea
4. South Korea 5. Japan 6. Taiwan

Applying Map Skills

1. middle latitudes

2. Eastern and Northern Hemispheres

3. (a) 23°N, 113°E (b) 39°N, 117°E (c) 31°N, 121°E (d) 35°N, 139°E (e) 37°N, 128°E

4. Taiwan, China

SUPPLEMENTARY MATERIALS

Books

Farley, Carol, *Korea: A Land Divided*, Dillon Press, 1984

Fencher, Ernest Barksdale, *War in Korea*, Franklin Watts, 1981

Journey into China, National Geographic 1982

Lawson, Don, *The Long March: Red China under Chairman Mao*, T.Y. Crowell, 1983

Rau, Margaret, *Holding Up the Sky: Young People in China*, Lodestar Books, 1983

The Minority People of China, Julian Messner, 1982

Yunagmei, Tang, *China, Here We Come*, B.P. Putnam's Sons, 1981

Other Media

China: An Emerging Giant NG: film/ video)

China: A Portrait of the Land (EB: film)

China's Changing Face (NG: film/video)

China's New Look (EEM: filmstrip)

Japan: Miracle in Asia (EB: film/video, available in Spanish)

Japan: Of Tradition and Change (NG: film/ video)

Japan: Technology and Tradition (SVE: 4 filmstrips, 4 cassettes, teacher's guide)

Japan—The Urban Life of Its People (AF: film)

15 South Asia *(pages 376–399)*

ASSIGNMENT GUIDE

■ **Text Features**

Map Workshop, p. 378   Spotlight, p. 394
Skill Workshop, p. 384   Chapter Review, pp. 398–399

■ **Teacher's Resource Binder**

Assign after
p. 378 Map Workshop: Using Scale WB p. 117
p. 381 Building Basics Worksheet 15.1
        Independent Practice Worksheet 15.1 WB p. 113
p. 384 Skill Workshop: Reading a Population Pyramid
           WB p. 118
p. 388 Building Basics Worksheet 15.2
        Independent Practice Worksheet 15.2 WB p. 114
p. 392 Building Basics Worksheet 15.3
        Independent Practice Worksheet 15.3 WB p. 115
p. 397 Building Basics Worksheet 15.4
        Independent Practice Worksheet 15.4 WB p. 116
p. 398 Map Test 15
        Chapter Test 15
        Enrichment Chapter 15 WB p. 119

■ **Geography Laboratory Manual: Investigating Chapter 15**

Use with pages 376–399

■ **Outline Maps 19 and 20**

Use with pages 376–399

■ **Overhead Transparencies 10, 48, 49, 50, 51, and Worksheets**

Use with pages 376–399
Chapter 15 South Asia (pages 376–399)

OVERVIEW

The chapter begins with an examination of the physical geography of South Asia which includes the Indian subcontinent and Southeast Asia. Differences in landforms that further subdivide the region are discussed. The chapter next highlights the cultural and religious diversity of the region and examines the impact of colonial rule and subsequent independence. In the final sections of the chapter, students learn about the political patterns and economic activities of the region.

INTRODUCING THE CHAPTER

Have the class locate South Asia on the map at the top of page 376. Point out that South Asia includes the Indian subcontinent as well as the islands lying between mainland Asia and Australia. What water bodies surround the region? (Indian Ocean, Pacific Ocean, Arabian Sea) Make a list of the countries of the region on the chalkboard. (India, Afghanistan, Pakistan, Nepal, Bhutan, Sri Lanka, Burma, Thailand, Kampuchea, Laos, Vietnam, Malaysia, Singapore, Brunei, Indonesia, Philippines) Ask students which country they think is the largest in population? In land area? The smallest in land area? In population? Do class members think of the region as a prosperous, industrial area or as mainly agricultural, developing region? After a brief discussion of student impressions, tell the class that in this chapter they will have a chance to check the accuracy of their ideas on South Asia.

15.1 The Physical Environment *(pages 377–381)*

MAIN IDEAS

- The Indian subcontinent and Southeast Asia comprise South Asia.
- The climate of the Indian subcontinent is influenced by the monsoon.

VOCABULARY

subcontinent, p. 377.

OBJECTIVES

Students should be able to:
- make a map of South Asia.
- identify landforms of South Asia
- explain how monsoons affect the climate.

TEACHING STRATEGIES

Using Outline Map 20 to Make a Map of the Region   Distribute copies of Outline Map 20, South Asia: Physical. With the help of the map on page 377, have students label the following rivers: Indus, Ganges, Brahmaputra, Godavari, Khrishna, Narmada, Sutlej Irrawaddy, Salween, Chao Phraya, and Mekong. Next have them label the following bodies of water: Indian Ocean, Bay of Bengal, South China Sea, Pacific Ocean, Java Sea, Arabian Sea. Then have students shade in the area of the Indian subcontinent in one color (India, Afghanistan, Pakistan, Bangladesh), the area of the two Himalayan countries of the western subregion in a second color (Nepal, Bhutan), and the Southeast Asian subregion in a third color.

Identifying Landforms of South Asia   Write the following terms on the chalkboard: *islands, archipelagoes, subcontinent, peninsula, mountains, plains, river valleys, delta, desert, plateau.* Ask each student to make a two-column chart on a sheet of paper. Have students label the first column *India and Its Neighbors* and the second column *Southeast Asia.* Have students list the terms from the board in one or both columns. Then have several class members read their charts, explaining why they placed each term as they did.

Understanding the Effects of Monsoons on Climate   Tell the class that climate patterns in South Asia are good examples of how wind patterns affect climate. Ask: What is the monsoon? (seasonal shifting of wind) Have a class member explain how the shifting of the winds creates a wet season from late spring to early fall and a dry season from October to May (In the spring, winds blow from the south, bringing moisture from the Indian Ocean. Beginning in October, the winds reverse direction. Since these winds do not travel over water, they do not carry moisture over the land.)

CHECK FOR UNDERSTANDING

Ask class members to explain why part of the region is called a "subcontinent." (large landmass that is part of a whole continent but separated from it by natural barriers and cultural differences) Then have class members name the major landforms associated with the western subregion and the major landforms associated with Southeast Asia. Ask students to indicate how the major rivers in the region have affected the physical environment of the lands through which they flow. (have created broad valleys, flat plains, and fertile farmland)

CORRECTIONS/EXTENSIONS

Reteaching   Divide the class into two groups. Ask each group to prepare an oral report on one of the subregions of South Asia. In their reports, groups should locate their subregion on the map on page 377, name the countries within the subregion, identify the landforms of the area, and describe the climates found within the subregion.

Enrichment   Tell students that one of the world's first civilizations began in the Indus River valley. Have students report to the class on the archaeological excavations at Harappa and Mohenjo-Daro.

15.2 The Human Imprint *(pages 382–388)*

MAIN IDEAS

- South Asia has great cultural and religious diversity.
- The region is densely populated with an increasing growth rate.
- Since independence from European colonial powers, many countries in South Asia have experienced political instability.
- Subsistence farming or herding are the chief means of earning a living.

VOCABULARY

Indochina, p. 385.

OBJECTIVES

Students should be able to:

- examine South Asia's cultural diversity.
- discuss population growth in South Asia.
- trace the political history of the nations of the region.
- analyze economic activities in South Asia.

TEACHING STRATEGIES

Examining South Asia's Cultural Diversity
Have students name the religions that are practiced in the region and list them on the chalkboard. (*India:* Buddhism, Hinduism, Islam; *Afghanistan, Pakistan, Bangladesh:* Islam; *Thailand, Burma:* Buddhism; *Malaysia, Singapore:* Islam, Hinduism, Taoism, Buddhism, Confucianism; *Nepal:* Hindu; *Vietnam:* Confucianism, Taoism, Catholicism; *Brunei:* Islam; *Philippines:* Roman Catholic) Have students give other ways that the region is culturally diverse. (hundreds of languages are spoken) Ask class members to identify factors that have contributed to diversity. (location as a crossroads)

Discussing Population Growth in South Asia
Direct students to the World Data Bank for South Asia on page 396. Have the class compare natural increase rates in South Asia with natural increase in East Asia. Which region has higher population growth rates? (South Asia) Higher per capita GNPs? (East Asia) Point out that India, with a population size second only to China, is growing more rapidly than China. Point out if its population continues to increase at the current rate, it will double in a little over thirty years.

Tracing the Political History of South Asia
Ask students to make a four-column chart. Have class members fill in these columns with information from the section: *Country, Colonial Ruler, Date of Independence, How Achieved.* Students should list all the countries of the region in the first column. When students have completed their charts, ask: Which country on the chart was never under colonial rule? (Thailand) When did most of the countries on the chart achieve independence? (after World War II) Which countries were originally part of India? (Pakistan and Bangladesh) What is similar about the way the countries of the region achieved independence? (Most fought in bloody conflicts before winning independence.)

Analyzing Economic Activities Have students use the land use map on page 386 to name the countries of the region that have some manufacturing. (India, Indonesia, Malaysia, the Philippines, Singapore) Judging by the map, what is the major economic activity throughout much of the region? (farming mostly for family use)

CHECK FOR UNDERSTANDING

Have students explain why the region is called an area of cultural diversity. Then ask students to describe settlement patterns in the region and give one example of ways in which ethnic, religious, or political differences have led to conflict among nations of the region.

CORRECTIONS/EXTENSIONS

Reteaching Divide the class into three groups. Ask each group to write three summary paragraphs. Each paragraph should summarize one of the subsections of Section 2: The People of South Asia, Political Patterns, Economic Patterns. Have the groups read their paragraphs aloud to the class. As a class, compare paragraphs to determine which main ideas each group considered important enough to include.

Enrichment Have students choose either of the following for a research report for presentation to the class: (a) the role played by Mahatma Gandhi in India's fight for (b) current political developments in Vietnam

15.3 India and Its Neighbors *(pages 388–392)*

MAIN IDEAS

- India is made up of a wide variety of ethnic groups.
- Afghanistan, Pakistan, and Bangladesh have experienced political unrest, which has slowed economic development.

VOCABULARY

caste, p. 388; Green Revolution, p. 389; cyclone, p. 391.

OBJECTIVES

Students should be able to:

- explain how India's cultural patterns have affected it's country's development.
- describe economic patterns in the region.

TEACHING STRATEGIES

Explaining Indian Cultural Patterns Write the terms *Hinduism* and *caste system* on the chalkboard. Have students define each of these terms and explain how each applies to life in India. Encourage class members to think about both positive and negative effects of Hinduism and the caste system on the Indian people. (A positive effect of Hinduism is that it has helped unify the nation and foster nationalism.)

Describing Economic Development in the Region Have students suggest reasons for the low standard of living in the countries of the subregion. (use of traditional farming methods; poor transportation linkages; political instability; lack of capital for the development of transportation linkages or manufacturing; rapid population growth in some countries) Make a list of these reasons on the chalkboard. Have class members explain how each factor has slowed development.

CHECK FOR UNDERSTANDING

Have students locate the countries of the subregion on a map of Asia and describe the main economic activities in each country.

CORRECTIONS/EXTENSIONS

Reteaching Make a three-column chart on the chalkboard. Label the columns *Country, Primary Economic Activities, Secondary Economic Activities*. In the first column list the following countries: India, Pakistan, Afghanistan, Bangladesh, Nepal, Bhutan, Sri Lanka. Have class members complete the chart by describing the specific primary and secondary economic activities important to each nation.

Enrichment Tell the class that while per capita GNP and population growth rates give some indication of standard of living, other social indicators are also important measures of human well-being. Have students use current almanacs to create a chart for the countries of the subregions. The chart can show literacy rates, infant mortality, life expectancy, and number of cars or televisions for each country.

15.4 Southeast Asia
(pages 392–397)

MAIN IDEAS

■ Rice is the major crop in Southeast Asia.

■ The economies of Vietnam, Kampuchea, and Laos have been hurt by years of warfare.

■ Singapore and Brunei are the wealthiest countries of Southeast Asia.

VOCABULARY

sultanate, p. 395.

OBJECTIVES

Students should be able to:

■ understand political patterns in Southeast Asia.

■ compare levels of economic development in South Asian nations.

TEACHING STRATEGIES

Understanding Political Patterns in Southeast Asia. Distribute **Outline Map 19, South Asia: Political.** Ask students to label the countries of the region and describe how each has or has not been affected by warfare in recent history. (Thailand receives refugees from Vietnam and Kampuchea; Kampuchea has been involved in war since the 1960's; Laos was engaged in civil war from the 1950's until 1975; Vietnam fought for its independence from France, then was engaged in a civil war at which time the United States came and sided with the south who eventually lost to the north. Vietnam is now engaged in Kampuchea aiding the government against rebels; Malaysia, Singapore, and Brunei have been unaffected; Indonesia saw a coup in 1965 and a civil war today on the island of Timor; Philippines is facing threats from rebels.)

Comparing Economies Development in South Asian Countries The countries of Thailand, Malaysia, and Singapore have achieved a higher standard of living than other countries in the region. Have class members review the information on Thailand, Malaysia, and Singapore in this section and suggest reasons for their economic successes.

CHECK FOR UNDERSTANDING

Have students name the most important agricultural crop in the region, give reasons for the slowed economic growth in Indochina, and identify the reasons for the higher level of economic development in Singapore, Brunei, and Malaysia.

CORRECTIONS/EXTENSIONS

Reteaching Divide the class into small groups. Have each group imagine that it has been asked to plan an advertising campaign to attract new businesses to the region. Each group should decide what countries and resources of the region it will highlight and create a poster that emphasizes these assets of the region.

Enrichment Have students research and report to the class on the ancient architechtural marvels of Angkor Wat and Angkor Thom in Kampuchea. Students may use any visual aids available to them.

Answers

MAP WORKSHOP (p. 378)

1. (a) about 265 miles (430 kilometers)
(b) about 700 miles (1,135 kilometers)
(c) 1,400 miles (2,300 kilometers)
2. the bottom map 3. the top map
4. the middle map
5. about 1,530 miles; by marking the distance on the middle map on the edge of a sheet of paper, then measuring the distance on the scale (or by finding that there is 2 3/16 inches between the two cities on the middle map, then multiplying this figure by the number of miles per inch, 700)

15.1 REVIEWING THE FACTS (p. 381)

Define
subcontinent: a large landmass that is part of a whole continent but separated from it by natural barriers and differences in culture

Answer
1. India and its neighbors to the west and Southeast Asia to the east
2. (a) in the Indus River Valley, on the Ganges Plain, and in the delta area formed by the Ganges and Brahmaputra rivers (b) the Deccan Plateau and some low hills, the Eastern and Western Ghats
3. the Irrawaddy, Salween, Chao Phraya, Mekong, and Red rivers

Locate
1. (a) the Irrawaddy, Salween, Krishna, Godavari, Ganges, and Brahmaputra rivers (b) the Indus and Narmada rivers
2. (a) Indonesia (b) Indonesia (c) Indonesia (d) Philippines (e) Indonesia (f) Philippines

SKILL WORKSHOP (p. 384)

1. (a) 0–4 years (b) 20–24 years
2. Answers will vary. 3. the industrial world

For a special challenge: A population explosion is more likely in the developing world. During the next 20 years, a large part of the population (those currently in the 0- to 14-year-old bracket) will reach childbearing ages. As a result, there will probably be many births.

15.2 REVIEWING THE FACTS (p. 388)

Define
Indochina: name given to Vietnam, Laos, and Kampuchea when the three countries were French colonies

Answer
1. Hinduism has no uniform set of beliefs. However, all Hindus worship many gods, each of whom is thought to be a form of a supreme being. Each Hindu has a duty, called dharma, to worship correctly and to follow proper conduct. Hindus also believe in karma. According to this belief, every soul is born over and over again until it is purified by good actions.
2. Economic growth cannot keep pace with rapid gains in population. The result is high unemployment and many hungry people.
3. the Philippines in 1946, India and Pakistan in 1947, Burma in 1948, Indonesia in 1949, Kampuchea and Laos in 1953, Vietnam in 1954, Malaysia in 1963, Singapore in 1965, Bangladesh in 1971
4. mainly rural population, low rate of literacy, primarily agricultural economies, low crop yields, limited access to modern agricultural technology, much subsistence farming, great need to import food and fuel, and little capital with which to develop industry

Locate
1. (a) Pakistan, Afghanistan
(b) Sri Lanka, Bangladesh, southern India, the area off the Malay Peninsula, the Philippines, and waters surrounding Indonesia
2. Karachi, Ahmadabad-Surat, Bombay-Pune, Asansol-Calcutta, Bangalore-Coimbatore-Madurai, Bangkok, Singapore, Jakarta, Surabaya, Manila

15.3 REVIEWING THE FACTS (p. 392)

Define
1. *caste:* a social group in India uniting people of a similar degree of religious purity
2. *Green Revolution:* the discovery and implementation in developing countries of better methods of growing rice and wheat
3. *cyclone:* a tropical hurricane or typhoon

Answer

1. Until recently, the caste system limited a person's choice of occupation and restricted an individual's contact with members of other castes. Although today a person's job and choice of spouse are no longer fixed by caste, in rural areas caste traditions remain strong.
2. Farmers use primitive methods, have little modern equipment, possess little or no land, and cannot afford fertilizer or seeds. In addition, locusts, droughts, and floods destroy crops from time to time. The impact of the Green Revolution has been undercut by poverty and the reluctance to break with tradition.
3. (a) herding, subsistence farming. (b) on the plain of the Indus River
4. Cyclones frequently sweep inland from the Indian Ocean across the Bay of Bengal, causing flooding and destroying homes and farmland.
5. (a) herding, subsistence farming (b) herding, subsistence farming (c) subsistence farming, commercial farming of such crops as coconuts, rubber, and tea

Locate

1. (a) Kabul (b) Islamabad
(c) New Delhi (d) Dhaka (e) Colombo
(f) Thimphu (g) Kathmandu
2. Karachi, Pakistan; Calcutta, India; Bombay, India; Delhi/New Delhi, India; Bangkok, Thailand; Jakarta, Indonesia; Manila, Philippines

15.4 REVIEWING THE FACTS (p. 397)

Define

sultanate: a country ruled by a Muslim monarch

Answer

1. rice, teakwood, rubber, coffee, tea, sugar, oil palms, tobacco, pineapples, coconuts
2. Thailand, Malaysia, Singapore
3. *On the Indochina Peninsula:* In Thailand, the government is controlled by the military and faces radical opposition and a serious refugee problem, caused by the conflict between Vietnam and Kampuchea. In Kampuchea, torn by war since the late 1960's, a coalition of rebel groups is fighting the government, which is backed by neighboring Vietnam. A civil war has been smoldering in Laos since the 1950's. Vietnam, which was unified only in 1975 after years of war, is still at war, with its troops fighting in Kampuchea and involved in periodic clashes with China along Vietnam's northern border. *In the island countries:* Since the 1970's, the government of the Philippines has been authoritarian; Communist guerillas as well as moderate groups oppose this government

Locate

1. Burma—Rangoon
   Thailand—Bangkok
   Laos—Vientiane
   Vietnam—Hanoi
   Kampuchea—Phnom Penh
   Malaysia—Kuala Lumpur
   Indonesia—Jakarta
   Philippines—Manila
   Singapore—Singapore
   Brunei—Bandar Seri Begawan
2. Barisan Mountains on Sumatra, Maoke Mountains on New Guinea, Annamite Mountains in Vietnam

GEOGRAPHY LABORATORY (pp. 398–399)

Speaking Geographically

1. cyclone 2. caste 3. subcontinent
4. Green Revolution 5. Indochina 6. sultanate

Testing Yourself

1. Deccan Plateau 2. Nepal 3. Ganges
4. Islam 5. Communist 6. Hindu
7. Laos 8. teak 9. Singapore 10. oil

Building Map Skills

1. Mekong River 2. Chao Phraya River
3. Salween River 4. Irrawaddy River
5. Brahmaputra River 6. Ganges River
7. Indus River

Applying Map Skills

1. 2,700 miles 2. 1,850 miles
3. 2,100 miles 4. 4,000 miles

SUPPLEMENTARY MATERIALS

Books

Haskins, James, *New Americans: Vietnamese Boat People,* Enslow, 1980

Lawson, Don, *The United States in the Vietnam War,* Harper & Row, 1981

Ogle, Carol and John, *Through the Year in India,* David & Charles, 1983

Peters, Richard O., *India: A Land of Contrasts,* Global Horizons, 1982

Smith, Dalus C., Jr., *The Land and People of Indonesia,* Harper & Row, 1983

Other Media

Families of Asia (EB: 6 filmstrips, 6 cassettes/ phonodiscs)

Indonesia: An Island Nation's Progress (UEVA: film)

South Asia: Region in Transition (EB: 5 filmstrips, 5 cassettes/phonodiscs)

Southeast Asia: Vietnam, Cambodia, Laos (CIM: film)

16 North Africa and the Middle East
(pages 400–423)

ASSIGNMENT GUIDE

■ Text Features

■ Teacher's Resource Binder

Assign after
p. 405 Building Basics Worksheet 16.1
         Independent Practice Worksheet 16.1 WB p. 120
p. 408 Map Workshop: Reading Maps and Tables of Oil
         Economics WB p. 124
p. 412 Building Basics Worksheet 16.2
         Independent Practice Worksheet 16.2 WB p. 121
p. 414 Building Basics Worksheet 16.3
         Independent Practice Worksheet 16.3 WB p. 122
p. 420 Skill Workshop: Distinguishing between Fact
         and Opinion WB p. 125
p. 421 Building Basics Worksheet 16.4
         Independent Practice Worksheet 16.4 WB p. 123
p. 423 Map Test 16
         Chapter Test 16
         Enrichment Chapter 16 WB p. 126

■ Geography Laboratory Manual: Investigating Chapter 16

Use with pages 400–423

■ Outline Map 21 and 22

Use with pages 400–423

■ Overhead Transparencies 11, 52, 53, 54, 55, and Worksheets

Use with pages 400–423

OVERVIEW

Chapter 16 stresses that North Africa and the Middle East is a dry land where people have learned to make the most of their environment. The region is important politically because of its location at the crossroads of Europe, Asia, and Africa and also because it has rich supplies of oil. Culturally, the region is important as the birthplace of three religions—Judaism, Christianity, and Islam. Finally, the chapter examines the two subregions—North Africa and the Middle East in greater detail. The chapter looks at economic activities in each subregion and the causes of political instability and conflict in the region.

INTRODUCING THE CHAPTER

Have the class read the Chapter Introduction on page 400 and locate the region on the locator map at the top of the page. According to the chapter introduction, what physical features do the countries of North Africa and the Middle East have in common? (extremely dry climate, few resources for industrial development except oil, and water shortages) What cultural feature gives the region a measure of unity? (Most people are Muslims—followers of Islam.) Then tell the class that in this chapter they will look at the ways these cultural and physical features have affected the development of the region.

16.1 The Physical Environment (pages 401–405)

MAIN IDEAS

- Most of the region is made up of desert plains and plateaus.
- Arid and semiarid conditions prevail in about 90 percent of the region.

VOCABULARY

Sahara, p. 401; dune, p. 401; Armenian Knot, p. 401; wadi, p. 401; flash flood, p. 401; sirocco, p. 402

OBJECTIVES

Students should be able to:
- locate the major landforms of North Africa and the Middle East on a map.
- identify major climate areas of the region.

TEACHING STRATEGIES

Using Outline Map 21 to Locate Landforms of the Region Distribute Outline Map 21 to the class. With the help of the physical map on pages 402–403, have students locate and mark each of the following landforms: Sahara, Rub Al Khali, Atlas Mountains, Asia and Hadramawi ranges, Armenian Knot, Zagros Mountains, Taurus Mountains, Pontic Mountains. Then have the class locate the narrow plains areas on the map. Ask students what bodies of water these lowlands are near. (Mediterranean Sea, Red Sea, Persian Gulf).

Identifying Climates of the Region Have students turn to the climate map on page 404 and note that there is little diversity of climates in the region. Ask: What two climates predominate in North Africa and the Middle East? (arid and semiarid) Which country of the region has the only area of humid subtropical climate? (Turkey) Along what bodies of water are the areas of Mediterranean subtropical climate located? (Mediterranean Sea, Caspian Sea, Black Sea) When do these coastal areas get rain? (winter months) Judging by the climate map, where would students expect the most densely settled areas of the region to be? (coastal areas with Mediterranean climate) most sparsely settled areas? (deserts)

CHECK FOR UNDERSTANDING

Have students describe the major landforms found in the region (plains and plateaus) and the areas that receive the most rain (coastal lowlands along Mediterranean and Caspian seas). Class members can also indicate the types of climate found in most of the region (desert, semidesert).

CORRECTIONS/EXTENSIONS

Reteaching Divide the class into small groups. Ask each group to imagine that its members are visitors to the region for the first time. Have each group write a letter to a friend in the United States describing the land and climate and explaining why North Africa and the Middle East are considered part of the same region. Have groups read their letters aloud to the class.

Enrichment Tell the class that the longest river in the world, the Nile, is located in this region. Ask students to research how the Nile influenced the development of early civilizations in the area.

16.2 The Human Imprint (pages 405–412)

MAIN IDEAS

- The most densely settled areas of the Middle East and North Africa lie along the coasts and in the river valleys.
- Three of the world's major religions—Judaism, Christianity, and Islam—began in the Middle East.
- With the exception of Israel, the countries of the region have authoritarian governments.
- Many people of North Africa and the Middle East live by farming.
- The export of oil has greatly improved the standard of living in some oil-rich countries.

VOCABULARY

monotheistic, p. 406; Palestine, p. 407; Sunni, p. 409; Shiite, p. 409; emir, p. 409

OBJECTIVES

Students should be able to:
- understand the population density of North Africa and the Middle East.
- explain how religion has affected political patterns in the region.
- identify the major economic activities in North Africa and the Middle East.

TEACHING STRATEGIES

Understanding Population Density in North Africa and the Middle East   As a class, compare the population density map on page 406 with the climate map on page 404. Have class members suggest relationships between climate and areas of heaviest settlement. (Population is heaviest in areas of greatest rainfall.) What country has the greatest population density? (Egypt) Where is the heaviest settlement found? (along the Nile) Have students suggest reasons why this area, despite the dryness of the climate, is able to support such heavy settlement. (fertile area due to the Nile river and greatest rainfall)

Understanding Political Patterns in the Middle East   Point out that in the Middle East religion and politics are often closely connected. Have students distinguish between the Sunni and Shiite sects of Islam. (*Sunni:* the largest branch of Islam; *Shiite:* concerned with strict adherence to traditional Islamic values and seeks the establishment of Islamic governments) Why have the political leaders of Saudi Arabia, Kuwait, and many other Arab states sided with Iraq in the conflict between Iran and Iraq? (They fear the spread of Shiite or fundamentalist Islam.) What is the relationship between Israel and the PLO? (continual conflict) What is the source of that conflict? (Palestinians do not want to be governed by Israelis nor have they wanted to accept Israel as a legitimate nation.)

Identifying the Major Economic Activities in the Region   Direct students to the land use map of the region on page 410. Ask: In what land areas is commercial farming a major land use? (coastal plains or lowlands areas where rainfall is more plentiful, along Nile River valley) In what countries is farming for family use important? (Morocco, Yemen, Turkey) What is the predominant land use in the region? (nomadic herding) Note that in large areas of the region there is little or no activity. Then refer the class to the World Data Bank on page 411. Point out that although in large areas of the Middle East and North Africa nomadic herding is the main occupation, many Middle Eastern countries such as Saudi Arabia and Kuwait have high per capita GNPs. Ask students what accounts for this? (oil resources)

CHECK FOR UNDERSTANDING

Have students describe the relationship between climate, landforms, and settlement patterns in the region and identify the three religions that began in the Middle East. (Judaism, Christianity, and Islam) Then ask class members to name the major religion in the region today (Islam), the countries in which Christianity or Judaism are the major religions (Lebanon, Israel), and the type of government found in most countries of the region (authoritarian).

CORRECTIONS/EXTENSIONS

Reteaching   Divide the class into two groups. Assign one group North Africa and the other group the Middle East. Tell each group to imagine it is being interviewed by a correspondent for an American television network. Have each group select a representative to interview the other members of the group in a short skit. In their skits, group members should address the reporter's interest in patterns of settlement, political patterns, and economic activities in the region.

Enrichment   Have students research the current operations of OPEC and ways in which oil wealth is helping Middle Eastern OPEC nations modernize.

16.3 North Africa
(pages 412–414)

MAIN IDEAS

■ The first people to settle North Africa were the Berbers—nomadic desert dwellers and herders.
■ Despite the dry climate, farming is important to North Africa's people.
■ Most cities in North Africa lie along the Mediterranean coast.

OBJECTIVES

Students should be able to:
■ relate the cultural patterns of the nomadic peoples of North Africa to the subregion's physical geography.
■ explain why coastal areas of North Africa are more heavily settled than inland areas.

TEACHING STRATEGIES

Relating Cultural Patterns to Physical Geography   Tell students that the North African subregion provides a good example of the ways that the physical environment can influence cultural patterns. Have students locate North Africa on the physical map of the region on page 403. Point out how the Sahara dominates the physical geography of the subregion. Have students speculate about the reasons a nomadic lifestyle developed among the Berbers and the Tuaregs. (The dryness of the subregion made it necessary for early peoples to develop methods of surviving other than farming. By raising herds of sheep and goats, North Africans were able to obtain food, clothing, and animal skins for shelter.)

Understanding Settlement Patterns in North Africa
Have students locate the largest cities of North Africa on the population density map on page 406. Have class members name the cities that are between 2 and 5 million (Casablanca, Algiers) and between 1 and 2 million (Tunis, Tripoli). What generalization can be made about the location of these cities? (All are located along the Mediterranean Coast of North Africa.) Have students suggest reasons for this. (lowland plains area with climate more suitable for human habitation than interiors of these countries; location in or near agricultural areas; location on the coast stimulated trade between Europe and North Africa)

CHECK FOR UNDERSTANDING

Have students describe the lifestyles of the Berbers and other nomadic peoples of North Africa. Then have class members name the crops grown in coastal areas (barley, wheat, millet, olives, figs, nuts) and in drier interior areas with the help of irrigation (citrus fruits, grapes, cotton, sugarcane, dates) Students can also explain why oil wealth has not helped all peoples of North Africa equally. (Benefits of oil wealth have gone to ruling groups or to increase military budgets rather than for economic development.)

CORRECTIONS/EXTENSIONS

Reteaching
Divide the class into an even number of small groups. Have groups write a series of questions on a notecard and answers to the questions on a separate notecard. Groups should then exchange question notecards answering them on the back. Have groups then return their cards back to the original group who should check them for accuracy.

Enrichment
Ask students to obtain travel brochures or magazine articles showing the ancient port cities of North Africa: Tangiers, Casablanca, Marrakech, Fez, and Tunis. Students should then prepare a report on these cities showing the *suq*, or marketplace, the mosque, and the traditional residential areas.

16.4 The Middle East
(pages 415–421)

MAIN IDEAS

- Israel's reliance on modern irrigation techniques has made it the most successful farming country in the region.
- Saudi Arabia and other smaller countries along the Persian Gulf have about half of the world's known oil reserves.
- War and conflict disrupt economic life and cause political instability in the region.

VOCABULARY

Bedouin, p. 415; kibbutz, p. 417; ayatollah, p. 421.

OBJECTIVES

- identify farming methods and agricultural problems in the Middle East.
- understand conflict in the Middle East.
- analyze economic patterns in the Middle East.

TEACHING STRATEGIES

Identifying Farming Methods in the Middle East
Ask the class what problems make farming a challenging occupation in the Middle East. (dryness of climate) Have students identify the Middle Eastern countries where farming is possible without irrigation. (coastal areas of countries bordering the Mediterranean) Then have students name the areas where irrigation is needed in order to grow crops. (on the Arabian Peninsula, Iraq, Iran, and inland areas of Mediterranean countries) What is the reason for the low productivity of many farms in the Middle East? (small plots; limited use of modern tools, seed, and fertilizers) Why are small farms generally less productive than large farms? (Small farms cannot take advantage of labor-saving farm machinery; small farmers tend to rely on traditional farming methods that are often inefficient.) How have some Middle Eastern governments attempted to solve this problem? (cooperative farms)

Understanding Conflict in the Middle East
Write the following words on the chalkboard: *Arab-Israeli conflict, Lebanese civil war, Iran-Iraq war.* Divide the class into three groups each representing one of the areas of conflict listed on the board. For each conflict, have a group prepare a short report indicating (a) the

main participants, (b) the issues, (c) the position each side has taken, (d) historical reasons, (e) and the effects of the conflict on the countries themselves and on other countries in the region. After each group has presented its report, the class can speculate on the future outcome.

Using Outline Map 21 to Analyze Economic Patterns in the Middle East Divide the class into small groups. Distribute copies of Outline Map 21, North Africa and the Middle East: Political. Have groups label the countries of the region. Then have groups use a different color to distinguish each of the following groups: countries with per capita GNPs of less than $1,000, countries with per capita GNPs between $1,000 and $5,000, countries with per capita GNPs between $5,000 and $10,000, and nations with per capita GNPs above $10,000. The World Data Bank on page 411 provides information for this activity. Remind groups to create keys for their maps. Then have each group speculate about the reasons for the varying income levels within the region.

CHECK FOR UNDERSTANDING

Have class members explain why low productivity is a problem for farmers in the Middle East and describe ways Israel and Egypt have improved farm productivity. Then have students explain how each of the following has contributed to tensions in the region: the PLO, the establishment of the state of Israel, Shiite control of Iran, and the arrival of Palestinian refugees in Lebanon.

CORRECTIONS/EXTENSIONS

Reteaching Have complete the activity labeled Reviewing the Facts on page 421.

Enrichment The following words came into the English language from Arabic or Persian. Have students find out why English borrowed these words from the Middle East: *alchemy., algebra, alkali, azimuth, caliber, camphor, cipher, damask, lemon, logarithm, orange, sherbert, sugar, zenith.*

Answers

16.1 REVIEWING THE FACTS (p. 405)

Define
1. *Sahara:* a large desert that extends across most of Morocco, Algeria, and Libya

2. *dune:* a ridge of sand piled up by the wind
3. *Armenian Knot:* a highlands region of the Middle East that includes the mountains of Iran and Turkey
4. *wadi:* an ancient streambed that is dry except during heavy rainfalls
5. *flash flood:* unexpected, rapid, short-lived flooding
6. *sirocco:* the hot, dry wind that blows over the Sahara from the interior of Africa

Answer
1. Most of the region is made up of vast desert plains and plateaus. The region also has a number of mountainous areas. Along coastal areas, there are narrow strips of coastal lowlands.
2. Arid and semiarid conditions prevail in about 90 percent of the region.
3. (a) coastal lowlands along the western and eastern Mediterranean and the southern shore of the Caspian Sea (b) winter
4. They receive enough rainfall during the winter wet season for farming.

Locate
1. Turkey, Iran 2. Cyprus, Bahrain

MAP WORKSHOP (p. 408)

1. Algeria, Iran, Iraq, Kuwait, Libya, Qatar, Saudi Arabia, United Arab Emirates
2. (a) Indonesia (b) Gabon, Nigeria (c) Ecuador, Venezuela.
3. (a) 1978 (b) 1979
4. less than half
5. By 1985, purchases from Arab OPEC had declined to about one sixth. Purchases from all OPEC members had declined to less than a third.

16.2 REVIEWING THE FACTS (p. 412)

Define
1. *monotheistic:* having a belief that there is one God
2. *Palestine:* early name for the land now occupied by Israel and part of Jordan
3. *Sunni:* the branch of Islam with the most followers
4. *Shiite:* a branch of Islam whose followers oppose efforts to modernize their religious practices
5. *emir:* the title for a monarch in some Middle Eastern countries

Answer
1. Judaism, Christianity, Islam
2. monarchies or other forms of authoritarian government

3. (a) In coastal areas with a Mediterranean climate, farmers grow fruits, olives, grapes, wheat, and tobacco. In inland areas with adequate rainfall, farmers grow barley and millet. Some dry lands that are irrigated grow corn, fruits, vegetables, and cotton. Where there is not enough rainfall and no irrigation, nomads herd animals.
(b) oil production and export

Locate
1. Turkey
2. Kuwait, Abadan, Manama, Doha, Dubayy, Abu Dhabi

16.3 REVIEWING THE FACTS (p. 414)

Answer
1. Berbers
2. (a) wheat, barley, millet, olives, figs, and nuts. (b) Citrus fruit, grapes, vegetables, cotton, sugarcane, and dates.
3. Mediterranean coast

Locate
1. Morocco—Rabat
   Algeria—Algiers
   Tunisia—Tunis
   Libya—Tripoli
2. Morocco

SKILL WORKSHOP (p. 420)

1. fact	6. opinion
2. opinion	7. fact
3. fact	8. opinion
4. fact	9. fact
5. fact	10. opinion

16.4 REVIEWING THE FACTS (p. 421)

Define
1. *Bedouin:* a member of a nomadic people of the Arabian Peninsula, Syria, or Jordan
2. *Kibbutz:* a cooperative farm community in Israel
3. *ayatollah:* a Shiite religious leader

Answer
1. Farm plots are small. Many farmers are tenant farmers, with little money for tools, seed, and fertilizer.
2. Standards of living have risen in many oil-rich countries. Governments have built schools, hospitals, and apartments. However, wealth has not been evenly distributed; it is concentrated in the hands of a few government officials and leading families.

3. The *Arab-Israeli conflict* stems from the refusal of Arab governments to recognize the state of Israel and from Palestinian claims to a homeland in Israel. War has broken out between Israel and its Arab neighbors in 1948, 1956, 1967, and 1973. A peace treaty was signed between Egypt and Israel in 1979, but trouble continues. Since 1975, the *conflict in Lebanon* has taken the form of a civil war between Christians and Muslims for control of the country. The *conflict in Iran* began in 1979 with the overthrow of the shah and the establishment of an authoritarian government led by Shiite religious leaders. In 1980, the *Iraq-Iran War* began. The two countries have been fighting ever since over a river on their mutual border; the war has been fueled by religious differences (Iran is Shiite, while Iraq is Sunni).

Locate
1. Bahrain—Manama
   Egypt—Cairo
   Iran—Tehran
   Iraq—Baghdad
   Israel—Jerusalem
   Jordan—Amman
   Kuwait—Kuwait
   Lebanon—Beirut
   Libya—Tripoli
   Oman—Muscat
   Qatar—Doha
   Saudi Arabia—Riyadh
   Syria—Damascus
   Turkey—Ankara
   United Arab Emirates—Abu Dhabi
   Yemen Arab Republic—Sanaa
   People's Democratic Republic of Yemen—Aden
2. parts of Iran, parts of southern Algeria, Libya, Egypt, Saudi Arabia

GEOGRAPHY LABORATORY (pp. 422–423)

Speaking Geographically

1. Sahara	5. Palestine
2. wadi	6. ayatollah
3. Armenian Knot	7. kibbutz
4. Sunni	8. sirocco

Testing Yourself
1. seas that border parts of North Africa or the Middle East
2. mountain ranges of North Africa and the Middle East
3. rivers of the Middle East
4. ancient cities and capitals of nations of the region

5. the holy books of the three major religions that originated in the Middle East

6. aspects of the Middle East's part in the production and export of oil

7. human-made bodies of water that have helped Egypt's economy

Building Map Skills
1. Turkey
2. Cyprus
3. Syria
4. Lebanon
5. Egypt
6. Israel
7. Jordan
8. Iraq
9. Iran
10. Saudi Arabia
11. Yemen
12. People's Democratic Republic of Yemen
13. Oman
14. Qatar
15. Kuwait
16. United Arab Emirates

A. Mediterranean Sea
B. Red Sea
C. Persian Gulf

Applying Map Skills
Answers will vary. Students should note that the region is a part of three continents—Europe, Africa, and Asia. It shares a southern border with the Sahara, an eastern border with Pakistan and Afghanistan in South Asia, a northeastern border with Central Asia, and a northwestern border with Europe. The bodies of water that surround the region are the Atlantic Ocean to the west, the Mediterranean Sea to the north, and the Arabian Sea to the east.

SUPPLEMENTARY MATERIALS

Books

Barlow, Christopher, *Islam*, David & Charles, 1983

Cross, Wilbur, *Egypt*, Children's Press, 1982

Doty, Rory, *Where Are You Going with That Oil?* Doubleday, 1976

Ingrams, Doreen, *New Ways for Ancient Lands*, EMC Corporation, 1974

Ofek, Uriel, *Smoke over Golan: A Novel of the 1973 Yom Kippur War in Israel*, Harper & Row, 1979

Spencer, William, *The Islamic States in Conflict*, Franklin Watts, 1983

Worth, Richard, *Israel and the Arab States*, Franklin Watts, 1983

17 Africa South of the Sahara *(pages 424–449)*

ASSIGNMENT GUIDE

■ Text Features

Map Workshop, p. 432   Skill Workshop, p. 446
Spotlight, p. 439   Chapter Review, pp. 448–449

■ Teacher's Resource Binder

Assign after
p. 428 Building Basics Worksheet 17.1
        Independent Practice Worksheet 17.1 WB p. 127
p. 432 Map Workshop: Interpreting a Map of Colonial
        Territories WB p. 131
p. 438 Building Basics Worksheet 17.2
        Independent Practice Worksheet 17.2 WB p. 128
p. 443 Building Basics Worksheet 17.3
        Independent Practice Worksheet 17.3 WB p. 129
p. 446 Skill Workshop: Using Graphs to Trace
        Literacy Rates WB p. 132
p. 447 Building Basics Worksheet 17.4
        Independent Practice Worksheet 17.4 WB p. 130
p. 449 Map Test 17
        Chapter Test 17
        Enrichment Chapter 17 WB p. 133

■ Geography Laboratory Manual: Investigating Chapter 17

Use with pages 424–449

■ Outline Map 23 and 24

Use with pages 424–449

■ Overhead Transparencies 11, 56, 57, 58, 59, and Worksheets

Use with pages 424–449

OVERVIEW

The chapter begins with an examination of the landforms of Africa south of the Sahara. Students learn that the land in Africa is generally flat, with a high plateau forming the center of the continent. The chapter looks next at sub-Saharan climates as well as ecosystems. The chapter also outlines population and settlement patterns in the region. It then traces Africa's history from ancient times through the period of European colonization to independence. An overview of the regional economy stresses the importance of subsistence farming and commercial agriculture. The final sections of the chapter examine four subregions: West Africa, Central Africa, East Africa, and Southern Africa.

INTRODUCING THE CHAPTER

Ask the class to locate sub-Saharan Africa on the map at the top of page 424. Point out that this region does not include all of Africa. Judging by the chapter title, what landform serves as a dividing line between the two regions of Africa? (Sahara) Ask students to speculate about why the two parts of the continent are usually considered different regions. (The desert has limited trade and communication. Thus the two regions developed different cultural patterns.)

Next have the class read the Chapter Introduction on page 424. Ask students to identify the characteristics that set North Africa apart from the rest of the continent. (Muslim, Arabic-speaking region closely tied to other countries around the Mediterranean Sea) From this description of North Africa, the class can begin to define what sub-Saharan Africa is *not*. (not closely tied to Mediterranean Sea, not entirely Muslim or Arab-speaking) Then tell the class that this chapter will describe the distinctive features of sub-Saharan Africa.

17.1 The Physical Environment *(pages 425–428)*

MAIN IDEAS

■ Most of Africa is a high, fairly level plateau. The only lowlands are narrow strips along the coast.

■ Tectonic activity that began millions of years ago formed the Great Rift Valley and the volcanic peaks of eastern Africa.

■ Africa lies almost entirely within the tropics, but its elevation gives much of the continent a moderate climate.

■ Rainfall varies widely, with the equatorial rain forests receiving the most and the savannas and deserts to the north and south receiving much less.

VOCABULARY

escarpment, p. 425.

OBJECTIVES

Students should be able to:

■ make a physical map of Africa south of the Sahara and identify major landforms and water bodies.

■ identify climates and ecosystems in sub-Saharan Africa.

TEACHING STRATEGIES

Using Outline Map 24 to Make a Physical Map of the Region
A distinctive feature of sub-Saharan Africa's geography is its low relief. To reinforce this fact, divide the class into groups. Distribute copies of Outline Map 24, Africa South of the Sahara: Physical. Ask each group to label the following water bodies: Lake Chad, Lake Victoria, White Nile, Blue Nile, Nile River, Lake Tanganyika, Lake Nyasa, Orange River, Limpopo River, Niger River, Zaire River, Zambezi River, Indian Ocean, Gulf of Guinea, Atlantic Ocean, Red Sea.

Then tell the groups to use the physical map on page 426 as a guide for coloring all areas

at sea level or below one color, all areas 700 to 1500 feet above sea level a second color, and all areas at 7000 feet or above a third color. When groups have completed their maps, tell the class that despite the region's flatness, sub-Saharan Africa has enormous hydroelectric potential. Ask them to pinpoint on their maps the points where the continent's rivers most likely have great waterfalls or rapids. (the escarpment) The hydroelectric potential of the region's rivers is discussed in subsequent sections of the chapter.

Relating Elevation to Climate in Sub-Saharan Africa
Write the following statement from page 425 on the chalkboard: "Despite its tropical latitude, much of Africa has a cool and comfortable climate because of high elevations." Ask students to explain this statement. What types of temperatures might they expect in tropical latitudes? (high temperatures year round) How does elevation affect climate? (the higher the elevation, the lower the temperature)

The effect of elevation on Africa's climate can be seen by comparing temperatures in Singapore and Nairobi, Kenya. Both areas have wet-and-dry tropical climates and have similar latitudes. In Singapore average temperatures range from 74°F to 87°F in October. In the same month, temperatures in Nairobi range from 55°F to 76°F.

Identifying Climates and Ecosystems of Sub-Saharan Africa
Direct students' attention to the climate map on page 427. Have class members name the countries that are on the equator and identify the two climates found in these countries. (wet tropical, wet-and-dry tropical) Then ask: What type of vegetation is found in the tropical wet and dry areas? (savanna) In the wet tropical areas? (rain forest) Have students note the similarities in the climates and vegetation zones found north and south of the savanna. What types of climates and vegetation zones are found at the Tropic of Cancer and the Tropic of Capricorn, both 23° from the equator? (arid and semiarid climates; steppe and desert ecosystems) Which country has the greatest diversity in climates? (South Africa)

CHECK FOR UNDERSTANDING

Ask students to draw rough cross-sections of sub-Saharan Africa, one from north to south and one from east to west, on the chalkboard. Both cross-sections should show land that rises sharply from the sea and then levels off. On the north-south cross-section, have students locate the equator and the various climate zones. On the east-west cross-section, ask them to identify areas where they might expect to find the warmest and the coolest temperatures. (warm at low elevations near the coast, cooler at high elevations)

CORRECTIONS/EXTENSIONS

Reteaching   List the following terms on the chalkboard: *African plateau, tectonic plate, Great Rift Valley, Nile River, Zaire River, Niger River, Zambezi River, tropical latitudes, rain forest, savanna, steppe, desert, arid, semiarid, equator.* Ask each student to write three paragraphs describing the landforms, climates, and ecosystems of Africa south of the Sahara. Have them use the terms listed on the chalkboard in their papers.

Enrichment   The famines in the Sahel region have been the subject of many newsmagazine articles in the past decade. Assign several students to report on the impact drought has had on the people of this area. Ask the class to consider the part nature has played and also the role of humans in causing these famines.

17.2 The Human Imprint *(pages 429–438)*

MAIN IDEAS

- Sub-Saharan Africa's population is unevenly distributed.
- Most people in the region live in rural villages, but cities are growing rapidly. Population growth rates are also high.
- The region's great ethnic diversity has contributed to political instability.
- Although good farmland is limited, 70 percent of the people are farmers. Most are subsistence farmers, but commercial crops are increasing in importance.
- Many African nations consider themselves to be nonaligned politically.

OBJECTIVES

Students should be able to:
- describe patterns of population distribution in sub-Saharan Africa.
- explain how ethnic differences have affected the ability of African nations to build unity.
- identify the major economic activities in sub-Saharan Africa.

TEACHING STRATEGIES

Describing Population Patterns   Begin by asking the class to explain why giving a single figure for Africa's population density, such as 50 persons per square mile, might be misleading. Make sure the class understands that such a statistic could imply that the population is evenly distributed, which is not true.

Have students identify the areas of heaviest settlement (tropical coast of western Africa, lake regions, river valleys, equatorial highlands of eastern Africa, subtropical part of southern Africa). What areas are thinly settled? (rain forests, deserts). What environmental factors appear to influence settlement patterns? (rainfall, water supply, fertility of soils)

Analyzing the Impact of Ethnic Differences on Political Patterns   Write the term "nationalism" on the board and ask a student to define this term. Have the class list factors that lead people to feel common bonds of loyalty and belonging. (shared language, beliefs, religion, customs, and cultural patterns; ties of kinship and history) To what groups do many Africans feel their strongest loyalties? (ethnic groups)

Then focus discussion on how colonial boundaries set by Europeans disrupted traditional groupings. Point out that Europeans used rivers, mountains, and other features of the land as a basis for borders. How have these boundaries made the problem of building national unity more difficult since independence? (National boundaries often separated members of the same ethnic group or forced together groups that historically were in conflict.) The results have been civil wars and secession movements in a number of nations.

Identifying Economic Activities   Direct students' attention to the land use map on page 434. Ask: What is the major land use in the area right along the equator? (hunting, fishing, and gathering) Why isn't the land there used for farming? (dense rain forest, heavy rains that wash nutrients out of the soil) Why is there little or no activity along the northern border of the region? (too dry, desert area) What activity is the major land use in the region as a whole? (farming for family use) Note that much of Africa is not suitable for farming. Have class members give reasons for the lack of good farmland. (too much or too little rainfall)

Then have students locate South Africa on the land use map and name its mineral resources. (diamonds, coal, gold, uranium, iron ore, copper) How does South Africa rank economically among the nations of the region?

(highest per capita income and GNP in the region) What is misleading about South Africa's per capita GNP statistics? (The nation's wealth is controlled almost entirely by the white minority.)

CHECK FOR UNDERSTANDING

Have students list the various economic activities of sub-Saharan Africa and explain which activities are linked to the highest and lowest population densities. (highest—manufacturing, mineral deposits; lowest—nomadic herding)

CORRECTIONS/EXTENSIONS

Reteaching Divide the class into small groups. Write the following phrases on the chalkboard: *Population and Settlement, Political Patterns, Economic Activities, Sub-Saharan Africa in the World.* Tell the class that African nations face challenges to their development in each of these areas. Have each group write several paragraphs that describe these challenges and the obstacles African nations face in overcoming them. The activity can conclude by having the class brainstorm ways African nations can work together to overcome these problems.

Enrichment Sub-Saharan Africa's history provides many topics for reports. Students might report on the ancient kingdoms of Kush, Ghana, Mali, Songhai, or Zimbabwe. The kingdoms of Benin and Ife were particularly noted for their bronze sculpture. A class member might prepare an illustrated report on this art.

17.3 West and Central Africa *(pages 440–443)*

MAIN IDEAS

- In both West and Central Africa, subsistence farming is the major means of making a living, but commercial farming is growing in West Africa.
- Both West and Central Africa have mineral wealth. Oil revenues have helped make Nigeria the most industrialized country in West Africa.
- Both regions need to develop better linkages for economic development.

VOCABULARY

slash-and-burn agriculture, p. 442.

OBJECTIVES

Students should be able to:
- compare settlement patterns and economic activities in West Africa and Central Africa.
- hypothesize about the benefits of education on a West African village.

TEACHING STRATEGIES

Comparing West and Central Africa The following activity will help students organize the information in this section. Make a three-column chart on the chalkboard. Label the columns *Areas of Comparison, West Africa,* and *Central Africa.* In the first column, list the following areas of comparison: area of heaviest settlement, natural resources, primary economic activities, secondary economic activities, plans for future development. Use the information in Section 3 to complete the chart. More able classes can also compare per capita GNPs and population growth rates of the two subregions, using the information in the World Data Bank on pages 436–437.

Hypothesizing about the Benefits of Education After the class has read the special feature "Spotlight on the Future" on page 439, have students discuss the importance of education to Africans. Ask class members to write short essays describing why they think Africans believe that education is their best hope for the future. What positive changes can better schools bring? What obstacles do Africans face in establishing and maintaining schools? villagers expect?

CHECK FOR UNDERSTANDING

Have students locate West Africa and Central Africa on a wall map of Africa and point out the areas of heaviest and sparsest settlement. Ask class members to describe the major economic activities in each subregion and describe the goals each subregion has for development.

CORRECTIONS/EXTENSIONS

Reteaching Divide the class into small groups. Have each group plan a two-week study tour through either West or Central Africa. The purpose of the tour is to educate American students about the people, the physical geography, and the economies of the area. The group can travel by bus and by air. Have groups list the places they would stop. Next to each place, have students write a brief explanation of why they chose that stop on the tour.

Enrichment In 1985 the population of Lagos, Nigeria, was slightly more than 6 million people. By the year 2000, twice that number of people will live in Lagos. Ask a class member to report on the ways the city has changed as a result of rapid growth.

17.4 East and Southern Africa (pages 443–447)

MAIN IDEAS

- While subsistence and commercial farming are the major economic activities in East Africa, tourism is also an important business in several East African countries.
- Southern Africa has more people of European ancestry than any other part of sub-Saharan Africa.
- South Africa is the only country in Africa still ruled by people of European ancestry. The government's apartheid policy keeps both economic and political power in the hands of the white minority.

VOCABULARY

apartheid, p. 445

OBJECTIVES

Students should be able to:
- identify factors that contribute to a nation's economic development.
- explain how apartheid affects life in South Africa.

TEACHING STRATEGIES

Identifying Needs for Economic Development Of the 35 poorest countries in the world, 23 are in Africa. The problems East Africa faces in its development are shared to some extent by almost all countries of the region. Some factors that have slowed East Africa's development are listed near the end of page 444. Have students name these factors as you write them on the chalkboard. (lack of metals and fuels; need for money, skilled workers, modern linkages, and political stability) Ask class members to explain how the absence of each factor hinders the building of a strong, modern economy.

Examining Apartheid in South Africa Ask students to define apartheid and explain how it affects society in South Africa. Focus discussion on the ways this policy affects where blacks and whites live, their ability to travel freely, and their ability to earn a living. Remind students that black South Africans have almost no political power, despite the fact that they outnumber whites about five to one. Ask students to give reasons why many black South Africans oppose the homelands policy. Have students suggest reasons why leaders of South Africa's white minority have resisted efforts to end apartheid.

CHECK FOR UNDERSTANDING

List the following economic activities on the chalkboard: mining, herding, subsistence farming, commercial farming, tourism. Ask students to give examples of countries in East and Southern Africa where each activity is important.

CORRECTIONS/EXTENSIONS

Reteaching Tell the class to imagine that they have a chance to meet with students their own age from East and Southern Africa. Among the students will be several from South Africa and Kenya. Ask each student to make a list of questions they would like to ask their African counterparts about the land, people, and political issues of the two subregions.

Enrichment Assign several students to prepare an itinerary for picture-taking safari through East Africa. Tourist agencies and guidebooks for Kenya and other East African countries are good resources for this activity.

Other class members can consult the *Reader's Guide* for articles on the mounting opposition to apartheid both within South Africa and throughout the region.

Answers

17.1 REVIEWING THE FACTS (p. 428)

Define
escarpment: a steep cliff that marks the edge of a plateau

Answer
1. (a) The entire center of the continent is a large, high plateau. Near the coasts are escarpments, cut by gorges through which rivers drain. The only lowlands are narrow strips along

the coasts. The Great Rift Valley lies in the eastern part of the African plateau. (b) Although most of Africa is in the tropics, much of the region has a cool climate because of the high elevation of the African plateau.

2. (a) A 40-mile-wide valley formed when two tectonic plates began pulling apart millions of years ago.

(b) Volcanic activity, which often occurs near the edges of tectonic plates, is still taking place along the rift.

3. (a) rain forest, savanna, semiarid steppe, desert (b) savanna

Locate

1. (a) Mozambique (b) Zaire (c) Nigeria (d) Mozambique
2. Kenya and Tanzania
3. (a) Mediterranean subtropical climate (b) wet-and-dry tropical climate (c) temperate marine climate

MAP WORKSHOP (p. 432)

1. Britain and France 2. Portugal
3. Zimbabwe, Zambia 4. Liberia, Ethiopia
5. Lesotho

17.2 REVIEWING THE FACTS (p. 438)

Answer

1. Most people live along the tropical coasts of western Africa or near lakes, in river valleys, in the equatorial highlands of eastern Africa, and in subtropical southern Africa. Large areas of desert and rain forest are sparsely settled. About 70 percent of the population lives in rural areas.
2. These cities based their power on their control of important trade routes, especially the north-south routes, over which salt and gold were traded.
3. The slave trade, managed by the Europeans, took the lives of thousands of Africans, led to wars among African groups taking part in the slave trade, and disrupted or destroyed many traditional African cultures. In later years, Europeans established colonies throughout most of Africa.
4. beginning in 1957 with Ghana and ending in 1980 with Zimbabwe; Most became independent during the late 1950's and early 1960's.
5. (a) Although two thirds of the region is unsuitable for farming, 70 percent of the people are farmers. Most are subsistence farmers, although such cash crops as bananas, cocoa, coconuts, kola nuts, palm oil, coffee, sugar, and cotton are cultivated.

(b) Mining of gold, copper, diamonds, manganese, uranium, and cobalt is important. These resources are exported in great quantity as well as used domestically to further industrial development. Nigeria is developing petroleum deposits. (c) Emerging industries include food processing, textiles, building materials, and production of pulp, paper, and wood products. However, with the exception of South Africa, which has been able to use its vast mineral wealth to become the most industrialized nation in the region, manufacturing remains the least developed aspect of the economy at present.

6. Most of the countries of the region consider themselves nonaligned. Some have experimented with socialist economic policies. For the most part, however, they do not feel that they must choose either Communism or democracy. They seek aid from both Communist and non-Communist countries.

Locate

1. (a) Atlantic Ocean (b) Red Sea (c) Gulf of Aden (d) Gulf of Guinea (e) Indian Ocean
2. (a) Lake Tanganyika (b) Lake Nyasa

17.3 REVIEWING THE FACTS (p. 443)

Define

slash-and-burn agriculture: the system of farming in which forest growth is cut down and burned to fertilize fields that will be used for only a few seasons

Answer

1. Going from north to south, the ecosystems change from desert to semiarid to savanna to rain forest to savanna again.
2. along the coast of the Gulf of Guinea
3. (a) oil (b) When world oil prices dropped suddenly in the early 1980's, Nigeria's income from trade was cut in half; its economy took a steep downturn.
4. Many Central African countries lack roads and other overland linkages, so the Zaire River is an important transportation artery. The river may also become an important source of hydroelectric power.

Locate

1. Mali, Burkina, Niger, Chad, Central African Republic 2. Chad, Niger, Nigeria, Cameroon

SKILL WORKSHOP (p. 446)

1. sub-Saharan Africa
2. sub-Saharan Africa

3. Latin America and the Caribbean
4. by about 17 percent
5. 44 percent

17.4 REVIEWING THE FACTS
(p. 447)

Define

apartheid: the South African government's policy of strict separation between blacks and whites

Answer

1. subsistence farming; production of such cash crops as coffee, cotton, sisal, tea, cloves, sugar, and peanuts
2. The policy has greatly restricted the civil rights of black South Africans. The white minority holds the economic and political power in South Africa. Black South Africans live in separate townships, often far from the cities in which they work. Members of some black ethnic groups have been forced to live in special homelands, established on poor, unproductive land. For many years, black South Africans had to carry special passes when they traveled. A black caught traveling without a pass could be jailed.

Locate

1. Kenya, Uganda, Tanzania
2. (a) Zimbabwe (b) Namibia (c) Tanzania (d) Ethiopia (e) Kenya (f) South Africa (g) Uganda

GEOGRAPHY LABORATORY
(pp. 448–449)

Speaking Geographically

1. escarpment
2. slash-and-burn agriculture
3. apartheid
4. nonaligned

Testing Yourself

1. plateau	9. Ethiopia
2. low	10. 1957 and 1980
3. savanna	11. agriculture
4. Sahel	12. hydroelectric power
5. high	13. South Africa
6. Bantu	14. linkages
7. Kush	15. ethnic diversity
8. 1800's	

Building Map Skills

1. Ethiopia	6. Madagascar
2. Sudan	7. Nigeria
3. Zaire	8. Kenya
4. Botswana	9. Zimbabwe
5. South Africa	10. Angola

A. Atlantic Ocean
B. Gulf of Guinea
C. Indian Ocean
D. Red Sea
E. Lake Victoria

Applying Map Skills

Answers will vary. Students' charts should indicate that parts of Ethiopia, particularly the Amhara Plateau, are at a higher elevation than South Africa. South Africa also has a desert area, while Ethiopia does not. The climate in Ethiopia is generally dry or semidesert. A cooler climate prevails only in the highlands of the plateau region. South Africa, on the other hand, has a great diversity of climate zones. Farming is the primary land use in Ethiopia, although there is also some nomadic herding. In South Africa, land use is more diversified. In addition to subsistence farming, there is an extensive coastal belt of commercial farming and stock raising as well as an area close to Pretoria and Johannesburg that is used for manufacturing. South Africa has a number of major population centers, while population generally seems to be more evenly distributed throughout Ethiopia. There are, however, two urban areas of high population density in Ethiopia.

SUPPLEMENTARY MATERIALS

Books

Elliot, Kitt, Benin: *An African Kingdom and Culture,* Lerner Publications, 1978

Foster, Blanche F., *East Central Africa,* Franklin Watts, 1981

Hornburger, *African Countries and Cultures,* David McKay and Company, 1981

Kerina, Jane, *African Crafts,* Lion Press, 1970

Laure, Jason, *South Africa: Coming of Age under Apartheid,* McGraw-Hill, 1980

Paton, Alan, *Cry the Beloved Country,* Charles A. Scribner's Sons, 1961

Smith, Rukshana, *Sumitra's Story,* Coward, McCann, Geoghegan, 1983

Other Media

Africa (NG: filmstrip, cassette, part of "Ancient Civilizations" series)

Africa before the Europeans (LF: film, covers A.D. 100–1500)

Africa: In Search of Itself (T-L: film)

Africa: Learning about the Continent, (SVE: 4 filmstrips, 4 cassettes, teacher's guide)

Africa: Living in Two Worlds (EB: film/video)

Afro-City: Abeokuta, Nigeria (AA: filmstrips cassettes, maps, 30 booklets, maps)

Ethiopia: A Way of Life (TA: 2 filmstrips, 2 cassettes, teacher's guide)

ASSIGNMENT GUIDE

- **Text Features**

  Map Workshop, p. 454   Skill Workshop, p. 466
  Spotlight, p. 464   Chapter Review, p. 470–471

- **Teacher's Resource Binder**

  Assign after
  p. 454 Map Workshop: Using a Polar Projection WB p. 138
  p. 456 Building Basics Worksheet 18.1
          Independent Practice Worksheet 18.1 WB p. 134
  p. 461 Building Basics Worksheet 18.2
          Independent Practice Worksheet 18.2 WB p. 135
  p. 465 Building Basics Worksheet 18.3
          Independent Practice Worksheet 18.3 WB p. 136
  p. 466 Skill Workshop: Using an Almanac WB p. 139
  p. 469 Building Basics Worksheet 18.4
          Independent Practice Worksheet 18.4 WB p. 137
  p. 471 Map Test 18
          Chapter Test 18
          Enrichment Chapter 18 WB p. 140

- **Geography Laboratory Manual: Investigating Chapter 18**

  Use with pages 450–471

- **Outline Maps 25 and 26**

  Use with pages 450–471

- **Overhead Transparencies 12, 60, 61, 62, 63, and 64**

  Use with pages 450–471

OVERVIEW

This chapter looks at the South Pacific, a region that has much more ocean water than land. Although the region includes two continents—Antarctica and Australia—as well as thousands of islands, it has fewer people than any other region.

The chapter traces the history of the region and outlines the political status of its many nations and territories. The chapter also examines the economic activities of the more developed parts of the region—Australia and New Zealand—as well as providing an economic overview of the less developed island nations.

INTRODUCING THE CHAPTER

Of all the regions of the world, the South Pacific is probably the one that students know least.

Have class members locate the region they think is the South Pacific on a world map. What countries do students think belong to this region? Tell the class that two continents are a part of this region. Have students guess which ones they are. (Australia, Antarctica) What landforms might be common in this region? (islands) What kinds of climates do students associate with the South Pacific? (Typically students think of tropical climates and ecosystems that include palm trees.) Point out that, in fact, all of Earth's climates and ecosystems occur someplace in the South Pacific region. Tell the class that a part of this region is sometimes referred to as the "land down under." What country do students associate with this phrase? (Australia) Have the class speculate about how Australia might have gotten this nickname.

Then have the class read the Chapter Introduction on page 450. According to the text, what is another name for this region? (Oceania) Why is this a fitting name for the region? (It has more water than people.) Have the class speculate about why the region has such a low population, compared to other regions. Among the factors that students might mention are the region's inaccessibility from other continents, the harshness of the climate in Antarctica, and the inability of small islands to support large populations.

18.1 The Physical Environment *(pages 451–456)*

MAIN IDEAS

- The Pacific Ocean varies greatly from place to place in depth, temperature, current, and ecosystem.
- The South Pacific region includes the continents of Australia and Antarctica and three large island groups—Melanesia, Micronesia, and Polynesia.
- Antarctica is an uninhabited continent made up of islands buried beneath an ice cap.
- Australia is the flattest and driest continent, with desert covering much of the broad western area known as the outback.
- All of Earth's climates and ecosystems occur someplace in the South Pacific region.

VOCABULARY

outback, p. 451; reef, p. 451; coral, p. 451

OBJECTIVES

Students should be able to:
- use latitude and longitude to locate places in the South Pacific region.
- describe and analyze the climates and ecosystems of the region.

TEACHING STRATEGIES

Using Latitude and Longitude to Locate Places Use the following activity to give students practice in using latitude and longitude and increase their familiarity with the countries of the South Pacific region. Divide the class into small groups. Ask each group to review the skill lesson "Using Latitude and Longitude" on pages 16–17. Then have each group pick five places shown on the map on pages 452–453. The places students select can be countries,

islands, water bodies, cities, or landforms such as mountains. Have the groups determine the latitude and longitude of each place they have selected and list these coordinates. Next to each set of coordinates, tell students to write a clue that helps identify the place. For example, a group might select Honiara in the Solomon Islands and use the following clues: 10°S, 160°N, capital city. Have groups take turns reading their locations and clues to the class. The group that correctly names each place first receives 5 points for its answer. The group with the most points at the end of the game wins.

Examining Climates and Ecosystems As the climates and ecosystems that predominate in Antarctica, Australia, and the islands are discussed, have students identify factors that influence climate in each area. Ask: How does latitude influence the climate in Antarctica? (Regions at high latitudes are cold because they receive no sun some of the year and only slanting rays during the rest of the year.) Which part of Australia lies within the tropical regions? (northern coast) What climate does it have? (humid tropical climate) What type of climate do the cities of Perth and Adelaide have? (Mediterranean subtropical) Which parts of Australia are the driest? (Australia's west coast and the interior of the continent) What types of ecosystems are found in this part of Australia? (desert and steppe) Why is rainfall plentiful along the southeastern coast but not on the west coast or inland? (The Great Dividing Range blocks moisture-bearing winds from reaching inland Australia.)

Contrast the climates of New Zealand and Australia. What accounts for the milder, marine climate in New Zealand? (moderating influence of water on the smaller island) Point out that the North Island of New Zealand is warmer than the South Island just as the northern coast of Australia is warmer than the southern coast of the continent. Ask students why this is so. Would this be the case if New Zealand were located north of the equator rather than south of the equator?

Conclude by having the class identify factors that create wet tropical climates and tropical rain forest ecosystems in Melanesia. On which islands does elevation influence climate? (volcanic islands that have mountainous areas)

CHECK FOR UNDERSTANDING

Ask each student to write the terms *Antarctica*, *Australia*, and *Islands* on a sheet of paper, leaving several lines of space between the terms.

Next to the name of each area, have class members write three or four sentences describing its landforms, climates, and ecosystems.

CORRECTIONS/EXTENSIONS

Reteaching   Write the following words and phrases on the chalkboard: *steppe, arid, dry plains and low plateaus, tropical climate, savanna, polar ice cap, coral, temperate marine climate, volcano, arid, desert, Great Dividing Range.* Have students identify which of the three areas in the South Pacific each term refers to, giving reasons for their choices. Several words fit more than one area.

Enrichment   The Great Barrier Reef provides some of the most exciting underwater sightseeing in the world. Ask a student to prepare an illustrated report on how the reef formed and the fishes, plants, and sea animals to be seen there.

18.2 The Human Imprint *(pages 456–461)*

MAIN IDEAS

- The traditional cultures of the South Pacific were a complex blend, including hunters and gatherers, farmers, and fishers; these cultures were severely disrupted by European colonization.
- Although the region as a whole is thinly populated, most of its population is concentrated in cities.
- The region has many independent nations, but some islands are controlled by the United States, Great Britain, or France.
- Australia and New Zealand were once British colonies and now belong to the British Commonwealth.
- The most economically developed nations of the region are Australia and New Zealand.

OBJECTIVES

Students should be able to:
- describe the effects of European colonial rule on the original settlers of the South Pacific.
- explain population patterns.
- analyze the relationship between economic activities and the physical geography of the region.

TEACHING STRATEGIES

Examining the Colonial Legacy   The plight of the Aborigines and Maoris following the arrival of Europeans has been compared to the fate of the American Indians after European colonization. Ask students to list some of the traditional ways of life in the South Pacific region. (hunting and gathering, subsistence farming, fishing) How did the arrival of Europeans disrupt these patterns? (brought new diseases, took over land, set up plantations for commercial farming) Focus discussion on the loss of cultural identity and traditions as well as actual losses of human life.

Surveying Population Patterns   Write the following statement on the chalkboard: "Although the people of Oceania are few in number and widely scattered, the region is very urbanized." Ask students for evidence to support this statement. (Nearly three out of four people of Oceania live in cities. About 85 percent of the people in Australia live in cities.) Ask why so many of the region's people live in cities. (Much of the land is unsuited for farming. People are drawn to cities by the greater economic, educational, and cultural opportunities.)

Relating Economic Patterns to the Physical Environment   As students examine economic patterns in Oceania, remind them to consider relationships between climates, landforms, and the types of economic activities that are prevalent in different areas.

Why is the raising of livestock, especially sheep, important in Australia? (Its semiarid ecosystem and flat land are well suited to grazing.) What resources have helped Australia develop its industry? (abundant mineral resources such as iron, zinc, tungsten, nickel, coal, and other energy fuels)

What aspects of its physical geography make New Zealand well suited to farming? (mild, humid, marine climate) Why is farming difficult on coral islands? (Soils are thin and poor; fresh water is scarce.) Why are volcanic islands better suited to farming than coral islands? (Volcanic soil is richer. Fresh water is more plentiful.)

What obstacles do the South Pacific islands face in industrializing? (isolation from world markets, small populations with little demand for manufactured goods) Discuss how these factors are barriers to economic development.

CHECK FOR UNDERSTANDING

Ask students to imagine that they are producing a video tape of life in the South Pacific at two periods of time—in 1500 and today. Ask different students to contribute sentences or phrases that are appropriate to each time period.

CORRECTIONS/EXTENSIONS

Reteaching   Divide the class into four groups. Tell one group to imagine its members are Australians, a second group South Pacific islanders, and a third group New Zealanders. Members of the fourth group are to be news reporters. Tell the first three groups that a they are to be interviewed by reporters for American television stations. The reporters will ask them about population patterns, political patterns, and economic activities in the South Pacific region. Have each group select a representative to be interviewed. Ask the fourth group to prepare a list of questions for a panel discussion of the topics mentioned above. Then hold a "Meet the Press" panel on the South Pacific region.

Enrichment   For years, the Australian Aborigines and the Maoris of New Zealand were often treated as second-class citizens in their respective countries. Assign several students to research and report to the class on the culture of the Aborigines or the Maoris and their status as minority groups today.

18.3 Australia
(pages 461–465)

MAIN IDEAS

- The most densely settled and economically developed part of Australia is the eastern and southeastern coast.
- Australia's most important economic is agriculture, especially sheep raising.
- Although manufacturing was slow to develop in Australia, World War II forced the nation to build its own industries. Today Australia is the leading industrial country of the South Pacific region.
- Australia is a parliamentary democracy.

VOCABULARY

artesian well, p. 461.

OBJECTIVES

Students should be able to:
- make a map of the regions of Australia.
- analyze economic development in Australia.

TEACHING STRATEGIES

Using Outline Map 26   Provide each student with a copy of Outline Map 26: *Australia: Physical*. Using the information on pages 461–462, have students map the three main regions of Australia described in the subsection "Australia's Regions." (southeastern coast between the Pacific Ocean and the Great Dividing Range; the Great Artesian Basin; the outback) Have groups make each region a different color and make a key for the map. Tell students to label the major geographic features and important cities in each region.

Analyzing Economic Development   Have class members list reasons for the slow development of industry in Australia before 1940. (Because it had a small population, Australia needed few manufactured goods. It was cheaper to import many manufactured goods than to produce them within the country.) How did World War II isolate Australia from its traditional trading partners? (The war disrupted shipping in the Pacific.) How did the war help Australia's industrial growth? (Cut off from their traditional trading partners, Australians were forced to build their own industries.) What nations are Australia's major trading partners today? (Japan, the United States)

CHECK FOR UNDERSTANDING

On a wall map of Australia, have students locate the major regions of the country. Then have students indicate the major economic activities for each region as you list them on the chalkboard. Ask class members to rank these activities in order of their importance to Australia's economy.

CORRECTIONS/EXTENSIONS

Reteaching   Divide the class into small groups. Have each group pick out the main ideas in the three subsections of Section 3. Ask group members to write the main ideas for each section on the chalkboard. Have the class compare main ideas and revise their own statements if necessary.

Enrichment   Some students might enjoy reporting to the class on Australian slang. They can translate the popular Australian song "Waltzing Matilda" for the class. Others might report on such animals as the kangaroo and the duckbill platypus that are found only in Australia. Reports should include a short explanation of the reasons for Australia's distinctive wildlife.

18.4 The Islands
(pages 465–469)

MAIN IDEAS

- Tourism and commercial fishing are expanding in economic importance for Oceania.
- New Zealand is the most developed of the island countries of the region, with most of its wealth coming from agriculture and sheep raising.
- New Zealand's abundant energy resources and minerals are helping its industry.
- Fishing and subsistence farming continue to be important for the region's island groups.

OBJECTIVES

Students should be able to:
- give examples of economic and political changes on the South Pacific Islands.
- make land use, population density, and climate maps for New Zealand.

TEACHING STRATEGIES

Analyzing Changes on the South Pacific Islands   Have the class describe the political and economic changes taking place on the islands of Oceania today. (increasing self-government, greater industrialization, growing tourism, development of commercial fishing, out-migration to more industrialized countries) Ask students to speculate on the factors that have led to each of these changes.

Making Maps of New Zealand   Divide the class into small groups. Each group can use the information in the subsection "New Zealand" to create its set of maps. Groups can begin by making an outline map of New Zealand, using the map on page 452 as a reference. Have each group make two copies of its completed outline map. Then have groups use their three outline maps to make a population map, a climate map, and a land use map showing agricultural, forest, and mineral resources. Both the world climate map on pages 64–65 and the world population map on pages 490–491 show New Zealand. Students can refer to these maps in making their climate and population maps. The land use map can be based on information in the text.

CHECK FOR UNDERSTANDING

Ask each student to write a statement that refers to New Zealand or one of the three major island groups. The statement should *not* name the island or island group it describes. Have pairs of students exchange their statements and try to identify the place their partner has described. If a statement is ambiguous, the writer should correct it.

CORRECTIONS/EXTENSIONS

Reteaching   Divide the class into small groups. Ask each group to imagine that its members work for a regional tourism commission. This board represents the island nations of the South Pacific. The job of this commission is to create an advertising campaign that will attract tourists to the islands. Have each group create a radio or television ad, a series of posters, or a travel brochure that will highlight the pleasures of vacationing in New Zealand or on other South Pacific islands.

Enrichment   More than 700 different languages are spoken by the peoples of Papua New Guinea. Some of these groups live much as their ancestors did thousands of years ago. Students might be assigned to report on the history of this largely undeveloped nation. Others might report on the early history of New Zealand and the part played by Abel Tasman and Captain James Cook in its exploration.

Answers

MAP WORKSHOP (p. 454)

1. (a) 90°S (b) 66½°S
2. (a) high latitudes (b) because the land area lies mainly in latitudes that are greater than latitude 66½° 3. about 65°W

For a special challenge: Because on a polar projection of the South Pole, the top, sides, and bottom of the map all lie north of the center of the map, which is the South Pole. A compass cannot show this. (On a polar projection of the North Pole, everything shown lies south of the center of the map, which is the North Pole.)

18.1 REVIEWING THE FACTS (p. 456)

Define
1. *outback:* the plains and plateaus of western Australia
2. *reef:* ridge that rises near the water's surface
3. *coral:* small sea animals whose skeletons may form islands

Answer

1. The South Pacific region has much more ocean water than land.

2. (a) Antarctica is made up of islands buried beneath an ice cap. These islands have mountains, valleys, plains, and an active volcano. (b) Australia is the flattest continent. It has a narrow plain on the southeastern coast, separated from plains and low plateaus to the west by low mountain ranges. (c) Some of the islands are volcanic, with steep, mountainous terrain. Some are atolls, which are generally flat, rising only a few feet above sea level.

3. The western two thirds of the continent is arid and semiarid. Only along the northern and eastern coasts is there much rain. Here, temperatures are mild.

Locate

(a) Canberra (b) Wellington
(c) Port Moresby (d) Port-Vila (e) Suva

18.2 REVIEWING THE FACTS (p. 461)

Answer

1. In Australia, Europeans drove the Aborigines from the best lands and killed many in fighting. Many other Aborigines died of diseases carried by Europeans. In New Zealand, many Maoris died fighting to hold onto their land. Both the Aborigines and the Maoris have made a place for themselves in modern society but have lost much of their traditional culture.

2. Population density is the average number of persons per square mile of land area. Since large areas of Oceania are sparsely settled, averages are misleading. When more heavily populated urban areas of Oceania are compared with urban areas in other parts of the world, densities appear higher than averages would suggest. Oceania has areas of high density.

3. (a) The lands of Oceania became targets of European nations competing to acquire colonies. Countries with colonies or territories in Oceania included England, Spain, the United States, Germany, and France. (b) independence for former colonies

4. (a) the raising of sheep and other livestock; the production of wool; the making of clothing, electronics, appliances, and precision instruments; the producing of steel; the processing of food (b) the production of wool, meat, and dairy products; the processing of other agricultural goods (c) fishing; subsistence farming (d) commercial farming of coconuts, coffee, and cacao; the processing of coconut meat to make copra

Locate

1. (a) the southeastern coast (b) Perth
2. There are several deserts and mountains.

18.3 REVIEWING THE FACTS (p. 465)

Define

artesian well: a well existing where a layer of groundwater is trapped between two hard layers of rock below the soil; water flows through the well to the surface by natural pressure

Answer

1. (a) The eastern and southeastern coast is the economic and cultural heartland of Australia. It is the most densely populated and most developed part of the country. Its climate is mild, moist, and pleasant. The land is well suited to farming in level areas and to grazing in highlands. (b) Many artesian wells and springs supply water for sheep and cattle ranches in the Great Artesian Basin of central Australia. (c) There is little development in the outback. Supplies of water are meager, vegetation is sparse, and there is little population.

2. Before World War II, few immigrants were accepted from countries other than the British Isles. After World War II, the Australian government encouraged immigration from other countries as well. Immigrants came from Germany, Austria, Poland, Italy, Greece, and Asia.

3. Australia is a parliamentary democracy. The head of state is the British monarch, who is represented by a governor general.

4. sheep and cattle raising; wheat farming; the growing of sugarcane, tropical fruits, and cotton

5. (a) large deposits of coal, petroleum, and natural gas to fuel industry (b) World War II cut off Australia from Europe and the Americas. Australians had no markets for their raw materials and no way to get manufactured goods. To cope, they built their own industries.

Locate

1. commercial farming and stock raising
2. Answers should include two of the following: Sydney, Adelaide, Melbourne.
3. hunting, fishing, and gathering along the north coast

SKILL WORKSHOP (p. 466)

1. (a) p. 544 (b) pp. 548 and 634
2. (a) Sydney (b) Sydney, Melbourne, Brisbane
3. (a) 15,345,000 (b) 47 4. Democratic, federal state system 5. SE of Asia
6. (a) Queen Elizabeth II (b) Ninian Martin Stephen

18.4 REVIEWING THE FACTS (p. 469)

Answer
1. development of commercial fishing, tourism
2. mutton, beef, wool
3. Melanesia, Micronesia, Polynesia

Locate
1. (a) 22°N, 158°W (b) 42°S, 175°E
2. Wake Island, Marshall Islands, Caroline Islands, Guam, Mariana Islands

Geography Laboratory   (pp. 470–471)
Speaking Geographically
1. b 2. d 3. a 4. c

Testing Yourself
1. Hawaii 2. Australia, New Zealand
3. Polynesia 4. Sydney, Melbourne 5. Antarctica 6. New Zealand 7. Australia
8. Micronesia 9. Canberra 10. New Guinea

Building Map Skills
1. Australia 2. Papua New Guinea
3. New Zealand 4. Hawaiian Islands
5. Mariana Islands

Applying Map Skills
1. (a) Temperate marine (b) Arid desert
(c) Wet-and-dry tropical
2. Western Australia, Northern Territory
3. bauxite
4. less than 2 persons per square mile
5. (a) Apia (b) Yaren, Tarawa

SUPPLEMENTARY MATERIALS
Books
Henderson, W.F., and R.A. Henderson, *Looking at Australia*, Lippincott, 1977
Kaula, Edna M., *The Land and People of New Zealand* (rev. ed.), Harper & Row, 1972
Leib, Amos P., *The Many Islands of Polynesia*, Charles Scribner's Sons, 1972

Other Media
Australia (2nd ed.) (EB: film/video, available in Spanish)
Australia and New Zealand (EB: 6 filmstrips)
Child of Papua New Guinea: The Same Today, the Same Tomorrow (EB: film/video)
The Pacific World (ED: 5 filmstrips) *Polynesia* (NG: film/video)

KEY TO SUPPLEMENTARY MATERIALS		
AA	*Abt Associates*, Cambridge, MA
AF	*Academy Films*, Venice, CA
AP/PH	*The Associated Press and Prentice-Hall Media*, Tarrytown, NY
AS	*The Asia Society*, New York, NY
BFA	*BFA Educational Media*, Santa Monica, CA
CAF	*Current Affairs Films*, Wilton, CT
CF	*Contemporary Films*, New York, NY
CIM	*Coronet Instructional Media*, Chicago, IL
D-G	*Dennoyer-Geppert Company*, Chicago, IL
E	*Encore*, Burbank, CA
EB	*Encyclopaedia Britannica Educational Corporation*, Chicago, IL
ED	*Educational Design*, New York, NY
EDNA	*E. David Neighbors and Associates*, Storrs, CT
EGM	*Eye Gate Media*, Jamaica, NY
EEM	*Educational Enrichment Materials*, Bedford Hills, NY
EMC	*EMC Corporation*, St. Paul, MN
EVE	*Encore Visual Education*, New York, NY
FI	*Films, Inc.*, Hollywood, CA
GA	*Guidance Associates*, Mount Kisco, NY
IER	*Imperial Education Resources*, Pleasantville, NY
IFB	*International Film Bureau*, Chicago, IL
KU	*Knowledge Unlimited*, Madison, WI
LF	*Landmark Films*, Falls Church, VA
M-Ed	*Micro-Ed*, Minneapolis, MN
NASA	*National Aeronautics and Space Administration*, Washington, DC
NG	*National Geographic Society, Educational Services*, Washington, DC
NYT	*New York Times*, New York, NY
PLP	*Projected Learning Programs, Inc.*, Chico, CA
R-McN	*Rand McNally*, Chicago, IL
ROP	*Right On Programs*, Huntington, NY
SSSS	*Social Studies School Service*, Culver City, CA
SVE	*Society for Visual Education*, Chicago, IL
TA	*Troll Associates*, Mahwah, NJ
TERF	*Teaching Resources Films*, Mount Kisco, NY
T-L	*Time-Life Films, Multi-Media Division*, Paramus, NJ
UEVA	*Universal Education and Visual Arts*, Universal City, CA
UL	*United Learning*, Niles, IL
UNRVS	*United Nations Radio and Visual Services*, New York, NY
USDA	*United States Department of Agriculture*, Washington, DC
WS	*Warren Schloat Publications, Inc.*, Tarrytown, NY

Heath
WORLD GEOGRAPHY

Heath

WORLD GEOGRAPHY

by Charles F. Gritzner

D.C. HEATH AND COMPANY
Lexington, Massachusetts / Toronto, Ontario

Charles F. Gritzner is Professor of Geography at South Dakota State University, Brookings, South Dakota. He was graduated from Arizona State University and received his Ph.D. from Louisiana State University. He was formerly Executive Director and President of the National Council for Geographic Education and has written more than 100 articles and books in the fields of cultural geography and geographic education.

Student activities were prepared by Linda K. Hillestad, who has taught geography for 16 years at the Brookings Middle School, Brookings, South Dakota, and has been a member of the Executive Board of the National Council for Geographic Education.

Executive Editor: Phyllis Goldstein; *Senior Editors:* Susan Belt Cogley, Margaret L. Kovar
Executive Designer: William Tenney; *Cover Design and Layout:* Jane Miron
Production Coordinator: Maureen Bisso LaRiccia
Manager, Editorial Services: Marianna Frew Palmer

Contents

v

UNIT 2   *The View from the Air*

UNIT 3 *The View from the Ground*

MAP WORKSHOPS

SKILL WORKSHOPS

SPOTLIGHT ON . . .

MAPS

xiii

ATLAS

WORLD DATA BANKS

xiv

DIAGRAMS, CHARTS, AND GRAPHS

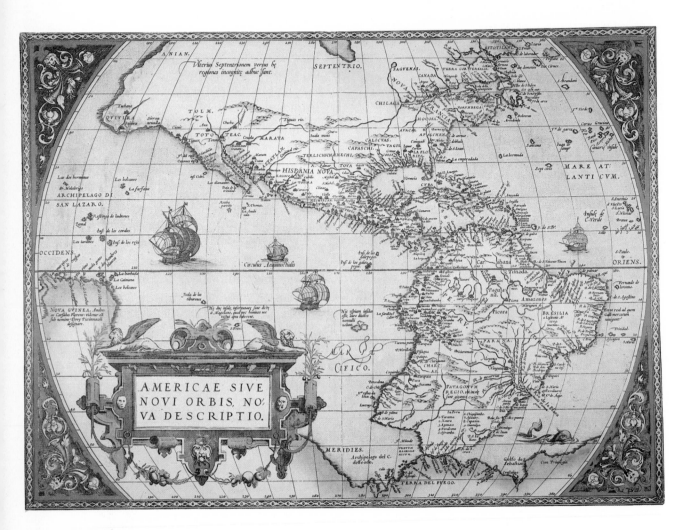

This map of the Western Hemisphere was drawn by Abraham Ortelius in 1570.

Reviewing Map and Globe Skills

Geography is the study of Earth's surface and human activities on Earth. The word *geography* comes from the Greek word *geographia,* which means "description of Earth." Scientists who study geography are **geographers**. Geographers study the physical conditions of the various places on Earth's surface. They try to understand how people and places influence one another.

Geographers use a number of tools to study and describe Earth. Among the newest tools are remote sensing images gathered from space by satellites. One of these is known as Landsat (Land satellite) images. Globes, maps, charts, graphs, and photographs also have important roles in the study of geography.

A mosaic of satellite images of Earth shows the 48 adjoining states of the United States.

Students will be using a wide variety of maps as they learn geography. It is important that a globe be made available so they can more fully understand the geographic relationships between the places they study and the place where they live. Make it a point to have students locate places on the globe as well as on maps.

1 Using Globes

A **globe** is a scale model of Earth. Like Earth, a globe is a sphere — shaped like a ball. It shows Earth's land and water areas and major geographic features. Globes can represent the size and shape of Earth's land and water areas accurately. They also show relative distances and directions accurately.

When you look at a globe, you may notice immediately that it has two poles — the North Pole and the South Pole. On a globe and on Earth, the poles help you tell direction. North is toward the North Pole. South is toward the South Pole. No matter what the starting point, a traveler going toward the North Pole on Earth is always headed north.

Geographers frequently refer to four hemispheres — the Northern, Southern, Eastern, and Western. The **equator,** an imaginary line halfway between the North and South Poles, divides Earth into the Northern and Southern Hemispheres. Two other imaginary lines divide Earth into the Eastern and Western Hemispheres. One of these lines is 0° longitude or the prime meridian. It stretches from the North Pole to the South Pole. The other line is exactly halfway around the world from there.

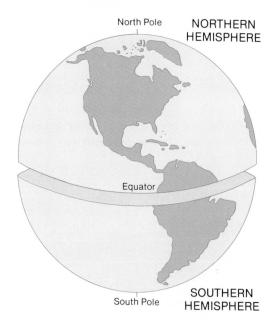

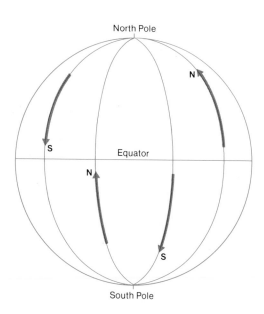

Holding and turning the globe gives you a number of different views of Earth. For example, no matter how you hold a globe, you will see only half of the sphere at one time. Each half is a **hemisphere,** or one half of Earth.

2

Students might be interested in four other hemispheres: (1) land hemisphere — centered on Paris, France; (2) water hemisphere — centered near New Zealand; (3) and (4) day and night hemispheres — created as Earth rotates on its axis.

The drawings on this page illustrate some important features of globes and the ways they represent Earth. Use the drawings to help you answer the following questions.

1. (a) Which has more land, the Northern Hemisphere or the Southern Hemisphere? (b) The Eastern Hemisphere or the Western Hemisphere?

2. In which two hemispheres is North America located?

3. Is Europe north or south of Africa? East or west of North America?

4. In which direction would you travel to get from Antarctica to Asia?

For a special challenge Which continent lies in all four hemispheres? Explain why.

NORTHERN
HEMISPHERE

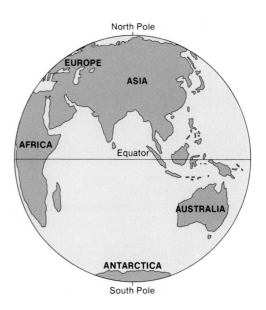

SOUTHERN
HEMISPHERE

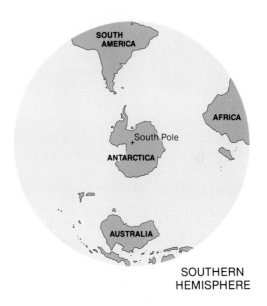

The line that divides Earth into the Eastern and Western Hemispheres is the prime meridian or longitude 0° and 180° longitude. Although the British Isles and a little bit of Africa are technically in the Western Hemisphere, geographers usually consider the lands of the Western Hemisphere to include North and South America and the islands near them.

3

2 Understanding Map Projections

A globe is the best way to represent Earth because a globe is round. Globes, however, are not handy to carry around. They also show few details of Earth's surface. For these reasons, geographers have found ways to make maps that show Earth. A **map** is a flat drawing of all or part of Earth. The different ways of drawing maps are called **projections.**

What happens when the round earth is drawn on a flat surface? Some land areas are changed in size and shape. Distances between land areas may be represented inaccurately. Some projections show the correct shape of land or water areas but make the areas look larger or smaller than they really are. Other projections show correct size but incorrect shape.

Each projection shown here has certain strengths and weaknesses. An interrupted projection shows both the size and shape of landmasses fairly accurately, but it divides the world into sections. This makes it hard to tell distances across water. A Mercator projection does not divide the world into sections, but it distorts sizes and shapes especially near the poles. The Robinson projection (pp. 34 – 35), which has minor distortions around the poles, is often used for world maps.

A polar projection shows how Earth would appear if you were looking down at one of the poles. It is accurate near the center but inaccurate toward the edges.

The Mollweide (môl vīd′ə) projection shows land and water areas drawn in true proportion to each other. The land shapes are not accurate, however, especially near the outer edges of the map.

Compare the maps shown on these pages. Then answer the questions.

1. On which projection does Greenland appear to be as large as South America?

2. Which projection shows Alaska as a small, narrow area of land?

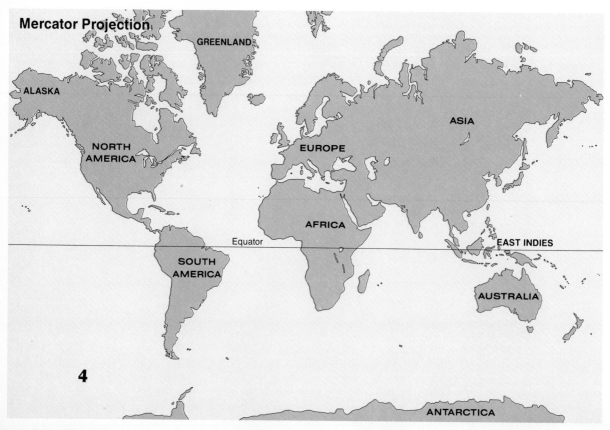

Mercator Projection

4

3. Which projection shows Alaska as a larger area, the Mercator projection or the interrupted projection?

4. How does the shape of Alaska on the Mercator projection compare with its shape on the interrupted projection?

5. (a) Which pole is shown on the polar projection? (b) What is the name of the land area shown on this projection?

Interrupted Projection

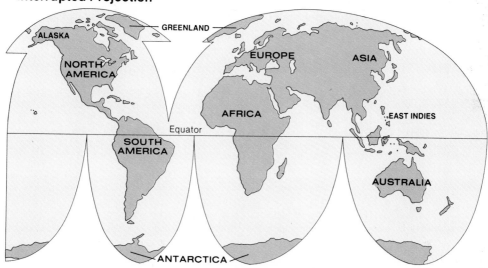

Mollweide Projection

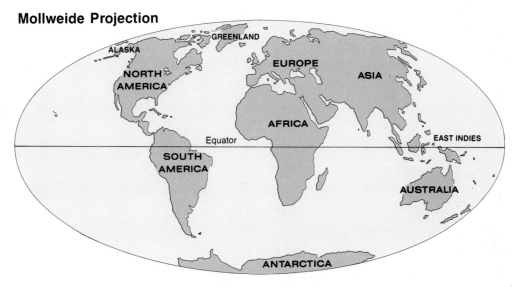

In the 1500's, the Flemish cartographer Gerardus Mercator used a picture of the Greek god Atlas on the title page of his books of maps. (In Greek mythology, Atlas was forced to hold up the heavens as a form of punishment.) Now all books of maps are called atlases.

3 Interpreting Map Symbols and Legends

Maps are alike in many ways. Most maps have a title that tells what the map is about. The title of the map on this page, for example, is "East Asia: Political." This tells you that the map gives political information about the region of East Asia. A **political map** shows the way people have divided the land. Political features include such things as cities and boundaries between countries and cities.

All maps have a special language of **symbols** to show information. A map symbol — a color, a line, a dot, or even a small picture — represents something on

Earth. A map's **legend,** sometimes called a **key,** shows the meaning of the symbols used on the map. The legend usually appears in a box. The map's title is frequently part of the legend.

Look at the legend for the map of East Asia. How many symbols does the legend explain? How does the use of color help you read this map?

Maps have a variety of purposes, depending on what they show. There are political maps, weather maps, road maps, population maps, and many others. Each map will have its own legend to unlock its information.

The map on page 7 is a resource map of states in the northeastern part of the

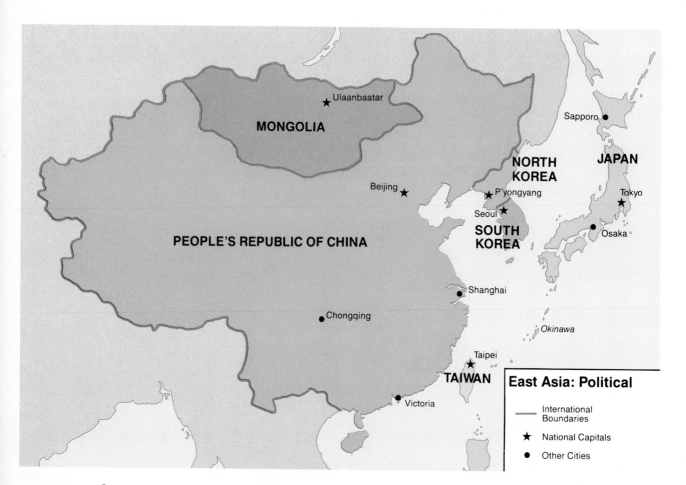

East Asia: Political

——— International Boundaries

★ National Capitals

● Other Cities

6

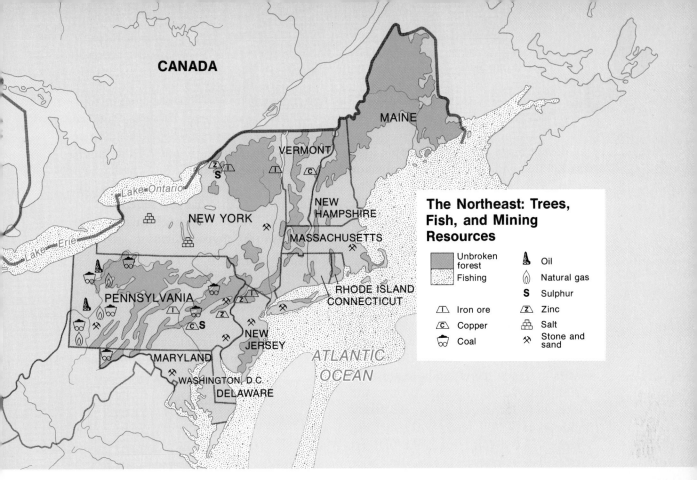

The Northeast: Trees, Fish, and Mining Resources

Legend:
- Unbroken forest
- Fishing
- Iron ore
- Copper
- Coal
- Oil
- Natural gas
- S Sulphur
- Z Zinc
- Salt
- Stone and sand

United States. Read the title of the map. What general kinds of resources does the map include? The legend tells you which symbols represent specific resources.

Notice the various boundary lines on this map. How do the boundaries between states differ from the international boundary line between the United States and Canada?

Before using a map, you always need to look at its title, legend, and symbols. Now use the maps on these two pages to help you answer the following questions.

1. (a) Name six countries of East Asia. (b) Which of the countries share international boundaries with the People's Republic of China?

2. What is the capital of Japan?

3. Which city is not a capital, Seoul, Taipei, or Shanghai?

4. (a) On the map of the northeastern part of the United States above, what resource is represented by the color green? (b) Which resource is represented by blue dotted areas?

5. (a) On this same map, how are the symbols for iron ore, copper, and zinc alike? (b) How are these symbols different?

6. Name five resources found in the state of New Jersey.

7. (a) In which state is there the greatest amount of unbroken forest? (b) In which state is there the least unbroken forest?

8. (a) Which two northeastern states have coal resources? (b) Which of the two has more coal? Explain your answer.

9. Which is located in New York's forest areas, iron ore or salt resources?

10. Which state has both oil and natural gas resources?

Answers to questions in column 1: In general, the map shows trees, fish, and mining resources. Mining resources are broken down into nine categories. The international boundary line is wider than the state boundary lines.
Answers to numbered questions are in the Teacher's Guide.

4 Reading a Physical Map

Political maps show how people have divided the land. **Physical maps** are concerned with land features that nature has determined. When you want to know about lakes, rivers, or the condition of the land in a certain place, you might use a physical map.

Colors on physical maps are especially important. They show land elevation. **Elevation** means height above **sea level.** Sea level is the surface of the ocean. Look at the elevation key for the map of Latin America. You will notice that three shades of green show lands lower than 7,000 feet (2,000 meters). Brown and white indicate lands with elevations higher than 7,000 feet (4,000 meters). There is also a color for lands that are lower than sea level. Areas like hills, mountains, and plateaus that stand higher than surrounding areas are called **highlands.** Areas like valleys and plains that are lower than surrounding areas are called **lowlands.**

You may have noticed the gray shading that also appears in the color blocks of the elevation key. The shading represents **relief.** Relief is the difference between the highest and lowest points of land in a certain area. A land area with frequent, sizable drops and rises in its surface has **high relief.** The rugged lands of mountain ranges have high relief. An area where the land rises or falls only slightly over a considerable distance has **low relief.**

The diagram on this page illustrates the relationship between elevation and relief. As you study the diagram, notice that lands at low elevations generally have low or moderate relief. Lands at high elevations, however, may have low, moderate, or high relief.

Use the map legend and its elevation key to answer the following questions.

1. What is the name of the land area with the highest elevation?

2. What is the name of the large lowland area in Brazil?

3. (a) What is the elevation of the Brazilian Highlands? (b) Would you say the land here has high, moderate, or low relief?

4. Give the elevation of (a) Bogota, Colombia, and (b) Brasília, Brazil.

5. Describe the elevation and relief of the country of Uruguay.

For a special challenge Describe elevation and relief in the country of Bolivia.

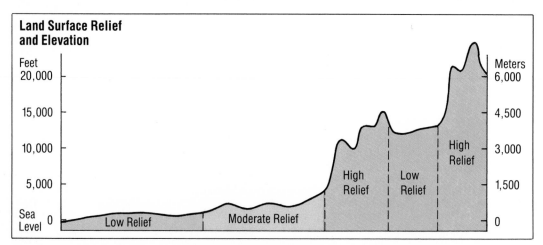

Land Surface Relief and Elevation

Answers to numbered questions are in the Teacher's Guide.
Assign the Workbook activity for Reviewing Map and Globe Skills 4.
Ask students: How can an area of highlands have low relief? (Even though the land is at a high elevation, it may be relatively flat, as in the case of a high plateau.)

Latin America: Physical

Elevation key

Feet	Meters
14,000	4,000
7,000	2,000
1,500	500
700	200
0	0
Below sea level	Below sea level

★ Capital city   ● Other city

Highest point—Mt. Aconcagua
Elevation: 22,834 ft/6,960 m

Lowest point—Salinas Grandes, Valdés Peninsula
Depth: -131 ft/-40 m

Longest river—Amazon River
Length: 4,082 mi/6,570 km

Largest lake—Lake Titicaca
Area: 3,200 sq. mi./8,288 sq. km

Area—7,935,269 sq. mi/20,552,366 sq. km

Population—421,260,000

ATLANTIC OCEAN

Tropic of Cancer

Gulf of Mexico

BAJA CALIFORNIA

WESTERN SIERRA MADRE

EASTERN SIERRA MADRE

Rio Grande

Monterrey

Guadalajara ●

MEXICO
Mexico City ★

YUCATAN PENINSULA

Havana ★

THE BAHAMAS
● Nassau

CUBA

DOMINICAN REPUBLIC

HAITI
Port-au-Prince

Santo Domingo

PUERTO RICO (U.S. COMM.)
VIRGIN ISLANDS (U.S.)
San Juan

ST. CHRISTOPHER AND NEVIS
Basseterre ★

ANTIGUA-BARBUDA
St. Johns

BELIZE
Belmopan ●

JAMAICA
Kingston ●

HONDURAS

GUATEMALA
Guatemala ★

EL SALVADOR
San Salvador ★

Tegucigalpa ★

NICARAGUA
Managua ★

CARIBBEAN SEA

DOMINICA
Roseau ★

ST. VINCENT AND THE GRENADINES
Kingstown

SAINT LUCIA
Castries

BARBADOS
Bridgetown

GRENADA
St. Georges

TRINIDAD AND TOBAGO
Port-of-Spain

Panama Canal

San José ★
COSTA RICA

PANAMA
Panama City ●

Maracaibo ●

Caracas ★

VENEZUELA

Medellín ●

LLANOS

Bogotá ●

Cali ●

COLOMBIA

Georgetown ★
GUYANA

Paramaribo ★
SURINAME

Cayenne ●
FRENCH GUIANA (FR.)

GUIANA HIGHLANDS

PACIFIC OCEAN

N

GALÁPAGOS ISLANDS (ECUADOR)

Quito ★
ECUADOR
Guayaquil ●

Equator

AMAZON BASIN

PERU

Lima ★

ANDES MOUNTAINS

Lake Titicaca

Arequipa ●

BOLIVIA
La Paz ★

Sucre ★

BRAZIL

Brasília ★

Recife ●

Salvador ●

BRAZILIAN HIGHLANDS

Belo Horizonte ●

GRAN CHACO

PARAGUAY
Asunción ★

Tucumán ●

São Paulo ●

Rio de Janeiro ●

Tropic of Capricorn

PAMPAS

CHILE

Córdoba ●

URUGUAY

Santiago ★
Mt. Aconcagua (22,834ft/6,960m)

Buenos Aires ★
Montevideo ★

Concepción ●

ARGENTINA

Río de la Plata

● Bahía Blanca

Salinas Grandes (-131ft/-40m)

PATAGONIA

| 0 | 500 | 1000 Miles |
| 0 | 500 | 1000 Kilometers |

FALKLAND ISLANDS (U.K.)
● Stanley

Tierra del Fuego

Cape Horn

SOUTH GEORGIA ISLANDS (U.K.)

30°N
20°N
10°N
0°
10°S
20°S
30°S
40°S
50°S

120°W 110°W 100°W 90°W 80°W 70°W 60°W 50°W 40°W 30°W 20°W

5 Telling Directions

If you want to tell someone where a place is or how to go to a certain address, you will almost certainly need to give the person directions. If you are using a map to travel through a city or across the country, you will need to tell directions. In order to follow the map correctly, you need to understand how maps show directions.

On Earth and on a globe, north is always toward the North Pole. As you might expect, north is always toward the North Pole on maps as well. Once you know which direction is north, you can figure out all the other directions. When you face north, south is always directly behind you. East is to your right. West is to your left. North, south, east, and west are the four main directions. They are called **cardinal directions.**

The North Pole does not appear on all maps. How, then, can you find north on a map? Many maps include a **direction arrow.** The arrow always points north.

Find the direction arrow on the map on this page. It tells you that north is toward the top of the map. This means that south is exactly the opposite, or toward the bottom of the map. East is toward the right side of the map, and west is toward the left.

Many maps are drawn so that north is toward the top of the map. If there is no direction arrow on the map, north will usually be toward the top. If the map is drawn with north in a different position, the direction arrow will tell you. Of course, all the other directions would also be in different positions.

Some maps have a **compass rose,** like the one shown on the world map on these pages. A compass rose shows all four cardinal directions plus the **intermediate directions.** Intermediate directions are the in-between directions. Northeast is an intermediate direction. This means that it is halfway between the cardinal directions north and east. The other intermediate directions are southeast, southwest, and northwest.

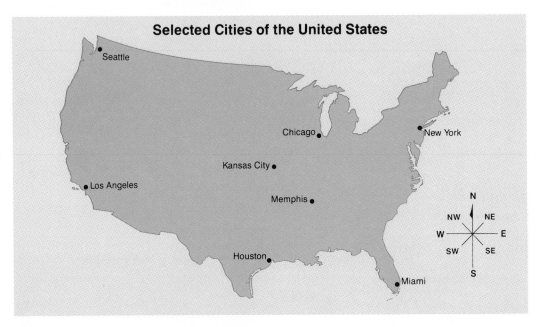

Selected Cities of the United States

10

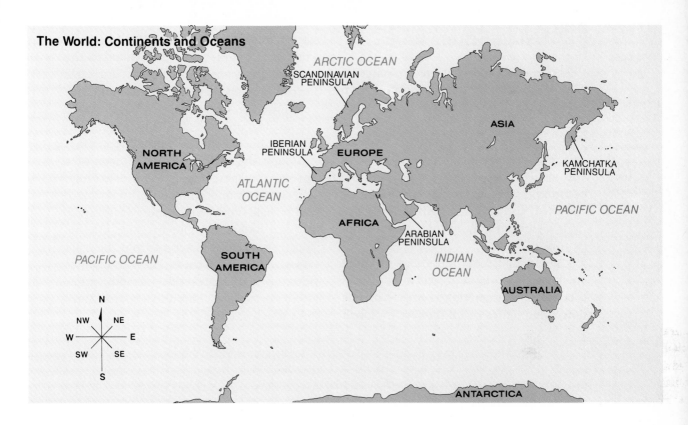

The World: Continents and Oceans

Use the map of cities in the United States to answer these questions.

1. Which city is almost directly north of Los Angeles?

2. Which city is almost directly south of Chicago?

3. Which is the closest city southwest of Chicago?

4. Which is the farthest city southwest of Chicago?

5. Use a cardinal direction to tell what direction Miami is from New York.

6. Use an intermediate direction to name the part of the country in which Seattle is located.

Now look at the map of the world.

7. Which continent is south of Europe?

8. What is the name of the peninsula in the northern part of Europe?

9. Which continent is northwest of South America?

10. If you were sailing straight across the Atlantic Ocean from North America to Europe, in what direction would you be going?

11. In what direction would you be going if you sailed straight from the Arabian Peninsula to Australia?

12. Use an intermediate direction to help you describe where Asia is in relation to Africa.

For a special challenge Look at the direction arrow shown here. Tell what direction would be at the top of the map.

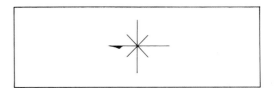

6 Using Scale

You can easily see that the two maps on these pages are the same size. They take up the same amount of space. But what about the areas the maps represent? How do they compare? If you say that the map on the left represents a larger area, you are correct. The map on the left shows all the countries on the whole continent of Africa. The map on the right shows Zaire (zä ir′), which is only one of Africa's many countries.

You can figure out how large or small an area really is by using the map's **scale.** The scale on a map is the line that tells how many miles or kilometers on Earth are represented by certain units on the map. Look at the scale line just below the legend for the map of Africa. This scale shows that on this map $1\frac{3}{4}$ inch (about $4\frac{1}{2}$ centimeters) represents about 2,000 miles (or about 3,200 kilometers) on Earth. One way to make measurements is to copy the scale line on the edge of a piece of paper. Then, to measure distances from one point to another, place your scale on the map where you want.

Now look at the map of Zaire. On this map, the scale is different from the scale on the map of Africa. The scale shows that $1\frac{1}{5}$ inch represents only 500 miles (810 kilometers). This tells you that Zaire is a much smaller area than Africa.

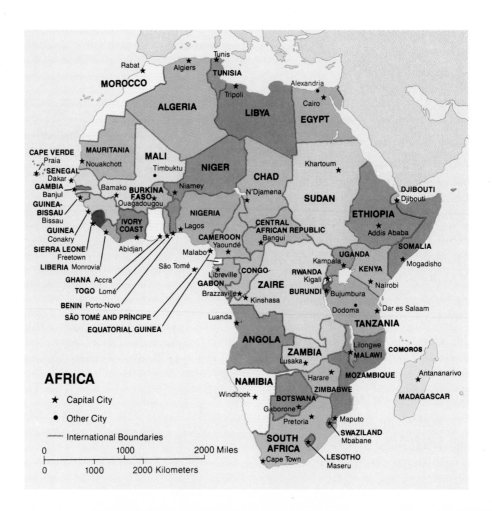

AFRICA

★ Capital City

● Other City

— International Boundaries

0   1000   2000 Miles

0   1000   2000 Kilometers

12

Find Zaire on the map of Africa. You will see that only one of Zaire's cities is named on that map. There would not be enough room to name many more cities. The map of Zaire, however, shows several cities as well as some important rivers and a large lake. Maps that show a large area in a small space are limited in the details they can show. Maps that show a small area in a large space can often show many details.

Use the scales on these maps to help you compare size and find distance.

1. The cities of Tunis and Cape Town are located near the northern and southern tips of Africa. Measure the distance between the two cities on the map. About how far does Africa reach in a north-south direction?

2. How far is Tripoli, Libya, from Cairo, Egypt?

3. Is the distance between Lusaka, Zambia, and Harare, Zimbabwe, greater or less than 600 miles (954 kilometers)?

4. How far is Zaire's capital, Kinshasa, from the city of Kananga?

5. Which is greater, the distance between Kisangani and Lubumbashi or the distance between the cities of Khartoum, Sudan, and Tripoli, Libya?

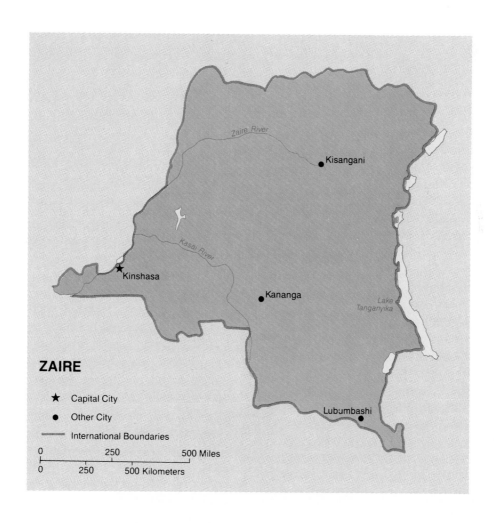

ZAIRE

★ Capital City

● Other City

— International Boundaries

0   250   500 Miles

0   250   500 Kilometers

13

7 Using a Grid

In this book, you will find a number of photographs of Earth taken from space. American astronauts took these photographs while they were on space missions. The astronauts probably received most of their training at the LBJ Space Center in Houston, Texas. The city of Houston is important to the space program in ways other than the training of astronauts. While the astronauts were in space, scientists working with computers directed their flights from the center at Houston.

Houston is one of the largest cities in the United States. It is a center for business and industry. In addition, Houston is a major port. A waterway called the Houston Ship Channel flows into larger waterways that connect the city's transportation routes with the Gulf of Mexico and the Atlantic Ocean.

If you were to visit Houston or any other city, you might use a map to help you find the places you want to see. The map would most likely include a **grid.** A grid is a pattern of regular sections identified by a system of numbering and lettering. The grid for the map of Houston on the opposite page uses both letters and numbers.

If you were to attend a sports event in an arena such as Houston's Astrodome, you would use a grid system to find your seat. You might walk down an aisle to find row S and then across row S to seat 35. Desks in a classroom arranged in rows could also be identified by a grid system. Map grids work in the same way.

Look at the grid for the map of Houston. Find the letters that go down the side of the map. Each letter identifies one of 7 rows that run horizontally across the map. Now find the numbers that run across the top of the map. These letters identify 7 rows dividing the map vertically. The rows meet to form blocks. The letters and numbers can be used to identify each block. For example, follow row G across the map as far as row 7. This is block G7. The Space Center is located in this block. Other points of interest can be located in the same way.

Below the map is an index. The index lists places of interest in alphabetical order. Beside each name, it lists the grid location according to the numbering and lettering system. A map index helps a visitor find the general area in which a certain place is found. Then the visitor can decide the best route for traveling to that point.

Use the index and the grid for the map of Houston to help you answer the questions that follow.

1. According to the index, in which block of the grid would you look to find the Astrodome?

2. One Shell Plaza and the Civic Center are located in the downtown area of Houston. (a) In which grid blocks, then, is downtown Houston? (b) Which major highways run through the downtown area?

3. Give the names and locations of two universities located in Houston.

4. (a) Through which blocks of the city grid does the Houston Ship Channel run? (b) In what block is the battleship *Texas* located?

5. After traveling up the channel, large oceanliners turn around in the Turning Basin at the western end of the channel. In which grid block is the Turning Basin located?

6. What transportation center is located in grid block E4?

14

Most students are familiar with highway maps, which provide excellent examples of index and grid systems. Have a highway map ready to show the class.

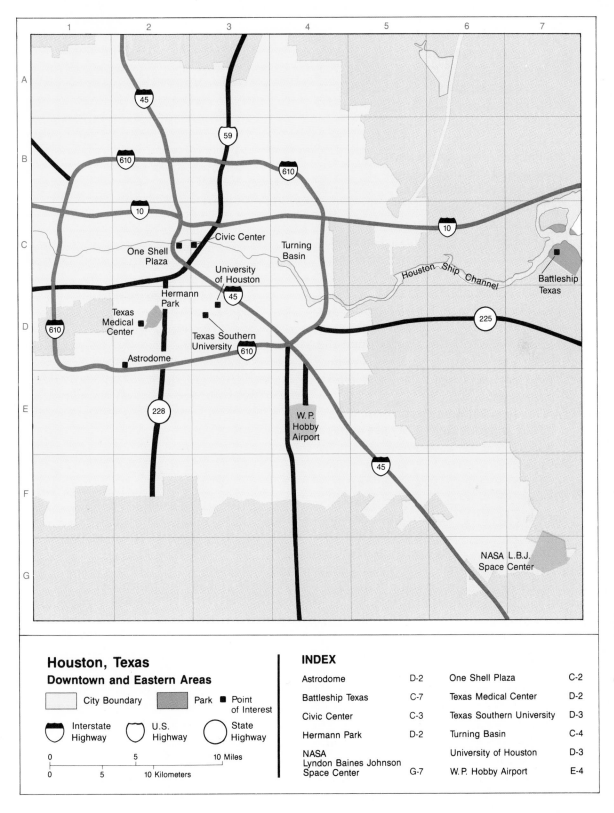

Houston, Texas
Downtown and Eastern Areas

City Boundary	Park ■ Point of Interest

Interstate Highway U.S. Highway State Highway

0   5   10 Miles

0   5   10 Kilometers

INDEX

8 Using Latitude and Longitude

Imagine a single dot on a table-tennis ball. How would you describe its location? You could not describe its location unless you had some additional markings on the ball. Geographers and mapmakers have solved the puzzle of locating places on the round Earth by using a **global grid.**

Two sets of lines make up the global grid. The lines of one set run all the way around the globe. They are called **parallels of latitude.** These lines never meet. Each one runs parallel to the equator.

A second set of lines on the global grid includes all the **meridians of longitude,** or simply **meridians.** Unlike parallels, each meridian goes only halfway around the globe. Meridians also come together. They meet at two points—the North Pole and the South Pole.

Geographers can measure distances of latitude and longitude. They use units of measurement called **degrees,** shown by the degrees symbol (°). Degrees of latitude start at the equator. The equator is latitude 0°. From the equator, degrees of latitude go as far north as the North Pole; they go as far south as the South Pole. The North Pole is latitude 90° north; the South Pole is latitude 90° south. Ninety degrees either north or south is the highest measurement for latitude.

There is also a 0° line used as the starting point for measuring longitude. The 0° meridian of longitude is known as the **prime meridian.** Degrees of longitude are counted either east or west of the prime meridian until the 180° meridian is reached. The 180° meridian is on the opposite side of the globe from the prime meridian and is the ending point for measuring longitude. Like the prime meridian, it is neither east nor west.

16

Lines of Longitude (Meridians)

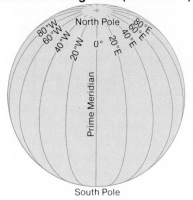

Lines of Latitude (Parallels)

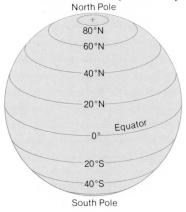

Parallels and Meridians

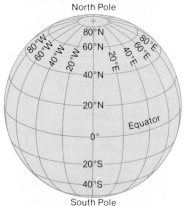

When parallels of latitude are combined with meridians of longitude, the grid on a globe or a map is complete. It is possible for geographers, pilots, and students to describe any location by finding where a parallel and a meridian meet.

Because of their size, maps and globes cannot show all the possible parallels and meridians. Instead, they show only regular intervals of latitude and longitude at perhaps 10, 15, or 20 degrees or more. When you describe a map location, therefore, you may have to estimate where additional parallels or meridians would fall. The city of Leningrad shown on the map here, for example, is approximately latitude 60° N, longitude 30° E.

Air and sea navigators use detailed charts and instruments to find exact locations. They may use Mercator projections because these maps are especially helpful for figuring latitude and longitude.

Now see how well you can use latitude and longitude to answer these questions.

1. (a) What two special lines meet at latitude 0° and longitude 0°? (b) In what ocean is this meeting point?

2. Find longitude 80° W on the map. Now find latitude 40° N. (a) On what continent is this point? (b) Find latitude 40° S at longitude 80° W. In what ocean is this point?

3. In which ocean is each of these points? (a) latitude 20° N, longitude 40° W (b) latitude 20° S at the 180° meridian

4. On which continent is each of these points? (a) latitude 60° N, longitude 85° E (b) latitude 20° S, longitude 20° E

5. (a) Across which continents does the prime meridian pass? (b) Name the continents that lie mainly east of the prime meridian. (c) Name the continents that lie mainly west of the prime meridian.

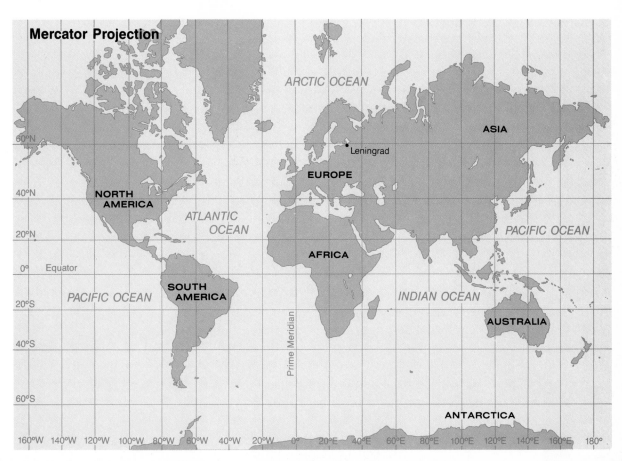

9 Following Circle Routes

Finding places on maps can suggest adventure — the possibility of traveling one day to distant places. By now, you can use latitude and longitude to give accurate descriptions of locations both near and far. You can follow a city map. You may have noticed that planning a route from one place to another takes some thought and skill.

Suppose you are planning a long trip by air. Perhaps you expect to fly from Philadelphia to Rome, Italy. You want to know the route the airplane will take. Most likely, the pilot will follow a **great circle route**. Great circle routes are the shortest distance between any two points on Earth.

A **great circle** is any imaginary line that circles Earth and divides it into hemispheres — equal halves. You already know that the equator divides the earth into the Northern and Southern hemispheres. The equator, then, is a great circle. No other parallel divides Earth into equal halves. The equator, therefore, is the *only* parallel that is a great circle.

The circle formed by the prime meridian and the 180° meridian is a great circle. Every meridian, in fact, when joined with its opposite meridian, forms a great circle. The polar map on page 19 shows part of the great circle formed by the 100° E and 80° W meridians. To see the rest of that great circle, you would need either a polar map of the South Pole or a globe.

Not all of the possible great circles pass over the poles or around Earth at the equator. If you tie a string around a globe

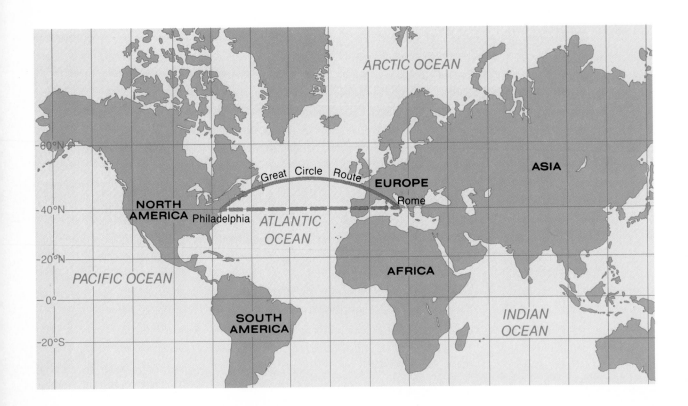

The 180° meridian is a special line. Do students know why? (*It is the international date line. By crossing it, you either gain or lose a day, depending on the direction in which you are traveling.*) Assign the Workbook activity for Reviewing Map and Globe Skills 9.

Students find the concept of circle routes difficult to grasp unless they actually try the globe-and-string experiment suggested below.

in such a way that it divides the globe into equal halves, you can move it anywhere around the globe and follow a great circle. The number of great circles and hemispheres into which Earth or a globe can be divided is unlimited.

A great circle route follows an arc, or segment, of a great circle. If you look at great circle routes on flat maps, it may be difficult to see the advantage they offer for air and sea travel. On the map on page 18, for example, the dotted line appears to be the shortest route between Philadelphia and Rome. Notice that the dotted line follows the 40° N parallel. The great circle route looks longer on this map. Now compare the two routes when shown on the map at the right. Notice that the dotted line again follows the 40° N parallel. Here the great circle route looks shorter.

By now, you may be wondering if mapmakers play tricks with great circle routes. The way to check up on them is to use a globe and a piece of string. Put one end of the string on Philadelphia. Follow the 40° N parallel across the Atlantic Ocean to Rome. Use a pen to mark the distance on the string. Use the same string and the globe to trace the great circle route shown on the map at the right. For which route did you need less string? Which route is shorter?

Now use the globe and a longer piece of string to see if you can complete the great circle that passes through both Philadelphia and Rome. How many more great circles can you trace between cities on the globe?

1. Study the four lettered lines on the bottom globe. Which are the great circle routes? Explain your choices.

2. Sea captains of the past were very pleased when wind conditions permitted them to "sail the meridian." Explain why.

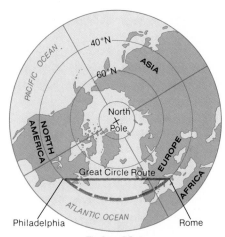

Polar Map

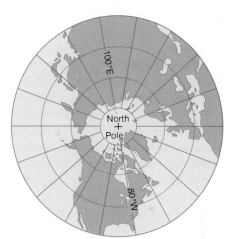

Great Circles: Meridians

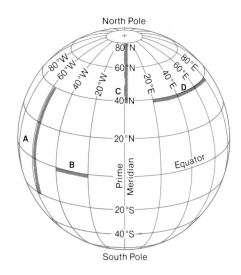

Answers are in the Teacher's Guide.

Assign Reviewing Map and Globe Skills Tests 1–9 once students have completed this unit.

Assign the final Workbook activity for Reviewing Map and Globe Skills in order to reinforce key map concepts and vocabulary.

19

Unit 1 examines the world as a whole. Physical features, climate, ecosystems, and resources are all discussed. Together they set the stage and provide the props for human life on this planet. A recurrent theme throughout these first four chapters is change, because Earth is not a static place.

THE VIEW FROM SPACE

"I can see it hanging there, surrounded by blackness, turning slowly in the relentless sunlight . . . It seems delicately poised in its circular journey around the sun."

Astronaut Michael Collins used these words to describe his view of Earth. He was looking at it from the lifeless surface of the moon. Thinking about the planet Earth as seen from space is one way to study geography. From this viewpoint, you can consider Earth's land and water, climates, environments, and natural resources. In Unit One, you will study all these geographic features. Photographs, Landsat images, and maps will help shape your space-eye view of Earth.

Students should be encouraged to make extensive use of the Atlas in their book as they read this and the following chapters. The names of many places are given as examples of various landforms, bodies of water, countries, cities, etc. Make it a point to have students locate each place-name on an Atlas map.

The Face of Earth

Imagine that you are an astronaut looking at Earth from your orbiting spacecraft. At this distance, the planet Earth appears very small and very fragile. Its round shape and beautiful colors contrast with the inky blackness of space beyond.

Three things about faraway Earth stand out. White clouds swirling around the planet make it look like a big marble. The deep shades of blue are mainly water. From space, it becomes clear that Earth's waters are connected. They form one vast ocean that covers much of the planet's surface. In places, you see masses of land interrupting the ocean. These are the continents. The surface conditions and plant life on the continents have a variety of colors. This variety suggests the differences that exist from place to place on Earth's surface.

Photographs and other images taken from space create a unique view of Earth, one unseen before the space exploration of the past 30 years. These pictures show Earth as a whole, yet made up of many regions. You can see that the land, water, and atmosphere are closely related.

From space, the surface of Earth appears still; yet it is constantly changing. The relationships between land, water, and atmosphere sometimes change suddenly and dramatically. More often they change in slow, unseen ways over millions of years. Either way, these relationships have special meanings for people everywhere.

1 Land and Water

Land and water together make up the surface of Earth. The land and water areas, however, are not evenly divided. Only 30 percent of Earth's surface is made up of land. Water covers about 70 percent of the planet.

Water on Earth

Two different types of water — salt and fresh — are found on the earth. Salt water is found in oceans and seas. It may also be found in inland waters, such as the Great Salt Lake in Utah. Fresh water fills rivers and most lakes.

Saltwater Areas The view from space shows a vast, connected ocean. Landmasses divide this world ocean into four main parts. These parts are the Atlantic, Pacific, Indian, and Arctic oceans. Most **seas** and **gulfs,** which are smaller than oceans, are also parts of the vast ocean system. Some seas — like the Caribbean Sea — are regions within an ocean. Others, such as the Red Sea, are connected to an ocean. (Saltwater seas that are surrounded by land, like the Caspian Sea, are really giant lakes.)

Most gulfs, like seas, are partially enclosed by land. The Gulf of Mexico is a very large gulf connecting with the Atlantic Ocean.

There are also other bodies of water connected with oceans and seas. Some are small while others are quite large. A **bay** is a body of water partly enclosed by land but having an opening to the sea. Because water in a bay is calm and free from strong currents, it is a natural harbor. San Francisco, California, and Tokyo (tō′kē ō), Japan, are both located on bays. Natural harbors have been important in the growth of both these cities.

Large sheltered areas make San Francisco Bay one of the world's best harbors.

A closer view of Earth from space would show places where a narrow channel of water connects two larger areas of water. This type of channel is called a **strait.** The Strait of Gibraltar (jə brôl′tər) between the Atlantic Ocean and the Mediterranean (med′ə tə rā′nē ən) Sea is an example of a strait.

Freshwater Areas Fresh water makes up only about 3 percent of Earth's water supply. Yet it provides the water needed by all things that live on land. Fresh water is found in lakes, streams, and rivers. It also lies under the surface as groundwater and in glaciers as ice.

A lake is a large body of water — usually fresh water — surrounded by land. Some lakes are quite small. Others are as large as seas. The Great Lakes in the United States are important water routes. Many large cities, such as Chicago and Cleveland, have grown up on their shores.

23

The Mississippi River and its tributaries provide an excellent example of a river system. Have students examine the Atlas map on pages 491–492 and name some of the tributaries of the Mississippi River.

A river is a large stream of water that empties into an ocean, lake, or some other body of water. Rivers begin as small streams. These streams, carrying water from springs, rain, or melted snow, join together to form a river. A river with all its streams, or **tributaries,** is called a **river system.**

Land on Earth

Thirty percent of Earth's surface is covered with land. Land areas, like those of water, differ in size and outline. Land also differs in the height and shape of its various surfaces.

Land Areas The largest landmasses on Earth are the **continents.** There are seven continents — Europe, Asia, Africa, North America, South America, Australia, and Antarctica. Three of the continents — Europe, Asia, and Africa — form a continuous landmass, sometimes called the Great World Island. Europe and Asia, which are part of the same land area, are connected to Africa by the Isthmus of Suez. An **isthmus** (is'məs) is a narrow strip of land joining two larger land areas.

The continents of North America and South America are also joined by an

This Landsat image shows Cape Cod, Massachusetts. A cape is a long strip of land shaped by ocean currents.

isthmus — the Isthmus of Panama. Australia and Antarctica are the only continents completely surrounded by water.

Landmasses smaller than continents and completely surrounded by water are called **islands.** Some islands are very small, and others are quite large. Some islands, like Iceland, are alone in the ocean. Others, like the Aleutian Islands of Alaska, are close to one another and form a chain. Such a chain of islands is called an **archipelago.**

Islands are formed in a number of ways. The Hawaiian (hə wī'yən) Islands were formed by volcanoes. Many islands of the South Pacific are coral reefs. Coral reefs are created by the buildup of skeletons of tiny ocean creatures. Other islands, often found at the mouths of rivers, are sandbars. Many islands along the Atlantic and Gulf coasts of the United States are of this kind.

Continents and islands have several kinds of land shapes formed by the meeting of land and water. One of these shapes is known as a **peninsula** (pə nin'sə lə). It is

The Sinai Peninsula joins Asia and Africa.

a finger of land jutting out from a landmass. Peninsulas are surrounded almost entirely by water. Florida and Nova Scotia (nō'və skō'shə) are both examples of peninsulas on the continent of North America. A **cape** is a point of land reaching into the sea. Cape Hatteras (hat'ər əs) and Cape Cod on the eastern coast of the United States and the Cape of Good Hope at the southern tip of Africa are examples of capes.

Landforms A closer look at Earth from space reveals the features on the surface of the land. This surface is made up of four major landforms—mountains, hills, plains, and plateaus (pla tōz'). These landforms differ in shape and **elevation**. Elevation is the height of land above the surface of the ocean—that is, above **sea level**.

The high, rugged landforms of **mountains** are the easiest to see from space. Some mountains are so high that their peaks are always capped with snow. This is true of the Himalayas (him'ə lā'əz) in Asia and parts of the Rocky Mountains in North America. Most mountains are lower, with their peaks free of snow for at least some of the year. The Appalachian (ap'ə lā'chən) Mountains in the eastern United States are an example.

Hills are raised areas of land that are lower than mountains. It can be hard to tell a hill from a mountain. What one person calls a hill, another may see as a low mountain. For example, the Black Hills of South Dakota have peaks that are called mountains.

Most people build their homes or plant their crops on the lower and more level places of the world. These are Earth's **plains** and **plateaus**. Unlike mountains and hills, they have low relief, or fairly even surfaces.

A plain is a large area with either level or rolling land. Plains may be located along a coast, such as the land that borders the eastern coast of North America, or within a continent's interior, such as North America's Great Plains.

Plateaus, like plains, have mostly level land surfaces. Plateaus are usually located at higher elevations than plains. A plateau may also have one or more steeply dropping edges that resemble steps. Rivers sometimes carve deep valleys into plateaus. The Grand Canyon, carved by the Colorado River, is an example of such a valley.

REVIEWING THE FACTS

Define

1. sea
2. gulf
3. bay
4. strait
5. tributary
6. river system
7. landform
8. continent
9. isthmus
10. island
11. archipelago
12. peninsula
13. cape
14. elevation
15. sea level
16. mountain
17. hill
18. plain
19. plateau

Answer

1. What two kinds of water are found on Earth?

2. (a) What is a continent? (b) Describe three ways islands are formed.

3. Which of the four major landforms best describes the area where you live?

Locate

Refer to the map of the world on pages 34–35.

1. Name two mountain ranges with peaks more than 14,000 feet (4,000 meters) above sea level. On which continent is each range located?

2. What body of water separates Europe from Africa?

You may wish to point out that this lesson introduces the study of physical geography. Physical geography is the study of the physical characteristics of Earth. Throughout the rest of this text, students will deepen their understanding of physical geography.

Answers are in the Teacher's Guide.

25

Texas Essential Elements 1B. Geographic terminology. 1C. Geographical tools and methodologies. 2B. Major landforms, regions, and features of the earth.

Interpreting a Diagram of Landforms and Bodies of Water

Geographers use special terms to identify the various landforms and bodies of water on Earth. Study the drawing on this page to learn what some of these terms are. Notice which terms apply to land and which to water. Look for ways in which certain features might be related to each other.

No single place on Earth, of course, would look like the drawing on this page. So many different features would never be found so close together. You will find all of them, however, symbolized on various kinds of maps. Turn to the maps in the atlas of this book. How many different kinds of landforms and bodies of water can you find?

1. What characteristics do a bay and a gulf have in common?

2. What similarities do a cape and a peninsula share?

3. Explain the difference between the source of a river and its mouth.

4. How is a tributary related to a river?

5. What is the difference between an isthmus and a peninsula?

For a special challenge Find and name the body of water that resulted from the work of people rather than nature. Explain how that body of water was formed.

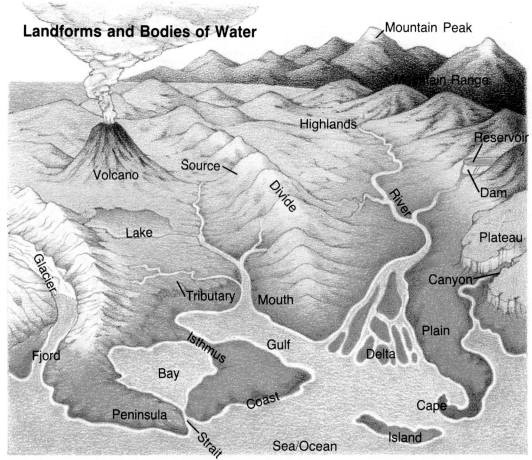

Landforms and Bodies of Water

Answers are in the Teacher's Guide.
Assign the Workbook activity for this chapter's Skill Workshop with this page.

Texas Essential Elements 1B. Geographic terminology. 1C. Geographical tools and methodologies. 2B. Major landforms, regions, and features of the earth. 2C. Physical and human forces that alter the earth's features.

2 The Changing Earth: Forces from Within

On your imaginary space trip, you saw Earth as it existed at one moment in the whole span of time. Changes in Earth's surface are always taking place. Some changes in the land, such as the crumbling of rock, happen so slowly that they are not noticed. Other changes, such as earthquakes or volcanic eruptions, are felt instantly. Over thousands of years, all these changes reshape Earth's landforms.

Moving Continents

Many changes in the land's surface are the result of forces within Earth itself. These forces may raise the land, creating mountains and hills. They may also lower it, creating level areas and lowlands. Day after day, land is raised, lowered, and even moved around. Very slowly but surely the face of Earth changes.

Look at the map on pages 34–35. Notice that the eastern side of South America looks as though it would fit against the curve of Africa's western coast. Parts of the Atlantic coast of North America might also fit against western Europe — like the pieces of a giant puzzle.

After looking at world maps in this way, some people began to wonder if the continents might once have been joined together in a single, huge landmass. Perhaps the continents had broken off and drifted apart over a long period of time. Sir Francis Bacon, an English scientist who lived more than 300 years ago, pointed out the matching coastlines. He was unable, however, to explain why the two continents seem to fit together.

Continental Drift In the past century, scientists have developed a **theory,** or idea, to explain the matching coastlines. This is the theory of **continental drift.** Many scientists think that about 200 million years ago the continents were joined together in one supercontinent, Pangaea (pan jē'ə). Slowly, pieces of the supercontinent moved apart. In time, these pieces of land reached their present locations — and they are still moving.

Scientists have found evidence that supports this theory. In studying rock formations of Africa and South America, they learned that some rock types on one continent match those on the other. This seems to suggest that the two continents were once joined. The scientists also compared fossils from both places. Fossils of ancient plants of one continent match those of the other. Yet Africa and South America are far apart and have quite different climates. The same plants could not have lived in two such different climates. So at one time, the continents may have been joined together and had similar climates.

Studies of the ocean floor gave scientists even more evidence that continents move. They show that the floor of the sea is actually spreading apart in some places. One such place is along a ridge that runs down the middle of the Atlantic Ocean. This area may be where the ancient continents moved apart over many years.

These maps show the world as it may have been 200 million years ago (left), as it is today (center), and as it may be in 10 million years (right).

Assign the Workbook activity for Chapter 1, Section 2, with pages 27–35.

Tectonic Plates

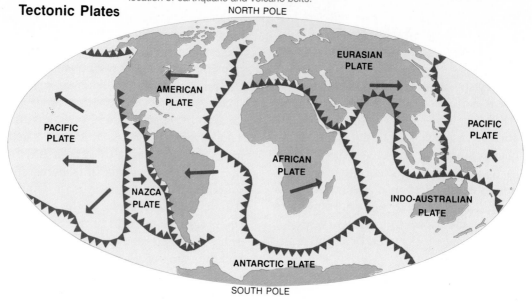

NORTH POLE

EURASIAN PLATE

AMERICAN PLATE

PACIFIC PLATE

PACIFIC PLATE

AFRICAN PLATE

NAZCA PLATE

INDO-AUSTRALIAN PLATE

ANTARCTIC PLATE

SOUTH POLE

Map Study   *Name the tectonic plate on which the United States is located.*

Answers to Map Study Question: American Plate

This diagram shows the parts of Earth's interior—the inner core, the outer core, and the mantle. Which is largest?

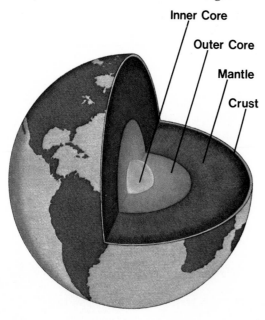

Inner Core

Outer Core

Mantle

Crust

Tectonic Activity   What do scientists think causes continents to drift? The answer lies in what is under Earth's surface. Beneath the land and water around you is a layer of rock. Scientists call this layer Earth's **crust**. The crust varies in thickness from 5 to 20 miles (8 to 32 kilometers). Compared with other layers inside Earth, the crust is very thin.

Below Earth's crust are layers of heavier rock and metal. This part is called the **mantle**. The mantle surrounds the center part, or **core**. The core has two sections. The outer core is liquid metal. The inner core is made of very hot, solid metal. Earth's crust floats on these heavier layers beneath it.

Because the crust floats, it can move around. Earth's crust does not move all in one piece but in separate sections. Scientists call these moving sections **tectonic** (tek ton'ik) **plates**. Think of them as plates of armor that overlap to cover the globe. These plates pull apart, drift, and sometimes collide. Their movement is called **tectonic activity**. Tectonic activity takes place very slowly. Tectonic plates

28

SPOTLIGHT ON EARTHQUAKES:

Can People Learn to Predict Them?

In 1985, a devastating earthquake hit Mexico City, the capital of Mexico. As the city's buildings swayed and toppled, thousands of people were caught in the rubble. Said one health expert, "It was like a war zone. There were fires; the smell of gas was everywhere." In about four minutes, 250 buildings collapsed. The quake was so strong that skyscrapers swayed as far away as Houston, Texas.

Mexico City, the world's most densely populated metropolitan area, has a shaky geological base. The city is built on soft sediment that was once a lake bed. In an earthquake, the city becomes like "a bowl full of jelly," said one expert.

Are people helpless against the forces of an earthquake? Many scientists think they can find ways to predict when and where this powerful force will hit. These scientists study seismology—a science that deals with earthquakes.

Seismologists analyze information on seismographs—special instruments that measure and record vibrations within the earth. They use these measurements to try to detect movements of the earth that might indicate that an earthquake is imminent. From testing well water, they also have learned that the concentration

of radon, a radioactive element, increases just before an earthquake. Many scientists have also observed that the behavior of certain animals changes before an earthquake. Bears and snakes may go into sudden hibernation. House cats may begin to meow and paw at the floor. So eager are people to learn to predict earthquakes that no possible clue is overlooked.

It is the hope of all people living in earthquake belts that scientists one day soon will be able to predict these natural disasters. If an earthquake is predicted, people may be able to leave before it strikes. This could save countless lives.

The Sierra Nevada (sē er'ə nə vad'ə) range in California is a good example of a group of mountains formed by the faulting of Earth's crust. The western edge of these mountains slopes gently into the Great Valley. The eastern edge rises 2.75 miles (more than 4 kilometers) above sea level and then drops sharply toward the Great Basin.

Volcanic Action A third way that mountains are formed is by volcanic action. This action, like folding and faulting, happens most often at the edge of tectonic plates.

A volcano is formed when tectonic forces cause Earth's interior mantle to explode outward. In such an explosion, melted rock escapes through Earth's

Almost 80 percent of all earthquakes occur around the edge of the Pacific Ocean.

crust. The rock that reaches the surface is called **lava** (lä′və). This **eruption** of a volcano causes the land to rise, often in a cone-shaped peak. Within the peak is an opening called a crater. Sometimes rivers of lava pour out of the crater and down a mountainside.

On May 18, 1980, Mount St. Helens, a volcano in the Cascade Range in the state of Washington, erupted. The eruption was so violent that the top of the mountain burst open. Great clouds of dust and ash blew into the air. Giant mud slides and a deep layer of ash devastated the countryside.

Volcanoes can create as well as destroy. Millions of years ago, magma poured out of an opening at the bottom of the Pacific Ocean. As the lava flowed out of the central cone, it spilled down the sides and cooled into solid rock. In time, volcanic activity created a mountain rising 29,700 feet (9,000 meters) from the ocean floor. Peaks of that mountain reached the surface of the ocean, forming many small islands. Those islands are known today as the Hawaiian Islands. One peak rises 13,800 feet (4,000 meters) above sea level. Called Mauna Kea (mou′nə kē′ə),

this mountain would be the tallest mountain in the world if measured from the ocean floor.

REVIEWING THE FACTS

Define

1. theory
2. continental drift
3. crust
4. mantle
5. core
6. tectonic plate
7. tectonic activity
8. rift
9. fold
10. faulting
11. fault
12. lava

Answer

1. What evidence have scientists found to support the theory of continental drift?

2. Name three ways mountains are formed. Give an example of mountains that were formed in each of these ways.

Locate

Refer to the map on pages 186–187.

1. In which four states are the Appalachian Mountains primarily found?

2. (a) Name the five largest islands of the state of Hawaii. (b) On which island is Mauna Kea located?

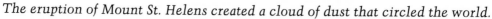

The eruption of Mount St. Helens created a cloud of dust that circled the world.

Reading a Contour Map

The physical map on page 9 shows elevation and relief by means of colors and shading. Elevation and relief can also be shown by the use of contour lines. A contour line is a line on a diagram or map connecting points of the same elevation. Study the diagram on this page. It shows a cross-section of an area in California. Each line drawn through this cross section is a contour line. As you can see, these lines are drawn at equal intervals. In this case, the distance between any two lines represents a rise or fall of 2,000 feet (610 meters).

Now look at the contour map on this page. The lines on this map are also contour lines. As you will notice, contour lines are not evenly spaced on the map.

Nevertheless, a pair of lines still represents a change in elevation of 2,000 feet. Where two contour lines are close together, the change in elevation occurs over a short distance. That is, the area has high relief. Where two contour lines are far apart, on the other hand, the change in elevation takes place over a long distance. That is, the area has low relief.

1. (a) Is Mt. Whitney steeper on its northern or southern slope? (b) Its eastern or western slope?

2. Compare the terrain around Mt. Whitney with the land around Owens Lake. In which area is there higher relief?

3. Compare the terrain around Owens Lake and that near the Kern River. In which area is there higher relief?

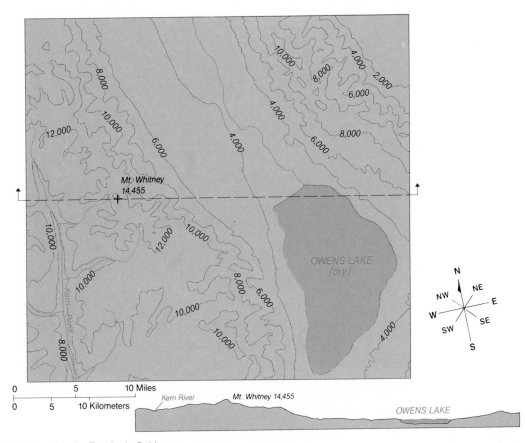

Answers are in the Teacher's Guide.
Assign the Workbook activity for this chapter's Map Workshop with this page.

33

World: Physical

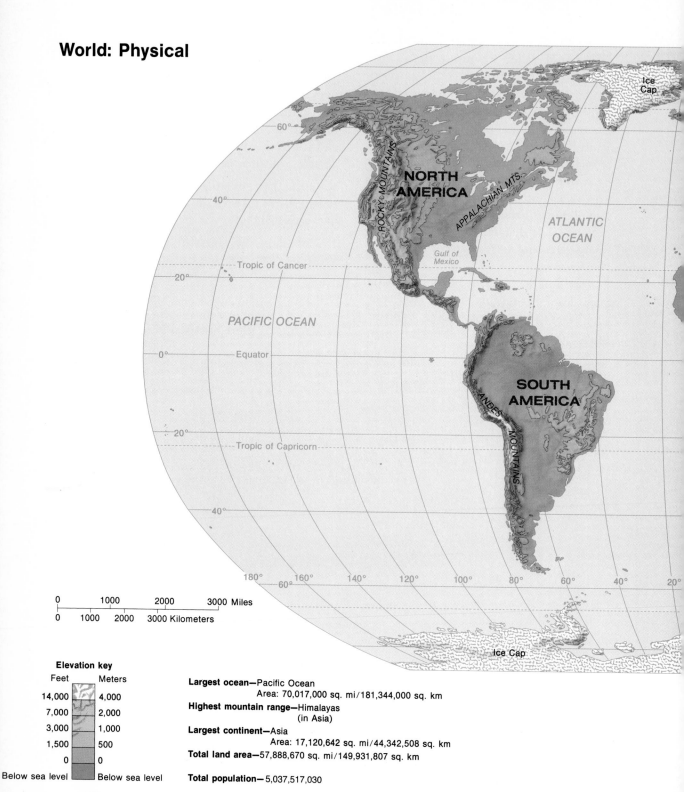

NORTH AMERICA

ROCKY MOUNTAINS

APPALACHIAN MTS.

Gulf of Mexico

ATLANTIC OCEAN

PACIFIC OCEAN

Tropic of Cancer

Equator

SOUTH AMERICA

ANDES MOUNTAINS

Tropic of Capricorn

Ice Cap

Ice Cap

60°

40°

20°

0°

20°

40°

180° 160° 140° 120° 100° 80° 60° 40° 20°
60°

0   1000   2000   3000 Miles
0   1000   2000   3000 Kilometers

Elevation key

Feet	Meters
14,000	4,000
7,000	2,000
3,000	1,000
1,500	500
0	0
Below sea level	Below sea level

Largest ocean—Pacific Ocean
  Area: 70,017,000 sq. mi/181,344,000 sq. km
Highest mountain range—Himalayas
  (in Asia)
Largest continent—Asia
  Area: 17,120,642 sq. mi/44,342,508 sq. km
Total land area—57,888,670 sq. mi/149,931,807 sq. km

Total population—5,037,517,030

Have students identify the major mountain ranges on Earth. Which continent has no mountains? (Australia) Sometimes this type of map is called a relief map.

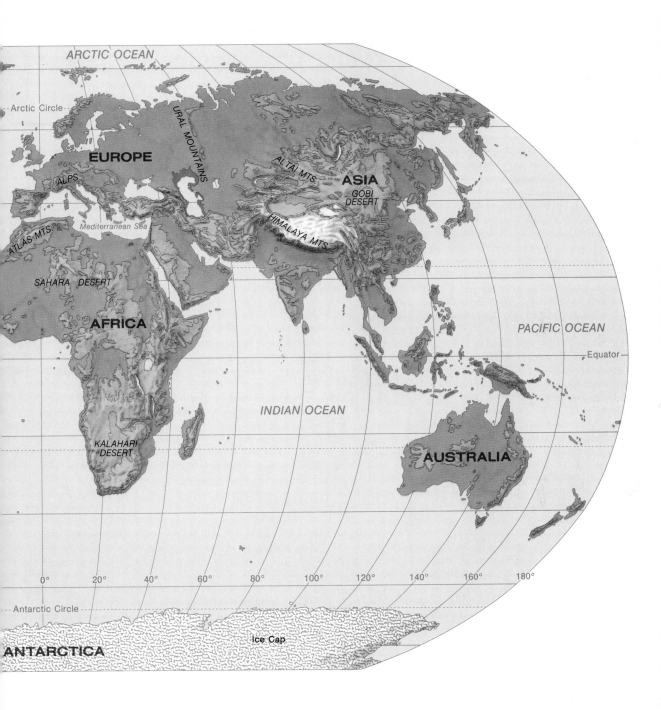

ARCTIC OCEAN

Arctic Circle

URAL MOUNTAINS

EUROPE

ALPS

ALTAI MTS

ASIA

GOBI
DESERT

Mediterranean Sea

ATLAS MTS.

HIMALAYA MTS.

SAHARA DESERT

AFRICA

PACIFIC OCEAN

Equator

INDIAN OCEAN

KALAHARI
DESERT

AUSTRALIA

0°   20°   40°   60°   80°   100°   120°   140°   160°   180°

Antarctic Circle

Ice Cap

ANTARCTICA

Map Study   *What are the names of the seven continents and four major oceans?*
What other land and water forms can you identify? In which hemisphere,
Northern or Southern, are the largest landmasses found? Through what
three continents does the equator run?

Answers to Map Study questions: Continents are North America, South America, Australia,
Asia, Africa, Europe, and Antarctica. Oceans are Pacific, Atlantic, Indian, and Arctic. The
largest landmasses are in the Northern Hemisphere. The equator runs through South America,
Africa, and Asia.

Erosion by the Rio Grande formed the Santa Elena Canyon in Texas's Big Bend National Park. The river carved the canyon out of a high plateau.

3 The Changing Earth: Forces from Without

Landforms are changed by forces from outside of Earth as well as from within. The forces making these changes are running water, glacial ice, wind, and ocean waves. They reshape the land by **erosion.** Erosion is the process by which rock and soil are stripped away from Earth's surface and moved to another place.

In time, erosion could wash most of the land into the ocean. The land would then be covered by sea water. The forces of folding, faulting, and volcanic action, however, balance the effects of erosion. These forces are always building up the land as erosion is wearing it away.

Running Water

The greatest cause of erosion is running water. The splash of a single raindrop on Earth's surface reshapes it. When rain hits the ground, it loosens the soil. Soft or sandy soil is quickly loosened by the hammer blows of raindrops.

Once a raindrop hits the earth, it begins its downhill journey to the ocean. As the fast-moving water slices into mountainsides, it carves a valley. As the land becomes less steep, the stream flows more slowly. Then it may join with other streams to form a larger river.

As it flows, the river changes color as well as size and rate of movement. The clear, fast-moving mountain stream becomes muddy brown from the tiny bits of earth it carries. As the current slows, the river leaves its eroded material, called **silt,** along the riverbank. When the river floods, it spreads silt all across the land of the lower valley. In time, these deposits create a plain along the river.

Moving toward a lake or ocean, the river continues to widen and lose speed. It also deposits more silt. These deposits build up the land near the mouth of the river. Such land may take the shape of a triangle or bird's foot and is called a **delta.** The delta continues to expand outward into the lake or ocean.

The silt deposited by a river is very rich. River valleys and deltas contain some of the most fertile land on Earth. Some of the richest farmland in the United States is in the Mississippi Valley. The deltas of

The wearing away of rock is known as weathering. Weathering takes place in two ways: mechanical weathering, in which rocks actually wear away or break apart; and chemical weathering, in which the chemicals interact to change rock from one kind of mineral to another.

Assign the Workbook activity for Chapter 1, Section 3, with pages 36–43.

Waves and Currents

Many of the changes that take place on the land's surface also happen on shorelines and lands under the oceans. The shoreline, where land and water meet, is directly changed by erosion. Waves crash against it. As waves wear away the shore in one place, currents deposit sand and build it up in another. The Atlantic Ocean is slowly eroding portions of the Cape Cod peninsula in Massachusetts. At the same time, it is building up the hook at the far end of the Cape. (See the photo on page 24.)

Lands under the ocean too are always changing. Long ago, people thought those lands were a level plain. However, underseas explorations have revealed that the same kinds of landforms lie beneath the ocean as above.

Underwater landforms are often similar to those of the nearby shore. A coastal plain that extends under the ocean is called a **continental shelf.** Along North

Thousands of square miles of farmland on the Great Plains of North America were destroyed by drought and wind erosion in the 1930's. ● *Ocean waves break against the rocks at Bailey's Beach, Maine. Erosion is slower here than on sandy Cape Cod, Massachusetts.*

41

A wave is a moving ridge or swell of water. A current is a moving stream of water in the ocean that is influenced by winds.

America's Atlantic coast, the continental shelf is very wide. Along the Pacific coast it is narrow, quickly sloping to the ocean deep.

In recent years, scientists have been able to map the ocean floor. And they have found many surprises. Beneath the Atlantic Ocean, a great mountain range called the Mid-Atlantic Ridge extends for 9,600 miles (16,000 kilometers). Dividing the range is a great valley, the Mid-Ocean Rift. Turn to the maps on pages 28 and 30. What might be causing this rift?

In other places, the ocean floor is cut by canyons, called trenches. The Mariana Trench in the Pacific Ocean is about 36,000 feet (more than 11,000 meters) deep. It reaches deeper below sea level than the highest mountain rises above sea level.

You have already read about volcanic activity that can create islands in the ocean. Earthquakes too can occur on the ocean floor. Such quakes may cause huge waves, called **tsunamis** (sü nä'mēz). These waves can travel thousands of miles across the ocean. When they reach land, they may sweep far up the shore, causing much damage and the loss of a great many lives.

Understanding Earth's Changes

Earth is not a simple place. All the forces you have read about in this chapter work together. The forces that raise Earth's surface and those that level it are never still. The balance swings in one direction or the other. In its swinging, it shapes the face of the planet.

Scientists have provided much information about Earth and the ways it changes. They continue to find new evidence and develop new theories. Some of the new theories help to explain how the edges and coastlines of continents took their present form.

Over thousands of years, tectonic activity thrusts up a mountain chain. At the same time, wind, water, and glacial ice begin to wear it down again. As these forces wear down one area, they help to build up another. Tectonic activity also moves whole continents from one place to another. Sometimes plates pull apart, and sometimes they collide. A volcano builds a mountain up from the floor of the sea. Wind and waves combine to start tearing it down again.

Look at just one area and think what may happen to it over millions of years. Folding may bend layers of Earth's crust.

The discovery of the Mid-Atlantic and the Mid-Ocean ridges has provided new information about changes in the surface and interior of Earth.

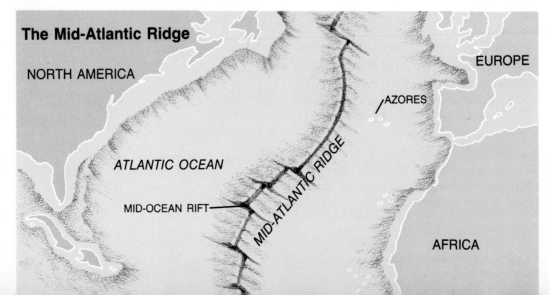

The Mid-Atlantic Ridge

NORTH AMERICA

EUROPE

ATLANTIC OCEAN

AZORES

MID-ATLANTIC RIDGE

MID-OCEAN RIFT

AFRICA

Discuss with students possible reasons for the changes seen in these photos.

These layers of rock tell how this land was formed. At one time, this part of Utah was under water.

Arizona's Monument Valley was once a high plateau. After erosion, tall buttes remain as a reminder of the past.

It may double them back over on top of themselves. Then perhaps a second folding takes place. The folded-over layers break, or fault. One section drops down an inch (2.5 centimeters), a foot (0.3 meter), or even 1,000 feet (300 meters). Then erosion—unnoticed over the centuries—wears down the surface even more.

Perhaps the ocean rises due to melting glacial ice and flows over the land. Rivers running into the ocean bring silt and build up the floor of the sea. Sand flows in and around the folded and faulted layers of rock.

Now the picture may get so complicated that even scientists find it hard to trace the sequence of changes. New tectonic activity may crack sections of Earth's crust apart. A volcano spouts lava up between the edges of the fault. Lava flows over the ocean floor, building up new land. And so it goes, again and again, century after century.

In this chapter, you have learned about the physical makeup of Earth—its land and water forms. You have studied the forces that change these forms. This knowledge provides a foundation for your study of geography.

REVIEWING THE FACTS

Define

1. erosion
2. silt
3. delta
4. glacier
5. moraine
6. fjord
7. Ice Age
8. loess
9. continental shelf
10. tsunami

Answer

1. (a) Name four outside forces that change Earth's surface. (b) How does each of these both create and destroy land?

2. Explain how rivers form valleys, plains, and deltas.

3. Describe similarities between the land surface and the ocean floor.

Locate

1. Refer to the map on pages 186–187. Name the states of the Mississippi River Valley south of the Ohio River.

2. Refer to the map on page 498. (a) Through what countries does the Nile River flow? (b) Into what body of water does it empty?

43

GEOGRAPHY LABORATORY

Highlighting the Chapter

1. Seventy percent of Earth's surface is water. Water is either salt or fresh. Salt water is found largely in oceans and seas. Fresh water is found in rivers and lakes. Thirty percent of Earth's surface is land. The largest landmasses are called continents. There are seven continents — Africa, Antarctica, Asia, Australia, Europe, North America, and South America. Smaller landmasses are known as islands. The surface of Earth has four major landforms: mountains, hills, plains, and plateaus.

2. Many scientists believe that the world's landmasses were once joined together in one supercontinent called Pangaea. Over millions of years, parts of that continent broke off and drifted away. This idea is known as the theory of continental drift.

Scientists also believe that Earth's surface is made up of sections, or tectonic plates. These plates may break, drift apart, and even collide. This action may bend and break Earth's crust, shaping Earth's surface. The movement of Earth's plates is still occurring.

Most tectonic activity takes place at the edges of tectonic plates. There, mountains are formed by tectonic activity, which folds and faults Earth's crust. Earthquakes and volcanoes are also the result of tectonic activity.

3. Earth's surface is continuously changing. The process by which Earth's surface wears down is called erosion. Erosion is caused by water, ice, wind, waves, and ocean currents. These forces not only wear away the soil but also carry it off and deposit it somewhere else.

Tectonic activity and erosion work together to build up, wear down, and redistribute Earth's surface. The one constant thing about Earth is that it is always changing. It has changed in the past, is still changing, and will continue to change in the future.

Speaking Geographically

In each group, two terms are related. Select the term that does not belong and explain why it is out of place.

1. island
   cape
   peninsula

2. bay
   gulf
   tributary

3. glacier
   moraine
   fjord

4. silt
   loess
   delta

5. folding
   faulting
   erosion

6. volcano
   tsunami
   eruption

7. plateau
   mountain
   hill

8. isthmus
   strait
   river

Testing Yourself

Complete the paragraphs with the correct terms from the list below.

erosion	mountains
plains	tectonic activity
folding	plateaus
elevation	volcanic action
continents	hills
faulting	continental drift
oceans	

Seventy percent of Earth's surface is made up of water. The largest bodies of water are called (1) ——. Land makes up the other 30% of Earth's surface. (2) —— are the largest landmasses. Landforms on Earth are measured in (3) ——, or height above sea level. The four major landforms are (4) ——, (5) ——, (6) ——, and (7) ——.

The idea that the location of the continents may have changed is a theory called (8) ——. This theory was supported by the discovery that Earth's crust moves in sections. This movement, called (9) ——,

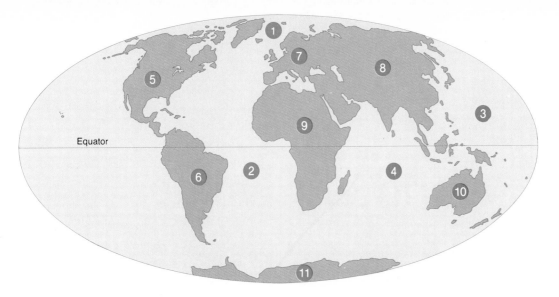

can produce mountains in three ways: (10) _____, (11) _____, and (12) _____. As these actions build up Earth's surface, water, wind, glacial ice, and waves wear away the surface through a process called (13) _____.

Building Map Skills

Study the map on this page. Then number a sheet of paper from 1 to 11. Write the name of the correct ocean or continent beside each number.

Applying Map Skills

Complete each sentence with the correct *cardinal* or *intermediate direction.*

1. Europe is _____ of Africa.

2. South America is _____ of Europe.

3. The Arctic Ocean is _____ of North America.

4. The continent of Antarctica is _____ of every other continent.

5. The Atlantic Ocean is on the _____ coasts of North and South America.

Exploring Further

1. Rock formations and fossils have offered evidence that the continents were at one time joined in a supercontinent. Do research on the topic of continental drift. Locate additional proof that the continents have changed position over millions of years and are still on the move.

2. Describe a problem, job, event, or activity related to knowledge of Earth's land and water areas. Ask your classmates to decide who might be best able to solve the problem or study that particular concern: a geographer, a cartographer, a seismologist, or a geologist.

3. Select an aerial photograph from your textbook. Draw a map of the same area. Make your map as accurate as you can. Then ask a classmate to identify the photograph that you have mapped. You may need to give your partner a 50-page searching area.

4. Choose a major earthquake or volcanic eruption and prepare a report describing the event. Tell when the event occurred and how people dealt with its effects. Conclude your report with information on the progress scientists are making toward predicting these violent acts of nature.

45

GEOGRAPHY LABORATORY

CHAPTER

A World of Climates

From space, astronauts can see the ever-shifting pattern of clouds above Earth. They can see "mares' tails," or cirrus (sir'əs) clouds, and "cotton puffs," or stratocumulus (strā'tō kyü'myə ləs) clouds. Sometimes they can see the spiral of hurricane clouds or a line of storms stretching halfway around the world.

Clouds are a sign of the moisture that is present in the air. They take shape and move in the atmosphere, the layer of air that surrounds Earth. They move with the changing patterns of the wind. Both cloud patterns and winds may change with the seasons.

Some parts of Earth are almost always free of clouds. These are the deserts, where there is too little moisture for clouds to form. Here few plants can grow in the sun-baked soil. On the other hand, some places may get more clouds than sunshine. To the astronauts, these places are likely to appear green because of their trees and grasses.

In this chapter you will learn how sun, water, and wind act together to create the world's climates and weather. You will learn what causes day and night and the seasons of the year. You will discover that there are many kinds of climate around the world. And you will find out which parts of the world have which kind of climate. First, however, you must understand the difference between climate and weather.

46

1 The Sun and Climate

Weather is the condition of the air at any one time. The weather report tells you how warm or cold, wet or dry, sunny or cloudy, windy or calm a place is on a given day. If you said that it was very cold in New York yesterday, with a heavy frost, you would be describing the weather. **Climate,** on the other hand, is the pattern of weather over a number of years. If you said that New York has hot, moist summers and cold, dry winters, you would be describing the climate.

Energy from the Sun

The sun has a great influence on Earth's climate and weather. Its energy is the source of Earth's warmth. It also warms the atmosphere surrounding Earth. This energy reaches Earth by means of the sun's rays, or **radiation.**

Earth receives only a small part of the huge amount of energy the sun radiates into space. The sun's rays travel 93 million miles (almost 150 million kilometers) through space to reach Earth. When these rays hit Earth's atmosphere, some of their energy is reflected back into space. Some is absorbed by the atmosphere, and some finally reaches Earth's surface.

The movement of heat between the sun, atmosphere, Earth, and space changes from one period of time to another. Sometimes more radiation remains in the ground, sea, or air than returns to space. At those times, the temperature rises. On the other hand, when more heat is reflected from a place than is stored, the temperature falls.

Day and night also affect temperature. The ground receives heat energy only when the sun is shining. The ground,

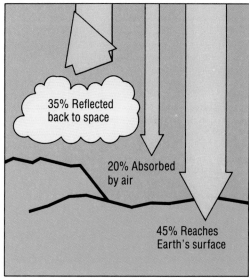

The sun's energy travels 93 million miles (150 million kilometers) through space to Earth. What portion of this energy does not reach Earth's surface? Why are some rays unable to reach Earth's surface?

however, loses heat to space all the time. At night, therefore, when Earth receives no heat energy, the ground cools quickly, and the temperature falls.

You can see by now that Earth's weather and climate depend on the heat of the sun. If the sun gave off 13 percent less heat, scientists predict that the entire planet would soon be covered with a layer of ice more than 1 mile (nearly 2 kilometers) thick. If the sun gave off 30 percent more heat, every form of life on Earth would burn up.

Earth's Movement and the Sun

The amount of the sun's energy a place receives varies because of the way Earth moves in space. Many places, including most of the United States, have warm and cold seasons. Other places may have hot weather or cold weather all year round. These differences are caused by changes in Earth's position in relation to the sun.

47

Answers to caption questions: 55 percent of the sun's energy does not reach the surface of Earth. Some is reflected back into space; some is absorbed by the atmosphere.

Assign the Workbook activity for Chapter 2, Section 1, with pages 47–52.

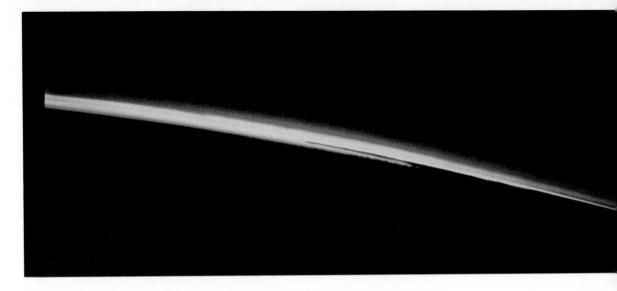

As a spacecraft approaches the daylight side of Earth, an astronaut sees an arc of bright light (top). ● *One rotation of Earth takes 24 hours, the length of a day. When it is noon on one side of Earth, what time is it on the side directly opposite (bottom)?*

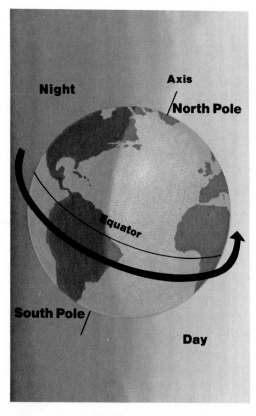

Rotation: Day and Night As Earth travels through space, it spins like a top. This spinning motion is called **rotation**. Earth rotates on its axis. The **axis** is an imaginary line through the center of Earth from pole to pole. It takes 24 hours for Earth to make one complete turn on its axis. When your part of Earth is turned toward the sun, you have daytime. As Earth continues to rotate, your part of the planet turns away from the sun. Then you have nighttime. Earth's rotation is the reason for day and night.

Revolution: The Seasons In addition to spinning on its axis, Earth travels around the sun. This motion, called **revolution**, takes Earth on a nearly circular path around the sun. This path is called an **orbit**. Earth makes one complete revolution in $365\frac{1}{4}$ days. This, of course, is one year. Earth's revolution around the sun determines how long a year is. It is also responsible for creating the seasons.

48

Reading a Weather Map

No matter what the season, people in most parts of the United States can expect the weather to vary from day to day. Daily weather maps on television and in newspapers show current weather conditions and patterns.

Like most maps, a weather map has a legend to unlock the meaning of its symbols. Study the key for the map on this page. Notice that it uses color and a variety of other symbols to show information. Find the three symbols that show fronts. A weather front is the edge of a mass of cold air as it meets a mass of warm air, or vice versa. A cold front is followed by colder weather. A warm front is followed by warmer weather. Unsettled or stormy weather often occurs along a front. Notice that one of the fronts on the map has arrowlike symbols.

These symbols indicate that the front is moving in a southeasterly direction. The stationary front is expected to remain in about the same place for a few days.

1. (a) For what day does this map show weather conditions? (b) In what season does this date occur?

2. (a) What color on the map represents average temperatures of 40°? (b) Average temperatures of 50°?

3. (a) Name three cities experiencing showers. (b) Name four cities with average temperatures in the 70° range.

4. Are there any occurrences of snow?

5. (a) Should a resident of Salt Lake City expect warmer or colder temperatures in the next few days? (b) How do you know?

6. Judging from the map, will the weather in and around Chicago stay the same or change in the next few days?

MAP WORKSHOP

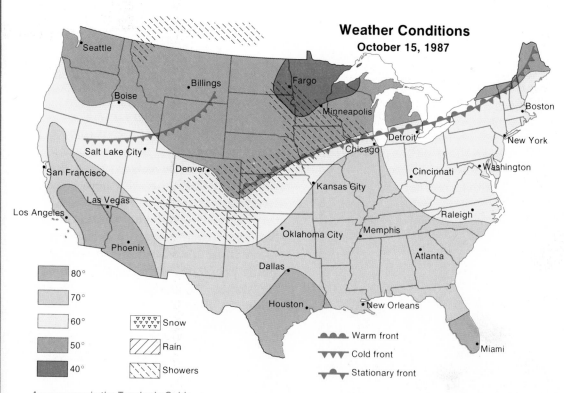

Weather Conditions
October 15, 1987

Legend:
- 80°
- 70°
- 60°
- 50°
- 40°
- Snow
- Rain
- Showers
- Warm front
- Cold front
- Stationary front

Answers are in the Teacher's Guide.
Assign the Workbook activity for this chapter's Map Workshop with this page.

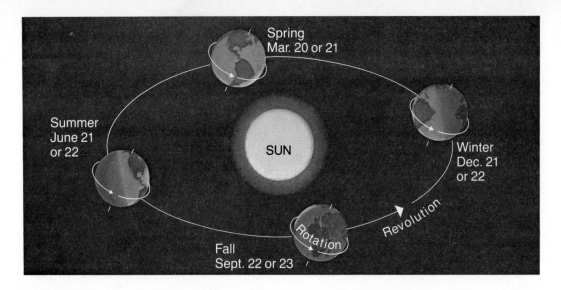

Earth's axis is shown by lines coming from the poles. Earth rotates on its axis as it revolves around the sun (top). ● *The seasons are created by the tilt of the Northern and Southern hemispheres (bottom).*

Seasons vary in different parts of the world because Earth's axis is tilted. Study the diagram above. It shows that Earth's axis is not straight up and down. It is tilted at an angle of $23\frac{1}{2}$ degrees.

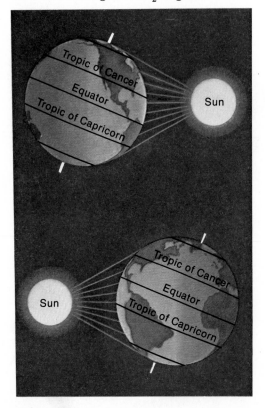

During Earth's journey around the sun, the Northern Hemisphere is tilted toward the sun from March until September. In these months it is spring and summer in the Northern Hemisphere. During the same period, the Southern Hemisphere is tilted away from the sun. There, it is fall and winter. While Americans are celebrating the Fourth of July with a picnic, Australians are having their coldest season.

Six months later Earth has traveled through half of its orbit around the sun. By now, the Northern Hemisphere is tilted away from the sun. Earth's Southern Hemisphere receives more direct sunlight, while the Northern Hemisphere gets only the very slanted rays. At this time it is fall and winter in the Northern Hemisphere and spring and summer in the Southern Hemisphere. While people in Vermont and Colorado are skiing, Australians are enjoying a summer swim.

During spring and summer, days are longer and nights are shorter. During fall and winter, nights are longer and days are shorter.

50

Revolution: Equinox and Solstice The change in seasons and daylight hours is so gradual that you may not notice it. Yet scientists know that these changes occur on a regular timetable.

Twice during the year—on March 20 or 21 and September 22 or 23—the number of daylight hours and the number of nighttime hours is exactly equal all around the world. The time when this happens is called an **equinox** (ē′kwə noks), from the Latin word meaning "equal night." At the time of an equinox, the noon sun is directly over the equator. Its rays touch Earth from pole to pole.

An equinox marks the start of both spring and fall. In the Northern Hemisphere, March 20 or 21 is the vernal (vėr′nl) equinox. There, it marks the beginning of spring. In the Southern Hemisphere, this same date is the beginning of fall. September 22 or 23 marks the beginning of fall in the Northern Hemisphere. It is known as the autumnal (ô tum′nəl) equinox. In the Southern Hemisphere, this date is the beginning of spring.

The times of year at which the difference in the length of day and night is at a maximum are **solstices** (sol′ stis əz). Solstice comes from Latin words that mean "when the sun stands still."

On June 21 or 22, the sun's rays reach their northernmost point. This brings the longest day of the year to the Northern Hemisphere. There, this day is called the summer solstice. During the next six months, the daylight hours in the Northern Hemisphere grow shorter and nights grow longer. About December 22, the sun's rays reach their southernmost point in the Southern Hemisphere. In the Northern Hemisphere, this is the shortest day and the longest night of the year. This time of year is known as the winter solstice. It marks the beginning of winter in the Northern Hemisphere.

Latitude and Climate

Why are some places on Earth always either hot or cold? The main reason for this is **latitude,** or how far north or south of the equator these places are. The amount of energy received from the sun changes with latitude. Places near the equator are hot because they get the most direct sunlight. Polar regions are cold because they receive far less sunlight.

Since Earth is always tilted $23\frac{1}{2}°$, the farthest point north to receive direct sunlight is $23\frac{1}{2}°$ north of the equator. Sun strikes this far north at the summer solstice. At this time, the sun shines directly overhead at latitude $23\frac{1}{2}°N$, known as the **Tropic of Cancer.**

The farthest point south ever to receive direct rays of the sun is $23\frac{1}{2}°$ south of the equator. The sun is directly overhead at this parallel, which is called the **Tropic of Capricorn,** during the winter solstice.

The area between the Tropic of Cancer and the Tropic of Capricorn is often called the **tropics,** or low latitudes. Because the tropics always receive the sun's most direct rays and have almost equal days and nights, most places there have a warm climate. The average annual temperature at the equator is 80°F (27°C).

Two special parallels are also drawn at $66\frac{1}{2}°$ north and south of the equator. The Arctic Circle is located at latitude $66\frac{1}{2}°N$ and the Antarctic Circle at latitude $66\frac{1}{2}°S$. The **polar regions,** or high latitudes, are located between these two parallels and the North and South poles. These areas receive no sun some of the year and, during the rest, only slanting rays. The climate there is cold, with short summers.

Between the tropics and the polar regions are the middle latitudes. Here, the sun's rays reach Earth at a high angle for part of the year and at a slant for the remaining months. Average temperatures

51

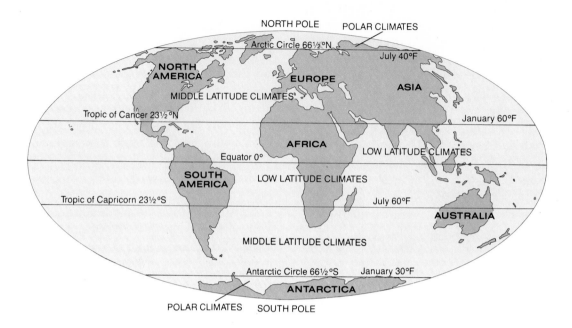

Map Study *This map shows the location of tropical (or low latitude) climates, temperate (or middle latitude) climates, and polar (or high latitude) climates. Find the Tropics of Cancer and Capricorn and the Arctic and Antarctic Circles.*

are cooler than in the tropics but warmer than in the polar regions. The climate of this region is called temperate. For this reason, this part of Earth is often called the **temperate zone.** Within this climate, temperatures vary greatly from one place or season to another.

REVIEWING THE FACTS

Define

1. weather
2. climate
3. radiation
4. rotation
5. axis
6. revolution
7. orbit
8. equinox
9. solstice
10. latitude
11. Tropic of Cancer
12. Tropic of Capricorn
13. tropics
14. polar region
15. temperate zone

Answer

1. (a) What causes day and night? (b) Seasons of the year?

2. (a) When the Northern Hemisphere is tilted toward the sun, what season is it there? (b) What season is it in the Southern Hemisphere at this time?

3. Where is the annual temperature usually the warmest — in the tropics, the temperate zone, or the polar regions? Give reasons for your answer.

Locate

Refer to the map on pages 494–495.

1. Through which large North American country does the Tropic of Cancer pass?

2. Name four South American countries through which the Tropic of Capricorn passes.

52

2 Water and Climate

The action of the sun and its effect upon Earth is only part of the story of climate. Another important part is water. Water exists in many forms. Besides its liquid form, it can occur as fog, mist, hail, sleet, snow, and ice. Earth's total quantity of water does not change. For all practical purposes, the same amount of water exists now as did millions of years ago. However, water changes in form as it goes from ocean to air to land and back again.

The Hydrologic Cycle

Water is constantly moving from ocean to air to land and back to ocean. This process is the **hydrologic** (hī'drə loj'ik) **cycle.** *Hydrologic* means "about the study of water." The hydrologic cycle is one way that water influences Earth's climate.

From Earth to Atmosphere In one part of the hydrologic cycle, water changes from a liquid to a gas. You have probably noticed that a puddle of water gradually dries up and disappears on a warm day. What actually happens is that the water, or liquid, in the puddle changes its form. It becomes a gas called **water vapor.** Like puddles, large bodies of water also give off water vapor. From the warm surface of the ocean, water vapor rises like steam from a teakettle. This process is called **evaporation** (i vap'ə rā'shən). Plants too give off water vapor. They lose it through their pores. This process is known as **transpiration** (tran'spə rā'shən).

The rates at which evaporation and transpiration occur are affected by temperature. Much water evaporates from a warm ocean, but very little from a cold ocean. Transpiration too increases when the temperature rises. You can see that changes in temperature make a great difference in the hydrologic cycle.

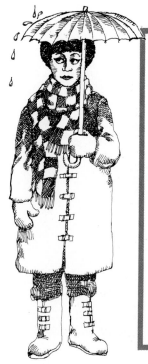

WEATHER ON THE RAMPAGE

DATE	LOCATION	DISASTER	DEATH TOLL
September 1900	Galveston, Texas	Hurricane	6,000
March 1925	South-central United States	Tornado	689
August 1931	Yellow River, China	Flood	3,700,000
February 1956	Western Europe	Blizzard	1,000
November 1970	Ganges Delta, Bangladesh	Hurricane	1,000,000
July 1981	Yangtze River, China	Flood	1,000
September 1984	Southern Philippines	Typhoon	10,000

Tell students that this lesson looks at precipitation. Ask students: When do we receive our precipitation? Does it come on a regular basis? All year round? In different forms? Some students might like to record highs and lows in precipitation for their area. Assign the Workbook activity for Chapter 2, Section 2, with pages 53–56.

SKILL WORKSHOP

Interpreting a Diagram

The water on Earth's surface is found in a variety of forms.

Oceans 97.000%
Glaciers and ice caps 2.000
Underground 0.500
Rivers and lakes. 0.020
Atmosphere 0.005

Total .99.525%

(As is the case with most measures, these percentages are not exact and may not add up to 100 percent.)

Study the diagram below. It shows how the hydrologic cycle works. On this dia-gram, you can trace the movement of water from the atmosphere to the earth and back to the atmosphere. Notice where water is found, what form it is in, and what happens to the water at each stage of the cycle. Then answer the following questions.

1. What are the four basic processes, or steps, in the water cycle?

2. (a) Name two sources of water in the air. (b) How much of Earth's water does the atmosphere usually hold?

3. What are four types of precipitation?

4. What happens to groundwater?

5. How does water get from land and ocean into the atmosphere?

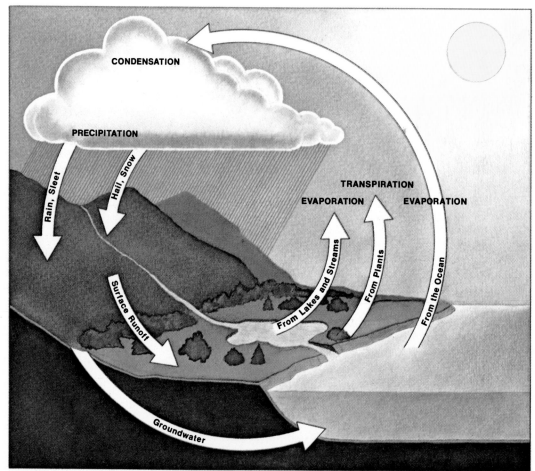

CONDENSATION
PRECIPITATION
Rain, Sleet
Hail, Snow
Surface Runoff
TRANSPIRATION
EVAPORATION
EVAPORATION
From Lakes and Streams
From Plants
From the Ocean
Groundwater

Point out that most of the water that falls on land evaporates before it can sink into the ground and that some of it runs into lakes, rivers, and streams. Only a small percentage of rainwater becomes groundwater. *Answers are in the Teacher's Guide.*

From Atmosphere to Earth When the temperature goes down, the air cannot hold as much water vapor as it can at higher temperatures. As air cools, therefore, the water vapor in it changes from a gas into tiny droplets of liquid. This process is known as **condensation** (kon'den sā'shən). These droplets gather to form water drops, which may then turn to rain, snow, sleet, or hail. Water that falls to the ground in any of these forms is known as **precipitation** (pri sip'ə tā'shən).

Some precipitation falls directly into oceans, lakes, and rivers. Some falls on the land. There, much of it runs off into streams and rivers. Some of it may also seep deep underground. There, it is stored as **groundwater.** It provides fresh water for springs and wells. All water that falls on land returns, sooner or later, to the ocean. Then the hydrologic cycle begins again.

The Water Balance

Each step of the hydrologic cycle works to balance the other steps of the cycle. The amount of precipitation is balanced by evaporation, storage, and runoff. These processes also balance one another. The balances that exist in any one place depend on the conditions there. The region of the Amazon River in South America is an example. Precipitation there is so heavy that the water cannot be stored. Instead, it empties into the Amazon River, making it the largest river in the world. The Amazon carries the runoff from the huge area back to the sea. Then the cycle begins anew.

Desert regions have a different type of balance. The balance there involves very little water. The climate there is too dry for most kinds of plants to survive. In fact, more water can evaporate from the desert than falls upon it. In hot desert areas, most rain actually evaporates before it hits the ground.

The balance within the hydrologic cycle may change as the seasons change. In St. Louis, Missouri, for example, floods often take place in early springtime. They are the result of melting snow, which adds to the amount of water in the Mississippi River. That extra water cannot be stored, because the ground is already filled with moisture. Neither can all this water evaporate. The temperature is still too cool for rapid evaporation to take place. Most plants are dead or inactive, so they take in little water. As a result, the water runs off. If the river cannot hold all the water, floods spread onto the land.

A different pattern often takes place in late summer and early fall. Many parts of the world have droughts during this season. The late summer heat causes fast evaporation. Plant life is at its height, using great amounts of water. If these changes are not balanced by rainfall, a drought begins. Rivers and streams dry up, crops wither and die, and forests and grasslands easily catch fire.

WOULD YOU LIKE TO BE . . .

A climatologist? A climatologist studies the climate by collecting information about weather over many years. These data help in predicting climate patterns and changes.

A meteorologist? A meteorologist studies the atmosphere and the weather and makes forecasts of future weather.

A navigator? A navigator determines the position and course of a ship or an airplane. The navigator must know about air and ocean currents.

55

REVIEWING THE FACTS

Define

1. hydrologic cycle
2. water vapor
3. evaporation
4. transpiration
5. condensation
6. precipitation
7. groundwater

Answer

1. (a) How does temperature affect the hydrologic cycle? (b) What may happen to precipitation after it reaches Earth?

2. (a) What balance exists within the hydrologic cycle? (b) How is this balance maintained in both wet and dry climates?

Locate

Refer to the map on pages 64–65.

1. Name the four oceans of the world.

2. (a) What ocean lies between Europe and North America? (b) Between Asia and North America?

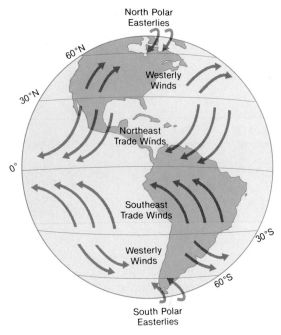

Map Study *Compare the prevailing wind patterns north and south of the equator.*

3 Other Factors Affecting Climate

Climate, as you have seen, depends largely on latitude, which influences heat, and moisture. Other things also affect climate. Winds and ocean currents distribute heat and moisture around the world. An area's nearness to water and its elevation are also important influences on its climate.

Winds

The view of Earth from space shows that clouds always surround the planet. Clouds move constantly because the air itself is moving. This movement of air is the wind.

Winds move the atmosphere's moisture. They also move warm or cold air, depending on the direction from which they blow. Winds blowing from the sea often bring moist air. In the United States, winds from the north bring cold air and winds from the south bring warm air.

Some winds blow almost constantly from a certain direction. These are the **prevailing winds.** Other winds, such as those that affect parts of southern Asia, change directions. They blow from one direction part of the year and the opposite direction the rest of the year. Winds that change direction seasonally are called **monsoons** (mon sünz′).

Study the drawing of the globe on this page. Notice the names of the prevailing winds and the direction in which they move. Winds are named for the direction from which they blow. So a polar wind brings icy air from a polar region. A northeasterly wind blows from the northeast. A westerly wind blows from the west.

Winds can be destructive. Tornadoes have wind speeds as high as 500 miles per hour. Hurricanes generally have slower winds (about 75 to 100 or more miles per hour), but last longer. *Answer to Map Study question:* Wind patterns north of the equator are a mirror image of those south of the equator. Other answers are in the Teacher's Guide.

SPOTLIGHT ON MONSOONS:

A Special Climate Pattern

In India and other countries of Southeast Asia, there are winds called monsoons. *Monsoon* is an Arabic word that means "season." The climate in India shifts between dry and rainy seasons. These changes are caused by seasonal shifts in the prevailing wind direction.

During winter months, winds blow from the north and bring cool, dry weather to the region. As the summer season approaches, wind patterns gradually change to a southerly flow. These winds originate over the tropical Indian Ocean and are very moist.

The winter months are cool and dry in most of India. With the arrival of spring, the area gets more and more direct sunlight. Day after day the sun shines without clouds or rain. India turns into a furnace. By late May, average daily temperatures are near 92°F (33°C), often with an afternoon high temperature of 109°F to 118°F (43°C to 48°C). The hot, dry days can seem endless and unbearable.

Then suddenly the weather pattern changes. Somewhat cooler, moist air from the Indian Ocean begins to blow over the dry land. Rain falls in torrents. The "wet monsoon" has arrived. People rejoice and hold festivals to celebrate the coming of the monsoon.

For about three months, it rains nearly every day. One village near the mountains gets an average rainfall of 449 inches (1,142 centimeters) a year! Almost all of that rain falls within about 90 days. Not all parts of India get this much rain, of course.

In September, the Northern Hemisphere begins to cool as the sun's rays strike at a lower and lower angle. The wet monsoon begins to break. Air over the ocean has become warmer than the air over land. Now the cool, dry winds from the north begin to blow once again. By November, this wind—the dry monsoon—has ended the rainy season. The dry season settles in once again.

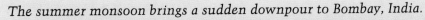

The summer monsoon brings a sudden downpour to Bombay, India.

Have students identify three warm ocean currents and three cold currents. Make sure they note where these currents begin.

Answers to Map Study questions: Oceans generally moderate the climate of nearby land areas. Cool currents at high latitudes make nearby areas colder.

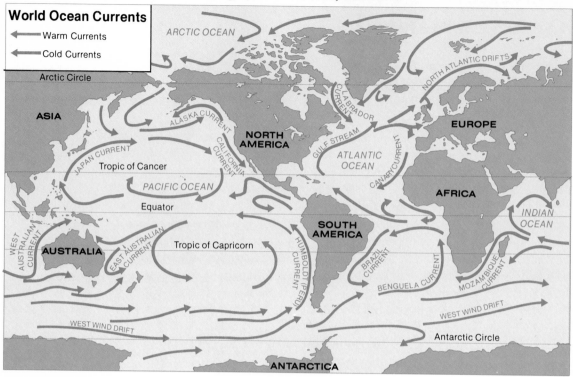

Map Study *How do oceans generally affect the climate of nearby land areas? How do cool currents affect land areas in high latitudes?*

Ocean Currents

While air in motion is called wind, water in motion is called a **current.** Ocean currents, like winds, distribute heat or cold and moisture in certain patterns throughout the world. In fact, ocean currents are in part pulled along by the prevailing winds. Their patterns are often the same as those of the winds.

Some ocean currents warm the lands they pass. One well-known warm current is the Gulf Stream. It starts in the Gulf of Mexico and runs along the eastern coast of the United States. (See the map on this page.) Then it crosses the Atlantic Ocean, branching off along western Europe as the North Atlantic Drift. It warms the continent as far north as Norway.

England's climate is one of those warmed by the Gulf Stream. The average January temperature in London is 40°F (4.5°C). By comparison, Montreal (mön trē ol') in Canada is at the same latitude. Montreal is not, however, warmed by the Gulf Stream. Its average January temperature is a cold 13°F (−10.5°C).

Another warm ocean current is the Japan Current, or Kuroshio. It starts in the northern Pacific Ocean and flows along the coast of southern Alaska. Without it, the harbor of Valdez (val dez'), Alaska, would be icebound in winter. Tankers carrying oil from the Alaska pipeline would not be able to leave port.

Currents from the North and South polar regions are cold. The Labrador (lab'rə dôr) Current starts in the Arctic Ocean. The Humboldt, or Peru, Current starts near Antarctica. Both currents cool nearby land areas.

58

Nearness to Water

Oceans and large lakes have a special effect on the climate of the land near them. These bodies of water moderate, or make milder, the temperature of the area.

Water has this effect on climate because large bodies of water do not gain or lose heat as quickly as nearby land does. For example, imagine going swimming in a pond on a warm summer morning. As you walk barefoot to the pond, the ground already feels warm from the sun. But as you wade into the pond, the water still feels cool from the night before. If you go swimming again in the evening, you will notice that the opposite is true. The ground will already have cooled off, but the water will still hold the day's heat.

Because the water was slower to gain heat during the day and slower to lose heat in the evening, its temperature throughout the day remained moderate compared to that of the land. Since air temperature is affected by the temperature of the land or water beneath it, the air over the pond also stayed moderate. As this air circulated, it spread its effect, moderating temperatures throughout the pond area.

In the same way but on a much larger scale, coastal areas have a moderate climate because ocean water is slow to change temperature with the seasons. In winter, the ocean holds the summer's heat long after the land has cooled. In summer, the ocean stays cold long after the land has grown warm. Climates moderated by the ocean are often described as **marine,** or oceanic.

Most inland climates are not moderated by nearness to water. In the middle of continents, the climate can be very cold in winter and very hot in summer. The climate in these areas is known as **continental.**

Elevation

A final factor that affects climate is the land's elevation. Temperatures change greatly with elevation. The higher you go, the colder it gets.

Elevation	Temperature
18,000 ft (5,400 m)	16°F (−9°C)
15,000 ft (4,500 m)	27°F (−3°C)
12,000 ft (3,600 m)	38°F (3°C)
9,000 ft (2,700 m)	49°F (9°C)
6,000 ft (1,800 m)	60°F (15°C)
3,000 ft (900 m)	70°F (21°C)
1,000 ft (300 m)	77°F (25°C)
Sea level	81°F (27°C)

Ask students if any of them have traveled in the mountains during the summer. What did they notice about the temperature as they climbed to higher elevations? Did they see snow in the mountains during the summer?

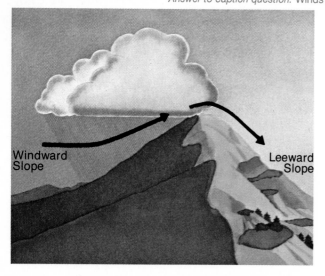

Windward Slope

Leeward Slope

Winds rise as they meet mountains. They also grow cool and lose their moisture. Why do leeward slopes get less rain than windward slopes?

This effect is clearly noticed in elevated areas near the equator. Without mountains or highlands, all lands near the equator would be hot. For example, much of Africa and South America are in the tropics. For the most part, they have very hot climates. In their highlands, however, the temperatures are moderate. For this reason, many Africans and South Americans live in highland areas. Even near the equator, both continents have mountain peaks with permanent snow and small glaciers.

Mountains also affect climate by blocking winds. The mountain ranges of the western United States, for example, keep the moderating influence of the Pacific Ocean from reaching the interior of the country. Areas east of the mountains, therefore, experience colder winters and hotter summers than do areas along the coast.

Mountains also influence rainfall. In the Pacific Northwest, for example,

coastal mountains block the prevailing winds. These winds have traveled over the warm Pacific waters, where they picked up moisture. As these moisture-carrying winds hit the steep western edge of the mountains, they are forced to rise. As the air rises, it cools. Cold air cannot hold as much moisture as warm air. So the clouds drop their water on the westward-facing slopes of the mountains below.

Mountain slopes that face the prevailing winds are called **windward** slopes. They often receive heavy rainfall. Slopes facing the other way are called **leeward** (lē′wərd) slopes. Much less rain falls there. In the United States, for example, the areas just east of the Cascades and the Sierra Nevada are desert.

REVIEWING THE FACTS

Define

1. prevailing wind
2. monsoon
3. current
4. marine
5. continental
6. windward
7. leeward

Answer

1. How do ocean currents and winds influence climate?

2. (a) What effects do large bodies of water have on the climate of lands nearby? (b) How is this effect created?

3. (a) In what ways do mountains influence the climate of land areas? (b) How may the climate on a mountain differ from that of the surrounding areas?

Locate

Refer to the map on page 58.

1. (a) Past which continent does the Humboldt Current flow? (b) Is this a warm or a cold current?

2. Past which continent does the Labrador Current flow?

60

Reading a Climate Graph

Temperature and precipitation are two of the most important factors in climate. Graphs provide an excellent way to show this information. The graphs on this page show the average monthly rainfall and average monthly temperatures for two major Asian cities — Bombay, India, and Singapore.

Each graph has 12 blue columns, one for each month. Starting at the left of the graph, the columns are labeled *J* for *January* through *D* for *December*. These columns show average rainfall in each month. To find the average rainfall each city receives in any month, use the scale on the right side of each graph. This scale shows the rainfall in inches.

Use the scale at the left of each graph to read the temperatures. Temperatures are shown in degrees Fahrenheit. Dots chart the average temperature for each month. The line connecting the dots shows the annual temperature range.

Refer to the graphs below to answer the following questions.

1. Which city receives more rainfall each year?

2. (a) In which month does Bombay receive its greatest amount of rain? (b) Singapore?

3. (a) Which city has the wider range in temperature each year? (b) In rainfall?

4. During which three months does Singapore receive about eight inches of rain?

5. In which five months does Bombay receive almost no rainfall?

6. Which city has higher annual temperatures?

7. (a) In which month(s) does Bombay have its highest average temperature? (b) Its lowest average temperature? (c) In which months does Singapore have its highest average temperatures? (d) Its lowest temperatures?

8. (a) In which months does Singapore average about 10 inches of rain? (b) In which month does Bombay?

9. Compare the two graphs to decide which city you would prefer to live in. Give reasons for your answer.

Singapore
Wet tropical

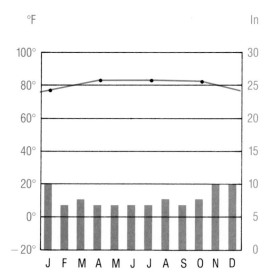

Bombay, India
Wet-and-dry tropical

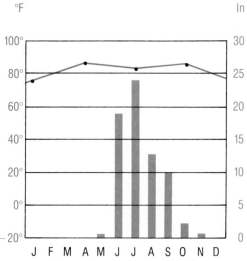

This kind of graph will be used throughout the rest of Chapter 2. Assign the Workbook activity for this chapter's Skill Workshop with this page. *Answers are in the Teacher's Guide.*

A year-round humid tropical climate means heavy runoff for the Zaire River in central Africa (top). ● *A dry-winter humid tropical climate is found in parts of India, including the east coast near Madras (bottom).*

4 Climates of the World

The patterns of temperature and moisture vary throughout the world. Latitude, winds, and ocean currents add to that variation. The result is a world of many different climates. They are sometimes divided into six major groups: humid tropical, subtropical, dry, mid-latitude, cold polar, and highland.

Humid Tropical Climates

Humid tropical climates are found in the tropical belt nearest the equator. **Humid** means that there is a lot of moisture in the air. Yearly average temperatures for these climates are high — at least 65°F (18°C) and much higher in some areas. There are two types of humid tropical climates: wet tropical and wet-and-dry tropical.

Wet Tropical This climate has heavy rainfall and high temperatures all year long. With plenty of rain and hot weather, plants thrive. Large rivers are common because of the great runoff of rainfall from the land.

Singapore has a wet tropical climate. Use that city's climate graph on page 61 to find out during which months it has more than 8 inches (20 centimeters) of rain. What is the average temperature during each of these months?

Wet-and-Dry Tropical This climate too has high temperatures. But there are definite wet and dry seasons. During the wet season, streams often overflow their banks and flood the land. As the weather becomes drier, streams become smaller and may dry up. In the driest months, the soil becomes parched. This climate has enough heat and moisture for grasses and some trees to grow. But there are rarely any large forests.

62

Palm trees and other tropical plants grow in the humid subtropical climate of Miami, Florida. Though frosts seldom occur in Florida, groves of orange trees may need protection during occasional winter cold waves.

Study the climate graph for Bombay, India, on page 61. What is the difference between the rainfall in January and that in July? What is the lowest average temperature, and during which months does it occur?

Subtropical Climates

Regions with subtropical climates have warm temperatures all year. There are two kinds of subtropical climates. One type is humid and has rain throughout the year. The other type has dry summers. Many people consider subtropical climates desirable places to live. They are also popular vacation spots.

Humid Subtropical Florida is a good example of an area with a humid subtropical climate. So are parts of Brazil, eastern Australia, and much of China. These places have mild winters and warm, humid summers. They are ideal for forests, many food crops, and fiber crops such as cotton.

On the climate graph for Jacksonville, Florida, which months have the greatest average rainfall? Which months have the least? What is the lowest average temperature, and when does it occur?

Jacksonville, Florida
Humid subtropical

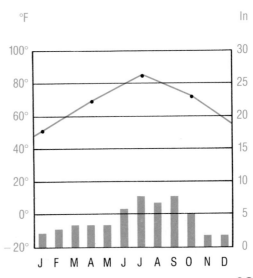

Answers to questions in column 1, paragraph 1: The difference between January and July rainfall is about 24 inches. The lowest average temperature is about 75°F, in January. *Column 2, paragraph 1:* July, August, and September have the most rainfall; November, December, and January have the least. The lowest average temperature, approximately 56°F, occurs in January.

63

World: Climates

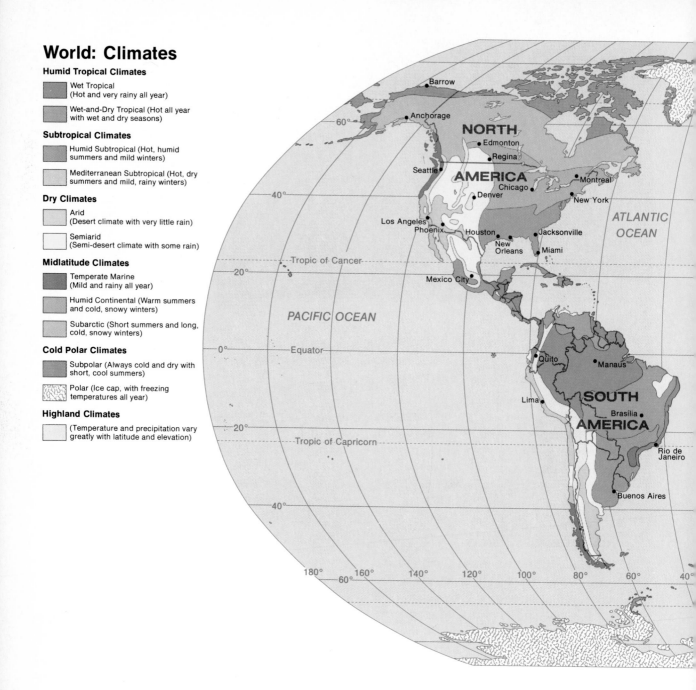

Humid Tropical Climates

- Wet Tropical (Hot and very rainy all year)
- Wet-and-Dry Tropical (Hot all year with wet and dry seasons)

Subtropical Climates

- Humid Subtropical (Hot, humid summers and mild winters)
- Mediterranean Subtropical (Hot, dry summers and mild, rainy winters)

Dry Climates

- Arid (Desert climate with very little rain)
- Semiarid (Semi-desert climate with some rain)

Midlatitude Climates

- Temperate Marine (Mild and rainy all year)
- Humid Continental (Warm summers and cold, snowy winters)
- Subarctic (Short summers and long, cold, snowy winters)

Cold Polar Climates

- Subpolar (Always cold and dry with short, cool summers)
- Polar (Ice cap, with freezing temperatures all year)

Highland Climates

- (Temperature and precipitation vary greatly with latitude and elevation)

Answers to Map Study questions: Climates at low latitudes are mainly wet tropical, wet-and-dry tropical, humid subtropical, Mediterranean subtropical, arid, and semiarid. Middle latitude climates are mainly humid subtropical, arid, semiarid, temperate marine, humid continental, and subarctic. High latitude climates are mainly subarctic, subpolar, and polar. Every climate is

ARCTIC OCEAN

Arctic Circle

Hammerfest

Reykjavík

Copenhagen

London

Leningrad

Moscow

Zurich

EUROPE

Rome

Lisbon

Algiers

Baghdad

Cairo

Riyadh

Mecca

Khartoum

Dakar

Lagos

AFRICA

Yaoundé

Nairobi

Kinshasa

INDIAN OCEAN

Johannesburg

Cape Town

Yakutsk

ASIA

Beijing

Seoul

Tokyo

Shanghai

Delhi

Calcutta

Bombay

Madras Bangkok

PACIFIC OCEAN

Equator

Singapore

Jakarta

Darwin

AUSTRALIA

Perth

Sydney

Melbourne

20° 0° 20° 40° 60° 80° 100° 120° 140° 160° 180°

Antarctic Circle

ANTARCTICA

Amundsen-Scott
Station (South Pole)

Map Study *What climates are found at low latitudes? Middle latitudes? High latitudes? What climates are found in more than one zone of latitude? Which continents have all kinds of climates? Why do parts of Europe at the same latitude as Yakutsk have warmer climates than Yakutsk?*

65

found in more than one zone. North America and Asia have nearly every climate. Parts of
Europe at the same latitude as Yakutsk are warmer than Yakutsk because they are warmed by
the Gulf Stream.

Olives and grapes grow well in areas with a Mediterranean climate. Here, fields of grapevines cover a valley on the island of Sicily, Italy.

Rome, Italy
Mediterranean subtropical

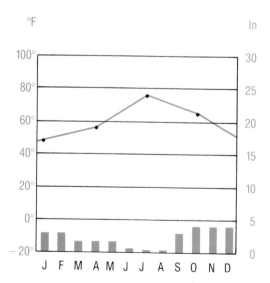

Mediterranean Subtropical This climate is common in California, southern France, Italy, and Greece. It is called a Mediterranean climate because it occurs in many places along the Mediterranean Sea. Winters there are warm and sunny, with a few storms and heavy rains. In the summer months, however, rainfall is slight. Most people consider this climate a very pleasant one to live in. It is good for growing many different types of fruits and vegetables.

On the climate graph for Rome, Italy, note the average rainfall during the month of July. Compare this amount with Jacksonville's average rainfall in July. Compare the average temperatures for the two places in July.

Dry Climates

All dry climates have little rainfall, but some get less rain than others. The seasonal patterns also differ.

66

Arid In a very dry, or **arid**, climate, little or no rain falls during the whole year. Arid climates often have the hottest daytime temperatures in the world. These climates, however, are not always hot. Because there is little moisture in the air to moderate temperatures, arid climates often have great changes in temperature. When the sun goes down, the earth and atmosphere cool quickly.

On the climate graph, what is the highest monthly rainfall for Khartoum (kär-tüm'), Sudan (sü dan')? How would you describe the average yearly temperature in Khartoum? How does it compare with that of Singapore?

Semiarid Like wet-and-dry tropical climates, **semiarid** climates have definite seasonal changes. There is a wet season and a dry season. Semiarid areas usually receive from 10 to 20 inches of precipitation a year. But the rain is not always reliable. In dry years, very little rain may fall,

The arid Sudan supports little plant life. Compare the vegetation in this area with that of Sicily, page 66, and with that of the Great Plains, page 68.

Khartoum, Sudan
Arid

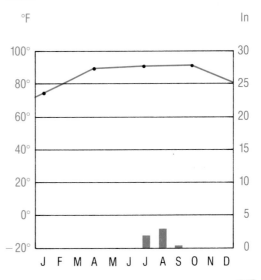

Answers to questions in column 1, paragraph 2: Khartoum's highest monthly rainfall occurs in August, when it reaches approximately 3 inches. Khartoum's average yearly temperature is very high. It is higher than that of Singapore.

Regina, Canada
Semiarid

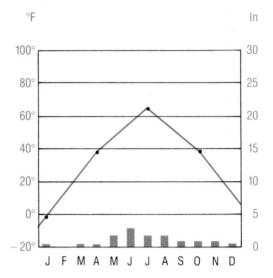

Wheat can be grown in the semiarid parts of the Great Plains of North America (top). ● *Temperate marine climates are known for their mists, fogs, and frequent rains. The moisture produces rich plant life like that of Ireland (bottom).*

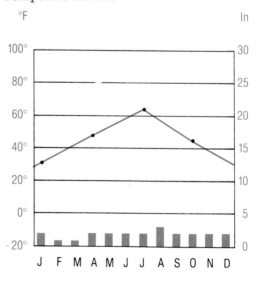

Copenhagen, Denmark
Temperate marine

Have students look at the map on pages 64–65 and locate areas with a humid oceanic climate. They should see that this kind of climate is usually found in the middle latitudes on the west sides of continents.

and drought conditions may parch the land.

With so little rain, trees and grasses do not grow as high as they do in more humid climates. Semiarid climates in the tropics do not have wide temperature variations. This climate in the middle latitudes, however, may have extreme summer and winter temperatures.

A semiarid climate is most likely to occur in the middle of a continent, far from the moderating influences of the ocean. In North America, a semiarid climate is found on the Great Plains, all the way from northern Mexico into Canada.

Study the climate graph for Regina (ri-jī′nə), Canada. What is the difference between the highest and lowest average temperatures? In what months do these extremes occur?

Mid-Latitude Climates

The higher middle latitudes contain three different types of climate. These differences are related to latitude and nearness to water.

Temperate Marine A temperate marine climate is near the ocean. You already know that water has a moderating effect on temperatures. Places with a temperate marine climate are therefore warmer than their latitude suggests. Northwestern Europe and the Pacific Northwest in the United States have a climate of this kind. Warm winds and ocean currents bring rain and moderate temperatures.

What are the highest and lowest average monthly temperatures for Copenhagen (kō′pen hā′gən)? What do you notice about the rainfall?

Humid Continental This climate is found in much of the northeastern United States, eastern Canada, and the Soviet (sō′vē et) Union. Rainfall in these areas is rather evenly spaced throughout

A forest with many kinds of trees grows in the humid continental climate near Moscow, U.S.S.R.

Moscow, U.S.S.R.
Humid continental

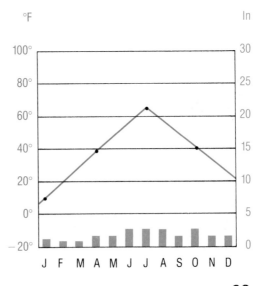

Answers to questions in column 1, paragraph 3: Regina's highest average temperature is approximately 65°F (July); its lowest average temperature is approximately −1°F (January). *Paragraph 6:* Copenhagen's highest average temperature is approximately 64°F; its lowest average temperature is approximately 33°F. Rainfall occurs fairly evenly throughout the year.

69

The subarctic climate of Soviet Siberia has long and bitterly cold winters. Evergreens are the chief plant life in the extreme temperatures of the region.

Yakutsk, U.S.S.R.
Subarctic

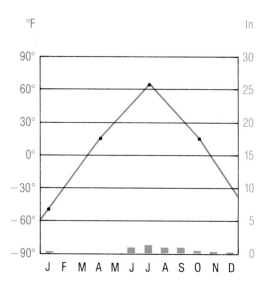

the year. Temperatures are colder in winter and warmer in summer than those in areas with a temperate marine climate. Humid continental climates are good for growing crops that are not damaged by sharp freezes.

Study the climate graph for Moscow on page 69. Notice the changes in temperature during the year. Also notice the precipitation pattern. In the spring, rain and melting ice and snow cause heavy runoff. Snow that falls in late fall and early winter stays on the ground until spring. What are the highest and lowest average temperature for Moscow?

Subarctic This type of climate is found only in parts of the Northern Hemisphere. A **subarctic** climate borders the Arctic Circle in Canada, Scandinavia (skan′də nā′vē ə), and the Soviet Union. Here, winters are long and very cold. Summers are short and cool. Precipitation is moderate — enough for forests of evergreens to grow. What are the highest and lowest average temperatures for Yakutsk (yə kütsk′) in the Soviet Union?

70

Answers to questions in column 2, paragraph 2: Moscow's highest average temperature is approximately 65°F; its lowest average temperature is approximately 15°F. *Column 2, paragraph 3:* The highest average temperature in Yakutsk is approximately 65°F. The lowest average temperature is approximately −59°F.

Subpolar climates are found only in the Northern Hemisphere. In general, areas with this climate border on the Arctic Ocean.

Cold Polar Climates

Two types of climate are found in the high-latitude polar regions. These differ only in their extremes of cold.

Subpolar Regions with this climate have very little precipitation but plenty of water. The water is usually frozen. When the summer thaw takes place, some melts turning the land into a marsh. Not far beneath the surface, however, is a layer, called **permafrost**, that never thaws. The summer season is too short for trees or other plants to grow very large.

On the climate graph for Barrow, Alaska, what is the highest average monthly precipitation? What is the highest average temperature, and in which month does it occur? Compare this with the temperature for Bombay, India (shown on page 61) during the same month.

Polar This climate is so cold that the land is always frozen. Most of Greenland and Antarctica are covered by permanent ice sheets. No plants grow, and no one lives on the ice sheets. Only a few scientists

Cool-summer polar climates have a short growing season. Though temperatures are no colder than in the subarctic, only small plants grow on the polar tundra.

Barrow, Alaska
Subpolar

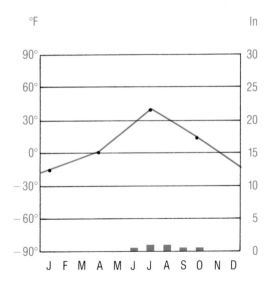

Answers to questions in column 1, paragraph 3: Barrow's highest monthly precipitation is approximately 1 inch. Its highest average temperature is approximately 39°F (July). Bombay's average temperature for July is approximately 82°F.

Answers to questions in column 2, paragraph 1: The lowest average temperature at Amundsen-Scott Station is approximately −76°F. It occurs in April and July. Precipitation is very evenly distributed throughout the year.

*Amundsen-Scott Station, Antarctica
Polar*

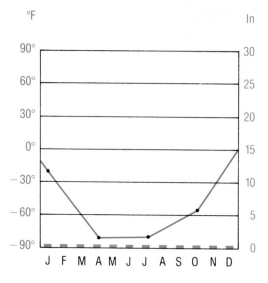

There is no plant life in polar areas. Only penguins feel comfortable on the permanent ice sheets of Antarctica.

visit. On the climate graph for Amundsen-Scott Station, Antarctica, what is the lowest average temperature? When does this temperature occur? Describe the precipitation pattern.

Highland Climates

The climates found in mountain, or highland, regions are different from others. The most important factor in a highland climate is the elevation of the land, not its latitude. The higher you go up a mountain, the cooler the temperature becomes. In India, for example, you can travel in just a few hours from a humid tropical climate to one like that of the arctic regions.

The plant life of highlands, like the temperature, changes with elevation. As you go up a mountain, you will find that different plants mark each climate zone. Near the base of a mountain, the climate is often moderate. There, dense broadleaf

Temperature and plant life change with elevation on these mountains in British Columbia, Canada.

and evergreen forests may reach up the slopes. Farther up, it is colder, with snows even in summer. Trees growing at these levels are smaller. Even higher up the mountain, it becomes too cold for trees to grow. This point is called the **tree line.** The climate near the tree line is like a subpolar climate. Even higher, you will often find a polar climate. The peak of Mount Kilimanjaro (kil'ə mən jä'rō) in East Africa is always snow-covered, although it is close to the equator.

In countries near the equator, many people may live in mountain areas. The lowlands are hot and humid, while the climate in the mountains is far more pleasant. Mexico, South America, and Africa have many places with highland climates. The climate of middle-latitude mountains is colder and less suitable for living.

The climate at very high elevations is usually cold everywhere. Often the cold is extreme, and violent storms are common. It is impossible to grow crops here, and animals have a hard time surviving. Few people live in this climate.

REVIEWING THE FACTS

Define

1. humid
2. arid
3. semiarid
4. subarctic
5. permafrost
6. tree line

Answer

1. (a) How are humid subtropical and Mediterranean subtropical climates alike? (b) How are they different?

2. What two kinds of arid climate are there?

3. What are the three types of climate found in the mid-latitudes? List the characteristics of each type.

4. (a) What kinds of climates are found in high latitudes? (b) In high elevations?

Locate

Refer to the map on pages 64–65.

1. Name a North American city with a Mediterranean subtropical climate.

2. Name four African cities with a wet-and-dry tropical climate.

73

Answers are in the Teacher's Guide.
Point out that in low latitudes, the tree line is often above 10,000 feet (3,000 meters). In middle latitudes, it occurs at lower elevations.

Highlighting the Chapter

1. Climate is the pattern of weather in a particular place over a long period of time. Weather is the condition of the atmosphere in a place at any one time. Climate and weather are mainly caused by changes in water and the atmosphere.

Earth is heated by the sun. During both day and night, Earth reflects some heat back into the atmosphere and space. The heat retained by Earth warms the land and water surfaces.

Night and day are caused by Earth's rotation on its axis. The changes in season and in the length of day and night are caused by Earth's tilt and its revolution around the sun.

Latitude is also an important factor affecting climate. Low latitudes, or the tropics, are generally warm. High latitudes, or the polar regions, are cold. Middle latitudes, called the temperate zone, have a wide range of climates. They can be hot in summer and cold in winter.

2. Water is continually cycled between the surface of Earth and the atmosphere. It falls to Earth's surface as precipitation. Water that falls inland flows to the oceans through river systems. Water returns to the atmosphere through evaporation and transpiration. There, it condenses and becomes precipitation again. This change of water from one form to another is called the hydrologic cycle.

3. Other factors also influence the world's climates. These include wind, ocean currents, and elevation. All these factors create certain predictable climate patterns.

4. The climates of the world can be divided into six major groups. These are humid tropical, subtropical, dry, midlatitude, cold polar, and highland. These groups differ from one another in average temperature, length of seasons, yearly precipitation, and humidity. Most of these groups are again divided into special types.

74

Speaking Geographically

Complete each sentence with the correct word or group of words from this chapter. The first letter of each word or group of words is given.

1. When people say that it was hot, humid, and clear yesterday, they are talking about the (w)_____.

2. (C)_____ is the pattern of weather in a particular place over a long period.

3. It takes Earth 24 hours to make one (r)_____.

4. The imaginary rod upon which Earth spins is called an (a)_____.

5. One (r)_____ of Earth around the sun takes $365\frac{1}{4}$ days.

6. The path Earth takes around the sun is called its (o)_____.

7. An (e)_____ occurs when there are equal hours of day and night around the world.

8. The times when the sun's direct rays reach the farthest point north or south of the equator are called (s)_____.

9. Distance north or south of the equator is called (l)_____.

10. (H)_____ climates have a lot of moisture in the air; in (a)_____ climates, the air is very dry.

Testing Yourself

Choose the term that best completes each sentence.

1. Earth has day and night because of the planet's (rotation, revolution, orbit).

2. Seasons are caused by Earth's revolution and (rotation, tilt, latitude).

3. The (solstices, equinoxes, axes) mark the beginning of summer or winter in the Northern and Southern hemispheres.

Equator

4. When the vernal equinox occurs in the Northern Hemisphere, it is the beginning of (fall, winter, spring) in the Southern Hemisphere.

5. The areas on Earth that receive the most direct rays of the sun are the (polar regions, middle latitudes, tropics).

6. The process by which water vapor changes from a gas to a liquid is given the name (evaporation, transpiration, condensation).

7. If you lived near the equator, your climate would most likely be (subarctic, Mediterranean, tropical).

Building Map Skills

Match the name of each country with the number that locates it correctly on the map on this page. Refer to the map on pages 486–487 when you need help.

_____India	_____Singapore
_____Brazil	_____China
_____France	_____Sudan
_____Canada	_____Soviet Union
_____United States	_____Australia

Applying Map Skills

1. (a) Give the capital city and its latitude for each country listed under "Building Map Skills" on this page. Refer to the Atlas maps on pages 492–493 and the Gazetteer for help. (b) Tell which capital is closest to the equator. (c) Which is farthest from the equator?

2. Refer to the world climate map on pages 64–65. Describe the climate pattern for the capital of the United States.

Exploring Further

1. Cities that have similar latitudes do not necessarily have the same climate. Choose cities of the same latitude (a) on different continents or (b) on opposite sides of the same continent. Describe the climate of each city and explain any differences.

2. Choose a country to which you would like to travel. Use the world climate map and Atlas maps to discover the type of climate it has. Then decide when during the year you would most like to visit the country and explain the reasons for your answer. Compare your choice and reasons with those of your classmates.

75

CHAPTER

3

Ecosystems: A Living Network

"From the moon, Earth appeared as a small, blue-green sphere, like a beautiful, fragile Christmas tree ornament I could cover with my thumb by holding it out at arm's length—very delicate and limited, the only color in the whole universe, the only friendly place we could see."

Astronaut William A. Anders

Among all the planets you can see from space, Earth is unique. The planets of Saturn and Jupiter have harsh environments. Saturn, shown with its rings, is very cold. Most of Jupiter's surface may be a hot liquid. Because both planets are hidden by clouds, scientists cannot be sure what the planets' surfaces are like.

Unlike Saturn and Jupiter, Earth provides an environment, or surroundings, in which life can exist. It alone has a thin blanket of atmosphere and a continually recycled supply of water. It alone has the special elements that support plant and animal life.

Earth actually has a number of different environments. You can see some of these from space. The white patches are layers of clouds. Light brown areas are deserts and treeless plains. You can see rivers winding across the land. Each of these environments stands alone. Yet each is also part of the whole—a network of environments spread around the world. In this chapter you will learn about Earth's different environments and the life within them.

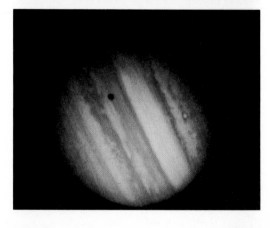

76

The top photo shows part of the Eastern Hemisphere as seen from the moon; the middle photo shows Saturn; the bottom photo shows Jupiter.

1 One Environment: A Network of Ecosystems

Every living thing has an environment within which it exists. Each life form depends upon its environment to sustain it. A water beetle has an environment. So does a stalk of wheat or a giant redwood. You too have an environment. Like all environments, yours includes both living and nonliving things.

Each of Earth's different environments is self-contained. That is, it includes the four nonliving elements — soil, air, water, and energy — needed for life. These life-sustaining elements together with living things — plants and animals — make up the **physical environment.** You share the physical environment with other living things. They also share it with you.

All Earth's environments are connected. In fact, Earth's surface is one vast and closely linked network of different environmental systems. Thus the global physical environment creates a complete unit, one worldwide system.

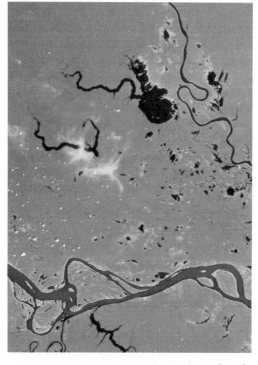

These Landsat images show three kinds of ecosystems. The Amazon River snakes through thick vegetation in Brazil's rain forest (top). ● *Desert dunes in China look like ocean waves. They are actually ridges 5 to 20 miles (8 to 32 kilometers) long (bottom right).* ● *Glaciers stand out against Iceland's mountains (bottom left).*

This chapter introduces students to the use of Landsat images. The key to these images appears on page 88. Here, the caption identifies the type of environment. Ask students to guess what the colors represent. Then use the key to find the correct answers.
Assign the Workbook activity for Chapter 3, Section 1, with pages 76–79.

77

WOULD YOU LIKE TO BE . . .

A biologist? A biologist studies the history, the life processes, and the environments of plants and animals.

A botanist? A botanist is a scientist who studies plants and plant life.

An ecologist? An ecologist studies the relationships among all the living and nonliving elements of an environment.

Ecosystems

A particular environment, its living and nonliving elements, and the ways they work together make up an **ecosystem** (ē′kō sis′təm). In other words, an ecosystem includes not only all the living and nonliving things in a certain place but also the ways in which they relate to one another.

The three most important factors in an ecosystem are climate, soil, and plant life, or **vegetation**. In Chapter 2, you learned that differences in temperature and rainfall create many different types of climate in the world. Climate, in turn, is the single most important factor in determining what plant and animal life develops in a certain place.

Another important factor in the forming of an ecosystem is **soil.** Soil is a mixture of rock particles and decayed plant matter. The kind of soil that a place has affects the plants that can grow there.

Plants help soil in two ways. First, they protect the soil from rains, from sunlight, and from winds. They do this simply by holding soil in place with their roots, providing shade, and depositing dead leaves and other matter on the soil. Second, when plants decay, they nourish the soil. Soil is actually changed by the plants that grow in it.

78

Development of Vegetation

Over hundreds of years, the plant life within a particular environment changes. Sometimes the change is the result of natural disasters, such as floods or fires. At other times, the change is caused by human activities. This gradual change is called **succession.**

In time, if left undisturbed, the plant life in an ecosystem will stop changing. This final stage is called **climax.** Vegetation at the climax stage may renew itself in the same form for thousands of years. The plant life at that state is called **climax vegetation.**

The stages of succession and climax can be seen after fire has destroyed a forest. First, plants that grow well in open spaces — mainly low-growing weeds — will cover the ground. Slowly, grasses and then small shrubs will begin to appear. Their protection and decayed matter will enrich the soil.

Near the edge of the burned area, where living trees drop seeds, pine trees will begin growing, gradually forming a forest

Shortly after a forest fire, weeds and other small plants begin to fill in the burned-out areas.

over many years. Pine trees, however, need full sunlight. As the forest floor becomes more and more shaded, trees that grow well in mixed sunlight and shade, such as birches and maples, will begin to replace the pines. These birch and maple trees will eventually be replaced by oak trees, which need the least sunlight. If the oaks were not replaced, they would become the permanent climax vegetation of this ecosystem.

In some environments, soil and climate conditions cannot support trees. Instead, grasses may be the climax vegetation. In other cases, drought-resistant plants such as cacti (kak′tī) may be the climax vegetation. (See the photograph on this page.) Whatever the climax vegetation is, it influences the other things that are able to live in the ecosystem.

REVIEWING THE FACTS

Define

1. physical environment
2. ecosystem
3. vegetation
4. soil
5. succession
6. climax
7. climax vegetation

Answer

1. (a) What are the three most important factors in any ecosystem? (b) How are the three major factors in an ecosystem related to one another?

2. What factors influence the growth of vegetation in an ecosystem?

Locate

Refer to the map of ecosystems on text pages 82–83.

1. (a) What ten ecosystems does the map show? (b) What color is used to show the mountain ecosystem?

2. What ecosystem covers the region that surrounds the Arctic Circle?

This needleleaf forest of sequoia trees in northern California is an example of climax vegetation. Heavy rainfall enables the trees to grow as tall as 306 feet (94 meters) (top). ● *The climax vegetation of this desert area is saguaro cactus. These plants grow in southern Arizona and northern Mexico (bottom).*

Texas Essential Elements 1C. Geographical tools and methodologies. 4B. Physical setting of world regions.

Reading an Annual Rainfall Map

The uneven distribution of rainfall over Earth's surface helps to account for the planet's many different climate regions. Yearly, or annual, rainfall can ranges from almost no rainfall in some desert areas to as much as 460 inches (1,150 centimeters) on Mount Waialeale (wī'ə lā ä'lā) in Hawaii.

The map on this page shows annual rainfall throughout the inhabited world. Examine the map's legend (key) and then study the map. The pattern you see will make it easy to identify areas where most of the rain falls as well as those areas that receive little precipitation.

Use the map below to answer the following questions.

1. Deserts occur in areas that receive little precipitation and where moisture loss through evaporation is great. Which continent has no deserts?

2. (a) Which part of Asia receives the most rainfall? (b) The least?

3. Near which parallel of latitude are the areas of heaviest rainfall found?

4. Describe the changing rainfall pattern that extends from west to east across Australia.

5. Which part of the United States is driest?

For a special challenge Compare the rainfall map on this page with the map of world ecosystems on pages 82–83. For each continent, name a large ecosystem that receives 40 to 60 inches (100 to 150 centimeters) of rain a year.

World: Average Annual Rainfall

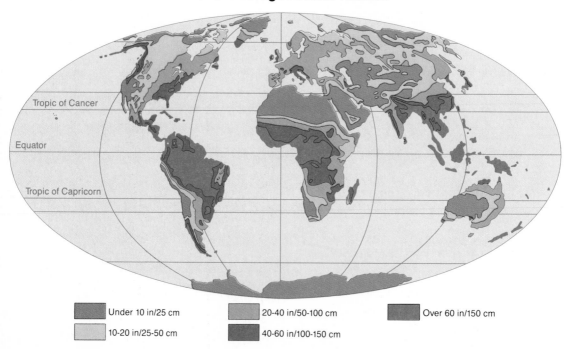

Tropic of Cancer

Equator

Tropic of Capricorn

Under 10 in/25 cm
10-20 in/25-50 cm
20-40 in/50-100 cm
40-60 in/100-150 cm
Over 60 in/150 cm

Answers are in the Teacher's Guide.
Assign the Workbook activity for this chapter's Map Workshop with this page.

2 Forest and Grassland Environments

The world contains many different ecosystems. In this section, you will study two major ecosystems, the forests and the grasslands. Of all Earth's ecosystems, the forests and the grasslands are the richest in plant and animal life. Therefore, most of the world's people live in these two ecosystems.

Forest Ecosystems

Trees are the main vegetation in a forest ecosystem. Forest ecosystems include needleleaf forests, broadleaf forests, and rain forests. Each of these environments has its own particular climate, soil, and vegetation. However, all forests receive at least 20 inches (51 centimeters) of rain a year—the minimum amount for the growth of large numbers of trees.

The Needleleaf Forest More than a third of all the world's forests are **needleleaf**. In such a forest, most trees keep their needle-shaped leaves throughout the entire year. Find the needleleaf forests on the map on pages 82–83.

The largest needleleaf forests are found in subarctic climates south of the Arctic Circle. These cold-climate needleleaf forests are called boreal (bôr'ē əl) forests. Precipitation falls year round. Snows are deep in winter. Most of the trees in boreal forests are spruce, larch, and fir. Summers last just long enough for these trees to grow. The winters, however, are so harsh that few other trees survive.

Several small needleleaf forest regions also occur farther south in the middle latitudes. Florida and other southeastern states have needleleaf pine forest areas. Many needleleaf forests cover mountains of the western United States.

Plenty of moisture supports the densely packed needleleaf trees of the swampy forests of Siberia.

Needleleaf forests provide a home for a variety of birds and animals. In many regions, they also provide a favorable environment for people. Needleleaf forests serve humans as valuable sources of lumber for building and of wood pulp for the making of paper.

The Broadleaf Forest Broadleaf forests have trees with wide leaves. Most of these trees lose their leaves every fall and grow new ones each spring. Such trees include oak, maple, birch, poplar, and elm. Find these forests on the map on page 82.

When Europeans first settled the eastern part of the United States in the 1600's, they found an almost solid forest stretching from the eastern coast to well past the Great Lakes and the Mississippi River. Much of that forest contained broadleaf trees. Over the years, the settlers cleared the forest for farming. Today most of that forest is gone.

Today about one third of the United States is covered with forests. Maine is the most heavily forested, with 90 percent of its land covered by trees. In contrast, only 1 percent of North Dakota is forested.

Assign the Workbook activity for Chapter 3, Section 2, with pages 81–87.

World: Ecosystems

- Tundra
- Evergreen forest
- Mid-Latitudes broadleaf forest
- Tropical rain forest
- Savanna
- Prairie
- Steppe
- Desert
- Ice cap
- Mountain

NORTH AMERICA

ATLANTIC OCEAN

Gulf of Mexico

PACIFIC OCEAN

SOUTH AMERICA

Tropic of Cancer

Equator

Tropic of Capricorn

60°
40°
20°
0°
20°
40°

180° 160° 140° 120° 100° 80° 60° 4
60°

Most ecosystems take their names from the kind of vegetation that grows in them. Have students compare this map with the climate map on pages 64–65. They will see that most ecosystems correspond to particular climate regions.

ARCTIC OCEAN

Arctic Circle

EUROPE

ASIA

Mediterranean Sea

AFRICA

PACIFIC OCEAN

Equator

INDIAN OCEAN

AUSTRALIA

20° 0° 20° 40° 60° 80° 100° 120° 140° 160° 180°

Antarctic Circle

ANTARCTICA

Map Study   Look at the natural ecosystems of North America,
Europe, and Asia. What has replaced some of these environments?
Locate the large natural ecosystems that still exist in Canada
and Alaska, the Soviet Union, Africa, and South America.

83

A path made by people runs through this broadleaf forest. How did many North American forests disappear (top)? ● *Most rain forests are in the tropics. Here is an example on the Hawaiian island of Oahu (bottom).*

Broadleaf forests are found mainly in moderate climates. Since large numbers of people choose to live in such areas, it is not surprising that many broadleaf forests have been cleared. People have used the wood both to build homes and furniture and to provide heat. Forests have also been cleared to make room for cities, farms, and roads.

Removing such large forests has changed the ecosystems of many areas. In some places, clearing the forests has brought the danger of widespread erosion.

The Rain Forest Almost half of all the world's forests are **rain forests.** Rain forests are located in the low latitudes, or tropics. Like trees in broadleaf forests, trees in rain forests have wide leaves. However, the trees of a rain forest are also evergreen, that is, they keep their leaves all year round.

Most areas in which there are rain forests get at least 60 inches of rain a year and have high temperatures. These conditions produce not only very tall trees but also thousands of other plants. These smaller plants cling to the trunks and branches of the trees. Where a dense overhead canopy of leaves blocks out the sunlight, the forest floor is often almost free of plant life. Where sunlight reaches the ground, as along streams, vegetation is a dense tangled mass, or jungle.

Some trees in tropical rain forests have hard and dark-colored woods, such as mahogany, teak, and rosewood. These woods are well suited to the making of furniture.

Rain forests serve a far more important purpose than just providing wood. The hot and humid climate creates a natural greenhouse. Using energy from the sun, the rain forests take carbon dioxide from the air. They combine the carbon dioxide with water from the soil to produce their own food. During this process they give

84

off oxygen, on which all life depends. In this way, dense tropical rain forests produce much of the world's supply of oxygen.

The soil and plant life of a rain forest are delicately balanced. The soil supports the plants. The dense growth and layers of decayed vegetation, in turn, protect the soil and help keep it fertile. If the vegetation is cleared away, that balance is upset. During the wet season, constant rain washes away the soil's **nutrients** — the food for plants. Then the tropical sun bakes the soil into a hard surface, where farm crops cannot grow.

Some people who live in the rain forest get their food by hunting wild animals and gathering wild plants. Others farm small fields cut free of the dense plant life. After several years, their fields lose nutrients, and farmers must abandon them. The forest then reclaims the land, and farmers clear new fields in other parts of the forest. Because the land in a rainforest ecosystem must be used in this way, it can support only a small number of farmers.

Grassland Ecosystems

Grasslands form another of Earth's major ecosystems. A grassland ecosystem may receive less rain than a forest. Its main vegetation is a variety of tall, medium, or short grasses. The height of the grasses depends on the amount of precipitation the area gets. Generally, those areas with the greatest precipitation have the tallest grasses and the most likelihood of supporting trees as well.

The Savanna The grasslands found in the tropical regions of the world are called **savannas** (sə van'əz). Find them on the map on pages 82 – 83. Most savannas receive 40 to 60 inches (101 to 152 centimeters) of rain a year. They are located where the climate is hot and moisture is seasonal. Because of the moisture, savannas have taller grasses and more trees than other grasslands.

One of the world's largest savannas is the Serengeti (ser'ən get'ē) Plain in East Africa. There, rainy summers and warm, dry winters produce thick grasses.

Herds of wild animals graze on the savannas of the Serengeti National Park in Tanzania, Africa.

Strange-looking trees—baobabs (bā'ō babz) and low, flat-topped acacias (ə kā'shəz)—dot the open land.

Most people of East Africa's Serengeti Plain do some farming and a great deal of cattle herding. A few miles from their villages live large herds of wild animals. This savanna ecosystem is the home of the last great herds of zebras, wildebeests, giraffes, and antelopes. Today many of Africa's savannas are being turned into farms and pastureland. As a result, herds of wildlife are beginning to disappear.

The Prairie Grasslands with tall and medium-height grasses are called **prairies** (prer'ēz). Most prairies receive 20 to 35 inches (51 to 90 centimeters) of precipitation a year. This rainfall is enough to support a few groups of trees, which are usually found along rivers.

In Argentina, grasslands are called **pampas.** They look much like the prairies of the United States and Canada. Find the prairie ecosystems in North and South America on the world ecosystems map.

Driving west across the northern United States offers a clear view of how differences in rainfall affect grasslands. In Illinois, where rainfall is moderate, natural grasses were once the climax vegetation. When the pioneers first settled there, the grass was so tall and abundant that people called it a sea of grass. Farther west, beyond the Mississippi River, the climate is drier and the natural grass grows a little shorter.

As recently as 150 years ago, antelope, bison, and elk grazed on the North American prairies. Rodents such as prairie dogs and gophers were common. Animal wastes made the soil richer. Wolves killed the grazing animals and left the remains. These added to the supply of decaying material. The grass kept the loose soil from blowing and washing away. The prairie ecosystem was in balance.

When Europeans came to this area, however, great changes took place. Settlers discovered that crops grew well in the soil. Many became farmers. They plowed the land, replacing the tall grass with corn (also a tall grass) and the shorter grass with wheat (a medium-height grass). Herds of livestock replaced the wildlife.

Few bison live on the North American prairie today. About 150 years ago herds numbered in the millions.

The Steppe   Much of the middle part of the United States is covered by the Great Plains. There, the grass is shorter than further east. This kind of grassland is called a **steppe** (step). Find the steppes on the world ecosystems map (pages 82 – 83).

The climate of the steppe is more severe than that of the prairie. Here, the inland climate brings hot summers and cold winters. Winds sweep across the open spaces, but they bring little precipitation — about 10 to 20 inches (25 to 51 centimeters) a year.

Vegetation on a steppe is sparse and slow-growing, with almost no trees. In most steppe lands, farming is difficult. The land is better suited to grazing. However, in some parts of the steppe, where the grass grows only in scattered bunches, even grazing is impossible.

In the late 1800's, farmers tried to plant crops on the steppe lands of the Great Plains in the United States. Problems quickly arose, mainly because rainfall varied greatly from year to year. In years of heavy rainfall, floods washed away the soil. In years of drought, crops withered and wind eroded the soil. Many farmers gave up and moved away.

Today some of these steppe lands are again producing farm crops. Farmers now plant rows of trees to slow the wind and prevent wind erosion. Plowing across slopes can help to stop water runoff and erosion. In many places, farmers also use **irrigation** in their fields so that crops will not wither and die in dry years. Irrigation is the bringing of water to fields through ditches, canals, or pipes.

Farmers in the Soviet Union too have turned the steppe into fields. They have had to deal with yet another problem: a short growing season. Crop failures in these lands have caused food shortages. Herding and grazing remain the most common uses of the world's steppes.

Cowboys take a moment to relax while driving cattle on the Soviet steppes.

REVIEWING THE FACTS

Define

1. needleleaf
2. broadleaf
3. rain forest
4. nutrient
5. savanna
6. prairie
7. pampa
8. steppe
9. irrigation

Answer

1. (a) How do people make use of needleleaf forests? (b) Why have many broadleaf forests been cleared? (c) Why is a rain forest not suited for large-scale farming?

2. (a) Which kind of grassland is most suitable for farming? Explain. (b) Which kind of grassland is the least suitable? Explain.

3. Which kinds of grasslands are there in the United States?

Locate

Refer to the map on pages 82 – 83.

1. (a) What part or parts of Africa does a rain forest cover? (b) What part or parts of South America?

2. Name the continent with steppe lands extending from its west coast to its east coast.

87

SKILL WORKSHOP

Interpreting Landsat Images

Landsat images taken of Earth from space are a valuable source of information. These images are made with computer-age technology. A mirror in an orbiting satellite captures light reflected from Earth. The satellite sends patterns of reflected light back to receiving stations on Earth. Then computers process the images into pictures that show sections of Earth's surface.

Landsat is important because it gives standardized pictures, taken at regular intervals, of Earth's entire surface. With Landsat, we can monitor changes that occur over large areas of Earth's surface. Landsat images show the movement of glaciers, the eruption of volcanoes, and the pollution of air and water. The Landsat image on this page shows the Himalaya Mountains in Asia.

Landsat images are like a new kind of art. Notice their fine details and vivid, rich colors. But as you study them, remember that these colors may be different from those that show elevation on maps. Landsat images have their own special color key. Many of the colors are related to vegetation or the lack of it.

To read Landsat images, you must know what the colors represent. Their meanings are summarized on this chart.

COLOR	MEANING
Shades of red	Growing vegetation, forests, grasslands, croplands
Light pink to light brown	Harvested croplands
Light brown to white	Dry land, no vegetation
Browns and yellows	Rocks and soil, rangelands
Pure white	Clouds or snow and ice
Bluish gray	Cities and towns
Bluish black in patterns	Cities and highways
Dark blue or black	Clear, deep water
Light blue	Muddy, silted, or polluted water, usually shallow

1. (a) What is the white area at the top of the photo? (b) What does that color tell you about the elevation?

2. What do the brown and yellow colors below the white represent?

3. What might the blue lines near the bottom of the photo show?

4. What does the bright red color near the bottom of the Landsat image show?

5. How would you describe this land area, based on the pattern of colors? Include reasons with your answer.

Answers are in the Teacher's Guide.
Assign the Workbook activity for this chapter's Skill Workshop with this page.

3 Polar, Desert, Mountain, and Oceanic Environments

The environments of the polar regions, deserts, and mountains contain more extreme conditions than grasslands and middle latitude climates. Their plant life is less abundant, and their climates are harsh. Yet people have learned to live in these environments. There is, of course, one environment people do not live in — the ocean. There, fish, plants, and a few mammals have adapted to the delicate salt-water ecosystem.

Polar Ecosystems

Polar ecosystems are found in Earth's coldest climates, near the North and South poles. The two main kinds of polar ecosystems are the polar ice cap and the tundra. Find these ecosystems on the map on pages 82–83.

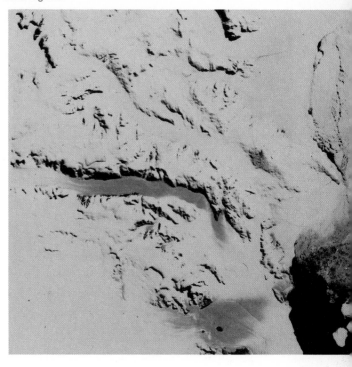

Landsat image of the Antarctic ice cap (top). ● *Polar bears hunt on the Arctic ice cap (bottom).*

Ask students if they remember why the polar regions are so cold. *(They receive only slanted sun rays most of the year and no sun part of the year.)*
Ask students to look at the map of world ecosystems on pages 82–83. Can they recognize any of the features on the Landsat image above? Compare it with the photo on page 91.
Assign the Workbook activity for Chapter 3, Section 3, with pages 89–96.

The Polar Ice Cap The term **polar ice cap** refers to the parts of the Arctic and Antarctic that are always covered with ice. As the world ecosystems map shows, Antarctica and most of Greenland have this kind of ecosystem.

The climate of the polar ice cap is forbidding. Temperatures are too cold for plants to grow. Yet wildlife is plentiful near the sea. Polar bears, seals, and walrus, together with penguins and a variety of other birds, live in this environment. They feed on other land creatures or on the rich sea life of the cold polar waters.

No matter where they live, plants and animals must adapt to their environment. This adjustment is called **adaptation.** The polar bear of the Arctic is a good example of adaptation to the ice-cap environment.

This Landsat image shows Baffin Island, lying off the northeast coast of Canada. Baffin Island has a typical short-summer polar climate.

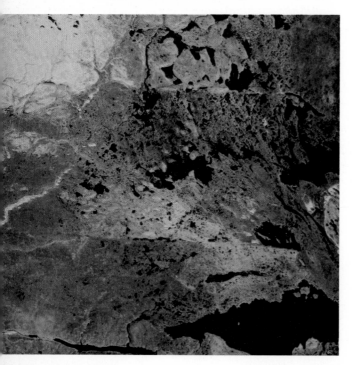

The polar bear's long white fur protects the bear by blending in with the snow. The bristly hair on the bottom of its feet keeps the animal from slipping on the ice. The polar bear's favorite food, seal meat, has a high fat content. This diet gives the bear a thick layer of fat for protection against the extreme cold.

Other animals have different ways of adjusting to the polar ecosystem. One of these is the arctic tern, a small sea gull. Twice each year this bird migrates as far south as the shores of Antarctica. It returns to the Arctic in summer to lay its eggs and raise its young. After hatching, these birds must grow very quickly. They have only a few days to learn how to fly. If they are not ready to migrate, they will be caught by the oncoming winter.

Very few people live in polar ice-cap regions. Some of those who live nearby may venture onto the arctic glaciers or sea ice to hunt from time to time. However, no one lives permanently on the polar ice. It is too harsh an environment.

The Tundra South of the ice-cap area in the arctic region lies the **tundra.** The tundra has a very short summer. However, even during the summer, the ground never thaws completely. A few feet under the surface is a layer of permanently frozen soil called permafrost.

Only the hardiest forms of plant life grow on the tundra. Those that survive best are mosses, lichens (lī′kənz), stunted flowers, and grasses. Their short root systems do not need to penetrate the permafrost. In addition, their short stems are strong enough to withstand the fierce polar winds.

Animals also live on the tundra. These include caribou, reindeer, musk-oxen, lemmings, and arctic foxes. The caribou, reindeer, and musk-ox feed on the short grasses of the region's climax vegetation.

Lemmings are small rodents. In Scandinavia and northwest Russia, they are famous for their migrations. Every eight to ten years huge numbers travel downhill from the overpopulated and food-scarce high country. If they reach the sea before the urge to migrate subsides, they plunge in and swim until they drown.

The tundra ecosystem is a fragile one. Tracks of vehicles will remain for years in the frozen ground. A plant or tree that is damaged takes a long time to recover. It may never reach its full growth.

Only a few people live off this harsh environment. Most are hunters and fishers. Because of their small numbers, their life-style is not a danger to the tundra ecosystem.

Desert Ecosystems

Deserts are the result of a very dry climate. They cover about one fifth of Earth's surface. Find the desert regions on the world ecosystems map.

At first glance, the desert may seem to be empty of all life. Actually it is alive with many different plants and animals. They are all adapted to their harsh environment. Desert plants have tough skins and few leaves, enabling them to keep what water they absorb. Large animals are scarce, but birds like mourning doves and rodents such as desert rats are numerous. Many desert animals are active at night when temperatures are cooler.

Not all desert ecosystems are the same. Although all deserts receive very little rainfall, some are hot while others are very cold.

Low vegetation covers the flat, treeless tundra in summer (left). Windblown furrows make patterns in the desert sand (right).

91

SPOTLIGHT ON DESERTS:

Survival Tactics

Living things in the desert must find ways to adjust to harsh conditions. For one thing, they must be able to get along with very little water. The kangaroo rat, for example, never actually takes a drink of water. It gets its water from the seeds it eats. Other animals, such as the camel, are able to go for long periods without taking in water.

Snakes do not control their own body temperature from within as humans do. Many snakes must sun themselves to raise their body temperature. If a snake stayed in the direct rays of the summer sun, however, its blood would boil and the snake would die. For this reason, snakes hide in shaded cracks and holes in the ground during much of the day.

Even plants are adapted to the desert environment. The saguaro (sə wär′ō) cactus of Arizona is an example. It expands like an accordion to take in water during the few rains each year. It can store many barrels of water to use sparingly during the long dry period.

Many desert plants enter a state similar to the hibernation of animals. When there is no rainfall, these plants simply wait. They are unchanged but still alive. When rain finally falls, the plants are able to reproduce. They blossom, put forth fruit, and then go to seed. This happens with great speed while the welcome moisture lasts.

Desert plants grow very slowly. They often cannot recover when animals feed on them. For this reason, many desert plants are protected by sharp spines and thorns that discourage animals from touching them. Within the protection of these thorns, cactus wrens build their nests. Here, their eggs and young are safe from animals and birds that try to eat them.

Thorny cactus plants thrive in the arid climate around Tucson, Arizona. How is this desert similar to the one shown on page 91? In what important way is it different?

Hot deserts are found mainly at low latitudes and low elevations. They are sometimes called tropical deserts. Among these deserts are the Sahara in North Africa and the Kalahari (kä′lä här′ē) in southern Africa.

Cold deserts, such as the Gobi (gō′bē) in Asia, the Great Basin in the United States, and Argentina's Patagonia (pat′ə gō′nē ə), are found at relatively high latitudes and high elevations. Winters are cold, and summers are warm or hot.

The desert, like the tundra, is a harsh yet fragile environment. Rain may cause severe erosion. A desert does not have enough vegetation to hold the moisture after a rain. During the occasional violent rainstorms, raging streams of muddy water cut deep trenches in the soil. Evaporation is quick, however. After a few hours of sunshine, a raging stream becomes a trickle or evaporates completely.

With little water and plant life, a desert cannot support many farming people. Some people, however, do grow crops or herd animals in the desert. Groups of

A Landsat image shows the shapes of the land in the Arabian desert.

herders in North Africa and Asia have called the desert home for centuries. They wander from place to place with their camels, goats, or sheep. Because the desert has few plants, herders must travel far to get enough food for their animals. The herders' lives revolve around the **oasis** (ō ā′sis), a place in the desert with a supply of fresh water. An oasis provides water, vegetation, and shade offering relief from the intense heat of the sun.

Here, nomadic herders come to an oasis in the North African desert to get water for their camels.

93

People who move from place to place in search of food for their animals are called nomads. An oasis may range in size from a small patch of land with a few palm trees to an area of several hundred square miles.

Other people farm in the desert. Desert soils, though dry, are often rich in nutrients. Because of the lack of rain, water has not washed the nutrients away. The rich soil and warm temperatures are favorable for farming. All that is lacking is enough water. With irrigation, therefore, some deserts can produce large amounts of crops. For example, people have been using water from Egypt's Nile River to farm the rich soils of the nearby desert for thousands of years.

Mountain Ecosystems

Mountain ecosystems can also have a harsh climate. The problem is not lack of water. Rather, mountain ecosystems may experience great changes in temperature and rainfall within a short period of time. Growing seasons are short. Strong winds, heavy snow, and severe rainstorms are common. Many mountain ecosystems are poorly suited for human life. Only a few people live in most mountain regions. Large numbers of people, however, make their homes in the Alps of Europe and the Andes of South America. Find the mountain ecosystems on the map on pages 82–83.

Mountain plant life is closely linked to elevation and temperature. Trees can grow on the slopes of mountains. They cannot, however, survive at very high elevations. Therefore, a line known as the tree line circles the sides of most tall mountains. Trees are found below this line but not above it.

Land above the tree line has thin soil and a short growing season. The surface may be very rocky. These conditions do not provide a favorable environment for large plants. The plants that do grow there are very small. They must be tough to survive the strong winds and great changes in temperature. These plants are able to live through long winters. They grow quickly during the short summer season, but then lie dormant during the long winter. In many ways, the plant life in a mountain ecosystem is like that of the tundra.

The slopes of the Sierra Nevada near Paintbrush, California, are colored red and yellow by delicate vegetation above the tree line.

Have students compare the population density map on pages 490–491 and the map of world ecosystems on pages 82–83. What relationship do they find between population density and desert, polar, and mountain ecosystems? *(Population density is lower in these ecosystems.)*

The oceans are home to the largest animal that has ever lived, the blue whale, as well as to some of the smallest. The food supply of the oceans is found in the upper layer of the water, where plants can receive the necessary sunlight.

The surefooted Dal sheep has a diet of twigs, leaves, and grasses.

Birds and small animals of the mountain ecosystem feed on the scant plant life. They also eat the insects that live on the plants. In winter the birds migrate to warmer places farther down the mountain or to more distant regions. Many small animals **hibernate,** or pass the winter in a sleepy, inactive condition. They survive on the stored-up fat within their bodies. Other animals get through the winter by eating the grasses they have stored away in their burrows.

Large animals of the mountain ecosystem are surefooted. They must be able to climb rocky crags and steep slopes. They feed on the short plants and the mosses that grow on rocks. They must have warm coats to withstand the cold.

Mountain ecosystems are fragile, even though they seem rugged. Any changes that upset the natural processes can bring permanent damage. A motorcycle wheel, for example, can cut a rut 2 inches (5 centimeters) deep in the thin soil. Once the soil is scraped loose from the rock, rain can wash it away. Soil that took thousands of years to form can be lost in a day.

Beautiful coral reefs are found mostly in tropical waters because the animals live only in water warmer than 65°F (18°C).

Oceanic Ecosystems

Oceanic ecosystems are a world unknown to most people. Yet the oceans produce an important part of the world's food supply. Fish is one of the greatest food resources. This resource will become even more important as the world's population increases.

Oceans have ecosystems, just as land areas do. Currents of cold water and currents of warm water create different ecosystems. Shallow areas have ecosystems that are different from those of deep areas.

Ocean ecosystems include a broad variety of living things. Microscopic plants and animals supply food for small fish. They in turn are eaten by larger fish. The fish population is able to survive because reproduction is fast and the number of

Fish swim along the edge of a coral reef in the Red Sea. Coral reefs are formed by millions of tiny, colorful sea animals, usually found in warm seas.

young, on which other fish feed, is huge. Some species of fish lay as many as a million eggs at one time. Less than one in a hundred thousand will live to maturity.

Fish-eating birds have adapted to catching fish in many ways. They dive after them and catch them in their saw-toothed or pouched beaks. Or they pull them out of the water while flying close to the surface. Most of this activity takes place in the waters close to shore.

The areas of the ocean that are closest to land have a particularly delicate ecosystem. Pollution can spread throughout the water and damage the food fish eat. If there is too much pollution, fish cannot survive.

REVIEWING THE FACTS

Define

1. polar ice cap
2. adaptation
3. tundra
4. desert
5. oasis
6. hibernate

Answer

1. (a) How have some people found ways to live in polar, desert, and mountain ecosystems? (b) In what different ways are plants adapted to polar, desert, and mountain ecosystems?

2. Why are arctic, desert, and mountain ecosystems considered fragile?

3. (a) Name four living or nonliving elements in an ocean ecosystem. (b) How is the oceanic ecosystem important to groups of people?

Locate

Refer to the map on pages 82–83.

1. Which continent has no mountain ecosystem?

2. Which two continents have the largest desert ecosystems?

4 Changes in Ecosystems

An ecosystem represents a balance worked out in nature. Sun, water, soil, vegetation, and living creatures all shape each ecosystem. Links among these elements become established over long periods of time.

Natural disasters may upset the delicate balance of an ecosystem. For example, a flash of lightning can set off a raging fire in the mountainside forests of Montana. Within days, thousands of acres may be burned bare. A drought on the Serengeti Plain of East Africa may destroy whole herds of wildlife.

Some changes may damage more than a single ecosystem. For example, dust from a volcanic eruption has sometimes changed the weather in distant parts of the world. The volcanic dust forms a cloud around Earth, blocking out the sun's energy and causing lowered temperatures. The climate in places thousands of miles from the volcano may be affected for months.

Human activity also alters the balance within and among ecosystems. More than any other form of life, humans are able to shape the environments they inhabit. They can also harm the environment. Such harm may be caused either knowingly or unknowingly. A person who takes wood from a forest for fuel may not know that this action, if done by thousands of people, will change the whole environment. People who dispose of rubbish in a river may see little immediate damage. But, if many other people also use the river as a dumping place, the river will one day become too polluted to support fish life. Even a small change, multiplied thousands of times, can damage an entire ecosystem.

Answers are in the Teacher's Guide.

Krakatoa, a famous volcano in Indonesia, erupted in 1883. It sent ash into the atmosphere that colored sunsets around the world for two years. It also caused temperatures to drop well below average throughout much of the world.

Problems in Land Use

Food is essential to the survival of human life. Most food comes from the land. People can gather plant life or grow crops. They can also hunt animals or raise livestock and poultry. People are always seeking ways to increase their supplies of food. This may mean making better use of present farmland or opening new lands for farming.

You already know what happened to steppe lands in the United States when they were opened to farming. Many of these farms failed when dust storms blew away the loose, dry soil. A similar problem arose in the Soviet Union when people tried to increase the food supply by growing wheat on the semiarid steppes.

Overgrazing may also harm an ecosystem. This is happening now in large areas of Africa south of the Sahara. Expanding herds of cattle are destroying the grasslands. Overgrazing may cause erosion and drought. The result is hunger for millions of people.

You have read before about how people can cause erosion by the cutting or burning of forests. Erosion is not the only result of these actions. When shade trees no longer line the banks of a river, sunlight raises the temperature of the water. Some fish will die because they cannot live in this warmer water. Because few seeds take root on the eroded land, new trees will not grow. An ecosystem that once produced lumber and wildlife will be gradually destroyed. By careful harvesting of forests, people can help protect the environment of a whole river system.

Problems in Water Use

People living near rivers must often deal with the problem of flooding. One way to control flooding is to build dams across rivers. Dams create reservoirs, which store the runoff and prevent floods. However, a new problem develops if deposits of silt fill up the reservoir. If that happens, the reservoir can no longer hold as much runoff as before.

A Landsat image shows a wheat-growing area in the Soviet Union during a year of average rainfall.

This image, taken in the same area a year later, shows a crop failure after a period of drought.

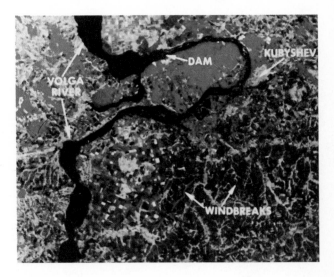

97

THE LAST PASSENGER PIGEON

A hundred years ago countless millions of passenger pigeons still lived in North America. Hunters would kill these beautiful birds and ship them to markets in big cities. There, the birds were sold for food at one or two cents each. In 1914, the last known passenger pigeon died in the Cincinnati Zoo.

Meantime the plains farther down the valley no longer receive their annual layer of silt. Over many years, this can hurt farming. They also get less moisture. As the land dries out, the ecosystem changes.

Irrigation too may change an ecosystem. Some of the changes — such as the increased water supply — are good. By making it possible to grow more crops, irrigation makes the land more productive. However, irrigation may also cause harm. It may reduce the supply of groundwater, on which future irrigation depends. Furthermore, most irrigation water contains dissolved mineral salts. As the water evaporates, these salts may build up in the soil and damage crops. This has happened on a large scale in Pakistan (pak'ə stan) in southern Asia as well as in a number of other places.

Problems in the Atmosphere

Air, like food, is essential to life. Human activities affect the quality of the air in many ways. Exhaust from cars and smoke from factories contain gases. These gases are dangerous to breathe in large quantities. Furthermore, when such gases combine with water in the atmosphere, they form acids, which fall to Earth as **acid rain**. Acid rain can pollute lake water, poison fish, and damage trees.

Nuclear radiation can also seriously harm the atmosphere. On April 26, 1986, the world's worst nuclear accident took place in the Soviet Union at the Chernobyl power plant in the Ukraine. The results of the accident were devastating. The explosion released a cloud of radiation that spread from soil to plants to cows to the milk supply. Nuclear contaminants from the Soviet Union drifted to north central Europe and eventually circled the globe. To this day, no one knows the full extent of the damage.

Problems in the Oceans

Oceans are Earth's great reservoir of water. You have learned that all water that falls on Earth eventually reaches the ocean through the hydrologic cycle. Pollution can also end up in the ocean. As it becomes more and more concentrated, pollution endangers the fish and plant life found there.

How does pollution reach the ocean? Pollution in the air is caught by rain and carried to the sea by rivers. Sea water evaporates and rises into the atmosphere. The pollutants remain behind, always increasing. People once thought that the oceans were too huge to be hurt by pollution. Today they know this is not true.

You have seen that human activity can be a danger to the ecosystems of the world, but it does not have to be. People

98

By the year 2000, it is predicted that six of every ten residents of the United States will live in the South and West. The arid Southwest is expected to grow the most, putting more pressure on an already limited water supply.
Answers are in the Teacher's Guide.

This beautiful lake in the Adirondack Mountains is dead. Because of the effects of acid rain, no living things survive in its waters.

The sinking of huge oil tankers and accidents at offshore oil wells can result in spills in the ocean. Such spills destroy sea plants and animals.

can find ways both to use and to protect Earth's environments. In recent years there has been growing concern about the environment. In the United States, for example, laws making it illegal to cause certain kinds of pollution have been passed. Today new cars must be equipped to use gasoline that has little or no lead. Factories must reduce the amounts of poisonous gases and particles they discharge into the atmosphere and bodies of water. Waste materials must be treated before being released into water. These and other changes have helped make the environment somewhat cleaner.

The view from space shows Earth as a place that is friendly to life. Protecting the balances in the big network of ecosystems can help to keep it that way.

REVIEWING THE FACTS

Define

acid rain

Answer

1. How have farming and industry sometimes harmed the environment?

2. How do flood control and irrigation sometimes change the balance of an ecosystem?

Locate

Refer to the map on pages 82–83.

1. On what continents are tundra ecosystems located?

2. Where is the world's largest ice-cap ecosystem?

99

GEOGRAPHY LABORATORY

Highlighting the Chapter

1. The world has many different ecosystems, which form a network covering Earth. As seen from space, the planet Earth is one large ecosystem. An ecosystem is the combination of parts of the physical environment together with the relationship among them. An ecosystem is influenced by such factors as climate, soil, water, plants, and animals. These combine in various ways to make different ecosystems.

2. The ecosystems most favorable to plant and animal life are forests and grasslands. These ecosystems also provide abundant resources for the support of human life.

3. Arctic, mountain, desert, and oceanic ecosystems are harsher environments than grasslands and middle latitude climates. While each supports plant and animal life, resources for human survival are sparse, and climate conditions are often extreme. Relatively few people live in most of these environments.

4. Human activity causes many changes in the world's ecosystems. Some of these changes are, in the short run, helpful to people. Certain changes are a danger to other living things and even to the ecosystem itself. People are learning that their well-being depends on protecting the balance of all ecosystems.

Speaking Geographically

Explain the relationship that exists between each pair of terms.

1. physical environment, ecosystem

2. vegetation, soil

3. succession, climax vegetation

4. needleleaf, broadleaf

5. prairie, savanna

6. desert, oasis

100

Testing Yourself

I. Match the description in Column A with the correct items in Column B. Two descriptions will not be used.

Column A
(a) threats to ecosystems
(b) deserts
(c) arctic animals
(d) types of forests
(e) fragile ecosystems
(f) results of natural disasters
(g) factors in ecosystems
(h) kinds of grasslands

Column B
1. soil, water, plants
2. needleleaf, broadleaf, rain
3. steppe, prairie, savanna
4. desert, tundra, mountain
5. Sahara, Atacama, Gobi
6. overgrazing, pollution, flooding

II. Choose the word or words that best complete each sentence.

1. Most trees in a needleleaf forest (lose their leaves every spring, keep their leaves all year long).

2. An oak tree is an example of a (needleleaf, broadleaf, rain forest) tree.

3. Rain forests are located in the (high, low, middle) latitudes.

4. Grasslands with the tallest grasses and most trees are called (savannas, prairies, steppes).

5. In a mountain ecosystem, the land above the tree line has (no trees, many trees, thick grasses and other vegetation).

6. The addition of salt to soil is a problem related to the use of (irrigation, reservoirs, contour farming).

7. When pollutants in the air, such as car exhausts and smoke from factories, combine with water in the atmosphere, they fall to earth as (nuclear radiation, oil spills, acid rain).

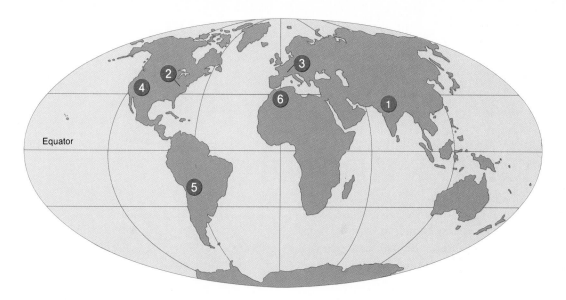

GEOGRAPHY LABORATORY

Building Map Skills

Each number on the above map refers to one of following mountain ranges.

Andes   Himalayas
Atlas   Appalachians
Rockies   Alps

Number your paper from 1 to 6. Beside each number, write the name of the correct mountain range and the continent on which it is found. (See pages 34 – 35.)

Applying Map Skills

Use the world ecosystems map on pages 82 – 83 to anwer these questions.

1. Which two ecosystems occupy the most land area in South America?

2. Which two ecosystems are found in most of eastern North America?

3. Name the seven ecosystems found in Africa between the Tropic of Cancer and the Tropic of Capricorn.

4. Using continent names and cardinal directions, describe the location of Earth's largest tundra and needleleaf-forest ecosystems.

Exploring Further

1. Locate the Amazon rain forest on the world ecosystems map, pages 82 – 83. Use the map to complete this activity.

Brazil is clearing large areas of the Amazon forest for farming and ranching. Hold a class discussion considering the advantages and disadvantages of such an undertaking. Take into account all you have learned about climate, environment, and the needs of people. How might the people of both North and South America be affected?

2. Choose one of the ecosystems described in the chapter. Pretend that you live in that ecosystem. Prepare a short description of your life and routine activities, your surroundings, and concerns. Have other class members name the ecosystem in which you live.

3. Divide the class into two groups. One group will do research on the Gobi Desert, the other on the Sahara. Each group should look for possibilities for the development of resources in its region. Compare the research findings in class. How are the two deserts alike? How are they different? What possibilities are there for development?

101

Earth's Resources

From space, you can view Earth's lands, waters, and atmosphere. You can also see signs of its different environments and ecosystems — the forests, grasslands, deserts, and ice caps. Together, these form a network of varied physical conditions on Earth's surface. What do these differences mean to humans?

Earth's environments provide a combination of elements that nourish plant and animal life. Humans also rely on ecosystems for the necessities of life. Of all the known places in the universe, only Earth provides the things people need to survive.

Any naturally occurring element that people depend upon for their survival — land, water, air, plant and animal life, soil, or minerals — is called a natural resource. Today people are becoming more aware of Earth's resources and their importance to human survival. They are learning that the supply of these riches is not endless. They are also discovering that the environment can be severely damaged when care is not taken in using resources. This damage can affect future generations.

Most resources are limited, and certain others can be destroyed. It is important to use all resources wisely. In this way, most of Earth's resources can be made to last.

In this chapter, you will learn about Earth's resources and how they are used. You will also see how people are learning to manage resources more wisely.

1 Resources: An Overview

A **natural resource** is any material or element from the environment that is used by humans. The things that form an ecosystem—climate, soil, water, minerals, and vegetation—are natural resources. They make it possible for animal life to exist. They also provide the means for human life. A resource, then, is anything that meets people's needs for living.

People and Resources

You must use Earth's resources in order to live. You drink water. The soil produces many of the foods you eat—fruits, vegetables, and grain for bread. Crops and natural vegetation also feed animals that provide your meat, eggs, and milk. The ocean provides not only fish but also the salt on your table. Your clothing, your home, and products you use everyday also are made from resources that come from the environment.

Only a few resources, such as water, are used in their original form. Most resources are changed before they can be used. Such resources are called **raw materials.** A raw material is any resource that can be made into a product. The paper in this book is made from the fibers of trees. The plastic cup you drink from is probably made from coal or petroleum. In each case, the original material has been changed so that you can use it. But without the cotton plant, the trees, and the coal or petroleum, you might not have a shirt, a book, or a cup.

Changes in Resource Needs People in every part of the world decide what resources are important to them. Some resources are used almost everywhere. For example, people have always relied on certain plants for food or for fibers that can be used to make clothing.

Changes in ways of living may change people's need for certain resources. Whales, for example, were once an important natural resource in the United States and Canada. Americans used whale oil as fuel for lamps. Then, in the late 1800's, people began using kerosene from petroleum to light their homes. It proved to be cheaper and less smoky than whale oil. As a result, whales became much less important as a resource.

Petroleum, a resource important in producing energy and making chemicals, is brought by pipeline from northern Alaska to a port on the North Pacific.

The Alaska pipeline was opened in 1977. It cost $7.7 billion to build. Have students find out about efforts to extend the line.

Assign the Workbook activity for Chapter 4, Section 1, with pages 103–104.

Changes in Resource Use Some resources grow in importance as people find additional ways to use them. Petroleum is a good example. As early as the 1500's, some Indian groups in North America noticed a black, oily substance seeping out of the ground in certain places. The Indians did not regard petroleum as a resource, however, because they did not have a use for it.

In the past hundred years, people have found many different uses for petroleum. At first, they used it mainly to light lamps and heat homes. Later, people found they could use electricity to light lamps. Petroleum was used then to produce electricity as well as to heat homes. Petroleum also became an oil for machines and a fuel for automobile engines. More recently, it has become a source of chemicals for making plastics, dyes, and many other products. All these uses have greatly increased the amount of petroleum needed. The result is that petroleum has become increasingly important as a resource.

Scientists are constantly searching for ways to turn other parts of the environment into resources. Fifty years ago uranium was considered worthless. Today it is a valuable resource. It is used to produce nuclear energy.

The Resource Base

Resources are divided into three groups — water and soil, plants and animals, and minerals. These groups provide the resource base that humans use.

Resources are not distributed evenly. Some parts of the world are rich in some resources and poor in others. You have seen that the amount and type of water, soil, plants, and animals differ from one ecosystem to another. Because of this, some ecosystems provide more resources for living than others do.

The supply of the different resources also varies. For example, Earth has a supply of water that cannot be increased or decreased. People use water over and over again without destroying it. Therefore, water is called a **recyclable resource.** On the other hand, soil, plants, and other living things can be used up. Yet they can also be replaced. Therefore, these resources are called **renewable resources.** Renewable resources can provide a continuous supply if they are wisely used.

Those resources that are limited in amount and cannot be replaced are called **nonrenewable resources.** Most of the metals and energy resources are nonrenewable. You can see, therefore, why using them carefully is so important.

REVIEWING THE FACTS

Define

1. natural resource
2. raw material
3. recyclable resource
4. renewable resource
5. nonrenewable resource

Answer

1. (a) Name two resources that have become important in the past hundred years. (b) What is each used for?

2. (a) What are the three main groups of resources? (b) How are they distributed throughout the world?

Locate

The Great Lakes form the largest body of fresh water in the world. Refer to the map on pages 492–493. Then name the lake that lies

1. totally within the United States

2. between New York and Ohio

3. north of the state of Michigan

104

2 Water and Soil Resources

Water and soil are two of the most important resources on Earth. They are essential to all life. Both resources are found all over the world. However, water and soil differ from place to place in quality, type, and use.

Water Resources

Water is the most common and widespread of all resources. Of Earth's total supply of water, 97 percent is found in the oceans. The other 3 percent is fresh water, found in glaciers, lakes, streams, and rivers.

The Need for Water Without water, there would be no life on Earth. You probably take water for granted. It is something you use every day for drinking, bathing, and cooking. The fact is that water is more important to life than food.

Most people could live for a week or more without food. They could not, however, survive 48 hours without fresh water to drink. Humans cannot drink salt water.

Because water is a recyclable resource, it is neither created nor destroyed by natural forces. In the hydrologic cycle, water moves from oceans to clouds to ground to plants to rivers, then back to oceans again. In the course of this cycle, water serves many uses, but it is never used up. The water that produces electricity can be used for irrigation, drinking water, swimming pools, and air conditioners before it goes on to another part of the cycle.

Distribution of Water The uneven distribution of water across the face of Earth can cause problems. In any place or at any time, there may be too much or too little water. For example, people who live near

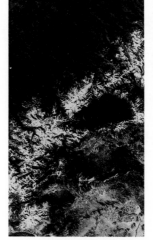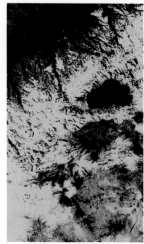

Landsat images from different years give information about snowfall in the Sierra Nevada. Runoff from melting snow affects California's water supply.

rivers must sometimes deal with floods. Many of the world's first farms and cities developed in river valleys because rivers provide fresh water and deposit rich soil along their banks. River valleys, however, are very likely to suffer badly during floods. Floods can destroy homes, crops, and human life. Still, after the waters recede, people often return to the same valley because of the good soil.

Floods occur when runoff is more than the land can absorb or rivers can carry.

Assign the Workbook activity for Chapter 4, Section 2, with pages 105–108.
Have students think back to the different climates discussed in Chapter 2. Which climate has plenty of water? *(rain forest)* Which one lacks water? *(desert)*

105

SPOTLIGHT ON SATELLITES:

Prospecting for Resources

Satellites constantly circle Earth, sending back information about every part of the world. This information is changed into maplike images. Today these images can be used to help locate new sources of minerals and other resources.

A hundred years ago a prospector riding a burro used a pick to look for copper deposits in the desert. Today satellites report on the presence of copper in a certain area. Veins of ore buried beneath the topsoil are seen by satellites that circle Earth. This development is leading to a new kind of prospecting. The opening of a big new copper mine in Arizona was made possible by satellite exploration.

How can a satellite find minerals buried beneath the surface? Some mineral deposits occur where, in the distant past, circulating hot water made a chemical change in rocks. These rocks now reflect sunlight differently from those around them. The satellite picks up these light reflections and sends the information back to Earth. There, the computer's record of light reflection is made into a picture called an image. Technicians study these images. They may then say, "It looks as if there might be some minerals in those rocks. That seems to be a good place to search for copper." Five copper-bearing deposits in a remote part of Pakistan were found in this way.

Satellites have other ways of finding underground fuel and mineral deposits. They identify features such as fault lines, rock types, and general land and water forms. Certain minerals or fuels have been found in the past near special geological formations. So prospectors look for parts of the world with similar features. Armed with information gathered by satellite, they go looking for Earth's riches.

Satellites are able to prospect for living resources also. They even help find schools of fish for commercial fishing. Satellite images locate ocean areas where temperatures and water depths make good fishing grounds. Knowing where to fish is half the secret of successful fishing.

A Landsat image of an Asian desert shows certain rock formations. From these, scientists can tell whether minerals may be found in this remote area.

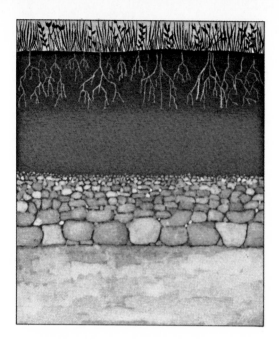

TOPSOIL
Gray to black;
Contains humus

SUBSOIL
Red, brown, or
yellow; Clayey

WEATHERED
BEDROCK
Contains pieces
of rock

BEDROCK
Parent material

The photo (left) and the diagram (right) show a cross section of soil, or a soil profile. Compare the four layers.

Soil Resources

Soil is another essential resource. It is used to produce most of the world's food. Crops are planted and grown in **topsoil**. Topsoil is the thin upper layer of the soil. It forms the surface of the land in most places on Earth. The average depth of topsoil is slightly less than 6 inches (15 centimeters).

The Content of Soil Soils are mainly composed of mineral particles. These particles start out as bits of rock, called **parent material,** which are broken off from larger rocks. Parent material is turned into small soil particles through two different processes. One process is called **mechanical weathering.** Mechanical weathering includes all the physical forces that break or wear away rock. The alternate heating and cooling of rock surfaces, pressure from ice or roots that creep into the cracks of rocks, the tread of animals — these are the kinds of forces that cause mechanical weathering.

As the parent material is broken into smaller and smaller pieces, it may also be changed by a process called **chemical weathering.** Chemical weathering is a process that dissolves rock material. A good example is the weathering of rocks in caves. The dissolved rock may eventually reform into small particles. These particles can form soils.

Along with mineral particles, soils contain **humus** (hyü'məs). Humus comes from plants. Plant life begins with seeds blown by the wind, carried by water, or dropped by birds and animals. Seeds fall between tiny bits of rock where they grow into plants. When plants die, they slowly decay and become humus. This decayed matter has nutrients that make the soil fertile.

Different combinations of mineral particles and humus form different types of soil. Soils with very little humus are often sandy or claylike. Soils with a larger percentage of humus tend to be dark and crumbly. Plants need both humus and mineral particles to grow. Farmers value the soils that are rich in humus because these are the best for growing most crops.

107

A DEEP SUBJECT

The world's deepest well hole was bored in Washita (wä'shə tô) County, Oklahoma, in 1974. Miners of the Loffland Brothers Drilling Company worked 503 days drilling for natural gas. They reached a depth of 5.7 miles (9.5 kilometers). The temperature at the bottom of the hole was 475°F (245°C).

Climate and Soil Climate plays an important part in creating soil. Heat and moisture act on mineral particles and humus. Therefore, both heat and moisture affect the type of soil that develops. Many months of sun and rain will cause heavy plant growth with plenty of humus. If too much rain falls, however, the soil may become **leached,** or drained of its nutrients. On the other hand, if rainfall is light, plant growth will be sparse, and little humus will be added to the soil. Still, the soil will not be leached. It will retain its mineral nutrients.

Comparing two different ecosystems shows how climate affects soil. In a desert ecosystem, few plants grow, because there is less than 10 inches (25 centimeters) of rainfall each year. Desert soil, therefore, has little humus. Yet, because there is little leaching, the soil is often rich in minerals that can provide nutrients for crops.

The soil of a rain-forest ecosystem is quite different from that of a desert. Temperatures are high, and rain falls every day. Plants grow quickly because of the great amounts of moisture and heat. Do you remember what happens when the rain forest is cleared of trees and crops are planted? When the rains come, the heavy rainfall erodes the soil. Rain also leaches nutrients from the soil.

REVIEWING THE FACTS

Define

1. topsoil
2. parent material
3. mechanical weathering
4. chemical weathering
5. humus
6. leach

Answer

1. Why is water an important resource?

2. (a) What accounts for differences among soils? (b) Explain how areas with great amounts of rainfall may not have good soil.

Locate

Use the map on pages 492–493 to help you name the United States river that

1. forms the southwest border of Texas;

2. flows through Montana, North Dakota, and South Dakota;

3. forms the boundary between California and Arizona;

4. forms the eastern boundary of Arkansas.

108

Texas Essential Elements 1B. Geographical terminology. 3D. Uses, abuses, and preservation of natural resources and the physical environment.

3 Biotic Resources

Soil provides the nutrients for living things, or **biotic** (bī ot'ik) **resources.** There are three main kinds of biotic resources. One is plants used for food. These plants include wild fruits and berries as well as crops like rice and wheat.

Many animals, both wild and tame, can also be used for food. These animals are a second type of biotic resource. Some animals also provide milk and eggs.

A third kind of biotic resource includes both plants and animals used as raw materials for manufacturing. For example, crops such as cotton and animal products such as wool are used to make cloth.

Biotic resources are renewable. Plants renew themselves by producing seeds for further plantings. In this way, new trees will eventually grow in a forest that has been cleared. Animals are another renewable resource. They produce young, which will in turn produce more animals. Similarly, millions of tons of fish can be removed from the ocean without exhausting the supply.

Wheat is an important biotic resource that provides food (top). ● *Sheep provide meat for food and wool for use in making clothing (bottom).*

Wood is a key biotic resource. It is used for fuel and as a raw material for making paper and other products (left). ● *The planting of seedlings will renew the supply of wood in this area (right).*

109

REVIEWING THE FACTS

Define

biotic resources

Answer

1. (a) Describe the three types of biotic resources. (b) Give an example of each.

2. Explain why biotic resources are considered renewable.

Locate

Five world leaders in fish production are identified below. Use the map on pages 486–487 to name them.

1. island country east of Korea

2. country that spans two continents and reaches to the Arctic Circle

3. second largest country on the continent of Asia

4. country bordered by Ecuador, Colombia, Brazil, Bolivia, and Chile

5. country whose northernmost point is approximately latitude 72°N and whose southernmost point is approximately latitude 19°N

Iron ore is processed to make steel.

4 Mineral Resources

Minerals are nonliving resources. They are found both on the land's surface and underground. Once removed from Earth's crust, most minerals have to be processed, or changed, before they can be used by people.

There are three main groups of minerals. One group is known as metals, or **metallic resources.** Iron and copper are of this kind. A second group is called **nonmetallic minerals.** They include such materials as stone, sand, and salt. The third group is made up of **energy fuels,** such as coal, petroleum, and natural gas.

Metals

Metals are found in Earth's crust, usually in the form of **ore.** Ore is rock that contains large amounts of metal. People process ore to extract the metal. In concentrated form, most metals are shiny and solid. They can be shaped or molded into many things. Metals are used in manufacturing and in building.

Iron is one of the most important metals. When iron is mixed with certain other minerals, it forms an even stronger material — steel. Steel is the basic material in tools and machines.

Other valuable metals are copper, lead, zinc, tin, and aluminum. Electric wire, hardware, and pipes are made of copper. Lead too can be molded into pipes. Lead is also used to make paint, dyes, and pottery glazes. Steel is coated with zinc to keep it from rusting. Tin is often mixed with other minerals and used in making lightweight metal objects, such as baking pans. Aluminum is made from bauxite (bôk′sīt). It is used in airplanes and cars, industrial products, building materials, household utensils, and food and drink containers.

Answers are in the Teacher's Guide.

Assign the Workbook activity for Chapter 4, Section 4, with pages 110–112.

Metallic minerals such as iron, aluminum, and gold are nonrenewable, but many of them can be used more than once. So the supply of these minerals can be protected by the process of recycling. Gold and silver, for example, are almost never thrown away. Rather, they are melted down and used again and again. Aluminum too can be recycled. For instance, aluminum cans are often melted down and made into new products. Unfortunately, no more than about 5 percent of the aluminum that could be reused gets recycled.

Nonmetallic Minerals

Not all minerals are metals. Nonmetallic minerals include both rare materials — such as diamonds and emeralds — and common materials — such as clay, gravel, and sand. Glass is made from sand, a nonmetallic mineral. Some sandpaper is made from feldspar (felds' spar). Fertilizer is made from potash (pot ash), which is another nonmetallic mineral.

Salt is the most important nonmetallic mineral. People cannot live without salt in their food. Since ancient times, salt has been used not only to season foods but also to preserve them. Many of the most important early trade routes were set up to transport salt to distant places. Long ago, Roman soldiers even received part of their pay in salt. The English word *salary* comes from the Latin word *salarium*, which means "salt."

Fossil Fuels

The energy fuels — coal, petroleum, and natural gas — are known as **fossil fuels**. Fossil fuels were formed from plants and animals that died millions of years ago. Through changes in Earth's surface, the remains of these plants and animals were buried deep underground.

Deposits of crude oil are found in the continental shelf, the underwater edge of continents. Here, an offshore rig drills for petroleum in the Gulf of Mexico.

There, intense pressure from the weight of Earth's crust brought about chemical changes in the plant and animal materials. Over the centuries, these materials were turned into coal, **petroleum**, or oil, and natural gas.

Now, millions of years later, fossil fuels are used to run furnaces, machinery, automobiles, airplanes, and ships. Chemicals manufactured from petroleum and coal are used to make plastics, drugs, dyes, fertilizers, and many other things. Heat provided by the burning of coal is part of the process of turning iron into steel. Much of the world's electricity is also produced with heat provided by burning coal.

Mineral resources are nonrenewable. Although the processes that formed coal still occur, people are using coal much

111

faster than it can be replaced. For all practical purposes, the supply is limited. The United States now has enough coal to last about 300 years at the present rate of use.

Supplies of petroleum are being used up at an even faster rate than supplies of coal. Petroleum, like coal, is nonrenewable. When it is pumped out of the ground, millions of years will pass before more will take its place. If the world goes on using petroleum at the present rate, the entire known supply will be gone in less than 50 years.

REVIEWING THE FACTS

Define

1. metallic resource
2. nonmetallic mineral
3. energy fuel
4. ore
5. fossil fuel
6. petroleum

Answer

1. (a) Name some important metals and tell how people use each. (b) What is the most important nonmetallic resource? (c) How is it used?

2. How were energy fuels, or fossil fuels, formed?

3. (a) How does recycling help to protect mineral resources? (b) Give examples of two mineral resources that can be neither recycled nor renewed.

Locate

Capital cities of the ten leading oil-producing countries are listed below. Use the Gazeteer on pages 501–514 to name the country in which each of these capitals is located.

1. Moscow
2. Riyadh
3. Washington, D.C.
4. Mexico City
5. Caracas
6. Beijing
7. London
8. Jakarta
9. Tehran
10. Lagos

5 Managing Resources

Hundreds of years ago resources seemed limitless. In the last 50 years, however, people's growing needs have seriously reduced the world's supply of such nonrenewable resources as petroleum and natural gas. Some scientists think that even many renewable resources are now threatened. How did this change occur? One reason is that there are more people in the world today than ever before. In addition, each person now uses many more resources than an individual did in the past.

The uneven distribution of resources adds to problems of scarcity. This uneven distribution can be offset by trade between countries rich in some resources and poor in others. But some countries do not have as much to trade as others.

People depend on Earth's resource base for their very survival. Preserving that resource base is, therefore, essential to human life everywhere. The careful use of resources is called **conservation**. To conserve resources means to use them wisely.

Managing Renewable Resources

People today are becoming more aware of the need to protect renewable resources. They are finding new ways of conserving the supplies.

Water There are a number of ways people can improve their use of water resources. As you know, the amount of water in the world does not change. Therefore, the secret of good management is learning how to redistribute water more efficiently.

For example, farmers have made the desert "bloom" by redistributing water from wet areas, that is, using irrigation.

Ask students how depletion of the world's petroleum might affect their lives.
Have the class make a list of ways their community is working to conserve resources.
Answers are in the Teacher's Guide.
Assign the Workbook activity for Chapter 4, Section 5, with pages 112–119.

However, if they use too much water, they can leach nutrients from the soil. If they do not properly drain irrigated fields, the water may evaporate, leaving behind mineral salts that can harm crops. Therefore, irrigation must be carefully managed.

Dams are another way of redistributing water. They store river water until it is needed. They can also prevent damage caused by flooding. At one time, people thought that big dams were best. They hoped the huge structures would hold back floods and protect the land downstream. They learned, however, that there are also disadvantages to a large dam. In a large dam, huge amounts of water as well as silt accumulate in the dam's reservoir. Downstream farmlands that depend on the river for silt deposits and moisture may suffer.

Many engineers now think that a small reservoir behind a small dam is a better way to manage water. Small dams still protect against floods. Yet, if one breaks, it is less destructive than a break in a big dam. Small dams on stream tributaries also allow more water to seep into the soil. They reduce erosion, which slows the rate of silt buildup in reservoirs behind larger dams.

People do not always agree about how water should be used. The use of water

The Bonneville Dam—which stands near Portland, Oregon—controls floods on the mighty Columbia River and provides irrigation for nearby farmlands in the states of Oregon and Washington.

from the Colorado River is a good example. In parts of the river's upper valley, in the state of Colorado, water is so cheap that farmers use more than is needed. The runoff from this overuse pours about 300,000 tons (270,000 metric tons) of mineral salts a year into the Colorado River. These salts cause serious problems in the lower valley. There, water from the Colorado River is drained off to provide irrigation for southern California, Ari-

Water sprinklers change an arid wasteland into a fertile field.

zona, and Mexico and drinking water for the city of Los Angeles.

Overuse of water also occurs in households. People may use more water than they need. Fixing leaky pipes and installing water-saving devices on faucets can save a surprising amount of water. Residents of Tucson, Arizona, for example, use water-saving devices that have reduced daily water use per person from as much as 177 gallons to 140 gallons, a drop of 37 gallons per person.

Fire is a danger to forests and wildlife (top). ● *Satellites help locate forest fires. Note the smoke and burned area in this Landsat image of an Alaskan forest (right).* ● *Water runoff from cleared land carves a deep gulley (bottom).*

Soil People in different parts of the world have found many ways to improve the use of soil. Long ago, people in the mountains of Asia needed more level lands on which to farm. Farmers built flat, steplike terraces on the mountain slopes. They held back the soil on the terraces with barriers of rocks. **Terracing** kept the rich soil from being washed away.

Farmers in the mountains of Europe and Latin America also use terracing to prevent erosion. On less mountainous land, farmers in the United States use **contour farming** to keep topsoil from washing away. Rather than plowing up and down hills, they plow across the slopes. The crosswise furrows keep soil from washing down the hill when it rains.

Crop rotation is yet another way of conserving soil. Crop rotation keeps any one crop from robbing all the nutrients from the soil. Farmers who practice crop rotation might grow cotton for several years and then plant a different crop. That crop might be peas or beans, both of which add nutrients, used up by cotton, to the soil.

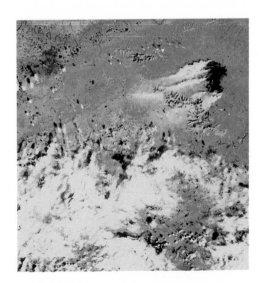

The use of fertilizers is another way to keep soil rich. Farmers have learned to apply humus, animal manure, or chemicals to the soil. These fertilizers put back nutrients taken from the soil by various plants. Fertilizers can also add nutrients missing from the soil.

People now realize that these fertilizers are not a cure-all. Some soils use up chemical fertilizers. The more they get, the more they need. In addition, many chemicals can poison the soil.

Protecting grasslands also helps to save soil. Some types of soil are too thin and poor for growing farm crops. Yet these soils can support grasses. Cattle, sheep, and other animals can graze on these lands. It is important, however, not to allow too many animals to graze on grasslands. Without grass to anchor the soil, the soil may be blown away by the wind.

Protecting forests is also important in managing soil, especially in countries where large numbers of people use the forests for fuel. In many parts of Asia, Africa, and South America, people have stripped even the steep hillsides bare. Now, when the streams rush down these hills, they carry away precious topsoil needed to grow food crops.

Contour farming prevents erosion on hillsides. What other examples of good resource management can be seen on this Wisconsin farm (top)? ● *These terraces in Nepal turn a rugged mountainside into valuable cropland. They also keep soil from washing away (bottom).*

Today's food production is highly dependent on chemical fertilizers. These will become more expensive as the nonrenewable materials from which they are made are used up.
Answer to caption question: alternating strips in fields, woodlots on steep hillsides, and a pond to contain runoff

Have students refer to the Spotlight on page 106 as a reminder of how satellites help locate fossil fuels.

Large-scale strip-mining operations — like these in Wright, Wyoming — can result in the removal of large amounts of topsoil.

Managing Nonrenewable Resources

Wise management and thoughtful planning are even more important for nonrenewable resources than for renewable ones. Once nonrenewable resources are gone, they are gone forever.

Minerals Minerals have been used throughout human existence. Supplies of some are dwindling. Finding substitutes for scarce minerals is one way to protect resources. Builders are using plentiful materials like concrete in place of scarce materials like steel.

WOULD YOU LIKE TO BE . . .

An agronomist? An agronomist is a scientist who studies crop production and economics.

An engineer? An engineer is a person who directs projects in a technical field. These might include the building of dams and waterways or the construction of mines.

A forester? A forester is a person who manages forest resources. A forester cares for trees and supervises control of forest fires. Keeping track of such activities as camping and skiing are other duties.

Fossil Fuels In modern times, inventions in industry, transportation, and modern comforts and conveniences have put heavy demands on energy resources. These demands are steadily growing.

Geologists and engineers are searching the world for new sources of natural gas and petroleum. Petroleum is often found in a type of rock called shale. It is also obtained from beneath the ocean on the continental shelf. Recently the search for petroleum and natural gas has been aided by satellites. A satellite can locate geologic structures that may have these fuels.

Even though new sources of petroleum and natural gas are being found, their supply remains limited. The more people use, the more important it becomes to conserve these resources. There are a number of ways to protect scarce energy resources. One is to use less of scarce resources like oil and more of plentiful ones like coal. In the future, more coal will probably be mined, because there is still much coal underground.

Widespread and heavy use of coal will require special controls to protect the environment. One type of pollution comes from coal mines underground. When coal is mined, air enters the mine shaft. The oxygen in the air combines with the sulphur and water in the mine and makes an acid. In places, the acid water may seep out of the rock and into nearby streams. Too much of it can kill fish and other life. Today mines are checked to prevent this problem.

A different threat to the environment develops when coal is taken directly from the surface of the earth. This process is called **strip-mining**. To get at the coal, big machines first rip off the topsoil. Mining one resource — the coal — harms another — the topsoil. Replacing the topsoil after the coal is gone helps to restore the land.

Coal is the world's most abundant and widely distributed nonrenewable energy source. Major reserves exist in Asia, North America, and Europe. The Soviet Union leads the world in coal production.

Comparing Information on Fuel Deposit Maps

Maps are useful tools for both showing information and evaluating how places are alike and different. The three maps on this page show the locations of the major fossil-fuel deposits in the United States. Use the map legends to find which map shows coalfields, which shows petroleum fields, and which shows natural-gas fields. These fossil fuels generally lie under Earth's surface in the areas shown.

Each map uses color to show where fuel deposits are located. What color is used for coalfields? Petroleum fields? Natural-gas fields?   *yellow, pink, green*

Study the maps to discover which states have supplies of these fossil fuels. If you need help with the names of states, refer to the map of the United States on pages 492 – 493 of the Atlas.

1. Which is greater in the central states — coal supplies or petroleum supplies?

2. A large area of petroleum deposits extends over four states in the central and southern portion of the United States. (a) Name the four states. (b) In which state does there appear to be the greatest deposits of petroleum?

3. Which fossil fuels are found in Alaska?

4. Which fossil fuel is deposited in a large area extending from Alabama northward to Pennsylvania?

5. Compare the locations of natural-gas fields with the locations of petroleum and coalfields. What relationship do you see?

6. Does your state have any fossil-fuel deposits? If so, name them.

For a Special Challenge What is the name of the mountain range in which fossil-fuel deposits extend from northern Alabama to Pennsylvania?

Answers are in the Teacher's Guide.

Assign the Workbook activity for this chapter's Map Workshop with this page.

United States: Fossil Fuel Supplies

Coal fields

Petroleum fields

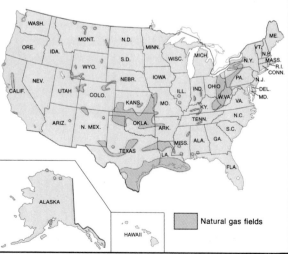

Natural gas fields

MAP WORKSHOP

Reading Energy Graphs

Information about energy resources is important for managing them. The three graphs on this page provide facts about energy sources and their use in the United States in a recent year.

Graph A is a pie, or circle, graph. The entire circle represents the country's total energy use. Each part of the circle shows the percentage of energy used for a certain kind of activity. The graph shows the relation of each part to the whole circle.

Graph B is a bar graph. Each bar stands for the percent of energy supplied by one source. "Hydro" means water. Domestic oil is oil produced in the United States. Imported oil is oil bought from other countries.

Graph C is a picture graph, or pictograph. It shows which states are the leading producers of petroleum in the United States. A barrel is the standard measure for oil. It is 42 gallons (about 636 liters).

1. What activity uses the largest amount of energy in the United States?

2. Which energy source provides more than half of the electricity in the United States?

3. Which produces more electricity — waterpower or oil?

4. Name two energy resources that are used to produce nearly equal amounts of electricity.

5. Which state is the leading producer of petroleum?

6. About how much more petroleum does Louisiana produce than Oklahoma?

7. About how much more petroleum does Texas produce than the states of Oklahoma and Wyoming combined?

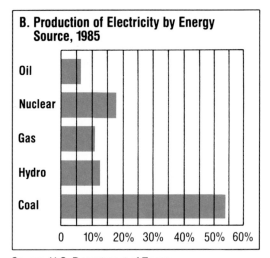

B. Production of Electricity by Energy Source, 1985

Source: U.S. Department of Energy

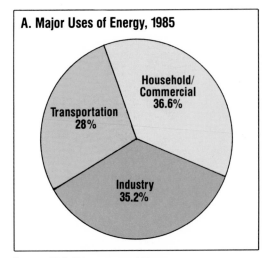

A. Major Uses of Energy, 1985

Source: U.S. Department of Energy

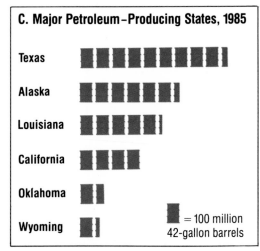

C. Major Petroleum–Producing States, 1985

Source: Statistical Abstract of the United States

Answers are in the Teacher's Guide.
Assign the Workbook activity for this chapter's Skill Workshop with this page.

Solar energy provides heat and hot water on this farm. Note the solar panels on the roof of the barn at the left.

The burning of coal can also harm the environment. When coal burns, poisonous sulphur gases are released into the air. Most factory chimneys now have scrubbers to filter out the sulphur. This stops pollution and saves the sulphur for other uses.

Finding alternative sources in place of fossil fuels is another way to conserve energy resources. One such alternative is **nuclear energy.** It is being used in many countries. A little nuclear fuel produces a lot of power. Nuclear energy also has disadvantages. Nuclear power plants need large amounts of water. As this water is used, some of it becomes radioactive. Radioactive water cannot be used by people. Nuclear power plants also produce radioactive waste materials. These materials are very dangerous and must be carefully stored for thousands of years.

Scientists are seeking ways to make electricity from wind power. This alternative may become an important source of energy. First, however, scientists must learn how to store the energy that windmills produce. This is also true of the energy from ocean tides and waves.

Solar energy could turn out to be the most important alternative source of energy. It comes from the heat of the sun. Solar-energy devices can store the sun's heat and produce energy even on a cloudy day. Solar energy is already used for heating and cooling. It can also be used to make electricity. Solar energy has the advantages of being reliable, simple, safe, and widely available. It does not harm the environment. However, at present it is used to produce only a small amount of power.

REVIEWING THE FACTS

Define

1. conservation
2. terracing
3. contour farming
4. crop rotation
5. strip-mining
6. nuclear energy
7. solar energy

Answer

1. What are some possible harmful effects of the overuse of water?

2. What have farmers done to improve soils?

3. (a) Why has the demand for energy and minerals increased in recent years? (b) What are some fossil-fuel alternatives?

Locate

Many states in the United States have nuclear power reactors. Use the map on pages 492–493 to name four, based on the clues below.

1. The capital is Montgomery.

2. It borders both the Pacific Ocean and Mexico.

3. Chicago is located there.

4. It borders Lake Ontario.

119

GEOGRAPHY LABORATORY

Highlighting the Chapter

1. A natural resource is any of Earth's materials that people use. People's needs for resources change over time. So do the ways in which resources are used.

The main types of resources are water and soil, plants and animals, and minerals. These resources are not evenly distributed on Earth. Those that are present in one place or country provide the resource base there. Some resources can be renewed or recycled, but other resources are nonrenewable.

2. Water is the most important resource because no living things could survive for long without it. Soil is made up of mineral particles from broken down rock and humus. Most of the world's food is grown in topsoil.

3. Plants and animals are biotic resources. Biotic resources are the living materials people use for food, clothing, and shelter.

4. Mineral resources include metallic and nonmetallic materials and fossil fuels. Many of these resources are limited in supply and are nonrenewable. Among the most important of the world's nonrenewable resources are coal, petroleum, and natural gas.

5. Conservation of resources helps to preserve the resource base. It encourages the renewing of resources and avoids the harmful effects of misuse. Conservation also includes recycling and finding alternative materials. These approaches can help to offset uneven distribution and population growth.

Speaking Geographically

Write the following headings across your paper.

Natural Resources
Nonliving
 Resources

Soil Conservation
Alternative Energy
 Resources

Then list the terms below in groups of three under the correct heading. Be prepared to briefly explain the meaning of each term.

recyclable
 resources
metallic resources
terracing
fossil fuels
nonrenewable
 resources
wind power

nonmetallic
 resources
crop rotation
solar energy
contour farming
renewable
 resources
nuclear energy

Testing Yourself

Complete each sentence with the correct word or words from the following list.

conservation
radioactive water
nutrients
natural resource
chemical
 weathering
strip-mining
fertilizers
petroleum

floods
salt
raw materials
scarcity
salt water
fresh water
rain
waves
metals

1. In the past hundred years, ____ has become an important fuel and source of new chemicals.

2. Lakes, glaciers, and rivers supply the world with much of its ____.

3. Leaching of soil can occur in areas with too much ____.

4. Desert soils may be poor in humus but rich in ____.

5. After people learned to make nuclear power, uranium became an important ____.

6. Cotton, flax, and wool are ____ from which useful products are manufactured.

7. ____ is a dangerous by-product of nuclear power plants.

120

8. _____, along with minerals such as clay, gravel, and diamonds, are taken from Earth's crust.

9. Through _____, people can both use and protect for the future their essential resource base.

10. Small dams with small reservoirs are sometimes favored as protection against soil erosion and _____.

11. Chemical _____ are frequent means for enriching soil in farming areas of the United States.

12. The process of _____ rips topsoil from the surface of the land.

13. Growing population and the uneven distribution of minerals, metals, and fossil fuels help produce a _____ of the world's resources.

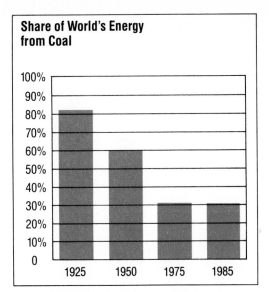

Share of World's Energy from Coal

Source: British Petroleum Review of Energy

Applying Geography Skills

1. The graph shows how much of the world's total energy was supplied by coal during selected years of this century. Construct a similar graph showing the percentage of the world's energy that was supplied by petroleum during the same years. Use the following information.

Year	Energy from Petroleum
1925	13%
1950	28%
1975	48%
1985	39%

2. Compare the graph you made with the one in the book. Describe the relationship between the use of coal and oil as sources of energy since 1925.

Exploring Further

Do library research on one of the topics listed below. Discover how each of them might contribute to the search for new or alternative resources.

Geothermal energy   Tidal energy

Solar energy   Wind energy

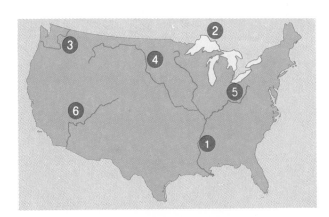

Building Map Skills

Match the name of each freshwater resource with the number that locates it correctly on the map on this page. Refer to the map on pages 186–187 for help.

___ Mississippi River   ___ Missouri River
___ Ohio River   ___ Great Lakes
___ Colorado River   ___ Columbia River

GEOGRAPHY LABORATORY

121

UNIT 2

THE VIEW FROM THE AIR

From space, you viewed the entire planet Earth. From this distance, you could consider the global patterns of landforms, climates, ecosystems, and resources. The view from the air now brings you closer to Earth's surface. From here, you can see the results of varied human activities on Earth.

As you pass over the eastern part of the United States on a clear night, you can see New York City. The city and its surrounding communities stretch out in a glowing network of electric lights that shine in buildings and along highways. This brilliant pattern is a dramatic reminder of the presence of humans on Earth. It is one among many examples of the imprint human beings have made on the planet.

CHAPTER

5

Does your community have old buildings or other structures that reveal some clues about earlier people who lived there? Some students may be interested in looking into the beginnings of their community and how it has changed over the years. What effects, both positive and negative, have humans had on the land?

The cave painting comes from Caveat Los Caballos in eastern Spain and dates from approximately 6,000 B.C. In it, hunters are ambushing deer.

Human Imprints of the Past

From the air, evidence of human activity is visible almost everywhere. Using resources from the physical environment, humans have changed the look of Earth. They have cleared forests, drained marshes, and leveled hillsides. They have created farms of varying sizes, opened grazing lands, and built crowded cities. They have constructed elaborate transportation systems over land, air, and water, and they have developed complicated communication networks that link people in distant parts of the planet. In many places, the human imprint is more evident than the natural environment itself.

That human imprint is not the same everywhere. In one region, many farmers are bent over a flooded rice field, tending the plants by hand. In another region, only one or two farmers using powerful machines work several large rice fields. In one part of a large city, skyscrapers line the streets. A few blocks away stand buildings many hundreds of years old. These older buildings are the imprints of people from the past.

In this chapter, you will learn about how people have changed the physical environment and why they have done so. You will also see how the human imprint has changed over time.

124

1 Culture: The Human Difference

Earth's physical environment includes a variety of landforms, climates, and ecosystems. These make up Earth's many different **habitats** (hab'ə tats). A habitat is a particular physical environment in which certain plants and animals grow or live naturally. These plants and animals are physically adapted, or suited, to their habitat. For example, an animal's methods for gathering food, protecting itself, and caring for its young are related to its habitat.

If plants or animals are removed from their natural habitat, or if their habitat changes greatly, they may not be able to survive. Scientists believe that many kinds of plants and animals have become extinct because of changes in the physical environment. Some such changes occurred naturally; others are the result of human actions.

Human Habitats and Cultures

Unlike plants and most animals, human beings are not physically adapted to their natural surroundings. People can change the physical environment to suit their many needs and wants. Human needs for food, water, shelter, and comfort can be met in a wide range of habitats. People have the ability to survive almost anywhere — even, for short periods of time, at the edges of outer space.

People everywhere on Earth change and adjust their environment through their **culture.** Culture is the total way of life followed by a group of people. Culture includes all the things the people of a society do, make, believe, value, and teach their young. People who share a way of life have a common culture.

Every Culture Is Unique

No two cultures are exactly the same. The distinctions among cultures may be quite large or very small. Many cultural differences are seen in the buildings people construct, the clothes they wear, and the ways they make and transport goods. Some cultural differences can be heard in the ways people speak and the music they play. You can taste cultural differences too. Every culture has its own special foods and dishes.

People of different cultures also have different points of view. Even when they act in similar ways, people may have different reasons for their actions. For example, a rancher on the pampas of South America protects and provides for cattle

(Above) shopping areas in Tokyo, Japan, and (below) Abidjan, Ivory Coast (Cote d'Ivoire), show some differences between cultures.

125

so that the animals will bring a good price when they are sold. Herding cattle is a way of earning a living for that rancher. In India, a follower of the Hindu religion protects cattle not because of the monetary value of cattle but because Hinduism teaches that these animals are sacred. An African herder on the Serengeti Plain protects cattle for yet another reason. In this culture, cattle are a sign of status. They show one's importance in society.

How do groups of people develop different ways of life? No one knows for sure. It is not surprising that people living in cold climates dress differently from people in warm climates, or that people in arid climates use water differently from people in rainy climates. But environment does not explain cultural differences. The rancher on the pampas and the African herder live in similar environments. Both make their home on grasslands. Their cultures differ because they have different values and beliefs.

WOULD YOU LIKE TO BE . . .

An archaeologist? An archaeologist is a scientist who searches for and studies tools, bones, buildings, and other remains of people from the past. Such articles give clues regarding the culture of the people who left them.

An anthropologist? An anthropologist studies customs, technology, beliefs, and other patterns of cultural behavior among people of both the past and the present.

A historian? A historian studies written records—such as letters and documents—created by people in the past. These records, along with early maps, artwork, drawings, and the like, help the historian learn about the past.

Cultures Have Common Elements

Cultural differences make the world an interesting place in which to live. However, in studying how people live, it is important to remember that all cultures have much in common. In every culture, for example, people live in family groups. Religious beliefs, language, and art are also important parts of every culture.

One of the most important jobs of every culture is caring for young people. Children everywhere learn the ways of life of their parents and grandparents. In many cultures, children attend schools to acquire this and other knowledge.

Every culture has leaders and laws. As a result, government is an important part of culture. So is a group's **economic system.** An economic system is the organized way in which people decide what and how much will be produced and how the output will be distributed.

Every culture also has a **technology.** A culture's technology includes all the tools, skills, and methods people use to produce goods and services.

Although every culture is unique, geographers divide Earth into **culture regions.** A culture region is a place where people's ways of living are similar. People within a culture region may have a common history, similar religious beliefs, or speak the same language. For example, Mexico and Central America, the Caribbean islands, and South America are considered parts of a culture region known as Latin America. Most countries there were once colonies of Spain and Portugal. Most Latin Americans are Roman Catholics. They also speak Spanish or Portuguese. Spanish and Portuguese developed from Latin, which was spoken in southern Europe about 2,000 years ago.

126

Cultures Change

All cultures change over time. Sometimes change occurs very rapidly. At other times, change takes place so slowly that few people are even aware of it. Some changes come about because young people do not always carry out customs and traditions exactly as their parents did. Other cultural changes come from new inventions and ideas. Most change, however, takes place as a result of contact with other cultures.

Since very early times, travelers carrying goods for trade have stimulated an exchange of ideas as well. The adopting of goods or practices from other cultures is known as **cultural borrowing.** A people that borrows from another culture rarely accepts ideas exactly as they are found. People usually alter the ideas they acquire to make them suit their own traditions or customs. As a result, cultures create new ideas through borrowing.

Whenever any new tool or idea is introduced into a culture, the people will first experiment with ways to fit it into their existing way of life. If they cannot find a satisfactory place for it, they will reject it, no matter how useful it might seem to outsiders.

Cultures Are Patterned

All the different elements that make up a culture fit together like the pieces of a jigsaw puzzle. A change in one part affects other parts. When people within a culture borrow an idea, invent something new, or discard a long-held custom, the action may be felt throughout their entire society.

The invention of the computer demonstrates how change in one part of a culture — its technology — can affect other parts. Computers are changing the kinds of jobs many people hold in the

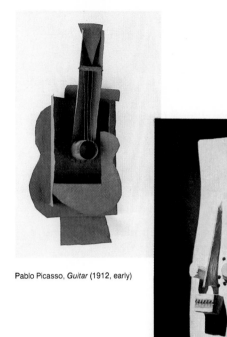

Pablo Picasso, *Guitar* (1912, early)

A sculpture by the twentieth-century European artist Pablo Picasso (top) shows the influence of masks made along Africa's west coast (bottom).

United States. Businesses equipped with computers need fewer file clerks and more word processors. Computers are also changing schools. Today students from grade school through college use computers to acquire skills and to prepare assignments. The invention of the computer has also led to new laws and new means of law enforcement, new forms of entertainment, and even new words in people's everyday speech.

In order to understand the world today, it is helpful to know how cultures have changed and adjusted to new ideas. The study of technology is a good place to start. It is through technology that human beings leave their most visible imprint on Earth.

REVIEWING THE FACTS

Define

1. habitat
2. culture
3. economic system
4. culture region
5. technology
6. cultural borrowing

Answer

1. What advantage do humans have over plants and animals in coping with their physical environment?

2. Give three examples of cultural differences and similarities.

3. Why do cultures change?

Locate

The way people use the land is part of their culture. Refer to the land use map on Atlas pages 488–489.

1. In what part or parts of North America is stock raising a major activity?

2. What color stands for nomadic herding?

Early people learned to make tools and weapons by flaking stones.

2 Early Technologies and Cultural Patterns

Scientists believe that the earliest technologies were developed by cultures in which people lived by hunting and gathering. **Hunters and gatherers** lived by killing animals and collecting plants that grew wild in their physical environment. Their most important technological achievements were the use of fire and the invention of hand tools.

Life during the Ice Age

Exactly how long ago hunters and gatherers flourished is not known. Scientists believe that such cultures were present during the Ice Age. During that time, people adjusted to the harsh, cold climate by using weapons to hunt animals. Scientists think that Ice Age people joined in small bands, often knit together by strong family bonds. Nearly everywhere, these bands developed simple weapons like spears.

Today only a few groups of hunters and gatherers remain. Most of them have changed, to one degree or another, in response to contact with modern cultures. Near the end of the last Ice Age—believed to be about 11,000 years ago—groups of hunters and gatherers were living on all continents except Antarctica. **Archaeologists** and other scientists who study past cultures have learned a great deal about these peoples by examining artifacts left by them.

Early Technology Large collections of bones from slain mammoths, reindeer, giant bears, and other mammals tell scientists about the tools used by early humans. From the quantity of the bones, scientists have concluded that many were skilled hunters. Shaped and worked

128

Students might be interested to know that there was a division of labor in hunter-gatherer societies—men hunted wild animals; women gathered roots, nuts, and fruits.

Answers are in the Teacher's Guide.

Assign the Workbook activity for Chapter 5, Section 2, with pages 128–131.

stones show that the people were also skilled in tool making. With their tools, they could make use of the many resources they took from their physical environment.

For hunting animals, the people made sharp stone points. Attached to wooden sticks, the stone points became spears for throwing. A stone with a notch chipped on one side might have been used to scrape the spear's pole smooth and straight. Early hunters also fashioned stone blades, which they probably used for cleaning and scraping the animal skins they wore for clothing.

Many early humans discovered how to start and use fire. One way of starting fire was very simple. People used two sticks that could be rubbed together to make heat. When flintstone was available, it was used as a firemaking tool.

Fire enabled people to adjust to their environment in a number of ways. In the warmth of campfires, people could survive in cold climates as well as in warm ones. Cooking over campfires increased the varieties of foods that could be eaten. It is also likely that the campfires brought people closer together. The night hours became a time to gather around the firelight and make tools. While huddled about their campfires, people may have used their spoken languages to plan hunting trips, share experiences, and pass on knowledge and beliefs.

Cave Art Some early humans lived in caves. The walls of their cave dwellings have scenes painted in red, yellow, and black colors. Cave dwellers mixed clay, minerals, and charcoal with animal fat to make their paints. The scenes they created show animals and sometimes hunters. Scientists think the paintings were made as part of ceremonies aimed at ensuring good hunting.

Evidence of Trade Many early peoples extended their resource base through trade with other groups. For example, some groups used obsidian (əb sid′ē ən), a black glass that could be worked easily into a number of useful tools. Obsidian occurs naturally in only a few places. Yet obsidian tools dating from the last Ice Age have been found hundreds of miles away from these places. From this fact, scientists have concluded that exchange occurred even among very early hunters and gatherers.

Huge, hairy mammoths were among the animals that Ice Age people hunted. Many mammoths had tusks 13 feet (4 meters) long.

129

When the ice sheets were at their largest, so much water was frozen that the level of the oceans dropped about 300 feet (92 meters). When it melted, the oceans returned to their present level. During the Ice Age, an estimated 30 percent of the land was covered with ice; today the figure is 10 percent.

Ice Age Populations and Movements

Compared to today, there were few people living on Earth as the end of the Ice Age approached. Groups were spread unevenly over Australia and the Americas as well as Africa, Europe, and Asia.

Hunters and gatherers usually lived in small bands. Sometimes a band became too large to live off the plants and animals in a particular area. At such times, a band divided. Some members remained in the area, while other members moved to new areas.

The amount of land needed by a group of hunters and gatherers depended on the plant and animal resources where it lived. A small area might be enough for a particular group if the wildlife there was densely concentrated. But in habitats where vegetation was spread out and animals were scarce, a much larger area would be needed by the same group.

Changing Lifestyles after the Ice Age

Scientists believe that the Ice Age glaciers retreated over many years, reaching their present locations about 11,000 years ago. The end of the Ice Age brought great changes in climate. These changes altered the nature of ecosystems in many parts of the world.

In much of the Northern Hemisphere, for instance, the climate grew warmer. Forests began to grow in places where cold during the Ice Age had prevented the growth of trees. Birds and smaller animals filled the forests. Many groups of hunters and gatherers created new technology to make use of the changed resources. They made bows and arrows for hunting swift forest animals. Canoes, nets, and traps helped them take fish from streams and lakes.

The technology of most early peoples did little to disturb the natural habitats in

Map Study *What part of Europe was almost entirely covered with glaciers during the Ice Age?*

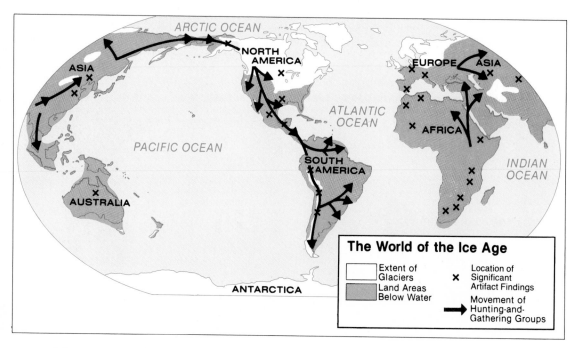

The World of the Ice Age

- ☐ Extent of Glaciers
- ▨ Land Areas Below Water
- ✕ Location of Significant Artifact Findings
- ➤ Movement of Hunting-and-Gathering Groups

Answer to Map Study question: the northern part

Texas Essential Elements 1A. Specialized fields of geography. 3A. Interrelationships of people and their environments. 3C. Agricultural base of regions. 3D. Uses, abuses, and preservation of natural resources and the physical environment. 4D. Major cultural, political, and economic activities within and among major world regions. 4E. Settlement patterns in terms of rural/urban location, structure, and function.

which they lived. One important exception was the burning of forests in some regions of the world. Scientists believe that the grasslands of North and South America, for example, developed after great forest fires burnt woodlands to the ground. Such fires may have been started by hunters seeking game.

In general, however, much of the imprint early peoples left on Earth is barely visible. The paintings on cave walls and the stone tools they left behind are among the signs that such people existed. As technologies advanced, people were able to make more lasting changes in the face of Earth.

REVIEWING THE FACTS

Define

1. hunters and gatherers
2. archaeologist

Answer

1. What evidence have archaeologists found in their study of early peoples?

2. What conclusions have they drawn from this evidence about how people lived?

3. Describe the technology, art, and trade of early peoples.

4. What factors influenced the size of groups of Ice Age people?

5. What imprint did the early humans leave on Earth's surface?

Locate

Refer to the map on page 130.

1. Which continents were partially covered or completely covered with ice during the Ice Age?

2. Along what route do scientists think early people moved from Asia to the Americas?

3 Fields and Cities

By working with stone, people in many parts of the world had found they could make better use of their environment than ever before. During the Ice Age, for example, people had invented simple tools to help them hunt and collect food. Gradually, additional ways to use tools were found. These changes in technology led to far-reaching changes in Earth's cultures.

From Collecting Food to Producing Food

After the Ice Age, people continued to work with stone to make hand tools. Some groups, however, adopted new methods to work with stone resources. In addition to making spears and other hunting weapons, they made pots, bowls, and other useful items by rubbing or grinding stones together. These objects became useful as people began to farm.

This ancient stone carving shows domesticated oxen pulling a cart.

Barley and millet seem to have been the first grains cultivated and eaten by human beings. Goats and sheep appear to have been the first domesticated animals, followed by pigs and dogs. Dogs were used for food as well as for hunting. Horses and camels were also used for food before they were used as a means of transportation.

ORIGINS OF DOMESTICATED PLANTS AND ANIMALS

Middle East and Central Asia

Apple	Grape	Camel
Barley	Millet	Cattle
Cabbage	Oats	Dog
Date	Olive	Goat
Fig	Onion	Horse
Flax	Peas	Sheep

South Asia

Cucumber
Lettuce
Millet
Cattle

North China

Apricot
Millet
Peach
Sorghum
Soybeans

Western Africa

Arrowroot
Oil palm
Rice
Yam

Eastern Africa

Coffee	Camel
Cotton	Donkey
Millet	
Sorghum	
Wheat	

Southeast Asia

Banana	Chicken
Coconut	Dog
Ginger and	Duck
other spices	Goose
Jute	Pig
Lemon	Water buffalo
Orange	
Tea	
Rice	
Sugarcane	

Middle America and South America

Avocado	Alpaca
Bean	Dog
Cacao	Guinea Pig
Corn	Llama
Plum	
Potato	
Squash	
Tomato	

The Beginnings of Farming Along with changes in toolmaking, people discovered new ways of handling animals and plants. While they still fished and hunted wild game, they now began keeping such animals as sheep, chickens, and pigs. These animals had become **domesticated**. A domesticated animal is one that depends on humans for protection and care. Domesticated animals do not find their own food and shelter in the wild. People have changed the animals' habits, so that these animals now look to humans to provide for them. People, in turn, depend on their domesticated animals for meat, skins, and milk.

Even more important than domesticated animals were domesticated plants. Rather than using only plants that grew wild, people also began to *raise* certain

132

plants. They probably started out by taking roots and replanting them in small garden plots. There, the plants could be protected from weeds and animals. In time, people developed domesticated crops that they could grow from seeds. These included grains like wheat, barley, rice, and corn.

Farming as a Way of Life Groups working with domesticated plants and animals gradually changed their economies from hunting and gathering to **agriculture**. Agriculture is the herding of animals and the farming of land. Groups that practiced agriculture produced much of their own food instead of collecting it from the physical environment.

Farming affected many aspects of people's cultures. For example, hunters and gatherers had moved from one area to another whenever their resources dwindled. But people who had crops to care for were likely to stay in a place for a long time. Many such groups built permanent dwellings in which they lived the year round. Their dwellings were usually built near one another in villages. Gardens and animal pens were kept nearby.

Early Farming in Southwest Asia

Farmers in different parts of the world lived in different environments. Therefore, they adopted varying practices. The chart on page 132 shows the varieties of plants and animals that were domesticated in different parts of the world. In addition, the map on page 135 shows where people first developed agriculture on their own.

Scientists have learned much about early agriculture from their study of sites in Southwest Asia. These sites, where the remains of very early farming peoples can be found, are located in the hills at the eastern end of the Mediterranean Sea and

THE SMALLEST DOMESTICATED ANIMAL

A full-grown silkworm is about three inches long. During its growing period, the silkworm eats day and night, feeding on mulberry leaves that the farmer provides every two or three hours. Then it enters a tiny wooden compartment provided by the farmer and spins a cocoon. The strands from the cocoons of several worms are connected to form one thread from which silk cloth is woven.

The Chinese first domesticated silkworms about 5,000 years ago. Chinese women cared for the silkworms and spun the silk. According to legend, it was an emperor's wife who first discovered silk.

in the region surrounding the Tigris and Euphrates rivers. By about 7,000 years ago, people living in this area, which stretched from what is now Turkey to present-day Iraq, had created permanent agricultural villages.

The villagers built houses of mud bricks, with stone fireplaces outside. Nearby they kept sheep and goats in low pens. They had many different tools made from stone and wood. Baskets and clay jars were used for storing food, especially grain. Grain could be kept for a long time without spoiling. The storing of grain helped the people keep a steady supply of food for everyone in the village.

133

SKILL WORKSHOP

Reading a Time Line

Time lines can help you understand the chronological relationship between events in the past. A time line shows when events took place and the order in which they happened.

The time line on this page reads from left to right. Find the markers that extend downward from this line. Notice the year for each marker.

Now look at the marker labeled B.C./A.D. This marker shows the approximate year of the birth of Jesus Christ. The letters B.C. stand for *before Christ*. The letters A.D. stand for the Latin words *anno domini*, which mean "in the year of the Lord." Events that occurred before the birth of Jesus are shown to the left of the B.C./A.D. marker. Events that took place after the birth of Jesus are shown to the right of the B.C./A.D. marker.

The lines that extend upward from the wide horizontal line show the years or dates of particular events. Notice that the letters B.C. are written *after* the numbers in a date. On the other hand, the letters A.D. are written *before* the numbers. When reading your textbook and other materials, you will find many years written in numbers only. When neither the letters B.C. nor A.D. appear with the numbers, the date is always an A.D. year.

The birth of Jesus was almost 2,000 years ago. About how long ago did the agricultural revolution begin? The time line shows 5000 B.C. as the approximate date for the first farming villages in Southwest Asia. If you add the almost 2,000 years since Jesus was born to 5,000 years, you find that these villages were formed about 7,000 years ago. By the same method, you can see that people began living in cities in the Tigris-Euphrates Valley about 5,000 years ago.

1. About how many years, from beginning to end, does the time line cover?

2. How many years separate one marker from the next on the time line?

3. Which year is earlier, 5000 B.C. or 4000 B.C.?

4. Which year is later, A.D. 1000 or 1492?

5. Were cities established in the Tigris-Euphrates Valley before or after the beginning of democracy in Greece?

6. About how many years ago was Rome founded?

7. In what year did Columbus sail to America? How many years ago was that?

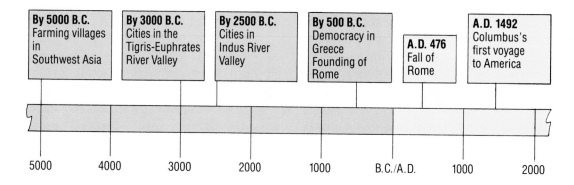

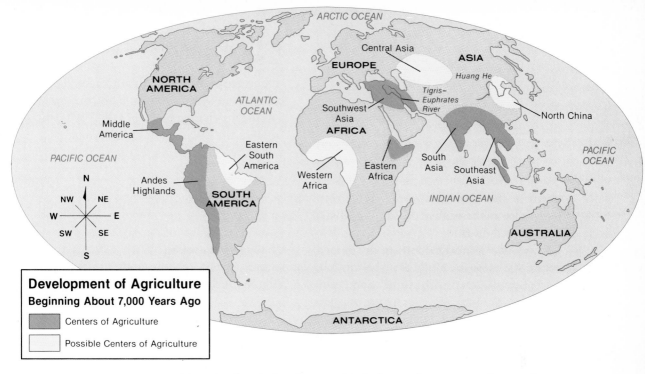

ARCTIC OCEAN

Central Asia
ASIA
EUROPE
Huang He
NORTH AMERICA
ATLANTIC OCEAN
Tigris–Euphrates River
North China
Middle America
Southwest Asia
AFRICA
PACIFIC OCEAN
Eastern South America
South Asia
PACIFIC OCEAN
Andes Highlands
SOUTH AMERICA
Western Africa
Eastern Africa
Southeast Asia
INDIAN OCEAN

N
NW NE
W E
SW SE
S

AUSTRALIA

ANTARCTICA

Development of Agriculture
Beginning About 7,000 Years Ago

Centers of Agriculture

Possible Centers of Agriculture

Map Study   *Why do you think the early centers of agriculture tended to be in the low and middle latitudes?*

Farming Cultures around the World

At various times, people in other parts of the world also began to farm. Every group of people who took up agriculture adopted it in its own way. How each group farmed depended on the culture's technology as well as the environment in its part of the world.

In North Africa   In the Nile River Valley of northern Africa, a farming culture began to develop thousands of years ago. The people settled close to the Nile River. Only along the river was there enough water to grow crops in the fertile soil.

Most of northern Africa, however, is very dry. Even today, farming is not possible in many parts of this region. In the dry areas of North Africa, therefore, other methods of surviving developed. Many people made use of domesticated animals instead of growing crops. These people kept herds of sheep and goats.

From their animals, North Africans produced food, clothing, and even shelter.

Herding required that people move often to graze their flocks. Therefore, the people of North Africa did not usually build permanent villages. Instead, they lived in tents that could be moved easily. These people were called **nomads.** Nomads are groups of people who wander from place to place and have no permanent dwellings.

As nomads traveled over dry grasslands, they used domesticated animals — donkeys, horses, or camels — to carry their tents and other belongings. Nomads also rode on the backs of these animals. Mounted nomads could cover greater distances than herders on foot. Riding camels and horses, nomads often helped to spread ideas and new technologies among more settled peoples.

In South Asia   About 5,000 years ago, a farming culture developed in what is now

Pakistan. This area is located along the Indus River in a dry valley. The plains in the Indus River Valley have fertile soils.

Once people learned how to bring water from the Indus river to their fields, population in the valley grew. Farming villages dotted about 1,000 miles (1,600 kilometers) of the valley floor. As in Southwest Asia, the people domesticated animals and planted a variety of crops. They also made many tools and utensils and carried on trade.

In East Asia Another culture developed in the Valley of the Huang He (hwäng hə), or Yellow River, in China. At about the time that the Indus River culture was beginning, people began to farm along the Huang He. There, conditions differed from those along the Indus. Rainfall was great at some times and scarce at others. This meant that the people had to deal with shortages of water as well as flooding. Under harsh conditions, they were able to grow crops of rice and millet.

In the Americas Archaeologists believe that people first came to America during the last Ice Age, perhaps 40,000 years ago. These people are believed to have crossed over a temporary land bridge joining Asia and Alaska in the Bering Strait. The people who came to America were hunters and gatherers. Over many years, they spread out through North and South America.

Early farming in this part of the world developed in several centers about 7,000 years ago. In what is now Mexico, early Indian farmers grew maize, or corn, and beans and squash. In the central Andes of South America, potatoes and small grains were the chief crops. Like other early farmers, American Indians settled in villages. During these years, however, most groups of people in the Americas lived mainly by hunting for food.

The Rise of Cities in Southwest Asia

The growth of agriculture affected cultures in many ways. Probably the most important change made possible by farming was the creation of cities. Archaeologists have learned a great deal about the growth of ancient cities and other cultural changes that took place among early farming groups in the Middle East and elsewhere.

Changes in Farming With a steady food supply to rely on, the population in the villages of the Southwest Asian hill country grew. Eventually, population exceeded available farmland, so farmers had to look elsewhere for land.

People searching for land spread onto the plains of the Tigris-Euphrates River Valley. The plains were level, and the soil was rich in nutrients. But the rains in the rivers' headwaters region were seasonal. During the spring months, the rivers flooded and overran the land. In summer, the sun baked the soil until it was dry and hard.

These conditions made it nearly impossible for the people to grow crops on the Tigris-Euphrates plains. Eventually, the farmers tried digging ditches to carry river water to thirsty plants during the dry season.

Irrigating the land on the plains made extensive farming possible. The people enlarged the small irrigation ditches into canals and built mud walls along the riverbanks to control flooding. Gardens became fields. Farmers used wooden plows pulled by oxen rather than hand hoes to turn and work the soil. At almost every harvest, farmers cut more barley and other grains than the villagers were able to use in a year's time. They were producing a **surplus,** or more than was required to meet their needs.

136

The map to the left is over 4,000 years old. Scribes in an ancient Sumerian city in the Tigris-Euphrates River Valley drew the map on a slab of wet clay. It shows the network of canals that the farmers of Sumer used to water their crops. The groups of wedge-shaped marks on the map show the region's ancient system of writing.

City Life Supported by large farming surpluses, the population in the Tigris-Euphrates River Valley grew larger. Some villages grew to the size of towns and cities. By the year 3000 B.C., there were a number of towns and cities near the Tigris and Euphrates rivers. These were among the first **urban** settlements in the world. *Urban* means "having to do with cities."

Because of large crop yields and grain surpluses, not everyone was needed to farm the fields. Many people worked full time in the cities. It is likely that the first full-time, nonfarming job was that of religious leader, or priest. In addition to leading worship, priests organized and oversaw the important work of building and maintaining irrigation systems. Priests supervised the large storehouses where grain surpluses were kept. They also devised a system for keeping records of how much went into the storehouses and how much was taken out.

From their methods of keeping records, the priests in the cities of the Tigris-Euphrates Valley developed a system of writing. They wrote on pieces of wet clay using sharpened reeds that made wedge-shaped marks. The priests also ran schools where some boys were taught how to read and write. These young men became **scribes.** The scribes made their living by writing letters and business contracts for merchants and other people in the urban centers.

The job of protecting the settlement was supervised and carried out by kings and warriors. Conflicts among the cities themselves sometimes broke out. At other times, invaders from the outside attacked and raided the cities.

Full-time merchants carried on trade with other places. They exchanged grain surpluses and other farm products for resources that were unavailable or scarce in the Tigris-Euphrates region.

There were also **artisans** in the cities. An artisan is a skilled worker who makes things by hand. In their workshops, artisans worked with wood, cloth, and leather. Like earlier peoples, they also used such metals as copper, gold, and silver. Urban artisans, however, increased the importance of metal as a resource. They mixed copper with tin to produce **bronze.** From bronze they could fashion weapons. They also crafted household items for wealthy families.

137

The Sumerians, who lived in the Tigris-Euphrates River Valley, made an important step in the development of writing when they used phonetization. This method of writing is similar to a rebus puzzle, in which words are expressed by pictures of objects whose names sound like the words or the syllables of which the words are composed.

SPOTLIGHT ON WRITING:

For the Record

Was one picture worth a thousand words to the priests of the cities of the Tigris-Euphrates River Valley? Probably not. But the priests did at first draw pictures to help them keep track of surplus grain in the temple storehouses. Working with a pointed stick and a piece of soft clay, a priest could draw a picture for each farmer who delivered grain to the temple. Beside each farmer's picture, he could draw pictures of baskets — one basket for every basket of grain the farmer brought.

Keeping picture records took a great amount of time, especially when harvests were large. To speed up their record keeping, the priests invented symbols to replace their drawings. One symbol stood for *five*, another for *six*, and so on.

As time went on, the priests invented many more symbols. They began to make symbols that stood for sounds, much as we use syllables that stand for certain sounds. With their symbols, the priests could put together words. They could use their system to send messages or tell about events in their cities.

Priests in both the Tigris-Euphrates region and in Egypt's Nile Valley were using symbols for writing by at least 5,000 years ago. Both writing systems had hundreds of symbols.

A group of people who worked in Egyptian mines did not like learning so many symbols in order to keep the records they needed. They invented a writing system of their own. Their system had only 22 symbols. Each symbol stood for a sound. They put the symbols together to form the words of their spoken language. They had created a kind of alphabet.

Nomads living near the Egyptian mines learned the workers' alphabet and introduced the idea to the Phoenician people. The Phoenicians were sea traders who traveled around the Mediterranean Sea. The Phoenicians made an alphabet of their own, from which other people of the Mediterranean world borrowed. The Greeks, for example, added a number of vowel sounds to their alphabet. The Romans in turn, borrowed from the Greeks to create an alphabet that fit their language. The English alphabet, used in many places today, is based on the Roman alphabet.

Symbols pressed into a clay tablet from the Tigris-Euphrates region (left) and painted hieroglyphics from Egypt (right) were two early systems of writing.

138

Cities around the World

Productive farming supported the growth of cities in a number of places outside the Middle East. These cities were built at different times in different parts of the world. In each place, cities took a shape of their own.

In North Africa As you have read, farming groups settled in the Nile River Valley to the southwest of the Tigris-Euphrates Valley. Farmers in this region learned to control the flooding of the Nile River. Over the years, irrigation systems were built. These systems made it possible for people to move into the dry lands at some distance from the river. On the fertile floodplain they began to produce large surpluses. Small villages grew into cities as farming could support more and more people. The Egyptians traded widely with other groups of people in their region of the world. Their merchants had ships equipped with sails to travel along the eastern coast of the Mediterranean Sea. These changes along the Nile, in what is known as Egypt, took place about the same time that cities developed in the Tigris-Euphrates region.

In South Asia Urban life developed early in the Indus River Valley. There, many villages and small cities were established as centers of learning and trade. The two largest cities, Mohenjo Daro (mō hen'jō da'rō) and Harappa (hə rap'ə), were most likely centers of government as well. Each was guarded by a large fortress. People in the two cities even built carefully planned streets and a drainage system to handle wastes and protect public health. The people also had a system of writing and produced many crafts.

In East Asia The first urban cultures in China probably began sometime after 2000 B.C. The people of the Huang He Valley built dikes and dredged the river

Thousands of years ago, Chinese civilization grew from thriving river-valley farms. Rice was the major crop of Chinese farmers. It was grown in the fertile soils on the floodplains of China's east-west flowing rivers.

bottom to prevent floods. Villages were built in the hills. The fertile lowland fields were irrigated so that rice could be grown there. From these beginnings, the Chinese established cities and a rich culture of their own. They developed a system of writing, building methods, government, and many inventions.

In the Americas Some farming groups in the Americas also developed urban cultures. The Olmec of Mexico built planned cities, which may have been religious centers. They also had a system of writing, a knowledge of mathematics, and a calendar. The Olmec cities disappeared around 200 B.C. South of Mexico, in what is now Guatemala, a new urban culture arose among the Maya in about 500 B.C. Like the cities of the Olmec, those of the Maya were centers for religion. About

139

The Olmec were the first people to tap rubber trees for sap. They were given their name by the Aztec, who came to them to get rubber. *Olmec* means "rubber people."

A.D. 1300, another group, the Aztec, created a large and advanced society in present-day Mexico. The Aztec built their capital city on an island in a lake. They grew grain and other farm crops on islands that they built in the lake around their capital. In South America, it was the Inca who created an urban culture. Their cities, high in the Andes, were connected by an elaborate system of roads.

In Africa South of the Sahara In the dense rain forests of Africa, farming surpluses were often difficult to produce. Farmers spent much of their time just keeping land cleared for farming. Therefore, cities did not develop in this region as early as in other parts of the world. The first large cities in Africa south of the Sahara were probably built in about A.D. 1000 to 1200. These cities were located in Mali, a kingdom in West Africa. Most of their wealth came from trade rather than agriculture. West Africa was a source of gold, ivory, dyed cloth, wood, and other valuable trade items. These were exchanged for goods from Europe, the Middle East, and parts of Asia. In addition to Mali, kingdoms elsewhere in West Africa and in East Africa grew wealthy from this trade.

The Achievements of Ancient Cultures

Most scientists believe that human beings have lived on Earth for several million years. Considering this span of time, the years following the last Ice Age were a brief period. Yet during this period, ancient cultures made remarkable leaps. Most of the plants and animals on which people today depend were first domesticated during those years. Early peoples used these plants and animals in their wild form to support their ways of living. For example, ancient peoples wove cloth from the hair of goats, sheep, and alpacas. From the silkworm, they took threads to make silk. From plant fibers, they wove cotton and linen fabrics.

Ancient builders made homes, temples, and palaces from brick, stone, wood, and reeds. Inventors in some parts of the world made paper and glass. People in the Middle East and elsewhere transported

Egyptians who lived almost 4,000 years ago built wooden boats like this model. Before sails were invented, oars propelled boats up and down the Nile. Later, Egyptian boats used sails.

140

Iron makes up about 5 percent of Earth's crust. It is found in nearly every country in the world and is so common that today people take it for granted. As late as colonial times, however, such things as iron nails and hoes were scarce and precious.

goods in wheeled carts pulled by domesticated animals. For river travel, merchants used wooden boats powered by men pulling on oars. The ancient invention of the sail captured winds to power boats on the seas.

One of the greatest achievements of ancient peoples was the discovery of how to use iron. Around 1500 B.C., warriors mounted on horseback and using iron weapons invaded the cities of Southwest Asia. They brought with them the knowledge of ironworking.

Iron soon became an important metal in the cities of Southwest Asia. It was more widely available and thus cheaper than bronze and other metals. Artisans found that they could make many ordinary objects from iron. Common people as well as the wealthy and powerful could at last afford these items. Ironworking also meant that kings and warriors had more weapons and could arm more soldiers.

Early accomplishments also extended into areas other than technology. In ancient Greece, people pioneered new forms of government. In some Greek cities, the citizens themselves — rather than the most powerful leaders — exercised authority. In these cities, citizens met in open meetings to vote on public matters.

In Rome, the people developed a complex system of written laws. Rome spread these laws over a large area. The parts of the world that fell under Roman control included much of North Africa, Southwest Asia, and Europe. These areas were conquered by Roman armies. Officials appointed by the rulers, who governed from the city of Rome, controlled the conquered areas. The Roman Empire lasted for hundreds of years.

Early cultures had their own forms of art and music. Works of literature and philosophy from the Chinese, East Indians, Greeks, and Romans are still read today. The chief religions of the modern world — Buddhism, Christianity, Hinduism, Islam, and Judaism — grew from the teachings of religious leaders who lived in ancient times.

The imprint of early farming peoples was more visible and longer lasting than that of hunters and gatherers. As ancient cultures grew, many forest and grassland areas were cleared for farms and cities. Roads, bridges, and canals became features of the landscape in many parts of the world. People were learning to control and change their environment in many ways.

REVIEWING THE FACTS

Define

1. domesticate
2. agriculture
3. nomad
4. urban
5. artisan
6. bronze
7. scribe

Answer

1. How does farming differ from hunting and gathering?

2. In what parts of the world did farming cultures first develop?

3. (a) What factors led to the building of ancient cities? (b) Where were cities built in the ancient world?

4. List some achievements of ancient urban cultures.

Locate

Refer to the map on page 142.

1. Name the present-day country in which the ancient city of Rome was located.

2. What sea was surrounded by the Roman Empire?

141

Texas Essential Elements 3B. Economic importance of water, energy sources, and other productive resources to regions. 3D. Uses, abuses, and preservation of natural resources and the physical environment. 4C. Population distribution, growth, and movements. 4D. Major cultural, political, and economic activities within and among major world regions. 4F. Geographic influences on various issues.

4 An Age of Trade and Expansion

For the most part, the cultures of the ancient world were cut off from one another. For example, the peoples of East Asia were separated by mountains, deserts, and seas from those of South and Southwest Asia. Deserts and rain forests surrounded many African culture centers. The early cultures of the Americas were separated from those elsewhere by two great oceans.

Early Trade

In the ancient world, people had not yet created the transportation and communications systems that would bring people of distant places into frequent contact with one another. Under these conditions, ancient cultures were nearly self-sufficient. Each had its own economy, government, and way of life. Contact with outside cultures was limited.

What trade did occur was carried out under difficult conditions. Because of poor roads and a lack of knowledge about navigation, travel was slow and dangerous. Weather, thieves, and wars often disrupted even short journeys.

Groups of people in some parts of the world braved these conditions so that they could trade with distant peoples. Nomads from central Asia and northern Africa, for instance, visited cities in Southwest Asia from time to time. They traded horses, metals, and fabrics for jewelry and weapons made by urban artisans. Eventually, trade became common in some regions. Traders leading caravans of pack animals made trips along well-traveled routes connecting Southwest Asia and parts of Africa, India, and China.

Before the 1400's, cultures changed slowly. Although there was trade among

Map Study *Name seven major bodies of water that bordered or flowed through the Roman Empire at its height.*

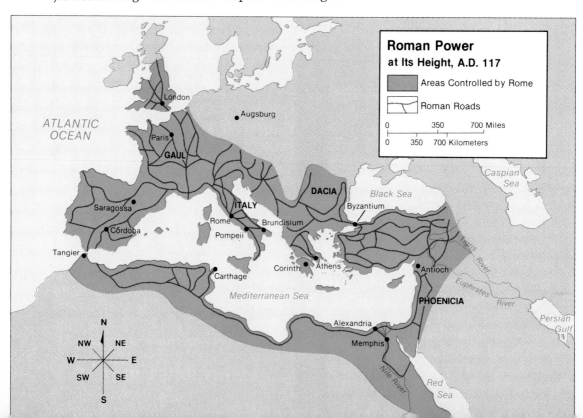

Assign the Workbook activity for Chapter 5,
Section 4, with pages 142–148.
Remind students that not only products but ideas
were exchanged when trade expanded.

countries, there was little direct contact among peoples. At one time, for example, the Romans traded with the Chinese for their silk. That trade, however, was indirect. Few Romans had any personal contact with the Chinese.

New Interest in Trade in Europe

One of the regions controlled by the Romans was Western Europe. By A.D. 476 Rome lost its power in this part of the world. Wars and conflicts followed the disappearance of Roman laws and armies. For more than five centuries, warriors and would-be rulers fought one another for power. The common people were left with little protection. Trade declined, and many people left the cities and returned to farming.

By the 1100's, a number of areas had been brought under the control of kings. Wars became less frequent. With longer periods of peace, people could travel more safely. Trade slowly revived. At first, merchants traveled only among nearby places. Gradually they journeyed farther and farther. As trade expanded, many people returned to the cities. There, they worked at jobs created by the rebirth of trade.

With these developments, Europe was about to enter a period of far-reaching and rapid change. Many people now had money with which to buy new goods. People became curious about the new places merchants told them about.

During the 1200's, Marco Polo, an Italian traveler and merchant, made a long overland trip from Europe to eastern Asia. After Marco Polo returned to Europe, the story of what he had seen in China was published in a book. Marco Polo had a great deal to tell Europeans about Chinese culture. He described ship canals, wide, tree-lined roadways, and

As trade revived in European cities at the end of the Middle Ages (top), merchants sought such goods as silk from China (bottom).

a communications system made up of messengers on horseback. He also told of gunpowder, paper, and magnetic compasses — all Chinese inventions unknown to Europeans at the time. He explained too how the Chinese burned "black stone," or coal, to warm their homes and bathwater. Europeans of Marco Polo's day burned only wood or charcoal as heating fuel.

Marco Polo, the first European to cross all of Asia, lived from about 1254 to 1324. His account of his trip to China, called *The Book of Marco Polo*, is probably the greatest travel book of all time.
Answer to Map Study question: Atlantic Ocean, Mediterranean Sea, Red Sea, Nile River, Black Sea, Tigris River, Euphrates River

In 1456, a German named Johannes Gutenberg invented a faster, less costly way of printing books than any that had been used before. As a result, books became much less expensive to buy, and larger numbers of people could afford them. For the first time, people without great wealth could afford books. Through reading, they could learn about distant places.

Many people in Europe read or heard about the new and wonderful things Marco Polo had seen. Not everyone believed what he reported. Yet his report marked the beginning of a new and strong European interest in trade with Asia. Over the next several centuries, the exchange of goods between European and Asian traders grew steadily.

European merchants generally traveled only as far as the Southwest Asian marketplaces on the eastern shores of the Mediterranean Sea. They carried wool, cloth, and other products to these markets. From these markets, they returned to Europe with spices, linens, sugar, and silk. These goods had come to Southwest Asia from China, India, and Southeast Asia. European merchants also obtained gold and ivory from Africa at the Mediterranean trading centers.

New Routes for Trade

Merchants and business leaders who handled Europe's trade with the places in Southwest Asia became very wealthy. Most of these people lived in port cities of Italy. Other Europeans, including the kings of European countries, wanted to share in the trade with Southwest Asia. But Italian merchants convinced their trading partners in Southwest Asia not to

deal with any other Europeans. Therefore, some countries of western Europe sought to buy Asian goods directly from Asia. They hoped to accomplish this by sailing all the way to India, Southeast Asia, and China by ocean ship.

Portugal's Voyages to Asia To make such a long trip, Europeans had to improve their ships and their knowledge of navigation. Prince Henry of Portugal led the way. He brought together mathematicians, geographers, and sea captains. These experts worked out charts that enabled sailors to find their latitude in open seas. The Portuguese also used earlier inventions — such as the magnetic compass, the astrolabe, and the quadrant — as navigation aids. The astrolabe and quadrant were devices that made it possible for sailors to find their location in relationship to the stars and the sun. The Portuguese were the first to design and build large, heavy vessels with more than one mast and several sails.

By A.D. 1500, sailors from Portugal had reached Asia. They had traveled all the way around the continent of Africa and across the Indian Ocean. As they had hoped, they soon established a rich trade with Asia.

Spain's Colonies in the Americas In an effort to match Portugal's successes, sailors from Spain landed in the Americas

144

in 1492. Christopher Columbus, who led the first Spanish voyage to reach America, had hoped to find East Asia by sailing west from Europe. Like other Europeans of that time, he had no knowledge that two continents, North and South America, stood in his path.

The Spaniards were at first disappointed that they had failed to reach Asia. Before many years passed, however, they found that the Americas, too, offered riches. In the Aztec cities of Mexico and the cities of the Inca in Peru there was a treasure of gold. There were also farm products as well as copper and other metals for mining.

The Europeans called the Aztec, Inca, and other inhabitants of the Americas **Indians**. This was what Columbus had called the first people he met after sailing to America. He chose this name under the mistaken belief that he had reached the East Indies.

During the 1500's and 1600's, the Spanish set up **colonies** in South America and the southern and western parts of North America, including nearly all of Middle America. A colony is a territory, settlement, or country governed by another country. Many Spanish people went to the Americas. The first were adventurers who sought to get rich from the gold and silver resources there. Spanish priests also made the journey. They did so to teach their Christian religion to the American Indians. Later, Spanish colonists left Europe to start new homes, farms, ranches, and mines in America. Indians did much of the work in Spain's early colonies.

Europeans Explore the World Other European countries joined in the Age of Exploration. The Netherlands became a successful trading country soon after Portugal had done so. Dutch traders set

In ships such as these, Columbus's crew sought Asia but discovered America.

out across the seas in the late 1500's. Like the Portuguese, the Dutch set up trading posts in various parts of the world.

By the early 1600's, the English also had foreign trading posts. Many were along the coasts of India. Farmers in India grew cotton, which villagers wove into fine cloth. English trading ships carried these beautiful, handcrafted cotton fabrics back to Europe for sale.

In addition, the Dutch and the English established colonies in North America and on several Caribbean islands. These colonies supplied the Netherlands and England with fish, timber, sugar, tobacco, molasses, and other goods.

Europeans also established trading posts in Southeast Asia. They gained access to coastal trading ports in China. The Chinese government, however, strictly controlled the amount of goods that Europeans took out of China.

145

MAP WORKSHOP

Reading a Map of Culture Regions

Geographers use regions as tools to study both people and their physical environment. A region is a place that is different in some way from the places around it. That difference can be anything that sets a region apart. A region can be a section of a country, like the Atlantic Coast or the Southwest. A region can also be set apart by the goods it produces, such as a wheat-growing region or an oil-producing region.

When geographers talk about how people live, they often talk about culture regions. (See page 126.) Culture regions are sometimes hard to define. Just as there is no clearly marked line where a desert region stops and a grassland region begins, there is no clearly marked line between two culture regions. North Africa is a good example. It has strong cultural ties both to Africa and to Southwest Asia, which is also known as the Middle East.

Some geographers regard North Africa as part of the Middle East. Others view it as part of Africa.

The map below shows one way of organizing the world into culture regions. Study the map and then answer the questions that follow.

1. (a) How many culture regions does the map show? (b) How many culture regions does the map show in the Western Hemisphere?

2. To what culture region does North Africa belong on this map?

3. To what culture region does each of the following countries belong? Use the map on pages 486–487 to help you. (a) India (b) China (c) Japan (d) France (e) Brazil (f) Canada (g) Saudi Arabia (h) Australia (i) Ghana

For a special challenge How does the map of the Roman Empire on page 142 help explain why England, France, Spain, Portugal, Italy, and Greece are part of the culture region known as Western Europe?

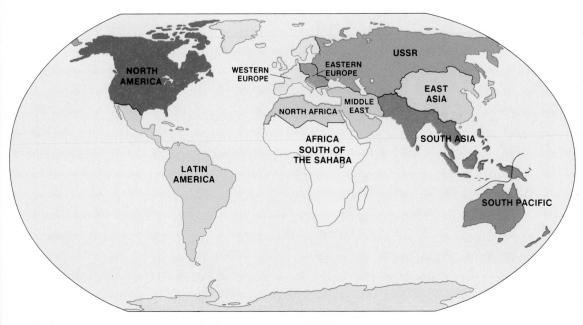

The Impact of Europe's Expansion

Europe's expansion across the seas brought Europeans into contact with peoples and cultures around the world. These contacts affected nearly every society in the world. Even among some agricultural and hunting-and-gathering societies, cultural patterns changed because of ideas introduced by Europeans. This was true especially in the Americas.

When the Aztec and Inca were conquered by Spanish guns, part of their culture was destroyed too. Many Aztec and Inca Indians adopted the religion of the Spanish — Christianity. The Spanish forced the Indians to adopt economies based on Spanish agriculture.

Spanish colonists also forced Indians to work in gold and silver mines and on farms. When Indians no longer supplied enough labor, the Spanish brought in Africans to serve as laborers. These Africans were enslaved. That is, they could be bought and sold and were bound to work for their owners. Other European colonists, including the English in North America and the Portuguese in Brazil, also used Africans as slaves. During the 1600's and 1700's, millions of people from the west coast of Africa were forced to come to the Americas to work on plantations and in mines.

Europeans started large sugar plantations on the islands of the Caribbean. Europeans found they could make more money by producing their own sugar in the Caribbean islands than by trading for it in Southeast Asia.

Europe's sea trade introduced American food crops to many parts of the world. Farmers in China, Africa, and southeastern Europe began to grow corn brought from the Americas. The Chinese also found that they could grow American sweet potatoes on lands that previously had gone unused. Potatoes from the Andes Mountains of South America became an important crop in Europe.

In some areas, contact with Europeans caused widespread disease. Without knowing it, Europeans were carrying diseases from their part of the world to new places. The Europeans themselves were immune to these diseases. But those who were not immune died by the millions. Diseases carried by Europeans were especially harmful to American Indians and people living in Pacific islands.

Today potatoes are an important crop in southwestern France and other parts of Europe. Potato farming began in South America.

Europe itself was changed in many ways by the Age of Exploration. Europeans came into direct contact with the many cultures and technologies of the world. The people of Europe borrowed ideas freely from other cultures. These borrowed ideas helped Europeans make new inventions and improve their own technologies.

The character of a people's culture has never been limited to their immediate geographical boundaries. New ideas have always spread from one location to another. This spreading of ideas occurred even during the last Ice Age. However, with the growth of overseas trade and colonization, ideas spread much more quickly than ever before. As the exchange of inventions and ways of life accelerated, so did the rate at which people were changing the face of Earth.

REVIEWING THE FACTS

Define

1. colonies
2. Indians

Answer

1. (a) Why was there little steady trade in the ancient world? (b) What factors led Europeans to trade during the Age of Exploration?

2. Describe the part played by each of the following countries in trade and colonization during the Age of Exploration: Portugal, the Netherlands, England.

3. What were some effects of Europe's trade on the world's cultures?

Locate

Refer to the map on page 142.

1. (a) What city, controlled by Rome, was located farthest east? (b) Farthest north?

2. List the Mediterranean ports under Rome's control.

5 The Industrial Revolution

Changes of many kinds took place within Europe during the Age of Exploration. Europeans gained immense wealth and wide knowledge about the world. They learned how to make use of a wide variety of inventions. And they acquired an interest in obtaining new goods and improving their own ways of making goods.

Population Changes

The Age of Exploration caused important shifts in population patterns in Europe. Many Europeans, for example, left their home countries to live in overseas colonies. In newly settled colonial areas, there was great opportunity for individuals to own farms or to set up businesses.

Despite the movement of people to colonies, the population of European countries grew rapidly during the Age of Exploration. Improvements in farming helped spur this growth. Better tools and methods for tilling the soil came into widespread use. Farmers could produce more food than in the past. The use of clover, for example, improved the fertility of the soil. Turnips provided food for livestock. Potatoes gave many people more nourishing diets.

Industrial Growth in England

Besides causing population growth, improvements in farming made it possible for Europeans to take up new kinds of work. In many parts of Europe, better roads and other means of transportation were built. In England, better transportation combined with riches from many colonies, gains in farming, and a series of

Before the Industrial Revolution, less than 10 percent of the people in Europe lived in cities. Today the figure for England is about 80 percent; France, 75 percent; Poland, 60 percent. *Answers are in the Teacher's Guide.*
Assign the Workbook activity for Chapter 5, Section 5, with pages 148–151.

This steam engine, designed by the English inventor James Watt, was used to pump water from coal mines.

inventions helped create the world's first industrial power.

In the 1600's and 1700's, changes and improvements in English agriculture reduced the number of people needed to work on farms. A great many displaced farmers moved to towns. This movement led to an increase in the number of people available for work in manufacturing.

At the same time, many business people, some of whom had made fortunes in overseas trade, had obtained enough money to pay for the building of factories. Money used to start or expand a business is called **capital.** The iron and coal needed for making and running machinery were also available in England. These conditions marked the beginnings of the **Industrial Revolution.** The Industrial Revolution was the change from manufacturing goods by hand to producing goods by power-driven machine. The Industrial Revolution was well under way in England by the middle 1700's.

In the early years of the Industrial Revolution, English inventors discovered a new way to make iron. They used coal-burning furnaces, called smelting furnaces, to produce iron from iron ore. With this technology, English industries eventually were able to make **steel.** Steel is a hard metal made from iron and carbon. It became the most important material in the production of machine parts. Machines made of steel eventually replaced the older wooden machines in English factories.

During the same years, other English inventors experimented with steam engines. These machines proved to be as important as the new ironworking technology. In 1769, James Watt introduced an engine, fueled by coal, that could produce steam pressure. Within only a few years, engines built according to Watt's design were running machines in factories and mines throughout England. Eventually, steam engines also powered locomotives and ships.

England's production of manufactured goods soared. Growing populations in Europe and the development of overseas trade provided markets for these goods. English goods were inexpensive compared to handmade goods. People throughout the world could afford to buy what English factories produced. The large world market helped bring great wealth to English factory owners. It also encouraged them to find ways to produce more and more goods and to create ever-newer products.

Many inventions required more horsepower than horses or waterwheels could provide. James Watt's steam engine provided a cheap, efficient source of power.

The Spread of Industrialization

Other countries were quick to borrow ideas for industrial production from England. The United States, which declared its independence from England shortly after the Industrial Revolution began, was one of the first. Almost all the countries in western Europe started to industrialize too. By 1900, the economies of England, the United States, and the countries of western Europe were no longer based on handmade goods and farming. They had become industrial economies. In them, agriculture was still necessary and important. But the largest amount of wealth in these countries came from goods produced in factories rather than on farms.

A New Colonization Period England, the United States, and western European countries built their industries throughout the 1800's. During those years, many European countries took a new interest in overseas colonies. Colonies could provide raw materials and large markets for factory products. Colonies could also give Europeans an opportunity to spread their own culture among other peoples of the world.

Large parts of the world came under the control of European countries. In Africa, Europeans pushed inland from their coastal trading posts. A number of European countries set up colonies. Eventually, they took control of almost the entire continent. In India, the English used force to gain control of farms, villages, and cities. Most of Southeast Asia was also colonized by European powers.

China did not become a European colony. Its government, however, lost control of its trade with European countries. In the 1800's, the British forced the Chinese to end restrictions on trade. Many industrial countries were then able to trade factory-made goods for Chinese pottery, tea, and silk.

Industrialization in Asia People in Japan saw that industrialization was changing the world. Japan's leaders feared that Japan might become a colony like other countries in Asia. They decided, therefore, that Japan must develop industries of its own. Even though it started at least 50 years later than Europe and the United States, Japan too was an industrialized country by 1900. It claimed Asian colonies of its own. These colonies provided Japan with raw materials needed for its industries.

The Asian country of Siam, today's Thailand, also started to industrialize during the late 1800's and early 1900's. In so doing, Siam, like Japan, avoided becoming the colony of another industrialized country.

The Impact of the Industrial Revolution

Unlike previous cultural changes, the effects of the Industrial Revolution were felt almost immediately throughout the entire world. Never before had the pace of change been so quick. Discoveries and inventions changed the ways of making things several times during a single person's lifetime. New inventions and industries built on themselves. For example, the use of electricity led to a whole new industry in copper for wire fittings. The introduction of the automobile promoted growth and change in petroleum and rubber industries.

On the darker side, people in industrialized countries experienced air pollution from the burning of coal in factories. As workers crowded into urban areas, unhealthful slums became widespread in many cities.

150

During the late 1800's, British companies mined diamonds in southern Africa.

Even cultures that did not industrialize felt the sudden impact of industrialization. Before the Industrial Revolution, village handweavers in India had no equals in the production of cotton cloth. Cotton cloth from English factories, however, put the Indian weavers out of business. Even in India itself, English cloth sold for lower prices than the handmade cottons. After the Industrial Revolution, India grew and supplied raw cotton for English factories. It no longer made great quantities of finished cloth.

Similar economic changes troubled other countries too. Chinese handmade porcelain, or chinaware, lost its value after the English copied it and began producing it in factories. Artisans in many other parts of the world also lost their markets to factory goods.

Industries require enormous quantities of resources and raw materials. Industrializing countries used up their mineral and soil resources at rapid rates. For example, some of the iron and coal fields that were opened in the Americas and Europe during the early years of industrialization are already exhausted.

During the 1800's and early 1900's, Europeans also drew heavily on the natural resources of their colonies. They shipped these resources to their home factories. Finished products were sold to the people living in the colonies. Under this system, colonial peoples rarely developed their own industries. Many African, Asian, and Latin American countries, therefore, have very little industry of their own even today.

The Industrial Revolution left a deeper imprint on Earth than earlier cultural changes. Human inventiveness had given people tremendous power to control and transform their physical surroundings. Resources were drawn from the environment in vast quantities and turned into a countless variety of goods. In many urban areas, the natural environment was greatly changed. More than ever before, human life was shaped by conditions that people had created themselves.

REVIEWING THE FACTS

Define

1. capital
2. Industrial Revolution
3. steel

Answer

1. (a) What changes in Europe made the Industrial Revolution possible? (b) Why was England the first country to develop large-scale industry?

2. What countries besides England rapidly adopted industry?

3. In what parts of the world did industrial countries establish colonies?

Locate

Refer to the map on page 498.

1. Name the African countries that are crossed by the equator.

2. Which African countries lie all or partly in the middle latitudes?

151

GEOGRAPHY LABORATORY

Highlighting the Chapter

1. Culture is the way of life followed by a people who share many things in common. The study of a people's culture reveals how they have chosen to use their physical environment to ensure their survival.

Although cultures around the world may differ widely, all have common elements. Every culture has a language, customs, beliefs, a government, and an economic system. Every culture also has technology, through which it develops its resources. One way of looking at the history of human culture is to trace the different levels of technology through which it has passed.

2. After the last Ice Age, people lived in groups that hunted wild animals and gathered wild plants for food. These people fashioned tools and weapons from stone, wood, and bone. They learned how to control fire. By the end of the Ice Age, hunting-and-gathering groups lived in nearly every part of the world.

3. Over many years, some groups of hunters and gatherers discovered how to control wild animals and plants. Domestication of plants and animals led to the development of farming cultures. Settled agricultural villages were established. In a number of places, farming produced food surpluses that supported urban settlements. These cities became centers of religion, craft making, and government. Artisans working there learned how to make objects from bronze and, eventually, iron.

4. The expansion of trade among peoples of Europe preceded the Industrial Revolution. Encouraged by trading opportunities, Europeans developed transportation systems, sources of power, machines, and new methods of producing goods. The trading and colonizing activities of industrialized countries helped bring countries in every part of the world in touch with one another.

Speaking Geographically

Number from 1 to 10 on a sheet of paper. Then use each of the following terms in a sentence to show that you know its meaning.

1. artisan
2. culture
3. culture region
4. economic system
5. habitat
6. nomad
7. technology
8. urban
9. bronze
10. agriculture

Testing Yourself

A. On a sheet of paper, arrange the events below in the order in which they occurred.

1. The discovery of ironworking

2. The domestication of animals and plants

3. The Industrial Revolution

4. Portugal's trading posts in Asia

5. European colonies in America

6. The rise of early cities

7. The use of simple stone tools

8. The industrialization of Japan

9. The fall of Rome

10. Columbus's discovery of America

B. Match each event in Column A with the event it caused in Column B.

Column A
1. The development of irrigation

2. Spain's search for trade routes to Asia

3. The keeping of records concerning crop harvests

4. The production of food surpluses

5. The invention of the steam engine

152

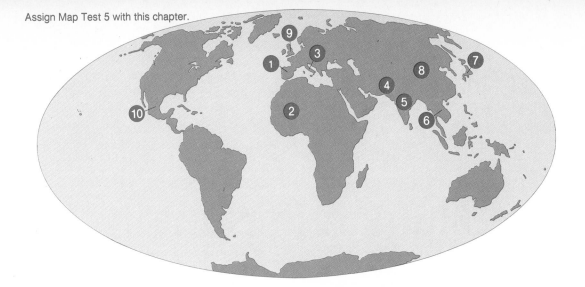

GEOGRAPHY LABORATORY

Column B

a. The development of writing

b. The farming of dry regions

c. Increased factory production

d. The discovery of America

e. The rise of early cities

Building Map Skills

Number your paper from 1 to 10. Write the name of each country listed below next to the number that identifies it on the map on this page.

China   Mali
United Kingdom   Mexico
India   Pakistan
Italy   Spain
Japan   Thailand

Applying Map Skills

Using maps in your textbook, find the following information about the rivers listed below: In which direction does each river flow? Through which countries does each river pass? Into what body of water does each river empty?

1. Tigris-
  Euphrates
2. Nile
3. Indus
4. Huang He

Exploring Further

1. Choose an island country in the tropics. Research the island's climate, population, economic system, and technology. Then write a report answering the following questions: If you moved to this island, how would your life be affected? What do you have now that might be useless in your new home? What new possessions might be useful? What differences between your present culture and the island's culture might you expect?

2. Trade has been important for thousands of years. How is trade important to the United States today? Using an encyclopedia, make a list of the goods that the United States obtains through trade. In addition, list the goods that the United States sells to other countries. What countries are the major trading partners of the United States today?

3. The Industrial Revolution would not have been possible without great changes in transportation. Even in recent years, the Transportation Revolution has continued. Report to the class on the changes in transportation in the United States between 1800 and 1970. Include information on how people traveled within towns, from town to town, and from country to country. Also tell how most goods were shipped.

153

CHAPTER

6

The Human Imprint in the Modern World

If you look to the ground from an airplane, you see not only airports but also highways, railroads, and harbors. All are used in the transportation of goods and passengers. You can see television and microwave antennas that provide almost instant communication across long distances. You can also see cities that spread beneath you for miles. Giant skyscrapers rise from the central parts of these cities into the air.

Even in less densely settled regions, the human imprint is visible. On the lower slopes of tall mountains, you may see bands of land that appear bare. In these places, foresters have planted young seedlings to replace older trees that have been removed with the help of powerful machines. Across arid lands, you may see rows of domesticated crops growing in irrigated fields claimed from the surrounding desert. Giant platforms and derricks stand along coastlines in many parts of the world. There, workers take oil from the ocean floor. All these scenes have their roots in the Industrial Revolution.

In this chapter, you will look more closely at the impact of industrial technology. In learning about Earth's cultures, you will consider how people today are governed, how countries develop their resources, and how countries work with one another.

154

The photograph is an aerial view of Atlanta, Georgia.

1 Population and Settlement

Toward the end of the Ice Age, the population of the world was no greater than 10 million. Today more than 15 million people live in the New York City area alone. New York is one of about 30 urban centers in the United States with more than 1 million residents. The United States is not the only country with such large cities. London in the United Kingdom, Tokyo in Japan, Mexico City in Mexico, and a number of other cities around the world have populations of 10 million or more. Today's large urban centers demonstrate the tremendous growth that has taken place in the world's population.

Growing Numbers of People

The population of the world is far greater today than ever before. Population has not expanded at a steady rate, however. For example, in A.D. 476—when Roman control over Europe and the Mediterranean region ended—there were about 200 million people on Earth. By the year 1700, over 12 centuries later, Earth's population had increased 3 times, to about 600 million. Yet, since the start of the Industrial Revolution—less than 3 centuries ago—the world's population has grown about 9 times. Today, there are over 5 billion people in the world, an increase of over 4.4 billion since 1700.

In some parts of the world, population is still growing rapidly. The recent increase in population has been so great that many geographers call it the population explosion. Some of the reasons for this burst of growth can be found in the changing technology of the industrial age.

HOW MUCH IS A BILLION?

You are offered a billion dollars—but on one condition: Before the money is yours, you must first count it—at the rate of 1 dollar a second for 8 hours a day. Will you accept this offer?

Figure it out. It will take 95 years to count it at this rate. You will be more than 100 years old before the billion dollars is yours!

Medical Advances The Industrial Revolution brought a revolution in science and medicine. Improved medical care has caused **death rates** to decline. The death rate is the yearly number of deaths for every 1,000 people. Sicknesses such as smallpox, scarlet fever, and cholera (ko'lər ə) once killed millions of people every year. Newly developed vaccines and medicines have cut down on these and other illnesses, increasing the number of years that most people live. As a result, populations around the world have grown. This growth has come despite wars and **famines** (severe food shortages), which have taken the lives of many people in some countries.

In many countries of the world, the **infant death rate** has declined dramatically. The infant death rate is the number of infants out of every 1,000 born each year who die before their first birthday. The **birth rate** is the number of live births each

Have students define the word *population. (the number of people living in a given place)* Urban refers to cities. An urban center includes both the city and its surrounding suburbs.
Students can get an idea of how large Earth's present population is by considering this fact: Almost 10 percent of all humans who ever lived are now living.

155

year for every 1,000 people. Even if the birth rate is high, population will not increase rapidly when the infant death rate is also high. A high birth rate combined with a low infant death rate, on the other hand, means that most children will live to adulthood. Where this is the case, population grows rapidly.

Improved Public Health Throughout history, impure water, improper treatment of wastes, and insects and rodents have spread diseases. During the 1300's, for instance, an outbreak of a disease known as the plague killed over one third of the people in Europe and Asia within 20 years. Modern water-treatment and waste-removal systems have reduced some of the threat of disease. Better

Health workers in Peru give children shots to prevent various illnesses. Disease control often results in longer life expectancy.

knowledge about sanitation has led to a decline in diseases spread by animals.

Increased Food Supplies The Industrial Revolution also led to improvements in diet. During the 1800's and 1900's, the use of power machines on farms enabled farmers to produce more food than ever before. The packaging of food in airtight containers and the use of refrigeration made it possible to store much of that food and ship it long distances. These changes have provided people with more reliable and varied food supplies. Better food supplies have meant, in turn, more healthy, longer-living people.

The effect of improved medicine, better public health practices, and increased amounts of food has been to lengthen **life expectancy.** Life expectancy is the number of years scientists expect the average person born in a given year to live. In most parts of the world, people born today have a longer life expectancy than people born at any previous time.

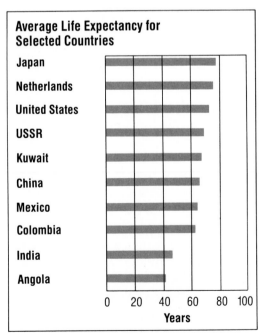

Average Life Expectancy for Selected Countries

Country	Years
Japan	
Netherlands	
United States	
USSR	
Kuwait	
China	
Mexico	
Colombia	
India	
Angola	

Source: World Development Report

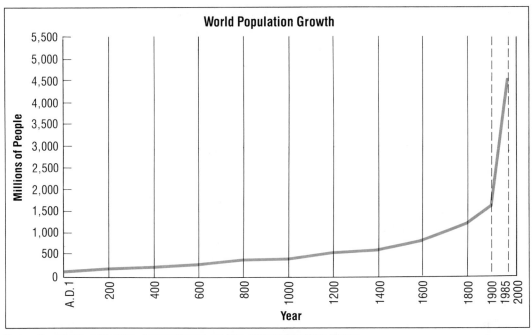

World Population Growth

Source: Compiled from World Development Report and Atlas of World Population History

Keeping Track of Population

Information about a country's population can help a country's leaders plan for the future. Nearly every modern country, therefore, has created a system for counting its residents. In counting population, the leaders try to learn far more than just how many people live in the country. They want to know about changes in the size of the population. They try to learn how many births and deaths there are each year, what kinds of jobs people have, how many people live in cities, and so on.

Countries often use the birth rate and death rate to help them keep track of changes in their populations. The difference between the birth rate and death rate is the rate at which population increases or decreases. The greater the amount by which a country's birth rate exceeds its death rate, the greater that country's rate of population growth will be. The birth rate in Mexico, for example, is 31, while the death rate is just 7. The population of Mexico is, therefore, increasing rapidly.

In the United States, on the other hand, the birth rate is 16 and the death rate is 9. The country's population is growing, but not as quickly as Mexico's.

A country that has about the same number of births and deaths each year has zero population growth. This means that its population remains about the same size from year to year. A number of countries — such as Austria, Belgium, and West Germany — have near zero population growth.

Migration

People sometimes move from one country to another or from one region within a country to another. This movement is called **migration**. The reasons for migration vary. As you learned in Chapter 5, people migrated to North America from Asia about 40,000 years ago. These people probably sought better hunting grounds. Another large movement of people occurred during the 1600's and 1700's. In these years, Europeans were

157

Brasília, the capital of Brazil, is a planned city. A model of modern architecture, it was built in the late 1950's and inaugurated in April 1960. Brasília is located some 600 miles (966 kilometers) inland from the heavily populated coast because of the Brazilian government's desire to promote development of the interior.

SPOTLIGHT ON NEW TOWNS:

Planned Communities

The idea of building "new" towns is almost as old as urban life itself. In recent years, many countries and private business investors all over the world have developed ideas for new, planned communities. These plans look for ways to make cities of the industrial age comfortable and pleasant places to live.

New-town plans differ widely and would result in cities that vary from one another. One plan, drawn up by Americans, calls for farms and factories to be mixed together. Downtown areas would be roofed over. People housed in huge structures would be served with computers for communication.

A new French city would place the city's traffic underground. Factory smoke would be carried off in underground channels, and garbage would be burned to help heat buildings. Homes and offices would all be soundproof.

Every new-town plan calls for control over the area the community is to occupy and the number of people who would live there. The new city in the American plan, for example, would be built on 50,000 acres and have a population of no more than 250,000.

High costs may prevent the plans for the most advanced new cities from leaving the drawing boards. But a number of new communities already in existence do put into practice many ideas meant to improve urban living. People in the new town of Reston, Virginia, with a planned population of no more than 75,000, live within walking distance of stores and places of work. They have a wide choice of recreational areas and activities. The new town of Tapiola, Finland, uses open areas of green grass and trees combined with blue water areas to create a beautiful community for 17,000 people.

Reston, Virginia

Tapiola, Finland

moving to colonies to find greater economic and political freedom. At the same time, European and colonial traders bought slaves along the west coast of Africa and shipped these captured Africans to America.

In the industrial age, people have migrated to find new jobs, improved living conditions, or greater freedom. During the late 1800's and early 1900's, millions of people from nearly every part of Europe, attracted mainly by economic opportunities, left their homelands. These Europeans resettled in colonies in the Americas, Africa, and Australia. There, they were able to obtain farmland, start businesses, or take jobs in factories.

In the late 1800's and early 1900's, immigration from Europe to the United States was especially heavy. **Immigrants** are people who leave one country to settle in another. Many of the immigrants coming to the United States settled in cities, where they took industrial jobs. In addition to those who settled in cities, many immigrants to the United States chose to live in the country. Here, they farmed or ran small businesses.

In recent years, immigration to the United States has continued. Thousands of people from Southeast Asia and Latin America have come to the United States. Like those who left their homelands for America in previous years, these immigrants dream of building a better life in their new country. Many have taken jobs in cities, while others have started businesses.

People also move from place to place within a country or area. This movement is called internal migration. During the industrial age, when millions of Europeans moved overseas, there was also great internal migration within Europe. Millions of people left villages in **rural** areas for cities. Like many of those who moved to other countries, these people hoped to find jobs created by the growing industries in urban areas. Sometimes, city population grew so large that many people could not find jobs.

There has also been great internal migration in the United States. In the middle and late 1800's, many people moved from the East Coast to settle in the central and western parts of the country. In the West, they found great expanses of land that could be farmed and mined. At the same time, large numbers of people moved to cities. The largest of these cities were located in the eastern and central parts of the United States.

During the early 1900's, there was a different pattern of population movement in the United States. People began moving to the South and Southwest, attracted by the warm climate and many job opportunities. They also moved out of cities to **suburbs**, the communities that surround cities.

WOULD YOU LIKE TO BE . . .

A census taker? A census taker collects information on the number and size of families in a given area. The information is gathered by mail and door-to-door survey.

An economist? An economist studies how wealth is produced, used, and distributed among the people of a country or throughout the world.

An interpreter? An interpreter translates the spoken word from one language into another. Interpreters translate speeches at meetings and conferences where people speak different languages.

A highway engineer? A highway engineer plans and designs the construction of major roads.

The United States has taken in more immigrants than any other nation in the world. In 1984, the six largest groups of immigrants to the United States were Mexicans, Filipinos, Vietnamese, Koreans, Indians, and Chinese. Do students know the meaning of the word *emigration?* *(movement of people out of a country)*

Reading a Road Map

Roads and highways are vital linkages throughout the states and cities of the United States. Millions of Americans use road maps to travel these routes every day of the year.

A road map shows the location of roads and highways. It can be used to discover which highways connect major cities and smaller towns. It lets people know in advance which roads have limited access. Cars are permitted to turn on to or leave limited-access highways only at certain marked entrances or exits, or interchanges. You can also use a road map to learn which highways have four lanes and which are paved, principal roads.

On this map, major highways are shown by thick blue and yellow lines. Route numbers are placed in circles and shields lying on the routes.

Thin red, blue, and black lines show other through highways. Interchanges are represented by squares. Cities appear as yellow areas, and towns are circles. One inch equals about 20 miles.

1. (a) Which highway leads north from Kalamazoo to Grand Rapids? (b) About how many miles would you travel between the two cities along this route?

2. Find Interstate 96 leading east from Grand Rapids toward Lansing. Follow this route from Grand Rapids to Interstate 69. (a) In what direction does Interstate 69 run? (b) How far is Lansing from Grand Rapids?

3. State Highway 37 leads south and east from Grand Rapids. Follow this route until you reach a city with an airport (shown by an airplane). Name this city.

4. Follow Interstate Highway 94 west from Jackson for about eighteen miles. What town will you reach?

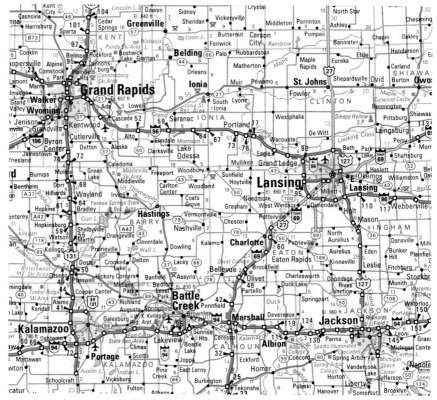

Answers are in the Teacher's Guide.

Assign the Workbook activity for this chapter's Map Workshop with this page.

Have students compare the world population density map (pages 490–491) with the maps showing climate (pages 64–65) and ecosystems (pages 82–83).

Where the World's People Live

The way people are spread out over the places in which they live is called population distribution. The worldwide distribution of people today is extremely uneven. In fact, almost half of the world's people live on only 5 percent of Earth's land.

Areas of the world can be compared according to their **population densities.** Population density for a given area is found by determining the average number of people living within each square mile (or square kilometer) of the area. For example, Detroit, Michigan, has about 1,200,000 residents and covers about 140 square miles (360 square kilometers). The city, therefore, has a population density of about 8,570 people per square mile (3,333 people per square kilometer). A population is said to be dense where many people live in a small area. A sparse population is found where few people inhabit a large area.

Mapping Population Distribution The map on pages 490–491 of the Atlas shows the population density throughout the world. The darkest shades of color show places with high population density. These places average at least 250 people per square mile. The largest areas of high population density are in East Asia, South Asia, and Europe. Smaller areas occur in parts of other continents, especially along the Nile River in Africa and the east coast of North America.

Much of the world has moderate population density. Density that averages from 25 to 250 persons per square mile is considered moderate. Almost all of Europe and about half of Asia are either moderately or densely populated. Roughly one third of North America and smaller parts of South America and Africa are also moderately populated.

Population density in Bombay, India (above), contrasts sharply with that of the Swiss village below.

Sparsely populated areas of the world have an average density of no more than 25 persons per square mile. The northern parts of North America and the central portion of South America are sparsely populated. So are Northern Africa, central and northern Asia, and most of Australia. In sparsely populated places, most of the people live in a few small settlements, with huge areas of uninhabited land nearby. On population maps, such as the one on pages 490–491, population density is shown as if the people are settled evenly throughout the area.

161

Texas Essential Element 4D. Major cultural, political, and economic activities within and among major world regions.

Interpreting a Cartoon

Most of the cartoons you read in your newspaper are meant to entertain and amuse. Some cartoons, however, have a more serious purpose. They try to influence public opinion, often by poking fun at someone or something.

Cartoons are a good means of communication. A simple drawing can deliver the same message as a long editorial. In this case, a picture really is worth a thousand words.

Political cartoons often are about government, people in government, political parties, or elections. One well-known political cartoonist is Herbert L. Block, winner of many awards and prizes for his work. "Herblock," as he signs his cartoons, has much to say about politics and the issues of the times.

1. What is the subject of the cartoon on this page?

2. What is its purpose?

3. (a) What symbols has the cartoonist used? (b) What do the symbols suggest?

4. What is the cartoonist's point of view?

5. Do you agree or disagree with the message of this cartoon? Explain your answer.

You may wish to bring in (or have students bring in) examples of political cartoons for class discussion.

Assign the Workbook activity for this chapter's Skill Workshop with this page.

"Help"

—from The Herblock Gallery (*Simon & Schuster, 1968*)

Urban Growth Before 1800, most people lived in rural areas. This was true even in Europe and other areas where cities had been built. By 1900, a big change had occurred. Industrialization had drawn millions of people to the cities of the United States and western Europe. By the early part of the 1900's, the urban population in the United States exceeded the rural population. Today nearly three quarters of the people of the United States live in urban areas.

The size as well as the number of cities has increased since the Industrial Revolution began. This growth has become even more rapid and widespread in the last 50 years. Before 1800, a place with 30,000 or 40,000 people was considered a large city. Only Tokyo, Paris, London, and Rome approached the million mark. By 1955, cities of a million or more people numbered 55. Only 20 years later, there were 161 such cities. Tokyo and London have grown so large that each has living in it about one fifth of the residents of its country.

Recent urban growth has been especially strong in the **developing countries.** Developing countries are those in which industries are still new and small. Most people live by farming or crafts work. These countries did not begin to industrialize until recently. In some of them, there was almost no industry until the 1950's.

Many developing countries have improved health care. As a result, their populations are growing. In some, farming areas have become too crowded to support all those who wish to farm. This has led more and more people to move to the cities to look for jobs. Despite tremendous growth in certain cities, however, there are still more people living in the rural areas of most developing countries than in their cities.

Trolleys like this one in Hong Kong enable people to live far from their jobs.

The Outward Spread of Cities In industrial countries, the pattern of cities has been transformed over the last 100 years or so. When the cities of industrial countries were first established, transportation was slow and expensive. People traveled mainly on foot, by horse, or by unpowered boat or ship. As a result, cities were compact. People's residences were built close to shops and workplaces. This enabled people to conduct their business by walking from one place to another.

Beginning in the 1800's, transportation in the industrial countries was revolutionized. Railroads, streetcars, and steam-powered boats made it possible for people to reach distant places quickly and easily. By the 1900's, the automobile made travel even faster and easier.

With improved transportation, the compact city became a thing of the past. People could now live miles from stores and businesses. At first, small numbers of city dwellers moved to greenbelts, which were suburbs just outside the limits of the city. Gradually, more and more people could afford to move to the suburbs. Within a few decades, large communities had grown up miles from the downtown parts of the city. While many people still lived within the original city, the focus of the downtown section's activity became business and shopping.

The pattern of wealth in cities of the United States has seen some drastic changes. Up to the nineteenth century, wealthy people lived in the inner city, while poor people lived on the outskirts. With the growth of suburbs, the wealthy began to move out, and the inner city became the home of low-income families.

Megalopolises in the United States

San Francisco • Oakland
San Jose
CALIF.
Los Angeles
San Diego

Chicago • Cleveland
Detroit
MICH.
ILL. IND.
OHIO
Pittsburgh
PA.

N.Y.
New York
Boston MASS.
R.I.
Hartford CONN.
N.J.
Philadelphia
Baltimore MD.
Washington, D.C.

Area of Megalopolis

0   300   600 Miles
0   300   600 Kilometers

N
NW NE
W   E
SW SE
S

Map Study *Use the map's scale to find out approximately how far the eastern megalopolis stretches along the coast.*

Today's cities are still being shaped by the transportation revolution. Complicated highway systems link people to the downtown area and the many outlying suburbs. Commuter railroads, subways, and bus systems also enable people to travel conveniently in many metropolitan areas. A **metropolitan area** is a city and its surrounding suburbs.

The communities that make up a metropolitan area have become linked in many ways. It is common for a person to live in one suburb, work in another, shop in still another, and visit the nearby city for entertainment and business.

Even more complex patterns result where the edges of one metropolitan area touch the edges of others. In such areas, the neighboring metropolitan areas may become one huge city made up of a number of smaller cities. Such a place is called a **megalopolis** (me'gə lo'pə ləs). The densely populated region from Boston to Washington, D.C., is the largest megalopolis in the United States. The areas between Chicago and Pittsburgh and between San Diego and San Francisco are other megalopolises. Western Europe and Japan also have megalopolises.

164

REVIEWING THE FACTS

Define

1. death rate
2. famine
3. infant death rate
4. birth rate
5. life expectancy
6. migration
7. immigrant
8. rural
9. suburb
10. population density
11. developing country
12. metropolitan area
13. megalopolis

Answer

1. (a) How has the world's population changed in the past three centuries? (b) What factors have caused this change?

2. To what areas of the world have large numbers of people migrated since the 1700's?

3. (a) What parts of the world are most densely settled? (b) Moderately settled? (c) Most sparsely settled?

4. How has the pattern of city settlement changed since the early 1900's?

Locate

Refer to the map above.

1. What city in Maryland is part of the megalopolis that extends from Boston to Washington, D.C.?

2. In what state is the megalopolis on the West Coast located?

2 Political Patterns

The view from the air brings Earth's mountains, deserts, and oceans into clear view. In the past, these natural features often acted as **frontiers**. A frontier is a stretch of unsettled territory. Until the twentieth century, every continent had frontiers. Today the last frontier on Earth is Antarctica. Many countries have laid claim to all or part of that frozen land.

From Frontiers to Borders

As the Industrial Revolution spread to countries around the world, frontiers disappeared on every continent. With more and more people to feed, many countries took a new interest in lands once thought unusable. New technology helped farmers turn wasteland into farmland. In the central part of North America, for example, farmers using steel-tipped plows turned the grasslands into fields of wheat and corn. In Europe, other farmers dredged marshes and even reclaimed land from the ocean itself.

The search for resources to power the new machines and keep factories humming also contributed to the disappearance of frontiers. People cleared the rain forests of valuable plants and trees. They drilled for oil in the world's deserts and mined for copper, iron, and other precious metals in mountain ranges on almost every continent. Even the oceans were combed for treasure.

The rush for land and other resources altered the way people thought about the boundaries between countries. In the past, natural barriers often separated countries. As the frontier began to disappear, however, groups of people living in one country came closer and closer to people living in other countries.

Often, neighboring countries wanted resources in the zone lying between them. To prevent disputes, it became necessary to establish recognized **borders**. During the 1800's in particular, many countries surveyed borders. These surveys were based on old claims put forth by neighboring countries.

Eventually, agreed-upon borders were established in most parts of the world. At times, a lake or river claimed by two countries was divided between them. The border was an imaginary line through the body of water. In addition, almost every country that touched the ocean claimed control over the sea that lies off its coast. The amount of ocean countries may claim is still a matter of dispute today.

Travelers between the United States and Canada must stop at stations along the border. There, officials regulate the movement of people between the countries.

You may wish to point out that this lesson introduces the study of political geography. Political geography is the study of how human political activities affect the size and boundaries of countries. Throughout the rest of this text, the students will deepen their understanding of political geography. Assign the Workbook activity for Chapter 6, Section 2, with pages 165–169.

165

The Political Map

There are over 160 countries in the world. Almost every one of those countries shares a border with one or more other countries. The exceptions are Australia, which is both a country and a continent, and island countries such as Japan, Sri Lanka, and Cuba.

A map of the world shows that countries today vary greatly in size and shape. The country with the greatest area is the Soviet Union. It is larger than the entire continent of South America. The Soviet Union contains one sixth of all the land on Earth. On the other hand, some countries are very small. Nauru, a tiny island country in the South Pacific, is about one sixtieth the size of the city of Los Angeles.

Countries vary in shape too. Some are compact. They may be shaped like a circle or a rectangle. Belgium, Kenya, and Rumania are good examples of such countries. Other countries are fragmented. Fragmented countries may have sections separated from one another by water or by the land of other countries. Japan and the Philippines are fragmented. The islands that make up each are separated from one another by ocean waters. The United States is another fragmented country. Two states, Alaska and Hawaii, are separated by land or water from the other 48 states.

Unitary versus Federal Government

Governing a compact country can be different from governing a more fragmented land. Yet every country has a government. In fact, governments have been part of culture at least since the rise of the world's first cities.

All but the very smallest countries are divided into smaller political units. These parts have different names in different countries. In the United States and India, they are known as states. Canadians call the parts of their country provinces. Parts of the Soviet Union are known as republics. France is divided into departments.

How much authority the parts of a country have varies greatly. Countries like France, Austria, and Sweden have **unitary governments.** In these countries, a central government makes basic decisions. Governments of the states or departments simply see that decisions of the central government are carried out. In France, for example, every school in the country uses the same textbooks. Teachers of every subject are expected to cover the same material on the same schedule.

Other countries, including the United States, have **federal governments.** Under a federal system, the central government shares power with states or provinces. In the United States, for example, each state is in charge of the schools within its borders. It is up to the states to decide how and when subjects will be covered in the schools. Some states even allow local schools to prepare their own courses of study.

Authoritarian versus Democratic Government

Whether unitary or federal, the governments of all countries have ways of making laws, of carrying out and enforcing laws, and of judging charges that laws have been broken. Although all governments carry out these tasks, no two of them do so in exactly the same way. In other words, forms of government differ from country to country. Most modern countries have either an authoritarian or a democratic government.

166

Authoritarian Government Under an authoritarian government, one person or a small group of people has complete authority for making and carrying out laws. Today most authoritarian governments are headed by dictators. A dictator has the power kings and queens held long ago. Unlike a king or queen, however, a dictator does not inherit power. He or she may get the authority to rule by winning control of the army or by imprisoning all opponents.

Many authoritarian governments today are under the control of a political party. For example, the Communist party has complete authority in the Soviet Union. No other political parties are allowed. In elections, the only candidates for office are those sponsored by the Communist party. Moreover, membership in the party is reserved for a small percentage of the people of the country. Yet it is party members who control the government.

There are many countries besides the Soviet Union with authoritarian governments. These countries differ in the amount of power given to the government. Highly authoritarian govern-ments, like those found in the Soviet Union and Cuba, are **totalitarian governments**. In countries with totalitarian governments, nearly every activity of citizens is subject to government control.

Democratic Government Countries with **democratic governments** are ruled by the people. Under such a government, citizens have ways of taking part in politics. Modern democracies use a method called **representative democracy**. In a representative democracy, the people elect leaders. Leaders are expected to represent the people by carrying out their wishes.

In countries with representative democracy, individuals have freedoms that the government may not take away. These freedoms include the right to choose leaders, to join political parties, and to state political opinions openly. In most democracies, individuals are also free to own property and seek jobs of their own choosing. In addition, people

Mikhail Gorbachev (left) speaks to leaders of the Communist party of the Soviet Union; these leaders control the Soviet government. ● *In New England towns such as Strafford, Vermont, citizens can take part in lawmaking at town meetings (right).*

167

The U.S. Constitution was signed in 1787.

may not be arrested unless authorities have good reason to suspect them of crimes.

There are many differences among countries with representative democracy. In some of these countries, the

Senegal, in Africa, has a representative government. Members of the National Assembly are elected to make laws.

government has greater authority than in others. The individual rights protected by a representative democracy also may differ from country to country. In addition, a representative democracy may have either a federal or unitary system. The United States is a representative democracy with a federal system of government. France also has a representative government. However, it has a unitary system of government. In both countries, the people have authority to govern.

A World of Nations

People have been living in countries for many centuries. The idea of a **nation,** however, is much older than the idea of a country. A nation is more than a group of people, the land they live on, and the government that rules them. It is a group of people who believe they belong together. They share similar values and beliefs.

Nations began to form in Europe during the troubled centuries that followed the collapse of Roman power. As some rulers won out over others, they built lasting kingdoms. People living under the same king or queen came to speak the same language, practice similar customs, and follow the same religion. After many years, the people living in a kingdom came to feel that they shared a history. These people had gained a sense that they belonged together. They had become a nation of peoples.

When Europeans colonized parts of the Americas, Africa, and Asia, they sometimes brought together people who had very different cultures. In time, these groups began to feel that they belonged together. Nations formed in such areas included a variety of cultures. The United States is an example of such a nation. It is made up of many different cultural and language groups.

168

Today many other nations are equally diverse. It was more difficult to create many of these nations than it was to create the United States. In some formerly colonized areas, people find themselves living among groups with whom they have little in common. There, national feeling does not come easily. Where people who feel common bonds have been separated, they may have little attachment to the countries they live in.

For these reasons, there has been turmoil in many countries that have recently become independent of European powers. Independence did not bring the kinds of changes that many hoped for. Civil war has been an outcome of independence in Nigeria, India, Uganda, and more recently in Zimbabwe.

Not all groups of people who believe themselves to be a nation have their own land. This situation can lead to conflict when these groups of people try to create a homeland. Since all the world's land is claimed by one nation or another, new countries must be carved from lands claimed by existing countries. Among the national groups seeking their own lands are the Palestinians in Southwest Asia, the Kurds in Iran, and the Basques in France and Spain. It is impossible to understand the world today without understanding the **nationalism** that motivates such groups. Nationalism is the belief that people who consider themselves a nation ought to have their own land and their own government.

The Arc de Triomphe is a symbol of France.

REVIEWING THE FACTS

Define

1. frontier
2. border
3. unitary government
4. federal government
5. authoritarian government
6. dictator
7. totalitarian government
8. democratic government
9. representative democracy
10. nation
11. nationalism

Answer

1. Why did frontiers disappear after the Industrial Revolution?

2. (a) Explain the difference between a unitary government and a federal government. (b) Between an authoritarian and a representative government.

3. What factors led to the formation of nations throughout the world?

Locate

Refer to the Atlas map of the world on pages 486–487.

1. Name three fragmented countries.

2. (a) What is the largest country in South America? (b) What countries share a border with France?

169

3 Using the Land and Its Resources

When geographers study the nations of the world, they look closely at people's economic activities. This tells them how the people use their land and develop its resources. Geographers also compare the levels of land use and resource development among the world's peoples.

Steps in Developing Resources

Economists divide the work involved in developing resources into primary, secondary, and tertiary economic activities. **Primary economic activities** are closely tied to the land and its plants, animal life, and mineral resources. People engaged in hunting and gathering, forestry, mining, and fishing take materials directly from the resource base. Farmers and livestock herders use the land directly to produce their products. All these people work in primary activities. Primary activities are the first step that people take in developing their land and resources.

Secondary economic activities are the next step people take in developing resources and raw materials. Few of the things people use every day are used in the form in which they are first found or produced. The wood a forester gathers must be processed before it becomes paper. The wheat a farmer grows is ground into flour and baked into bread. Manufacturing, of course, is the way people process raw materials into paper, bread, and other finished products. Most manufacturing takes place in factories.

The next step in land and resource development is to distribute products to people. The distribution of products involves **tertiary economic activities.** These activities are often referred to as **services.** People who work in services do not actually make goods. Instead, they make sure that people are able to get and use products.

In industrial countries, service industries are large and varied. The operation of transportation systems is one of the most important services. It would be difficult for people to obtain goods without fast highways, well-kept harbors, and

Have students give examples of the major kinds of economic activity evident in or near their community. Have them indicate whether each kind of activity is primary, secondary, or tertiary. Assign the Workbook activity for Chapter 6, Section 3, with pages 170–176.

safe railroads and airlines. Modern economies also depend on rapid and efficient communications. Telephone, television, and satellite operators all offer services that bring information to people. Both transportation and communications are **linkages** that help get products to people and bring people together.

There are many services besides transportation and communications. All help people in some way. The supplying of energy helps people make things. An example of this kind of activity is the operation of power plants. People who work in such places as department stores, repair shops, cleaning businesses, banks, insurance companies, and government also supply vital services.

The gathering of resources, such as trees (left), is a primary economic activity.
• Turning resources into products is a secondary economic activity. Here wood is made into paper (center).
• Providing a service, such as managing a hospital staff, is a tertiary economic activity (below).

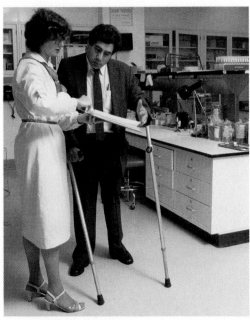

Organizing Economic Activities

Economic activities may be carried out in various ways. That is, the production and distribution of goods and services may be organized according to different principles.

Just as political systems differ in how much authority they give to individuals, economic systems also differ in how much individual freedom they permit. To understand a nation's economic system, you must first ask who owns and controls its resources, technology, and businesses.

Free Enterprise In a system practicing **free enterprise,** private citizens own most of the resources, technology, and businesses. Under free enterprise, any individual is free to start a business of his or her own. Business owners may use their resources and equipment largely as they see fit. Competition among businesses determines the prices of goods and services.

Workers also have great freedom in a free-enterprise economy. They can decide for themselves what jobs to seek. No one can be forced to work at a particular job.

Free-enterprise economies are not subject to many controls by the government. The government may make regulations to ensure that competition is fair. It does not, however, decide what products businesses will produce or how businesses will be managed. The economic systems of the United States and Canada are based on free enterprise.

Socialism Under **socialism**, the government owns such basic resources as coal and iron. The government may also own many businesses. In most socialist economies, for example, large and important industries—such as automobile plants and steel mills—are likely to be owned

Free enterprise is based on competition.

by the government. Private individuals own and operate most smaller businesses and industries. These privately owned businesses may be subject to many government controls. While the government's controls are extensive, workers are still free to choose among jobs. Sweden is a nation that has an economy organized under socialist principles.

Communism The system of **communism** provides for government ownership of nearly all resources and businesses. Under communism, the government owns and operates almost every industry. It plans and directs the use of resources. The government chooses what products to make and in what quantities they will be made. Prices for goods and services are set by the government. The government also determines what jobs most workers will do. The Soviet Union and Cuba are examples of countries whose economies are based on communist principles.

Economic Levels in Industrialized Countries

Nearly all economic activity in industrialized countries is **commercial activity**. That is, in these countries, most people produce goods in order to sell them. For example, farmers in many parts of the world use modern machines to produce large amounts of food. They grow far more than they and their families can eat. The surplus is sold in exchange for money. In industrial nations, economic activity is usually quite varied. Factories make many kinds of goods, often in large quantities. Farmers may grow a variety of crops, with huge surpluses. **Consumers,** or those who buy goods and services, can shop in department stores, supermarkets, and specialty stores. There, they are able to make their selections from a seemingly endless array of products.

Economic Choices Highly industrialized nations are able to choose which economic activities to emphasize. England, for example, has the technology to produce the food its people need. Nevertheless, it imports most of its food. The English have chosen to concentrate on manufacturing and trade instead of farming. Much of the countryside in England is left free for the grazing of sheep that provide wool for the cloth industry.

Development of Linkages Most industrial nations have or are building modern systems of transportation and communication. These systems enable people to take part in commercial economic activity. A nation's harbors, railways, airlines, roads, and pipelines make it possible for people to receive things from far away. The gasoline a Californian buys at the neighborhood gas station may have come from Saudi Arabia or Venezuela. A Vermonter's watch or audio headset may have been made in Japan or Taiwan.

172

In industrialized countries such as the United States, modern equipment allows farmers to produce huge crops.

People's daily life in industrial countries depends on transportation and communication linkages. Life can change suddenly if something happens to even one network. On several occasions, for example, unexpected shutdowns of nearby power plants cut off New York City's electricity. During these blackouts, buildings and streets darkened. Subways stopped, and traffic lights went out. Telephones and computers went dead. Refrigeration units shut down. Loss of power brought nearly all business to a standstill in this huge city of the industrial age.

Growing Service Industries Most industrial countries are constantly improving their ways of making products. One important result of improvements in technology has been that fewer and fewer workers can make more and more goods. While the need for workers in factories and on farms has fallen, services have required increasing numbers of workers. In the United States, Japan, and many Western European countries, services have become a basic part of the economy. Millions of people are employed in providing health care, operating computers, making sales, and other such activities.

A Comfortable Standard of Living People in industrial countries generally have a higher **standard of living** than do people in developing nations. The standard of living of a group of people is a measure of how well off that group of people is. In industrial countries, there are many goods and services available. What a country does not make can generally be obtained through trade. Moreover, people in many industrial nations can afford more than the necessities. In some industrial nations, large numbers of people take for granted conveniences not even dreamed of a century ago.

In today's automobile factories, robots replace assembly workers for some jobs.

Economic Levels in Developing Countries

In developing nations, many people engage in **subsistence activity**. They do not produce goods for sale. Instead, they grow crops, raise animals, and make crafts to meet their own needs. They produce just enough for their own use.

In many ways, life in developing nations is similar to what it was like before the Industrial Revolution. The work people do is much like that done by their ancestors. Incomes are low. Most farmers and laborers have trouble obtaining even basic necessities.

Important Mineral Resources Developing countries have little choice of what economic activities to pursue. Some are fortunate in having mineral resources needed by other countries. Such nations do not have the means to develop or make use of these resources on their own. They may, however, sell them to industrial countries.

Selling resources can make a big difference in a developing nation's living standards. Kuwait and the United Arab Emirates, for example, used to be among the poorest countries in the world. Then they discovered large deposits of petroleum, from which oil and gasoline are made. Industrial countries need petroleum to fuel factories, heat homes, and power motor vehicles. Kuwait and the United Arab Emirates, among other nations, have grown rich selling petroleum to industrial countries. This money is used to provide education and medical care. It is also used to build factories.

Growing Populations In many developing countries, population is growing rapidly. When such nations have little industry and few resources, they must concentrate on providing food, clothing, and shelter for their people. What resources exist, then, are devoted to the supplying of necessities. Little is left over for the development of industry. As a result, large populations have prevented a number of countries from industrializing. Under these conditions, the standard of living in these countries remains low. People lack comforts and even many items considered essential in industrial countries.

Little Modern Technology Developing nations do not manufacture many modern tools or much modern machinery. They have little money with which to buy tools and machines from industrial nations. Therefore, farmers and laborers work with old-fashioned equipment. Many villagers, for example, till the soil by hand. Even draft animals like oxen — used in the place of tractors — are in short supply. Under these conditions, it takes many hours to plow, plant, and harvest crops. Yields are often low, barely enough to feed a single family.

A Need for Linkages Transportation and communications differ from one developing nation to the next. The least-developed nations have few telephones, television sets, and radios. Those that do

In Sri Lanka, many farmers still raise rice almost entirely by hand.

174

Nearly one half of the world's people live in countries with an average per capita GNP of $275 or less.

The per capita GNP for each of the world's nations is included with the World Data Banks for the regional chapters in Unit 3.

exist are often in poor repair. Few people own cars. In fact, bicycles and mopeds may be the most numerous vehicles in the cities. In the countryside, people may travel by foot. While cities may have paved streets, there are likely to be no more than a few dirt roads in rural areas. There may be no railroads, and the nation's airports may be small and poorly kept up. Sometimes rivers still serve as the most important linkages.

Poorly developed linkages can stand in the way of industrial development. Modern linkages are often too costly for poor countries to build and maintain. Yet without such linkages, it is hard to get goods to market. Contact with other nations is difficult.

Despite these difficulties, almost every part of the world has some contact with other parts. A village in Bangladesh, for example, may have just one unpaved road. That road, however, connects the village to the nation's capital. The capital, moreover, is connected to other Asian cities by many similar roads. Sea routes may link the capital to other countries and continents. Communication linkages also join faraway places. Radio and television offer information to people who cannot read.

Measuring Economic Conditions

Nations keep track of their economies just as they keep track of their populations. They need to know if their economies are strong and will be able to provide for their people's wants and needs.

The most common measure of economic activity is **gross national product,** or GNP. The GNP is the total value of all goods and services produced by a country in a year. If a nation's GNP is rising from one year to the next, the nation's economy is usually in good condition.

Another measure of how a nation's economy is doing is the **per capita GNP.** *Per capita* means "for each person." A nation's per capita GNP is its gross national product divided by its population. The per capita GNP gives the average value of products and services produced for each person in a given year. A nation's economy is considered healthy when its GNP is growing faster than its population. This means that both its GNP and its per capita GNP are rising.

Per capita GNP is a good guide to a nation's standard of living. For example, India and the Netherlands have nearly equal GNP's. That is, they produce roughly the same amounts of goods and

Although families in this village in India cannot afford TV's, a service organization provides one for the whole community.

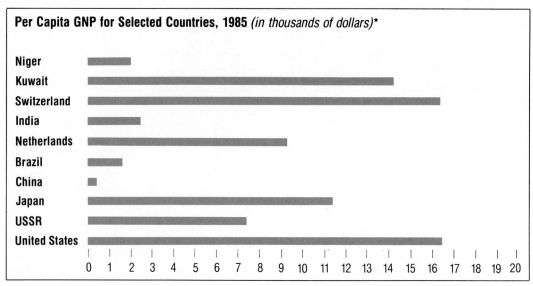

Per Capita GNP for Selected Countries, 1985 *(in thousands of dollars)**

Niger	
Kuwait	
Switzerland	
India	
Netherlands	
Brazil	
China	
Japan	
USSR	
United States	

0 1 2 3 4 5 6 7 8 9 10 11 12 13 14 15 16 17 18 19 20

* Source: Population Reference Bureau

Representative GNP's for Selected Countries, 1985*	
Country	**Billions of Dollars**
Niger	1.4
Kuwait	27.0
Switzerland	108.0
India	200.0
Netherlands	134.0
Brazil	232.0
People's Republic of China	329.0
Japan	1,384.5
USSR	2,101.6
United States	3,998.0

REVIEWING THE FACTS

Define

1. primary economic activity
2. secondary economic activity
3. tertiary economic activity
4. service
5. linkage
6. free enterprise
7. socialism
8. communism
9. commercial activity
10. consumer
11. standard of living
12. subsistence activity
13. gross national product
14. per capita GNP

Answer

1. Compare the economic levels of industrial and developing countries.

2. How is the performance of an economic system measured?

Locate

Using the map on pages 488–489, name the two continents with the largest areas of (a) manufacturing, (b) nomadic herding, (c) commercial farming and stock grazing.

services. The population of India, however, is more than 50 times greater than that of the Netherlands. India must divide what it produces among many more people than the Netherlands does. Therefore, each person living in India has far less wealth than each person living in the Netherlands. Per capita GNP is far lower in India. Developing countries like India generally have lower per capita GNP's than more industrialized countries.

176

2. *Nations:* (a) Asia, (b) United Kingdom, (c) Nauru.

3. *Population explosion:* (a) medical advances, (b) increased food, (c) famine.

4. *Migration:* (a) nationalism, (b) political freedom, (c) economic opportunity.

5. *Governments:* (a) unitary, (b) federal, (c) fragmented.

6. *Democracies:* (a) France, (b) the Soviet Union, (c) the United States.

7. *Linkages:* (a) factories, (b) highways, (c) telephones.

8. *Economic systems:* (a) representative democracy, (b) socialism, (c) free enterprise.

9. *Trade:* (a) exports, (b) immigration, (c) tariffs.

10. *Developing countries:* (a) subsistence farming, (b) advanced technology, (c) mineral resources.

11. *Megalopolis:* (a) Chicago to Pittsburgh, (b) Denver to Phoenix, (c) Boston to Washington, D.C.

Building Map Skills

Number your paper from 1 to 14. Identify the countries numbered on the map at the right. These countries — along with the United States and Canada — are the members of the North Atlantic Treaty Organization (NATO).

Applying Map Skills

Compare the world maps showing population density (pages 490–491), climate (pages 64–65), and ecosystems (pages 82–83). What generalizations can you make about the most sparsely populated areas?

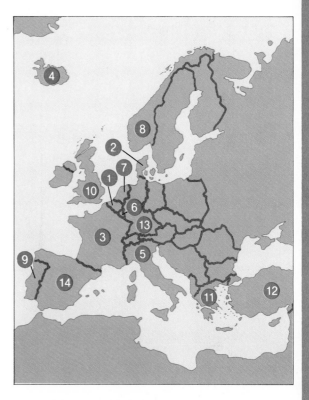

Exploring Further

1. In 1987, for the first time in modern history, the growth rate of the world's population declined. Even at slower growth rates, world population is expected to reach 6.2 billion by the year 2000. Think about the effects this growth might have on your life. Write an editorial expressing your views on population growth.

2. For one week, take note of the kinds of clothes that you wear, foods that you eat, appliances and machines that you use, and sources from which you get information. Find out which items are imports. Clothing and appliances often have special labels giving place of manufacture.

3. List the economic activities in or near your community. Your local newspaper can be of some help. So can your community library. List examples of primary, secondary, and tertiary activities. Which kind of activity seems most important?

181

GEOGRAPHY LABORATORY

UNIT 3

THE VIEW FROM THE GROUND

The view from the ground gives you a close-up look at Earth. Now you can see how the daily actions of people shape the 12 regions they inhabit. From the ground, you will examine these regions. You will discover the landforms, climate, and ecosystems of each. In studying each region, you will compare the ways that people use their resources, the communities that people live in, and the ways that nations are governed. You will visit some of the world's smallest villages, highest mountains, and thickest forests. You will also travel to large and thriving cities, such as Tokyo, Japan, shown on the opposite page.

In this chapter, students will study the physical environment of the United States, which has been divided into five major landform regions. The section on the human imprint will reveal the importance of immigration and economic development to the nation's growth. The United States is then broken into four cultural regions. Students will learn where people live, what they do, and what trends are currently affecting each of the four regions.

The United States

The United States stretches across the middle of North America. About 500 years ago this area was sparsely settled. Groups of Indians were scattered across the land. These groups lived differently from one another, in the vast wilderness. Along the Pacific coast, for example, Chinook took salmon and other fish from the ocean. Iroquois of the eastern woodlands hunted deer in vast forests and raised crops in small fields nestled in the woodlands.

By 1650, the face of the continent had changed little. European newcomers had built a few settlements on the eastern coast and in the southwestern desert. At first, the Europeans lived in small areas within the great wilderness. Gradually, however, in search of wealth or trade or better land, they expanded their settlements. Over the next few centuries, continued expansion and the growing use of resources would change the face of North America on a scale never equaled in human history.

Today neither the Indians nor the European settlers of the 1600's would recognize the land they lived in. Where there were once millions of bison running wild, there are now but a few thousand, herded largely onto government lands. Their home — the plains area — is now a place for the grazing of domesticated cattle and the farming of grain. City skyscrapers and factories rise where forests and prairies once covered the land.

The photo shows Houston, Texas.

184

Texas Essential Elements 1B. Geographic terminology. 1C. Geographical tools and methodologies. 2B. Major landforms, regions, and features of the earth. 4A. Criteria for determining regions. 4B. Physical setting of world regions. 4F. Geographic influences on various issues.

1 The Physical Environment

In no part of North America have the changes been as rapid and as great as in the part that became the United States. There are a number of reasons for the unparalleled changes in this region. Industrious and daring people came from all over the world to settle in the United States. These people brought the skills and knowledge needed to farm, to trade, and to make many kinds of goods. America's economic and political systems gave them great freedom.

The people who came to North America found a large land, rich in resources. Before learning about the American people, you should consider the country's environments and ecosystems.

Landforms

In terms of area, the United States is the fourth largest country in the world. The landforms in this vast area offer remarkable contrasts. To take just one example, the peak of Alaska's Mount McKinley, with an elevation of 20,320 feet (6,194 meters), is the highest point in the United States. The lowest spot is Death Valley, California, where the surface of the land is 282 feet (89 meters) *below* sea level.

The Coastal Plains The eastern coast of the United States is a long, gently rolling lowland area. These **coastal plains** reach from Maine to Texas. The lowlands along the Atlantic Ocean are known as the Atlantic Coastal Plain. Those that border the Gulf of Mexico are called the Gulf Coastal Plain. The southern part of the coastal plains reaches many miles inland. This inland area has fertile soil, which makes the plain well suited to farming. In the northern portion, the plain is narrower and less suited to farming.

A ranger makes her rounds in a valley in Yellowstone National Park, Wyoming.

The Appalachian Mountains At the western edge of the Atlantic Coastal Plain, the land rises to form the hills of the Piedmont (pēd'mont'). The Appalachian (ap'ə lā'chən) Mountains lie to the west of the Piedmont. The Appalachians run from the northern part of Maine southwest into Alabama. They have different names in different parts of the country. The mountains hold an abundance of minerals, especially coal.

The Appalachians form a natural barrier between the coastal plains and the interior part of the United States. But the Appalachians have been worn down by erosion and are not very high. Rivers have carved out a number of narrow valleys, called gaps. These gaps create east-west openings in the mountains.

185

PACIFIC OCEAN

130°W
45°N
40°N
35°N
30°N
125°W
120°W

Strait of Juan de Fuca
Cape Flattery
Puget Sound
Seattle
Olympia
Portland
Salem
Cape Mendocino
Cape
San Francisco Bay
San Francisco
San Jose
Point Conception
Los Angeles
San Diego

WASHINGTON
OREGON
CASCADE RANGE
COASTAL RANGES
COLUMBIA PLATEAU
F.D. Roosevelt Lake
Pend Oreille Lake
Flathead Lake
ROCKY
LEWIS RANGE
BITTERROOT RANGE
Columbia R.
Goose Lake
Klamath R.
Pit R.
Snake R.
Boise
IDAHO
SNAKE RIVER PLAIN
Helena
MONTANA
Milk R.
Fort Peck Lake
Missouri R.
Yellowstone R.
Powder R.
ABSAROKA RANGE
BIGHORN MOUNTAINS
Bighorn R.
RANGE
WYOMING
M
O
U
N
T
A
I
N
S
Lake Sakakawea
NORTH DAKOTA
Bismarck
Lake Oahe
SOUTH DAKOTA
Pierre
BLACK HILLS
BADLANDS
White R.
MINNESOTA
Lower Red Lake
Lake of the Woods
Minnesota R.
Des Moines R.
IOWA
Des Moines
SIERRA NEVADA
CENTRAL VALLEY
Pyramid Lake
Lake Tahoe
GREAT BASIN
NEVADA
Great Salt Lake
GREAT SALT LAKE DESERT
Salt Lake City
WASATCH RANGE
UINTA MOUNTAINS
UTAH
Green R.
Lake Powell
Lake Mead
Carson City
Sacramento
Mt. Whitney (14,494 ft/4,418 m)
Death Valley (-282 ft/-89 m)
CALIFORNIA
MOJAVE DESERT
IMPERIAL VALLEY
Salton Sea
CHANNEL ISLANDS
Cheyenne
FRONT RANGE
Denver
North Platte R.
South Platte R.
COLORADO
COLORADO
SAN JUAN MOUNTAINS
PLATEAU
GRAND CANYON
PAINTED DESERT
ARIZONA
Phoenix
SONORA DESERT
Tucson
Santa Fe
SANGRE DE CRISTO MOUNTAINS
NEW MEXICO
SACRAMENTO MOUNTAINS
El Paso
Rio Grande
Pecos R.
GREAT PLAINS
SAND HILLS
NEBRASKA
Platte R.
Lincoln
Republican R.
Smoky Hill R.
KANSAS
Topeka
Kansas City
Canadian R.
OKLAHOMA
Oklahoma City
Tulsa
Lake Eufaula
Red R.
OUACHITA MOUNTAINS
Lake Texoma
LLANO ESTACADO
Colorado R.
TEXAS
Dallas
EDWARDS PLATEAU
Austin
Houston
San Antonio
GULF
Galveston Bay
Padre
125°W
95°W

HAWAII (13,796 ft/4,205 m)
PACIFIC OCEAN
160°W
Kauai
Oahu
Honolulu
Molokai
Lanai
Maui
Mauna Kea
Hawaii
Hilo
20°N
155°W
0   50   100 Miles
0 50 100 Kilometers

ARCTIC OCEAN
70°N
Point Barrow
130°W
BEAUFORT SEA
Arctic Circle
BROOKS RANGE
Bering Strait
St. Lawrence
ALASKA
Tanana R.
ALASKA RANGE
Mt. McKinley (20,320 ft/6,194 m)
Anchorage
Valdez
Gulf of Alaska
Juneau
COAST MOUNTAINS
BERING SEA
Kodiak
ALASKA PENINSULA
Attu
0   250   500 Miles
0 250 500 Kilometers
180°
170°W
ALEUTIAN ISLANDS
60°N
50°N
PACIFIC OCEAN
160°W
150°W
140°W

N

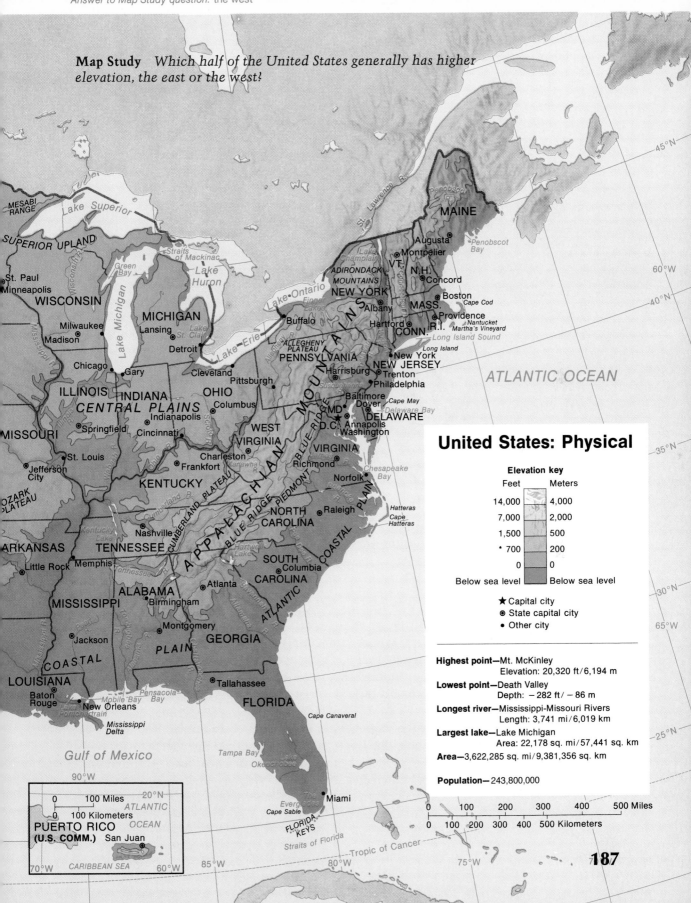

Map Study *Which half of the United States generally has higher elevation, the east or the west?*

United States: Physical

Elevation key

Feet		Meters
14,000		4,000
7,000		2,000
1,500		500
700		200
0		0
Below sea level		Below sea level

★ Capital city
◎ State capital city
● Other city

Highest point—Mt. McKinley
    Elevation: 20,320 ft / 6,194 m
Lowest point—Death Valley
    Depth: − 282 ft / − 86 m
Longest river—Mississippi-Missouri Rivers
    Length: 3,741 mi / 6,019 km
Largest lake—Lake Michigan
    Area: 22,178 sq. mi / 57,441 sq. km
Area—3,622,285 sq. mi / 9,381,356 sq. km

Population—243,800,000

187

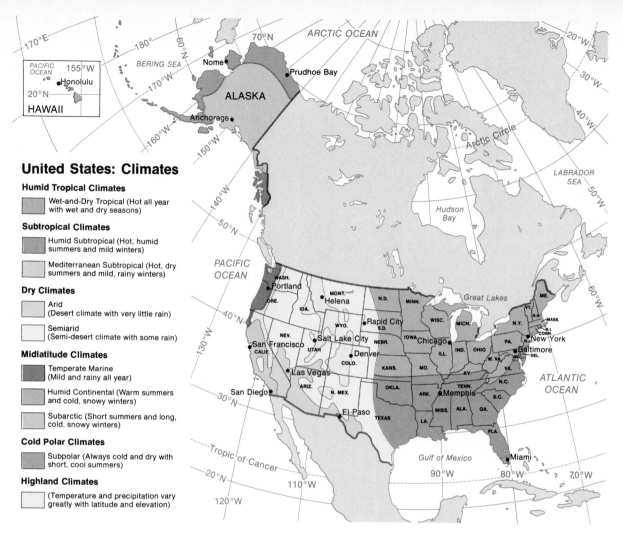

United States: Climates

Humid Tropical Climates

Wet-and-Dry Tropical (Hot all year with wet and dry seasons)

Subtropical Climates

Humid Subtropical (Hot, humid summers and mild winters)

Mediterranean Subtropical (Hot, dry summers and mild, rainy winters)

Dry Climates

Arid (Desert climate with very little rain)

Semiarid (Semi-desert climate with some rain)

Midlatitude Climates

Temperate Marine (Mild and rainy all year)

Humid Continental (Warm summers and cold, snowy winters)

Subarctic (Short summers and long, cold, snowy winters)

Cold Polar Climates

Subpolar (Always cold and dry with short, cool summers)

Highland Climates

(Temperature and precipitation vary greatly with latitude and elevation)

Map Study *What is the climate like in your state? Which is the coldest state? What city has a humid-tropical climate?*

The Interior Plains The middle section of the United States is a vast plain. This region extends westward from the Appalachian Mountains to the Rocky Mountains. Among the few highlands that break the plains are the Superior Upland and the Black Hills in the north and the Ozark Plateau in the south.

The plains are divided into two major parts. The wetter, eastern portion is called the **Central Plains.** The western portion of the interior plains is known as the **Great Plains.** Both parts of the plains have good soil. Vast deposits of energy resources lie in the southern plains.

The Rocky Mountains and the Western Plateaus At the western edge of the Great Plains, the Rocky Mountains rise sharply. The Rockies are actually a series of ranges. Among them are the Bitterroot in Montana and Idaho and the Sangre de Cristo (san'grē də kris'to) in Colorado and New Mexico.

Geologists consider the Rockies to be young mountains. They were formed too recently to be worn down through erosion. The Rockies are marked by towering peaks and steep-sided valleys among the high ridges. Large needleleaf forests spread across the valleys and lower

188

slopes. In addition, many important metals and other resources lie within these rugged mountains.

A large plateau region lies just west of the Rocky Mountains. The land here has steep cliffs and canyons, isolated mountains, and **basins,** or low-lying areas into which rivers drain. Many basins are rich in such resources as oil and natural gas.

The Pacific West The Pacific West is made up of the western coast of the 48 adjoining states, Alaska, and the Hawaiian islands. In the adjoining states, the Pacific Coast has high mountains, among which are broad, fertile valleys. The most important ranges are the Sierra Nevada (sē er′ə nə vad′ə) and the Cascades in the eastern portion of the region and the Coastal Ranges along the western coast. The valleys lying between the eastern and western ranges include the Willamette Valley in Oregon and the Central and Imperial valleys in California. The mountains are rich in timber, while the valleys are suited to farming.

Much of Alaska and Hawaii are also mountainous. The Rocky Mountains extend north into Alaska. The Hawaiian islands were formed by volcanic activity. There are still a number of active volcanoes on the islands.

Climates and Ecosystems

Most of the United States is in the middle latitudes. The climate is mainly moderate. There is, however, great variety within the United States. In fact, nearly every kind of climate is found within the United States. The same is true of the ecosystems within the country.

Most of the eastern part of the country has a humid continental climate. Broadleaf forests and areas of mixed broadleaf and needleleaf forests cover much of this region. The climate is similar, though

drier, in the middle part of the country. Tall grass covered this area before it was cleared away by settlers. Further west, the plains are still drier. Shorter grass was the natural vegetation.

In the Rockies, the climate is dry, with harsh, cold winters. Desert areas lie southwest of the Rockies, especially in Arizona and Nevada.

The heavy rainfall along the Pacific Coast supports thick needleleaf forests. These forests extend from central California into Alaska. Mosses, grasses, and short bushes are the vegetation in northern Alaska, an area of tundra.

The island state of Hawaii has a great deal of variety in a relatively small area. Dense tropical forests cling to rain-swept mountain slopes. Only a few miles away it may be so dry that cacti dot an area of semidesert.

REVIEWING THE FACTS

Define

1. coastal plains
2. Central Plains
3. Great Plains
4. basin

Answer

1. (a) Describe the landforms along the eastern coast of the United States. (b) Of the interior plains. (c) In the Rocky Mountain area. (d) In the Pacific West.

2. (a) Describe the ecosystems along the eastern coast of the United States. (b) In the interior plains. (c) In the Rocky Mountain area. (d) In the Pacific West.

Locate

Refer to the map on pages 186–187.

1. Name four ranges that are part of the Rocky Mountains.

2. (a) In what state is most of the Great Basin located? (b) The Grand Canyon? (c) The Great Salt Lake?

189

2 The Human Imprint

Today the United States is the world's leading producer of both farm products and industrial goods. Its form of government and economic system have been imitated by many other countries. Its inventors and scientists have given the world a host of new products.

The American People

The United States is one of the most diverse nations in the world. Its many different people are united, however, in the value they give to representative democracy, personal freedom, and economic opportunity.

The First Americans Scientists believe that the first people to migrate to North America were Asian hunters. During the Ice Age — 20,000 to 30,000 years ago — so much water was frozen as glacial ice that the sea level was lower than it is today. As the sea level fell, a bridge of land appeared, connecting North America and Asia at the Bering Strait. Most scholars believe that Asians crossed this land bridge into North America while pursuing game beginning about 40,000 years ago. Over thousands of years, large numbers of such hunters may have made America their home.

At the end of the Ice Age, about 11,000 years ago, the seas rose as glaciers melted. The land bridge disappeared. At this time, experts believe, hundreds of groups of hunters were scattered throughout North and South America. Each group had its own language, customs, religious beliefs, and way of life. Although each group had its own name, these first Americans are referred to as Indians today.

Early European Settlers Today there are about 1.5 million Americans who are descendants of the early Indians. Most

Today many American Indians live and work in cities.

Americans, however, have ancestors who migrated to America within the last 400 years.

Large numbers of these immigrants came from Europe between 1600 and 1700. Most were from the British Isles, France, the Netherlands, and Germany. Many settled along the eastern coast of what is now the United States. By the mid-1700's, these settlers lived in a group of colonies controlled by England.

Large numbers of **Hispanics,** or people of Spanish ancestry, have also lived in North America since the 1600's. Most of the land settled by people from Spain lay in South America. Spanish adventurers explored as far north as Colorado and Kansas. They even traveled up the Mississippi River. Eventually there were Spanish settlements in the southwestern part of what is now the United States. Areas where large numbers of Spanish-speaking people settled included the lands stretching from Texas to southern California.

Lands settled by the Spanish were not part of the United States at its founding.

The section entitled "The Human Imprint" gives students an overview of the population and settlement patterns as well as the political and economic patterns of each region.
Assign the Workbook activity for Chapter 7, Section 2, with pages 190–197.

Some areas, however, were acquired by the United States during the 1800's. People in Texas, for example, became citizens of the United States in 1845. In that year, Texas was added as the twenty-eighth state. Hispanics in other parts of the southwestern region became American citizens after the United States took over a vast area from Mexico in 1848. These lands cover most of the southwestern portion of the United States.

The Arrival of Africans Millions of Africans also came to America. The first were explorers. For example, an African named Estevanico helped lead Spanish expeditions during the early 1500's. Then, in the early 1600's, Europeans began bringing Africans to America by force. By the mid-1600's, many European settlers were buying slaves that traders brought from Africa. Although slavery was practiced throughout the English colonies, it gradually died out in the northern colonies. In the southern colonies, however, labor was needed to work the many tobacco, rice, and — in the 1800's — cotton farms. Slavery continued there long after the United States had become independent.

The slave trade became illegal in 1808, and few Africans came to America after that year. At the end of the Civil War, in 1865, slavery was outlawed.

Most black Americans continued to work on farms after gaining freedom. In the twentieth century, however, great changes took place. For example, many blacks moved from the rural parts of southern states to cities in both southern and northern states. There, they took jobs in services and in such industries as automaking and steelmaking. Today blacks are represented in nearly every occupation. The areas of the greatest black population are still in the southern states and in the cities of the Northeast, the Midwest, and the West Coast.

Recent Immigration There have been three great waves of immigration since 1840. The first lasted from 1840 to 1860. This wave brought large numbers of Irish, English, German, and Scandinavian immigrants to the country. Many of these newcomers became farmers on the interior plains. Others took jobs in city stores and workshops. Still others became laborers, building canals and railroads.

As American industry grew in the late 1800's, the country needed more and more people to work in its factories. The second great wave of immigration brought workers from Europe to fill industrial jobs. From 1880 to 1930, millions of southern and eastern Europeans entered the country. The greatest numbers came from Italy, Russia, Poland, and Hungary. Most of them moved to industrial cities. They worked in factories, mills, stockyards, and railroad yards.

Those who became U.S. citizens during the second wave of immigration often settled in the country's growing cities.

191

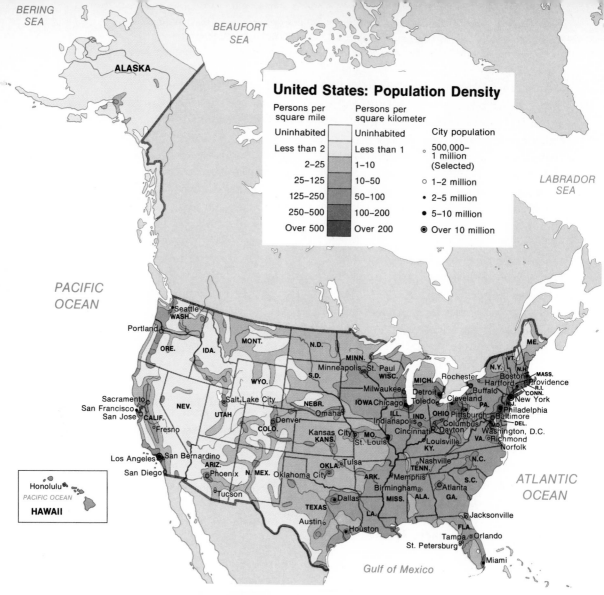

United States: Population Density

Persons per square mile	Persons per square kilometer
Uninhabited	Uninhabited
Less than 2	Less than 1
2–25	1–10
25–125	10–50
125–250	50–100
250–500	100–200
Over 500	Over 200

City population

- ○ 500,000– 1 million (Selected)
- ○ 1–2 million
- • 2–5 million
- ● 5–10 million
- ◉ Over 10 million

Map Study   *Which state has the lowest population density? How does population density vary within California? Florida?*

Large numbers of Chinese also came to America during the 1800's. They moved mainly to California and other western states. Many Chinese took jobs building railroads or mining copper and silver.

The third wave of immigration began in the 1950's. It is still going on. In recent years, millions have emigrated from Mexico and other countries of Latin America. Many immigrants have also come from Asia — especially the Philippines and Korea — and the West Indies.

Settlement Patterns

During most of the nation's history, the American people have been **mobile**. People who are mobile move often.
Settling the Continent At first, there was little need for European settlers to move westward. But as the population grew and land became scarce, hardy pioneers left the region along the eastern coast and struck out westward. By the 1860's Americans had settled lands reaching

Answers to Map Study questions: Alaska has the lowest population density. Population density in California varies from less than 2 to over 500 people per square mile (less than 1 person to over 200 people per square kilometer). Population density in Florida varies from 2 to 500 people per square mile (1 person to 200 people per square kilometer).

well beyond the Mississippi River. During the same years, the western coast, from Oregon to southern California, was also attracting settlers.

Moving to Urban Areas As industry grew in the late 1800's, many Americans left rural areas for cities. The midwestern and northeastern areas gained population as their cities expanded.

More than 240 million people live in the United States today. About 75 percent of them live in cities, suburbs, towns, and villages. Such places, however, take up only about 2 percent of the country's land area. This means that much of the population is found in crowded areas. These areas lie mainly along the Atlantic and Pacific Oceans, the Gulf of Mexico, and the Great Lakes.

Recently, however, there has been great growth in the sunbelt, the southern and southwestern states with year-round warm climates. Many people and businesses have moved from the snowbelt, or northern industrial states, to these areas. Many Americans have also moved from large metropolitan areas to smaller cities and towns. Some have even moved back to the country.

Political Patterns

The United States is a representative democracy. Its lawmakers and many government officials are elected by the people. Nearly every citizen 18 years of age and over has the right to vote. The powers of the government are listed in a written document called the Constitution of the United States.

The Constitution was approved by the people of the original 13 states between 1787 and 1790. It established a federal system of government. The national government has the power to make the nation's laws, to regulate trade between the states, to maintain armed forces to defend the country, and to conduct relations with other nations.

There are three branches of the national government. The **legislative branch** makes the laws. This branch is made up of a **bicameral,** or two-part, lawmaking body called Congress. The **executive branch,** headed by the President, carries out laws made by Congress. The **judicial branch,** or the nation's courts, judges whether people's actions are in accord with the laws.

The Government of the United States

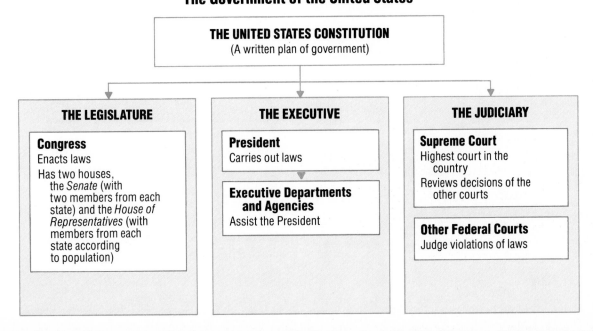

THE UNITED STATES CONSTITUTION
(A written plan of government)

THE LEGISLATURE

Congress
Enacts laws
Has two houses,
the *Senate* (with two members from each state) and the *House of Representatives* (with members from each state according to population)

THE EXECUTIVE

President
Carries out laws

Executive Departments and Agencies
Assist the President

THE JUDICIARY

Supreme Court
Highest court in the country
Reviews decisions of the other courts

Other Federal Courts
Judge violations of laws

In addition to listing the powers of the federal government, the Constitution protects the rights of the people. It guarantees freedom of worship, free speech and a free press, and freedom of petition and assembly. Under the Constitution, the government may not take people's property without a fair reason. The Constitution also gives every American equal protection of the law. It protects citizens from unfair arrest and punishment.

Under the federal system, each state has its own government. Each state has a constitution that provides for three branches of government. The powers of the states include punishing criminals, establishing public schools, chartering businesses, issuing drivers' licenses, and regulating traffic.

The U.S. Congress meets in the Capitol.

Economic Patterns

The United States has 5 percent of the world's people and about 6 percent of the world's land area. Yet it produces about 30 percent of the world's manufactured products. The country's GNP is trillions of dollars.

The Development of Farming   In the early days of the nation, most Americans worked in farming. This remained the case until about 1880. By that time, new farm machines had begun to make it possible for decreasing numbers of farmers to grow ever-larger crops. Later, farmers began to use chemicals that protected their crops from harmful insects. They used better seeds and improved the soil with fertilizers. They also used such scientific methods as crop rotation and contour farming.

An Industrial Giant   By the late 1800's, the United States had become an industrial giant. America's industrial success depended in part on the availability of resources. For example, the growing steel industry needed vast amounts of iron ore, coal, and limestone. In the late 1800's, as the United States entered the Steel Age, it found these resources in plentiful supply in the Great Lakes region. The early mining and quarrying industries grew along with the steel industry, which was located in the same area. Mining also developed in the late 1800's and early 1900's in the Rockies. There, valuable metals like lead, zinc, copper, gold, and silver were mined. Today coal and other resources are also found in the Rockies.

Energy Supplies   Another important factor in the growth of industry has been supplies of energy. The first American factories were built along rivers in Massachusetts and nearby states. The machines ran on water power. They turned out textiles and shoes.

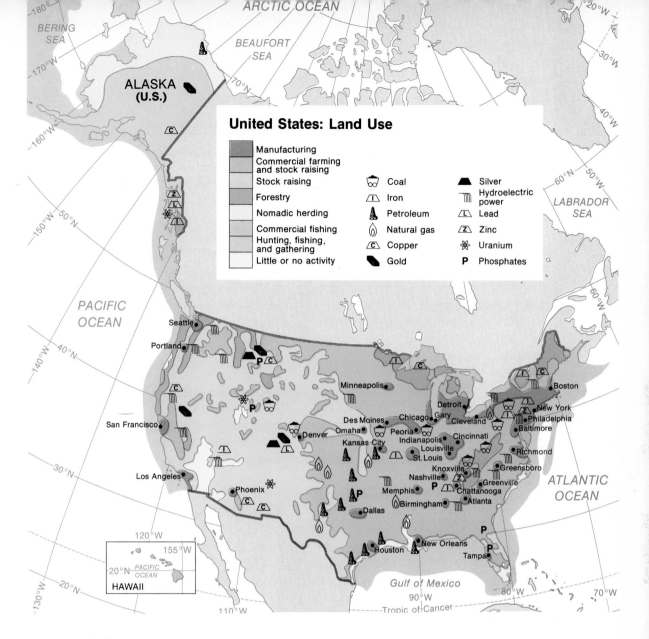

United States: Land Use

Manufacturing
Commercial farming and stock raising
Stock raising
Forestry
Nomadic herding
Commercial fishing
Hunting, fishing, and gathering
Little or no activity

Coal
Iron
Petroleum
Natural gas
Copper
Gold

Silver
Hydroelectric power
Lead
Zinc
Uranium
Phosphates

Map Study *Where in the United States does most of the farming take place? Compare this map with the climate map on page 188. What connection can you see between climate and farming?*

Coal became an important fuel in the mid-1800's. It was burned to make steam to drive locomotives and factory machines. Later it was used by power plants in generating electricity.

In the 1900's, new ways of producing power were developed. Oil and natural gas became the most important fuels. Large oil and natural gas fields are found in Texas, Louisiana, Oklahoma, and Alaska. Despite large deposits of these fuels, in recent years the United States has had to import large quantities of oil to meet the huge demand.

In addition, nuclear power is used in many places. Nuclear energy is fueled mostly by uranium. Uranium is mined in the Rocky Mountain states.

What type of land use is predominant in your community? Does your state or region have any of the important resources identified on the map?

195

Answers to Map Study questions: Most farming takes place in the eastern half of the country. This half has most of the country's mild, moist climate areas.

WORLD DATA BANK

Country	Area in Square Miles	Population/Natural Increase*		Per Capita GNP
United States	3,622,285	243,800,000	(0.7%)	$16,400

Natural Increase does not include immigration.

The source for the World Data Banks is the 1987 World Population Data Sheet published by the Population Reference Bureau.

Good Linkages Industrialization also depends on good linkages. Natural waterways and rugged overland trails provided the earliest travel routes in the United States. As the nation's economy grew, ways to carry more goods farther and faster had to be found.

In the early 1800's, Americans built a network of canals in the northeastern states. These canals linked farming valleys with distant cities. Later an extensive rail system was created. By the late 1860's, a person could travel from the Atlantic Coast to the Pacific Coast entirely by rail. The nation's canals and railroads helped the growth of industry during the 1800's.

In the twentieth century, transportation has been further improved. Cars and trucks became the most important method of travel in the early part of the century. The states, with help from the nation's government, have built better and better roads. Beginning in the 1950's, an interstate highway system was built. Today it provides a route to nearly every major city. Another improvement in transportation has been the building of the air-travel system. Modern harbor facilities and pipelines, which carry oil products, are also key parts of the nation's transportation network.

Telephones, radios, and television sets in virtually every household bring people into close contact throughout the country. Communications satellites carry a variety of programs around the world. Computers provide communication for business and have given the United States the lead in building the newest linkages.

American Free Enterprise Another important factor in developing industry has been the skills of managers and workers. American business owners, like the pioneers of the early 1800's, had the courage to take risks in new fields. Talented inventors sought better ways of doing things. The large labor force possessed many skills and was willing to work hard.

Under the free-enterprise system, people can profit from their efforts. In the United States, the rewards people can earn from hard work are great. Free enterprise encourages people to develop their resources, to expand their factories, and to innovate in countless ways.

Foreign Trade Today the United States has more foreign trade than any other nation. Canada, Japan, and Mexico are its chief trading partners. Major exports are cars, aircraft, office machines, computers, chemicals, and food. The United States imports large amounts of steel, clothing, electrical appliances, cars, and oil.

In recent years, the United States has had an unfavorable balance of trade. Americans are buying a great many goods from some nations that buy far less from the United States. Japan is one of these nations. Americans buy large numbers of cars and electronics products from

Japanese companies each year. However, the Japanese buy few American products in return. Canada is another nation with whom the United States has a large trade imbalance.

A Changing Economy Like some other industrial nations, the United States is entering what economists call the post-industrial age. In post-industrial countries, the importance of industrial production is falling while the importance of services is growing. Yet, in spite of this change in the American economy, the United States remains the world's greatest maker of industrial goods.

REVIEWING THE FACTS

Define

1. Hispanic
2. mobile
3. legislative branch
4. bicameral
5. executive branch
6. judicial branch

Answer

1. (a) What groups of people lived in America before the first Europeans arrived? (b) What groups of people settled in North America during the period of early European settlement?

2. Describe the three waves of immigration that have occurred since 1840.

3. Explain the system of government in the United States.

4. What factors have helped make the American economy strong?

Locate

Refer to the map on page 195.

1. (a) In which areas of the country are there deposits of coal? (b) Of petroleum? (c) Of natural gas? (d) Of iron ore?

2. (a) Which areas have timber resources? (b) Lands for grazing livestock?

3 The Northeast

The Northeast includes many of the areas first settled by Europeans. The northern part of this area is known as **New England.** The adjoining part, to the west and the south, is often referred to as the **Middle Atlantic states.** When Europeans settled this region, most made their living from the sea or from farming. Today the Northeast is one of the most heavily urbanized and industrialized parts of the world.

Where People Live

Find the Northeast on the population density map on page 192. You should notice that the Northeast is densely populated. The Northeast has only about one twentieth of the nation's land area. Yet nearly one fourth of the American people live in the Northeast.

Settlement is especially dense along the Atlantic coast. In fact, a megalopolis known as BosWash extends from Boston, Massachusetts, to Washington, D.C. Additional metropolitan centers cluster along some rivers and the Great Lakes.

New York City is part of the BosWash megalopolis.

In the remainder of this chapter, the United States is divided into four regions—the Northeast, the Midwest, the South, and the West. The people, economy, and current trends in each region are then discussed.

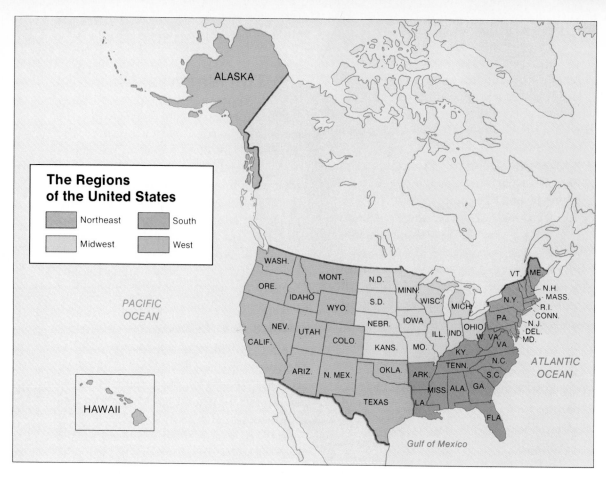

The Regions
of the United States

- Northeast
- South
- Midwest
- West

Map Study *Which region has no states that border an ocean? Which region has the largest area? the smallest area?* • *Southern Pennsylvania has large areas of good farmland.*

In northern New England—Maine, Vermont, and parts of New Hampshire—most people live in rural areas. There are also areas in west central New York and central Pennsylvania that are largely rural.

How People Work

The Northeast is a place of varied economic activity. People who live there work on farms and fishing boats, in factories and stores, and in offices and banks.
Farming Little of New England is suited to large-scale farming. Poor soil, long winters, and hilly land make farming there difficult. To the south—in Pennsylvania, New Jersey, and Maryland—

198

The map on this page should be used as students are learning about the four regions of the United States. In which of the four regions do your students live?
Students can refer to the land use map on page 195 as they read about work in the Northeast.
Answers to Map Study questions: the Midwest; the West; the Northeast

the growing season is longer and the soil is better. Today's farmers in this area specialize in **dairy** and **truck farming.** Dairy farmers produce milk and cheese from cows. Truck farmers raise poultry and grow fruits and vegetables. Products from dairy and truck farms are sold in the large cities nearby.

Fishing and Forestry Since colonial times, people of the Northeast have turned to activities other than farming. Many who lived along the Atlantic coast fished and built ships. Today fishing is still an important activity in the Northeast. In addition, forests have supplied great amounts of timber for building and furniture making.

Mining and Manufacturing The Northeast has been heavily industrialized since the late 1800's. The first factories were textile mills and shoe factories built in the 1830's. By 1900, the Pittsburgh, Pennsylvania, area had become the center for the nation's steel industry. Bituminous coal is mined in the same area.

Electrical machinery and transportation equipment, consumer goods, metals, processed foods, paper, and chemicals are important products of the Northeast today. Cities along the coasts of New Jersey and Delaware have refineries that process petroleum to make gasoline. These refineries also supply petroleum products to the many chemical plants located in the area. Electronics products, medical equipment, and computers are made in a number of places, especially the area around Boston.

Providing Services Service industries employ a great many workers in the Northeast. New York City is the nation's center for banking. With its large harbor and modern port facilities, it is also the scene of great foreign trade. New York and nearby Connecticut together are the insurance capital of the United States.

Boston, New York, and Philadelphia have some of the nation's best-known colleges and universities. Boston is also a leader in the development of computer software and in medical research. Entertainment, tourism, and recreation also are important industries in the Northeast.

Recent Changes

In the 1970's, some manufacturing companies in the Northeast fell on hard times. Many had old, inefficient equipment. As a result, they lost business to companies with modern machines. Clothing and shoe factories closed down. Steel firms also cut back production. In the years since, state and local governments have tried to find ways to keep factories working and to bring in new businesses where possible.

In addition, a number of northeastern cities lost population in the 1960's and

Nearby coal, iron ore, and limestone helped western Pennsylvania become a steelmaking center. Today foreign competition is hurting the industry.

199

1970's. Some businesses and factories left large urban centers for rural areas. For example, southern New Hampshire attracted many new businesses and large numbers of people during those years. Many businesses also moved south to the sunbelt.

While many northeastern cities are still losing population, some are not. Boston, for example, grew slightly in the mid-1980's. New York City remains the nation's largest city. Immigration has brought many new residents to New York and other urban areas. The largest numbers of immigrants have come from such islands of the West Indies as Haiti and the Dominican Republic.

REVIEWING THE FACTS

Define

1. New England
2. Middle Atlantic states
3. dairy farming
4. truck farming

Answer

1. Which parts of the Northeast are densely populated?

2. (a) Why is large-scale farming difficult in New England? (b) What kind of farming is most important in the Northeast?

3. (a) What are the Northeast's leading manufactured goods? (b) What are some of the service industries that are important in the region?

4. Why did many clothing and shoe factories in the Northeast close down during the 1970's?

Locate

Refer to the map on page 198.

1. Name the states of the Northeast.

2. Which northeastern states border the Atlantic or connect with the Atlantic by a bay?

200

4 The Midwest

The 12 states of the Midwest take up almost the entire northern part of the interior plains. These states cover about one fifth of the nation's land area. They are home to one fourth of its people.

Where People Live

Looking at the population density map on page 192, you can see that the area of high density in the Northeast extends into the Midwest. The cities around the Great Lakes are part of a megalopolis called ChiPitts, which reaches from Chicago, Illinois, to Pittsburgh in the Northeast. Rail, water, and air routes link this area to the industrial and trade centers of the Northeast. Together, the urbanized areas of the Midwest and Northeast are often called the nation's industrial heartland.

The western and southern portions of the Midwest are not as densely settled as the Great Lakes area. To the west are fertile farmlands surrounding a number of large cities like Kansas City, Missouri; St. Louis, Missouri; and Minneapolis, Minnesota. Throughout most of the Midwest, there is also good farmland. Large farms, small towns, and many medium-sized cities are located there.

How People Work

The Midwest has level fields, excellent waterways, and abundant minerals and other resources. This combination of advantages makes the Midwest one of the most varied and productive regions in the world.

Farming Most farming in the Midwest is done on a large scale, often by corporations. These corporations are called **agribusinesses.** Midwestern growers

Grain elevators store grain grown on midwestern farms. Corn, wheat, and other crops are later shipped to city markets or fed to livestock.

use such machinery as cultivators, planters, and combines. Farmers add chemical fertilizers to the soil.

The results are staggering. In few nations do farmers grow as much as do midwestern farmers. The average midwestern farmer produces enough to feed about 80 people each year. The Midwest's farm production is almost twice as much as the American people can consume.

Corn, wheat, soybeans, meat, and dairy goods are the Midwest's most important agricultural products. The corn belt stretches from western Ohio into Minnesota and eastern Kansas. Most midwestern corn is grown as feed for livestock. Raising livestock is the chief activity in the western part of the Midwest.

Wheat grows well in the dry climate of the Great Plains, which begin in the Midwest. In the Dakotas, where winters are cold and long, farmers grow mainly spring wheat, which is harvested in the fall. In Kansas and Nebraska, where winters are milder, farmers grow winter wheat, harvested in the spring.

Farmers in Wisconsin, Minnesota, and Michigan specialize in dairy and truck farming. Like farmers in the Northeast, they sell many of their goods in nearby urban centers.

Mining and Manufacturing Most of the Midwest's manufacturing is located east of the Mississippi River. The nation's largest steelmaking area is the Great Lakes region. This area extends from Chicago, Illinois, through Gary, Indiana, to Pittsburgh.

The region's steelmakers have sources of iron ore, limestone, and coal close by. During the 1800's, the Mesabi (mə säb'ē) Range in northern Minnesota supplied the nation's steel industry with iron ore. The Mesabi deposits were used up by the middle of the 1900's. Today taconite (tak'ə nīt'), a useful low-grade ore, is still mined in the Mesabi area. Indiana is the nation's leading producer of limestone. Coal is mined in a number of midwestern states. The most important deposits are found in Ohio, Indiana, and Illinois.

Transportation equipment is another important manufactured product. The city of Detroit and its surrounding area are considered the world capital of automaking. In addition, midwestern factories make tractors, combines, reapers, and other farm equipment. Important

Mastering What You Read

Understanding and remembering what you read is the key to being a successful student. Use the following steps to help you get the most from this and other books.

Preview the chapter Before reading the chapter, skim the chapter opening and the summary. Take note of headings and look for maps, graphs, and photographs to get a general impression of the content.

Read each lesson carefully One way to get the most out of your reading is to turn each lesson and section heading into one or more *who, what, when, where,* or *why* questions. As you read, look for answers to your questions.

Take notes Jot down the answers to your questions in note format or record the main ideas in outline form.

Reread the lesson After you have finished taking notes, reread the lesson. You will gain a better understanding of any section that may have seemed confusing to you.

Review the material Use the chapter summary to help you review the main ideas. Compare the summary to your notes. Have you picked out the main ideas of the chapter?

This chapter looks at the United States, its land and people. The headings from the first section of the chapter appear below. On a separate sheet of paper, turn each heading into a question. Then answer your questions with main ideas from the chapter. The first few headings have been done for you as a sample.

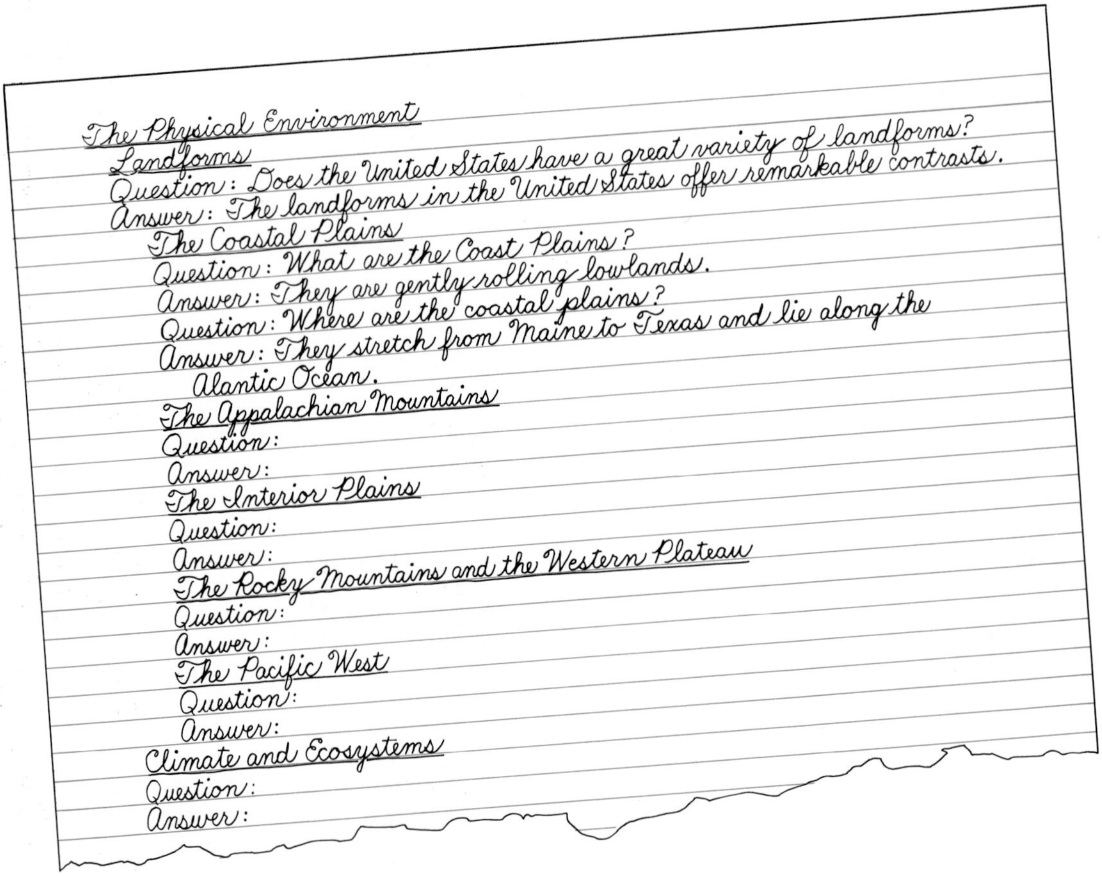

The Physical Environment
Landforms
Question: Does the United States have a great variety of landforms?
Answer: The landforms in the United States offer remarkable contrasts.
The Coastal Plains
Question: What are the Coast Plains?
Answer: They are gently rolling lowlands.
Question: Where are the coastal plains?
Answer: They stretch from Maine to Texas and lie along the
  Alantic Ocean.
The Appalachian Mountains
Question:
Answer:
The Interior Plains
Question:
Answer:
The Rocky Mountains and the Western Plateau
Question:
Answer:
The Pacific West
Question:
Answer:
Climate and Ecosystems
Question:
Answer:

Answers are in the Teacher's Guide.

Assign the Workbook activity for this chapter's Skill Workshop with this page.

For many years, steelmaking in the United States was identified with the name Andrew Carnegie and the city of Pittsburgh. Carnegie, originally a penniless Scottish immigrant, built a steel mill in Pittsburgh in 1873. When he sold his company to U.S. Steel in 1901, it was worth $250 million.

Computer-run robots can build dishwashers. As industrial jobs have disappeared, more workers are learning skills needed for technical jobs.

products also include machine parts, washers, dryers, and refrigerators. Many agricultural products also come to cities of the Midwest for processing.

Providing Services Many services are provided in the region. For example, the transportation hub of the region is Chicago. Located at the southern tip of Lake Michigan, Chicago is an excellent place from which to ship goods by water. It also has the world's busiest airport and extensive rail facilities. A network of highways connects it with distant cities.

Recent Changes

The Midwest, like the Northeast, has lost some of its businesses and residents to the sunbelt. At the same time, many factories — especially steel mills — have lost business to foreign competition. The people of the Midwest are adjusting to these changes. Auto factories, for example, have installed new technology. Robots and computers are widely used in making cars today. Some steel factories, especially in the Chicago area, use the latest equipment. In addition, a number of state and city governments are working to get companies from other countries to build factories in the Midwest.

Additional changes are taking place in the Midwest. For example, many farmers are unable to sell all they produce. Grain growers in particular find it hard to locate markets for their large harvests. The income of farmers is falling. Many farmers cannot afford the equipment and supplies they need. Some have had to look for additional sources of income. A few have given up their land to larger growers.

REVIEWING THE FACTS

Define

agribusiness

Answer

1. (a) Where do most midwesterners live? (b) Which parts of the Midwest have the lowest population density?

2. What are the most important goods produced in the Midwest?

3. Describe the recent challenges faced by midwestern factories and farmers.

Locate

Refer to the map on page 198.

1. Name the states of the Midwest.

2. Which states border the Great Lakes?

203

Texas Essential Elements 1C. Geographical tools and methodologies. 4C. Population distribution, growth, and movements.

Using a Baseball Map to Interpret Population Trends

Baseball is a spectator sport that attracts millions of Americans each year. It is also big business. To make a profit, a baseball team must draw large numbers of fans to its home games. Only a metropolitan area can support a major-league baseball team.

In 1950, there were 8 National League teams and 8 American League teams. All these teams were located in cities of the Northeast and the Midwest. Since 1950, a number of cities have acquired expansion, or new, baseball teams. A number of teams have also relocated to new cities. By 1977, the National League had 12 teams and the American League 14. In 1985, plans were made to add 2 teams to the National League.

As the leagues have expanded, it has become clear that teams follow population trends. When a team moves or a city acquires an expansion team, it is usually a sign of a population shift.

1. How many teams in existence before 1950 are still located in their original cities?

2. (a) Which two Canadian cities have acquired baseball teams? (b) Were the teams they acquired expansion teams or transferred teams?

3. (a) How many expansion teams have been acquired by cities in the United States? (b) How many teams have transferred from one city to another?

4. Which state has acquired the greatest number of teams since 1950?

5. Based on the information on the map, make a statement describing the pattern of population growth in the United States since 1950.

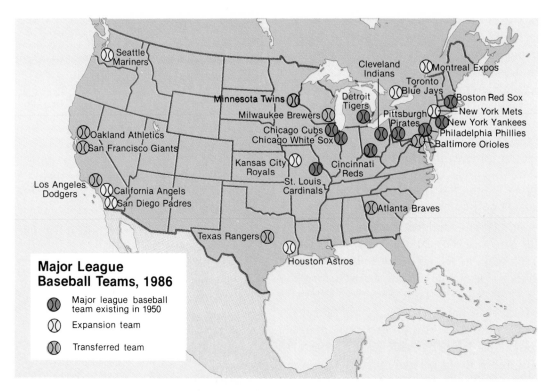

Major League Baseball Teams, 1986

- Major league baseball team existing in 1950
- Expansion team
- Transferred team

Answers are in the Teacher's Guide.
Assign the Workbook activity for this chapter's Map Workshop with this page.

5 The South

The first British settlers in the southern English colonies found the climate and soils ideal for farming. Colonists grew tobacco and other crops for export to England. After the United States became independent, the South remained a largely rural region. Today it is the scene of rapid, exciting changes.

Where People Live

Well into the early 1900's, most southerners lived on farms or in small towns. Even today the percentage of people living in towns and cities is lower in the South than in any other region. Still, about two thirds of the people of the South live in urban areas.

In the early years, the largest southern cities were ports. New Orleans, Louisiana, for example, was located on the Mississippi River near the Gulf of Mexico.

Several other southern cities — including Richmond, Virginia, and Columbia, South Carolina — were built in an area known as the **fall line.** The fall line is the point at which the Atlantic Coastal Plain and the Piedmont meet. Rivers flowing toward the ocean break into waterfalls and rapids at the fall line. Boats traveling inland from the ocean could not navigate these churning waters. In colonial times, goods going west were transferred from boats to wagons at the fall line. Gradually cities grew up at these points. In later years, energy provided by the falls in the rivers encouraged manufacturing and thus population growth in these cities.

Today large, fast-growing urban areas extend along the Atlantic and Gulf coasts of Florida. In addition, there is heavy population density in and around Atlanta,

Near New Orleans, the Mississippi River flows into the Gulf of Mexico. Its location has made the city a major port.

Georgia; Memphis and Nashville, Tennessee; and Birmingham, Alabama. Areas of rapid growth include the arc from Greenville, South Carolina, to Raleigh, North Carolina, and the area around Norfolk, Virginia.

How People Work

Large forests, extensive mineral deposits, fertile soils, and long growing seasons help make the South the strong and varied economic region that it is today.

Farming Since colonial days, agriculture has been a key part of the South's economy. Cotton became the major crop of the region in the 1800's. It was grown on both farms and **plantations,** large farms worked by slave laborers. Even after the abolition of slavery, the South remained a farming area. It grew cotton and other crops much as before.

Until the late 1700's, cotton was not very important because it was too expensive to produce. Then, in 1793, Eli Whitney invented the cotton gin (gin is short for *engine*), which made cotton production profitable, and the industry grew rapidly. At one time, the South produced two thirds of the world's cotton.

Tell students to note the diversity of the South's economy.
Do students understand the meaning of the word *textile*? *(a woven fabric)* Ask them
why the South would be a logical place for this type of industry. *(cotton growing)*

This scene has been changing steadily since the early 1900's. Today most southern farmers use modern methods and equipment to grow cotton and other crops. These include peanuts, peaches, apples, oranges, grapefruits, soybeans, corn, and winter vegetables. Poultry farms supply consumers in many parts of the country with broiler chickens and turkeys. Southern farmers also engage in dairy farming and the raising of beef cattle.

Forestry and Fishing A great deal of pine is cut in the South. The warm, moist climate enables pine trees to grow to cutting size in just 20 to 30 years. The South's thick forests also supply nearly half the nation's hardwood.

The South also takes in a large part of the nation's annual catch of fish. The Atlantic catch is used partly for animal feed and partly for human consumption. Gulf fishers harvest shrimp and other fish, and the South's rivers yield catfish.

Mining and Manufacturing The South has a wealth of natural resources and raw materials. Huge petroleum and natural-gas reserves lie along the Louisiana coast. Enormous coalfields stretch for more than 650 miles (1,040 kilometers) through the Appalachian Mountains. Deposits of iron ore are mined in Alabama, Georgia, and Tennessee.

Manufacturing has become an important economic activity in the South. Textile making was the first major industry in the region. In the late 1800's, many textile mills—some relocating from New England—were built in the fall-line cities. Waterfalls provided power to run the machines. Today clothing factories continue to operate in Virginia, Georgia, and the Carolinas. They specialize in work clothes, sportswear, and children's clothing. The center of southern steel production is Birmingham.

These bales of jute are being shipped to one of the South's textile mills. Fibers from jute plants are spun into threads and then woven into many different kinds of cloth.

Auto factories are located in many parts of the South. Several of these factories are owned by foreign automakers, who find the South a good place to build cars. Large plants also produce dyes, insect sprays, and other chemical products.

Food processing is another major industry in the region. Products include cooking oils, poultry, and canned fruits and vegetables.

Services A moderate climate, sandy beaches, and forest-covered mountains make many parts of the South favorite vacation and recreation spots. Tourism is especially important in Florida. Millions of visitors from all over the United States, Latin America, and Europe vacation in Florida each year. They visit beach resorts, amusement parks, and camping sites. Historic cities such as New Orleans, Louisiana, also draw tourists.

206

Several cities are mentioned in this lesson. Students should find their
location on maps either in this chapter or in the Atlas.
Assign the Workbook activity for Chapter 7, Section 5, with pages 205–207.

Recent Changes

Experts believe that the South will continue to grow. Businesses are attracted by low wages, low land prices, and low taxes. In addition, the work force is better educated and more skilled than ever before. The warm climate and low energy costs appeal to many residents of the Northeast and Midwest.

As people move to the South, its urban areas grow larger. With growth come new challenges. For example, Tyson's Corner, Virginia, was little more than a crossroads with a service station in the 1940's. Today it is a bustling community of over 60,000 people. It has large office buildings, modern highways, and shopping areas. In many southern communities, busy streets, heavy demand for services, and industrial pollution have accompanied growth.

REVIEWING THE FACTS

Define

1. fall line 2. plantation

Answer

1. How does urbanization in the South compare with that in other regions of the United States?

2. (a) What was the major crop of the South before the Civil War? (b) What are the major crops in the region today?

3. What manufactured goods are produced in the South?

4. Why have businesses and people relocated to the South?

Locate

Refer to the map on page 198.

1. Name the states of the South.

2. (a) Which southern states border the Atlantic Ocean? (b) The Gulf of Mexico?

6 The West

Much of the western coast was settled during the years when pioneers and farming families spread through the Midwest and inland South. The area lying between the Midwest and the Pacific coast, however, was not settled until years later. In fact, large parts of the Rockies and the plateau region have few residents today. The West as a whole remains sparsely populated compared with other regions. Even so, population is growing faster in the West than in any other part of the United States.

Where People Live

A little over half the land area of the United States lies within the West. Few people live on the Great Plains and in the mountain areas of the West. Widely scattered ranches and farms cover much

San Francisco lies at the northern end of California's megalopolis. That megalopolis is the largest area of dense population in the West. The city's skyscrapers overlook the San Francisco-Oakland Bay Bridge.

Have students examine the Western states on the physical, climate, land use, and population density maps in this chapter. What conclusions can be drawn about this region of the United States?
Assign the Workbook activity for Chapter 7, Section 6, with pages 207–211.

SPOTLIGHT ON HERITAGE:

The Fifty States

State Name	Origin/Meaning	State Name	Origin/Meaning
Alabama	Choctaw; from *Alba Ayamule*, "one who clears the land"	Montana	Spanish; "mountainous"
Alaska	Eskimo; from *Alakshak* or *Alayeksa*, "great land"	Nebraska	Omaha; from *Ni-bthaska*, "river in the flatness"
Arizona	Papago; from *Arizonac*, "place of the small spring"	Nevada	Spanish; "snowy, snowed upon"
Arkansas	Sioux; from *Arkansaw*, "south wind people"	New Hampshire	English; after Hampshire County, England
California	Spanish; "an earthly paradise"	New Jersey	English; after the Isle of Jersey
Colorado	Spanish; "red land, red earth"	New Mexico	Spanish; after Mexico
Connecticut	Mohican; from *Quinnituk-qut*, "at the long tidal river"	New York	English; after the Duke of York
Delaware	English; after Governor Lord de la Warr	North Carolina	English; after King Charles II
Florida	Spanish; "land of flowers"	North Dakota	Sioux name for themselves, "friend, ally"
Georgia	English; after King George II	Ohio	Iroquois; from *Oheo*, "beautiful, beautiful water"
Hawaii	Native name; *Hawaiki*, or *Owykee*, "homeland"	Oklahoma	Choctaw: "the red people"
Idaho	Shoshone; "light on the mountains"	Oregon	Algonquin; from *Waure-gan*, "beautiful water"
Illinois	Algonquian; from *Iliniwek*, "men, warriors"	Pennsylvania	American; after William Penn plus Latin *sylva*, "woodland"
Indiana	American; "land of the Indians"	Rhode Island	Dutch; "red clay island"
Iowa	Dakota; from *Ayuba*, "the sleepy one"	South Carolina	English; after King Charles II
Kansas	Sioux; "south wind people"	South Dakota	Sioux name for themselves, "friend, ally"
Kentucky	Iroquois; from *Kentake*, "meadow land"	Tennessee	Cherokee; after a Cherokee settlement
Louisiana	French; after King Louis XIV	Texas	Spanish; from *Tejas*, from a local Indian word *Texia* for "friend, ally"
Maine	French; after a French province		
Maryland	English; after Henrietta Maria, queen consort of Charles I	Utah	Navaho; "the upper land" or "land of the Ute"
Massachusetts	Algonquian; "at the big hill"	Vermont	French; from *Vert*, "green" plus *Mont*, "mountain"
Michigan	Chippewa; from *Mica Gama*, "big water"	Virginia	English; after the Virgin Queen, Elizabeth I
Minnesota	Dakota Sioux; "sky tinted winter"	Washington	American; after George Washington
Mississippi	Chippewa; from *Mici Sibi*, "big river"	West Virginia	English; after the state of Virginia
Missouri	Algonquian; "muddy water"	Wisconsin	Algonquian; "grassy place" or "place of the beaver"
		Wyoming	Algonquian; from *Mache-weaming*, "at the big flats"

of the plains area. Small mining towns and tourist centers dot the Rockies. In Alaska, great forests and tundra extend unbroken for thousands of square miles. Alaska's population density—just 0.7 people per square mile (0.3 per square kilometer)—is lower than that of any other state.

There are, however, major centers of population throughout the West. A megalopolis known as SanSan extends along the California coast from San Francisco to San Diego. A number of large and growing cities—among them Dallas and Houston—are located in central and eastern Texas. Even high in the Rockies and in the hot, dry desert basins there are pockets of dense population. Denver, Colorado—the mile-high city—is a major center for trade and energy production. Both Salt Lake City, Utah, and the rapidly growing city of Phoenix, Arizona, are attracting new industries.

How People Work

The West is an area of contrasts. Economic activities on the Pacific Coast and in eastern Texas are varied, with many industries and services and large-scale farming. In the Great Plains and the Rockies, however, there is a great deal of specialization.

Farming The West has three major farming areas. One is in the Great Plains, where huge farms and ranches are common. Farmers in this area grow wheat, corn, other grains, and hay. In some parts of the plains, ranching is more important than crop growing.

The fertile valleys of the states that border the Pacific are the second major agricultural area in the West. In these valleys are huge orchards and farms. Major crops include vegetables, strawberries, apples, pears, grapes, and nuts.

WHEN CAMELS ROAMED THE RANGE

In 1865, 75 seasick camels from North Africa arrived in Indianola, Texas. The United States Army hoped to use these animals to carry equipment in the western desert. But the camels' wide hooves, so well adapted to the Sahara, were not suited to the rocky land of American deserts. The unusual appearance of the camels caused horses and cattle to stampede. In the end, most of the camels were sold to circuses. Canada took a few of them to work on road building. The rest were left to roam the desertland of the Southwest.

A smaller farming area also exists in the Hawaiian islands. There, on large, plantationlike farms, growers produce sugarcane, pineapple, and other tropical crops. Factories in Hawaii process many of these crops.

209

Forestry and Fishing Forestry is one of the most important economic activities in the Pacific Coast region. In Oregon, Washington, and northern California, thick evergreen forests support large-scale lumbering operations. Fishing, especially for salmon and tuna, is also an important industry in the Pacific states. Over half the nation's fish catch is taken in western waters.

Producing Minerals The West has large deposits of minerals and other resources. Oil wells in Texas alone produce more oil than many of the world's oil-rich countries. Oklahoma also has tens of thousands of oil wells. A large amount of crude oil is shipped out of these states for processing. Still, many of the jobs in such cities as Houston and Dallas, Texas, and Oklahoma City and Tulsa, Oklahoma are related to the oil industry.

The Rockies have valuable deposits of coal and some recently discovered

About three fifths of the copper mined in the United States comes from Arizona.

deposits of petroleum. Large quantities of copper ore are strip-mined in western states, including Arizona. Other metals are found throughout the Rocky Mountains. Among them are zinc, manganese, silver, molybdenum (mə lib′də nəm), and lead. Manganese is used to harden special steels. Molybdenum can be used to harden steels or, on its own, to make X-ray tubes and missile parts.

California is another major mineral-producing area. It has large petroleum-refining and natural-gas industries. Its mines produce gold, sulphur, lead, and other minerals.

Petroleum is by far Alaska's most important resource. A pipeline built during the 1970's transports crude oil from the Arctic coast across the state to the ice-free port of Valdez (val dēz′). Tankers take the oil to refineries in California or to buyers in Japan. There are plans to build another pipeline that will carry oil across Canada to a port on the Great Lakes. New jobs created by the petroleum industry and by pipeline construction have caused Alaska's population nearly to double since 1960.

Manufacturing Many kinds of factories are located in the West, especially on the Pacific Coast. Seattle, Washington, has huge aircraft-manufacturing plants. So do Los Angeles and other southern California cities. An area known as Silicon Valley, just outside of San Francisco, is the country's leading electronics and computer-making center. In California, food-processing plants can fruits and vegetables grown in local farming valleys and fish caught in the Pacific. Plants in Portland, Oregon, process wood from northwestern forests and food from farms and fisheries. As in other parts of the country, chemical plants are located near the refining centers.

Ski resorts in the Rocky Mountains make tourism an important industry in Colorado. The population of Puerto Rico is Hispanic, and nearly 40 percent of the people live in the capital city of San Juan.

Services The services of the West are varied. Foreign trade, for example, developed because of the good ports and the abundant raw materials and finished goods that could be exported. Seattle, Portland, San Francisco, and San Diego are all major cities with excellent harbors. A large portion of the nation's import-export business, especially with Asian countries, passes through these cities.

The year-round mild climate and the beauty of the Pacific area have helped build other services. Tourism is a major business in Hawaii and California. National parks in the scenic Rockies also attract millions of visitors each year. The nation's filmmaking and television industries are based in the Los Angeles area.

Outlying Possessions

The United States has a number of possessions in the Caribbean Sea and the Pacific Ocean. Puerto Rico, a Caribbean island, is one of these possessions. Puerto Rico was ceded to the United States by Spain in 1898. It became a territory of the United States in 1917. Today Puerto Rico is known as a free commonwealth. It is self-governing but is part of the United States. Puerto Rico has a representative in Congress who can speak for its residents but cannot vote. Puerto Ricans are citizens of the United States.

The Panama Canal Zone, at the southern tip of Central America, is another territory of the United States. By the year 2000, the Canal Zone will belong entirely to the country of Panama.

Recent Changes

Parts of the West are short of a vital natural resource — water. With a growing population, some parts of the West are having a hard time finding adequate water supplies. Two rivers in particular are the lifelines of the dry southern part of the West. Starting high in the mountains, the Colorado River passes through parts of Colorado, Utah, Arizona, and California. The Rio Grande flows through New Mexico and along the southern border of Texas. But these rivers do not reach every place in which people live.

Existing aqueducts and irrigation systems must be constantly expanded to keep pace with the growing demand for water. The construction of dams, reservoirs, and aqueducts has helped make living in these places possible. For example, the cities of Phoenix and Tucson, in Arizona, have attracted new businesses, workers seeking jobs, and many retired people from other states.

As in the South, population in the West is expected to keep growing. Immigration is a major factor. People from Mexico have entered southern California and Texas in great numbers. California is home to growing numbers of Asians, especially Koreans and Filipinos.

REVIEWING THE FACTS

Answer

1. What kinds of farming are practiced in each of the West's agricultural areas?

2. In what resources is the West rich?

3. What major resource challenge do some parts of the West face?

Locate

Refer to the map on page 198.

1. Name the states of the West.

2. (a) Which states border the Pacific Ocean? (b) Which western state borders the Gulf of Mexico?

211

GEOGRAPHY LABORATORY

Highlighting the Chapter

1. The five major landform areas of the United States are the coastal plains of the East; the Appalachian Mountains; the interior plains (the Central Plains and the Great Plains); the mountains and plateaus of the Rockies; and the mountains and valleys of the Pacific West. Climates vary greatly, but most of the United States has a moderate climate.

2. The United States population is over 240 million. Americans trace their ancestry to nearly every part of the world. Today the United States is a representative democracy with a free-enterprise economy. It has many resources for farming and industry. It is the world's most industrialized nation, and it has the world's largest foreign trade.

3. The Northeast covers a relatively small area of the United States. It is the most heavily industrialized and most densely populated part of the country. It also has dairy and truck farming and is developing computers and other advanced technologies.

4. The Midwest covers most of the Central Plains and the eastern part of the Great Plains. It produces large quantities of corn, wheat, and meat and dairy products. In urban areas, steel, farm machinery, and automobiles are produced. Food processing is also important.

5. Traditionally an agricultural region, the South is changing rapidly. Farm products include soybeans, tobacco, corn, cotton, a variety of fruits and vegetables, and livestock. There are many growing urban areas with a variety of industries.

6. The West is the fastest-growing region of the United States. Ranchers raise cattle, and farmers grow wheat. Mining companies produce valuable metals and minerals. Rich oil deposits are found in the West. Manufacturing and the growing of fruit and vegetables are leading industries along the Pacific Coast.

212

Speaking Geographically

Some terms from the chapter are defined below. Number your paper from 1 to 8. For each definition, write the proper term.

1. Semiarid region east of the Rockies

2. Large farms worked by slave laborers

3. Six states in the northeast corner of the United States

4. Growing of vegetables and fruit

5. Corporations that run farms

6. Zone in which rivers and streams have many falls and rapids

7. The branch of the government directed by the President

8. Lawmaking branch of the government, also called Congress

Testing Yourself

Several traits of the different United States regions are listed below. Number your paper from 1 to 10. After each number, write the name of the region or regions to which the phrase given applies.

1. Has a megalopolis

2. Grows cotton and peanuts

3. Has mountain valleys with intensive fruit and vegetable farming

4. Is the center of the auto industry

5. Has many cattle ranches

6. Has the nation's fastest population growth

7. Is the most sparsely populated region

8. Contains the nation's largest city

9. Has vast iron ore and taconite ranges

10. Contains the Appalachians

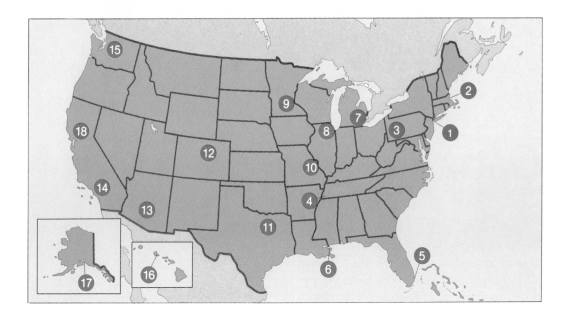

Building Map Skills

Number your paper from 1 to 18. Then write the name of the proper city for each number on the map above.

Applying Map Skills

Number your paper from 1 to 10. Then use the following clues to identify ten states. Write the name of the proper state beside each number. When you have finished, underline the first letter of each state. You should be able to spell the name of an important American city by unscrambling these letters. What is this city?

1. This state borders New England.

2. Its southern boundary is formed by the Rio Grande.

3. This state lies between Vermont and Maine.

4. Most of Yellowstone National Park is in this state.

5. It lies between Illinois and Ohio.

6. It is the newest state.

7. The Black Hills are in this state.

8. The center of the South's steel industry is here.

9. It is the largest state east of the Mississippi River.

10. This state lies north of Texas.

Exploring Further

1. Make a report on the production of bread in the United States. Include these topics: the crops used in making bread, how and where these crops are grown, the transporting of crops to processing centers, how and where the crops are processed, the delivery of the bread to consumers.

2. Imagine that you take a trip down the Mississippi River. You start at its source and end your trip in the Gulf of Mexico. Keep a diary of the sights you might see each day of the trip.

3. Select a national park for a research project. Report on the main attractions in the park.

213

GEOGRAPHY LABORATORY

Canada

To the north of the United States lies a large and friendly neighbor—Canada. Canada covers almost the entire northern part of North America. It is a vast country, taking up about one fifteenth of Earth's surface. Only one other country—the Soviet Union—is larger.

Canada and the United States share the world's longest unguarded border. At some places along this border, the two countries are so much alike that a visitor can have trouble telling one from the other.

There are indeed many similarities between Canada and the United States. Both nations were settled mostly by European immigrants. Both were once colonies of Great Britain. Both have a representative government and a free-enterprise economy. The standard of living is high in both Canada and the United States. Each country has a great wealth of minerals, vast forestlands, abundant waters for fishing, fertile soil for farming, and many other natural resources.

Canada is, however, different from the United States in many important ways. Canada's population is sparser. Its climate is colder than that of most of the United States. Canada also has far greater expanses of undeveloped land. In this chapter, you will read about the land and the people of Canada. You will learn about the many ways in which Canada and the United States are alike and different.

214

The photograph is an aerial view of Hopedale, Labrador.

Texas Essential Elements 1B. Geographic terminology. 2B.
Major landforms, regions, and features of the earth. 2C. Physical
and human forces that alter the earth's features.

1 The Physical Environment

Study the map of Canada on page 216. You should notice that Canada's coastline is very long. Much of it lies along icy, Arctic waters. To the south, Canada borders the United States. The western part of the Canadian-United States border is formed by the 49°N parallel. On the east, the border is dominated by the Great Lakes.

Landforms

There are five major land regions in Canada. Several of these regions are also found in the United States.

The Appalachian Highlands The Appalachians extend across the eastern coast of Canada. These highlands create a jagged, rugged shoreline with many natural harbors. They also form a number of large islands in the Atlantic Ocean.

The Appalachian area, like most of Canada, was covered by the great ice sheets of the last Ice Age. The action of glaciers eroded this northern part of the Appalachian Mountain system. As a result, the hills and mountains of eastern Canada are low and rounded in appearance.

The St. Lawrence-Great Lakes Lowlands The lowlands around the St. Lawrence River and the Great Lakes are the smallest of Canada's land regions. They were shaped during the Ice Age. At that time, glaciers leveled hills and scoured out basins in the lands just west of the Appalachians.

When the glacial ice began to melt — 12 to 14 thousand years ago — some of the glacial basins were filled with water. Among the many lakes formed in this way were the five Great Lakes. Together, these lakes make up the largest

Many lakes in the Canadian Shield were formed by glaciers.

body of fresh water in the world. During the Ice Age, the St. Lawrence Valley was a great channel carrying glacial runoff northeastward into the Gulf of St. Lawrence. Today, the St. Lawrence is a broad, deep river. In addition, the lowlands along the St. Lawrence have rich, brown soil.

The Canadian Shield A horseshoe-shaped area of hills and plateaus covers about half of Canada's land. Known as the **Canadian Shield**, this area is believed to be the oldest part of North America. Over millions of years, its ancient rocks have been worn down by ice and water.

The Canadian Shield is a rugged, forested region with poor soils. It is dotted with glacial lakes. Rivers flowing from these lakes have many falls and rapids. They are, therefore, not good for navigation. Because of their falls, however, these rivers have become sources of **hydroelectric power,** or electricity created by water-driven turbines. Deposits of such minerals as copper, iron, nickel, and silver are found in abundance in the Canadian Shield.

215

Have students use the physical map of Canada on page 216 to locate
each of the land regions as it is discussed.
Assign the Workbook activity for Chapter 8, Section 1, with pages 215–218.

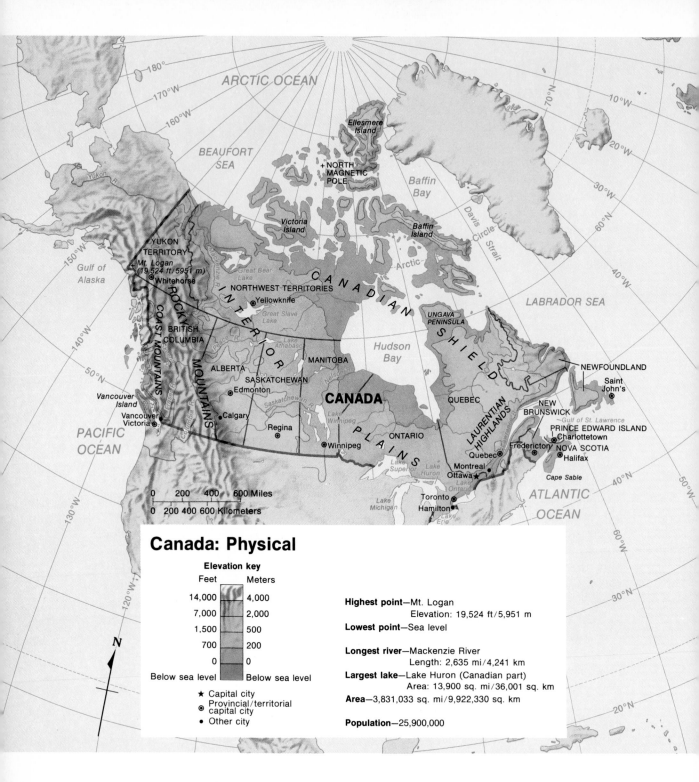

Canada: Physical

Elevation key

Feet	Meters
14,000	4,000
7,000	2,000
1,500	500
700	200
0	0
Below sea level	Below sea level

★ Capital city
◉ Provincial/territorial capital city
● Other city

Highest point—Mt. Logan
      Elevation: 19,524 ft/5,951 m
Lowest point—Sea level

Longest river—Mackenzie River
      Length: 2,635 mi/4,241 km
Largest lake—Lake Huron (Canadian part)
      Area: 13,900 sq. mi/36,001 sq. km
Area—3,831,033 sq. mi/9,922,330 sq. km

Population—25,900,000

Map Study   *Which province of Canada is the most mountainous?
At what elevation is Montreal? Winnipeg? Regina?*   ● *Which area
of British Columbia is milder, the northwest coast or the
central region? What is the reason?*

216

Answers to Map Study questions: British Columbia; 0–700 feet (0–200 meters); 700–1,500
feet (200–500 meters); 1,500–7,000 feet (500–2,000 meters); the northwest coast; the Pacific
Ocean moderates temperatures along the coast.

Glaciers and glacial lakes can still be seen in Glacier National Park, which lies on the border between western Montana and Canada. This park is part of the Waterton-Glacier International Peace Park established by Canada and the United States in 1932.

The Western Interior Plains There is a large plains region in the interior of Canada. The Western Interior Plains are part of the same expanse of plains that is found in the United States. Like those in the United States, the Canadian plains are a broad, gently rolling prairie. Their black soil is very fertile. The plains also have deposits of valuable minerals.

The Western Mountains The Rockies and the Coastal Mountains form a narrower area in Canada than they do in the United States. As in the United States, however, these ranges are separated by a rugged strip of valleys, basins, and plateaus.

Alpine, or mountain, glaciers formed in the Western Mountains during the Ice Age. Because of the cold temperatures of the area, many of these glaciers did not disappear when the Ice Age ended. They are still at work, carving out deep U-shaped valleys and sharp peaks.

Climates and Ecosystems

Because it lies so far north, most of Canada is cold, with long, harsh winters and short, cool summers. Only a small area mostly along the southern border, is good farmland. Much of the rest of Canada is wilderness.

Northern Canada Northern Canada has a subarctic climate. In the far north is a vast tundra where mainly short grasses, mosses, and tiny flowering plants grow. South of the tundra, there is the **taiga** (tī′gə), an extensive needleleaf forest.

In large parts of northern Canada, there is permafrost. Only the surface layer of soil thaws during the summer; water is not able to seep into the frozen layers beneath. Therefore, swamps, marshes, and ponds form as the snow melts.

Southeastern Canada Most Canadians live in a narrow band of land in the southern part of the country. This area has a humid continental climate. The weather

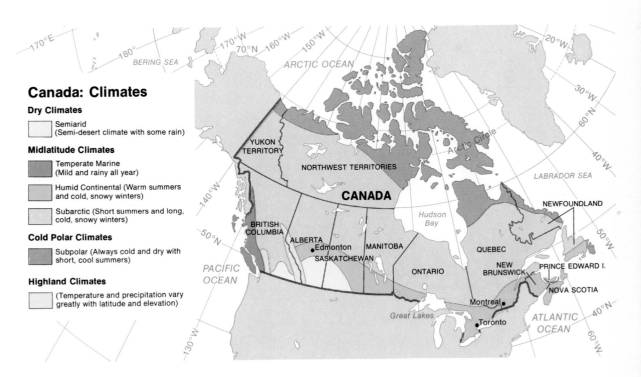

Canada: Climates

Dry Climates

Semiarid (Semi-desert climate with some rain)

Midlatitude Climates

Temperate Marine (Mild and rainy all year)

Humid Continental (Warm summers and cold, snowy winters)

Subarctic (Short summers and long, cold, snowy winters)

Cold Polar Climates

Subpolar (Always cold and dry with short, cool summers)

Highland Climates

(Temperature and precipitation vary greatly with latitude and elevation)

is moderated by the ocean. Even so, the winters in this region are cold with heavy snowfalls.

The natural vegetation of the region is forest. In the southernmost areas, some of the forest has been cleared away. The St. Lawrence-Great Lakes Lowlands are the best part of the region for farming.

Central Canada The central part of southern Canada is drier than the eastern part of the region. On the plains, the winters are bitterly cold and dry. The summers are short, but they last long enough and have enough rainfall to support wheat farming and grazing.

Southwestern Canada Along the Pacific Coast, the ocean helps create a temperate marine climate. For example, the coastal city of Vancouver is warmer in January than Albuquerque, New Mexico. As in the northwestern United States, evergreen forests cover much of western Canada.

REVIEWING THE FACTS

Define

1. Canadian Shield
2. hydroelectric power
3. alpine
4. taiga

Answer

1. (a) Describe the landforms in the Appalachian region. (b) In the St. Lawrence-Great Lakes region. (c) In the Canadian Shield. (d) In the Western Interior region. (e) In the west.

2. What climates and ecosystems prevail in various parts of Canada?

Locate

Refer to the map on page 216.
1. Name the upland area on the eastern part of the Canadian Shield.

2. Name four lakes northwest of the Great Lakes.

218

2 The Human Imprint

Most of the vast, bitterly cold northern part of Canada is wilderness. Settlement and economic development have taken place only in a relatively small area in the south. Yet the people of Canada have turned their country into one of the world's leading industrial democracies. Canada produces a wide variety of factory and farm goods. It has modern services, good linkages, and large cities.

The Canadian People

Scientists believe that people first came to Canada thousands of years ago. Groups of migrating hunters from Asia may have settled there during the Ice Age (page 190). Indians settled in diverse groups across the interior. Other groups of hunters made their homes along northern coastal waters. These people — who have a common language and customs — are the **Inuit** (in'yə wət). (They are also known as the Eskimo.)

There are slightly more than 20,000 Inuit in Canada today. As in the past, they live in the Arctic regions, mostly by hunting and fishing. Almost 300,000 members of Indian groups also live in Canada today.

Most of Canada's people have ancestors who emigrated from Europe sometime after 1600. Because of Canada's cold climate and poor soil, however, fewer European settlers went there than to the United States.

Most of the earliest European settlers were French. During the 1600's and 1700's, thousands of them settled in a French colony called New France. The area around Hudson Bay was in the hands of the British.

By the mid-1700's, England and France were struggling to gain power in Europe and to control colonial lands in many parts of the world. Both countries wanted to win control over Canada's vast forest-land and the profitable fur trade. By 1763, the British had defeated the French. As a result, Great Britain took over France's lands in Canada.

Very few immigrants came from France after Britain took control of Canada. English-speaking people, however, began to come in greater numbers than before. By the early 1800's, there were more people of British ancestry than of French ancestry in Canada.

Not until after World War II, however, did large numbers of people enter Canada from abroad. Since 1945, more than two million new residents have come to Canada. These recent immigrants are from Caribbean and Asian nations as well as from European nations.

The English and French heritages remain strongest among the Canadian people. More than half of all Canadians are descendants of English-speaking people. A third are descendants of French speakers. About 80 percent of all French Canadians live in Quebec.

Each language group retains its own culture. English-speaking Canadians, for example, are mostly Protestants. Most French Canadians are Roman Catholics. Differences between the two groups can also be seen in the styles of architecture and in the farming methods of English-speaking and French-speaking areas.

A country in which there are two principal languages is called **bilingual** (bī lin'gwəl). Canada is such a country. French and English are its official languages; each is spoken by millions of Canadians. Both languages are used on postage stamps, official documents, and money. Labels on products and signs are often printed in both French and English.

In Toronto, Ontario (above), most people are of British ancestry and speak only English. • *In Quebec City, Quebec (below), most people are of French ancestry and speak French.*

219

MAP WORKSHOP

Reading a Subway Map

In 1954, Toronto became the site of Canada's first subway. Today this subway, like those in other large cities, serves many commuters, or people who travel to and from work each day. It is also used by shoppers, students, and visitors. Toronto's subway system has 34 miles of track. People can get to a subway by entering any of about 60 stations in various parts of the city.

Like other subway systems, Toronto's provides maps to help riders reach their destinations easily. Subway maps show the routes taken by the various subways that make up the Toronto system. They also give the location of stations.

The map on this page shows a portion of the Toronto subway system. It covers just the downtown area of the city. Use it in answering the following questions.

1. What are the names of the three subway routes shown on this map?

2. What stations are located between Museum Station and Osgoode Station?

3. Name the station where the Bloor and Yonge subways meet.

4. Suppose you work at City Hall and need to go to the CN Tower. (a) Which station would you most likely use to gain entrance to the subway? (b) Which subway would you most likely ride? (c) At which station would you be most likely to leave the subway?

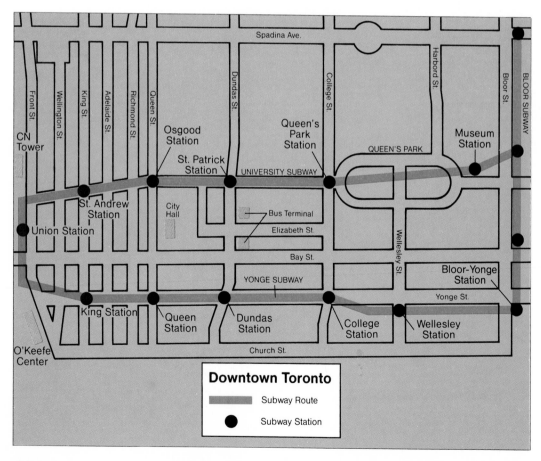

Downtown Toronto

▬▬▬ Subway Route

● Subway Station

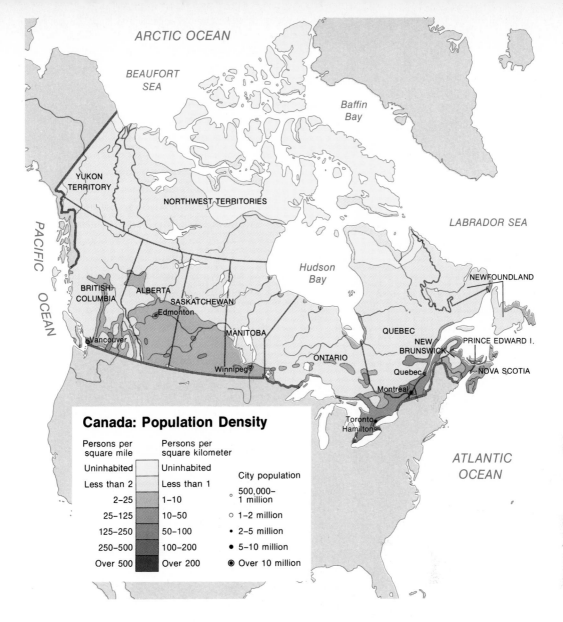

Canada: Population Density

Persons per square mile	Persons per square kilometer
Uninhabited	Uninhabited
Less than 2	Less than 1
2–25	1–10
25–125	10–50
125–250	50–100
250–500	100–200
Over 500	Over 200

City population
- ○ 500,000–1 million
- ○ 1–2 million
- • 2–5 million
- • 5–10 million
- ◉ Over 10 million

Map Study *What areas of Canada have the highest population density? Compare this map with the climate map on page 217. What is the climate like where most of the people in Canada live?*

Settlement Patterns

While Canada has more land than the United States, its population is far smaller. Canada has only about one tenth as many residents as the United States.

More than 90 percent of Canada's people live on 10 percent of its land — the densely settled lowlands of the St. Lawrence-Great Lakes region. The greatest number of large cities is located in this part of Canada. These cities are close to the Canadian-United States border. They include Toronto, Canada's leading industrial and commercial city, and Montreal, the second largest French-speaking city in the world. The rest of the country is sparsely populated.

221

You might have students compare this map to the United States population map on page 192.
Does Canada have any cities of over ten million people? *(no)*
Answers to Map Study questions: southern Canada; humid continental

Political Patterns

Canada's road to independence was quite different from that of the United States. In addition, its form of government borrows as much from European countries as it does from the United States.

An Independent Canada Canada remained under British control long after the United States had won its independence. In 1867, however, with Great Britain's approval, four colonies formed the **confederation** of Canada. A confederation is a loose association under a common government. The members of the confederation of Canada were called **provinces**. Gradually new provinces

The changing-of-the-guard ceremony in Ottawa, Canada's capital, is a tradition that began in Great Britain. Canada was once ruled by Great Britain.

were added, and the central government gained increased powers.

Although it could make its own laws, Canada remained a part of Great Britain. Canada continued to recognize the authority of the British monarch. Changes in Canada's constitution had to be approved by the British government. Until 1918, Canada's relations with foreign nations were controlled by Great Britain.

In 1931, Canada became one of the original members of the British Commonwealth of Nations. The Commonwealth is an association made up of Great Britain, nations under the control of Great Britain, and independent countries that were once controlled by Great Britain. The members give one another trade advantages and assistance with defense.

Like most members of the Commonwealth, Canada has complete independence. Its government is equal in standing and powers to the government of Great Britain. Under the Commonwealth, however, the British monarch is the **head of state,** or symbolic leader, of each member nation.

In 1982, Great Britain granted Canada a new constitution. Unlike the constitution of 1867, the new constitution can be changed by the Canadian people without the approval of the British government. The new constitution also lists the basic freedoms of the Canadian people.

A Parliamentary Democracy Canada has a form of government — **parliamentary** (pär′lə ment′ə rē) **democracy** — much like that of Great Britain. A parliamentary democracy has two branches of government. A body called the **parliament** makes the nation's laws. A national court system decides cases arising under the laws.

In a parliamentary democracy, the legislative and executive powers are not di-

222

The Government of Canada

THE MONARCH OF GREAT BRITAIN
(Represented by the Governor General of Canada)

THE LEGISLATURE	THE EXECUTIVE	THE JUDICIARY
Parliament Enacts laws Chooses executive officials Has two houses, one elected and one appointed	**Prime Minister** Carries out laws Is responsible to parliament **Cabinet** Assists prime minister	**Supreme Court and Other Courts** Judge violations of laws

vided between separate branches. Instead, the parliament has authority both to make laws and to see that they are carried out. The majority in parliament chooses a member of the parliament as **prime minister.** As the leading official in the government, the prime minister is often called the **head of government.** The prime minister is expected to carry out the laws as the members of the parliament wish.

The prime minister is assisted by a **cabinet,** or group of advisers for matters such as defense, justice, and the environment. Cabinet ministers are members of the parliament and, like the prime minister, are responsible to the parliament. If the prime minister and cabinet lose the support of the parliament, elections for parliament are held. The new parliament may select a new prime minister.

The British monarch is represented by a **governor general.** The monarch can appoint a citizen of either Great Britain or Canada to this position. The governor general appears at official ceremonies and has other symbolic duties.

A Federal System Canada has ten provinces. Find them on the map on page 216. These provinces are part of a federal system. Like the states of the United States, each province has its own government. The provinces of Canada, however, have greater powers than the states of the United States.

In northern Canada, there are two territories. Find them on the map on page 216. Because they have few residents, the territories are administered directly by the national government.

Current Political Issues Most Canadians support a united Canada. They cannot, however, ignore the cultural and regional differences in Canada. At times, for example, some French Canadians living in Quebec have sought to make their province an independent country. They believe separation from the rest of Canada is the best way to preserve their traditional culture.

Many French Canadians, however, are not in favor of a separate Quebec. Most English-speaking Canadians also want Quebec to remain a province of Canada.

223

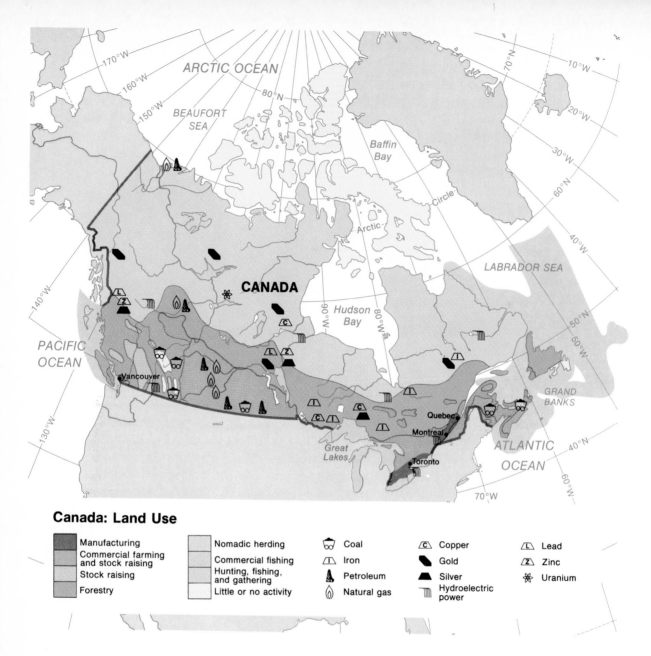

Canada: Land Use

Land Use		Resources			
Manufacturing	Nomadic herding	Coal	Copper	Lead	
Commercial farming and stock raising	Commercial fishing	Iron	Gold	Zinc	
Stock raising	Hunting, fishing, and gathering	Petroleum	Silver	Uranium	
Forestry	Little or no activity	Natural gas	Hydroelectric power		

Map Study *In what area are most of Canada's energy resources found? What minerals are mined in Canada? Where is hydroelectric power generated?*

Economic Patterns

Canada has a free-enterprise economy. It has grown especially rapidly in the last 30 years. Today Canada's GNP is among the ten highest in the world.

A major difference between the economy of Canada and that of the United States is the extent of government ownership of business. Almost all businesses in the United States are privately owned. On the other hand, the government of Canada owns one of the two major airlines and most telephone and telegraph operations. Canada's largest television network is financed by the national

224

Have students locate these regions and the provinces found within each on the map on page 228.
Point out that there is a city of Quebec in the province of Quebec.

Quiet bays in Nova Scotia offer scenic beauty as well as fishing resources. Many tourists vacation in this province.

The St. Lawrence-Great Lakes Lowlands

The small, narrow strip of lowlands in the area around the St. Lawrence River and the Great Lakes is the heartland of Canada. The lowlands lie in the southern part of Quebec and Ontario. Most of Canada's residents live in these lowlands. Canada's industry is also concentrated in the region. Urban areas have steel mills, metal factories, food-processing plants, and car plants. Outside the cities, there is dairy and truck farming. Produce is shipped to lowland cities and to the United States.

The St. Lawrence River and Seaway have been important to the development of this region. The river is a source of hydroelectric power. The waters of the St. Lawrence are also used in the manufacturing processes of many of the region's factories. The river and seaway provide an excellent shipping route. Such St. Lawrence port cities as Toronto and Montreal have grown into large commercial and industrial centers.

The Canadian Shield

The northern part of Quebec, Ontario, and Manitoba as well as parts of the Northwest Territories lie on the Canadian Shield. In the far north, the Shield is frozen and snowbound much of the year. There are few residents.

Farther south, in the subarctic areas, population is still sparse. There are, however, abundant natural resources. Dense needleleaf forests make lumbering a major industry. The ancient rocks hold a treasure chest of minerals. There are large deposits of iron, silver, zinc, copper, lead, gold, and uranium. Small mining towns have been formed near recently opened mines.

Canadians call the Shield their storehouse of minerals. It is a key to the country's future. Many experts believe that even the northern reaches of the Shield will soon be developed.

Much of Labrador, part of the province of Newfoundland, is covered with snow from September to June.

229

The Canadian Shield actually extends as far south as northern New York, Michigan, Wisconsin, and Minnesota. It was the first part of North America to be permanently elevated above sea level by natural forces, making it the oldest geologic formation on the continent.

SPOTLIGHT ON A NORSE SETTLEMENT:

A Bull That Changed History

A thousand years ago the Norse lived in Scandinavia, a coastal region of northern Europe. Expert sailors and navigators, the Norse were traders and adventurers. They were also good storytellers. Some of their stories, or sagas, tell of trips the Norse made from their colony in Greenland to the shores of North America.

According to these sagas, a trader named Leif Ericsson reached the North American mainland around A.D. 1000. Many grapevines grew along the shore. The land was heavily forested, and fish and animals were plentiful. Leif Ericsson named the place Vineland the Good. When he returned to the Norse colony on Greenland, he had high praise for Vineland.

In the summer of 1003, Thorfinn Karlsefni (thôr fin′ kärl sev′ne) and about 160 other Norse men and women from Greenland set sail for Vineland. Their ships carried supplies that included livestock. One of the animals they brought was a bull belonging to Karlsefni.

Karlsefni and his group of explorers searched for the land of grapes described by Leif Ericsson. After nearly a year, they found an area that seemed to be like the place Leif Ericsson's group had visited. In springtime, Karlsefni's group built a settlement on a river and called the place Hop. They planned to start a permanent colony there.

In the spring of the following year, a group of strangers, paddling skin canoes, began to visit the Norse. The Norse traded with these visitors, whom they called Scraelings. All went well until one day the bull belonging to Karlsefni suddenly ran bellowing from the forest. The Scraelings, who evidently had never seen cattle before, fled in fright.

Several weeks later a larger group of Scraelings returned. This time they attacked the Norse settlement. They killed two people and wounded others. After this attack, the Norse knew that they would never feel safe in Vineland. With some sadness, they abandoned their settlement and returned to Greenland.

Norse attempts to colonize North America probably ended with Karlsefni's return to Greenland. His ill-tempered bull may have influenced history. Permanent European settlement of North America — and Canada — did not begin for another 500 years.

Tourists visit reconstructed Viking sod houses at L'Anse aux Meadows, the site of the earliest Norse settlements in North America.

Petroleum from Alberta's rich deposits is treated at this refinery in Edmonton.

The Western Interior Plains

The Western Interior Plains extend across Manitoba, Saskatchewan, Alberta, and the Northwest Territories. Most of the region is thinly populated. Small, scattered towns serve the distantly spaced farms and ranches. The major crop of the region is wheat. Even more important than the growing of wheat is livestock ranching.

During the past 30 years, fossil fuels and other minerals have been discovered on the plains. There are especially large fields of coal, natural gas, and petroleum. More than 85 percent of Canada's oil and coal comes from Alberta alone. There are vast deposits near Regina, Saskatchewan.

With the development of the plains' mineral wealth has come a population and building boom. Forty years ago, for instance, Edmonton and Calgary, Alberta, were little more than cow towns. Today they are modern cities with wide streets, large businesses, new sports arenas, and many tall buildings.

The Western Mountains

Canada's Western Mountains are located mainly in British Columbia and the Yukon Territory. Thick forests of fir, spruce, and cedar cover much of the region. Along with wood pulp, these forests supply lumber for building and for export. More than half of British Columbia's income comes from lumbering and forestry.

Like the Canadian Shield, the Western Mountains have rich mineral deposits. Mining companies dig out lead, zinc, gold, copper, and molybdenum.

Mountain rivers, with steep falls, are ideal for generating power. A number of factories have located near rivers in the Vancouver, British Columbia, area. These factories turn out many different kinds of wood and paper products, refine crude oil, and assemble automobiles and ships.

REVIEWING THE FACTS

Define

1. Atlantic provinces
2. Grand Banks

Answer

1. (a) Describe the economy of the Atlantic provinces. (b) The Western Interior. (c) The Western Mountains.

2. What economic changes are taking place on the Canadian Shield?

3. How is the St. Lawrence River important to southern Quebec and Ontario?

Locate

Refer to the map on page 216.

1. On a sheet of paper, write the names of the ten provinces and two territories.

2. After each entry, write the name of the capital city for that province or territory.

231

Vancouver is only 15 miles from the United States border. It is the third largest city in Canada and the country's busiest port.

Answers are in the Teacher's Guide.

GEOGRAPHY LABORATORY

Highlighting the Chapter

1. Most of Canada's major land regions are parts of landforms also found in the United States. Much of Canada's land was shaped by glaciers during the last Ice Age. Today a cold climate marks most of Canada. Canada's population and industrial centers are in the St. Lawrence-Great Lakes Lowlands. The Canadian Shield has valuable mineral deposits. So do the Western Interior Plains, where rich soil is also found in the southern areas. Permafrost makes the far north a difficult place in which to build.

2. Like the United States, Canada is a land of immigrants. Its population is small. There are two major population groups — people with English ancestry and descendants of the French. Canada is a parliamentary democracy that has remained a member of the British Commonwealth of Nations. There are ten provinces and two territories in Canada. The importance of mineral production has grown in recent years, but manufacturing is still the most important economic activity.

3. The people of the Appalachian Highlands carry on extensive fishing in the Grand Banks, which lie in the North Atlantic off the coast of the Atlantic provinces. There is little manufacturing and farming in this region. The industrial and commercial heartland of Canada is the St. Lawrence-Great Lakes Lowlands. Truck farming, manufacturing, and trade are well developed there. The Canadian Shield is a storehouse of minerals. It is being developed for its iron, silver, uranium, and other resources. On the Western Interior Plains, there is large-scale wheat farming and ranching. Large deposits of coal, natural gas, and petroleum are found in the plains region. The Western Mountains have vast forests that provide lumber. In this region, there is also a variety of mineral resources and extensive fishing grounds.

232

Speaking Geographically

Use each of the following words or terms in a sentence to show that you understand its meaning.

1. alpine
2. bilingual
3. cabinet
4. confederation
5. Grand Banks
6. hydroelectric power
7. parliament
8. prime minister
9. province
10. pulp

Testing Yourself

In each sentence below, the *italicized* word makes the statement false. Number your paper from 1 to 11. Beside each number, write the word that would make the statement true.

1. Canada is the *fourth* largest country in the world.

2. One of Canada's *provinces* is the Yukon.

3. *All* of the Great Lakes are shared by Canada and the United States.

4. The two official languages of Canada are English and *Spanish*.

5. Most French Canadian people live in *Ontario*.

6. The capital of Canada is *Montreal*.

7. Canada has a *president* at the head of its government.

8. Most of Canada's oil and coal comes from *Manitoba*.

9. The Rocky Mountain range extends through *eastern* Canada.

10. Most Canadians live in *northwestern* Canada.

11. Most of Canada's manufacturing is found in the *Canadian Shield*.

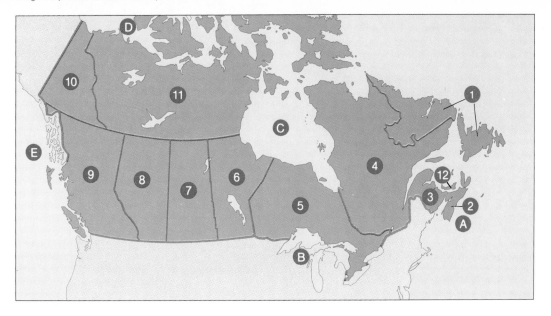

Building Map Skills

On the map above, provinces and territories are numbered. Bodies of water are lettered. Number your paper from 1 to 12; also write the letters A through E on your paper. Then write the name of the correct province or territory for each number. Write the name of each body of water beside the letter that identifies it.

Applying Map Skills

A. Arrange the following cities, land features, and bodies of water in order from east to west.

Winnipeg	Vancouver
Montreal	Laurentian
Hudson Bay	Highlands
Newfoundland	Great Slave Lake
Island	Lake Ontario
Rocky Mountains	Regina

B. Arrange the following land features and bodies of water in order from north to south.

Baffin Island	Baffin Bay
St. Lawrence River	Ellesmere Island
Labrador	Lake Erie

Exploring Further

1. Write an itinerary, or plan of places to visit, for a trip around the largest lake in North America, Lake Superior. Describe the highlights of this trip. Include cities, provinces, and states that can be seen. Do research to find out what preparations are necessary for crossing the border between Canada and the United States. Finally, make a map to show the region. It should give the route and the location of places you will visit.

2. Agriculture is important to the economy of both Canada and the United States. Compare and contrast farming in these two countries.

3. Research the way of life of the Inuit — past and present. Report your findings to the class.

4. When tides rush up narrow bodies of water, they have great power. France has built a power plant to produce electricity from such tides. The Bay of Fundy, in eastern Canada, has some of the greatest tides in the world. Has anything been done, or are plans being made, to harness this source of energy? Check into this topic, and write a report on what you find out.

233

GEOGRAPHY LABORATORY

The culture region of Latin America has been divided into two parts for discussion in this book. Middle America is described in Chapter 9; South America in Chapter 10. In the first of these chapters, students take a close look at Mexico, Central America, and the Caribbean islands. Make sure students know where these places are in relation to their community.
This area of the world is frequently in the news. Before you begin reading, lead a class discussion to find out what students know about these countries and the people who live in them.

Middle America

Middle America includes three distinct areas — Mexico, Central America, and the islands of the Caribbean Sea. Geographically, Middle America is part of the North American continent, but culturally the region is Latin American. The map on page 9 shows Latin America. As you can see, Latin America is made up of Middle and South America. The term *Latin* refers to the Spanish and Portuguese languages, which grew out of Latin, the language of ancient Rome. For more than 300 years, most of Latin America was colonized by Spain and Portugal. Portugal controlled Brazil in South America, while Spain held most of the rest of South America as well as Middle America. The heritage of Middle America is, therefore, in great part a Spanish heritage.

While Spanish influence is strong, Middle America is shaped by many cultures. A strong Indian imprint can be seen in farming practices, clothing, language, and arts. A variety of European cultures also helped create today's Middle America. During the colonial period, the English, French, and Dutch established colonies there. Each European group left its own imprint. In addition, because many Africans were brought to parts of Middle America, African cultures played an important part in shaping life in the region. In some locations today, East Asians and people from India add still further diversity to the cultural pattern.

234

1 The Physical Environment

Middle America is far smaller than either the United States or Canada. It has fewer mineral resources. Much of its land has rugged mountains or thick rain forest. Little of it is suitable for farming. Yet the people of the region have found and developed valuable deposits of gold, silver, copper, and petroleum. In the narrow mountain valleys and on the plains along the seacoast, people grow a variety of crops in the fertile soil. There are huge cities high on mountain plateaus and in some coastal areas.

Landforms

Find Middle America on the map on page 236. You should observe that the region is made up of a funnel-shaped strip of land and an arc of islands. The strip of land appears to be a land bridge connecting southern North America and South America. Actually, north of the Isthmus of Panama, the mainland is part of the continent of North America. The mainland is widest in northern Mexico. The narrowest point on the mainland is in the south, near Panama City, Panama, where the isthmus is only about 40 miles (64 kilometers) wide.

Coastal plains extend along both the Pacific and Caribbean coasts of the mainland. Most of the mainland, however, is mountainous. The mountains are Y shaped. In the north, the Western Sierra Madre (sē er'ə mäd'rē) and the Eastern Sierra Madre form the upper part of the Y. Between these ranges is an area of plateaus called the Mesa Central (mā'sə). It is there that most of Mexico's people live.

Just south of Mexico City, the Western and Eastern Sierra Madre join to form a single mountain range. This range makes

THE CORNFIELD THAT SMOKED AND . . .

One day in 1943, a farmer near Mexico City was startled to see a column of smoke spiraling upward from a small hole in his field. Unable to cover the hole and stop the smoke with rocks, the farmer rushed to his village to warn the townspeople. Three hours later the farmer and some friends returned to find a very deep hole and dense clouds of black smoke. That night, after a violent explosion, a volcanic mountain began to rise in the field. The mountain continued to grow for nine years. Today Mount Paricutín (pə rē'kə tēn') rises more than 1,500 feet (457 meters) above its original base, covering the field where corn once grew.

up the lower part of the Y. There, volcanoes rise more than 17,000 feet (5,100 meters) above the Valley of Mexico. From this area, a mountainous backbone extends southward. It joins the Andes Mountains in South America. Together these mountains are part of the Rim (or Ring) of Fire, which encircles the Pacific Ocean. Earthquakes and volcanic eruptions are common throughout this zone.

When speaking of North America, most people think only of the United States, Canada, and Mexico. Few realize that the countries of Central America are also part of the continent. About 500 volcanoes have erupted in historical times. Two thirds of them are in the Northern Hemisphere. About 60 percent of active volcanoes are on the perimeter of the Pacific Ocean.

235

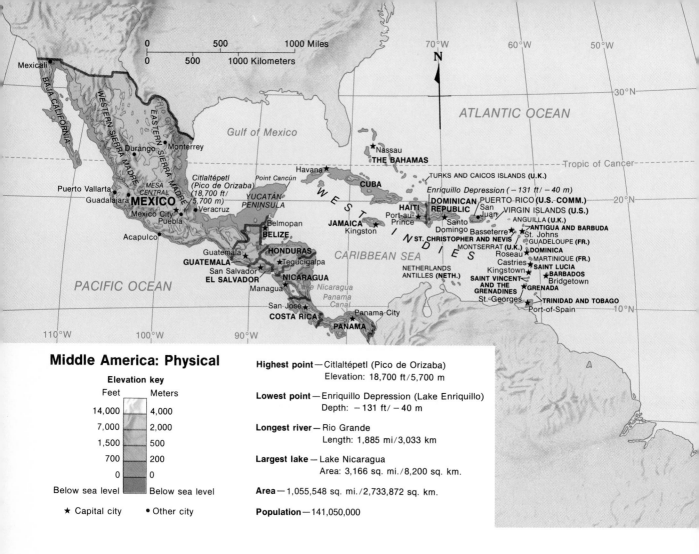

Middle America: Physical

Elevation key

Feet	Meters
14,000	4,000
7,000	2,000
1,500	500
700	200
0	0
Below sea level	Below sea level

★ Capital city   • Other city

Highest point — Citlaltépetl (Pico de Orizaba)
Elevation: 18,700 ft/5,700 m

Lowest point — Enriquillo Depression (Lake Enriquillo)
Depth: −131 ft/−40 m

Longest river — Rio Grande
Length: 1,885 mi/3,033 km

Largest lake — Lake Nicaragua
Area: 3,166 sq. mi./8,200 sq. km.

Area — 1,055,548 sq. mi./2,733,872 sq. km.

Population — 141,050,000

Map Study   *Which country contains the highest point in Middle America? Name the two largest peninsulas in the region.*

Many Middle American cities have been damaged by earthquakes, some many times. For example, plate movements along Mexico's west coast caused a catastrophic earthquake in Central Mexico in 1985. In Mexico City, thousands of people lost their lives, and many buildings were destroyed.

Much of the soil in the region was formed by erosion of the mountains. Streams and rivers have carried silt to valleys and to coastal plains. In some places, the soil is the product of volcanic ash. The most fertile soil is found in the mountain valleys and on the coastal plains.

The island area of Middle America is located mainly in the Caribbean Sea. The Caribbean islands are scattered in a wide curve across a distance of nearly 2,000 miles (3,200 kilometers). The northernmost islands lie just off the coast of Florida. The southernmost islands lie near the coast of Venezuela.

The Caribbean islands are part of a chain of mountains, the tops of which rise above sea level in a number of places. Some of these mountains are steep sided and volcanic. Others are limestone shelves that have been lifted above the sea by geologic forces.

236

Climate and Ecosystems

Most of Middle America lies south of the Tropic of Cancer. The region, therefore, has mainly tropical conditions. Even in the most northern parts of Mexico, summers are extremely hot and winters quite mild. Nearly all the rest of the region has a humid tropical climate.

Of course, climates in mountain areas vary with elevation. Over just a few miles, conditions can change from steamy and humid to cool and dry as the land rises.

Most of the region gets a great deal of rainfall. The exception is northern Mexico, which has semiarid and arid desert areas. The rainfall pattern in the wet areas

Hundreds of buildings toppled when an earthquake shook Mexico City in 1985.

Map Study *What changes in climate would you experience if you moved from northwestern to southeastern Mexico?*

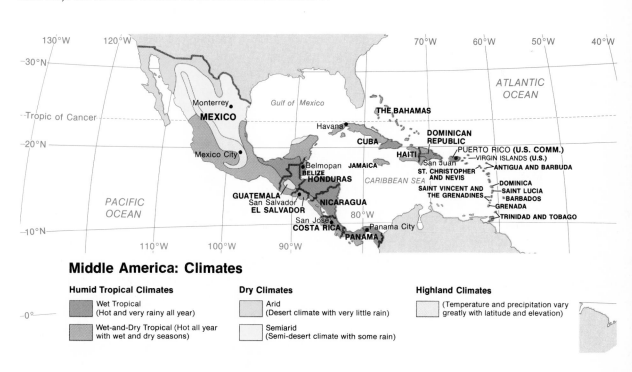

Middle America: Climates

Humid Tropical Climates
- Wet Tropical (Hot and very rainy all year)
- Wet-and-Dry Tropical (Hot all year with wet and dry seasons)

Dry Climates
- Arid (Desert climate with very little rain)
- Semiarid (Semi-desert climate with some rain)

Highland Climates
- (Temperature and precipitation vary greatly with latitude and elevation)

237

is created in part by the **trade winds.** The northeast trade winds blow southwestward across the Atlantic Ocean and the Caribbean. They bring moisture from the ocean to the north shore of the Caribbean islands and the east coast of the mainland of Middle America. Rains are heavy in these areas much of the year. Dense rain forests grow on the coastal plain and lower mountain slopes.

The high mountains of the mainland cut off the trade winds from the west coast. The west coast, therefore, does not have as much precipitation as the east coast. In fact, there is very little precipitation on the western side of the mountains during the winter. Because rainfall there is more moderate, the main ecosystem is savanna.

REVIEWING THE FACTS

Define

trade winds

Answer

1. Describe the mountains of the mainland of Middle America.

2. How were the island areas of Middle America formed?

3. (a) What is the climate of most of Middle America? (b) Describe precipitation patterns in Middle America. (c) How does elevation affect the climate?

Locate

Refer to the map on page 236.

1. What body of water lies west of Central America?

2. What body of water is just east of Mexico?

3. What body of water is east of the Bahamas?

2 The Human Imprint

The lands of Middle America were at one time colonies of European powers. Today nearly all countries of Middle America are independent. These countries have found it hard to change past patterns. Most people still earn their living through agriculture. But in many ways, Middle America is changing. One sign of today's changes is the movement of people to cities.

The People of Middle America

The Spanish first came to the Caribbean islands in the late 1400's. By the early 1500's, Spanish adventurers were exploring the mainland of Middle America. At that time, the islands and mainland were both occupied by Indians.

Today most people of the mainland have Indian or Spanish ancestry. On the islands, there is a different pattern. Most of the people are of African or European ancestry.

Early People of Middle America Indians lived in Middle America for thousands of years before the Europeans explored the region. Farming was common since about 6500 B.C. Farmers grew maize, beans, squash, sweet potatoes, cacao (from which cocoa and chocolate can be made), pineapples, tomatoes, and other crops.

Between A.D. 300 and 900, a great Indian civilization developed in parts of present-day Mexico and Guatemala. This was the civilization of the Maya. Most of the Maya lived in farming villages. However, the Maya also built large cities that served as religious centers. Their priests created an advanced system of mathematics and an accurate calendar.

In the 1400's, the warlike Aztec conquered much of Mexico. The Aztec developed another great civilization. They

Answers are in the Teacher's Guide.
The Caribbean islands are frequently hit by hurricanes. Ask a student to learn more about these natural disasters and report back to the class.
More than half of Guatemala's population is Indian, descended from the Maya.

established their capital, Tenochtitlán (tä nòch'tē tlän'), on an island in Lake Texcoco (tes kō'kō'). In the center of the city stood a pyramid. Around it were roads, bridges, plazas, and a variety of buildings. The Aztec even grew crops in Tenochtitlán by building islands from the mud that lay at the bottom of Lake Texcoco. From their capital, the Aztec ruled Indian groups throughout Mexico. Conquered peoples worked for the Aztec, paying tribute in farm goods or luxury items such as gold.

The Colonial Period Early in the 1500's, with the help of Indians who wanted to end Aztec rule, the Spanish defeated the Aztec empire. They built Mexico City at the site of Tenochtitlán.

Eventually the Spanish controlled all of the mainland except a small British colony in what is today Belize. As Spanish power spread, so did Spanish culture. The Spaniards built well-planned towns. They placed a Catholic church at the center of each town. Catholic priests made journeys to mountain villages to convert Indians to Christianity. Many Indians learned Spanish. Some adopted Spanish customs. Some colonial Spanish men married Indian women. The descendants of such couples are known as **mestizos** (me stē'zōz'), or persons of mixed European and Indian ancestry.

In the Caribbean islands, the pattern of colonization was different. Many European nations besides Spain established colonies. The Dutch, French, Portuguese, and English were among these nations. Today people on Caribbean islands generally speak the language of the nation that colonized their island. They practice many of that nation's customs as well.

On the islands and in coastal areas, the Europeans built plantations. At first, they used Indians, some of whom were forced to work on the plantations as slaves.

Ranches started by Spanish settlers in Mexico usually included a large house, or hacienda, built in the style of houses in Spain.

Within a century, however, the Europeans turned to a new source of labor. They began bringing captives from Africa to serve as slaves.

The Europeans also mined gold and other minerals. Both Indians and Africans worked in the mines.

The Colonial Legacy One consequence of colonization was a tragedy that caused the Indian population of Middle America to decline sharply. Indians lacked immunity to smallpox, typhoid fever, measles, influenza, and other diseases carried by Europeans. These diseases killed millions of Indians. Africans also carried diseases, such as malaria and yellow fever, that ravaged the Indians. As a result, the Indian population of the region dropped by about 90 percent during the first century of European settlement.

239

Another result of colonization was the concentration of wealth in the hands of a very few people. Under the European colonial system, Spanish colonies in Middle America were governed largely by officials who had been born in Spain. These officials and their families held large tracts of good farmland. For all others, the right to own land and take part in politics was greatly restricted. For example, people of Spanish ancestry born in the colonies, who were called **Creoles,** could hold only lower positions in the government.

People of Indian, African, or mixed ancestry generally owned little property. Most of these people worked in some way for European colonists. The result was a wide gap between the laborers and the wealthy owners of land and businesses. Modern Middle America has yet to escape this heritage.

Modern Settlement Patterns Middle America has population problems. More than 135 million people live there today. This is more than half the population of the United States. The area these people live in is one third as large as the United States. Today birth rates in the region are higher than in most other parts of the world. Population is growing rapidly.

The population of Middle America is distributed very unevenly. Not long ago the great majority of Middle American people lived on farms or in small villages. These farms and villages were located mainly in mountain valleys or plateaus and along the coast.

In recent years, great numbers of people have moved to cities. Today, in many countries, over half the people live in one or two large cities. However, some people cannot find jobs once they move to the

Map Study *What is the population density of northern Mexico? Of central Guatemala? What is the approximate difference in population between Mexico City and Havana?*

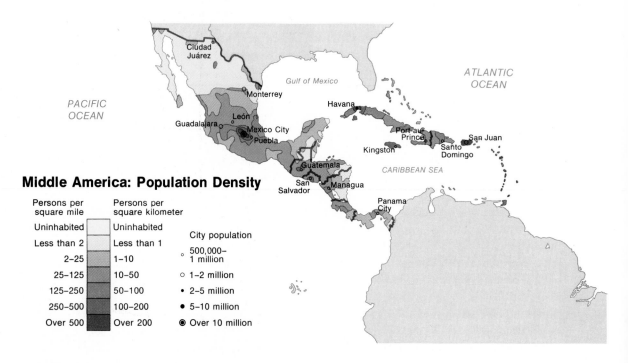

Middle America: Population Density

Persons per square mile	Persons per square kilometer
Uninhabited	Uninhabited
Less than 2	Less than 1
2–25	1–10
25–125	10–50
125–250	50–100
250–500	100–200
Over 500	Over 200

City population
- 500,000– 1 million
- 1–2 million
- 2–5 million
- 5–10 million
- Over 10 million

240

city. Others find only low-wage jobs. As a result, cities have many residents who cannot afford good food and shelter. Slums encircle nearly every city. Cities have trouble providing services for their booming populations.

Political Patterns

Spain's colonies won their independence in the early 1800's. During the same years, France lost some of its Caribbean colonies. British colonies gained their independence later — for example, Jamaica and Trinidad and Tobago in 1962, Barbados in 1966, Grenada in 1974, and Belize in 1981. The United States, England, France, and the Netherlands still control a number of small island territories in the Caribbean.

After winning their independence, most countries of Middle America found it hard to create stable governments. Wealthy landowners controlled each government. The people had little or no say in how they were governed. Those who had little money and little farmland came to feel that their rulers acted only to protect selfish interests.

As a result of these conditions, there were many rebellions and uprisings in the new nations of Middle America. During the 1800's and early 1900's, rebels tried to set up democratic governments in these countries. For the most part, their efforts failed.

The pattern of dictatorial rule and rebellion continued well into recent years. For example, Cuba went through a revolution in 1959. For many years, Cuba had been led by a harsh dictator, Fulgencio Batista. In the 1950's, some Cubans took up arms to oust Batista. A rebel leader named Fidel Castro became premier after Batista fled the country in 1959. Castro's government soon became a Communist

dictatorship. It is the Soviet Union's major ally in the Americas.

More recently, Nicaragua and El Salvador, have experienced serious unrest. In 1979, a group of rebels known as the Sandinistas overthrew a dictatorship in Nicaragua. The new government of Nicaragua has friendly ties with both Cuba and the Soviet Union. Fighting has continued in Nicaragua because the Sandinista government is being challenged by a rebel group known as the Contras. Since the mid-1970's, rebels in El Salvador have been fighting to overthrow the government of that country. Fearful that a rebel victory would increase Cuba's influence in the region, the United States has extended aid to El Salvador's government.

In recent years, Central American governments have become more democratic. Previously, control of the governments of the region's countries had shifted back and forth between rival groups of military leaders and elected civilians. In 1982, however, the people of Honduras restored parliamentary democracy. De-

José Napoleón Duarte addresses a crowd during his 1984 campaign to become president of El Salvador.

Students might be interested in knowing that the United States governed Cuba between 1898 and 1902. Up to 1959, when Castro overthrew the Batista government, the United States maintained close political and economic ties with Cuba. Since 1959, relations between the two nations have been severely strained.

241

MAP WORKSHOP

Using Latitude and Longitude

The map below shows some of the islands in the West Indies known as the Lesser Antilles. Some, like Saint Christopher, are easy to spot on the map. Others, like Redonda, look like tiny specs.

Each of these islands, no matter what its size, has an exact location. That location is expressed on maps by means of latitude and longitude. (See pages 16–17.)

Geographers describe parallels of latitude in terms of degrees, minutes, and even seconds. There are 60 minutes (written as 60′) within each degree of latitude. Within each minute, there are 60 seconds (written as 60″). So latitude 22°30′ N is halfway between 22° N and 23° N. The same is true for meridians of longitude. Longitude 79°30′ W is exactly halfway between 79° W and 80° W.

What difference does a minute make? Quite a bit if you are a captain sailing through the Caribbean. One minute of latitude or longitude is equal to one nautical mile. A mistake of one mile may cause you to miss your destination.

1. Use the map to tell the island that lies at each of these locations.
   (a) latitude 17°56′N, longitude 62°20′W
   (b) latitude 18°15′N, longitude 63°05′W
   (c) latitude 17°55′N, longitude 62°50′W
   (d) latitude 17°39′N, longitude 63°16′W

2. Give the approximate latitude and longitude of each of the following cities.
   (a) Charlestown
   (b) Plymouth
   (c) Basseterre
   (d) Sandy Point

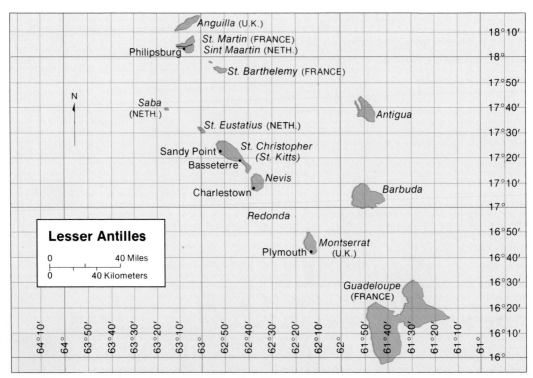

Lesser Antilles

0   40 Miles

0   40 Kilometers

WORLD DATA BANK

Country	Area in Square Miles	Population/Natural Increase		Per Capita GNP
Antigua and Barbuda	170	100,000	(1.0%)	$2,030
Bahamas	5,382	200,000	(1.8%)	7,150
Barbados	166	300,000	(0.9%)	4,680
Belize	8,865	200,000	(2.7%)	1,130
Costa Rica	19,575	2,800,000	(2.7%)	1,290
Cuba	42,803	10,300,000	(1.2%)	NA
Dominica	290	100,000	(1.7%)	1,160
Dominican Republic	18,815	6,500,000	(2.5%)	810
El Salvador	8,124	5,300,000	(2.5%)	710
Grenada	131	100,000	(1.9%)	970
Guatemala	42,042	8,400,000	(3.2%)	1,240
Haiti	10,714	6,200,000	(2.3%)	350
Honduras	43,278	4,700,000	(3.1%)	730
Jamaica	4,243	2,500,000	(2.0%)	940
Mexico	761,602	81,900,000	(2.5%)	2,080
Nicaragua	50,193	3,500,000	(3.4%)	850
Panama	29,761	2,300,000	(2.2%)	2,020
Saint Lucia	239	100,000	(2.5%)	1,210
Saint Vincent and the Grenadines	150	100,000	(2.0%)	840
Trinidad and Tobago	1,981	1,300,000	(2.0%)	6,010

spite civil war, El Salvador held presidential elections in 1984. José Napoleón Duarte, who had been removed as head of a ruling council just two years before, won. In 1985 — under a new, democratic constitution — an elected president also took office in Guatemala.

Costa Rica, on the other hand, has had more stable government. Like other countries in the region, it had authoritarian governments in the 1800's and early 1900's. Since 1918, however, the country has been a democracy. Today it has a presidential system. In 1987, Costa Rican President Oscar Arias Sanchez won the Nobel Peace Prize for his plan to end fighting in Central America.

Economic Patterns

The countries of Middle America have economies based on primary activities. Except in Mexico, there is little manufacturing. Tourism is important, but agriculture, the production of oil, and mining are the key activities in the region.

This focus on primary activities leaves Middle America dependent on other nations. Countries sell their resources to earn money to pay for finished goods made in industrial countries. Changes in prices for such goods as sugar, coffee, and oil, therefore, have a great impact on Middle America. Rising prices can bring sudden wealth, while falling prices can cause a large drop in income.

243

Costa Rica was discovered by Columbus on his last voyage to America, in 1502. He named it Costa Rica, which means "rich coast," beause he hoped to find gold there.

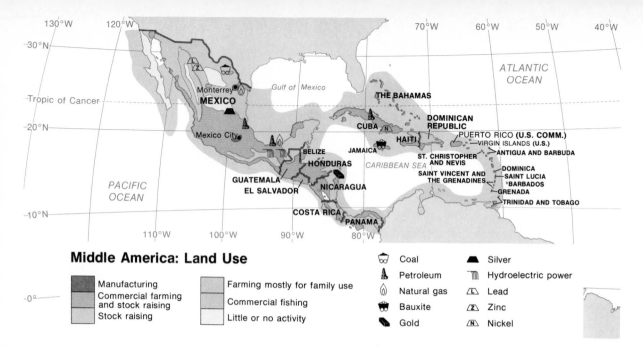

Middle America: Land Use

Manufacturing
Commercial farming and stock raising
Stock raising

Farming mostly for family use
Commercial fishing
Little or no activity

Coal
Petroleum
Natural gas
Bauxite
Gold

Silver
Hydroelectric power
Lead
Zinc
Nickel

Map Study *In which Middle American countries is the land used almost entirely for commercial farming and stock raising?*

Developing Mineral Resources Gold and silver first attracted Spanish colonists to Middle America. However, Middle America's mineral wealth is neither great nor widely distributed. Therefore, mining is quite limited today.

Agriculture Middle America is an important region for commercial agriculture. Sugar, cacao, bananas, and coffee are raised on plantations. Many of these plantations are owned by American companies. There is some cattle ranching along the west coast of the mainland.

Most people in the region, however, earn a living on small farms. They grow corn, beans, fruits, and other crops. Farmers use these crops to feed their families. They also sell some of their produce in the markets of nearby towns.

Linkages Poor linkages have hindered trade in Middle America. Mountains, deep valleys, tropical forests, wide rivers, and the ocean created natural barriers throughout the region. In the past, therefore, much of Middle America's trade was by sea. Most trade was with the United States. The same is true today.

Only in the last fifty or so years have good north-south land routes been constructed within the region. The Pan American Highway was begun in the 1920's. Today it extends from the Rio Grande through Central America to Puerto Montt, Chile, on the west coast of South America and Buenos Aires, Argentina, on the east coast of South America.

Middle America in the World

The United States has had a special interest in Middle America's development. For example, shortly after the nations won their independence, both France and Great Britain tried to gain influence over the region and its trade. To prevent this, President James Monroe wrote a message in 1823 warning European nations not to interfere with the new nations. This policy became known as the Monroe Doctrine.

In the years since the 1820's, the United States has grown more involved in the region. On a number of occasions, the United States has sent troops to help

244

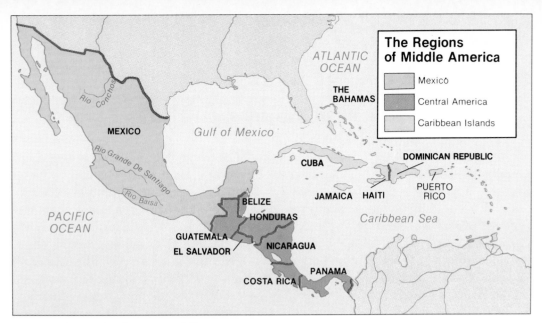

Map Study *Which two Middle American countries share the same island?*

Answer to Map Study question: Dominican Republic, Haiti

governments stop rebellions. In a few cases, the United States has given aid to groups of rebels. In recent years, the United States has been especially concerned about efforts by the Soviet Union and Cuba to gain influence in Middle America. It has been willing to help countries resist this influence. For example, in 1984, armed forces of the United States invaded the island nation of Grenada to prevent Grenada's Communist rulers from stockpiling weapons and building an airstrip with the assistance of Cuba. The people of Grenada then established a new, democratic government.

Some people in Middle America have resented involvement by the United States in their countries. They feel that this involvement may make them dependent on the United States.

Today, however, several governments in the region have good relations with the United States. United States businesses have millions of dollars invested in Middle America. The United States government gives financial and military assistance to many countries of Middle America.

REVIEWING THE FACTS

Define

1. mestizo

2. Creole

Answer

1. Describe Middle American Indian cultures before the arrival of Europeans.

2. (a) Which European country had the greatest influence on the mainland of Middle America? (b) What cultures have influenced life in the Caribbean islands?

3. What kinds of governments are there in the region?

4. What are the chief economic activities in Middle American countries?

5. How has the United States played a role in Middle America?

Locate

In each pair of nations below, which nation is closer to the United States?

1. Cuba, Belize

2. El Salvador, Panama

3. Nicaragua, Jamaica

245

SPOTLIGHT ON HERITAGE:

Celebrating the History of Barbados

Every July, the people of Barbados dance in the streets in celebration of their nation's rich heritage. Although Barbados did not gain independence until 1966, people have been living on the tiny Caribbean island since 1625. The islanders are proud of their past and eager to teach their children about it.

Like many islands in the Caribbean, Barbados's heritage reflects the contributions of several different cultures. For over 300 years, the island was a part of the British Empire. The British claimed the island after discovering that its soil and climate were well-suited to growing sugarcane. Sugar was a valuable cash crop in the 1600's and 1700's. Therefore, it drew a number of people from England and Scotland to the island. By the late 1600's, Barbados was covered with large sugar plantations.

The owners of the island's plantations lived in great luxury. The hard work of growing sugarcane was done by slaves from West Africa. Even after slavery was abolished in 1838, the former slaves continued to work in the sugarcane fields.

Over the years, a new culture arose on Barbados. It was a mixture of British and West African customs. One of the most popular of the new traditions was a holiday known as Crop Over. It marked the end of the sugarcane harvest. For plantation owners, Crop Over was a time to anticipate the profits of the harvest. For slaves, it was a time of rest.

In 1973, Bajans decided to recreate that celebration even though sugar was no longer central to the island's economy. Since then, it has become an annual event.

As in the old days, the holiday begins on a Saturday with the traditional delivery of the last load of sugarcane. Over the next three weeks, people enjoy calypso music, cane-cutting contests, and specially prepared foods like pudding n'sous —a spicy pork sausage made with onions and pepper.

The celebration also includes parties, concerts, parades, and tours of old plantations. Some islanders reenact life in the 1700's and 1800's. Others practice stick licking (fencing with rounded tree limbs) or sew costumes for the carnival that marks the final weekend of Crop Over.

July has become a time to retell old stories, sing old songs, and rediscover long-forgotten customs and traditions. It has also become a time of homecoming. Many people who have emigrated from Barbados return to the island each July to remember their past.

3 Mexico

Mexico is the most powerful nation in Middle America. In terms of area, it is the largest country in the region. Its population is larger than that of all the rest of the nations of Middle America combined. Mexico has many natural resources, and its GNP is the highest in the region.

Mexicans are mainly of Spanish and Indian ancestry. There are about 80 different Indian languages spoken in Mexico. Most Mexicans, however, speak Spanish. Most are also Roman Catholics. European and Indian customs have blended to create a culture that is uniquely Mexican.

Economic Development

Mexico's economic system is a combination of free enterprise and socialism. Most businesses are owned and operated by private companies. On the other hand, the government owns auto and steel plants, the nation's oil company, its air and rail companies, its radio and television stations, and its power plants.

Farming and Ranching Most of Mexico's farming takes place in the Mesa Central, where the soil is fertile and the climate is mild. There are both large commercial farms and small plots in this area.

Before the 1900's, most land was owned by a few wealthy ranchers. It was worked by **peons,** poor, landless farmers, who settled near ranches. Most peons lived in extreme poverty. In 1915, the government began to break up large land holdings. Farmland was turned over to rural communities known as **ejidos** (e hē'dōs), which exist to this day. In an ejido, the land belongs to the whole community, but each family works a plot of its own. The family may use the land as long as it lives in the ejido.

Just over 10 percent of the land in Mexico is arable, yet 40 percent of the people are engaged in agriculture. Both commercial and subsistence farming are found in Mexico.

Father Hidalgo was a brave leader in Mexico's fight for independence.

The ejido system has not put an end to Mexico's rural poverty. Therefore, the government has sponsored a variety of programs to help small farmers. It provides education, money, irrigation, and some transportation services.

Some parts of the Mexican countryside have large-scale commercial agriculture. In the arid northern section of Mexico,

Many people live by farming in Mexico's high central plateau.

for example, there are large cattle ranches. The northern end of Baja California has large farms. In this area, fields are irrigated, and there is intensive farming as in southern California. Plantations on the Yucatán Peninsula produce agave (ə gäv′ē) plants. The yellow fiber from agave, called henequen (hen′i kən), is used in making cord and rope.

Mineral Resources Mining was the most important economic activity in Mexico during the colonial period. Today mining is still important. Gold, silver, copper, sulfur, lead, and zinc are mined in the Sierra Madre. Iron and other minerals are also mined on the plateaus of northern Mexico.

In 1978, huge oil reserves were discovered along Mexico's Gulf coast. Mexico has since become one of the world's leading exporters of oil. During the 1980's, however, the world experienced an oil glut. This situation caused a drop in oil prices. As a result, Mexico's oil income fell drastically.

Industry Although farming employs the most people, manufacturing accounts for the largest part of Mexico's GNP. Even so, workers' wages are low in comparison to those paid in the United States and other industrialized countries.

Oil refining and the production of chemicals are the major industries along the Gulf coast. Other Mexican industries are located on the Mesa Central. Mexico City, at the southern tip of the mesa, is the nation's industrial center. Its products include cars, chemicals, clothing, and electrical appliances. Guadalajara, Puebla, Monterrey, and Juárez are also large manufacturing cities. Monterrey is the center of Mexico's iron and steel industry. Many companies from the United States have located in Juárez and other cities near the Mexican border. They produce clothing, electronic goods, and other items that require much hand labor.

Tourism Mexico's natural beauty, tropical beaches, and historical sites lure many tourists. Spectacular Maya ruins draw thousands of visitors to the Yucatán Peninsula each year. A recently developed tourist center at Cancún on the northeastern tip of the peninsula offers warm tropical breezes and sparkling clear Caribbean waters. Puerto Vallarta and Acapulco are among the popular tourist spots on Mexico's Pacific Coast.

Prospects for the Future

Mexico's two most pressing problems are population growth and foreign debt. The nation's population is expected to double over the next 25 years. If the economy does not expand equally, unemployment and poverty will continue to be widespread.

Nowhere is population growth more visible than in Mexico City. Hoping to find jobs, more than 2,000 people move to the city each day. The metropolitan area is one of the world's largest. It had 18 million residents by the mid-1980's. Experts predict that it will have 26 million residents by the year 2000. Joblessness, vast slums, dense smog, and tangled traffic jams are among the city's problems.

The rapid economic growth experienced during the 1970's has slowed. Much of this growth was based on Mexico's income from foreign oil sales. At the time, the nation borrowed heavily from other nations to pay for the development of new industries. It expected that future oil income would help pay these debts. When world oil prices dropped in the 1980's, Mexico found it hard to repay its loans. Today it suffers from one of the world's highest foreign debts. This debt may take years to repay, even if demand for Mexico's oil picks up.

248

5 The Caribbean Islands

The Caribbean islands, also known as the West Indies, curve through the Atlantic Ocean, the Caribbean Sea, and the Gulf of Mexico. There are three groups of islands. The group of islands lying farthest north is the Bahamas. Southwest of the Bahamas are the Greater Antilles (an til′ēz). The Greater Antilles include the large islands of Cuba, Jamaica, Puerto Rico, and Hispaniola. Hispaniola is the island on which Haiti and the Dominican Republic are located. The third group of islands is called the Lesser Antilles. These small islands curve eastward and southward from Puerto Rico to Venezuela. The islands of Trinidad and Tobago are only 7 miles (11 kilometers) from Venezuela.

The earliest inhabitants of the Caribbean islands were Indians. Few Indians survived the first century of colonization. Today most residents of the islands are descendants of English, French, Dutch, and Spanish colonists and Africans who were brought to America as slaves.

On most islands, there is a black majority. In these places, styles of dress, food, music, and building all reflect African culture. On the other hand, about half the residents of Cuba and the Dominican Republic are descendants of Europeans. In these countries, the culture is largely Spanish.

Other cultures have also helped shape Caribbean life. Because Haiti once belonged to France, people there speak French. French is also spoken in Guadaloupe and Martinique, overseas departments of France. Residents of former British colonies—Barbados, the Bahamas, Grenada, Jamaica, and Trinidad and Tobago—speak English. English is

Tropical beauty and balmy weather draw tourists to San Juan, Puerto Rico. Tourism is one of the Caribbean's leading industries. Wide beaches, sparkling waters, and modern resorts are big attractions.

also spoken in a few other current British colonies. Because of emigration from India, East Indian languages and culture are also found in Trinidad and Tobago. The Netherlands Antilles—the islands of Aruba, Bonaire, and Curaçao—are still under the control of the Netherlands. People there speak mainly Dutch.

The Caribbean Economy

By and large, the nations of the West Indies are poor. The region's poverty is partly a result of one-sided economic development. Most Caribbean nations depend on farming. However, the islands are mountainous and good farmland is scarce.

Students should locate the Caribbean islands on the map on page 236. One of the most interesting aspects of these islands is the diversity of cultures found on them. As overseas departments, Martinique and Guadaloupe are each represented in the French Parliament by two senators and three deputies.

251

Texas Essential Element 1C. Geographical tools and methodologies.

Using a Gazetteer

If you were asked to write a report on the Galapagos Islands, the first thing you might do is check a gazetteer. A gazetteer is a geographical dictionary that lists countries, cities, rivers, mountains, and other geographical features in alphabetical order. Gazetteers provide a variety of information about places, including location, size, population figures, and occasionally some historical information.

An atlas and a gazetteer are often found at the back of a geography book. The atlas contains maps of countries and continents. The gazetteer lists in alphabetical order the place names from those maps.

The *G* entries from the *Heath World Geography* gazetteer (pages 501–514) appear below. Find the Galapagos Islands in the sample. At what degrees of latitude and longitude are the islands located? To what country do they belong? Notice that they are shown on the Atlas map on page 495. If you turn to that map, you will find the Galápagos Islands at latitude 0°10′ S and longitude 87°45′ W.

Look over the sample below. Then use the information to answer the following questions.

1. On what page will you find the map showing the latitude and longitude for Galveston Bay?

2. On what page will you find the map showing the latitude and longitude for Ghana?

3. What is the latitude and longitude for Goose Lake, California?

4. (a) What is Gibraltar? (b) What is its latitude and longitude?

5. What lake is located at latitude 66°10′ N and longitude 119°53′ W?

6. Use the Gazetteer to locate the Green River in the United States. Through what two states does it flow?

G

Name	Latitude	Longitude	Page(s)
Gabon, country in Africa	0°30′ S	10°45′ E	498
Gaborone, capital of Botswana	24°28′ S	25°59′ E	498
Galápagos Islands, part of Ecuador	0°10′ S	87°45′ W	495
Galveston Bay, Texas	29°39′ N	94°45′ W	492
Gambia, country in Africa	13°38′ N	19°38′ W	498
Ganges River, India	34°32′ N	87°58′ E	497
Gdansk, city in Poland	54°20′ N	18°40′ E	496
Geelong, city in Australia	38°6′ S	144°13′ E	499
Geneva, Lake, Switzerland	46°28′ N	6°30′ E	496
Genoa, city in Italy	44°23′ N	9°52′ E	496
Georgetown, capital of Guyana	7°45′ N	58°4′ W	495
Georgia, state in the United States	32°40′ N	83°50′ W	493
Germany, East, country in Europe	53°30′ N	12°30′ E	496
Germany, West, country in Europe	51°45′ N	8°30′ E	496
Ghana, country in Africa	8° N	2° W	498
Gibraltar, territory of the United Kingdom in Southern Europe	36°8′ N	5°22′ W	496
Gibraltar, Strait of, between Africa and Europe	35°55′ N	5°45′ W	496
Gila River, Arizona	32°41′ N	113°50′ W	492
Glasgow, city in Scotland	55°54′ N	4°25′ W	496
Godthab, capital of Greenland	64°10′ N	51°32′ W	494, 500
Gold Coast, city in Australia	28°5′ S	153°25′ E	499
Goose Lake, California	41°56′ N	120°35′ W	492
Gor'kiy, city in the U.S.S.R.	56°15′ N	44°5′ E	496
Goteborg, city in Sweden	57°39′ N	11°56′ E	496
Gotland, island off Sweden	57°35′ N	17°35′ E	496

Name	Latitude	Longitude	Page(s)
Great Australian Bight, bay in Australia	33°30′ S	127° E	499
Great Bear Lake, Canada	66°10′ N	119°53′ W	494, 500
Great Salt Lake, Utah	41°19′ N	112°48′ W	492, 494
Great Slave Lake, Canada	61°37′ N	114°58′ W	494, 500
Greece, country in Europe	39° N	21°30′ E	496
Green Bay, Wisconsin	44°55′ N	88°4′ W	493
Greenland, country in North America	74° N	40° W	494, 500
Green River, United States	38°30′ N	110°10′ W	492
Greensboro, city in North Carolina	36°4′ N	79°45′ W	493
Greenville, city in South Carolina	34°50′ N	82°25′ W	493
Grenada, country in the Caribbean Sea	12°2′ N	61°27′ W	494
Guadalajara, city in Mexico	20°41′ N	103°21′ W	494
Guadeloupe, island of France, in the Caribbean Sea	16°7′ N	61°19′ W	494
Guangzhou, city in China	23°7′ N	113°15′ E	497
Guatemala, capital of Guatemala	15°45′ N	91°45′ W	494
Guatemala, country in Central America	15°45′ N	91°45′ W	494
Guayaquil, city in Ecuador	2°16′ S	79°53′ W	495
Guinea, country in Africa	10°48′ N	12°28′ W	498
Guinea-Bissau, country in Africa	12° N	20° W	498
Guinea, Gulf of, Africa	2° N	1° E	498
Guyana, country in South America	7°45′ N	59° W	495

Answers are in the Teacher's Guide.

Assign the Workbook activity for this chapter's Skill Workshop with this page.

Since colonial days, sugar has been the most important crop of the region. Today sugar farmers in the Caribbean face many hardships. Prices for sugar are low, and foreign competition makes it hard for Caribbean farmers to sell their crops.

Other crops produced in the West Indies include tobacco, bananas, coconuts, and fruits. Some islands produce spices. Coffee is Haiti's most important cash crop. Jamaica produces small amounts of a high-quality coffee known as Blue Mountain.

Minerals are less abundant on the islands than on the mainland of Middle America. Jamaica mines bauxite, a mineral used in making aluminum. Cuba has deposits of both nickel and manganese. Petroleum and natural gas are produced in Trinidad and Tobago.

Because of low prices for raw materials, many nations of the Caribbean have fallen into deep debt. They have little capital with which to develop industry. Manufacturing in the Caribbean is largely limited to refining or processing agricultural crops. Sugar refining is a major industry. Both Cuba and Jamaica also have plants for processing minerals. Trinidad and Tobago has large oil refineries; Cuba, Jamaica, and Puerto Rico have some smaller oil refineries. Alcoholic beverages, clothing and textiles, chemicals, fertilizer, and machinery are also produced in the Caribbean. Most of the baseballs used in the United States are made in Haiti.

The United States is the major trading partner for most of the Caribbean nations. Cuba is the one exception. Before the Cuban revolution, Cuba exported large amounts of sugar to the United States. After the revolution, Cuba abolished free enterprise. Today it is the only nation in the West Indies with a communist economy. Cuba depends on its trade

Sugarcane is a major Caribbean crop.

with and financial assistance from the Soviet Union.

Because of their moderate climate, sunny beaches, and natural beauty, the Caribbean islands have become a favorite destination for tourists. Winter is the busiest season, but many tourists come during the summer. The cooling trade winds and ocean breezes make summer in the West Indies a pleasant change from hotter weather in many parts of the world.

REVIEWING THE FACTS

Answer

1. What three groups of islands make up the West Indies?

2. What cultures have influenced life in the West Indies?

3. (a) What are the chief products of the Caribbean nations? (b) What economic challenges do these nations face?

Locate

Refer to the map on page 236 to identify the country of which each city below is a capital.

1. Havana
2. Kingston
3. Santo Domingo
4. Port-au-Prince

253

Highlighting the Chapter

1. Middle America includes Mexico, Central America, and the islands of the Caribbean Sea. The mainland is the southern part of North America. It is largely mountainous, with high, rugged highlands extending southward in a Y shape. Along the coasts are fertile plains. Good soil is also found in mountain valleys and in the plateau region of the north. The Caribbean islands are also mountainous.

2. Middle America was colonized by Spain and other European countries. On the mainland, Indian cultures and Spanish culture have shaped most nations. The Caribbean cultures were influenced by colonial nations as well as by Africans. There are few nations with a history of stable democratic government in the region. Most Middle American economies are still based on farming. Most nations export farm goods or natural resources to earn cash to pay for finished goods. Even in oil-rich Mexico, there is a lack of capital and extensive poverty.

3. Mexico, one of the world's major oil producers, is the most industrialized nation of Middle America. It also has important mineral resources that are mined. Mexico distributed land among many of its rural people during the 1900's. As in other parts of Middle America, tourism is a vital part of its economy.

4. Central America is a largely agricultural region with little manufacturing or mining. Bananas, sugarcane, cacao, and coffee are grown on plantations. Subsistence farmers grow corn, wheat, and beans in the highlands.

5. The West Indies have a mixture of cultural and population patterns. Agriculture is the mainstay of the Caribbean economy. Plantations produce sugarcane, coffee, and tropical fruits. There is some petroleum and mineral production as well as a number of large natural gas and oil refineries. Tourism is another important economic activity.

254

Speaking Geographically

Number a sheet of paper from 1 to 5. Beside each number, write the correct term for the definition given below.

1. Poor farm laborer who settles near and works the land of a landowner

2. Farmland belonging to a rural community, on which plots are given to families

3. Person of mixed European and Indian ancestry

4. Winds that blow westward across the Caribbean toward the equator

5. Person of Spanish ancestry born in Latin America

Testing Yourself

Number your paper from 1 to 9. Then fill in the blanks in the sentences below.

1. The large plateau region between the Eastern and Western Sierra Madre in Mexico is called the _____.

2. Many of the mountains of Middle America are active _____.

3. The only country in the Caribbean with a communist government is _____.

4. _____ has a stable, two-party, democratic government.

5. The major waterway connecting the Pacific and Atlantic oceans is the _____.

6. The European nation that had the greatest influence on the culture of Middle America is _____.

7. Nearly every nation of the Caribbean has important trade ties with the _____.

8. Haiti, Jamaica, and most nations of Central America produce fine _____.

9. _____ is a major linkage connecting Mexico, Central America, and South America.

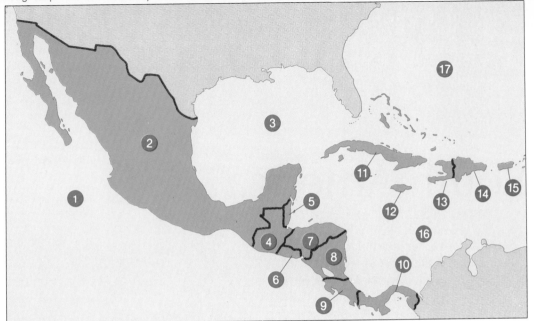

Building Map Skills

Number your paper from 1 to 17. After each number, write the name of the country or body of water identified by that number on the map above.

Applying Map Skills

Each of the clues below identifies a place in Middle America. Number your paper from 1 to 10. Write the name of the place each phrase identifies beside its number.

1. Peninsula that borders California

2. Central American country that has no Caribbean coast

3. Central American country that has no Pacific coast

4. Mountains of eastern Mexico

5. Countries bordered by the largest Middle American country

6. Smallest country in Central America

7. Largest island in the West Indies

8. Largest lake in Central America

9. Countries in Middle America lying on the Tropic of Cancer

10. Country in Middle America with southernmost point

Exploring Further

1. Two fascinating peoples of Middle America were the Maya and the Aztec. Compare their civilizations. Include information on the location of each, the years they flourished, their economies, their religion, and their artistic and scientific accomplishments.

2. Nicaragua, Honduras, El Salvador, and Guatemala are undergoing conflict and change. Events in these nations are often reported in the news media. Keep a file of newspaper or magazine articles covering developments in these nations.

3. Tourism has long been important in Middle America. Choose an island or country you would like to visit. Consult a travel agency to learn about the place you have chosen. Prepare a report describing your proposed trip. Tell what you will need to take along, how much your trip will cost, and what special arrangements you must make.

255

In this chapter, students will become acquainted with the continent of South America. In Sections 1 and 2, the continent will be considered as a whole. In Sections 3 through 6, the continent is broken up into four regions.

South America

South America, the fourth largest continent, lies to the southeast of North America. It is connected to North America by a narrow strip of land—the Isthmus of Panama. Like Middle America, South America is part of the Latin American culture region. The region's governments, religious practices, arts, and economics have been shaped by many of the same factors that shaped Middle America.

South America, however, is larger and more varied than Middle America. For example, the continent measures about 4,750 miles (7,640 kilometers) from Cape Horn, Chile, in the south to Punta Gallinas, Colombia, in the north. It extends nearly 3,300 miles (5,300 kilometers) east to west. It has dense rain forest, towering mountain ranges, vast plains, and parched deserts.

Many South American countries have modern cities and industries that differ little from those of Europe or North America. In many large cities, there are densely packed skyscrapers housing corporate offices. Many South American countries have auto, steel, and chemical companies, where skilled workers use the latest technology. Within these same countries, however, there are many people living in grinding poverty. Farming is hard throughout much of the region. In some parts of the continent, land travel is nearly impossible. Political conflict and the slow pace of change in many isolated areas hold back economic development.

256

The photograph shows a Sunday market in Colombia.

1 The Physical Environment

The South American continent is shaped roughly like a triangle pointing toward the South Pole. Its northern side is the Caribbean coastline. Its western side borders the Pacific. Its eastern side extends along the Atlantic. Across the northern coast are the countries of Colombia, Venezuela, Guyana (gī an'ə), Suriname (sùr'ə näm'ə), and the French possession of French Guiana (gē an'ə). Ecuador, Peru, Chile, and the western part of Colombia lie on the west coast. Brazil, Uruguay (ur'ə gwī'), and Argentina are on the east coast. In the interior, there are two landlocked countries—Bolivia and Paraguay (par'ə gwī').

Landforms

South America has seven different landform areas. There are four highland areas and three areas of plains.

Mountains The Andes Mountains lie along the Pacific coast. Their towering peaks and high ridges form a barrier between a sliver of coastal plain next to the Pacific and the interior plains.

The Andes were probably formed as South America drifted apart from Africa (page 28). As the continent collided with the Nazca plate, which lies under the Pacific, rocks were folded and thrust high above sea level. The continental plate is still moving west, slowly grinding over the sea floor. As a result, earthquakes, volcanoes, and folding continue in the region. In 1985, for instance, Nevado del Ruiz, a volcano in Colombia, erupted. It wiped out the city of Armero and three nearby towns.

Much of eastern South America is also mountainous. Over millions of years, the peaks of the Eastern Highlands have been worn down. Today much of their area is only about 1,000 to 3,000 feet (300 to 900 meters) above sea level. The largest upland is the Brazilian Highlands. Along with a plateau region to their west, these highlands cover most of southern Brazil.

Another highland area is in the northeast. The Guiana Highlands lie between the Orinoco (ōr'ə nō'kō) and Amazon rivers. The highest waterfall in the world, called Angel Falls, is located in this area.

At the southern tip of South America is the continent's largest plateau, Patagonia. It touches both the pampas to the northeast and the Andes to the west. Patagonia is a dry, windswept area. It has many deep canyons carved by rivers flowing from the Andes to the Atlantic Ocean.

Plains East of the Andes, a series of plains runs through the center of the continent. In the north is the llanos (yä'nōs). The llanos are drained by the Orinoco River, which flows from the Andean highlands into the Atlantic.

South of the llanos lies the Amazon Basin. The giant Amazon River flows from high in the Andes eastward into the Atlantic. It is the world's second longest river but carries more water than any other river. The plains in the basin cover an area almost as large as the United States.

A third large plains area is located in the south-central part of the continent. There, the Paraná (par'ə nä') and Paraguay rivers and their tributaries have created a vast lowland area. This area includes Paraguay, Uruguay, and the fertile pampas of Argentina.

Climates and Ecosystems

Because it extends through 67 degrees of latitude, South America has a great variety of climates. The continent is widest

The Amazon begins as a tiny brook 17,000 feet (5,182 meters) up in the Andes of Peru, only 120 miles (193 kilometers) from the Pacific Ocean. It flows east, gathering strength, until it reaches the Atlantic, about 4,000 miles (6,436 kilometers) away. Its mouth is 200 miles (322 kilometers) wide, and it can be navigated 2,300 miles (3,701 kilometers) inland.

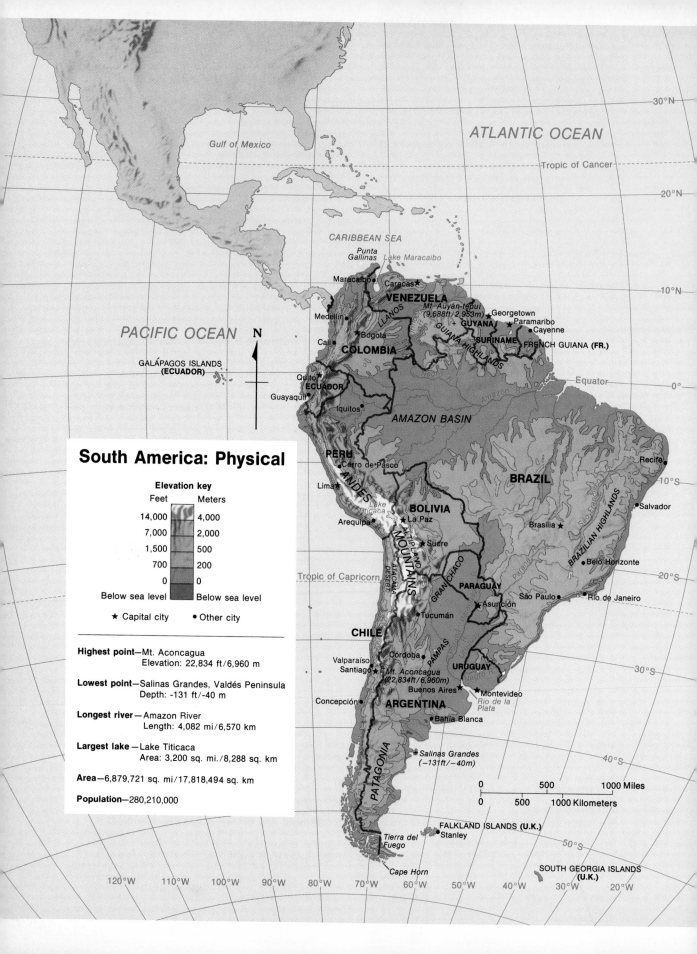

ATLANTIC OCEAN

Tropic of Cancer — 30°N

20°N

Gulf of Mexico

10°N

CARIBBEAN SEA

Punta
Gallinas   Lake Maracaibo

Maracaibo •
Caracas ★

PACIFIC OCEAN   N   VENEZUELA   Mt. Auyán-tepuí   Georgetown •
                                       (9,688ft/2,953m)   Paramaribo •
Medellín •   LLANOS   GUYANA   • Cayenne
GALÁPAGOS ISLANDS   • Bogotá   SURINAME   FRENCH GUIANA (FR.)
(ECUADOR)   Cali •   COLOMBIA   GUIANA HIGHLANDS

Quito ★   Equator — 0°
ECUADOR
Guayaquil •   Negro
                    Iquitos •   Amazon
                        AMAZON BASIN

PERU   • Recife

Cerro de Pasco •   BRAZIL   10°S
Lima ★   ANDES   São Francisco
        Lake
        Titicaca   • Salvador
Arequipa •   BOLIVIA   BRAZILIAN HIGHLANDS
            ★ La Paz
        ALTIPLANO   ★ Sucre   Brasília ★
        ATACAMA DESERT
        MOUNTAINS   • Belo Horizonte   20°S
Tropic of Capricorn   GRAN CHACO   Paraná
            PARAGUAY   São Paulo •
            Asunción ★   • Rio de Janeiro
        Tucumán •

CHILE   PAMPAS   URUGUAY
        Córdoba •
Valparaíso •   Mt. Aconcagua
Santiago ★   (22,834ft/6,960m)   Montevideo ★   30°S
        Buenos Aires ★   Río de la
Concepción •   ARGENTINA   Plata
        • Bahía Blanca

        PATAGONIA   Salinas Grandes   40°S
                (−131ft/−40m)

                0   500   1000 Miles
                0   500   1000 Kilometers

            FALKLAND ISLANDS (U.K.)
Tierra del   • Stanley
Fuego   50°S

Cape Horn   SOUTH GEORGIA ISLANDS
                        (U.K.)

120°W   110°W   100°W   90°W   80°W   70°W   60°W   50°W   40°W   30°W   20°W

South America: Physical

Elevation key

Feet	Meters
14,000	4,000
7,000	2,000
1,500	500
700	200
0	0
Below sea level	Below sea level

★ Capital city   • Other city

Highest point—Mt. Aconcagua
    Elevation: 22,834 ft/6,960 m

Lowest point—Salinas Grandes, Valdés Peninsula
    Depth: -131 ft/-40 m

Longest river — Amazon River
    Length: 4,082 mi/6,570 km

Largest lake — Lake Titicaca
    Area: 3,200 sq. mi./8,288 sq. km

Area—6,879,721 sq. mi/17,818,494 sq. km

Population—280,210,000

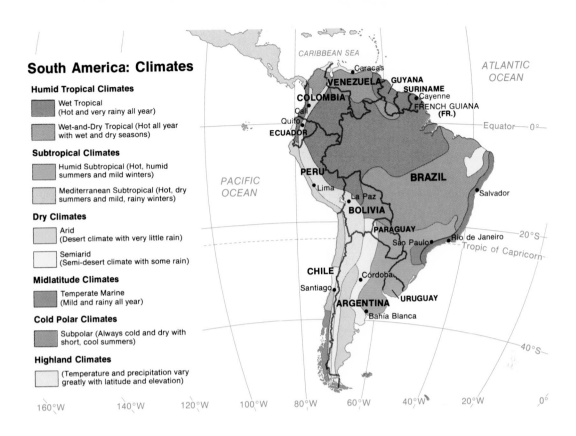

South America: Climates

Humid Tropical Climates

Wet Tropical (Hot and very rainy all year)

Wet-and-Dry Tropical (Hot all year with wet and dry seasons)

Subtropical Climates

Humid Subtropical (Hot, humid summers and mild winters)

Mediterranean Subtropical (Hot, dry summers and mild, rainy winters)

Dry Climates

Arid (Desert climate with very little rain)

Semiarid (Semi-desert climate with some rain)

Midlatitude Climates

Temperate Marine (Mild and rainy all year)

Cold Polar Climates

Subpolar (Always cold and dry with short, cool summers)

Highland Climates

(Temperature and precipitation vary greatly with latitude and elevation)

Map Study *Which South American countries lie in the Andes Mountains? In which countries are there lowlands drained by the Amazon River system? • Which part of South America has a hotter, moister climate, the east or the west? Which South American countries have both dry and tropical climates? Where are the continent's temperate zones? Describe the changes in Chile's climate from north to south.*

between the equator and the Tropic of Capricorn. This vast area is mostly tropical. The Amazon Basin is hot and rainy all year round. Apart from the Andes region, the rest of the tropical area is hot all year, with a rainy season and a dry season.

The Amazon Basin, where it rains nearly every day, is the world's largest area of tropical forest. There, some trees rise over 200 feet above the forest floor. Overhead, the trees' crowns form a dense canopy. Little plant life survives beneath these trees. However, in sunlit spots — where trees have fallen, or along streams

and in clearings — there is thick, tangled vegetation called jungle.

Many kinds of animals live in the Amazon forest. The tapir, which resembles the horse and the rhinoceros, is the largest land animal native to the region. The tropical rivers abound with fish (including the deadly piranha), snakes, rodents, and alligatorlike caimans.

As in other mountain areas, the climate of the Andes changes from hot to cold as elevation increases. In the southern Andes, the climate is moist and cool. Forests that are like those of the Pacific

259

Northwest in the United States are found in the area. North of these forests, along the western slopes of the mountains, is the Atacama (at'ə käm'ə) Desert. Rich in many minerals, this desert is the driest in the world. Parts of it have gone more than 20 years without a drop of rain.

Grasslands stretch for hundreds of miles in the northern and southern plains areas. Scientists believe that tall trees once gave shade to these expanses. Then, thousands of years ago, hunters set fires to clear trees and shrubs, where game was concealed. These fires may have destroyed the original ecosystem of the plains. In the absence of shade trees, tall grasses flourished, forming savanna ecosystems. The soil on these plains, especially on the pampas, has proved to be good for farming.

REVIEWING THE FACTS

Answer

1. What are the landform regions of South America?

2. What signs of continental drift are evident in South America?

3. Describe the climates and ecosystems of South America.

4. Why is there so great a variety of climates in South America?

Locate

Refer to the map on page 259.

1. Which South American countries are entirely north of the equator?

2. In which countries is there a year-round hot and rainy climate?

3. Name the countries in which there is a desert or semi-desert.

4. What is the major climate of the South American countries that lie along the equator?

2 The Human Imprint

South America has been shaped by a variety of cultures. The first people to live on the continent were Indians. Later, Europeans, Africans, and Asians settled in South America. As in Mexico and Central America, Spanish culture has been very important. There is, however, greater cultural diversity in this region than in Mexico and Central America.

The People of South America

South America as a whole is sparsely settled. In fact, the vast interior of the continent has few people and little economic development. Even so, experts talk of population pressures on the continent. For one thing, population is growing by about 2.3 percent a year. This rate makes South America one of the world's fastest-growing regions. In addition, people are crowded into places where climate is moderated by the ocean or by elevation. The majority of the population is found along the Atlantic coast. There are also areas of dense settlement in the central and northern Andes. Three of every four South Americans lives in a city.

Indians As in Middle America and North America, groups of Indians lived in South America long before 1500. The Indians of the Amazon Basin lived in scattered riverside villages, from which they fished and hunted. They also grew sweet potatoes, beans, and potatolike roots, called Manioc.

By contrast, high in the Andes, the Inca created a great empire. Its people practiced intensive farming, with mountainside terraces and irrigation for growing potatoes, beans, corn, and other crops. Inca artisans made beautiful pottery and gold jewelry. The Inca domesticated

260

Quito, Ecuador, and Manaus, Brazil (along the Amazon River), are both located near the equator, but their climates are very different. Ask students to explain why. (elevation) Assign the Workbook activity for Chapter 10, Section 1, with pages 257–260 and for Chapter 10, Section 2, with pages 260–267. Answers are in the Teacher's Guide.

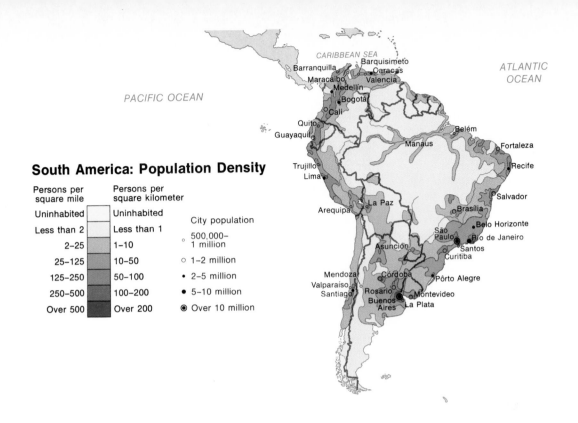

South America: Population Density

Persons per square mile	Persons per square kilometer
Uninhabited	Uninhabited
Less than 2	Less than 1
2–25	1–10
25–125	10–50
125–250	50–100
250–500	100–200
Over 500	Over 200

City population

○ 500,000–1 million

○ 1–2 million

• 2–5 million

• 5–10 million

◉ Over 10 million

Map Study *Where is South America's population most sparse? Most dense?* • *La Paz, Bolivia, is high in the Andes. Indians live on the mountainsides, overlooking modern residences and government high rises.*

the llama and the alpaca. Both of these animals were a source of woolen fiber. Llamas were also used as pack animals on roads connecting small villages with cities. In the cities, there were magnificent temples and other public buildings. The Inca emperor ruled as an absolute king.

Indian influence continues to be strong in South America. Although the Inca and other groups were conquered by Europeans, they did not vanish. In the mountains of Peru, for example, some Indians farm today much as the Inca did five centuries ago. Many of these Indians speak the language of their ancestors. They dress in traditional clothes, follow ancient religions, and eat foods that are like those of their ancestors.

261

The Colonial Impact Europeans began to colonize South America in the 1500's. As in Middle America, colonists came to find wealth and to spread Christianity. The Portuguese settled in Brazil. The Spanish moved into the Andean region and southeastern South America. In addition, France, Great Britain, and the Netherlands set up colonies along the coast of the Caribbean Sea in an area that became known as the **Guianas.**

Spanish colonies in South America, like those in Mexico and Central America, had a pyramidlike system of social class. At the top of the pyramid was a small group of people from Spain. Only these people held government posts. They also owned mines, ranches, and plantations. Below those born in Europe were the Creoles, people of European ancestry born in the colonies. A larger group, the mestizos, had both Spanish and Indian ancestors. They ranked lower than the Creoles. Most mestizos were laborers on farms or skilled workers in towns. At the bottom of the social pyramid were Indians and, in some areas, blacks brought from Africa. Both groups served as slaves in mines and on plantations.

Portugal's colony, Brazil, was ruled very much like the colonies of Spain. As elsewhere, colonists there owned and managed plantations. In Brazil, however, Indians were scattered in the remote interior and did not work well as slaves on plantations. Therefore, when the colonists sought workers for their farms, they imported large numbers of Africans. Slavery became an important part of Brazil's economic life. People of African ancestry became a large group within the population. Brazil did not abolish slavery until 1888.

Slavery was also important in the colonies held by France, Great Britain, and the Netherlands. When African slaves were freed during the mid-1800's, each of these colonies turned to a new source of labor. British Guiana—now called Guyana—looked to the British colony of India. Nearly half the population of Guyana today traces its ancestry to India. Laborers from the Netherlands' East Asian colony of Indonesia came to Dutch Guiana, which is the country of Suriname today. Immigrants from Europe and China added still further to the mix of people in the Guianas.

Political Patterns

Independence came to most of South America in the first part of the 1800's. Only the Guianas remained European colonies after the 1820's (page 273).

Winning Independence In Spanish South America, the road to independence was long and hard. The most famous patriot was a wealthy young Creole named Simón Bolívar (bə lē' vär'). In 1817, Bolívar took command of a rugged army in the north. After five years of bitter war in

Bolívar is known as the Liberator.

262

wet river basins and frigid mountain passes, Bolívar's army freed what is now Venezuela, Colombia, and Ecuador.

During the same years, José de San Martín (san'mär tēn') led an army fighting for independence in the southern part of the continent. San Martín, who was born in Argentina, had served for years in the Spanish army. He returned to Argentina, his homeland, in 1810 after it became independent. Like Bolívar, San Martín was inspired by the idea of freedom for all of Latin America. In 1817, San Martín took charge of an army in what is now Chile. After defeating the Spanish in Chile, he moved his troops into Peru. There, he linked up with Bolívar's army. Bolívar took command of both armies and led the final battles for independence. By 1824, Spain no longer controlled any lands on the continent.

Independence came much more easily in Brazil. In 1807, the king of Portugal, King João (zhwoun), was forced to flee Europe as French troops swept through his country. King João took his court to Brazil, Portugal's large colony in South America. During his stay there, many Brazilians came to resent the king's riches and the privileges given those who had come with him from Portugal.

In 1821, with the return of peace in Europe, King João went back to Portugal. He left his son, Dom Pedro, behind to rule Brazil. Once back in Portugal, King João began to tighten his control over Brazil. When Brazilians protested, Dom Pedro sided with them and declared the country independent. He became its emperor.

The South American Republics In the 1820's, the former Spanish colonies adopted constitutions providing for representative government. By the late 1880's, Brazil had also become a republic. These new countries modeled their governments on that of the United States. As

Many churches and other public buildings in South American cities show the influence of Spanish and Portuguese architecture. This influence can be seen in this view of the city of Bahia, Brazil.

in Middle America, however, small groups of wealthy families and military leaders often gained real political power.

In most countries of South America, representative governments have often been replaced with dictatorships in **coups** (küz). A coup is a sudden, and sometimes violent, overthrow of an existing government by a small group, usually of military officers. South American dictatorships usually ignore the constitution and courts, end elections, and abolish the legislature. With a few exceptions, military governments help to keep wealth in the hands of the few. Under dictatorships, the landless and the poor have little chance to improve their lives or take part in government. People who protest may be jailed, kidnapped, or killed.

263

Economic Patterns

Most countries of South America have free-enterprise economies. There are, however, important differences between free enterprise in South America and many other parts of the world. Strong dictatorships in some Latin countries have **nationalized** major industries. To nationalize a business is to place it under government control. Oil production, communications, mining, steelmaking, and meat-packing are among the industries that are owned by South American governments.

Producing Minerals and Fuels Many South American countries have large and valuable mineral deposits. Tin, copper, iron, gold, and silver are mined throughout the Andes. Nitrates, used to make fertilizers, are found in the Atacama Desert. Along the Caribbean coast are supplies of bauxite and iron. Iron, quartz crystals, gemstones, and manganese are also mined in Brazil.

Venezuela has the biggest oil deposits on the continent. Colombia also produces oil and coal. Coal is also mined in Brazil.

Farming Very little of South America has fertile soil. One of the best farming areas is the pampas of Argentina. There, farmers grow wheat, corn, and flax. Ranchers have large herds of cattle. Colombia and Brazil, where coffee is grown in the highlands, produce 40 percent of the world's coffee. In the Brazilian lowlands, sugarcane is produced on large plantations. Ecuador grows more than 25 percent of the world's bananas in its lowlands.

Throughout much of South America, however, farmers grow little more than their families need. The chief crops of such farmers are corn, wheat, and potatoes. These farmers have small plots of land. Fertilizers, pesticides, and high-yield seeds are virtually unknown to them. Crop yields are so low that even with many people engaged in farming, some nations must import food. The governments of many South American nations are trying to improve farming by introducing new crops and modern methods.

Industry Spain and Portugal did little to develop industry in their South American

WORLD DATA BANK

Country	Area in Square Miles	Population/Natural Increase		Per Capita GNP
Argentina	1,068,297	31,500,000	(1.6%)	$2,130
Bolivia	424,162	6,500,000	(2.6%)	470
Brazil	3,286,475	141,500,000	(2.1%)	1,640
Chile	292,259	12,400,000	(1.6%)	1,440
Colombia	439,734	29,900,000	(2.1%)	1,320
Ecuador	109,483	10,000,000	(2.8%)	1,160
Guyana	83,000	800,000	(2.0%)	570
Paraguay	157,046	4,300,000	(2.9%)	940
Peru	496,224	20,700,000	(2.5%)	960
Suriname	63,039	400,000	(2.1%)	2,570
Uruguay	68,039	3,100,000	(0.8%)	1,660
Venezuela	352,143	18,300,000	(2.7%)	3,110

Have students study the map on page 265 to identify the patterns of land use and the distribution of natural resources in South America. They should note the low number of manufacturing areas on the continent.

South America: Land Use

Legend:
- Manufacturing
- Commercial farming and stock raising
- Stock raising
- Forestry
- Farming mostly for family use
- Hunting, fishing, and gathering
- Commercial fishing
- Little or no activity

Coal	Diamonds
Iron	Hydroelectric power
Petroleum	Tin
Natural gas	Lead
Copper	Zinc
Bauxite	Uranium
Gold	Tungsten
Silver	

Map Study *What are South America's main centers of manufacturing? What countries have manufacturing centers? In what countries are there hydroelectric power stations?*

colonies. As a result, the countries of South America had few factories until recently. Even today, manufacturing is largely limited to food processing and textile making for local markets.

However, some countries—particularly Brazil and Argentina—have become industrialized. Steelmaking, metal production, and chemical refining are large industries in these countries.

Linkages Rain forests, mountains, and other natural barriers make transportation and communication difficult in South America. Only Argentina, Brazil, and Uruguay have good highway systems. Even in these countries, there are areas with no paved roads. Nearly half the Pan American Highway (page 244), for instance, is not paved. In addition, railroads are in poor repair and offer only slow transportation to the inland.

Most of the continent's rivers are poor for navigation. The Paraná, Orinoco, and Amazon are exceptions. Shippers can send large vessels up the mighty Amazon as far inland as Iquitos, Peru—nearly 1,900 miles (3,065 kilometers) from its mouth.

Because of the barriers to ground and water travel, air travel is very important. Nearly every country has government-owned or government-supported airlines. Airlines connect the continent's major cities with Europe and the United States. Charter air service links many isolated locations within the continent.

265

Comparing Employment Graphs

The level of economic development in a country influences the kinds of jobs its people hold. The more developed a country is, the more likely it is that a high percentage of its work force will hold industrial and service jobs. In a less developed country, a greater part of the work force will be in agriculture.

The graphs on this page show the percentages of people holding agricultural, industrial, service, and other kinds of jobs in five South American countries. As you study the graphs, remember that industrial work includes mining. Services include government work. Keep in mind too that the percentages refer only to the number of employed people in each country, not to the total population.

Use the graphs to help in answering the following questions.

1. (a) What percentage of Argentina's work force is engaged in agriculture? (b) In industry? (c) In services?

2. Compare the percentages of agricultural workers for all five countries. (a) Which country has the lowest percentage? (b) The highest percentage?

3. (a) Which country has the highest percentage of service workers? (b) The lowest percentage?

4. Which country has the highest percentage of workers in both industry and services?

5. (a) How are Chile and Paraguay alike? (b) How are they different?

For a special challenge Use the graphs to decide which country has the most developed economy.

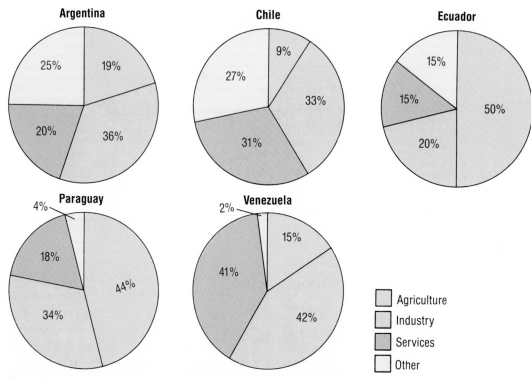

Source: Compiled from World Almanac and Book of Facts/World Development Report

Assign the Workbook activity for this chapter's Skill Workshop with this page.

Encourage students to watch for new developments in South America as they read newspapers and magazines.
Answer to Map Study question: Chile, Argentina, Paraguay, Uruguay
Answers to Reviewing the Facts are in the Teacher's Guide.

Prospects for Growth   Even though some of its countries are industrialized, South America is growing at a slow rate. Its economic development is much like that of the rest of the developing world. In many countries, a large part of the population can barely support itself. Throughout the region, land is poorly distributed. A few wealthy families hold vast estates, while the majority of the people have little land or wealth. The economies of many countries in South America continue to depend on income from just a few crops or mineral resources.

As in Middle America, foreign debt is a brake on economic growth. During the 1970's, some countries borrowed large amounts of money from foreign countries to pay for new projects. As income from their exports has fallen (page 243), these countries have found it hard to pay back their loans. As a result of their debts, they now have less money with which to pay for new businesses and to raise living standards.

REVIEWING THE FACTS

Define

1. Guianas   3. nationalize
2. coup

Answer

1. (a) Which countries colonized most of South America? (b) By which country was Brazil colonized?

2. (a) When did most South American countries become independent? (b) How do dictatorships affect life in South America?

3. What economic activities are important in South America?

Locate

Refer to the map on this page.

1. What two countries of South America cover the greatest distance north and south?

2. Name the continent's two landlocked countries.

Map Study   *What countries lie in Southern South America?*

The Regions of South America

- Brazil
- Colombia, Venezuela and the Guianas
- Andean South America
- Southern South America

3 Brazil

The largest country in South America is Brazil. The fifth largest country in the world, it dominates the eastern part of the continent. Just over half of all South Americans live in Brazil. Brazil's GNP is almost twice as large as that of Mexico, the country with the second largest GNP in Latin America.

People and Settlement Patterns

In remote areas of Brazil, small groups of Indians still live in traditional ways.

During Carnival, a yearly festival, dancers whirl through Rio de Janeiro.

For the most part, however, Brazilian culture is a blend. Most Brazilians are descended from Europeans. In addition, many Brazilians have African ancestors, and a large part of the population is of mixed European and African ancestry. Apart from a few Indian groups in the Amazon Basin, nearly all Brazilians speak Portuguese.

Nine of 10 Brazilians live within 200 miles of the Atlantic Ocean. Most of Brazil's large cities are in this region, located on the narrow coastal plain and its bordering uplands. The two largest cities are São Paulo (saùⁿ paù'lù), the fifth biggest city in the world, and Rio de Janeiro (rē'ō dä'zhə ner'ō). The coastal cities are seaports linked to one another by coastal shipping, an important form of transportation in Brazil.

Brazil's inland has a tropical climate. Most of the Amazon region is a steamy rain forest. The northeast has hot weather all year round, and severe droughts are common. Even so, the northeast is crowded.

The population in temperate southern Brazil is growing. This is a land of rugged hills, low mountains, and gently rolling plains. There, farmers grow coffee, and ranchers raise cattle. Newly started factories have begun to turn out a variety of goods.

To reduce crowding, Brazil's government has encouraged people to settle in sparsely populated areas. Most important among these is the Amazon area. In addition, the government has tried to attract people to the central highlands. For example, the country's capital was moved in 1960 from Rio de Janeiro to Brasília, 600 miles (970 kilometers) inland. The government has built roads, offered settlers land and money, and taken other measures to speed development of the interior region.

Brazil's land surface is somewhat unusual because its highest elevations lie just west of the Atlantic Ocean. Most of its rivers flow toward the interior.
During the 1960's, the Brazilian government instituted programs (building reservoirs, developing drought-resistant plants, etc.) to improve conditions in the northeast.

SPOTLIGHT ON THE AMAZON BASIN:

An Endangered Ecosystem

The largest rain forest in the world covers the Amazon Basin. It stretches across half of Brazil as well as parts of Venezuela, Ecuador, Peru, and Bolivia. Like tropical rain forests on other continents, the Amazon Basin is in danger. Every year settlers cut, burn, and clear over a million trees to open land for farming and ranching. That destruction has consequences not only for South Americans but also for people on every other continent.

In a rain forest, trees and plants keep the constant rain from washing away valuable topsoil. The plants, in turn, obtain nutrients — the minerals and water they need to grow — from the soil. Those nutrients come from decaying leaves and fruits of trees and shrubs.

Once the trees and shrubs are gone, the thin forest soil is quickly eroded by heavy rains and then baked by the tropical sun. Within a few years, the nutrients in the soil are gone. Then farmers and ranchers move deeper into the forest, leaving behind a near-desert. If present patterns continue, by the year 2000 the Amazon Basin will lose about 63 million acres of rain forest (an area three times the size of Portugal).

Such a loss could have disastrous effects. About one fourth of the medicines that doctors prescribe contain at least one ingredient from the rain forest. In fact, about 70 percent of the drugs identified as having anti-cancer properties grow only in the rain forest.

Scientists fear that deforestation may also affect climate. Half of the Amazon's rainfall comes from water given off by plants. When those trees and other plants are gone, there will be less rain throughout the Americas.

Deforestation has yet another consequence. When hundreds of thousands of trees are burned in the rain forest each year, carbon dioxide accumulates in the atmosphere and traps heat. As a result, temperatures rise around the globe, causing polar ice to melt, raising the level of the oceans, and changing climate patterns everywhere.

Brazil's Economy

During most of its past, Brazil depended on a handful of products. For example, in the late 1800's, the Amazon Basin had a flourishing rubber industry. But then European colonies in Southeast Asia began producing large rubber crops. Brazil's rubber boom collapsed.

At other times in Brazil's history, sugar, gold, or coffee has been the most important product. As with rubber, the sale of each of these products led to a boom. Then, increased competition or a drop in prices brought hard times. During these years, most Brazilians remained poor. A few plantation and business owners, however, made large profits.

Since 1970, Brazil has tried to produce a better variety of goods. During these years, Brazil has become an industrial power. Today Brazil has new economic problems. Like other Latin American

269

countries, Brazil paid for industrial growth by borrowing from foreign banks. Its foreign debt in the mid-1980's was among the highest in the world.

A rapidly increasing population also strains Brazil's economy. Many Brazilians are without jobs, and there is widespread poverty. The rural poor have not shared in the recent economic growth. In some isolated areas, people are undernourished and poorly educated. Government and business leaders now face the challenge of raising the standard of living for nearly half of Brazil's people.

Builders are busy extending roadways into Brazil's interior rain forests. • *Workers tend the coffee crop on a plantation.*

Resource Development

For many centuries, Brazil was an agricultural country. Today the largest part of Brazil's GNP comes from manufacturing and services. The development of energy resources has helped industrialization. Coal is now mined in the highlands near São Paulo. In the 1970's, oil was discovered off the Atlantic coast and in the Amazon region. According to some experts, Brazil may soon have enough oil for its own needs.

The energy picture is brightened by the low oil needs of the country. About 80 percent of Brazil's motor vehicles run on **gasohol,** a mixture of gasoline and alcohol made from agricultural crops. Nuclear and hydroelectric power are used widely in industry. Brazil mines uranium for its nuclear power plants. Electricity is generated by several giant power dams. For example, the Itaipu (i tä'pü) power station, built by Brazil and Paraguay on the

270

Paraná River, is the world's largest hydro-electric dam.

Brazil has some of the largest iron-ore deposits in the world. It also has manganese and other minerals used in making high-quality steel. Today Brazil is an important maker of parts for automobiles, airplanes, and military equipment. Its factories also produce finished cars, computers, chemicals, foods, textiles, and a variety of consumer goods for a growing population.

While agriculture accounts for only about 10 percent of what Brazil sells, nearly a third of all Brazilians work in agriculture. Brazil is the world's leading exporter of coffee and sugar. It is South America's largest cattle producer. Except for wheat, Brazil produces enough food to feed its own people.

Among the forestry products from the Amazon region are lumber, pulp, carnauba wax (used as a polish and in making candles), and nuts. Many forest products provide raw materials for Brazil's furniture, paper, and tire factories. Others are sold abroad.

REVIEWING THE FACTS

Define

gasohol

Answer

1. Where do most Brazilians live?

2. What are some of Brazil's current economic problems?

3. Brazil is the world's leading exporter of two goods. Name them.

Locate

Refer to the map on page 258.

1. Name Brazil's capital.

2. Only two South American countries do not border Brazil. What are they?

A BRAZILIAN GHOST TOWN REBORN

In the late 1800's, the Amazon Basin was the center of a booming rubber empire. Cities like Manaus (mə naʉs') thrived. Manaus even had an opera house, where famous singers from Europe and North America came to entertain. The rubber boom ended when rubber plants were smuggled out of Brazil to Southeast Asia. The Asians grew the trees on plantations and sold rubber at cheaper prices than the Brazilians could. By 1910, cities like Manaus had almost become ghost towns.

Unlike most ghost towns, Manaus came to life again. In 1966, the Brazilian government made the city a free port, removing all tariffs and taxes. Manaus is a major trade center, served by river, air, and highway transport. Once an island of settlement in a vast wilderness, Manaus is now a thriving city in the midst of Brazil's growing interior.

271

Texas Essential Elements 3B. Economic importance of water, energy sources, and other productive resources to regions. 3D. Uses, abuses, and preservation of natural resources and the physical environment. 4D. Major cultural, political, and economic activities within and among major world regions. 4E. Settlement patterns in terms of rural/urban location, structure, and function.

4 Colombia, Venezuela, and the Guianas

Located on South America's northern coast are four countries and a department, or political division, of France. The countries are Colombia, Venezuela, Guyana, and Suriname. French Guiana is part of France. As you have read, Guyana, Suriname, and French Guiana are known as the Guianas. They are the only part of South America not once colonized by Spain or Portugal.

Colombia

Colombia is made up of many mountain villages and a few large towns and cities. Because of poor transportation, the rural villages of Colombia are isolated. It is hard to make a living in the hills. Therefore, people are flocking to the cities. The population of Bogotá (bō'gə tȯ'), for instance, doubles about every ten years. Combined with the country's fast rate of population growth, the move to cities has created serious urban problems.

The Colombian people are divided along lines of ancestry and class. Most Colombians are mestizos. Generally, mestizos are poor farmers or agricultural workers. Many live in mountain valleys. They grow coffee on small hillside plots. There are also blacks living along the Caribbean coast. Some Indians still live in the mountains of southern Colombia.

About a fifth of the population is of European ancestry. In general, this group is wealthier than the rest. In fact, most of Colombia's wealth is owned by a few families of European descent.

Colombia's economy was long based on the export of coffee. Besides coffee, bananas and cacao are important crops. Yields are often low because of poor soil, seeds, and equipment. Fertilizer is too expensive for most Colombian farmers to buy.

The growth and export of illegal drugs is a means of livelihood for many rural farmers. In recent years, the government of Colombia has tried to end this activity.

Today the country's economy is more varied than it was in the past. Colombia has a number of minerals and fuels. It mines coal, iron ore, and limestone and has several oil fields. These resources supply textile mills, steel plants, shoe factories, and chemical refineries.

Families raise crops on small farms in Colombia's highlands.

Venezuela

Colombia's neighbor to the east is Venezuela. It has one of the highest standards of living in Latin America. Both per capita GNP and per capita income are higher in Venezuela than in any other country of the region. But wealth is concentrated in the hands of a few.

Much of Venezuela's wealth comes from oil. There are large oil deposits along the Caribbean coast. The giant derricks in Lake Maracaibo (mar'ə kï'bō), which is really an inlet of the Caribbean, look like a forest of steel.

The eruption of Nevado del Ruiz in November 1985 killed 25,000 Colombians and buried a large area in which coffee had been grown. Colombia is second only to Brazil in world coffee production.

Oil was discovered in Venezuela early in the 1900's. For many years, foreign companies — especially those of the United States — controlled oil production in Venezuela. The government of Venezuela gradually bought out the foreign companies. By 1976, the industry had become nationalized. That is, it was completely owned by the government of Venezuela.

Since the 1960's, the government has encouraged farm production. Today there is large-scale commercial ranching on the Orinoco Plain. The government gave farmland in the region to landless farmers. In addition, new irrigation works are now providing water for crops during the dry season. Venezuela has a democratic government. There are no rigid class differences. The country has a middle class. The poor receive government aid to help with housing, health care, and jobs.

The Guianas

Guyana, Suriname, and French Guiana are located along the Atlantic, east of Venezuela. Each has a narrow coastal plain — where most of its people live — and hot, wet highlands covered with rain forest. Guyana is a world leader in the export of bauxite. Guyana also exports sugarcane and rice, grown on coastal plantations. Suriname grows rice, bananas, and sugarcane. Like Guyana, it has large bauxite deposits. French Guiana is the poorest of the three places. Its economy was boosted in the 1960's when France decided to build a launching site for rockets and satellites there.

Guyana won its independence from Britain in 1966, while Suriname became independent of the Netherlands in 1975. Since independence, both have had unstable governments. Cultural divisions have

Oil products, processed at modern plants like this one, are important to Venezuela's economy.

been responsible for at least some of the political turmoil. In Guyana, for instance, Europeans and blacks usually vote against East Indian candidates for office.

After independence, many East Indians fled Suriname. This flight robbed the new country of much-needed managerial and technical workers. In recent years, there has been a series of coups.

REVIEWING THE FACTS

Answer

1. (a) What groups make up most of the population of Colombia? (b) What population divisions are there in the Guianas?

2. (a) In what ways is Colombia's economy changing? (b) What factors help explain Venezuela's economic success?

Locate

Refer to the map on page 258.

1. Name the capitals of Colombia, Venezuela, and each of the Guianas.

2. What bodies of water does Colombia border?

273

5 Andean South America

Ecuador, Peru, and Bolivia are located on the west coast of South America, in the Andes. Cultural patterns in this area differ in many ways from those in the north and the east. For example, people in Brazil and the Caribbean countries live mainly on the coastal lowlands. In the Andean countries, however, most centers of population are in the highlands. Lowland areas have attracted development only recently.

People of the Andes

The Andean countries share a strong Indian heritage. Today almost 5 of every 10 residents are Indians. About 4 in 10 are mestizos. Only about 1 in 10 is of pure Spanish descent. In Ecuador, there is also a large black population.

Most people in the area speak Spanish. Many Peruvians and Bolivians, however, speak an Indian language. Peru is the only South American country with two official languages — Quechua, a language of the ancient Inca, and Spanish. About 10 percent of the Peruvian people speak only Quechua. Some Peruvian Indians speak Aymara, another ancient language.

In all three Andean countries, a large part of the population lives in the mountains and upland valleys. In both Ecuador and Peru, about half of the people live at elevations of more than a mile (1.6 kilometers). In Bolivia, nearly 80 percent of the people live on the **altiplano,** a high plateau over 2 miles (3.2 kilometers) above sea level. In Ecuador and Bolivia, some of the largest cities are located in the mountains.

Most of the remainder of the population lives along the coastal plain of Peru and Ecuador. The Humboldt Current — a cold Pacific current — moderates temperatures along the coast, making the region extremely arid. The major urban center of the region is Lima, Peru.

Until recently, the hot, humid eastern lowlands — lying in the Amazon Basin — had almost no residents. But the discovery of oil has brought people to this area.

There is great poverty in the Andes. In the highlands, Indians and mestizos grow barely enough to feed their families. People of European ancestry, on the other hand, are generally middle or upper class. Most of them live in cities in the coastal lowlands. A few wealthy city families own much farmland. In addition, a very few people own most of each country's businesses.

Lima is Peru's capital and most important city.

Economic Development

Most of those who live in the Andes are subsistence farmers. They raise potatoes, beans, and other crops. Andean governments are trying to get farmers to grow a wider variety of crops and to increase their yields. Farmers are urged to irrigate, to relocate to tropical lowland areas, and to use fertilizers, pesticides, and modern tools. In some areas, these efforts have paid off. For example, large crops of bananas and coffee are grown on Ecuador's hot, humid northern coast.

For the most part, however, farms remain unproductive. In Bolivia, for instance, most farmers still live in the arid altiplano, and few use modern methods. As a result, Bolivia, a country in which two thirds of the people are involved in agriculture, must import food.

Peru Of all the Andean countries, Peru has had the most economic success. Today Peru exports cotton and sugarcane grown on the coast and coffee grown in the highlands. Minerals — including copper, iron, lead, zinc, and silver — make up more than half of Peru's exports. Among the newest sources of income are oil and timber production in the Amazon lowlands east of the Andes. In addition, Peru has plants that process agricultural products and refine metals and oil. It is also trying to draw tourists to its lofty mountains, sandy deserts, tropical forests, and ancient Inca ruins.

As Peru has developed new businesses, older industries have been kept alive. Fishing is a traditional business. In recent years, however, overharvesting has reduced Peru's catch of tuna and other fish. The export of fish meal and guano, however, is still important. Fish meal is made from dried anchovettas, fish caught in the Pacific. Guano, a rich fertilizer, comes from the droppings of birds that feed on schools of small fish in the cool waters of the Humboldt Current.

Ecuador Ecuador's economy is less diverse than that of Peru. The country once depended on the export of bananas. Today, however, Ecuador has new industries. Since the 1970's, the importance of mining has grown. Oil is produced in the Amazon lowlands and has become Ecuador's leading export. Ecuador also has large mineral deposits, fertile farmland, and rich timber reserves that remain to be developed.

Bolivia Bolivia is one of the poorest countries of South America. In mountain areas, subsistence farmers grow crops much as their ancestors did centuries ago. There is little industry. Nearly 60 percent of the country's export income comes from one product — tin. Oil is exported

Tin is Bolivia's most important export. The country produces about 13 percent of the world's supply of this metal. Heavy equipment is in operation at the mine at Cerro Rico, Bolivia, high in the Andes.

275

Machu Picchu is one of the Inca's best-preserved cities, hidden 9,000 feet (2,700 meters) up in the Andes of Peru. It was rediscovered in 1911. A student may wish to do research and report to the class on this ancient city.

as well. Like other countries that depend on the export of a few goods, Bolivia has fallen into deep debt in recent years.

Linkages Development in the Andean countries has been held back by the difficulty of moving goods in the region. The Andes Mountains and the dense rain forest of the eastern lowlands make it hard to build good roads and railroads. This has hurt economic efforts. For example, the mountain mining center of Cerro de Pasco, Peru, is but 110 miles (177 kilometers) from the Pacific port of Lima. A train trip from one of these cities to the other, however, takes a winding route that nearly doubles the distance. Traveling from Lima, a train must climb almost 15,500 feet (4,650 meters). It must go through 67 tunnels, across 63 bridges, and around 11 hairpin turns. On level terrain, the trip might take 3 hours. Through the mountains, it takes 10 hours. As a result of such difficulties, Peru ships forest products and oil on the Amazon to Atlantic ports about 2,000 miles away.

REVIEWING THE FACTS

Define

altiplano

Answer

1. Where do most people of Peru, Ecuador, and Bolivia live?

2. How are Andean countries developing their economies?

3. Why are linkages in the Andean region poor?

Locate

Refer to the map on page 258.

1. Name the capitals of Peru, Ecuador, and Bolivia.

2. Which country in the Andean region lies on the equator?

6 Southern South America

Four countries—Chile, Argentina, Paraguay, and Uruguay—lie in the southern part of South America. The long, narrow country of Chile covers nearly half the continent's Pacific coast. The towering Andes—with snow-capped peaks, few valleys, and passes closed almost year round—form Chile's boundary with Argentina. Argentina is the second largest country in South America in terms of area and population. Paraguay and Uruguay are located just north of Argentina, in lowlands formed by the Uruguay, Paraguay, and Paraná rivers.

People of Southern South America

In contrast to the people of the northern Andes, few people live in the highlands of southern South America. The biggest population concentrations are in the plains areas. These include the plains along the coast of central Chile, the lowlands along the Paraná River, and the pampas of Argentina with their neighboring plains of Uruguay.

Other parts of the region have very few residents. Not many people live in the high Andes. The flat, scrub- and marsh-covered Gran Chaco area of northern Argentina and western Paraguay is thinly settled. Patagonia, a barren, windswept plateau, is an even larger area of sparse population.

The cultural patterns of southern South America have been shaped in large part by people whose ancestors came from Europe. Most Argentines are of Spanish or Italian ancestry. Virtually everyone living in Uruguay has European ancestry.

276

There, too, the largest groups trace their heritage to Spain and Italy. While many Chileans are mestizos, most are descendants of Spaniards. Paraguay, on the other hand, is nearly all mestizo. The Indian imprint in Paraguay is so strong that over half the people speak Guaraní, an Indian language, rather than the official language, Spanish. Paraguay also has the highest rate of population growth in South America. Population growth in the other three countries is the lowest in all of mainland Latin America.

Economic Development

Southern South America is one of the more prosperous areas of Latin America. While there is poverty in the region, fertile land and abundant minerals give the region a strong economic base. Thriving farms and ranches, large mining operations, and some important manufacturing industries produce a variety of goods for home use and for export.

Argentina In the late 1800's, as demand for food grew in Europe's booming cities, Argentina became an important agricultural supplier. On the pampas, farmers grew wheat for export. Ranchers produced beef cattle on large **estancias.** Cowhands called **gauchos** worked the herds for wealthy landowners. Tenant farmers, working small plots, grew feed crops for the cattle raised on estancias.

Today Argentina is still a major producer of agricultural goods. The level terrain, long growing season, and fertile soil of the pampas make these plains suitable for growing crops besides wheat. Corn and flax are two crops grown on the pampas and exported in large quantities. In Patagonia, ranchers produce wool and mutton.

Argentina's leading industries are meat-packing and textiles. The country also produces cars, cement, and chemicals. Enough oil is produced within Argentina to meet the country's needs.

Some people think that Argentina has the potential to become one of the world's great economic powers. Political troubles, however, have held the country back. During the twentieth century, conflicts between competing groups have often turned violent. Military councils called **juntas** (hun'təz) have ruled for long periods. The dictators have sharply limited freedom of speech and the press. Many who spoke out against the government simply "disappeared." That is, they were kidnapped and killed by secret army units.

While democracy returned in 1985, many Argentines have been reluctant to invest in the nation's economy. Today Argentina depends on borrowed money. Its foreign debt is one of the highest in the world.

Chile Chile is another country whose economy has been hurt by political

A gaucho herds cattle to pasture.

277

Interpreting a Transportation Map

Uruguay's economy depends on good land transportation. The map on this page shows how land transportation routes serve the country.

Use the map to help in answering the following questions.

1. (a) Name three forms of transportation that the map illustrates. (b) Judging from this map, which city is the major international port and shipment center?

2. A wheat farmer, marked with a W on the map, sells a crop that is to be exported to Europe. (a) To which local town will the farmer most likely deliver the wheat? (b) Where will the wheat be shipped on its route to Europe? (c) How will the wheat be transported?

3. The town of Salto is a meat-processing center. (a) By what form of transportation will rancher C's cattle shipment probably arrive at Salto? (b) If the processed meat is trucked by the most direct route from Salto to Montevideo, through what five towns will it pass?

4. Rancher S has a shipment of raw wool to send by rail to a textile mill in Canelones. (a) To which town might he take his wool? (b) How many miles will the wool travel from there?

5. A shipment of imported manufactured goods must go from Montevideo to Río Branco. Describe the route and distances the goods will probably travel.

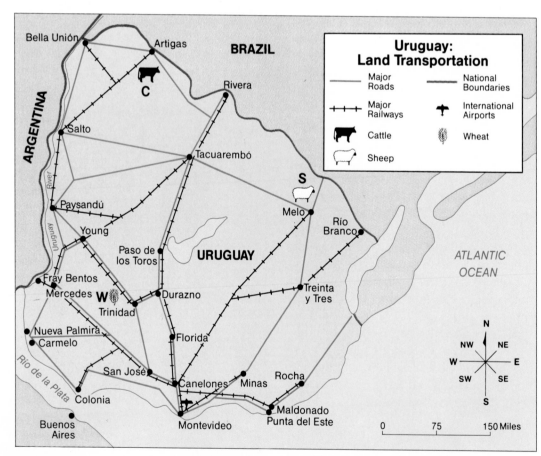

problems. During most of the 1900's, Chile had a democratic government. After the election of a socialist government in 1970, prices skyrocketed, strikes rocked the economy, and investment fell off. In 1973, promising to restore order, military leaders overthrew the socialist government. Serious inflation and unemployment, however, have continued.

Chile's key economic activity is mining. Before World War II, the major export was nitrate, which was mined in the Atacama Desert. With the introduction of synthetic fertilizers, nitrate production fell off. Copper then became Chile's leading export.

Chile must import many goods. It needs machine parts for its mining operations and its growing steel and other industries. However, its biggest need is food. Much of Chile is dry desert or rugged mountains. Soil is poor, and farms are not productive. Therefore, Chile cannot raise enough food for its people. Money earned by exporting minerals must be used to buy food abroad.

Paraguay For many years, Paraguay was the poorest country in South America. Isolated and landlocked, it produced food for its people and a few timber products — like tannin, a quebracho tree extract, used in the tanning of leather. The country has some advantages. It has grazing lands, rich farming areas, and a number of rivers. Today, Paraguay is building dams on the Paraná River to harness water power. Now that the Itaipu Dam (pages 270–271) and two others have been completed, Paraguay is likely to become the world's largest exporter of hydroelectric power. Income from this activity will help the country begin to develop other economic activities.

Uruguay The Uruguayan lowlands lie just across the Río de la Plata from the pampas. Like the pampas, Uruguay has prosperous sheep and cattle ranches and farms. Near Montevideo (mänt'ə və dā'ō), farmers grow vegetables and fruit. Wheat and feed crops are grown in the west, along the Río de la Plata. Farm goods are shipped to the leading port, Montevideo, which is the hub of Uruguay's efficient highway and railroad system.

Because Uruguay produces mainly farm goods, it imports its manufactured goods and energy. With few fuels or metals, it is unlikely that Uruguay will ever have much industry. Still, income from wool, hides, grain, meat, and leather exports exceeds the costs of imports. In this respect, the economy of Uruguay is more stable than that of many other Latin American nations.

REVIEWING THE FACTS

Define

1. gaucho
2. estancia
3. junta

Answer

1. How does population growth in southern South America compare to that of the rest of the continent?

2. (a) What are Argentina's leading agricultural products? (b) Manufactured goods?

3. On what export does Chile's economy depend?

4. (a) What economic changes are taking place in Paraguay? (b) Why is Uruguay economically stable?

Locate

Refer to the map on page 258.

1. Name the capitals of Argentina, Chile, Paraguay, and Uruguay.

2. Which of the southern South American countries lies entirely in the middle latitudes?

279

Highlighting the Chapter

1. South America has a variety of landforms. The Andes Mountains extend along the Pacific coast. In the central part of the continent are a series of river basins and plains. To the east are highlands. Much of the continent has hot, humid weather year round and a rain-forest ecosystem. There are also large areas of desert and grasslands.

2. The people of the region trace their ancestry to European settlers from Spain, Portugal, and other countries and to the Indians who lived in the region before Europeans settled there. There are also a large number of descendants of Africans. Class and other social divisions have made politics unstable. Most countries in the region are only beginning to industrialize. Large numbers of people are still subsistence farmers.

3. Brazil dominates the continent in both size and population. Its GNP is the largest in Latin America. Since 1970, Brazil has built roads, factories, dams, and power plants. It has diversified its economy through iron and steel production and agricultural development.

4. The countries of the northern coast differ in many ways. Colombia is a poor, farming country. It has, however, begun to develop its huge coal deposits. Venezuela's oil reserves help give it a high per capita income. It is also moving ahead with agricultural and mining development. The Guianas, while rich in mineral resources, have yet to develop their economies.

5. The Andean countries are poor. Most people live by subsistence farming. However, Peru has had recent success in developing its forest and oil industries. Bolivia mines valuable minerals, particularly tin. Ecuador has a growing oil industry.

6. Southern South America has a generally higher standard of living than the region as a whole. Argentina has strong manufacturing and varied commercial agriculture. Chile relies on its copper exports. In both Argentina and Chile, recent political turmoil has hampered economic growth. Paraguay, though mainly an agricultural country, is becoming a major hydroelectric-power producer. Uruguay has a stable economy based on grain and livestock exports.

Speaking Geographically

Number a sheet of paper from 1 to 5. Use the following words to fill in the blanks below.

altiplano	llanos
estancias	pampas
gauchos	

In contrast to Chile, which has great deserts and rocky mountains, and Bolivia, where most people live high on the (1) _____, Argentina and Venezuela have excellent agricultural lands. One of the most productive plains regions of the world is the (2) _____ of Argentina. In this region, (3) _____ herd cattle on large ranches called (4) _____. Venezuela's plains region, the (5) _____, is another ideal place for cattle raising.

Testing Yourself

Number your paper from 1 to 7. Write the correct choice for each sentence on your paper.

1. The largest country in South America is (Brazil, Argentina).

2. Much of Venezuela's wealth comes from the export of (lumber, oil).

3. Brazil's population is sparse (in the interior, along the Atlantic coast).

4. The country that had the greatest impact on South American culture was (Britain, Spain).

5. The country with the greater Indian population is (Bolivia, Uruguay).

6. Tin is the most important export of (Paraguay, Bolivia).

7. (Uruguay, Chile) pays for its food imports by exporting copper.

Building Map Skills

Number your paper from 1 to 13. Beside each number, write the name of the country it identifies on the map on this page. After each country, write the name of its capital.

Applying Map Skills

Buenos Aires, Argentina, and Valparaiso, Chile, are important South American port cities. Buenos Aires is on the eastern coast, and Valparaiso is on the western coast. Ships sailing from these cities to Houston in the United States take far different routes. Using the maps on pages 9, 186–187, and 265, tell which bodies of water and waterways a ship would pass through on its way to Houston from each of these cities.

Exploring Further

1. "Down to the sea and away to the north" is a popular saying in South America. "The north" refers to the United States. The saying refers to South America's trade pattern. Few goods produced in the region are sold to other South American countries. Most exports go to the United States. Select three South American products. Find out how these products are made, how they reach their markets, and to which countries they are exported.

2. Brazil's production of gasohol has helped ease its dependence on oil. Find out about the production of gasohol in the United States. To what extent is this form of energy being used in the United States?

3. Choose an animal that is native to South America. Report to the class on the habitat of this animal, its food sources, and how the animal is used by people. Make drawings to illustrate your presentation. The drawings should help you describe the animal's appearance and habits.

281

Europe is made up of three distinct regions: Western Europe, Eastern Europe, and the Soviet Union, each of which is discussed in a separate chapter. Refer students to the world map in the Atlas and explain that Europe extends as far west as Iceland and as far east as the Ural Mountains. The democratic countries of Western Europe are studied in Chapter 11. Many Americans trace their ancestry back to a country or countries in Europe. Ask students whether any of them knows that his or her ancestors came to America from Europe.

Western Europe

Europe is the western part of the Eurasian landmass. It is a small continent. Yet for centuries it has been a center for new ideas about science and religion, for artistic achievement, and for new technology.

Europe extends from the subarctic island of Iceland east across the European mainland. Its easternmost part, the Ural Mountains of the Soviet Union, borders Asia. The northern parts of Europe reach beyond the frigid Arctic Circle. Southern Europe, on the other hand, lies in the subtropical Mediterranean region.

Europe is divided into three separate regions — Western Europe, Eastern Europe, and the Soviet Union. Each part is covered in its own chapter. The first chapter on this region covers Western Europe. Western Europe is not separated from Eastern Europe by natural features, such as mountains. In fact, some countries of Eastern Europe were once part of countries in Western Europe. In addition, Greece — which is considered part of Western Europe — lies to the east of some Eastern European countries.

The countries of Western Europe are united by political and cultural ties. The region is made up of the European countries that have democratic governments. Eastern Europe consists of the countries with Communist governments. This division dates back to the end of World War II, a war that involved nearly every country of Europe.

282

The photo shows Rotterdam harbor in the Netherlands. Rotterdam, which is located on a tributary of the Rhine River, is one of the busiest ports in the world. Use this information to discuss Europe's close connection to the sea and the continent's worldwide economic importance.

1 The Physical Environment

Geographers call Europe a peninsula of peninsulas. The continent itself is much like a peninsula reaching westward from the huge Eurasian landmass. Many smaller peninsulas extend from Europe, especially from the western part. Notice the number of peninsulas shown on the map of Western Europe on page 284. Among the larger ones are the Scandinavian (skan'də nā'vē ən) and Jutland peninsulas in the north. Extending south are the Iberian, Apennine (ap'ə nīn'), and Balkan peninsulas.

Now look at Western Europe's ragged coastline. You will see seas, gulfs, bays, inlets, small fjords (fē ordz'), and thousands of islands. These features give Europe more miles of coastline than any other continent. They also create some of the world's best natural harbors.

Landforms

Europe's landforms fall into four regions. The heart of Europe is a rich lowland region, the Great European Plain. This region lies on the northern coast of the continent. It extends from the Ural Mountains all the way to France. Its broad rolling fields are fertile. In Western Europe, the plain is drained by the Elbe (el'bə), Rhine, Seine (sān), and Loire (lə wär') rivers. With its large rivers and relatively flat land, this area is a center for transportation, trade, and cultural exchange.

South of the Great European Plain is a highlands region. Called the Central Uplands, it extends from Spain across the middle of the continent. Elevations range from 1,000 feet (300 meters) to 6,000 feet (1,800 meters). Except in river valleys, the Central Uplands has thin, rocky soil. It is a poor place for farming.

South of the Central Uplands is a mountainous region. It is dominated by one of the world's great mountain systems, the Alpine Mountains. Geologically the tall, rugged Alps are young. The region south of the Alps is still shaken by earthquakes and volcanoes.

Many of Europe's river systems including the Rhone, the Seine, and the Po — drain the Alps. These rivers have carved deep valleys. Because of their many passes and gaps, the Alps are not a major barrier to trade and other contacts between countries.

In Europe's northwest, there is another highlands region. The Northwest Mountains include the Normandy Hills of France, the Cambrian Mountains and the Pennines on the British Isles, and the Kjølen Mountains in Scandinavia. On their steep slopes, these mountains have thin, poor soil.

Much of Europe's land shows signs of glacial activity. Mountain glaciers have scoured valleys and peaks in the Alps and other mountain areas. Along the coast of Norway, glaciers made deep trenches that extended below sea level, leaving a ragged coastline of fjords.

The Swiss Alps attract many skiers and other vacationers.

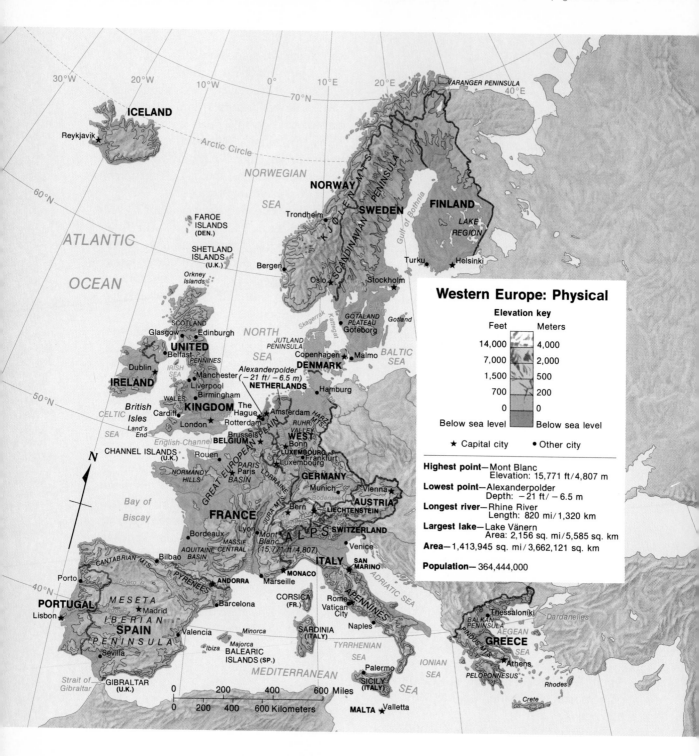

Western Europe: Physical

Elevation key

Feet		Meters
14,000		4,000
7,000		2,000
1,500		500
700		200
0		0
Below sea level		Below sea level

★ Capital city   • Other city

Highest point—Mont Blanc
 Elevation: 15,771 ft / 4,807 m
Lowest point—Alexanderpolder
 Depth: −21 ft / −6.5 m
Longest river—Rhine River
 Length: 820 mi / 1,320 km
Largest lake—Lake Vänern
 Area: 2,156 sq. mi / 5,585 sq. km
Area—1,413,945 sq. mi / 3,662,121 sq. km

Population—364,444,000

Map Study   *Which country takes up most of the Iberian Peninsula?*
Which countries share the Scandinavian Peninsula? Which country
occupies a single island?

Have students find the Gulf Stream on the map on page 58. One of its most spectacular
effects is found along the coast of Norway. Although much of the coast is within the Arctic
region, it remains free of ice and snow even during the winter.

Climates and Ecosystems

Most of Western Europe lies at the same latitude as Canada. Yet Western Europe's climate is milder than that of Canada. Why this difference? The answer lies in a current called the Gulf Stream. The Gulf Stream carries warm water from the Gulf of Mexico across the Atlantic where it joins the North Atlantic Drift along the coast of Western Europe. The warmth from the Gulf Stream helps to warm the land nearby.

These conditions give the area north of the Alps and south of the Scandinavian Peninsula a temperate marine climate. Winter days are often cloudy, rainy, and humid. Although the weather can be cool, it is rarely very cold.

The southern and northern parts of Europe lie outside the temperate area. South of the Alps, the climate is subtropical. In the northernmost parts of Western Europe, on the other hand, there are subarctic conditions.

Forests once covered much of Western Europe. Today very little forest is left in the southern part of Western Europe. Great expanses of trees were cleared for use as fuel or to make room for farms, towns, and cities. Large needleleaf forests remain in the Alps and in the north. Even these forests have been affected by human activity. The Black Forest of West Germany, for example, has been severely damaged by acid rain.

Western Europe: Climates

Subtropical Climates

Humid Subtropical (Hot, humid summers and mild winters)

Mediterranean Subtropical (Hot, dry summers and mild, rainy winters)

Dry Climates

Semiarid (Semi-desert climate with some rain)

Midlatitude Climates

Temperate Marine (Mild and rainy all year)

Humid Continental (Warm summers and cold, snowy winters)

Subarctic (Short summers and long, cold, snowy winters)

Cold Polar Climates

Subpolar (Always cold and dry with short, cool summers)

Polar (Ice cap, with freezing temperatures all year)

Highland Climates

(Temperature and precipitation vary greatly with latitude and elevation)

Map Study *What is the climate like in most of France? Portugal? Southern Italy?*

REVIEWING THE FACTS

Answer

1. Describe the major land features of Western Europe.

2. Tell why the climate of Europe is warmer than the climate of parts of Canada that lie at the same latitude.

Locate

Refer to the map on page 284.

1. (a) Name the mountain range in central Italy. (b) Between Spain and France. (c) In northern Italy.

2. Through what three countries does the Arctic Circle pass?

2 The Human Imprint

People have left an imprint on nearly every part of Europe's land. The influence of the people of Europe extends even further. It has been felt across almost the entire globe. Beginning in 1500, Europeans revolutionized trade and transportation. New land and water routes led to European contacts with nearly every part of the world. Western European religious beliefs, legal and political ideas, scientific discoveries, and arts and literature affected people in many regions. In turn, Western Europe changed as it learned more about the rest of the world. Today European cultures show the effects of this long history and of recent changes.

Population Distribution

Western Europe is home to about 380 million people. It is one of the most densely populated regions on Earth. The Netherlands, which lies on the coast of the North Sea, is the most crowded country in Europe. It has nearly 900 people per square mile (346 per square kilometer). South of the Netherlands, the area of dense settlement extends into the Ruhr Valley. It continues along either side of the Rhine River, reaching as far south as Munich, West Germany.

The southern part of the British Isles is also very crowded. There are smaller pockets of high population density in Italy and Spain. Only in parts of the Alps, in the arid highlands of Spain, and in subarctic Scandinavia and Iceland are there few residents.

Over 75 percent of all Western Europeans live in towns or cities. Paris, London, Madrid, Athens, and Rome are large urban areas, each having several million residents. About 50 other cities, many of them in the lowlands bordering the En-

Western Europe: Population Density

Persons per square mile	Persons per square kilometer	
Uninhabited	Uninhabited	
Less than 2	Less than 1	
2–25	1–10	City population
25–125	10–50	○ 1–2 million
125–250	50–100	• 2–5 million
250–500	100–200	● 5–10 million
Over 500	Over 200	◉ Over 10 million

Map Study *Name the largest city in Western Europe.*

glish Channel and the North Sea, have populations of over a million. The region has two megalopolises—one around London in England and the other in the Ruhr Valley of West Germany.

Despite its great population, Western Europe has the lowest rate of population growth in the world. The number of people in Europe is increasing by less than 1 percent a year. Many Western European countries are not growing at all. The population in some, like Denmark and West Germany, is actually declining.

Have students turn to the world population density map on pages 490–491 and find Europe. Ask them to compare it with other continents. They should see that there are fewer areas of sparse population here than on any other continent.
Answer to Map Study question: London

Students will have the opportunity to take a closer look at the diversity of European languages in the Map Workshop on page 288.

Cultures of Western Europe

The cultures of Western Europe have roots that date back hundreds and, in some cases, thousands of years. Until the age of trade and exploration, these cultures developed in relative isolation from one another. The result is a history of cultural differences in the region.

Language More than 50 languages are spoken on the European continent. Linguists, or those who study the origins and uses of language, group languages into families and branches. A language family is a group of languages that grew from a common language. In Europe, most languages belong to the **Indo-European** family.

Two branches of the Indo-European family are most important in Western Europe. In the south and the east, Romance languages — or those based on Latin, the language of the ancient Romans (page 141) — are most common. Romance languages include French, Italian, Portuguese, and Spanish. To the north and west, people speak Germanic languages. English, German, and Swedish are examples of Germanic tongues.

Education Europeans are among the best-educated people in the world. Their universities are centers of scientific achievement and learning in many subject areas. Today Europe's literacy rates are high. Throughout the region, about 95 percent of the people are **literate,** or able to read and write. Few other areas of the world publish as many magazines, newspapers, and books per capita as Western Europe.

There are important regional differences in European education. The standard of living of southern European countries is lower than that of northern European countries. As a result, it is hard for southern European countries to af-

Banners in four languages — Dutch, French, English, and German — hang outside this Amsterdam concert hall.

ford the kind of schools that northern European countries have. The literacy rate in southern Europe, therefore, is below that of other countries of the region.

Religion Although Christianity is the most common religion, parts of Western Europe differ in their religious practices and beliefs. In the south, most of the people are Roman Catholics. The Catholic Church took shape during the time of the Roman empire. The spiritual leader of the Church is the pope. With the assistance of the Roman Curia — a group of administrative offices — the pope governs the Church from Vatican City, an independent country located in Rome, Italy.

Most northern Europeans belong to a different branch of Christianity. Their churches were formed during the 1500's, when a number of reformers broke away from the Catholic Church. Because these groups protested certain practices and rituals of the Catholic Church, they became known as **Protestants.** There are many

287

Texas Essential Elements 1C. Geographical tools and methodologies. 4D. Major cultural, political, and economic activities within and among major world regions.

Interpreting a Language Map

Look at the map on this page. Its legend shows many of the languages spoken in Europe today. Linguists believe that each of Europe's languages belongs to one of three different language families — Indo-European, Ural-Altaic, or Basque. All the languages of a family are based on a single, ancient language.

The legend also shows the branches of each language family in a separate color. The languages of each branch, shown by numbers, are closely related. The Indo-European family has five branches in Europe — the Germanic, Romance, Celtic (kel'tik), Greek, Albanian, and Slavic languages.

Use the legend to interpret the language map. To identify country names, turn to pages 284 and 309.

1. (a) How many modern European languages are members of the Ural-Altaic family? (b) The Indo-European? (c) The Basque?

2. (a) To which language family does English belong? (b) To which branch?

3. Name five large countries in which people speak Romance languages.

4. To which family and branch do the majority of languages spoken in the eastern part of Europe belong?

For a special challenge Use what you have learned from the language map and your reading to write a statement describing the cultural diversity of Europe.

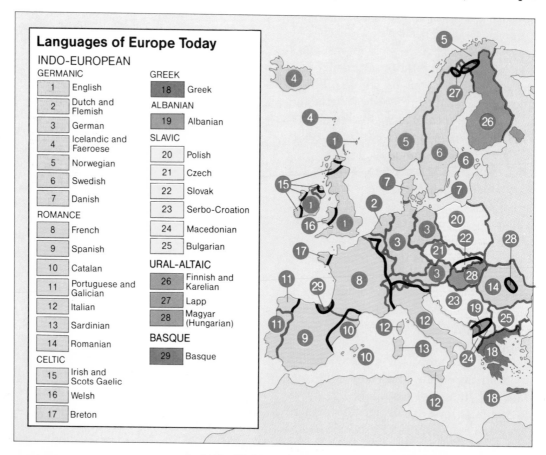

Languages of Europe Today

INDO-EUROPEAN

GERMANIC
1	English
2	Dutch and Flemish
3	German
4	Icelandic and Faeroese
5	Norwegian
6	Swedish
7	Danish

ROMANCE
8	French
9	Spanish
10	Catalan
11	Portuguese and Galician
12	Italian
13	Sardinian
14	Romanian

CELTIC
15	Irish and Scots Gaelic
16	Welsh
17	Breton

GREEK
| 18 | Greek |

ALBANIAN
| 19 | Albanian |

SLAVIC
20	Polish
21	Czech
22	Slovak
23	Serbo-Croation
24	Macedonian
25	Bulgarian

URAL-ALTAIC
26	Finnish and Karelian
27	Lapp
28	Magyar (Hungarian)

BASQUE
| 29 | Basque |

Assign the Workbook activity for this chapter's Map Workshop with this page.
Answers are in the Teacher's Guide.

Today there are over 17 million Jews in the world. Most of them live in North America. The Jews are a people, or national group, as well as a religion. Judaism was probably the first monotheistic religion. (Monotheism is belief in one God.) The beliefs of Jews are described on pages 406–407 of Chapter 16.

denominations, or organizations, of Protestant churches. Each denomination is independent.

Many non-Christians also live in Western Europe. In recent years, Hindus from India and Muslims from Turkey have come to the region for work. But historically Jews have been the largest group of non-Christians in Europe. Their religion, Judaism, developed in the Middle East centuries before Christianity.

After the breakup of the Roman empire around A.D. 500, many Jews left the Middle East for Europe. Large numbers lived in what is now Spain, France, Germany, and Poland. The Christian majority often persecuted Jews. Jews could hold only certain jobs. Some countries expelled Jewish residents.

Despite these hardships, more than ten million Jews lived in Europe by the 1930's. Most lived in Eastern Europe, particularly in Poland and the Soviet Union. But many lived in France, Germany, and other countries of Western Europe.

When the Nazis took control of Germany in 1933 (page 298), persecution of the Jews there increased sharply. Many Jews were sent to concentration and forced-labor camps. After the Nazis launched World War II, their leader, Adolf Hitler, set in motion a plan to wipe out all the Jews of Europe. At first, special units of the German army rounded up and killed Jews in conquered areas of Eastern Europe. Later, Jews from throughout Eastern Europe were sent to death camps. Jews from Western Europe were also sent to these camps and killed. By 1945, the Nazis had killed about six million Jews. These events are known as the **Holocaust.** After the war, many of the Jews who had survived left Europe for Israel and the United States.

Political Patterns

For most of Western Europe, the fall of the Nazis and their allies in 1945 marked the end of a brief, terrible period of totalitarian rule. Today all countries of the region have democratic governments. In addition, in every country the government plays a key part in providing for people's well-being. Most governments of Western European countries own some major businesses and provide such free services as medical care and old-age insurance. Because their governments provide so many services to improve public welfare, they are sometimes called **welfare states.**

Forms of Government In a few countries of Western Europe, voters elect members of a legislature and a president. France, for example, has a presidential system. For the most part, however, Western European countries are parliamentary democracies. Voters elect members of a parliament. The majority in parliament then chooses one of its members as prime minister.

Ten countries of Western Europe are **constitutional monarchies.** Among them are the United Kingdom, Belgium, Sweden, and Norway. In these countries, the head of state is a king or queen. Under the constitution, the monarch has little if any governing authority. The powers of government belong to parliament and the prime minister, who is the head of government. The monarch performs such symbolic duties as accepting appointments of officials and greeting foreign leaders.

Political Parties In contrast to the United States, most Western European countries have several parties. Italy, for example, has ten political parties. While candidates from every party run for office, usually two or three parties have the

289

largest following. Thus, these parties have the best chance of winning.

Under the parliamentary system, political parties play an important part in governing. The party that wins the most seats in parliament chooses the prime minister. If no party wins a majority, a group of parties — representing a majority — can agree to act together. This group then selects the prime minister.

Political Unity Western Europe is made up of many countries in a relatively small area. Throughout its history, Europe has been the scene of conflict and warfare. Countries have clashed over religion, trade, and territory. The two most catastrophic wars of the twentieth century — World War I and World War II — began as conflicts among European countries.

Europe continues to be divided by international rivalries. The most serious division today is that between the democratic countries of Western Europe and the communist countries of Eastern Europe. Most countries of Western Europe cooperate on military matters, travel, and trade. For example, since 1949 countries of Western Europe have sent delegates to the Council of Europe. The Council of Europe works for legal and cultural cooperation and human rights. In addition, most Western European countries are members of NATO (North Atlantic Treaty Organization). Through NATO, they act with Canada and the United States to guard against aggression from other countries (page 179).

Some countries of Western Europe are **neutral.** This means that they do not take sides in international conflicts. In Switzerland, the policy of neutrality dates back to the 1500's. Finland and Austria established similar policies in the 1950's. None of these three countries belongs to NATO.

Economic Patterns

Western Europe was the home of the Industrial Revolution. By the late 1800's, England and Germany were the world's leading industrial powers. Today Western European countries are among the top ten manufacturing countries in the world. The countries in the southern part of the region are generally less industrialized than the northern countries.

The Role of Government Most Western European countries have mixed free enterprise systems. That is, they have elements of free enterprise and elements of socialism. Most businesses are in private hands. However, the governments own the countries' coal-mining operations, steel plants, rail systems, and some other industries. High taxes limit the wealth of those with high incomes. Government programs transfer wealth to those with low incomes. The result is that nearly everyone shares in the countries' high standard of living.

Resources Europe's resources are varied and extensive. The region has important desposits of natural gas, iron ore, coal, and bauxite. In addition, earnings from manufactured exports — planes, ships, railroad equipment, and the like — enable Western Europe to import raw materials that are lacking.

Coal and natural gas have long been the major sources of energy in the region. But Western Europe has had to import large amounts of oil to fuel its industry. Recent finds of oil in the North Sea have made Europe less dependent on energy imports than in the past. Some countries are developing hydroelectric and nuclear energy. Europeans are also trying to use less energy at home and in businesses.

Agriculture In crowded regions, people often make intensive use of the land and its resources. In Western Europe, for

290

Coal from West Germany's Ruhr Valley is used in local steel mills.

example, farmers produce two or three times as much food per acre as farmers in the United States. In many areas, they use chemical fertilizers, pesticides, and modern machinery. In northern Europe, farmers grow potatoes, rye, wheat, and oats. In France, Germany, and the southern parts of Europe, grapes for wine are grown on hillsides. In many parts of Western Europe, farmers raise livestock.

Linkages Ocean shipping and airlines link Western Europe with most of the world's other countries. Western Europe also has a dense network of rivers and canals, highways, railroads, and pipelines. Almost every part of Western Europe is served by some form of modern transportation. The railroads are especially fast and easy to use. In fact, customs officers ride trains so that the passports of passengers traveling from one country to another can be checked during their trip.

Economic Unity Just as Western Europe has achieved a high degree of political cooperation, so too have efforts to create economic unity paid off. Twelve countries of Western Europe belong to the **European Economic Community,** often referred to as the **Common Market.** The

Western Europe: Land Use

■ Manufacturing	⛏ Coal ◣ Silver
Commercial farming and stock raising	△ Iron ✳ Uranium
Stock raising	⚗ Petroleum ▽ Tungsten
Forestry	◊ Natural gas 〰 Hydroelectric power
Nomadic herding	⬡ Copper
Commercial fishing	⛏ Bauxite
Little or no activity	◣ Gold

Map Study *In what countries of Western Europe is forestry a major activity? Manufacturing?*

Common Market countries allow workers to move back and forth between member nations. They have eliminated tariffs and other trade restrictions on goods traded among member countries. These measures help create a unified economy for Western Europe.

The North Sea is one of the world's great fishing areas. Over three million tons of fish are caught there each year, mostly by people from Denmark, Norway, and Britain.

291

Answers to Map Study questions: Norway, Sweden, Finland, Iceland; France, the United Kingdom, West Germany, the Netherlands, Luxembourg

WORLD DATA BANK

Country	Area in Square Miles	Population/Natural Increase		Per Capita GNP
Andorra	188	47,000	(5.4%)	NA
Austria	32,375	7,600,000	(0.0%)	$ 9,150
Belgium	11,749	9,900,000	(0.0%)	8,450
Denmark	16,629	5,100,000	(−0.1%)	11,240
Finland	130,127	4,900,000	(0.3%)	10,870
France	211,208	55,600,000	(0.4%)	9,550
Greece	50,942	10,000,000	(0.2%)	3,550
Iceland	39,768	200,000	(0.9%)	10,720
Ireland	27,135	3,500,000	(0.8%)	4,840
Italy	116,305	57,400,000	(0.1%)	6,520
Liechtenstein	62	28,000	(1.8%)	16,900
Luxembourg	992	400,000	(0.0%)	13,380
Malta	124	400,000	(0.8%)	3,300
Monaco	.73	28,000	(1.2%)	NA
Netherlands	14,405	14,600,000	(0.4%)	9,180
Norway	125,181	4,200,000	(0.2%)	13,890
Portugal	35,552	10,300,000	(0.3%)	1,970
San Marino	24	23,000	(1.6%)	NA
Spain	194,896	39,000,000	(0.5%)	4,360
Sweden	173,730	8,400,000	(0.1%)	11,890
Switzerland	15,942	6,600,000	(0.2%)	16,380
United Kingdom	94,525	56,800,000	(0.2%)	8,390
Vatican City	108.7 (acres)	1,000	(0.1%)	NA
West Germany	95,977	61,000,000	(−0.2%)	10,940

REVIEWING THE FACTS

Define

1. Indo-European
2. literate
3. Protestant
4. Holocaust
5. welfare state
6. constitutional monarchy
7. neutral
8. European Economic Community
9. Common Market

Answer

1. Describe settlement patterns in Western Europe.

2. What are some of the cultural divisions in Western Europe?

3. What forms of government are most common in Western Europe?

4. What are Western Europe's main economic activities?

Locate

Refer to the map on page 284.

(a) Name the sea between Iceland and Norway. (b) Between England and Norway. (c) East of Greece. (d) South of Europe.

292

3 The British Isles and Northern Europe

The British Isles and much of Northern Europe are separated from the rest of Europe by water. The United Kingdom—made up of England, Wales, Scotland, and Northern Ireland—and Ireland occupy the British Isles. England, Wales, and Scotland are located on a single island, Great Britain. This entire area has a mild climate because of the influence of the Gulf Stream.

Iceland, Finland, and the countries of Scandinavia—Sweden, Norway, and Denmark—lie to the north of most of the British Isles. Known as **Norden**, these countries are isolated from the parts of Europe lying to the south. Generally their coastal lowlands are warmed by ocean currents and breezes, but inland the winter weather is bitterly cold.

The People

With more than 55 million people, the United Kingdom is one of the most densely populated countries in the world. The countries of Norden, on the other hand, have small, sparse populations. There, people live mainly along the coastal lowlands. The frigid interior highlands of these countries have very few residents.

People living in Norden and the British Isles have a generally high standard of living. For example, the per capita income in Norway, Sweden, and Denmark is higher than that in the United States. Norway, Sweden, and Denmark were among the first countries in the world to have large-scale social-welfare programs. Government services are paid for by taxes that are far higher than those paid by residents of the United States and Canada.

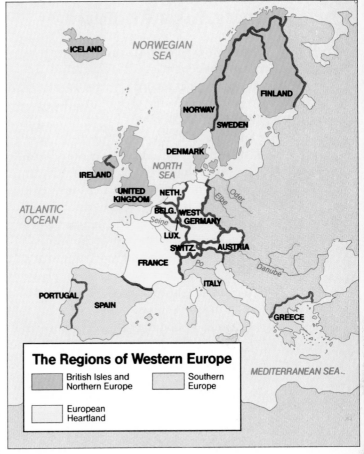

The Regions of Western Europe

- British Isles and Northern Europe
- Southern Europe
- European Heartland

Map Study *What bodies of water border the British Isles and Northern Europe? The European Heartland? Southern Europe?*

Economic Development

Most countries of northern Europe and the British Isles have a great deal of manufacturing. Fishing, farming, mining, and forestry are also important. As in other industrial regions, many people work in service industries. In the United Kingdom, Sweden, and Norway, more than 50 percent of the workers are employed by the government and other services.

Ocean Resources All northern Europe is located on islands or peninsulas. As a result, the people of the region have learned

293

SKILL WORKSHOP

Analyzing a Photograph

A photograph captures a moment in time and keeps it as a visual record. To understand that record, you need to study the photograph and ask yourself questions about it.

First, you should ask about the subject of the photograph. Then study the details to see what they show about the subject. What kind of general statements can you make about the subject after looking at the details in the picture? Can you detect a point of view on the part of the photographer? Does the photograph support or illustrate information you already know? What can the photograph show you that a map or drawing might not show?

The photograph here shows the city of Bergen which lies on the western coast of Norway. Use information from the photograph to answer these questions.

1. What are the landforms near Bergen?

2. What economic activity or activities do you see in the photograph?

3. In what season was the photo taken?

4. Explain how the photograph illustrates or supports each of the following statements from the text. (a) People living in Norway have a generally high standard of living. (b) The people of Norway depend on the sea for a living. (c) The coast of Norway is warmed by ocean currents and breezes.

5. In general, what feeling about Norway does this photograph convey?

294

Answers are in the Teacher's Guide.
Assign the Workbook activity for this chapter's Skill Workshop with this page.

how to make use of the sea. For one thing, the sea has been a natural barrier protecting the British Isles and northern Europe. It has made invasion by outsiders difficult and enabled the people to develop their own lands.

Fishing has also been important in the region for hundreds of years. Fishers from northern Europe have taken catches from waters stretching from the Baltic and North Seas to Iceland and Newfoundland. More than 75 percent of Iceland's exports are fish or fish products.

The United Kingdom and Norway have profited from the sea in still another way. Starting in the 1970's, both countries began to produce oil from wells in the North Sea. In a region in which the high price of oil imports has checked growth, these countries have enjoyed an advantage by having their own sources of oil.

Agriculture Even farming in the British Isles and northern Europe depends on nearness to the sea. Warmth from the Gulf Stream allows people to grow crops farther north than they could otherwise. Winds from the sea bring plenty of rain to fields and grasslands.

However, the region has little farmland. Much of the interior of the northern countries has rocky land with poor soil. Farming, therefore, is concentrated on the coastal lowlands. Farms are generally very small. Most countries of the region must import food. The United Kingdom, for example, buys more than half its food abroad. No other country in the world imports so great a share.

Ireland has a greater part of its land available for farming than other countries in the region. About two thirds of Ireland's land is farmed. Grains, potatoes, cabbages, and sugar beets all grow well. Ireland's farmers grow enough to feed the country's people without importing food.

Norway's fjords—deep, glacier-scoured inlets of the sea—create a ragged coastline with many natural harbors. Along the steep cliffs of the fjords lies fertile soil, where small farms have been located.

Most of Denmark is also suited to agriculture. The Danes grow barley, oats, rye, and wheat. Other important agricultural activities are dairy farming and the raising of livestock. Meat, milk, butter, and cheese, as well as barley, are exported in large quantities.

The inland areas of Norway, Sweden, and Finland are cold and forested. Therefore, little farming can take place there. On the other hand, lumber, wood pulp, and paper products are produced. Much of Wales, Scotland, and the north of England is not suited for growing crops. These areas are, however, good for grazing sheep. The animals' wool provides the raw material for the United Kingdom's many textile mills.

295

THE WORLD'S LONGEST PLACE-NAME?

LLANFAIRPWLLGWYNGYLLGOGER-YCHWYRNDROBWLLLLANTISILIOG-OGOGOCH is the longest place-name in Wales. It may be the longest in the world. In Welsh, it means "the Church of St. Mary by the white pool of the hazel trees near the fierce whirlpool of the church of St. Tysiliog by the red cave." People who live there, when asked where they live, usually say "Llanfair P.G."

Industry By the late 1700's, England was the world's greatest industrial power. By the 1900's, its position had slipped. One important factor in this decline was its factories. As other countries industrialized, they built new, highly efficient plants. Many factories in the United Kingdom were built years ago. The machinery and processes in these older factories cannot turn out goods as quickly as those in new plants. Even so, the United Kingdom today is among the top ten manufacturing countries. It also ranks as a leading center of finance and banking.

Factories in the United Kingdom rely mainly on imports of raw materials. The country's coal deposits, for example, have been mined for many years. The remaining coal lies deep below the surface and is difficult to mine. Iron ore, cotton, and such chemicals as sulfur must be imported in large amounts. To pay for these, businesses in the United Kingdom sell machinery, chemicals, steel, cars, textiles, and clothing abroad.

Other countries of the region also depend on imported raw materials. Finland, for example, buys cotton and metals from other countries. It uses these raw materials in its clothing and textile mills, farm-machinery factories, electric-motors works, and shipyards.

Because of its lack of energy resources and minerals, Norway did not begin to industrialize until after most countries of the region. By developing hydroelectricity and importing coal, Norway was able to build manufacturing plants by the early 1900's. Today, using imported bauxite, the country is one of the world's leading producers of aluminum.

Sweden has rich deposits of iron ore and other resources. But, like Norway, it relies on imports of coal and oil. Sweden's most important manufactured goods include ball bearings, automobiles, farm machinery, aircraft, and other precision equipment.

Linkages The linkages in the British Isles and much of northern Europe are especially good. They enable the countries of the region to transport raw materials and finished goods within their borders, throughout Europe, and to faraway parts of the world. The region has many rivers and harbors suited to shipping. The heavily populated areas of the region are served by roads and highways. In the United Kingdom, most roads are paved.

296

Texas Essential Elements 3C. Agricultural base of regions. 3D. Uses, abuses, and preservation of natural resources and the physical environment. 4D. Major cultural, political, and economic activities within and among major world regions.

The Concorde, *built by Great Britain and France, is a passenger plane that flies faster than the speed of sound.*

Only the major roads of the other countries of the region have paved surfaces. Railroads serve the region's population centers, including mining and manufacturing areas. Airlines handle most long-distance passenger travel.

REVIEWING THE FACTS

Define

Norden

Answer

1. Where in Norden and the British Isles is population density greatest?

2. Describe the standard of living in Scandinavia.

3. How has nearness to the ocean affected countries of northern Europe?

4. What are the major economic activities of the region?

Locate

Refer to the map on page 284.

1. Name the countries for which these cities are capitals: (a) London, (b) Dublin, (c) Oslo, (d) Stockholm, (e) Helsinki, (f) Copenhagen, (g) Reykjavik.

2. Name the mountains in Norway and Sweden.

4 The European Heartland

The heartland of Europe is an area of dense settlement. It has great cities, busy factories and railroads, and productive farms. The heartland covers the western end of Europe's Great European Plain and the inland hills and low mountains that rise gradually to the Alps. A number of rivers — including the Elbe, Meuse (myüz), Seine, and Rhine — flow north across this region.

The people of the heartland are diverse. They practice a variety of religions and speak a variety of languages. In addition, they are divided into a number of countries. These countries include France and West Germany, which dominate the central part of the heartland. Sandwiched between France and West Germany in the north are three small countries — Belgium, the Netherlands, and Luxembourg. Three other small countries — Switzerland, Liechtenstein (lik′tən stīn′), and Austria — lie to the southeast.

Despite the number of countries in the heartland, there are strong links among the people of the region. Highways, railroads, rivers, canals, and airlines make travel throughout the region easy. For centuries, goods and ideas have been exchanged across the borders separating the people of the region.

France

In terms of area, France is the largest country in Western Europe. However, it ranks third — behind West Germany and the United Kingdom — in population. Today France has a well-balanced economy. It has strong mining, farming, and manufacturing. Its people have a high standard of living, though not as high as

Have students locate these eight countries on the map on page 284. Ask them why this area would be called the heartland of Europe.
Answers are in the Teacher's Guide.
Assign the Workbook activity for Chapter 11, Section 4, with pages 297–302.

297

Paris is the largest city in France.

the people of the United States and the Scandinavian countries.

Agriculture Most of France lies on fertile plains. Today about a third of the land is used for growing crops. The climate is moderate, and there is plenty of rainfall.

Most French farmers live in towns or villages. They go to their fields each morning and return home each night. Many still use draft animals and hand methods to work small plots.

In recent years, the government has taken steps to combine small farms into larger ones. Modern equipment has been introduced. As a result, France has a diverse, thriving farm economy. Leading products are wheat, meat, cheese, and feed for livestock. Grapes are grown to make wines that are considered the best in the world.

Manufacturing Skilled artisans in France made shoes, china, and linen and other textiles well before the Industrial Revolution. Modern French industries still depend on skilled labor. The emphasis is on high quality rather than on large quantities. Top-quality goods produced in France range from designer fashions to powerful computers.

France has rich deposits of such resources as iron ore, coal, and bauxite. These resources are used in France's **heavy industry.** Heavy industry is manufacturing that uses large amounts of raw materials and large machines. It produces bulky goods that can be transported only by rail or ship. The heavy industry of the Paris region includes the making of cars, aircraft, steel, and aluminum. Near Rouen (rü än') and in southern France, there are large chemical plants.

The Paris region also has **light industry.** Light industry uses small quantities of raw materials and small tools. Goods made in light industries are easily shipped by truck. In the Paris area, factories produce computers and television sets. Using textiles made in the Lyons (lē ōn') region, Parisian factories also produce clothing. Another important product in the area is perfume, made from flowers grown in southern France.

West Germany

While France has been united under a single government for centuries, Germany became a country more recently, in 1871. In the years that followed, Germany became one of the world's leading industrial and political powers. During the 1930's, a totalitarian government—led by the Nazi party—ruled Germany with an iron hand.

The Nazis launched World War II in 1939. Their attempt to conquer large parts of Europe ended in bitter defeat in 1945. The victorious powers, known as the Allies, were the United States, the United Kingdom, France, and the Soviet Union. At the end of the war, Germany was split in two. The eastern part, occupied by the Soviet army at the end of the war, became the Communist country of East Germany. The western part became

298

International trade has become very important to the economy of West Germany. Through its membership in the Common Market and the tremendous volume and value of its trade, it has become a keen commercial rival of the United States. West Germany and the United States remain political and military allies.

The Berlin Wall, built by East Germany in 1961, separates West and East Berlin. (See feature, page 312.)

West Germany. With the permission of the United States, France, and the United Kingdom, West Germany also controls the western part of the former capital of Germany, Berlin. This city is located far within the borders of East Germany. West Berlin is separated from Communist East Berlin by a high, guarded wall topped with barbed wire.

West Germany is a democratic country. It has a free-enterprise economy. Germans have long been among the world leaders in science and technology. West Germany's production of manufactured goods places it among the world's top industrial countries. It has the highest GNP in Western Europe, and its people have a high standard of living.

Agriculture Considering the amount of good land and the size of the population, West Germany's farm production is outstanding. The country produces about three fourths of the food its people eat. Potatoes, rye, and wheat are the chief food crops. Exports of finished goods help pay for food imports. Only a very small part of the country's GNP comes from agriculture.

Manufacturing West Germany is the world's fourth largest producer of iron and steel. Only the Soviet Union, the United States, and Japan produce more. The center of heavy industry is the Ruhr Valley. There, starting in the late 1800's, iron ore and coal were mined for shipment to nearby steel mills. The Saar Valley, near the French border, also supplied mills with coal. Later, plants producing heavy machinery and cars were built near the steel mills.

Today West Germany relies on imports for its raw materials and energy resources. The Ruhr Valley is still one of the world's major industrial and urban areas. Several other industrial centers are scattered throughout the country. Leading products include steel, machinery, cars, tools and instruments, and electrical equipment.

Making railroad cars is an example of the heavy industry in West Germany's Ruhr Valley. Here, a welder joins sections of a railway car.

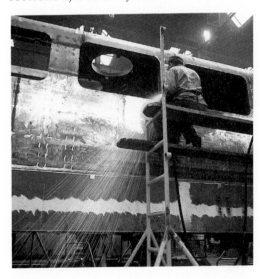

299

The Low Countries

Belgium, the Netherlands, and Luxembourg lie on the low plain between France and West Germany. Almost the entire expanse of this plain is near sea level. Because of this, Belgium, the Netherlands, and Luxembourg are known as the **Low Countries**. These countries are also known as **Benelux**. *Benelux* is made up of the first letters of each country's name.

The Netherlands and Belgium both border the North Sea. Much of the Netherlands was once covered by sea and lake water. Land below sea level was reclaimed by large draining and pumping projects. The biggest cities, best farmland, and main commercial centers of the Netherlands are on lands that were once covered with water.

Agriculture Farmers in the Low Countries produce a variety of crops. In Belgium, they raise horses and cattle. The Netherlands produces cheese and other dairy products. Its other leading farm goods are beef cattle, hogs, barley, flax,

It took the Dutch five years to reclaim this land from the sea. Now it is a valuable farming area.

and flower bulbs. Flower bulbs grown in the Netherlands, particularly tulip bulbs, are exported to many parts of the world.

Industry and Commerce The Benelux countries make up one of the most heavily urbanized areas of the world. Not much land remains for farming. Most people work in commerce or industry. The Dutch, as residents of the Netherlands are known, were for a time Europe's leading traders. During the 1600's, the Dutch controlled a vast colonial empire and produced large amounts of textiles. Banks thrived in Amsterdam by lending money to merchants and factory owners. Trading companies built offices and warehouses in Amsterdam and other Dutch cities.

In the 1600's, Belgium also became a trading center. Hundreds of companies had offices in Antwerp and in Brussels, the Belgian capital. As in the Netherlands, there were large banks in Belgium.

By the 1700's, the English and the French had defeated the Dutch in a series of wars. No longer the world leaders, the Dutch remained a strongly commercial and industrial people. Belgium also continued its manufacturing and foreign trade. Today both countries produce steel, textiles, and chemicals. Luxembourg too is heavily industrialized. It makes more iron and steel per capita than any other country in the world.

The region continues to have a lively foreign trade. In fact, Rotterdam in the Netherlands and Antwerp in Belgium are the first and second busiest seaports in the world. From them, most of the region's manufactured goods — as well as goods made in other parts of Europe — are shipped to ports throughout the world. Rotterdam and Antwerp also handle raw materials and fuels for the Low Countries and central Europe.

More information on the Netherlands' efforts to reclaim land from the sea can be found in the Spotlight feature on page 301.

SPOTLIGHT ON POLDERS:

Claiming Land from the Sea

A dramatic example of how people can shape their environment is found in the Netherlands. With hard work, determination, and ingenuity, the Dutch have actually created the land on which much of their country lies. Over the centuries, the Dutch have taken about 20 percent of their country's land from the sea and other bodies of water. They began draining lands for farming and grazing nearly 800 years ago. By 1600, large-scale reclamation projects were under way, and the process continues today. Future projects will convert into agricultural land much of the sea around Zeeland (zē′lənd) and the IJsselmeer (ī′səl mer′) and Wadden Zee (väd′ən zā′).

To reclaim land, the Dutch built dikes, or long earthern dams. Then they used pumps to drain water from behind the dikes. At first, wind power was used to drive the pumps. Today, however, modern engines have replaced the windmills of the past.

The Dutch call the drained lands polders. A network of drainage canals, dikes, and pumping stations surrounds the polders and protects them from flooding. Livestock graze and crops now grow on the fertile polders themselves. Because the reclaimed land is so valuable for farming, the Dutch often build their villages and roads atop dikes or on less fertile land.

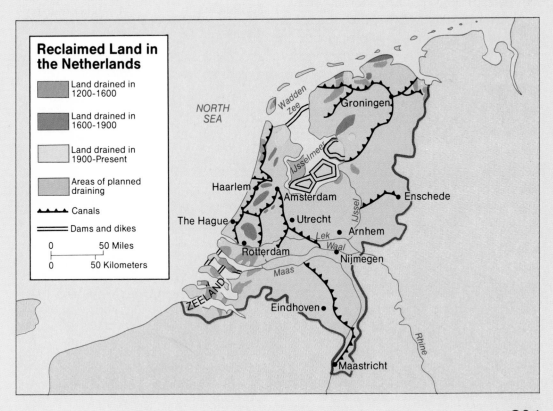

Reclaimed Land in the Netherlands

- Land drained in 1200-1600
- Land drained in 1600-1900
- Land drained in 1900-Present
- Areas of planned draining
- Canals
- Dams and dikes

0   50 Miles
0   50 Kilometers

NORTH SEA

Wadden Zee

Groningen

IJsselmeer

Haarlem

Amsterdam

Enschede

The Hague

Utrecht

IJssel

Arnhem

Lek

Rotterdam

Waal

Nijmegen

Maas

ZEELAND

Eindhoven

Rhine

Maastricht

The Countries of the Alps

Austria, Switzerland, and Liechtenstein lie in the Alps. This is a hard place in which to develop agriculture and industry. Good farming areas are limited to a few valleys and high plateaus. There are no major fuel or mineral deposits. In addition, the Alpine countries are landlocked. Their imports and exports must be transported across other countries and over high mountains. Despite these limits, the countries of the Alps are industrialized and have a high standard of living. In fact, the Swiss enjoy the highest per capita GNP in the world. When the rest of Europe industrialized, Switzerland became an important banking center. By providing banking services, the Swiss profited from Europe's industrial development. Later the Swiss became skilled in the making of complex instruments. Mountain streams provided hydroelectric power. Raw materials were imported. Finished goods were shipped on narrow, winding mountain roads.

To overcome these conditions, the Swiss specialized in light industry. Today

Swiss watchmakers are skilled workers, able to produce precision instruments.

Swiss workshops make fine watches, high-quality chocolates, premium textiles, and precision instruments. Such goods can be made only by highly skilled workers. The skills of its artisans may be Switzerland's greatest resource. The Swiss also farm the rugged hillsides and highlands. They produce meat, wine, and cheese and other dairy products.

Austria has more resources than Switzerland. There is more good land for farming and grazing. As well as light industries, Austria has iron and steel works in the Vienna area. Even so, Austria's economy has not been as successful as Switzerland's.

REVIEWING THE FACTS

Define

1. Low Countries
2. Benelux
3. heavy industry
4. light industry

Answer

1. How does French farming differ from most farming in the United States?

2. (a) Explain how Germany became divided into West Germany and East Germany. (b) Where is the industrial center of West Germany?

3. What are the most important economic activities of the Low Countries?

4. Why do the countries of the Alps specialize in light industries?

Locate

Refer to the map on page 284.

1. Name the countries for which these cities are capitals: (a) Paris, (b) Bonn, (c) Brussels, (d) Amsterdam, (e) Bern, (f) Vienna.

2. (a) Name the river that flows through Paris. (b) On which the capital of West Germany lies.

302

5 Southern Europe

Southern Europe includes most of the countries that border the northern part of the Mediterranean Sea. Portugal, which borders the Atlantic Ocean, is also part of southern Europe. The region's major countries are Italy, Greece, Portugal, and Spain. There are also a number of very small countries — Andorra, Monaco, Malta, San Marino, and Vatican City.

Most of the lands of southern Europe are mountainous. The mountains are broken in places by fertile river valleys and coastal plains. The area has a Mediterranean climate. Its summers are warm and dry; winters are wet and mild. The waters of the Mediterranean, Adriatic, and Aegean seas link the countries to one another, to other European countries, and to Asia and Africa.

Throughout the region, people in remote rural areas still follow traditional ways. There, farming, family life, religious practices, and trade have been little affected by the Industrial Revolution. In other places, the people have tapped their limited resources and capital to develop thriving industries. Economically, however, the region lags behind the rest of Europe. The per capita GNP of southern European countries averages about half that of the other countries of Western Europe.

Portugal

Portugal is one of the least industrialized countries of Europe. Nearly half its people farm or fish to earn a living. Wine from grapes and cork from tree bark are leading exports. Canned sardines are also exported. Farmers also produce grain and olive oil. Despite its production of farm exports, Portugal must import much of its food, including wheat.

Portugal makes such goods as textiles and shoes. It has also fuel and mineral resources that include coal, copper, tin, slate, and sulfur. These resources will be of use in the future as Portugal expands its industry.

Spain

Spain is a rapidly changing country. Once the proud ruler of the world's greatest empire, Spain was weakened by wars with other countries and internal conflict during the late 1500's. It eventually lost nearly all of its empire and became a poor country. During the 1930's, a dictator named Francisco Franco took power in Spain. Under his rule, Spain made little progress. In the 1970's, however, the dictatorship was replaced by a constitutional monarchy. Under the new government, industry and commerce have grown in importance.

However, the old and the new continue to stand in sharp contrast. Much of Spain is covered by the dry Meseta, a highland area in the center of the country. There,

Farmers in Spain's Basque region, along the border of France, use their land mainly for raising livestock.

During the fifteenth century, Spain was the foremost power in Europe, with an overflowing treasury (income from the colonies) and a powerful navy. In 1588, the navy — known as the Invincible Armada — launched an attack on England and lost. This was the beginning of Spain's decline as a world power.

303

farmers grow crops only with great difficulty. Lacking money for irrigation, machines, and fertilizer, they work with hand tools. Their efforts yield meager crops. Many graze livestock to produce meat. Yet in a few places, farmers have been able to use modern methods. Irrigation, fertilizer, and tractors have turned parts of the Meseta into fertile wheat fields.

Spain also has two great urban areas — Madrid in the center of the country and Barcelona on the Mediterranean coast. Madrid is the capital and largest city. Barcelona is the center of Spain's growing industry.

Other industrial areas are located in Spain's northern regions, where there are deposits of iron ore and coal. Jobs in the car and ship industries have attracted many workers to these areas. As a result of these changes, Spain is becoming more and more urbanized and industrialized.

An office worker enters information on a computer at one of Turin's giant auto factories.

Italy

Italy has the most developed economy of southern Europe. The center of Italy's industry lies in the Po River Valley. North of the Po Valley, tunnels through the Alps shorten routes that lead to France, Switzerland, and Austria. South of the Po Valley, the Apennines stretch across the central part of Italy. These mountains are a barrier between the more rural, southern part of Italy and the industrialized northern plains. Therefore, the Po Valley is more closely linked to the European heartland than to southern Italy.

Italy is not rich in minerals and other resources. It does, however, have Alpine rivers and streams that are a source of hydroelectric power. Italy imports iron ore and scrap metal to supply its steel industry. With such efforts, factories in the Po Valley make a variety of goods. The city of Turin has become one of the world's leading producers of cars, trucks, and tractors. Milan is a booming city, with tall modern buildings, important banks, and many company offices. These and other cities also make medicines, television sets, silk, typewriters, sewing machines, and motor scooters. Food processing and the making of textiles, shoes, and chemicals are also important industries.

The fertile, well-irrigated Po Valley is also a rich farming area. Its grapes place Italy among the world's leading producers of inexpensive wines. Wheat, olives, citrus fruits, and vegetables are other major crops.

There is little good farmland in southern Italy. People practice subsistence farming on steep hillsides. Light industries provide some jobs in textile mills, food-processing plants, and clothing factories. The standard of living is much

The world's longest road tunnel, 7 miles (11.2 kilometers), runs through Mt. Blanc, the highest peak in the Alps, and connects France with Italy.

You might encourage a few students to find out more about famous tourist attractions in
Greece and then report back to the class.
Assign the Workbook activity for Chapter 11, Section 5, with pages 303–305.

lower in this region than in northern Italy. Many people leave the region for jobs in the Po Valley or other European countries.

The capital of Italy is Rome, located on a plain on the western side of the southern peninsula. Rome continues to be one of the world's leading cultural, educational, and tourist centers.

Greece

Greece is a fragmented country. The northern mainland has wooded hills and some fertile cropland. To the south, the Peloponnesus (pel ə pə nē′ səs) is a peninsula covered with dry, rocky highlands. Hundreds of small islands dot the Aegean and Ionian seas.

Nearly 75 percent of the people live in urban areas. Athens is the capital and largest urban center of the nation. Nearby

Tourists in Greece view the ruins of a culture whose influence has not died.

is Piraeus (pi rē′əs), the leading port. Shipping is one of the country's largest industries. Its commercial fleet is one of the largest in the world.

Even in urban areas, Greece has little manufacturing. In fact, the second largest industry is tourism. Visitors come to see the ruins of the ancient Greek civilization at Athens and other cities. Resort areas are located on many of the Greek islands.

A short while ago most Greeks were subsistence farmers. Greek farmers still graze cattle and sheep or grow grapes and olives on the scarce farmland. Where they can, they grow tobacco, cotton, or wheat as well. Poor rocky soil and a lack of modern tools and irrigation keep Greek farming from becoming productive. Many young people leave rural areas for Athens and industrial cities of the European heartland.

REVIEWING THE FACTS

Answer

1. How does southern Europe compare with the European heartland in terms of standard of living?

2. In what ways has Spain changed in recent years?

3. Along what river is most of Italy's industry located?

4. What are the two chief economic activities of Greece?

Locate

Refer to the map on page 284.

1. Name the countries of which these cities are capitals: (a) Lisbon, (b) Madrid, (c) Rome, (d) Athens.

2. (a) Name the island lying off the southern tip of Italy. (b) Southeast of Peloponnesus. (c) Directly west of Rome.

Have students locate the countries of Southern Europe on the map on page 284.
Portugal is one of Europe's poorest countries. About two thirds of its people live in rural areas.
One of its main economic problems is a lack of energy and mineral resources.
Answers are in the Teacher's Guide.

GEOGRAPHY LABORATORY

Highlighting the Chapter

1. Western Europe is made up of the democratic countries of Europe. On the mainland, it reaches from the Iberian Peninsula to the eastern borders of West Germany and Austria. It occupies a portion of the continent's Great European Plain and includes the Alps as well as the mountains and highlands of the Iberian and Italian peninsulas. Its climate is moderated by the warm, moist air blown inland from the Gulf Stream in the Atlantic Ocean.

2. Though comparatively small in area, Western Europe is one of the most heavily industrialized, urbanized, and populated places in the world. Its people have a high standard of living and are well educated. They are also culturally diverse, living in many different countries and speaking many different languages. Parliamentary democracy is the most common form of government. While the economies of the region are based on free enterprise, there is a great deal of government ownership of major transportation and communication linkages as well as of some other industries.

3. The British Isles and Norden have strong ties with the sea. Besides fishing, these countries have valuable commerce. The United Kingdom and Scandinavia have industrial economies. Despite its recent production of oil from the North Sea, the United Kingdom relies on imports of energy. It must also import food. Agriculture is important in Ireland and Denmark, and forestry adds to the economies of Finland and Scandinavia.

4. The European heartland is made up of France, Germany, the Low Countries, and the countries of the Alps. France is a major industrial and farming country. West Germany has the highest GNP in Western Europe. It is a major producer of steel, cars, and other similar products. The economies of the densely populated Low Countries depend to a great extent on banking and shipping as well as on manufacturing. The Alpine countries are limited in natural resources. Yet they have a high standard of living. Countries of the Alps are leading makers of precision instruments and other products of light industry.

5. Southern Europe is less developed than most of northern Europe and the European heartland. Portugal is largely a farming country. Spain is just beginning to industrialize. The most highly industrialized country of the region is Italy. Its steel and auto plants and factories are located in the northern plains of the Po River Valley. Greece has little manufacturing. However, it is the world's leading ocean-shipping nation.

Speaking Geographically

Number from 1 to 9 on a sheet of paper. Then match the following terms to their meanings.

Benelux
Common Market
constitutional
   monarchy
Holocaust
Indo-European
literate
neutral
Norden
welfare state

1. Able to read and write

2. Scandinavia, Finland, and Iceland

3. Government that provides many programs to assist citizens with such matters as health care and pensions

4. Democratic country in which there is a king or queen

5. The Low Countries

6. Not taking sides in international disputes

7. An organization that promotes economic unity in Western Europe

8. The Nazi party's brutal persecution of European Jews

9. The major language family in Europe

Testing Yourself

Write the following places across the top of a sheet of paper: Low Countries, Scandinavia, West Germany, Southern Europe

Now put the words and phrases from the list below under the correct heading.

reclaimed land
Po Valley
Appennines
Ruhr Valley
olive oil
busiest ports in
  the world

Mediterranean
  climate
North Sea oil
subarctic climate
Iberian Peninsula
Saar Valley

Building Map Skills

Number your paper from 1 to 18. After each number, write the name of the country identified by that number on the map on this page.

Applying Map Skills

On your paper, list the following capital cities in north-south order, beginning with the northernmost city.

Amsterdam
Athens
Bern
Bonn
Copenhagen

London
Madrid
Paris
Rome
Stockholm

Exploring Further

1. Languages within a branch of a language family are alike in many ways. You can see some likenesses by comparing the words for *mother*, *father*, *brother*, and *sister* in the Romance languages — French, Spanish, Italian, and Portuguese. Also compare words with the same

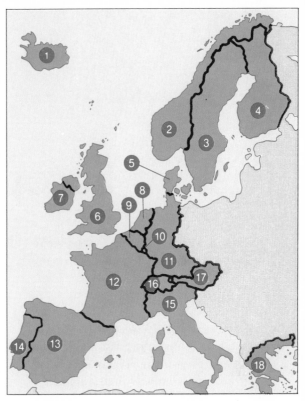

meanings in the Germanic languages. Are there similarities within the language family as well as within each branch of it?

2. Iceland is sometimes called the Land of Fire and Frost. Do research and prepare a report explaining why this description is appropriate.

3. Andorra, Malta, Monaco, San Marino, and Vatican City are tiny countries in Europe. Gather information on their location, size, population, physical features, economy, and form of government.

4. Many Americans trace their heritage to Europe. Using a telephone book or directory of community organizations, find the names of associations of people with a European heritage in your community. Choose one such organization and interview an officer. Find out what country its members emigrated from, the number of people from that country in your community, and when and why people from that country came to the United States.

307

In this chapter, students will be learning about the countries located between Western Europe and the Soviet Union. Although some of the Soviet Union is located in the eastern part of the European continent, that nation is discussed separately in Chapter 13. Ask students what happens to something if it is shattered. Tell them to watch for clues as they read this chapter that will explain why this term is so often used to describe Eastern Europe.

Eastern Europe

Have you ever heard it said that someone is between a rock and a hard place? In many ways, this phrase might describe the location and problems of Eastern Europe.

Eastern Europe lies between two very powerful regions. To its west is Western Europe, with its democratic governments and high standards of living. To the east is the powerful Soviet Union, with its authoritarian government and controlled socialist economy.

Eastern Europe has long been a meeting place — and a battleground — for different groups of people. In past centuries, waves of migrating people swept into the area from the east, south, northwest, and northeast. As a result of these pressures, Eastern Europe is often called a "shatter belt." Pressures from outside and divisions within the region have made it difficult for Eastern Europeans to form strong, stable countries. Political boundaries have shifted many times. Wars have been frequent.

Eastern Europe has historic ties with both Western Europe and the Soviet Union. During the 1800's, however, the links between Eastern Europe and Western Europe grew weaker. The Industrial Revolution and democracy were growing stronger in Western Europe, but these trends made little headway in the countries of Eastern Europe. Today most Eastern European countries are closely tied to the Soviet Union, both politically and economically.

308

Answers to Map Study questions: Great European Plain, Great Hungarian Plain, Walachian Plain; Hungary, Poland, East Germany; Dinaric Alps; Transylvanian Alps
Assign the Workbook activity for Chapter 12, Section 1, with pages 309–310.

1 The Physical Environment

Eastern Europe is made up of eight countries — East Germany, Poland, Czechoslovakia (chek'ə slō väk'ē ə), Hungary, Romania, Bulgaria, Yugoslavia, and Albania. The physical geography of Eastern Europe is marked by a complex interweaving of mountains, plains, and river basins.

Landforms

Eastern Europe has only one large area of unbroken flatlands. In the north, the Great European Plain stretches broad and level across East Germany and Poland toward the Soviet Union. This is the same plain that covers the northern part of Western Europe.

South of the Great European Plain, Eastern Europe becomes a tangle of small mountain ranges and plains. The Erzgebirge (erts'gə bir'gə) and Sudeten (sü dāt'ən) mountains mark the southern borders of East Germany and Poland. The Carpathian (kär pā'thē ən) Mountains swing southward from Poland into Romania. There they meet the Transylvanian Alps, forming a curve of mountains that looks like a giant fishhook. Along the Adriatic Sea, the Dinaric (də nar'ik) Alps extend through Yugoslavia and Albania. In Bulgaria, the Balkan and Rhodope (räd'ə pē) mountains run eastward toward the Black Sea.

Within this maze of mountains lie two sizable plains. The Great Hungarian Plain spreads across most of Hungary extending southward into Yugoslavia. In southern Romania and northern Bulgaria,

Map Study *Name the two large plains areas of Eastern Europe. Which three countries lie mainly in lowlands? What mountain system dominates Yugoslavia? What mountains lie in the heart of Romania?*

Eastern Europe: Climates

Subtropical Climates

Humid Subtropical (Hot, humid summers and mild winters)

Mediterranean Subtropical (Hot, dry summers and mild, rainy winters)

Midlatitude Climates

Temperate Marine (Mild and rainy all year)

Humid Continental (Warm summers and cold, snowy winters)

Map Study *Which countries of Eastern Europe lie entirely in subtropical climate areas?*

the Walachian (wä lā'kē ən) Plain reaches to the coast of the Black Sea.

Linking these two plains is the greatest waterway of Eastern Europe, the Danube (dan'yüb) River. The Danube flows through or along the borders of five Eastern European countries: Czechoslovakia, Hungary, Yugoslavia, Romania, and Bulgaria. The second-longest river in Europe, the Danube is a busy transportation route. Port cities dot its banks, and freight barges move through its waters.

310

Climate and Ecosystems

Located far from the Atlantic Ocean and its Gulf Stream, Eastern Europe's climate is colder and drier than Western Europe's. Most of Eastern Europe has the type of climate called humid continental. Its winters are longer and its growing seasons shorter than those in the marine climates of Western Europe.

Only the southern part of Eastern Europe has a mild climate. Along the Black and Adriatic seas, the climate is Mediterranean, with dry summers, mild wet winters, and a longer growing season.

Tall grasses once covered the Hungarian and Walachian plains. Mixed forests originally grew on much of the remaining lands in Eastern Europe. Today farms and cities have replaced the original vegetation on most of the lowlands, but large forests still cover many mountainous areas.

REVIEWING THE FACTS

Answer

1. Why has Eastern Europe been called a shatter belt?

2. (a) Describe the landforms of the northern part of Eastern Europe. (b) Of the southern part.

3. (a) What types of climate are found in Eastern Europe? (b) Where is each type found?

Locate

Refer to the map on page 309.

1. Name the country to which each of the following capitals belongs. (a) East Berlin (b) Warsaw (c) Prague (d) Budapest (e) Bucharest (f) Belgrade (g) Sofia (h) Tirana

2. (a) Name the sea north of Poland. (b) East of Bulgaria and Romania. (c) West of Yugoslavia.

Texas Essential Elements 4C. Population distribution, growth, and movements. 4D. Major cultural, political, and economic activities within and among major world regions.

2 The Human Imprint

Eastern Europe includes many different **ethnic groups.** Members of an ethnic group share customs and traditions that give them a feeling of identity. Often they are united by language, religious beliefs, historical traditions, and a common ancestry. Many people in Eastern Europe have strong loyalties to their own ethnic group. Dislike and distrust among ethnic groups have played a large part in making Eastern Europe a cultural shatter belt.

Traditional occupations, like the herding of sheep, are still common in many parts of Eastern Europe.

The People of Eastern Europe

Eastern Europe is a densely settled area. Its overall population density is about three times higher than that of the United States.

Settlement and Growth Patterns For centuries, there were few large cities in Eastern Europe. Most Eastern Europeans were farmers who lived in small towns. Since 1950, however, industrialization has spread in the region, and industrial cities have grown. These changes have led to a sharp decline in the population of rural areas and small towns. Today nearly two out of every three Eastern Europeans live in cities.

In most East European countries, the population is growing very slowly, if at all. In Hungary and East Germany, the population is actually declining. Only Albania, with a yearly growth rate of more than 2 percent, has a rapidly expanding population.

Language Differences The majority of Eastern Europeans speak Slavic languages. About 1,500 years ago, the Slavic peoples migrated into Europe from areas

Eastern Europe: Population Density

Persons per square mile	Persons per square kilometer	
2–25	1–10	
25–125	10–50	City population
125–250	50–100	○ 1–2 million
250–500	100–200	• 2–5 million

Map Study *Name the five largest cities of Eastern Europe. Which country has no large cities?*

Answers to Map Study questions: Berlin, Warsaw, Katowice, Bucharest, Budapest; Albania

Assign the Workbook activity for Chapter 12, Section 2, with pages 311–320.

SPOTLIGHT ON THE BERLIN WALL:

A City Divided

Over 25 years ago, in August of 1961, East German soldiers and workers labored through the night. They were building a wall to separate East Berlin from West Berlin. The next day East Berlin officials announced that the purpose of the wall was to keep the West out. In reality, it was built to keep East Germans in. In the week before the wall went up, 2000 East Germans fled to West Berlin in a single day. Over the next 25 years, only about 5000 successfully escaped to the West through Berlin.

In the beginning, the wall was little more than a crude barrier of cinder blocks, mortar, and barbed wire. Over the years, it was constantly improved. Today there are two walls. The outer wall stands 13 feet high and is 28 miles long. It is separated from the inner wall by a desolate patch of earth.

After the wall was built, East German officials called it the "antifascist protection wall." In West Berlin, it is known as the "wall of shame." It is a constant reminder that friends, families, and neighbors have been separated.

As the years have passed, the governments of East and West Berlin have gone separate ways. Yet people on both sides of the wall continue to dream of a day when their city will be one again. Recently, a visitor to East Berlin was studying a city map when an elderly East Berlin woman asked if she could look. "We can't get maps that show the West," she explained, "and I just wanted to see the whole thing again."

In recent years, the two governments have worked together on projects important to both halves of the city. For example, East and West Berlin have cooperated on waste disposal and pollution. Still, East German officials insist that the "German question" is closed forever. The wall will not come down, and the city will never be reunited.

Berliners disagree. They still feel that they are one city, not two. When West Germany scored its second goal in the World Cup soccer finals in June of 1986, a volley of flares and rockets lit the East Berlin sky. The city, although politically divided, remains united in the hearts of its people. As one West Berlin official stated, "One Berlin is Communist; the other is not. But when we speak, it is Berliner to Berliner."

---

farther east. The Slavic language group includes many different languages. The people of Bulgaria, Poland, Czechoslovakia, and Yugoslavia speak Slavic languages. (Russian too is a Slavic language.)

Eastern Europe also includes non-Slavic languages. The people of East Germany speak German. Romanian is a Romance language, more closely related to Italian and French than to the language of its Slavic neighbors.

Hungary's language has its own distinctive history. Many people in Hungary are descended from a group known as the Magyars (mag'yärz'). The Magyars were nomadic herders who moved westward from southern Russia about 1,000 years ago. The Magyars (Hungarians) are more closely related to the peoples of Asia than to the Slavic and other European peoples. The Hungarian language belongs to the **Ural-Altaic** (yûr′əl al tā′ik) family rather than to the Indo-European family.

Religious Differences Religious differences have also helped to make Eastern Europe a cultural shatter belt. In the western and northern parts of the region, most people are Roman Catholics. The Roman Catholic Church is especially strong in Poland. In the east and southeast, the Eastern Orthodox Church is the traditional preference. The Eastern Orthodox Church is a branch of Christianity that split from the Roman Catholic Church in 1054. In Albania, the Islamic religion took hold many years ago when the area was under Turkish rule. Islam is a religion that began in Arabia in A.D. 622. Its followers are known as Muslims.

Before World War II, Jews formed large communities in many parts of Eastern Europe, especially in Poland. When Nazi Germany conquered Eastern Europe, millions of Jews were killed in the Holocaust (page 289).

Today it is difficult to estimate the number of people who belong to each religious group in Eastern Europe. The Communist governments in the region discourage all religious beliefs and practices. Many people, however, continue to follow their religious traditions.

The Role of Minorities Almost every country of Eastern Europe has ethnic or religious minorities living within its borders. A **minority** is any small group within a country that differs from most of the population.

Yugoslavia has the greatest ethnic mix of all countries in Eastern Europe. Its population is a collection of minorities. The Slavic peoples of Yugoslavia include Serbs, Croatians (krō ā′ shənz), Slovaks, Bulgarians, and Macedonians. In fact, the name *Yugoslavia* means "land of the South Slavs." The country also includes non-Slavic groups such as Hungarians and Turks. Yugoslavia has at least three official languages. The presence of many groups has made it difficult for Yugoslavia to build a single nation.

The presence of minorities has made it difficult for countries in Eastern Europe to agree on boundaries. During the 1970's, for example, a Slavic minority living in southern Austria felt uncomfortable among the German-speaking majority of the country. They quarreled with the Austrian government and appealed to the government of Yugoslavia for support. In the dispute that followed, Yugoslavia considered taking over the part of Austria where the Slavic people lived. Such incidents have been frequent in the history of Eastern Europe.

Political Patterns

Ethnic groups throughout Eastern Europe have often felt that people who share a common way of life should live together as one nation, with their own government and their own political boundaries. This belief, as you have read, is called nationalism. Feelings of nationalism among the region's ethnic groups have been a powerful force in Eastern Europe's political development.

During the late 1800's, when nations and nationalism were very powerful in Western Europe, most of Eastern Europe was under the rule of two large empires (see map on page 316). One was the Austro-Hungarian empire, which controlled much of what is now Hungary, Czechoslovakia, Poland, Romania, and Yugoslavia. The ruling group in that empire was the German-speaking Austrians, with some special rights given to the large Hungarian minority. The second large

313

empire was the Ottoman empire, which controlled land in the Balkans and along the Black Sea. Under these two empires, the Slavic peoples of Eastern Europe had little opportunity for self-rule.

Around 1900, many Slavs struggled to form their own nations. Some groups won their freedom from the weak Ottoman empire. One such group formed the small independent country of Serbia (today part of Yugoslavia). Serbia encouraged Slavic nationalists elsewhere.

Nationalist Movements and World War I
In June 1914, a Slavic nationalist assassinated the heir to the throne of the Austro-Hungarian empire. Austria immediately declared war against Serbia. These events were the sparks that ignited World War I. Soon the war had spread to most countries of Europe and to others beyond the continent.

When World War I ended in 1918, the old empires of Eastern Europe had been destroyed. Political boundaries then changed, and the map of Europe was completely redrawn. Instead of large empires, Eastern Europe became a region of many small countries. Yet some ethnic groups remained dissatisfied.

World War II World War II began in Europe in 1939 and lasted until 1945. Because of the rivalries and hostilities within Eastern Europe, some countries there fought on the side of Germany and Italy, and others fought for the Allies (the United States, the United Kingdom, France, and the Soviet Union).

German forces overran much of Eastern Europe early in the war. Later, however, the German armies were forced to retreat. As they withdrew, Soviet armies advanced westward across Eastern Europe. By 1945, Soviet forces had occupied much of Eastern Europe. The Soviet Union was in a position to control events in those countries.

Czechs fought bravely against invading Soviet troops during August, 1968. Within a few days, however, the Soviets replaced the country's reform-minded government.

314

Soviet Domination Since 1945, the countries of Eastern Europe have had Communist governments modeled on that of the Soviet Union. Small non-Communist political parties lost their power as communism gained strength during the late 1940's. In other countries, the Soviet Union used force to set up a Communist government.

Each Eastern European country has its own Communist party, which dominates the government of that country. In several countries, including Hungary and Romania, the Communist party is the only political party allowed by law. East Germany, Poland, Yugoslavia, and some other countries have two or more political parties, but the Communist party is the one in firm control.

Most national Communist parties in Eastern Europe have close ties with the Soviet Communist party. The Soviet Union is, in fact, the real power behind most of Eastern Europe's governments. Eastern European countries are often called Soviet **satellites,** meaning that they have little independence.

The Soviet Union and all the Eastern European countries except Albania and Yugoslavia belong to a treaty organization called the Warsaw Pact. The Warsaw Pact is a Communist defense agreement, under which member nations agree to come to one another's aid in the event of an attack.

Resistance to Soviet Power Many Eastern Europeans have resented Soviet influence. Resistance to Soviet power has taken many forms.

In 1956, many Hungarians rebelled against their Communist government, but the Soviet Union used tanks and troops to put a bloody end to the revolt. The Soviet Union also invaded Czechoslovakia in 1968 when its government tried to make changes that challenged Soviet control.

During the 1980's, many workers in Poland banded together in the Solidarity movement. Through Solidarity, Polish workers tried to win better wages and working conditions from their government. The Soviet Union responded by forcing the Polish government to impose **martial law.** Under martial law, the military has the authority to rule a country.

Some Eastern European countries have succeeded in reducing Soviet influence. As early as 1948, Yugoslavia began to throw off some Soviet controls. Unlike Hungary, Czechoslovakia, and Poland, Yugoslavia shares no border with the Soviet Union. Moreover, Yugoslavia has the advantage of a long seacoast on the Adriatic Sea, by which the country could easily get supplies from Western Europe

In the 1980's, Poles rallied behind the Solidarity movement in an effort to win reforms. The government eventually banned Solidarity.

Texas Essential Elements 1C. Geographical tools and methodologies. 4D. Major cultural, political, and economic activities within and among major world regions.

Using Maps for History

Between 1871 and 1923, many political changes took place in Eastern Europe. The ethnic groups of the region were struggling to win national homelands. Two large but weakening empires — the Ottoman and the Austro-Hungarian — were struggling to hold on to their power. The maps on this page show the political outcome of 50 years of war and diplomacy. Use the maps to answer the questions that follow.

1. What was the only independent nation on the Balkan Peninsula in 1871?

2. In 1871, through what empire did the Danube River flow?

3. (a) Name three groups that live in Eastern Europe today who were ruled by the Ottoman empire in 1871. (b) Name three groups whose territory was ruled by Austria-Hungary.

4. In 1871, what three empires controlled the land where the Polish people lived?

5. Name a city in the Russian Empire that became part of Poland.

6. Name a city in the Austro-Hungarian Empire that later became part of the country of Yugoslavia.

7. (a) What countries bordered the Adriatic Sea in 1871? (b) In 1923, what countries bordered the Adriatic Sea?

8. By 1923, what nations made up Eastern Europe?

9. (a) In 1871, who controlled the city of Constantinople at the southern outlet of the Black Sea? (b) What country controlled this city in 1923?

10. Compare the map of Eastern Europe in 1923 to the map on page 309 of Eastern Europe today. How have the location and territory of Poland changed since 1923? (These changes took place in 1945 as a result of World War II.)

For a special challenge Compare this map to the map of languages on page 288. Name at least two groups in Eastern Europe that did not win countries of their own.

Answers are in the Teacher's Guide.

Assign the Workbook activity for this chapter's Map Workshop with this page.

in case of conflict with the Soviet Union. Albania too has broken away from the Soviet Union. Both Albania and Yugoslavia, however, remain firmly Communist in their governments.

Even though all countries in Eastern Europe have a Communist government, it is clear that there is still unrest and political dissatisfaction within Eastern Europe. The region's ethnic groups have not forgotten their identities and long-felt national goals. Resentment against Soviet dominance is strong in Poland, Hungary, Czechoslovakia, and Romania.

Economic Patterns

The Soviet Union has drawn most Eastern European countries under its economic as well as its political control. Eastern Europe's economic background is different from that of Western Europe. During the late 1700's and the 1800's, Eastern Europe remained cut off from the Industrial Revolution that was taking hold in Western Europe. For most parts of Eastern Europe, industrialization did not begin until after 1900, and even then its progress was slow.

Economic Development since 1945 One goal of the Communist governments has been to build industry. Under communism, the government owns and operates factories, mines, communication and transportation systems, and some large farms.

Eastern European governments have placed the greatest importance on the production of **capital goods.** Capital goods are products used mainly by other industries or for transportation. Examples of capital goods are heavy machinery, trucks, railroad equipment, and ships. Eastern European factories do not produce many **consumer goods.** Consumer goods are products such as refrigerators, radios, and cameras — products that are used by individuals.

Having few consumer goods to sell has hurt Eastern Europe's export trade. It has also kept Eastern Europe's standard of living rather low, compared to that of Western Europe.

Farming too is less developed in Eastern Europe than in Western Europe. Many Eastern Europeans live and work on small farms. In many cases, these farmers grow crops and raise livestock using methods that are centuries old. Crop yields are generally low.

The system of communism itself has discouraged economic gains. Although government control of the economy has led to growth in heavy industry, government planning often has resulted in

Basic necessities are in short supply in many Eastern European countries. Here, Poles line up at a food store.

317

Using Graphs to Interpret Economic Trade Patterns

Graphs are a convenient way of showing economic activities and trends in countries. These circle graphs show the kinds of imports and exports traded by two Eastern European countries, Hungary and Poland. The graphs also show what percentage of the country's total trade each category of imports or exports represents. The lists of trading partners show the countries with which Hungary and Poland each carry on most of their trade. Careful study of the graphs will help you form a general picture of trade patterns in these two countries.

1. Compare Hungary's exports and imports. (a) Into what category does the greatest percent of its imports fall? (b) What category makes up the smallest percent of its imports? (c) Its exports?

2. (a) What kinds of items make up more than half the total value of Poland's exports? (b) Which two categories make up more than 70 percent of its imports?

3. Which country is more dependent on fuels and raw materials from outside its own borders?

4. Which country probably has more large factories to manufacture heavy machinery?

5. How does trade reflect the two countries' ties with the Soviet Union and its satellites?

6. Which of the two countries carries on trade with the greater number of non-Communist countries?

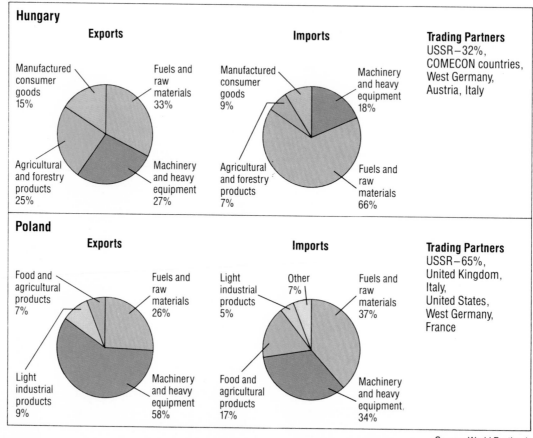

Hungary

Exports

Manufactured consumer goods 15%

Fuels and raw materials 33%

Agricultural and forestry products 25%

Machinery and heavy equipment 27%

Imports

Manufactured consumer goods 9%

Machinery and heavy equipment 18%

Agricultural and forestry products 7%

Fuels and raw materials 66%

Trading Partners
USSR–32%, COMECON countries, West Germany, Austria, Italy

Poland

Exports

Food and agricultural products 7%

Fuels and raw materials 26%

Light industrial products 9%

Machinery and heavy equipment 58%

Imports

Light industrial products 5%

Other 7%

Fuels and raw materials 37%

Food and agricultural products 17%

Machinery and heavy equipment 34%

Trading Partners
USSR–65%, United Kingdom, Italy, United States, West Germany, France

Source: World Factbook

inefficiency. During the early years of communism, all workers received equal wages, no matter how hard they worked or how much they produced. Many workers found little motive to do their best. In recent years, some Communist governments have begun giving the best workers higher pay to encourage production.

Providing Mutual Economic Assistance
The countries of Eastern Europe carry on trade mostly among themselves and with the Soviet Union. All the Eastern European countries except Yugoslavia and Albania are members of the Council for Mutual Economic Assistance, called **COMECON.** As in Western Europe's Common Market, COMECON countries exchange products, with few tariffs or other barriers to free trade among member nations.

Map Study *In what countries of Eastern Europe are there supplies of natural gas? Of oil? Near what cities in Poland is coal mined? What resource is mined along Yugoslavia's Adriatic coast?*

Eastern Europe: Land Use

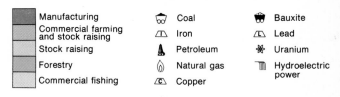

Manufacturing	Coal	Bauxite
Commercial farming and stock raising	Iron	Lead
Stock raising	Petroleum	Uranium
Forestry	Natural gas	Hydroelectric power
Commercial fishing	Copper	

WORLD DATA BANK

Country	Area in Square Miles	Population/Natural Increase		Per Capita GNP
Albania	11,100	3,100,000	(2.0%)	$ NA
Bulgaria	42,822	9,000,000	(0.1%)	NA
Czechoslovakia	49,371	15,600,000	(0.3%)	NA
East Germany	41,826	16,700,000	(0.0%)	NA
Hungary	35,919	10,600,000	(−0.2%)	1,940
Poland	120,726	37,800,000	(0.8%)	2,120
Romania	91,699	22,900,000	(0.5%)	4,860
Yugoslavia	98,764	23,400,000	(0.7%)	2,070

319

The Soviet Union is the most powerful member of COMECON. The Soviet plan is for each member nation to specialize in the goods it can produce best. Then each country is to market its products in the Soviet Union and other Eastern European countries. Some COMECON members, however, have protested that this plan hurts their economies. For example, Romania complains that it is expected to produce wood products and farm goods, rather than to develop its own industry.

REVIEWING THE FACTS

Define

1. ethnic group
2. Ural-Altaic
3. minority
4. satellite
5. martial law
6. capital goods
7. consumer goods
8. COMECON

Answer

1. How have settlement patterns in Eastern Europe changed since 1950?

2. (a) What are the major language groups in Eastern Europe? (b) The major religious groups?

3. Why has political stability been difficult to achieve in Eastern Europe?

4. What is the Warsaw Pact?

5. Give three examples of ways in which the Soviet Union dominates Eastern Europe today.

Locate

Refer to the map on page 309.

1. Which two countries of Eastern Europe are landlocked?

2. Name three capital cities that lie on or near the Danube River.

3. Where is Eastern Europe's largest lowland area?

3 Nations of Eastern Europe

Some 40 years of Communist rule have brought a variety of changes to Eastern Europe. Compared with the period before World War II, Eastern European industries and economies have grown stronger under communism. People in Eastern Europe recognize these gains, yet some of them long for the personal freedoms and greater economic benefits enjoyed by their neighbors in Western Europe.

East Germany

East Germany's official name is the German Democratic Republic. It became a separate country after World War II when Germany was divided (pages 298–299). The separation of East and West Germany is an unsettled question. West Germany's government has long favored the reunion of the two countries. Only in the 1980's has East Germany's government extended any hope for a future reunited Germany.

East Berlin is the capital of East Germany. As you read in Chapter 11, Berlin is a divided city. Between 1945 and 1961, many refugees fled from East Germany by going first to East Berlin and then crossing into West Berlin. To close that escape route, the Communists built a heavily guarded wall—which still stands—between the two sections of the city.

East Germany has one of the strongest economies in Eastern Europe. It has more heavy industry than any other Eastern European country. It also has the best-developed railway, highway, and waterway linkages. East Berlin, Leipzig (līp'sig), and Dresden are the major centers of industry, transportation, and commerce.

Encourage students to compare information on the two Germanies by studying the World Data Banks on pages 292 and 319.
Answers are in the Teacher's Guide.
Assign the Workbook activity for Chapter 12, Section 3, with pages 320–325.

Students from nearby Dresden harvest grapes on one of East Germany's many government-owned farms.

East Germany manufactures machinery, cars, ships, chemicals, electronics, textiles, and a variety of other goods. The country is poor in resources, and therefore it must import most of the raw materials for its factories. Its most important exports are engineering goods and chemicals.

Agriculture makes up a small but important share of East Germany's economy. Most of East Germany's land lies on the Great European Plain, and good soils are widespread. Nearly all East Germany's farms are large **collective farms** or **state farms.** Collective farms are run by groups of farmers under government direction. All farmers on the collective work together and earn a share in the farm's income. State farms are run as government-owned businesses, and the farmers who work on them are paid wages by the government. East Germany's largest crops are potatoes, rye, wheat, barley, and sugar beets.

Poland

Poland's population and land area are the largest in all of Eastern Europe. Its industry has developed rapidly since 1945. The government owns nearly all the industry. Mining, steelmaking, and heavy industry are concentrated in the Silesia (sī lē′zhə) district, between the cities of Wroclaw (vrȯt′släf′) and Krakow.

Warsaw, Poland's capital, is also the economic, cultural, and transportation center of Poland. The city produces automobiles, machinery, appliances, chemicals, and textiles. The city of Gdansk (gə dansk′), on the Baltic coast, is a shipbuilding center. As with other Eastern European countries, the Soviet Union is Poland's largest trading partner.

Most of Poland is on the Great European Plain. Because the land is mostly flat, it is easy to farm. Poland is the world's second leading producer of potatoes and rye. It is also Eastern Europe's leading producer of beef and pork.

321

Today's cities of Eastern Europe have farmers' markets. In Krakow, Poland, women sell potatoes, grown on their own land, in the city market. The money they earn is an important addition to their wages.

Poland's farm production is not all that it could be. Much of the soil needs fertilizer, and many farmers use outdated methods to work their small plots. In the late 1940's, Poland's Communist government tried to set up collective farms, but the Polish farmers wanted to keep their own land. They rebelled, and the collective plan failed. Today nearly all of Poland's farms are privately owned.

The Polish people have protested often and sometimes violently against their Communist government. They have called strikes and rallies to protest low wages, food shortages, high consumer prices, oppression of personal freedoms, and Soviet control. Shipyard workers at Gdansk, who formed Solidarity, have led the most recent protests. The Polish people have also held firmly to their Roman Catholic faith despite many struggles between the Church and the Communists.

Czechoslovakia

The nation of Czechoslovakia was first formed in 1918 at the end of World War I. It takes its name from two Slavic groups —the Czechs, who lived mostly in the western part of the country, and the Slovaks, who lived in the east.

Czechoslovakia is a landscape of hills, mountains, narrow valleys, and upland plains, with little flat land suitable for agriculture. Western Czechoslovakia is one of Eastern Europe's most heavily industrialized areas. The Czechs had close ties with Western Europe, and they shared in early developments in industry and technology. In addition, Czechoslovakia has many industrial resources, including coal, copper, lead, and zinc.

Prague (präg) is the nation's cultural and industrial center as well its capital. It is famous for high-quality glassware, textiles, and leather goods. In addition, machinery, automobiles, and military goods are produced there. One of Europe's largest iron and steel works is located at Plzen (pəl'zen'). This city also manufactures military goods for the Soviet Union.

Compared to other countries of Eastern Europe, Czechoslovakia has a high standard of living. More consumer goods are available in Czechoslovakia than in the Soviet Union itself or other COMECON countries.

Hungary

Much of Hungary lies on the broad, flat, fertile plain of the Danube River. As a result, Hungary exports large quantities of food. Wheat, corn, barley, rye, sugar beets, and wine from grapes are its major products. Livestock fattened on locally grown grains provide beef and pork. Nearly 80 percent of Hungary's agriculture is operated under a collective-farm system.

322

Soviet domination of Hungary has met with resistance. In October 1956, demonstrations against the government developed into open revolt. On November 4, Soviet forces launched a massive attack on Budapest to quell the uprising. Thousands of Hungarians were killed in the fighting that followed; thousands more were deported; 200,000 fled.

After a long lag, industry in Hungary is beginning to grow. The country has some coal, and it has exported bauxite to the Soviet Union and Czechoslovakia for many years. Hungary is now developing its own steel industry, using imported iron ore. However, the country lacks the energy resources needed for much heavy industry, so Hungarians concentrate on light industries. Their leading products in this field are fine tools and medicines.

Since the late 1960's, the Hungarian government has launched a number of reforms. No other Soviet satellite country offers its citizens more cultural and economic freedoms. Beginning in 1980, the government has experimented with small-scale free enterprise. Today perhaps three out of every four Hungarian workers make extra money by farming private plots, working in small shops, making handicrafts, or working after hours in factories. There is hope that the reforms will bring long-term prosperity to Hungary.

Even though they work on government-owned farms, Hungarian farmers can grow and sell some produce on their own.

DISTINGUISHED DRIVERS

Czechs are proud and considered fortunate to own more automobiles than almost any other people in Eastern Europe. But there are some disadvantages to their prized luxury and status symbol. New-car prices may run higher than two years' wages. Once purchased, cars require hard-to-find service and scarce parts. Most Czech owners are resigned to being their own mechanics. Do-it-yourself owners have set up shop in parking lots, yards, and streets all over the capital city of Prague.

323

Over 90 percent of Hungary's population is Magyar (also the name of their language). About two thirds of the people are Roman Catholic, and over 50 percent live in urban areas.

Romania and Bulgaria

Romania and Bulgaria both border the Black Sea. They share the Danube River as a common boundary.

The overall standard of living in Romania and Bulgaria is lower than in most other parts of Europe. Agriculture is a major activity in both countries. About 90 percent of the farming takes place on state farms or collectives. Both countries produce corn, wheat, oats, and other small grains. Bulgaria's Maritsa (mə rēt'sə) River valley is famous for growing roses used to make perfume. Sheep raising is important in central highland areas.

Romania and Bulgaria have a variety of mineral resources, many of which are untapped. Romania's most developed resource is petroleum. The largest oil field on the European mainland is located in the Carpathians, near the Romanian city of Ploesti (plō yesht'ē). The Soviet Union is the major buyer of Romanian oil. Other COMECON countries buy Romanian oil and natural gas as well.

Although Bulgaria and Romania are similar in some ways, their political outlooks differ. Romania has a long history of quarrels with the Soviet Union. For example, Romania refused to support the Soviet Union during its quarrel with China in the 1960's. Romania has also attempted to strengthen its ties to non-Communist countries by increasing trade with Western Europe. The closeness of the Soviet Union, however, puts strict limits on Romania's freedom of action.

Bulgaria, on the other hand, is more closely linked to the Soviet Union than any other Eastern European satellite. Its ties date back for more than a century and are cultural, historical, and economic as well as political.

Yugoslavia and Albania

The large country of Yugoslavia and the small country of Albania lie along the eastern side of the Adriatic Sea. The coastal areas of both countries enjoy a warm, sunny, subtropical Mediterranean climate. Palm trees line scenic beaches, with mountains rising inland.

The climate, the seacoast, and the beautiful off-shore islands make tourism an important industry in Yugoslavia. Yugoslavia's mountain ski resorts also attract thousands of tourists every winter. Albania, on the other hand, is a closed country that permits almost no foreign visitors. It is the most isolated country of Eastern Europe. Even though it is a Communist country, it has poor relations with its neighbors, the Soviet Union, and China.

The most important economic activity in both Yugoslavia and Albania is farming. Yugoslavia has some collectives, but most farms are privately owned. Along the Adriatic coast, Yugoslav farmers grow Mediterranean crops such as grapes, olives, and other fruits and vegetables. In the country's major farming area, on the

Roses, used in making perfumes, are harvested in Bulgaria's Maritsa Valley.

324

Vacationers bask in the sun in the resort area along Yugoslavia's Adriatic coast.

plains along the Danube River, grain crops thrive in the fertile soil. Compared to other countries in both Eastern and Western Europe, farming methods in Yugoslavia are simple, and productivity is low.

Most Albanians are subsistence farmers or shepherds. In the Albanian countryside, poor linkages and rugged mountains isolate villages and peoples.

The two countries both have important mineral deposits, but neither has well-developed industries. Albania has petroleum and natural-gas deposits, yet it is still the least developed country in all of Europe. Yugoslavia has a rich variety of mineral resources, including lead, bauxite, iron, coal, zinc, mercury, copper, and antimony. However, Yugoslavia has little manufacturing as yet. Instead, it exports its raw materials and imports finished goods.

Politically, Yugoslavia and Albania are unique among the countries of Eastern Europe. Neither country has close ties with the Soviet Union. They are not members of either the Warsaw Pact or COMECON (although Yugoslavia is an associate member of the latter).

Though still under a Communist government, Yugoslavia has developed its own social, economic, and political systems without Soviet controls. The country has good relations with Western Europe and other democratic nations.

In the early 1960's, Albania broke relations with the Soviet Union in favor of China, the other large Communist country. In recent years, the Chinese and the Albanians have also had disagreements, but Albania has not returned to the Soviet camp.

REVIEWING THE FACTS

Define

1. collective farm
2. state farm

Answer

1. Name the three countries of Eastern Europe that lead the region in industrial development.

2. What efforts have been made by each of the following countries to limit Soviet influence? (a) Romania (b) Yugoslavia (c) Albania

3. (a) What changes or reforms are workers seeking in Poland? (b) What reforms have been achieved in Hungary?

Locate

Refer to the map on page 309.

1. Name six Eastern European countries that share borders with countries of Western Europe.

2. (a) Which Eastern European country is the largest? (b) The smallest?

Answers are in the Teacher's Guide. **325**

Albanians call their country *Shqiperia*, which means "eagle's land." Albania has the fastest-growing population in all of Europe. The people are divided into two main groups, the Ghegs in the north and the Tosks in the south.

GEOGRAPHY LABORATORY

Highlighting the Chapter

1. The eight countries of Eastern Europe are East Germany, Poland, Czechoslovakia, Hungary, Romania, Bulgaria, Yugoslavia, and Albania. Because of the frequent conflicts that have arisen among the region's peoples, Eastern Europe has been called a geographical shatter belt. Cultural and political differences have been reinforced by mountain ranges that break up the region's several plains. Most of Eastern Europe has a humid continental climate. However, the southernmost portion has a Mediterranean climate. Farms and cities cover most of the lowland areas, but large forests are found in the mountains.

2. Densely populated, Eastern Europe is a mixture of many ethnic groups. People of Slavic descent are in the majority, but there are sizable non-Slavic minorities. The different groups have strong nationalistic identities and outlooks, and some are still not satisfied with their divided groupings among present nations. Since the end of World War II, Soviet-style communism has dominated Eastern Europe, despite outbreaks of resistance. Communist governments in each country have worked to develop modern agriculture and heavy industry. Most of the Eastern European nations trade largely with each other and the Soviet Union under a trade agreement known as COMECON.

3. East Germany is the most industrialized of the Eastern European countries. Poland's new industries also produce many goods. Western and central Czechoslovakia have some well-developed industries, while the eastern half remains more agricultural. Hungary, Poland, and East Germany have the largest and most productive agricultural areas. Yugoslavia and Albania, both of which have loosened ties with the Soviet Union, are — with Romania and Bulgaria — among the least developed countries in all of Europe.

326

Speaking Geographically

Use each of the following terms in a sentence to show that you understand how the term applies to Eastern Europe.

1. ethnic group
2. Ural-Altaic
3. Eastern Orthodox
4. Islam
5. minority
6. satellite
7. martial law
8. capital goods
9. consumer goods
10. COMECON
11. collective farm
12. state farm

Testing Yourself

Number a paper from 1 to 11. For each phrase or pair of phrases below, name the Eastern European country they describe.

1. Has a divided capital city

2. Least developed; once had close ties with China's Communist government

3. Relatively high standard of living; named for its two largest ethnic groups

4. Today has most cultural and economic freedom

5. Closest ties to the USSR over many years; grows roses for making perfume

6. Large oil field; mostly agricultural

7. Large producer of potatoes and rye; strong Roman Catholic faith

8. Active tourist industry; does not have close ties with the Soviet Union

9. Has recently experienced protests against the government led by Solidarity, an organization that began among shipyard workers

10. Little land suitable for agriculture; famous for glassware, textiles, and leather goods

11. Most farms privately owned; produces Mediterranean crops such as olives

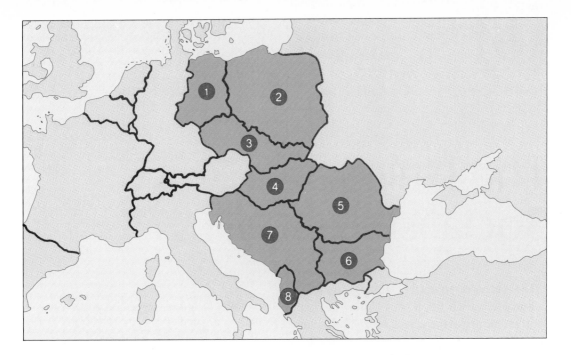

Building Map Skills

Number your paper from 1 to 8. After each number, write the name of the country labeled with that number on the map above.

Applying Geographic Skills

Use the World Data Bank on page 319 or a current almanac to make a chart comparing the countries of Eastern Europe. On your chart, provide the following information:

• The countries that have the largest and smallest populations
• The countries that have the highest and lowest population densities
• The countries that have the largest and smallest land areas
• The countries that have the fastest and slowest population growth rates

Beside each country's name, also provide the appropriate figure.

Exploring Further

1. Do further research on the Solidarity movement in Poland. Prepare a report on its leaders, goals, and activities. How did the Polish government respond to it? How did the Soviet Union respond? What is Solidarity's current status? How is the movement viewed in other parts of the world? Look in newspapers and magazines for up-to-date information.

2. Yugoslavia is one of the most culturally diverse countries in Europe. Prepare a display or a report on the country's various ethnic groups, languages, and religions. What problems has this diversity created? What role did the political leader Tito (Josip Broz) play in uniting the country? How is Yugoslavia's government organized to give different ethnic groups some independence?

3. Do research to find out what events surrounded the building of the wall that separates East Berlin from West Berlin. What country initiated the building, and why? What were the reactions of the German people and others throughout the world? Write a report.

327

The Soviet Union, one of the world's two super-powers, is described in this chapter. Students will look at the physical setting of the world's largest country in Part 1. Part 2 examines the life of the people and their political and economic systems. In Part 3, the Soviet Union is divided into five separate regions for further study.

The Union of Soviet Socialist Republics

The Union of Soviet Socialist Republics, commonly called the Soviet Union, is the largest country in the world. More than one sixth of the world's land area lies within its borders. The second largest country, Canada, is only about half the size of the Soviet Union.

This vast nation spreads across two continents, Europe and Asia. A third of the Soviet Union lies in Europe. Cities, farms, and factories are concentrated in the European part of the Soviet Union. The rest of the country is in Asia, separated from the European section by the Ural Mountains. The Asian part of the country gives the Soviet Union a resource base unmatched by any other country in the world.

One consequence of the Soviet Union's size is that it has many neighbors. In fact, no other country in the world has so many. Some neighbors — like most countries of Eastern Europe — are friendly. But the Soviet Union has difficult relations with many of its neighbors. China, for example, shares a long border — and a long rivalry — with the Soviet Union.

In the twentieth century, the Soviet Union became a world power. Today its industrial production places it among the world's leaders. How the Soviet Union uses its environment and its power will play a large part in shaping the future world.

328

1 The Physical Environment

The Soviet Union is enormous. Yet it lies entirely in the middle and high latitudes. Almost half the country is as far north as the unsettled Canadian frontier. Because of its northern location, the Soviet Union's climates and ecosystems are less varied than one would expect in so vast an area.

Landforms

The Soviet Union has six major landform regions. In the west, the *Great European Plain* extends from Eastern Europe into the Soviet Union. This plain sweeps east as far as the Ural Mountains. Its broad expanse is interrupted by only a few highland areas. In the past, invaders from Europe found that the Great European Plain provided them with an easy route into Russia.

Map Study *Which has a higher elevation, the Caucasus or Ural mountains? The Central Siberian Plateau or the Lena Plateau? What major rivers and landforms does the Trans-Siberian railroad cross?*

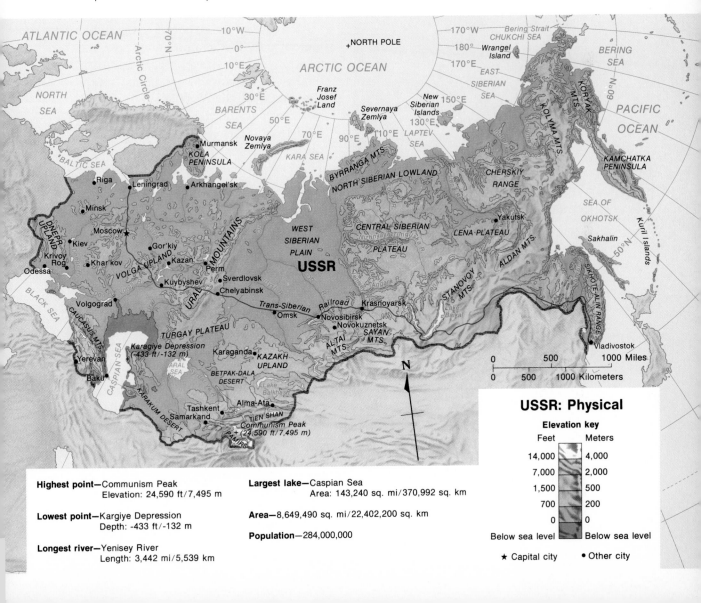

Highest point—Communism Peak
Elevation: 24,590 ft/7,495 m

Lowest point—Kargiye Depression
Depth: -433 ft/-132 m

Longest river—Yenisey River
Length: 3,442 mi/5,539 km

Largest lake—Caspian Sea
Area: 143,240 sq. mi/370,992 sq. km

Area—8,649,490 sq. mi/22,402,200 sq. km

Population—284,000,000

USSR: Physical

Elevation key

Feet		Meters
14,000		4,000
7,000		2,000
1,500		500
700		200
0		0
Below sea level		Below sea level

★ Capital city   ● Other city

The *Ural Mountains* rise from the European plain where the continents of Asia and Europe meet. These highlands run northward from the Aral Sea to the Arctic Ocean. Because they are low and rounded, they are easy to cross and do not form a major barrier to travel.

Four regions lie in the vast lands of **Siberia**. Siberia is the part of the Soviet Union that lies east of the Ural Mountains. The *West Siberian Plain* is immediately east of the Urals. Drained by the Ob River, it is one of the world's largest lowlands. Much of it is swamp and marsh.

GLOBAL RECORD SETTERS

Largest country: *The Soviet Union, with 8,600,383 square miles (22,274,900 square kilometers).*

Deepest lake: *Lake Baikal, with a depth of 5,712 feet (1,741 meters).*

Largest plain: *The West Siberian Plain, with an area of nearly 1,000,000 square miles (2,600,000 square kilometers).*

Lowest temperatures outside Antarctica: *Official reading of -90°F (-65°C) at Verkhoyansk, Siberia, and unofficial temperature of -108°F (-78°C) in Oymyakon, Siberia.*

Largest forest: *The taiga, in the northern Soviet Union, with 2,500,000,000 acres (1,000,000,000 hectares).*

Farther east, between the Yenisey (yen'ə sā') and Lena rivers, is the *Central Siberian Plateau.* A rugged frontier area, its highlands rise to about 2,000 feet (1,500 meters) above sea level.

Along the Pacific Ocean is a mountainous region. It is called the *East Siberia Uplands.* These uplands include the Stanovoy, Cherskiy, and Kolyma mountains. The mountains form a giant horseshoe around the Central Siberian Plateau. This horseshoe is a region of towering peaks and wind-swept plateaus intermixed with low basins. Lake Baikal (bī kȯl') is in the Baikal Mountains, just south of the Central Siberian Plateau. It is the world's deepest lake.

Along the southern border of the Soviet Union is another mountainous area, the *Central Asian Ranges.* The Caucasus (kȯ'kə səs) Mountains are in the southwest, between the Black Sea and the Caspian Sea. They reach elevations of greater than 18,500 feet (5,550 meters). East of the Caucasus are the Pamirs (pə mirz'). These are the tallest mountains in the Soviet Union. Communism Peak is 24,590 feet (7,495 meters) high. To the east of the Pamirs are the Altai (al'tī), Sayan (sə yän'), and other ranges of central Asia. The mountain ranges continue along the Soviet-Chinese border all the way to the Pacific.

Climates

Although large parts of the Soviet Union are no farther north than Western Europe, the Soviet Union has a far colder climate. Western Europe blocks the Soviet Union from the warming effect of the Gulf Stream. The European part of the country has a humid continental climate, with cool summers and cold winters. Rivers are frozen about three months a year.

330

USSR: Climates

Subtropical Climates

Humid Subtropical (Hot, humid summers and mild winters)

Mediterranean Subtropical (Hot, dry summers and mild, rainy winters)

Dry Climates

Arid (Desert climate with very little rain)

Semiarid (Semi-desert climate with some rain)

Midlatitude Climates

Humid Continental (Warm summers and cold, snowy winters)

Subarctic (Short summers and long, cold, snowy winters)

Cold Polar Climates

Subpolar (Always cold and dry with short, cool summers)

Highland Climates

(Temperature and precipitation vary greatly with latitude and elevation)

Map Study *What Soviet cities lie in an area with a desert climate? What is the climate of Moscow? Irkutsk? Anadyr?*

To the east, Siberia has long, bitterly cold winters and very short summers. Rivers freeze for seven to nine months of the year. Winter temperatures are commonly as low as -60°F (-51°C).

Many parts of the Soviet Union do not get enough precipitation for farming. In the northwest, rain and snow are plentiful. However, in the southwest and south central regions — where there are fertile soils and a longer growing season — precipitation is meager. Much of Siberia is also dry.

Ecosystems

As a result of the extreme cold, half the Soviet Union is covered with snow six months of the year. In the far north, extending from the Barents Sea to the Pacific, is tundra. Permafrost underlies the entire area. Only hardy mosses, lichens, grasses, and other small plants survive. South of the tundra, a great needleleaf forest called the taiga reaches from the European plain all the way to the eastern mountains. The Soviet taiga is the largest forest region in the world.

Point out that land use in much of the Soviet Union is greatly affected by cold temperatures, a short growing season, and lack of adequate rainfall. These factors limit the production of food.

331

Answers to Map Study questions: desert — Kungrad, Balkhash; Moscow — humid continental; Irkutsk — subarctic; Anadyr — subpolar

Texas Essential Elements 1C. Geographical tools and methodologies. 2A. Earth-sun relationship.

Understanding World Time Zones

What time is it? If someone in the Soviet Union and someone in France were to answer that question at the same moment, each person would give a different but correct answer. How can this be?

As you know, Earth rotates on its axis. In making one complete rotation, Earth turns 360°. It does this once each day, every 24 hours. Dividing 360° by 24 hours, you find that Earth rotates 15° each hour. In 1884, most nations agreed to use one system of world time zones. The system divided Earth into 24 time zones, 15° apart.

The map shows the time zones recognized today. Because Earth rotates from west to east, the hours grow earlier from east to west. When it is 7:00 A.M. in New York, it is 4:00 A.M. in Los Angeles. A traveler going west subtracts an hour for each time zone he or she crosses. Going east, the traveler adds an hour.

Look at the time-zone map. The numbers along the top of the map show what time it is in each of the other time zones when it is noon at the prime meridian. Use the map to answer the following questions.

1. (a) When it is noon at the prime meridian, what time is it in Los Angeles? (b) What time is it in Beijing?

2. How many time zones run through the Soviet Union?

3. If it is 3:00 P.M. in Moscow, what time is it in Tashkent?

4. How many hours' difference is there between Buenos Aires and Novosibirsk?

5. If it is 7:00 P.M. in London, what time is it in Washington, D.C.?

6. Notice that the boundaries of the time zones zigzag across land areas. Why do you suppose this is so?

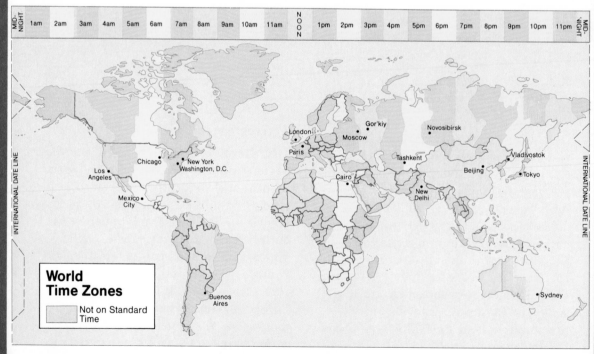

World Time Zones

Not on Standard Time

Answers are in the Teacher's Guide.
Assign the Workbook activity for this chapter's Map Workshop with this page.

South of the taiga, in the western and central parts of the country, is a zone of mixed needleleaf and broadleaf forests. There, winters are milder and growing seasons are longer than in the taiga region. Soil is more fertile, too.

Still further south, in the central portion of the Soviet Union, lies the Soviet steppe. Once, a sea of grass covered the whole area. Now much of the land has been developed for agriculture. Scattered trees grow on hills and in river valleys. The steppe has rich, black soil. Rainfall is, however, scant.

To the west of the steppe, in the European part of the Soviet Union, the climate is more humid. There, prairie grasses are the natural vegetation. Together with the steppe, this prairie forms the heartland of Soviet farming.

To the south and east of the steppe are deserts with large dunes and salt flats. There is little plant life.

REVIEWING THE FACTS

Define

Siberia

Answer

1. (a) List the major landform regions of the Soviet Union. (b) Describe the chief features of each.

2. How does the climate of the Soviet Union compare with that of Europe?

3. What are the ecosystems of the Soviet Union?

Locate

Refer to the map on page 329.

1. What two oceans border the Soviet Union?

2. Name the river and the mountains that separate the European and Asian parts of the Soviet Union.

2 The Human Imprint

Before the 1920's, the Soviet Union was called Russia. Russia was an absolute monarchy under a ruler called a **tsar** (zär). Although it was large, Russia had a weak economy. The great majority of its people were peasant farmers. During the twentieth century, Russia became the world's first Communist country. The Communist government has made far-reaching changes in Russia and altered world relations in many ways.

The Soviet People

The Soviet Union is the third most populous country, behind only China and India. Within this large population, there is much variety.

Ethnic Groups The Soviet population is made up of people belonging to some 90 ethnic groups. Each major ethnic group has a historic homeland of its own. Language, customs, and economic development vary from region to region.

About half the Soviet people are Russians. Russians are Slavs. No one knows for certain where Slavs came from. They may have migrated from Asia to the eastern part of Europe about 1,500 years ago. Eventually they became the major group in what is now the Ukraine (yü krān') (see map, page 336).

During the 800's, the Slavs in the Ukraine were ruled by traders from Scandinavia, some of whom were known as the **Russ**. The Russ organized the Slavic peasant farmers under a central government. Establishing their capital in Kiev (kē'ev), they made their kingdom a strong power. The Slavs became known as Russians — people who lived in the land of the Russ.

The area under the control of the Russians steadily expanded. Today Russians

333

Answers are in the Teacher's Guide.
When beginning Section 2, have students locate the city of Kiev on the map on page 329.
Assign the Workbook activity for Chapter 13, Section 2, with pages 333–343.

Registan Square, ringed by Muslim-style buildings, lies in the heart of Samarkand, in Uzbekistan. Muslim architecture is common in Soviet Central Asia.

dominate a large region that extends from the Black Sea north to Finland and from west of the Don River across Siberia. Large numbers of Russians also live in other parts of the Soviet Union.

As the Russians expanded their empire, they brought other ethnic groups under their control. Other Slavic peoples in the Soviet Union include the Ukrainians and the Belorussians (bel'ō rush' ənz). These groups live mainly along the western border. They speak Slavic languages much like Russian.

Turkic peoples live in much of **Soviet Central Asia.** This region stretches from the Caspian Sea to China. The Uzbeks, Kazakhs, Kirghiz (kir gēz'), and other Turkic peoples speak related languages.

Various other ethnic groups also live in the Soviet Union. Latvians, Lithuanians, and Estonians live near the Baltic Sea. In the area around the Black Sea there are

Georgians and Armenians. Across Siberia, there are scattered groups of people whose languages and customs resemble those of American Indians and Inuit.

Although many of the Soviet people hold religious beliefs, religion is discouraged by the Communist government. Because of government controls, many believers do not attend church. The major religion in the country is the Russian Orthodox religion — a branch of Christianity. In the southwest, the chief faith is Eastern Orthodox, while Protestants are numerous in the region near the Baltic Sea. In Soviet Central Asia, many people are followers of Islam.

Where People Live Most Soviet people live in the western, European part of the country. The area of dense settlement is cone-shaped. The wide end of the cone is in the west, extending from the Caspian Sea along the Black Sea and the western border all the way to Finland. The pointed end of the cone lies across the Urals, past the city of Omsk. Settlement is also dense south of the Aral Sea in parts of Soviet Central Asia. Most of Siberia remains an unsettled, forbidding frontier.

As recently as the 1920's, more than 80 percent of the Soviet people lived in rural villages. Since then, the country has undergone dramatic industrialization and urbanization. Now about two thirds of the people live in urban areas.

The population is growing at about 1 percent a year. The Soviet government believes that population growth can help develop the sparsely populated east. After World War II, a war in which 27 million Soviets died, the government urged people to have large families. Today the government offers good housing and high wages to families willing to move east. Areas of recent growth lie mainly near the eastern tip of the cone of dense settlement (see map, page 335).

334

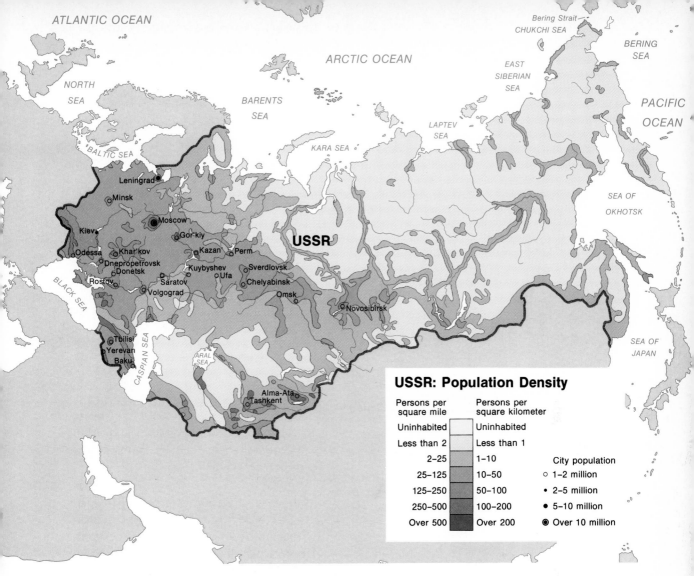

ATLANTIC OCEAN

ARCTIC OCEAN

NORTH SEA

BARENTS SEA

BALTIC SEA

Bering Strait
CHUKCHI SEA

BERING SEA

PACIFIC OCEAN

EAST SIBERIAN SEA

LAPTEV SEA

KARA SEA

SEA OF OKHOTSK

Leningrad
Minsk
Moscow
Kiev
Gor'kiy
Odessa
Khar'kov
Kazan'
Perm
Dnepropetrovsk
Donetsk
Kuybyshev
Sverdlovsk
Rostov
Saratov
Ufa
Chelyabinsk
Volgograd
Omsk
Novosibirsk
USSR

BLACK SEA
CASPIAN SEA
ARAL SEA

Tbilisi
Yerevan
Baku

Alma-Ata
Tashkent

SEA OF JAPAN

USSR: Population Density

Persons per square mile	Persons per square kilometer
Uninhabited	Uninhabited
Less than 2	Less than 1
2–25	1–10
25–125	10–50
125–250	50–100
250–500	100–200
Over 500	Over 200

City population
○ 1–2 million
• 2–5 million
● 5–10 million
◎ Over 10 million

Map Study *Name the Soviet Union's three largest cities in order of size from largest to smallest. Around which sea—the Black or the Aral—is population denser?*

Political Patterns

From the 1300's until 1917, Russia was ruled by the tsars. The capital of the tsarist government was St. Petersburg (now called Leningrad). Under the tsars, Russia gained control of an empire. The vast majority of the Russian people, however, were extremely poor. Most were peasants obliged to work for large landowners.

In the early 1900's, Russia began to develop industry. Large numbers of peasants came to St. Petersburg, Moscow, and the Baku oil fields. Wealth and power still rested with the tsarist government, the military, and upper-class landowners. The government, which was corrupt and cruel, had little popular support.

Establishing Communist Rule World War I brought a crisis in Russia. Millions of Russians died in the fighting, and Russia lost much land to Germany. The economy collapsed. Tsar Nicholas II responded to criticisms of his rule by exiling opponents to Siberia.

335

Republics of the Soviet Union

― Republic Boundary ★ National Capital

Map Study *What is the largest of the Soviet republics? Which republic lies furthest south? Which border the Caspian Sea?*

In 1917, the crisis became a revolution. Strikes and riots led by various groups of revolutionaries raged across the country. No longer able to rule, Nicholas resigned. A new republican government took power, but it proved weak. Within months, a group of Communists known as the **Bolsheviks** were able to overthrow this government.

The leader of the Bolsheviks was a young lawyer turned revolutionary named Vladimir Ilyich Ulyanov. Taking the name Lenin, he spread the doctrine of a German philosopher named Karl Marx. Marx had written that capitalism exploited the industrial working class. If society as a whole owned the means of production, Marx argued, then everyone would share equally in the wealth that was produced.

The Bolsheviks adapted Marx's theories to Russia. Lenin emphasized those parts of Marx's writings that called for violent revolution and dictatorial rule by the Communists. Impatient and bold, it was Lenin who urged the Bolsheviks to take power by force in 1917.

Lenin was the first head of Russia's Communist government. He gave his Bolsheviks a new name, the Communist party. This party quickly became the most powerful political group in Russia. During a bitter civil war that ended in 1920, they defeated their remaining rivals. They have ruled the country ever since.

The Communist System The Soviet Union's current constitution was written in 1977. Power to make laws is given to the Supreme Soviet, which is the highest

336

legislative body of the Soviet Union. Its members are elected by voters. The Supreme Soviet, however, is not often in session. Most legislative duties are carried out instead by the Presidium, a permanent executive committee. Members of the Presidium are chosen by the Supreme Soviet. Executive powers belong to the Council of Ministers, whose members are also selected by the Supreme Soviet. The head of this council is the **premier,** or head of the government.

The constitution does not specify the powers of the Communist party. Even so, the Communist party is the real power in Soviet government. Only party members may run for office. No other political parties are permitted to exist. In nearly all cases, only one name for each office appears on election ballots. Voters can vote for this candidate or no candidate at all. Once in office, party members carry out party policies.

Leningrad's Hermitage, once a palace of the tsars, is now a museum (top). St. Basil's Cathedral (bottom) is on Red Square.

The Government of the Soviet Union

THE COMMUNIST PARTY
Has no official powers under the constitution
Chooses candidates for the Supreme Soviet
Proposes top leaders of the government
Proposes laws

THE NATIONAL LEGISLATURE

Chairman of the Presidium of the Supreme Soviet
Serves as head of state
(May also serve as premier)

Presidium of the Supreme Soviet
Enacts laws between sessions of the Supreme Soviet

Supreme Soviet
Meets twice a year
Approves laws proposed by the Communist party
Has two houses, one representing districts and one representing nationalities

THE EXECUTIVE

Premier
Serves as chief executive
(Is often chairman of the Communist party)

Council of Ministers
Acts as the cabinet
Assists the premier

337

Two important leaders of the Soviet Union were Joseph Stalin and Nikita Khrushchev.

The first day of May, May Day, is a major holiday in the Soviet Union. In Moscow, a river of red flags—carried by delegations from various parts of the country—flows beneath leaders on a reviewing stand.

The Communist party exercises totalitarian control over life in the Soviet Union. All the country's newpapers and broadcast stations are owned by either the Communist party or the government. The party does not permit citizens to speak or write freely. Criticism of the party or government can lead to arrest and imprisonment. Citizens may not form organizations without the party's approval. Thus it is nearly impossible for those who disagree with the Communist party to influence politics.

Only about 10 percent of the Soviet people are members of the Communist party. To join, a citizen must be nominated by current party members who know her or him well. The person must perform work under the party's guidance for at least a year before becoming a member. The process ensures that only those who agree with Communist policies and are dedicated to the party will become members.

The top bodies of the Communist party are the Politburo and the Secretariat. The Politburo establishes the country's policies. The Secretariat carries out daily party work. It is directed by the single most powerful official in the country, the **general secretary**. In most cases, the general secretary is also the premier.

The Soviet Union has a federal system of government. There are 15 political divisions called republics. In 1922, Russia was renamed the Union of Soviet Socialist Republics to reflect the makeup of the country.

Each republic in the Soviet Union is based on the homeland of a major ethnic group. The Russian Soviet Federated Socialist Republic, for example, has a majority of Russians. Each republic has its own governing council called a soviet. As with the national government, all local officials are members of the Communist party.

The federal system is supposed to ensure that each ethnic group has its own territory and some privileges of self-government. However, absolute control belongs to the national government. In addition, the government has Russified the republics. That is, Russians who migrate to non-Russian republics receive special privileges. Because of this policy, Russians hold many good factory jobs and top positions in local government.

The official language of the Soviet Union is Russian. Members of all ethnic groups must learn Russian as well as their own language. Most Russians learn only their own language.

338

When protestors in Hungary, Czechoslovakia, and Poland sought more control over their own countries, the Soviet Union used military threats or actual intervention to prevent change. In Hungary and Czechoslovakia, Soviet troops were sent in to crush the protest movement. Popular, reform-minded leaders were removed from office with the help of the Soviet troops.

In recent years, the Soviet Union has assisted rebel groups in Latin American, African, and Asian countries. In most cases, these rebels were trying to replace a government friendly to the United States with one that would not be friendly to the United States. Two examples of such actions are Soviet aid for rebels who took power in Angola and Ethiopia in the 1970's.

In 1979, the Soviet Union acted to save a Communist government in its neighbor Afghanistan. Soviet troops invaded the country to battle an uprising by Afghans who opposed their government. The United States warned that this invasion was part of the Soviet Union's efforts to increase its control in the country and the region.

The Soviet Union has also had tense relations with China. Like the Soviet Union, China is a Communist country. The two countries share a long border. Once an ally of the Soviet Union, China disputes Soviet claims to lands along their border. Soviet and Chinese troops clashed over these lands in the 1960's and 1970's. China's quarrels with the Soviet Union are complicated by its disagreements with the Soviet Union over how to carry out Communist ideas. The Chinese agree with the United States that the Soviet Union is trying to gain control over less powerful countries. In recent years, however, Chinese and Soviet officials have met to discuss their differences.

Smaller and developing nations have often been drawn into the competition between the Soviet Union and the United States. Some countries align themselves with the Soviet Union. That is, they take the Soviet side on issues. Other countries usually are aligned with the United States. Many developing countries, however, have remained **nonaligned.** That is, they do not wish to link themselves with either superpower. China has encouraged countries to become nonaligned.

REVIEWING THE FACTS

Define

1. tsar
2. Russ
3. Soviet Central Asia
4. Bolsheviks
5. premier
6. general secretary
7. kolkhoz
8. sovkhoz
9. nonaligned

Answer

1. What is the largest ethnic group in the Soviet Union?

2. (a) In what part of the Soviet Union is population densest? (b) Sparsest?

3. Describe the role of the Communist party in the Soviet government.

4. (a) What are some factors in the weakness of Soviet agriculture? (b) What industrial products has the Soviet Union emphasized?

5. Why have Soviet relations with the United States and China been difficult?

Locate

Refer to the map on page 329.

Name the river on which each of the following cities lies: (a) Kiev, (b) Gor'kiy, (c) Omsk, (d) Novosibirsk, (e) Krasnoyarsk, (f) Yakutsk.

343

SPOTLIGHT ON SOVIET TEENS:

Growing Up in the Soviet Union

Six mornings a week, Monday through Saturday, students throughout the Soviet Union rush off to school. Like their counterparts in other countries, they study their native language, mathematics, science, and social studies. Many also learn a foreign language. English is the most popular choice.

After school, students do their homework. They also play soccer, listen to music, go to movies, and visit with friends. Rock music and American films are as popular in the Soviet Union as they are in Western Europe and the United States. So are jeans, tennis shoes, and T-shirts. Yet growing up in the Soviet Union is very different from growing up in the United States or Western Europe.

Some differences are cultural. Other differences are a result of the Soviet system of government. The government affects every part of Soviet life. It chooses which television programs will be aired and when, and what their content will be. It also controls the goods offered for sale in local stores.

Unlike Western students, Soviet teens cannot buy their jeans, tennis shoes, and tapes at a store. The government owns the stores, and it refuses to stock Western fashions or music. Shoppers can legally acquire such goods only by trading with an American or European tourist. For those who live in remote areas where few tourists venture, it is almost impossible to legally buy a pair of jeans. As a result, an illegal, or underground, trade has developed in the Soviet Union. The farther a place is from Moscow the higher the prices of Western goods. A pair of brand-name jeans, for example, may cost a So-viet teenager as much as $400 in Siberia.

The Soviet government controls more than TV viewing and shopping. It has a say in almost every part of a student's life. It determines what courses students may take, how their teachers teach those courses, and even what books they may read. The government even decides what kind of high school a student will attend.

At the end of eighth grade, everyone takes a series of tests. Those who score low must go to vocational or trade schools. Those who score high go to a high school that offers college preparatory courses. The government also selects a few students for special training. Many of those students show talent in athletics, dance, music, or theatre. Other students have extraordinary ability in science or mathematics.

Although higher education is free in the Soviet Union, not everyone who wants to go to college can do so. Students have to pass five qualifying tests before they are admitted to a university. They must also show their support for their country's system of government. One way to do so is by joining Komsomol, or the Young Communist League. Although membership does not guarantee a student a place at a university or technical institute, those who fail to join often have trouble getting in no matter how high their test scores are.

The government's involvement in a student's life does not end with graduation. The government assigns every graduate a job. Students must accept the job they are assigned and hold it for at least three years. Only then can Soviet citizens change jobs.

Map Study *In which regions is the Russian republic?*

3 Regions of the Soviet Union

The western part of the Soviet Union has long been the most developed region of the country. In recent years, however, the government has made plans to push eastward. Many Soviets feel that the eastern section, once regarded as a barren wasteland and place of exile for prisoners, will provide industrial opportunities in coming years.

Western Soviet Union

The heartland of the Soviet Union is made up of the western part of the Russian republic and the six republics lying between the Baltic and the Black seas. Early Russia took shape in this region. Today the western Soviet Union remains the center of the country's politics, population, and production.

The Richest Farming Area The western part of the Soviet Union lies in the fertile triangle. The Ukraine prairie has the best farmland in the Soviet Union. The growing season is long enough, and there is usually enough moisture to grow wheat, corn, sugar beets, sunflower seeds, and other crops. Farms in Belorussia and Moldavia are also productive. They grow various grains, potatoes, flax, sugar beets, and such fruits as grapes.

Rainfall is a major problem for these farmers. Except in the southern Ukraine,

345

Students should refer to this map as they read about the five regions of the Soviet Union.
Answer to Map Study question: Western Soviet Union, Western Siberia, and Eastern Siberia
Assign the Workbook activity for Chapter 13, Section 3, with pages 345–349.

The Soviet government has combined small farms into large ones and has encouraged the use of heavy machinery.

the western Soviet Union has frequent shortages of rainfall. Crops have failed because of droughts many times in recent years.

The center of the Soviet livestock industry is in the Ukraine. However, farmers there killed millions of cattle and sheep during the 1930's in protest against the creation of collective farms. As a result, Soviet ranching lagged for a time.

The Soviet diet is high in carbohydrates, especially bread and potatoes. Soviet planners have tried to increase the role of meats and dairy foods. They have encouraged farms to raise livestock. In the 1950's and 1960's, corn — to be used as feed for livestock — was planted in the warm, wet areas of the fertile triangle.

Steel is made in the Donets Basin.

Following World War I, attempts were begun to decentralize industry and develop new centers farther from the vulnerable western borders.

Industrial Areas The western Soviet Union has a number of major industrial areas. The Moscow Region surrounds the Soviet Union's capital city. Textile, chemical, and electronics factories are located there. The area is densely populated with factory workers and highly skilled professionals.

The Donets Basin lies near the Black Sea in the eastern Ukraine. This area has the Soviet Union's most productive coalfields. Less than 200 miles (320 kilometers) from the Donets Basin's coalfields are the vast iron-ore ranges of Krivoy Rog. Drawing on these resources, nearby cities, including Donetsk and Lugansk, produce iron and steel.

East of the Donets Basin, along the Volga River, is a newly developed industrial center. Its major cities are Kazin and Kuybyshev. More important to this region than the great Volga is the oil and gas field at Perm. This field is one of the Soviet Union's major sources of fuels. Since World War II, this area has developed oil and chemical refining, fertilizer making, and auto manufacturing.

Still farther east is the rich Ural mining district. There, great mines yield iron, copper, nickel, and other metals. Factories turn out steel and heavy machinery. The region is also a major oil-producing center.

Transcaucasia

Transcaucasia lies between the Black and Caspian seas. *Transcaucasia* means "across the Caucasus Mountains." Indeed, this towering range cuts off the region from the rest of the Soviet Union. The smallest of the five Soviet regions, Transcaucasia includes the republics of Georgia, Azerbaidzhan (az'ər bī jän') and Armenia. Transcaucasia has a warmer climate than any other part of the Soviet Union.

Industrial strength is often measured by iron and steel production. Since 1945, the Soviet Union has ranked second to the United States as the world's largest producer of both.

Most people who live in Transcaucasia are not Slavs. Rather, there is a mix of many different peoples. In the past, small bands of oppressed people from various places found refuge in the many valleys of Transcaucasia. Today a traveler in this region can hear many languages besides Russian.

A great deal of development has taken place in Transcaucasia under Soviet guidance. From Georgia and Azerbaidzhan come cotton, tobacco, olives, and almonds. Farmers in Georgia grow citrus fruits, tea, and grapes for wine. Such crops will not grow well anywhere else in the country.

Mineral and energy resources are also important. The world's largest manganese deposits are in Georgia. For a time, Azerbaidzhan was the world's largest oil producer. Many oil derricks dot the Caspian Sea near the republic's capital, Baku. Azerbaidzhan's reserves of petroleum have declined in recent years, so oil production has fallen off.

Economic activity in Armenia centers around the capital, Yerevan (yer'ə vän'). Synthetic rubber, textiles, tobacco products, and machinery are produced in the city's factories. Mining, crop growing, and livestock production thrive in the outlying areas.

Soviet Central Asia

The republic of Kazakhstan dominates Soviet Central Asia. South of this large republic are four smaller republics — Kirghizia (kir gē'zhē ə), Uzbekistan, Tadzhikistan (tä jik'i stan'), and Turkmenistan. Most people of the region are Muslims who speak Turkic languages. Traditional culture influences the celebration of holidays, music and arts, marriage customs, and other aspects of life in the region.

Soviet planners are in the process of developing Soviet Central Asia. In recent years, large parts of the Kazakhstan steppe, north of the Caspian Sea, have

Because of the housing shortage, grandparents often live with their children's families. Here, a grandmother and grandfather take care of their grandchildren. ● *Throughout Soviet Central Asia, farm women sell their produce at markets like this one in Frunze, Kirghizia.*

been plowed, planted, and irrigated. Farms are very large; most are kolkhozes. Major crops are wheat, oats, rye, and barley. In the driest areas, near the Caspian Sea, there is cattle and sheep grazing.

Turkmenistan and Uzbekistan, which lie in the southwest part of the region, are chiefly desert plains. With the help of irrigation, collectives there grow cotton, fruit, and vegetables. Goats and sheep graze on the steppe.

To the southwest, Tadzhikistan and Kirghizia are almost entirely mountainous. Traditionally areas of sheep raising, they too have croplands today. They produce cotton, rice and other grains, and fruits and vegetables.

When rainfall is good, the land of Soviet Central Asia is productive. In years of little rainfall, wheat and other crops fail. When vegetation withers, winds blow away the topsoil.

Mining and manufacturing have become key parts of the Soviet Central Asian economy in recent years. Kazakhstan is rich in minerals. It produces coal, lead, zinc, tungsten, and uranium. Before World War II, minerals from Kazakhstan

Novosibirsk is a center for art, science, and industry in Western Siberia.

were sent to the Urals to be used in factories there. Today, however, factories in Kazakhstan turn out many goods. Iron and steel, chemicals, and related manufactures are made near the city of Karaganda. The city of Alma-Ata is also a thriving industrial and commercial center. With the growth of industry, people have moved to the cities of Kazakhstan. More than half the republic's population lives in urban areas.

Western Siberia

The Western Siberian region is part of the giant Russian republic. It lies between the Urals and the Yenisey River. Most of the people of Western Siberia live in the taiga and steppe area. This area lies between tundra to the north and the Altai Mountains to the south. Even in the taiga and steppe, population is sparse. Villages are sometimes hundreds of miles apart. The vast northern tundra has almost no inhabitants. The Altai Mountains too have few people. Much of this range is a nature preserve. It is a protected park for antelope, deer, and the rare snow leopard.

The main agricultural area of Western Siberia lies in the steppe. There, soil is fertile. This area was first planted in recent years as part of the Soviet policy of expanding eastward.

Western Siberia fits into the Soviet government's plan to develop industries in the east. Because of its great expanse, the rugged terrain, and the extreme cold, development is not easy. Yet much of Western Siberia is rich in oil deposits. To tap these deposits, the Soviet government has invested great sums of money in the region.

Western Siberia has coal as well as natural gas. In fact, the region may have enough natural gas in reserve to supply the entire world for thousands of years at present rates of use. There are plans for

Soviet Central Asia is one of the warmer regions of the Soviet Union. Have students look at the physical map on page 329 and the climate map on page 331. What type of climate is predominant in this region? *(arid)* Have them name two deserts in this region. *(Karakum and Betpak-Dala.)*

the construction of a pipeline to carry gas to cities west of the Urals. The pipeline will eventually be linked with Western Europe, enabling the Soviets to sell natural gas to many countries, including Italy, France, and West Germany.

Just east of Novosibirsk (nō'vō sə birsk'), Western Siberia's largest city, is a mining and industrial area called the Kuznetsk Basin. Like the Donets Basin, it has large deposits of high-quality coal and iron ore. It produces steel, aluminum, and heavy transportation goods like railroad cars and locomotives.

Eastern Siberia

Eastern Siberia is a land of plains, plateaus, and mountains. To the north, there is tundra. To the south are thick forests. Reaching from the Yenisey River to the Pacific, Eastern Siberia is the largest, least populated, and least developed of all Soviet regions.

The Trans-Siberian Railroad, running close to the southern Soviet border, threads together the isolated villages of Eastern Siberia and connects the region with the western Soviet Union. The Soviets have built a new railroad in Eastern Siberia to link up with the Trans-Siberian Railroad and the port of Vladivostok. With the new railroad, Soviet planners hope to promote the further development of Eastern Siberia's resources for shipment to industrialized parts of the country.

Eastern Siberia has coal, natural gas, and waterpower resources. Wood, fish, gold, and tin are also plentiful. Soviet plans for developing Eastern Siberia have moved slowly so far. Workers are in short supply. Therefore, the government has offered higher wages and extra benefits to people who move to the area. Even so, most people who venture to Eastern

The Pacific Ocean port of Vladivostok lies about 4,000 miles east of Moscow.

Siberia stay there only a short time. They return to the west, putting the long, harsh winters and frontier living conditions behind them.

REVIEWING THE FACTS

Answer

1. Why is the western Soviet Union considered the country's heartland?

2. What economic development has occurred in Transcaucasia?

3. What has been done to improve the economy of Soviet Central Asia?

4. In what ways is Siberia important to the future of the Soviet Union?

Locate

Refer to the maps on pages 336 and 486–487.

Identify the following neighbors of the Soviet Union: (a) country lying northwest of Leningrad, (b) country lying south of Uzbekistan, (c) country lying west of Vladivostok, (d) country lying south of Kamchatka.

349

Highlighting the Chapter

1. The Union of Soviet Socialist Republics, or the Soviet Union, is the world's largest country. Its western portion lies on the Great European Plain. The great taiga — the world's largest forest — begins on this plain. The region's climate is moist and cold in the north, warmer and drier in the south. The plains end at the Ural Mountains. To the east of the Urals is Siberia, a vast region of plains, plateaus, mountains, and basins. The southern part of the country has prairie in the west and steppe in the central parts. Mountain ranges rim most of the extreme southern edges.

2. The Soviet Union includes a population of great ethnic diversity. Each of its 15 republics is based on a homeland of one of the country's major ethnic groups. The Russians, a Slavic people, make up the largest group. The Soviet Communist party controls the government, the economy, and the lives of citizens. Freedom of speech and religion are severely restricted. Under the party's rule, the Soviet Union went from a farming nation to a major industrial power.

3. The regions of the Soviet Union differ in their economic development. The western Soviet Union is the most highly developed region. It includes heavy industry and mining centers in the Moscow Region, the Donets Basin, and other areas. Large farms in the Ukraine and neighboring republics grow grains and other crops. In Transcaucasia, there are large farms, mines, oil wells, and thriving factories. Soviet Central Asia has recently become an important agricultural center. It also has rich deposits of minerals and growing iron and steel, chemical, and other industries. In Western Siberia, factories in the Kuznetsk Basin manufacture steel and heavy equipment. The Soviet Union is also producing oil and natural gas from its unequaled Siberian storehouse.

350

Speaking Geographically

Number your paper from 1 to 7. Then write the letter of the correct definition for each of the terms below.

1. kolkhoz
2. general secretary
3. tsar
4. Soviet Central Asia
5. sovkhoz
6. Russ
7. Bolsheviks

a. state farm, land of which is owned by the Soviet government

b. group of Russian revolutionaries later known as the Communist party

c. absolute monarch of Russia

d. collective farm, land of which is owned by a group of farmers

e. top official in the Soviet Communist party

f. Scandinavian people that dominated Slavs in the Ukraine in the 800's

g. area of the Soviet Union lying between the Caspian Sea and China

Testing Yourself

Number your paper from 1 to 5. Write the term that best completes each sentence below.

1. The (Ural, Altai, Caucasus) Mountains stand between the European and Asian parts of the Soviet Union.

2. The Soviet Union's system of government is (tsarist, unitary, Communist).

3. (Ukrainian, Belorussian, Russian) is the official language of the Soviet Union.

4. The best farming area of the Soviet Union lies in (Siberia, the Ukraine, the Sayan Mountains).

5. The (Donets Basin, Kuznetsk Basin, taiga) is a mining and industrial area in Siberia.

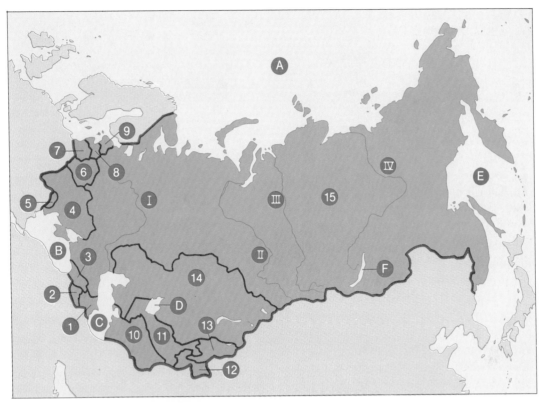

Building Map Skills

The map on this page shows a number of geographic features of the Soviet Union. Each number on the map represents a political subdivision; each letter represents a body of water; and each Roman numeral represents a river. On your paper, write the numbers 1 to 15, the letters A to F, and the Roman numerals I to IV. Beside each, write the correct name of the geographic feature it represents.

Applying Map Skills

On your paper, list the following cities in west-to-east order.

Archangel'sk
Leningrad
Moscow
Murmansk
Novosibirsk

Odessa
Sverdlovsk
Tashkent
Vladivostok
Volgograd

Exploring Further

1. For a week, collect articles from newspapers and magazines dealing with Soviet-American relations. Pay special attention to such matters as nuclear-arms-limitation talks. Do you find more examples of rivalry or cooperation?

2. Choose one of the following ethnic groups living in the Soviet Union: Armenians, Latvians, Lithuanians, Estonians. Research the history, customs, language, and religion of the group you have selected. Present your findings so that your classmates will understand the group and its way of life.

3. One of the best-known examples of music written by a Russian composer is the "1812 Overture," by Peter Tchaikovsky. Locate a copy of the overture and listen to it in class. Then have various students report on Tchaikovsky's life and the historical event on which the "1812 Overture" is based.

351

The photograph shows Xi'an Province of Shanxi, China.

East Asia

Eight countries make up East Asia. On the mainland of Asia are China, Mongolia, North Korea, and South Korea. There are also two small mainland territories— Macau, which is a province of Portugal, and Hong Kong, a British colony. Japan and Taiwan are island countries lying off Asia's eastern coast. China has far more land than all the other countries of the region combined.

The most striking feature of East Asia is its huge population. About a fourth of Earth's population live in the region. China alone has over a billion residents.

East Asia was the home of ancient civilizations in China, Korea, and Japan. Until this century, most of its people lived by farming. Their tools and methods had changed little since ancient times.

Today East Asia is experiencing exciting changes in both economics and politics. Its countries are among the world's leaders in manufacturing and trade. Japan's production of manufactured goods is surpassed only by the United States and the Soviet Union. In China, a time of turbulence has brought surprising changes. After 30 years of strict government control, a new group of leaders is experimenting with a blend of Communism and capitalism. The country is also ending its isolation from the rest of the world. In this chapter, you will learn more about the changing face of East Asia.

352

1 The Physical Environment

East Asia is divided into two distinct areas. There is a vast mainland area, from which juts a large peninsula to the south of the Yalu River. Three groups of islands lie to the east of the mainland. They are the archipelago of Japan, an island arc known as the Ryuku (rē ü′kü′) Islands, and Taiwan (tī′wän′) with its neighboring islands.

Map Study   *What desert does the Great Wall of China cross? What East Asian countries are islands? In what country are East Asia's highest landforms located? Name these landforms.*

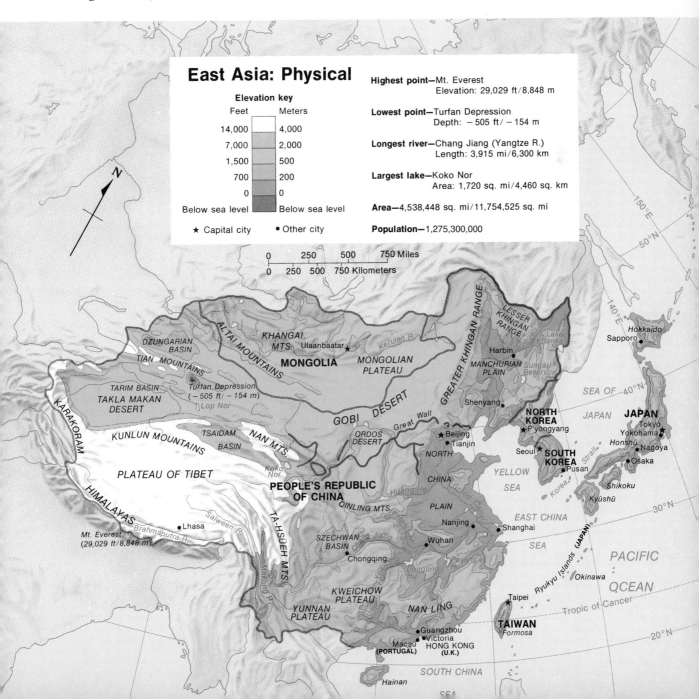

East Asia: Physical

Elevation key

Feet	Meters
14,000	4,000
7,000	2,000
1,500	500
700	200
0	0
Below sea level	Below sea level

★ Capital city   • Other city

Highest point—Mt. Everest
Elevation: 29,029 ft / 8,848 m

Lowest point—Turfan Depression
Depth: −505 ft / −154 m

Longest river—Chang Jiang (Yangtze R.)
Length: 3,915 mi / 6,300 km

Largest lake—Koko Nor
Area: 1,720 sq. mi / 4,460 sq. km

Area—4,538,448 sq. mi / 11,754,525 sq. mi

Population—1,275,300,000

Landforms

The East Asian mainland has mountains that are among the highest in the world. These mountains circle the interior of the region and its coastal lowlands.

Several ranges of low mountains rise along China's southern border. In the southeast, there is a series of plateaus along the boundary with Southeast Asia. To the west are the Himalaya (him'ə lā'ə) Mountains, the high Plateau of Tibet, and the Karakoram (kar'ə kōr'əm) Mountains. People call this high area the roof of the world. *Himalaya*, which means "house of snow," is a reminder that these mountains are always snowcapped. Much of Tibet is also snow-covered year round.

China's northwest is separated from the Soviet Union by the Tian Mountains. This range lies between two low-lying basins—the Tarim (dä'rēm') Basin and the Dzungarian (zung'gar'ē ən) Basin. East of these basins is central China, a region of mountains and plateaus.

The region's northern boundary with the Soviet Union is also a highland area. The Altai Mountains extend from the Soviet Union into western Mongolia. In the extreme northeast, highlands cross the Korean Peninsula.

The mainland's only plains lie in the eastern part of China. To the north, the Manchurian Plain is wedged between interior uplands and coastal highlands. A larger lowland area, the North China Plain, extends southward from the Beijing region well past the Huang He, also called the Yellow River. Just north of the Yangzi River (now called the Chang Jiang), rugged hills break up the North China Plain. Aside from coastal plains and a lowland along the Xi (shē) River, this southeastern area is hilly.

East Asia is part of the Rim of Fire, an area of volcanoes and earthquakes that circles much of the Pacific Ocean (pages 235–237). Earthquakes are a constant hazard. The two deadliest earthquakes in history, for example, struck in China. More than 800,000 people lost their lives in an earthquake there in 1556. A quake in 1976 claimed about the same number of victims.

The islands scattered off the eastern coast of Asia are especially prone to earthquakes and volcanic activity. These islands were formed millions of years ago by volcanoes that erupted as the Pacific plate was driven under a deep trench off the coast of Asia. Tall, volcanic mountains with snow-covered peaks rise from the center of the islands. These mountains slope downward to narrow coastal plains.

Climate and Ecosystems

East Asia lies at latitudes similar to much of the United States. Its climate patterns too are like those of the United States.

The northern and western part of the mainland are arid and semiarid areas. Tibet is dry and cold because of its high elevation. Three great deserts—the parched Gobi, the Ordos, and the Takla Makan—extend across much of the west-central mainland. To the northwest is a large steppe region in the Dzungarian Basin.

If not for the Himalayas and the Plateau of Tibet, these arid parts of central China would be wet. As it is, the southern highlands block the moist, warm air moving north from the Indian Ocean.

In the east, the mainland has a climate a bit like that of the eastern United States. The southeast is humid subtropical. Temperatures are moderate all year, and there is abundant rainfall. The northeast has a humid continental climate. There is

354

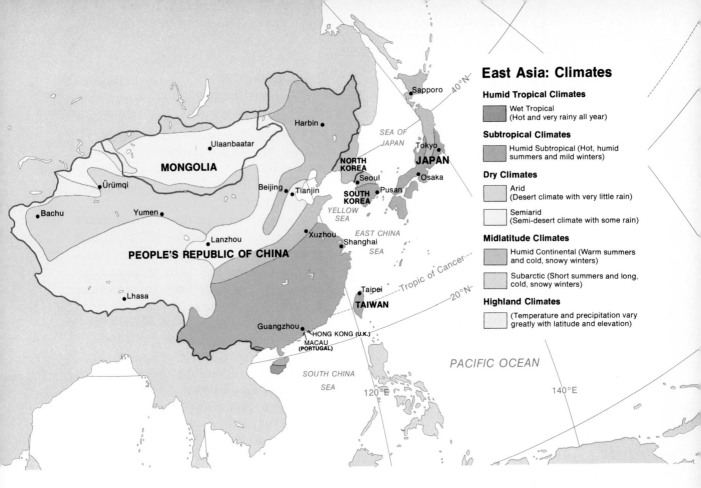

East Asia: Climates

Humid Tropical Climates

Wet Tropical
(Hot and very rainy all year)

Subtropical Climates

Humid Subtropical (Hot, humid
summers and mild winters)

Dry Climates

Arid
(Desert climate with very little rain)

Semiarid
(Semi-desert climate with some rain)

Midlatitude Climates

Humid Continental (Warm summers
and cold, snowy winters)

Subarctic (Short summers and long,
cold, snowy winters)

Highland Climates

(Temperature and precipitation vary
greatly with latitude and elevation)

Map Study *What is the climate in most of Mongolia? Where in China
is it hot and rainy throughout the year? What East Asian countries
have mid-latitude climate regions? Regions with dry climates? Areas
of highland climate?*

enough rainfall for farming, but the
winters are long and cold.

Monsoons affect the weather of Korea,
Taiwan, and parts of Japan. During the
summer, the monsoon comes from the
Pacific. It brings heavy rains and hot temperatures. The monsoon shifts during
winter, carrying cold, dry air from inland
areas. The area's weather can then become bitterly cold.

East Asia's largest forests are in China,
in the highlands just northwest of Korea.
Forested lands also cover hillsides in
Korea, Japan, and Taiwan. On the mainland, the coastal lowlands have been
cleared of forests.

REVIEWING THE FACTS

Answer

1. Where are East Asia's lowlands found?

2. (a) Describe the effects of the Himalaya Mountains and the Plateau of Tibet
on the climate of west-central China.
(b) Of monsoons on the climate of Korea,
Japan, and Taiwan.

Locate

Refer to the map on page 353.

1. (a) Name the river that flows through
the Ordos. (b) The Szechwan Basin.

2. Into what sea does the Xi River drain?

Answers to Map Study questions: Mongolia—semiarid; always hot and rainy—Southeast
China; midlatitude climates—China, North and South Korea, Japan, Mongolia; dry climates—
China and Mongolia; highland climate—China and Mongolia
Answers to numbered questions are in the Teacher's Guide.

355

2 The Human Imprint

The physical features of East Asia tend to isolate its people from other regions of the world. The lowland plains, where most people of the region live, are thousands of miles from other population centers. To the east is the great Pacific Ocean. The southern, western, and northern boundaries of the mainland are mountainous. For hundreds of years, the countries of the region deliberately kept themselves apart from the industrialized nations of Western Europe and North America. Since World War II, however, East Asia has undergone rapid change. It now has many links with the world community of nations.

The People of East Asia

Most of East Asia's people live on less than a fifth of the region's land. The most heavily populated areas are the temperate and moist lands on the eastern part of the mainland and the coastal plains on the islands. In these areas, population is extremely dense. Large expanses of the region, however, have few people. There, the land is too high, too wet, too dry, or too cold to support farming or large settlements.

Population East Asia has a great many large cities. In fact, China has more cities with over a million residents than any other country in the world. Despite its many cities, however, China has a mostly rural population. Over 80 percent of its people live in farming villages. The Manchurian Plain, the Huang He Valley, the Szechwan (sech wan) Basin, and the North China Plain are the most densely settled farming areas of the world.

In the rest of East Asia, the proportion of people living in cities is greater. Nearly 90 percent of the people of Hong Kong, for example, are city dwellers. Japan's population is about three quarters urban.

Settlement in some parts of Japan is very dense. Japan is about the size of California, but its population is about half that of the United States. Nearly 25 million people live in Tokyo and nearby Yokohama alone.

In spite of its great density, East Asia's population is growing slowly. The annual growth rate for the region is about 1 percent. However, a 1 percent annual increase in China's population of more than 1 billion results in an addition of more than 10 million people each year. Therefore, China's government discourages large families. Couples are penalized if they have more than one child.

Ethnic Groups Each country of East Asia is dominated by a single ethnic group. In China, for example, the largest group by far is the Han, who make up about 94 percent of the population. Nearly the entire population of the eastern half of China is Han. In addition to the Han, however, China has over 50 other peoples. These smaller ethnic groups are scattered around China's northern, western, and southern borders.

Most of China's people speak one of the Sino-Tibetan languages. The Han speak various **dialects** of Han Chinese. Dialects are forms of a language that differ from one another in vocabulary, pronunciation, and grammar. Speakers of one Chinese dialect may not understand those who speak another. The great majority of Han Chinese speak the Mandarin dialect. *Mandarin* means "commonly understood language." The Mandarin dialect is the official form of the Chinese language.

All of China's languages are written in the same way. Instead of an alphabet, the Chinese use thousands of **characters**. Each character is a series of pen or brush

356

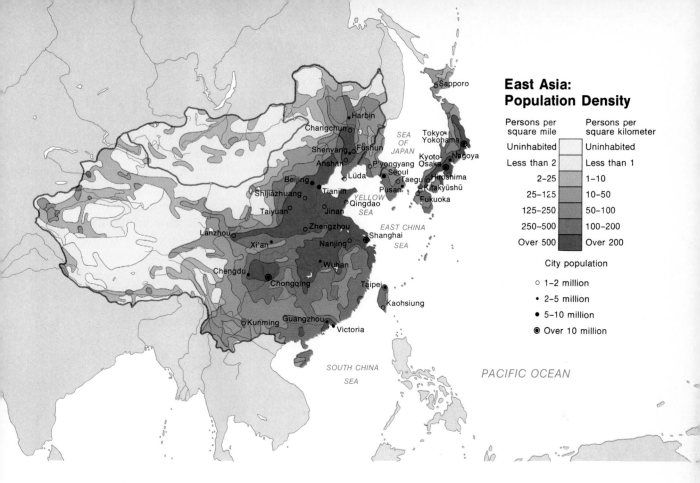

**East Asia:
Population Density**

Persons per square mile	Persons per square kilometer
Uninhabited	Uninhabited
Less than 2	Less than 1
2–25	1–10
25–125	10–50
125–250	50–100
250–500	100–200
Over 500	Over 200

City population

○ 1–2 million
• 2–5 million
● 5–10 million
◉ Over 10 million

Map Study   *In what part of East Asia is population concentrated?
What areas are uninhabited? Name East Asia's four largest cities.*

strokes representing a word or syllable. (In this textbook and in English-language newspapers and magazines, Chinese words are written by means of the English alphabet. Letters spell the sounds of the spoken Chinese words.)

As in China, nearly all the people of Japan belong to one ethnic group. Ancestors of the Japanese probably included ancient inhabitants of Japan as well as those who had migrated from the mainland and from islands to the south. Japanese is the country's chief language. Like Chinese, it is written in characters. Japanese characters were borrowed from the Chinese in the sixth century. Over the years, the Japanese have adapted the characters so that they are now distinct from those of the Chinese.

East Asia's Religions   Religion has played an important part in shaping the cultures of East Asia. Three major religions — Confucianism (kən fyü′shə niz′əm), Taoism (daú′iz′əm), and Shintoism — began in the region. In addition, religions from other parts of the world spread to East Asia. There, religious practices and beliefs often blended. Today the region's main religions have many elements in common.

Most influential in China was Confucianism. Confucianism began as a set of teachings based on the sayings of Confucius, a philosopher born in China about 550 B.C. Confucius lived at a time of great disorder. He believed that China's unrest would end only when people learned to treat one another with respect. He taught

357

Using a Graph to Make Comparisons

Texas Essential Element 1C. Geographical tools and methodologies.

The world is constantly changing. Tectonic plates move gradually, altering the appearance of Earth's surface. Climate patterns shift, bringing changes in temperature and rainfall across Earth.

Some changes can be quantified. For example, scientists can record temperatures in degrees Fahrenheit or Celsius. They can measure rainfall in inches or centimeters. A line graph presents a picture of such changes over a given period of time.

The line graph on this page shows information on changes in birth rates in four countries during a 12-year period. The birth rate is the number of births in a country for every 1,000 people that live there. Three of the countries on the graph are in Asia. The fourth, Costa Rica, is in Middle America. The graph's legend tells you which line on the graph represents the birth rate in each country.

The numbers along the left side, or vertical axis, show the birth rate. The numbers along the bottom of the graph, or the horizontal axis, indicate individual years for which information on birth rates was recorded. By using these two axes and the four lines on the graph, you can see how the birth rate changed in each country from 1962 to 1984. Because information for all four countries is plotted together on one graph, making comparisons is much easier.

1. Which country had the highest birth rate for the years 1974–1984?

2. During which years was the birth rate in China and Taiwan the same?

3. How did birth rates in all four countries change during the years 1968–1970?

4. (a) Describe the overall pattern of China's birth rate from 1962 to 1984. (b) Contrast this pattern with that of Costa Rica.   *Answers are in the Teacher's Guide.*

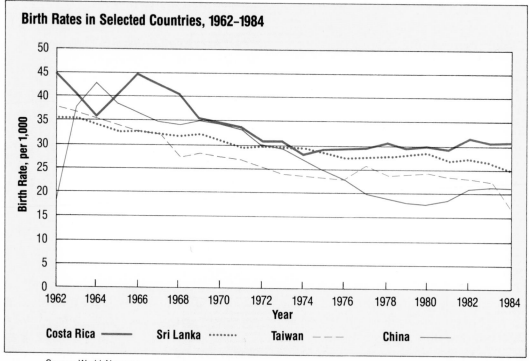

Birth Rates in Selected Countries, 1962–1984

Costa Rica ———   Sri Lanka ·······   Taiwan – – –   China ———

Source: World Almanac

that children should honor their parents and that citizens should obey their rulers. Parents and rulers should exercise their responsibilities in a just way. In later years, books of Confucian thought became the basis for China's educational system. While the practice of Confucian religion has declined in recent years, Confucian ideas still affect the thinking of many Chinese.

Another religion that began in China is Taoism. It developed about 2,000 years ago. Taoism emphasizes the importance of living in harmony with nature.

About 500 years before the birth of Taoism, one of Asia's great religions, Buddhism, originated in India. Buddhism stresses meditation, withdrawal from worldly desires, and respect for all forms of life. By the first century A.D., Indian traders had brought Buddhism to China. It steadily gained followers and spread to Tibet, Korea, and Japan.

A religion known as Shintoism developed in ancient Japan. Shintoists worshiped many nature gods and goddesses and revered the emperor of Japan as the offspring of the sun goddess. Those who practiced Shinto altered the religion as they came into contact with Buddhism and Confucianism. Today many Shintoists still worship the kami — or gods and goddesses — in simple wooden shrines.

Political Patterns

With the exception of Mongolia, every country in East Asia adopted its present form of government after World War II. Only Japan has a truly representative government. The rest of the region's countries have authoritarian governments. Mongolia, North Korea, and China have Communist systems. Until recently, both Taiwan and South Korea had one-party governments.

A temple in Kyoto, the old capital of Japan, shows the love for tradition and natural beauty that marks Japanese culture.

Japanese Democracy For hundreds of years before World War II, Japan was ruled by authoritarian leaders. Control of the government shifted between powerful families and strong military leaders. These leaders tried to keep foreign influences — particularly those brought by Western European traders and missionaries — out of Japan. As a result, Japan was isolated from outside developments like the Industrial Revolution.

In 1868, a group of reformers won control of the emperor's government. With the cooperation of the young emperor, these reformers strengthened the central government and urged Japan to learn from the industrialized countries of Western Europe. This time of reform is known as the Meiji (mā′jē′) period. *Meiji* means "enlightened rule." The reformers also gave Japan its first written constitution in 1890. The constitution provided for a government in which the emperor was to be the highest authority. He was assisted by a prime minister and a legislative body called the Diet.

359

You may wish to have students review the discussion of democratic, authoritarian, and totalitarian forms of government on pages 166–168.

During the early twentieth century, Japan joined other world powers in a quest for empire. After a brief war with Russia in 1904 and 1905, Japan seized territory in Manchuria, as northeastern China is known, and took all of Korea.

A group of military leaders and industrialists pushed for larger conquests. Japan attacked China in 1931. By the late 1930's, Japan and China were fighting a full-scale war. China fell into Japan's hands in 1940.

During World War II, Japan was allied with Germany. The Japanese overran islands in the South Pacific and several countries in Southeast Asia. Japan also attacked the United States at Pearl Harbor, Hawaii, in December 1941. This attack led to a bitter war against the United States and its allies. Japan surrendered in 1945, a few weeks after the United States had dropped nuclear bombs on the cities of Hiroshima and Nagasaki.

This park in Hiroshima is a memorial to those who died or were injured in the atomic bombing of the city in 1945.

Japan's defeat in World War II led to big changes in the country. The Japanese lost the lands they had taken before and during World War II. Under the orders of the United States, Japan adopted a new constitution. The government became parliamentary in form. The emperor's role was reduced to that of symbolic head of state. In the words of the constitution, "land, sea, and air forces, as well as other war potential, will never be maintained" by Japan. That is, Japan pledged to seek peaceful relations with other countries.

Under the new constitution, Japan has been a stable democracy. It now maintains only enough military forces to defend itself. Although Japan and the United States compete economically, the two countries have been firm allies since the 1950's.

China For thousands of years, China was an empire ruled by a series of royal families. The country had a rich and complex culture. Its art and technology were highly developed. For example, the Chinese created fine paintings, bronze bowls, and porcelain (a fired clay called china). They were the first people to make paper, the magnetic compass, gunpowder, and movable type.

The Chinese strictly limited trade and contacts with outsiders. China's leaders did not believe that other cultures had much to offer. However, in the 1800's the government allowed European companies to trade in China. Portugal took over the port of Macau (mə kau'), and Great Britain made Hong Kong a colony.

The people of China still did not want foreigners in their country. In 1911, rebels overthrew China's rulers, the Manchus, and set up a republic. A military government replaced the new republic in 1912.

By the 1920's, China was engulfed in a bitter civil war. On one side were feudal

360

warlords and supporters of military rule. The other side included a group called the Nationalists, led by Chiang Kai-shek (jē äng' kī'shek'), and the tiny Chinese Communist party, whose leader was Mao Zedong (maù'zə dùng').

In 1928, the Nationalists won control of China's government. By this time, the Nationalists and the Communists had become bitter enemies. Chiang's group set up a one-party dictatorship. The Communists fled to the countryside. There, they began a long war against Chiang's government.

Both the Nationalists and the Communists fought against Japanese invaders during the 1930's and 1940's. After the defeat of the Japanese, however, the civil war intensified. In 1949, the Communists drove the Nationalists off the mainland of China. The Nationalists set up a government on the island of Taiwan, where many Chinese already lived.

The Communists proclaimed the People's Republic of China on the mainland. As in other Communist countries, the government of the People's Republic is controlled by the Communist party. Today the People's Republic is recognized by the United Nations as the official representative of the Chinese people.

Until the 1960's, the People's Republic had close ties with the Soviet Union. During the 1960's, the Chinese and the Soviets had several sharp quarrels. Troops clashed along the heavily armed border. Eventually, the Soviet Union cut off aid to China.

About the same time, China went through the **Cultural Revolution.** The Cultural Revolution was an effort by radical leaders to speed up change in China. The radicals believed that China could not achieve the aims of Communism without violently attacking old ways of life. They tried to keep out foreign ideas.

Between 1976 and 1987, Deng Xiao-ping worked to modernize China.

Many top leaders of the Chinese Communist party were accused of spreading old ideas. Radicals removed thousands of these leaders from their positions. Many of them were jailed or killed. Violent street clashes erupted between radicals and their opponents.

The hold of the radicals weakened during the 1970's. China began to seek ties with foreign countries. Finally, after Mao Zedong died in 1976, moderates gained control of the Communist party and the government. Led by Deng Xiao-ping (dəng' shaù'ping') until mid-1987, this group relaxed government controls and tried to improve the economy.

The Two Koreas Before World War II, Korea was a single country controlled by Japan. As the war ended, the Soviet army held northern Korea. Southern Korea was occupied by the United States armed forces. The Soviets blocked elections that would have reunited Korea. In 1948, two separate governments were set up.

North Korea invaded South Korea in 1950. The fighting ended after three years, with Korea still divided. In 1972, the two governments agreed that the country should be reunited. However, relations remain strained, and the two

361

WORLD DATA BANK

Country	Area in Square Miles	Population/Natural Increase		Per Capita GNP
China	3,705,390	1,062,000,000	(1.3%)	$ 310
Japan	143,749	122,200,000	(0.6%)	11,330
North Korea	46,541	21,400,000	(2.5%)	NA
South Korea	38,023	42,100,000	(1.4%)	2,180
Mongolia	604,247	2,000,000	(2.6%)	NA
Taiwan	12,456	19,600,000	(1.2%)	NA

countries distrust each other. Today both Koreas keep troops along their border.

The Communist government of North Korea is extremely harsh. For example, home radios have dials fixed to government broadcasts. The secret police keep close track of people's activities. North Koreans have almost no voice in governing. The government tells people where they may live and work.

South Korea is strongly anti-Communist. Since 1948, it has had a constitutional government. However, most of the power rested with the president. Over the years, there have been military coups aimed at increasing the power of the president. Until recently, people risked arrest if they spoke out. Yet South Koreans continued to demand greater freedom.

In 1987, the Korean people voted in favor of a new constitution, which the government wrote under pressure. The government has also approved a free, direct presidential election scheduled for December 1987, the first since 1971.

Mongolia China's neighbor to the north, Mongols, nomadic warriors, ruled an area reaching from western Russia to Korea during the 1200's. In the 1680's, China conquered Mongolia.

Outer Mongolia, the northern part of Mongolia, gained independence from China in 1924. It set up a Communist government and became known officially as the Mongolian People's Republic. Mongolia is a close ally of the Soviet Union. Many Soviet troops are stationed in the country today.

Economic Patterns

Despite the growth of manufacturing in much of East Asia, economic activities vary greatly from country to country. Some East Asian nations are industrial powers, while in others most people farm much as their ancestors did.

Agriculture In the wet, densely peopled areas of East Asia, farming is intensive. Rice has been the major crop since ancient times. It is grown in fields called **paddies.** The best places for growing rice are flat lands with heavy rains and a warm climate. The major rice-growing areas, therefore, are the southern parts of the region. In lowlands, farmers flood their paddies to keep weeds from growing. Rice is also grown on terraced hillsides. There, by flooding terraced paddies and planting several crops a year, farmers get large harvests from even small plots of land.

In areas with less water, farmers grow wheat and other grains. Wheat is the chief crop in northern China. Where there is too little rainfall to support farming, crops are sometimes grown with the help of irrigation. In Mongolia and parts of central and western China, people raise flocks of sheep and goats.

East Asians turn to the sea as a source of protein. China and Japan together account for more than a fourth of the world's annual catch of ocean fish. Fishing is an important activity in all other East Asian countries except landlocked Mongolia. In addition to ocean fishing, there is widespread fish-farming, or the raising of fish in ponds.

Modern Industry and Trade East Asia sells manufactured goods all over the world. Anyone living in the United States can readily understand the impact of East Asia's trade. Think of the typical consumer goods that Americans buy. Clothing labels often read, "Made in Korea" or "Made in Taiwan." Many Americans drive Japanese-made cars. Tableware and

Map Study *What is North Korea's major energy resource? How is most land used in Mongolia? In Eastern China?*

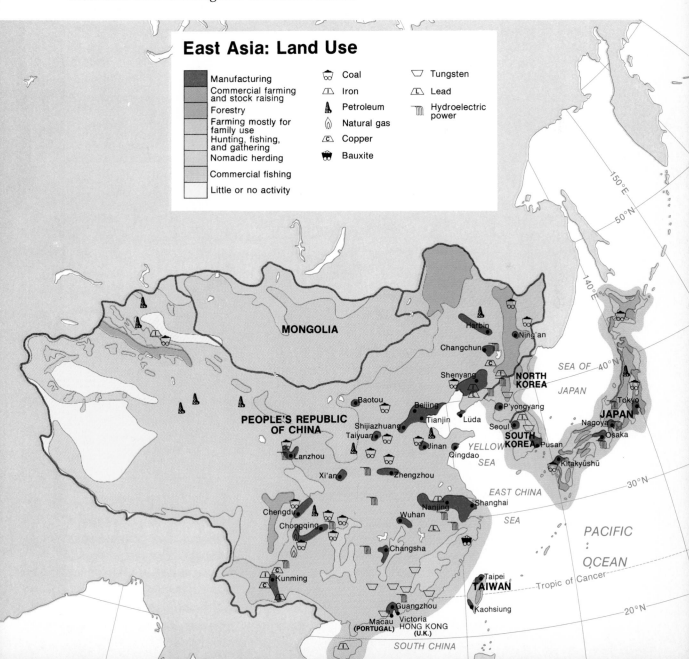

Texas Essential Elements 1C. Geographical tools and methodologies. 4C. Population distribution, growth, and movements.

Reading a Cartogram

As you have learned, maps are drawn according to scale. The sizes at which areas are shown depends on the scale used by the mapmaker.

Some special maps use a special kind of scale. For example, a mapmaker might want to show how countries differ in steel production, in per capita GNP, in oil use, or in some other way. To do so, the mapmaker can use a cartogram, in which the sizes at which countries are shown varies—not according to their areas—but according to how much steel they produce, to how high their per capital GNP's are, to how much oil they use, or to any other measure that is chosen.

The map on this page is a population cartogram. It shows the countries of the world at sizes determined by how large their populations are.

Use the population cartogram to answer the following questions.

1. Turn to the world map on pages 486–487. Canada is the world's second largest country in area. Compare Canada as it appears on the world map with Canada as it appears on the cartogram on this page. How does Canada's size on the cartogram differ from its size on the world map?

2. Look again at the map on pages 486–487. (a) Which country is largest in area? (b) Which country is largest on the map on this page?

3. Compare Japan on the two maps.

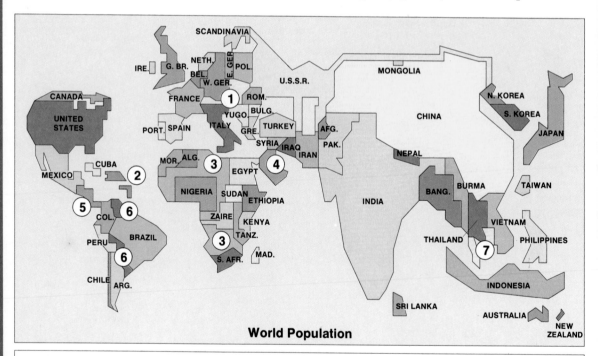

World Population

1 Other European nations

2 Other Caribbean nations

3 Other African nations

4 Other Middle Eastern nations

5 Central American nations

6 Other South American nations

7 Other Southeast Asian nations

Answers are in the Teacher's Guide.

Assign the Workbook activity for this chapter's Map Workshop with this page.

cookware, microwave ovens, radios, televisions, and stereo equipment are all imported from East Asia.

East Asia's growing trade is part of a remarkable change in the world's economy. For nearly 400 years, from the 1600's to the 1970's, most trade and manufacturing took place in countries that border the Atlantic Ocean. They include the countries of Western Europe, the United States, and Canada. Since the late 1970's, the **Pacific Rim** has become the leading industrial and trade area. The Pacific Rim includes those countries that border or lie in the Pacific Ocean. The United States and Canada are part of the Pacific Rim. So are New Zealand, Australia, the countries of Southeast Asia, and the nations of East Asia. The countries of the Pacific Rim produce over half the world's goods and services today.

REVIEWING THE FACTS

Define

1. dialect
2. character
3. Cultural Revolution
4. paddy
5. Pacific Rim

Answer

1. What is the largest, most important ethnic group in China?

2. What are the chief religions of East Asia?

3. List the Communist countries of East Asia.

4. How are East Asia's economic patterns changing?

Locate

Refer to the map on page 364.

Which East Asian country is most sparsely populated?

3 The East Asian Mainland

China, the third largest country in the world, occupies most of mainland East Asia. Its neighbors are Mongolia to the north, North and South Korea to the northeast, and the tiny colonies of Macau and Hong Kong to the southeast.

The People's Republic of China

China dominates East Asia. It has the most people and the largest area. Its religious practices, form of government, and system of writing have influenced other countries in the region. Yet until recently, China's economy has grown very slowly. Since ancient times, China's greatest effort has gone toward raising food for its huge population. Even today the country is largely agricultural, and the standard of living is not high.

Recent Changes As you learned, China's leaders changed course in the late 1970's. During the 1950's and 1960's, China's leaders tightly controlled nearly every aspect of life in the country. They banned

Family life is an important part of Chinese culture.

365

music, art, movies, and books from capitalist countries. They directed China's economy through five-year plans. State-owned factories were told what goods to produce and at what prices to sell their products. During these years, China's economy improved, but there were long periods of hardship and many setbacks.

The new policies of the 1970's provide for greater economic freedom. Although the government still owns and runs most businesses, people may now own small businesses. China seeks investments from foreign countries. The government also is making large investments in heavy

industry and educational programs to train scientists, managers, and technicians. China's GNP has become one of the fastest growing in the world. China is no longer an isolated giant. Today the country is actively involved in world trade, travel, and the exchange of ideas.

Yet China remains Communist. The Communist party controls the country's government. As in the Soviet Union, only a small fraction of the people belong to the Communist party. Personal freedoms — such as the right to speak and publish freely — are restricted. Most people have few ways in which to influence the government.

Agriculture About three fourths of the people of China are farmers. After taking power in 1949, the Communists ended private ownership of the land. They set up two types of farms — state farms, run like those in the Soviet Union (page 340), and **communes.** The communes were very important in China.

YAKS, SHEEP, AND SALT ARE NOT ENOUGH

The ambitions of the local officials in China's remote Qinghai province are not easily satisfied. Until just a few years ago, the province had far more yaks and sheep than it had people. Its economic activities consisted of selling a bit of salt and raising livestock. But in 1983, Qinghai got the central government's permission to try new ways to develop its economy. It began to deal directly with foreign business leaders in starting new enterprises. Plans call for the construction of new linkages to enable the province to develop its riches of oil, potash, asbestos, lead, zinc, and magnesium.

Communes varied greatly in size. Some had a few thousand members, while others had as many as 100,000. The members of a commune jointly owned and farmed commune land. They elected leaders. These leaders decided what crops to produce and how to divide the work. However, communes had to sell a set amount of their output to the government. Only what was left after sales to the government could be sold in local markets. Commune members were paid from the earnings of the commune.

The commune system has ended under China's new economic policy. Peasants may now plant and harvest their own crops on assigned plots. Although they cannot sell their plots, they can buy their own equipment and even hire workers. Under the new system, farm output has risen every year. The country is now the

366

China's Chang Jiang River carries deposits of fertile silt as it flows to the East China Sea. ● *Chinese farmers plant rice on a commune in the south.*

world's leading producer of rice, wheat, cotton, and tobacco.

China's most productive farming area lies in the humid river valleys and plains of the east. More than 90 percent of China's people live in these lowlands. From ancient times, this region has been China's heartland.

In the southeast, farmers grow rice and other crops in the fertile soil of the Xi River Valley. This warm, moist area has a year-round growing season. The mighty **Chang Jiang River** in central China is also bordered by great farmlands. The Yangzi Valley, China's "rice bowl," has one of the highest population densities on Earth. To the north is the valley of the **Huang He.** The Huang He gets its other name, the **Yellow River,** from the tiny particles of yellowish-brown **loess** carried in its water. The Huang He Valley too is a major farming region. But temperatures are too cold for rice. Wheat, millet, and **kaoling** (a type of sorghum) are the major crops in the area.

China's rivers can bring severe damage. Sometimes silt clogs riverbeds, making the water rise over the banks. Great floods then wash over the lowlands. These floods wipe out crops and cause

death and destruction. The Huang He has caused so much suffering that people call it China's river of sorrow. To guard against flooding, the Chinese for centuries have built **dikes,** or levees, along the riverbanks. But somehow many of the rivers have always broken through.

The Development of Industry Because the need for food is so great, China's Communist government for many years stressed farming. But the government is now promoting industry. China has deposits of many minerals. Its resources provide a base for the making of steel, chemicals, and oil products.

Today China produces mainly capital goods and heavy equipment. Many consumer goods are imported. But China is making growing quantities of such things as clothing and appliances.

The chief industrial center is in Manchuria, in northeast China. Manchuria is rich in iron ore and coal. The areas around Beijing and Shanghai are also important manufacturing centers.

As industry has grown, China's living standard has improved. The government has tried to spread the benefits from urban, industrial areas to the countryside. Farm income has risen quickly in

367

Huang He floods killed at least two million persons in 1887 and nearly four million in 1931.
Agricultural production has increased 2 to 3 percent a year, despite the fact that the government
has continued to emphasize industrial over agricultural development.

recent years. Some peasants now have items like washing machines, tape recorders, and refrigerators. The government hopes that improved conditions in rural areas will make peasants less eager to move to the already crowded cities.

The Western Regions China's west is little developed. Temperatures in the west can be very hot in the summer and freezing cold in the winter. Few people live in this dry and rugged region. However, efforts to farm and extract mineral resources in the west are under way. For example, farmers now grow wheat and cotton in irrigated fields in the Tarim Basin. A pipeline carries oil from the Dzungarian Basin to the eastern industrial area.

Mongolia

Mongolia is one of the world's most remote countries. It lies landlocked between the Soviet Union and China. High mountains, parched deserts, and vast distances separate Mongolia from the heartlands of its two giant neighbors.

A statue of Sükh Baatar, a leader of Mongolia's independence movement in the early 1900's, stands near government buildings in Ulaanbaatar's main square.

Mongolia is a **buffer state,** a country that lies between rival countries. Historically and culturally Mongolia has links to China. But today it has a Communist government with ties to the Soviet Union.

Most of Mongolia is sparsely populated. There are large areas of desert in the south and steppe in the rest of the country. On the steppe, nomads have long herded cattle, sheep, camels, and horses.

Even today live animals and animal products such as meat, wool, hides, and furs make up the bulk of Mongolia's exports. In recent years, however, with Soviet help, other economic activities have been developed. Coal and copper mining, food processing, textiles, and chemicals are some of the new industries. Better linkages, also built with Soviet help, are helping to transport raw materials and finished products. The Trans-Mongolian Railroad links both Moscow and Beijing to Mongolia's capital and largest city, Ulaanbaatar (ü'län bä'tȯr').

Other changes have come to the country during recent years. Trucks have largely replaced camels as means of transporting products. Modern houses are replacing the beehive-shaped tents called yurts that have served as homes for Mongol peoples for centuries. Still, Mongolia is isolated by distance and surrounded by two powerful neighbors.

North and South Korea

Korea has been a divided country since 1948. Before that time, most Koreans were farmers. Since 1948, both North and South Korea have built new industries. Today both countries — despite their many differences — have rapidly growing economies that are based on manufacturing.

South Korea South Korea has had special success. Its GNP is one of the fastest growing in the world. This achievement

South Korean factory workers make baseball gloves for export.

is remarkable because most of Korea's resources are in the north. Apart from some coal and iron, South Korea has few resources for industry. Its leading manufactured goods include textiles, food products, and electronics items. South Korea attracts foreign investors, who make use of the country's many skilled workers.

Even though wages are low, South Korea's standard of living is rising. Per capita income is about double that of North Korea. Almost every South Korean family has a radio. Many families have television sets.

The government has helped private industry sell products abroad. South Korea exports its products all over the world. Leading trade partners include the United States and Japan.

South Korea's farmland is better than North Korea's. Rice is the chief crop. South Korea can raise almost enough food to feed its population.

North Korea Communist North Korea has a wealth of resources. These include gold, coal, and molybdenum; some large forests; and sites for hydroelectric plants. The country has much heavy industry. Its chief products are iron and steel, farm machinery, and textiles. About 80 percent of North Korea's trade is with the Soviet Union and China.

Farming is done on collectives. As in South Korea, rice, corn, and wheat are the major crops. However, North Korea must import large amounts of food.

Hong Kong and Macau

At the mouth of the Xi River in southeastern China are two tiny European colonies. On the east side of the Xi lies Hong Kong. Thirty miles away, on the west bank, is Macau. Macau is the oldest surviving European colony in Asia. It became a territory of Portugal in 1542. Hong Kong was established as a British colony in 1842. Both Portugal and Great Britain used their small colonies as ports for trade with China.

Before the Communists came to power in China in 1949, many goods flowed between China and the rest of the world through part of Hong Kong. But trade slowed almost to a standstill when the Communists gained control of China. So Hong Kong turned to other activities. For one thing, it began to make and export consumer goods. Today leading products are textiles and clothing, toys, plastics, and watches and clocks. Hong Kong is also a financial center.

Despite prosperity, the colony faces an uncertain future. China and Great Britain have agreed that Hong Kong will become a part of China in 1997. There is worry that Hong Kong's economic success will be threatened when it comes under Communist rule. To reduce fears, the Chinese have promised that Hong Kong can keep its capitalist economy.

369

Hong Kong and Macau are both very urbanized—92 percent and 97 percent respectively. With a population of over 5.5 million living on 409 square miles of land, Hong Kong is one of the most densely populated places on Earth.

Goods made in Asia are shipped from Hong Kong's busy port to Europe and the United States.

Macau is much smaller than Hong Kong. Unlike Hong Kong, which has one of the world's finest natural harbors, Macau's harbor is too shallow for today's large ships. Tourism and some textile production support the people of Macau.

REVIEWING THE FACTS

Define

1. commune   2. buffer state

Answer

1. How have recent policy changes affected economic growth in China?

2. What part of China is the country's agricultural heartland?

3. (a) List the chief economic activities in Mongolia. (b) South Korea. (c) North Korea. (d) Hong Kong. (e) Macau.

Locate

Refer to the map on page 353.

1. (a) Name the capital city of China. (b) Mongolia. (c) South Korea. (d) North Korea. (e) Hong Kong. (f) Macau.

2. What river flows along the border between China and the Soviet Union?

4 The Pacific Islands of East Asia

A number of islands lie off the eastern coast of Asia. Between these islands and the coast of China are several seas — the Sea of Japan, the Yellow Sea (named for the yellow-brown silt brought to the sea by the Huang He), and the East China Sea. Beyond the islands lie the vast expanses of the Pacific Ocean. Japan and Taiwan are the two island nations of Pacific East Asia.

Japan

Japan is the most developed country in Asia. It is highly urbanized. It has a great deal of heavy and light industry. Its people enjoy a standard of living like that of people living in Western Europe and the United States. Japan's economic success, however, has been recent. Before 1900, few people would have imagined that the country would become an industrial giant within the next 50 years.

Japanese Industry Japan is often called the miracle of Asia. Its growth has come despite many obstacles. For example, Japan has few resources. It is a small country made up of many separate islands. About four fifths of its land is mountainous. Much of the flat land is occupied by towns and cities. The Japanese islands are often shaken by earthquakes and have many active volcanoes. Japan is located far from the major industrial countries with their huge markets.

Japan overcame the obstacles that faced it. Today a network of excellent air and water linkages joins the individual islands. Japan now leads the world in shipbuilding, accounting for more than one third of all vessels built. Its merchant fleet, one of the world's largest, ships its goods all over the world. To make up for

Answers are in the Teacher's Guide.
Only about 13 percent of Japan's land is level enough for cultivation.
Education is extremely important in Japanese society—approximately a third of all high school students go on for further education.

its lack of resources, Japan imports nearly 97 percent of the minerals and fuels it uses. It is the world's largest oil importer. Every few hours a huge tanker carrying oil arrives at a Japanese port. Japan also imports large amounts of iron ore, coal, and other raw materials.

The country specializes in making high-value, lightweight manufactured goods. Japanese companies learned how to make such goods by studying factories in developed countries. They altered their own methods to improve efficiency and quality.

Japanese companies have developed their own ways of doing business. Most firms take a strong interest in the well-being of employees. Some promise their workers lifetime employment. The work force is well educated and receives good wages. The government has closer ties with business than do most governments in other countries with free-enterprise systems. In Japan, workers, companies, and government all work together closely.

The fact that Japan's cities and industries were destroyed during World War II actually helped the nation's economy. In Europe, the Soviet Union, and even in the United States, many factories and much

of the equipment used in them are old. After the war, however, Japan built new factories, furnished with the most modern equipment available. Japan's industries are therefore very efficient.

Population density in Japan is high. Tokyo's building patterns reflect the city's dense settlement. ● *One of Japan's high-speed trains rushes past Mount Fuji, a sacred peak.*

Assign the Workbook activity for Chapter 14, Section 4, with pages 370–373.

371

SPOTLIGHT ON EDUCATION:

Exams Japanese Style

The Japanese believe that to excel a student must work hard. Exceptional ability is not required, only effort. The pressure to excel begins early. Many Japanese mothers spend hours teaching their preschoolers. Other parents send their three and four-year-olds to special schools designed to help children qualify for the best kindergartens.

Once in school, the competition becomes more intense. Students compete to get into the best junior high schools, then the best high schools, and finally the best universities. To help their children boost their scores, many parents send their children to *juku*, privately-run cram schools. Here, after a full day at school, students spend another three or four hours getting the extra help they need to pass their exams.

In an article that appeared in *U.S. News and World Report*, a reporter described how the pressure to excell affects high school seniors.

"A year ago, Ikuko Yoshimizu watched her senior friends at Mita High turn into book-weary zombies, losing sleep and weight as they disappeared into the stage of intense cramming that the Japanese call *shiken jigoku*, or exam hell. 'Their faces got thinner and thinner,' Ikuko recalls. 'I remember thinking, I don't want to be like that.'

"Now, herself a senior and only weeks shy of the grueling college-entrance tests, seventeen-year-old Ikuko has managed better than most to balance study with play and to keep a healthy sense of self. To be sure, her schedule is demanding, with 12-hour days the norm. Monday through Saturday, she is up at 7 A.M., gobbles breakfast, and pedals her bike to school, usually getting in just before the 8:30 bell. Afternoons, she meets with a singing club to rehearse rock tunes. For months, she went to a cram school to prepare for February's college entrance exam. Now she hits the library. She gets home at 7 P.M., usually with 20 pounds of textbooks, studies 4 to 5 hours and turns the light off at 2 A.M. 'Everybody does like that,' she notes. 'It's tiring, but I only have a bit more to go, so I can stick it out.'"

Once Ikuko is admitted to a university, the years of intense competition will be over. Life will become easier for her. Tests will be few and papers almost unheard of. Students know that when they graduate, they will be recruited for jobs almost solely on the basis of their university's prestige.

Japanese farms are also very productive. Farmers use machines, chemical fertilizers, and irrigation to improve yields. Rice is the major crop. Other important crops include barley, sugarcane, and fruits and vegetables. Farmers also raise livestock. Through intensive farming, farmers produce about two thirds of the food the country needs.

Japan exports much of its industrial production. Key products are watches, cameras, and electronics goods — such as

Japan's auto industry is highly successful. Several major auto companies produce small- and medium-sized cars for export. Here, newly made cars await shipment abroad.

radio and television sets and computers. These goods sell for high prices but are small, light, and easy to ship. Japan also makes cars. Even with the need to import food and raw materials, Japan has one of the world's most favorable trade balances.

Taiwan

Taiwan is a mountainous island in the East China Sea. The island was settled by people from the mainland of China in the 1400's. In the 1600's, the Portuguese arrived and named the island Formosa. But the Chinese soon conquered the island and expelled all foreigners. When the Chinese Communists defeated the Nationalists in 1949, the Nationalist leader Chiang Kai-shek led his supporters to Taiwan. There Chiang set up an authoritarian government. Today the country is called the Republic of China.

Taiwan, like China, was by tradition a farming country. Farms in Taiwan are small. They produce mainly rice and sugar. In recent years, however, Taiwan has emphasized industry. Its factories produce a variety of goods for export. They include textiles, clothing, electronics products, and processed foods. Taiwan has a thriving trade with industrialized countries. Because of its very rapid economic growth, Taiwan — along with Hong Kong, South Korea, and the South Asian country of Singapore — is often described as one of the four new Japans.

REVIEWING THE FACTS

Answer

1. Describe the obstacles to economic growth in Japan.

2. What measures did Japan take to make up for its late start in developing its economy?

3. How has Taiwan's economy changed in recent years?

Locate

Refer to the map on page 353.

1. (a) What is the capital of Japan? (b) Of Taiwan?

2. Name the four largest of the Japanese islands.

373

GEOGRAPHY LABORATORY

Highlighting the Chapter

1. East Asia is divided into a mainland area and groups of mainly volcanic islands lying off the eastern coast of the mainland. The mainland is circled by towering mountains and dry plateaus. Moist lowlands lie along the eastern coast. On both the mainland and the islands, there is frequent earthquake activity.

2. For centuries, the cultures of East Asia were isolated from developments in the rest of the world. During this time, complex civilizations arose on both the mainland and the islands. These civilizations were based on farming. By 1900, East Asia was on the threshold of great changes. The region had begun trading with outside countries, and the old forms of government were giving way to newer forms. Today the countries of East Asia are leaders in manufacturing and trade. Even Communist China, which still has a farm-based economy, is beginning to industrialize.

3. The countries of the mainland include China, Mongolia, North and South Korea, and the colonies of Hong Kong and Macau. China is experiencing especially rapid change. Its Communist leaders have ended a period of isolation and strict controls. Under relaxed rules, the Chinese are making great strides in economic development. The Communist government of Mongolia is changing Mongolia from a nomadic, rural country to one that has modern economic activities. Communist North Korea has many resources and produces a variety of industrial goods. South Korea, which has a free-enterprise economy, has become an important exporter of factory-made products. Tiny Hong Kong specializes in making small, lightweight products for export.

4. Japan is one of the world's top industrial powers. In spite of many disadvantages and a late start, Japan has built modern, efficient factories. Its excellent linkages enable Japanese companies to export their products all over the world. Taiwan has also built a strong manufacturing economy. It too exports large quantities of goods.

Speaking Geographically

Use each of the following words or terms in a sentence to show that you understand its meaning.

1. commune
2. paddy
3. Pacific Rim
4. buffer state
5. Cultural Revolution
6. dialect
7. character

Testing Yourself

Number your paper from 1 to 14. List three names, places, or facts that belong under each category below.

1. Mountain ranges bordering China
2. Rivers in China
3. Dense farming areas of China
4. Communist countries of East Asia
5. Pacific Rim countries
6. Major crops of East Asia
7. Resources that Japan must import
8. Industrialized countries of East Asia
9. Religions that began in East Asia
10. Climate areas on the mainland of East Asia
11. Deserts of China
12. Island groups in East Asia
13. New policies in China
14. Changes in Japan that occurred after World War II

374

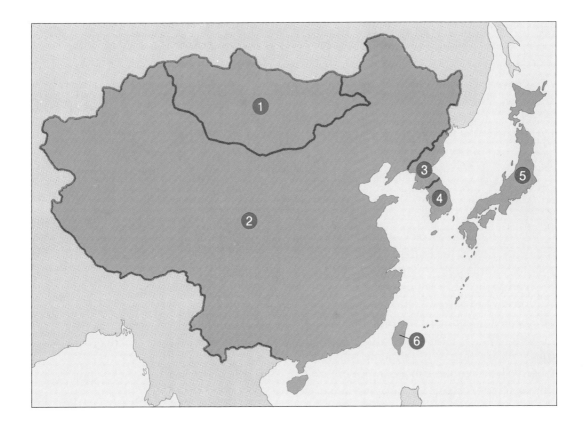

Building Map Skills

Number your paper from 1 to 6. After each number, write the name of the country identified by that number on the map on this page.

Applying Map Skills

1. Is East Asia mostly in the high, middle, or low latitudes?

2. In which hemisphere is all of East Asia's land located?

3. Give the approximate latitude and longitude of each of the following cities: (a) Guangzhou, (b) Beijing, (c) Shanghai, (d) Tokyo, (e) Seoul.

4. Through which East Asian countries does the Tropic of Cancer pass?

Exploring Further

1. From far out in space, astronauts can clearly see the Great Wall of China, a structure built many years ago across north-central China. Prepare a report on the Great Wall and the circumstances under which it was built.

2. Imagine that you are on a trip from Lhasa, in Tibet, to Shanghai, on China's east coast. Write a series of letters to a friend, describing what you see. (Supplement information from the text with an encyclopedia article on the regions of China.)

3. Japan's economic achievements are often in the news. Start a file of newspaper clippings on the Japanese economy. What challenges do Japanese companies pose to companies of the United States? What lessons have American businesses learned from Japanese businesses?

In this chapter, students will be learning about one of the most densely populated areas of Earth and the many problems it faces. Again, you might begin by asking them to identify things they think of when they hear of India, Vietnam, Singapore, or any of the other nations discussed in this chapter. Ask about products, types of government, and religions.

The photograph shows Singapore.

South Asia

Nearly one out of every three people in the world lives in the southern part of Asia. Among the region's countries are four of the world's top ten in population. Overpopulation and poverty are key problems in nearly every country of the region.

South Asia is a region of striking contrasts. It has areas of grinding poverty where change comes slowly. In the hills of Burma, farmers stoop to plant rice in paddies, using tools and methods like those used hundreds of years ago. In the isolated mountain villages of Laos, craftsworkers make goods their ancestors made. Far from cities and far from modern means of transportation, monks in Nepal practice Buddhism in traditional ways. Miles to the south, street vendors in Delhi, India, sell curried rice from handcarts, and tiny shops display handcrafted fabric.

On the other hand, parts of South Asia are lively centers of trade and industry. Teams of sweltering workers harvest the rubber crop on Indonesia's vast commercial plantations. Factory workers in Malaysia's leading city of Kuala Lumpur solder circuit boards for electronics equipment. In Singapore, huge cranes load cargoes onto giant ocean vessels. Factory workers sew clothing, make shoes and sporting goods, and assemble appliances in the Philippines. In tiny Brunei and in vast Indonesia, oil wells pump black gold for sale to industrial countries.

376

1 The Physical Environment

South Asia occupies most of the southern mainland of Asia as well as the islands lying between mainland Asia and Australia. The region's western border is formed by Iran's boundary with Afghanistan and Pakistan. The eastern border is formed by groups of islands, or archipelagoes, lying south and southeast of the mainland.

South Asia is divided into two subregions. India and its neighbors lie to the west, and Southeast Asia is in the east.

India and Its Neighbors

The western subregion lies south of the Hindu Kush, Karakoram, and Himalayan mountains. This area includes India and its neighbors — Afghanistan, Pakistan, and Bangladesh. It also includes the Himalayan countries of Nepal and Bhutan (bü tan') and the island country of Sri Lanka (srē' län'kə).

The part of Asia south of the Himalayas is called the Indian **subcontinent**. A subcontinent is a large landmass that is part of a whole continent but separated from it by natural barriers and differences in

Map Study *What is the most mountainous portion of South Asia? Name three rivers that drain India's Deccan Plateau? What is the name of the easternmost island in South Asia? On what land feature do Laos, Kampuchea, Thailand, and Vietnam lie?*

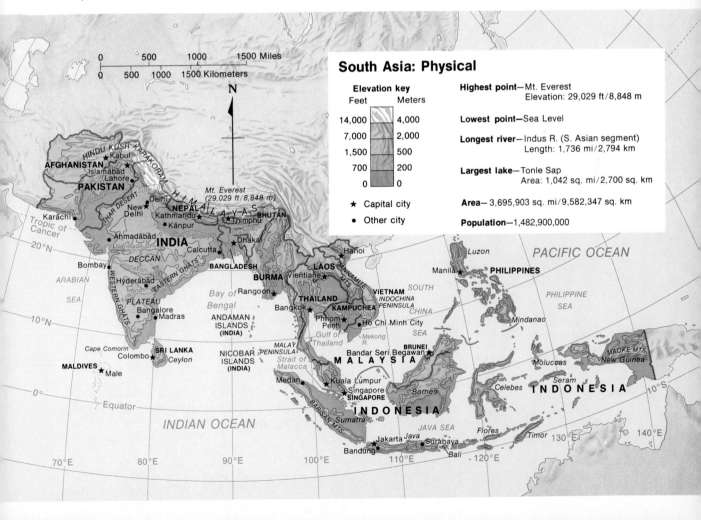

South Asia: Physical

Elevation key

Feet	Meters
14,000	4,000
7,000	2,000
1,500	500
700	200
0	0

★ Capital city
● Other city

Highest point—Mt. Everest
Elevation: 29,029 ft/8,848 m

Lowest point—Sea Level

Longest river—Indus R. (S. Asian segment)
Length: 1,736 mi/2,794 km

Largest lake—Tonle Sap
Area: 1,042 sq. mi/2,700 sq. km

Area—3,695,903 sq. mi/9,582,347 sq. km

Population—1,482,900,000

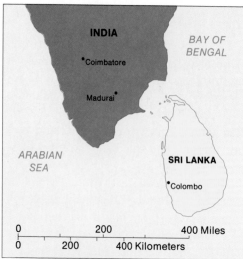

Using Scale

Each of the three maps on this page shows Sri Lanka. The size of this island country differs from map to map. What can explain this difference in size?

As you have learned, the size of features on a map is determined by scale. Scale is the relationship between distances as they are measured on Earth and as they are shown on a map. Every map is drawn to a particular scale.

Mapmakers cannot show features at their true sizes. So they choose to make a given unit of measurement on Earth's surface a certain length on the map's surface. A mile on Earth, for example, might be shown as an inch on a map. Most map scales are expressed in both miles and kilometers. The scale a mapmaker chooses for a map depends on the amount of detail to be shown and the desired size of the map.

Because they use different scales, the three maps on this page show Sri Lanka at different sizes. Compare the maps and read the scale for each. Then answer the following questions.

1. (a) How many miles and kilometers are represented by one inch on the top map? (b) On the middle map? (c) On the bottom map?

2. Which map best shows Sri Lanka's location in Asia?

3. Which map makes it easiest to find how long Sri Lanka is from north to south?

4. You could use two of these maps to figure the distance from Dhaka, Bangladesh, to Colombo, Sri Lanka. Which would be more accurate?

5. Give the distance in miles from Delhi, India, to Colombo, Sri Lanka, and tell how you calculated it.

Answer to question in column 2, paragraph 1: The maps are drawn to a different scale.
Answers to numbered questions are in the Teacher's Guide.
Assign the Workbook activity for this chapter's Map Workshop with this page.

culture. The Indian subcontinent extends in a large, triangle-shaped peninsula southward into the Indian Ocean.

Landforms Towering mountains rise at the northern edge of the Indian subcontinent. They are the highest mountains in the world, part of a huge mountain region called the roof of the world (page 352). Nearly all of Afghanistan is made up of arid highlands. The northern part of Pakistan is also a region of high mountains and plateaus. So is northern India, where elevations reach more than 28,000 feet (8,600 meters). Both Nepal and Bhutan are mountain countries, nestled high in the Himalayas along India's northern border. Mount Everest, lying in Nepal near the border with China's province of Tibet, is the world's highest mountain (29,028 feet, or 8,848 meters).

At the foot of the northern mountains are two great rivers. Southwest from the snowcapped Karakoram Mountains flow the tributaries that form the Indus River. The Indus River creates a broad valley in the southern part of Pakistan. This valley has fertile soil and flat land. The world's largest system of irrigation canals distributes water from the Indus to dry lowlands along the river.

The Ganges (gan'jēz') River also forms a broad and fertile plain. This plain extends southeastward from the northern mountains. It has both good soil and ample rainfall. The most densely populated part of India is found in the Ganges lowland. The area is also one of South Asia's most productive farming regions, supplying much of India's wheat and rice. The southeastern part of the Ganges Plain is a large floodplain. There, the Ganges and the Brahmaputra (bräm'ə pü'trə) rivers meet. The delta area, crisscrossed by ribbons of river water, is one of the world's most fertile areas. It also is one of the wettest. North of the delta, the town

of Cherrapunji, in India, receives about 450 inches (1,143 centimeters) of rain each year. And in one 12-month period, 1,042 inches (2,646 centimeters) of rain fell. This is almost 87 feet!

There is a large desert area — the Thar (tär), or Great Indian, Desert — southeast of the Indus River Valley. The Thar Desert extends from southern Pakistan into northwestern India. It is a region with few people and little activity.

South of the Thar Desert and Ganges Plain is a triangle of high, rolling land in the center of the Indian peninsula. This is the Deccan Plateau. The eastern part of the Deccan is an area of heavy rainfall. To the south and the west, the Deccan gets only moderate rainfall. Rivers flow across the Deccan eastward into the Bay of Bengal. Farmers use these rivers to irrigate dry parts of the upland. Forests blanket large parts of the Deccan, and the area has a variety of minerals.

The Eastern and Western Ghats (or Hills) border the Deccan Plateau on both coasts. Between the hills and the ocean are fertile coastal plains. On the western coastal plains, there is plenty of rainfall. On both coasts, population is dense, and rice farms are productive.

The Monsoon The climate of the Indian subcontinent is influenced by the monsoon (page 57). The word *monsoon* comes from *mausim*, the Arabic word for season. The seasonal shifting of the winds creates a dry season and a wet season. The wet season lasts from late spring through early fall. During these months, winds blow from the south, bringing moisture from the tropical waters of the Indian Ocean. Rain falls in torrents when the wet winds reach land. Heavy rains come almost daily.

From October to May, the winds reverse direction, blowing from the continental interior of Asia. The heavy rains

South Asia is subject to tropical storms called typhoons and cyclones. In 1977, a typhoon struck southern India, killing an estimated 20,000. In 1970, a cyclone of great magnitude hit present-day Bangladesh, killing at least 200,000. One or two students may wish to report to the class on these types of storms.

379

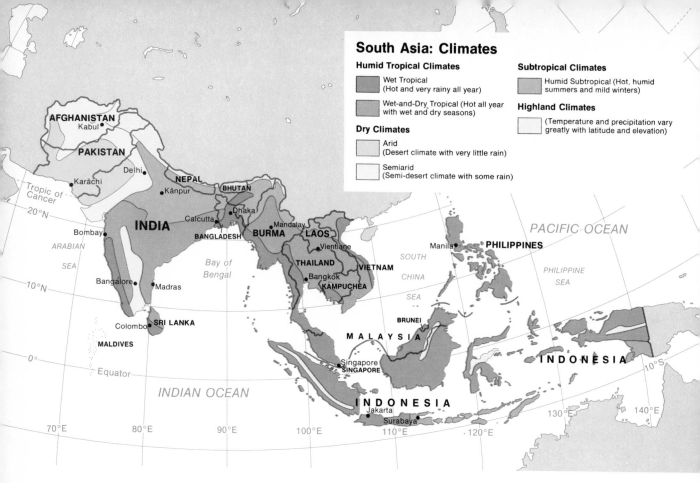

South Asia: Climates

Humid Tropical Climates

Wet Tropical
(Hot and very rainy all year)

Wet-and-Dry Tropical (Hot all year
with wet and dry seasons)

Dry Climates

Arid
(Desert climate with very little rain)

Semiarid
(Semi-desert climate with some rain)

Subtropical Climates

Humid Subtropical (Hot, humid
summers and mild winters)

Highland Climates

(Temperature and precipitation vary
greatly with latitude and elevation)

Map Study *What country has almost entirely desert climate conditions? What country has virtually no variation in climate? Where is the driest part of India?*

cease. Total rainfall during the dry season amounts to no more than several inches. The land becomes parched. Small streams and water holes dry up, and vegetation becomes dry as tinder.

Southeast Asia

Southeast Asia forms the eastern subregion of South Asia. This subregion includes the troubled mainland countries of Burma, Thailand (tī'land'), Kampuchea (kam'pə chē'ə), Laos, and Vietnam. Malaysia lies partly on the mainland and partly on the island of Borneo. Other countries in Southeast Asia lie entirely on islands. They are Indonesia and the Philippines and the tiny nations of Singapore and Brunei (brü'nī').

Much of Southeast Asia is hot year round. Unlike the Indian subcontinent, this region has heavy rains all year long. More than 80 inches (203 centimeters) of rain falls each year nearly everywhere in Southeast Asia. Many places get over 150 inches (381 centimeters) of precipitation a year.

Mainland Southeast Asia is dominated by forest-covered mountains. At the northern tip of Burma, peaks reach heights of 19,000 feet (5,900 meters). But for the most part, the highlands of Southeast Asia are lower than those to the west.

Mountain chains reach southward along the Malay and Indochina peninsulas. Dense broadleaf forests and tropical rain forests cover much of the land. In some mountain valleys and gaps, forests

380

Ask students to name the latitudinal belt in which most of these countries are located. *(low latitudes or tropics)* In addition to being near the equator, the climate of these countries is also affected by the proximity of large bodies of water.

have been cleared. In these places, people have small farms and villages. In Burma and Thailand, there are large savanna areas.

Among Southeast Asia's mountains are deep valleys created by five great river systems. The Irrawaddy and Salween rivers flow from Burma's northern highlands across the southern plains into the Bay of Bengal. Central Thailand is drained by the Chao Phraya (chaù prī'ə) River. The mighty Mekong River flows along Laos's border with Thailand, through Kampuchea, and across a delta at the southern tip of Vietnam. The Red River flows eastward across northern Vietnam. Except for the Salween, each of these rivers has created a broad valley, flat plains, and fertile farmland. Southeast Asia's river valleys are rice-growing areas with very dense settlement.

The islands of Southeast Asia lie in groups, or archipelagoes. The islands of Indonesia form one archipelago, and the Philippines occupy another. The islands are mountainous. Many are volcanic in origin. Most people live in highland valleys and on coastal plains.

Indonesia occupies the world's largest archipelago — more than 13,500 islands. These islands reach from just off the coast of mainland Malaysia almost to Australia. Indonesia has more active volcanoes than any other country in the world. Unlike the other island countries of the region, Indonesia has many broad plains. Streams, swamps, and dense tropical forests, however, make travel difficult.

The Philippine archipelago stretches 1,100 miles (1,774 kilometers) along the southeastern edge of Asia. It includes more than 7,000 islands, nearly all of which are mountainous. Only about 150 of the islands are larger than 5 square miles. Over 95 percent of the country's people live on just 11 of the islands.

HOW DEEP IS THE OCEAN?

The deepest place on Earth is the Mariana Trench. It is located on the floor of the Pacific Ocean to the east of the Philippines. With a depth of 36,419 feet (11,036 meters), the trench is even deeper than Mount Everest is high.

REVIEWING THE FACTS

Define

subcontinent

Answer

1. What are the two subregions of South Asia?

2. (a) In what parts of the Indian subcontinent are there lowlands? (b) What landforms make up the interior of the Indian peninsula?

3. What are the major rivers of Southeast Asia?

Locate

Refer to the map on page 377.

1. (a) Name the rivers that empty into the Bay of Bengal. (b) Into the Arabian Sea.

2. Name the country to which each of the following islands belongs: (a) Java, (b) Bali, (c) Sumatra, (d) Luzon, (e) Timor, (f) Mindanao.

381

Texas Essential Elements 3A. Interrelationships of people and their environments. 3D. Uses, abuses, and preservation of natural resources and the physical environment. 4C. Population distribution, growth, and movements. 4D. Major cultural, political, and economic activities within and among major world regions. 4F. Geographic influences on various issues.

2 The Human Imprint

Like other regions of the world, South Asia has features that set it off from nearby areas. South Asia is isolated by mountains, deserts, and oceans. Its climate differs from that found elsewhere in Asia. The region's cultural geography also stands in sharp contrast to that of bordering countries.

The People of South Asia

South Asia is a crossroads. Traders, explorers, and adventurers who came from other parts of the world influenced the region's cultures. These outsiders brought new languages, religions, and ways of using the environment.

Cultural Diversity South Asia is a patchwork quilt of ethnic groups with different customs. Hundreds of languages are spoken in the region.

South Asia also has a variety of religions. Both Buddhism (page 357) and Hinduism began in India. Hinduism is one of the world's oldest religions. Unlike many other religions, Hinduism has no single founder and no uniform set of beliefs. Hindus worship many gods, all of whom are thought to be forms of a supreme being. Each Hindu has a duty, called dharma (där′mə), to worship correctly and to follow proper conduct. A

Map Study *Compare this map with the map on page 377. What is the most densely populated island in South Asia? What is the population density of the area extending from Delhi to Calcutta?*

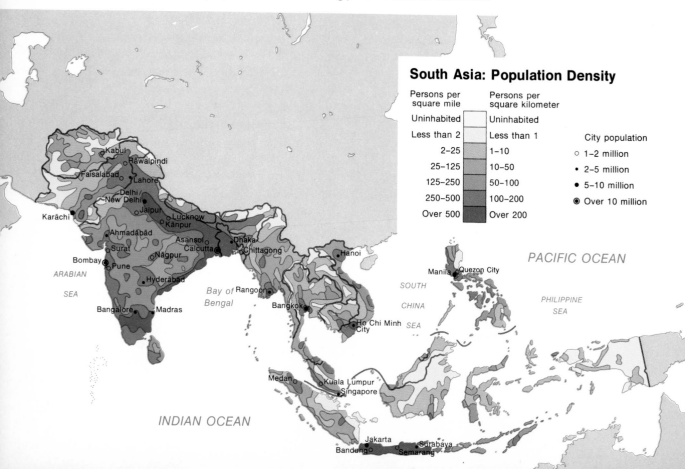

South Asia: Population Density

Persons per square mile	Persons per square kilometer
Uninhabited	Uninhabited
Less than 2	Less than 1
2–25	1–10
25–125	10–50
125–250	50–100
250–500	100–200
Over 500	Over 200

City population
○ 1–2 million
• 2–5 million
● 5–10 million
◉ Over 10 million

person's dharma depends on his or her situation in life. A peasant farmer's dharma, for example, differs from that of a landlord. The duties of young students are not the same as those of older people with jobs.

Hindus also believe in karma. According to this belief, every soul is born over and over again until it is purified by good actions.

About 83 percent of the people of India are Hindus. More than 10 percent of the Indian people are Muslims, while about 2 percent are Sikhs (sēks), who follow a religion blending Hinduism and Islam. Sikhs are concentrated in northern India. Christians make up about 3 percent of the Indian population.

Religious beliefs in other countries of the subcontinent have been influenced by borrowings from the Middle East, India, and China. Afghanistan, for example, lies on the boundary of South Asia and the Middle East. As a result, nearly all its people are Muslims. Pakistan too is almost entirely Muslim. So is Bangladesh. The mountain country of Bhutan and the island of Sri Lanka are Buddhist. Nepal, on the other hand, is mainly Hindu.

There are many religions in Southeast Asia. Buddhism has many followers on the mainland. The influence of China, which for many years ruled Vietnam, can also be seen in the number of Confucians and Taoists in that country. The chief religion of Indonesia, Malaysia, and Brunei is Islam. It was brought by Arab traders about 500 years ago. The Philippines, on the other hand, were colonized by Spain and are largely Roman Catholic. There are many Catholics in Vietnam as well.

Settlement Patterns In South Asia, about 30 percent of the world's people are crowded into an area no bigger than the United States. The region's population is growing rapidly. With a 2.3 percent

annual increase, each year the population grows by more than 33 million.

India, for example, has the second largest population in the world today. In 1900, India had 250 million people. Since then, birth rates have remained high, but death rates fell because of improved sanitation and health care. By the 1960's, India's population had doubled. Since then, it has grown by another 150 million. By the year 2000, India may have more than 1 billion people.

Governments on the subcontinent and in Southeast Asia have tried to encourage lower birth rates. These efforts have met with little success. People have been reluctant to give up traditional customs, which include large families with many children to help work the land.

It is nearly impossible for economic growth to keep pace with such gains in population. Although development has brought India much more food and many more jobs, the standard of living has improved little because of the growing numbers of people. Most other countries of South Asia have similar pressures.

Political Patterns

Ethnic, religious, and national differences in South Asia have complicated the region's politics. Countries with many distinct groups of peoples find achieving unity to be difficult. In addition, disagreements between countries in the region have led to deep-rooted hostility and many wars.

Ancient Cultures South Asia was the scene of ancient kingdoms. An early civilization developed in the Indus River Valley (page 136). Later, Aryan invaders established a series of kingdoms in northern India. Other empires, notably the Mauryan and Mogul, followed that of the Aryans.

383

Texas Essential Elements 1C. Geographical tools and methodologies. 4C. Population distribution, growth, and movements.

Reading a Population Pyramid

The graph on this page is called a population pyramid. Such a graph shows the percentage of a region's or nation's population that falls into various age groups. It also compares the distribution of age groups by sex, ethnic background, nationality, or some other category.

By looking at the population pyramid on this page, you can compare the age distribution of the population of developing countries and industrial countries. The shape of the pyramid is determined by the relationship between births and deaths and migration. As you can see, the two sides of the pyramid form contrasting patterns. These patterns show differences in population growth rates and life expectancy in the developing world and the industrial countries.

To find the percentage of population in any one age group in the developing countries, first locate the age group in the center column. Then examine the bar that extends to the left. The percentage is read by checking the length of the bar against the percentage scale across the bottom of the pyramid. To read the percentage of people in the same age group in the industrial countries, repeat the same steps, using the bar extending to the right.

Answer the following questions based on the population pyramid on this page.

1. (a) Which age group shown on the graph is the largest for the developing countries? (b) Which is the largest for the industrial countries?

2. Find the bar for industrial countries that includes your age. What percentage of the population falls into your age group?

3. Which has the greater part of its population over 65 years of age, the developing world or the industrial world?

For a special challenge Based on the population pyramid, in which countries — developing or industrial — does a great increase in population over the next 20 years seem more likely?

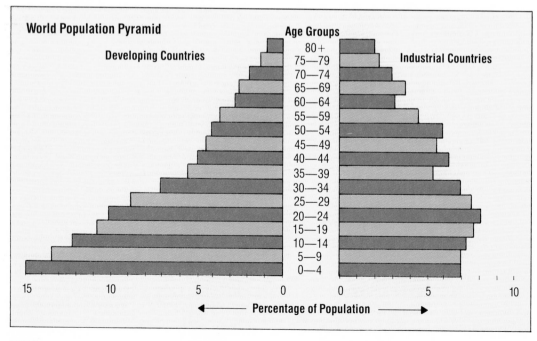

384

Developed countries emphasize secondary and tertiary economic activities and have a generally high standard of living. Developing countries have a generally lower standard of living and largely agricultural economies. Sometimes developing countries are referred to as Third World countries.

To the east, the Khmers (kə merz') built an empire that included much of present-day Kampuchea, Thailand, Laos, and southern Vietnam. Indian culture had a strong influence on Southeast Asia. Indian merchants settled along trade routes in Burma, southern Thailand, Kampuchea, Malaysia, and Indonesia. Indian religions, laws, literature, and arts spread to much of the region.

Colonization Europeans began sailing to South Asia in the late 1400's, about the same time that Columbus reached the Americas. At first, they were interested in little more than the lucrative trade in spices, silks, cotton, and gemstones. Eventually, however, European countries began to take control of South Asia's resources and governments.

Every country in the region except Thailand came under the rule of a European power. India and Pakistan became a colony of England's. England also controlled Burma and Malaysia. **Indochina** — as Vietnam, Laos, and Kampuchea were known — fell under French control. Indonesia was a Dutch colonial outpost. First Spain, and later the United States, held the Philippines. The Portuguese had small possessions that were used as shipping and trade centers.

During colonial times, European companies controlled the land and resources of Southeast Asia. They built large plantations and earned vast profits from rubber, sugar, and other crops. The people of the region, however, were left with little. Most were subsistence farmers.

Winning Independence Colonial rule lasted until the mid-1900's. India became an independent country in 1947. At that time, Hindu and Muslim leaders fought for control of the new country. Pitched street battles between rival groups marred the winning of independence. To prevent further conflict, Great Britain

Built by the Khmers in the 1100's, Angkor Wat is a magnificent temple.

divided India into two independent nations, India and Pakistan. Present-day India is made up of areas that were mainly Hindu. India is the world's largest democratic state. It is a federal republic with divisions called states. Many of its states are based on language groups, and ethnic conflict continues in the country.

Pakistan is made up of areas that were mainly Muslim. Pakistan was itself divided into a western region and a region lying at the mouth of the Ganges, over 1,000 miles to the east. In 1971, East Pakistan and West Pakistan fought a bloody war. Eventually, East Pakistan established its independence as the country of Bangladesh. In recent years, Pakistan has been ruled by a military dictatorship. Bangladesh is also a military dictatorship, but it has close ties to India and the Soviet Union.

Many other countries of South Asia have also become independent since World War II. The United States granted independence to the Philippines in 1946. After a four-year war for freedom, Indonesia gained its independence from the

385

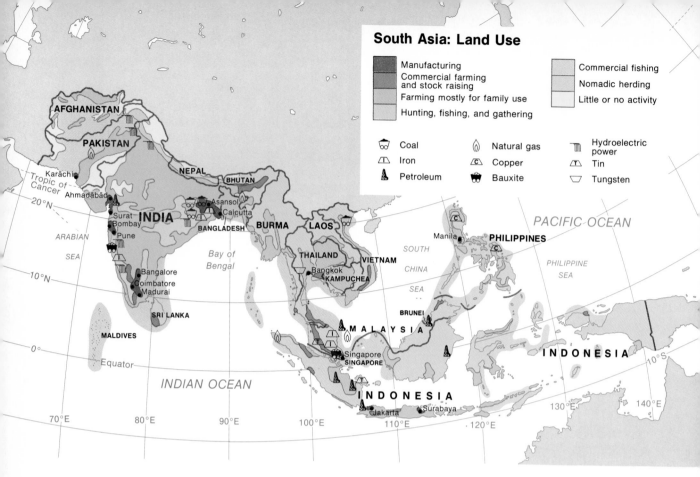

South Asia: Land Use

Manufacturing

Commercial farming
and stock raising

Farming mostly for family use

Hunting, fishing, and gathering

Commercial fishing

Nomadic herding

Little or no activity

🗛 Coal   🗛 Natural gas   🗛 Hydroelectric power

🗛 Iron   🗛 Copper   🗛 Tin

🗛 Petroleum   🗛 Bauxite   🗛 Tungsten

Map Study *What country has the greatest coal resources in South Asia? Petroleum? Name the country with the most manufacturing.*

Dutch in 1949. The British ended their control of Burma in 1948, of Malaysia in 1963, and of Singapore in 1965. Tiny Brunei, on the island of Borneo, won its freedom from British rule in 1983.

The countries of French Indochina fought hard for independence. These countries lie next to one another on the Indochina Peninsula. Kampuchea and Laos won their freedom from France in 1953. In Laos, a Communist movement fought first against the French and then against the new government of Laos. In Vietnam, the Communist movement called the Viet Minh fought a long war for independence. In 1954, France gave up control over Vietnam. The country was divided into North Vietnam, under Communist rule, and South Vietnam. The

independence agreement called for elections to reunite the country in 1955. However, bitterness between the two sides was so strong that the elections were not held. Rebels, supported by North Vietnamese equipment and troops, began trying to overthrow the government of South Vietnam.

The United States supported the South Vietnamese with aid and military advice. By the mid-1960's, large numbers of American soldiers were fighting in South Vietnam. In 1973, the United States signed a peace agreement and withdrew its troops. However, the war continued. In 1975, North Vietnamese troops swept south, toppling the government of South Vietnam. The country was reunited under a Communist government and

Answers to Map Study questions: India has the most coal; Indonesia has the most petroleum; India has the most manufacturing.

More that 8 million Americans served in the Vietnam War; approximately 50,000 died.

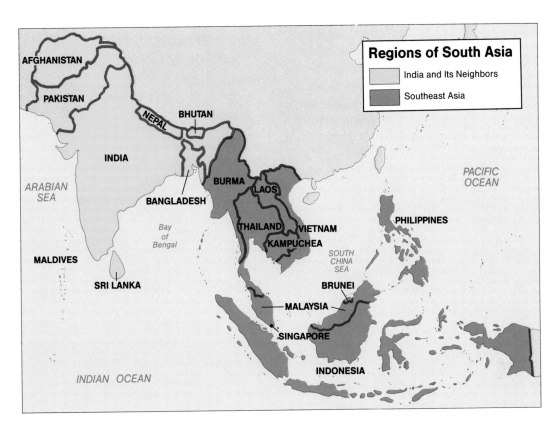

Map Study *Name the mainland countries of Southeast Asia. What is an island country near India?*

took the name of the Socialist Republic of Vietnam.

In neighboring Laos, the Communists also won a long war in 1975. They set up a government friendly to that of Vietnam.

In Kampuchea, the Khmer Rouge (which means "Red, or Communist, Khmers") also took power in 1975. The Khmer Rouge wanted all Kampucheans to work the land, without any distinction among individuals. The government forced millions of people out of urban areas to farms. Thousands of doctors, writers, and other educated people were jailed or killed. In the upheaval, millions of Kampucheans were put to death or died of starvation.

In contrast to the government of Laos, the Khmer Rouge government quarreled with the leaders of Vietnam. In 1978, a border clash between Kampuchea and Vietnam led to war. After a series of short battles, Vietnamese troops drove the Khmer Rouge government from power. They installed a new Communist government, friendly to Vietnam. As a result, all of Indochina is ruled by Communist governments that have close ties.

Economic Patterns

The countries of South Asia are mainly developing nations. Most of the people live in rural areas. Few can read and write. Farming is the chief way of earning a living, but crop yields are low. In much of South Asia, nearly all the available land is farmed. People in remote mountain areas still use ancient farming methods. Some

387

Pol Pot was the leader of the Khmer Rouge. Today Kampuchean rebels, including many Khmer Rouge guerrillas, are fighting to overthrow the government installed by Vietnamese troops.

people are nomadic herders. Others are subsistence farmers on river plains, eeking out a meager living for their families. Still others are involved in the modern commercial farming of grains or tropical plantation crops. In the Communist countries, collectives and state farms are common.

Despite the number of people involved in farming, some of the countries of South Asia must import large amounts of food. Most also rely on imports of fuel. After paying for food and fuel, these countries have little money left. Thus, they cannot afford to pay for the development of industry. The only countries with much manufacturing are India, Indonesia, Malaysia, the Philippines, and Singapore.

REVIEWING THE FACTS

Define

Indochina

Answer

1. Describe the religious beliefs of the Hindus.

2. Why is population a serious problem in South Asia?

3. When did the countries of South Asia gain their independence from European countries?

4. What economic patterns does South Asia have in common with other developing countries?

Locate

Refer to the map on page 386.

1. (a) What countries of South Asia have large areas of nomadic herding? (b) Where is commercial fishing important?

2. Near what cities are South Asia's manufacturing regions?

3 India and Its Neighbors

The Indian subcontinent is a vast peninsula. It includes dusty villages far from modern linkages and conveniences. But it also has modern cities teeming with activities and ideas. Farming is the most important occupation, but there is growing manufacturing and commerce. Recent turmoil, however, has held back the area's economic development.

India — The Giant of South Asia

India is made up of a wide variety of ethnic groups. Most Indians, however, are Hindus. Hinduism has helped unify the people of India by creating common customs and goals. For example, the Hindu religion discourages the killing of animals and the eating of animal flesh. As a result, the people of India cherish and protect animals. The country has more domestic animals than any other country in the world. Many of India's animals are used in economic activities. Water buffalo pull carts and plows. Cows provide dung for fertilizer. But many animals serve no economic purpose. They roam at will.

The Indian social system is also affected by Hindu beliefs. Under Hinduism, people are grouped by religious purity, not by personal wealth. People who are equal in purity belong to the same **caste**. The purest people are priests. Below the priestly caste are about 3,000 other castes. The lowest is made up of servants. Below the bottom caste is a large group of untouchables.

In the past, a person's occupation was based on his or her caste. Each caste also was like a community for people of similar rank. Contact between individuals in

Answers are in the Teacher's Guide.
Students should be encouraged to refer to the World Data Bank on page 396 for statistics on each of the countries they study in Section 3.
Assign the Workbook activity for Chapter 15, Section 3, with pages 388–392.

different castes was restricted. A priest could not accept food prepared by a member of a lower caste. People from different castes did not marry.

Today the caste system is not as strong as it was in the past. For example, recent laws prohibit mistreatment of untouchables. In cities, a person's job and choice of spouse are no longer fixed by caste. However, many people still follow caste tradition, especially in rural areas.

Nearly three fourths of India's people live by farming. Most still use primitive methods. They have little equipment and own little or no land. Many farmers are tenants who pay part of their crops to landlords as rent. Few farmers can afford to buy fertilizer or good seeds. Locusts, droughts, or floods destroy crops from time to time. As a result, many of India's farmers cannot grow enough to feed even their own families.

Few Indians have an adequate diet. Because of religious beliefs and poverty, people eat little meat. Most crops grown in India do not provide much protein. Rice, wheat, and millet are India's leading food crops. India has the largest acreage of rice of any country in the world. But because of poor farming practices, rice yields are among the lowest in the world.

During the 1960s, research led to better ways of growing rice and wheat. These changes, called the **Green Revolution**, promised to increase crop yields in many Third World countries. These hopes were not realized in India. The Green Revolution meant using fertilizers, more water, larger fields, and heavy equipment run by oil products. India's poverty and the reluctance of people to change traditions limited its impact. Although crop yields improved, the gains did not keep pace with the country's population growth.

India has some mineral deposits. The most important of these are coal and

Every year, thousands of people visit Benares to bathe in the Ganges, whose waters Hindus consider to be holy.

iron. They form the basis of the country's growing steel industry. Steel mills and related factories are concentrated in the east, near the city of Jamshedpur (jäm'shed'pur'). In addition to coal and a small amount of petroleum, India has many dams that provide hydroelectric power. The country has developed its own nuclear energy.

Jamshedpur is the center of India's steelmaking and heavy industry.

389

Calcutta, which lies near Bangladesh, is India's largest city. Its major product is a fiber plant called jute, from which twine and burlap sacking are made. The city also has large cotton mills, construction companies, and chemical factories. Other large cities are Madras, a center for cotton textiles in southeastern India, and Bombay, an industrial city on India's west coast. India's capital, New Delhi, is part of a sprawling metropolitan area that includes the city of Delhi in the northern part of the country.

Afghanistan and Pakistan

Neither Afghanistan nor Pakistan has a developed economy. Afghanistan is land-locked and extremely poor. It has few resources, and only about 10 percent of its land is cultivated. Eighty percent of its people are either herders or subsistence farmers. The small valleys in which most farmers live are isolated from one another. Kabul (käb'əl), the capital and only large city, has poor links to the countryside. Even in Kabul, there are very few industries.

Afghanistan is wracked by civil war. Since 1979, Islamic fighters have challenged the rule of the Communist government. Massive aid from the Soviet Union—including tens of thousands of troops—has helped keep the Afghan government in power. The civil war has hurt the economy, making growth in the near future unlikely.

Pakistan is also a poor country. It has scant mineral resources and few fuels. There is, however, fertile farmland on the plain of the Indus River. With the help of irrigation, such food crops as rice and wheat are grown. Pakistan grows and exports cotton. In recent years, Pakistan has built a cotton textile industry. Karāchi, a port city on the Arabian Sea, is Pakistan's major population and industrial center.

A worker tends a water-turned grinding wheel in an Afghan corn mill. ● In the dry highlands of Pakistan, raising sheep is a common way of earning a living.

390

Bangladesh

Bangladesh is one of the world's poorest and most troubled nations. The country's government is corrupt and unstable. Terrorism and riots are common. Few countries have as great a population problem as Bangladesh. In addition, the bitter war for independence left the economy in shambles. Even today Bangladesh has one of the lowest per capita GNP's in the world.

Eighty-five percent of Bangladesh's people live in rural areas. Rice is the leading crop. In some places, three crops of this grain can be grown each year in the fertile soils of the Ganges floodplain. However, jute and tea are the chief cash crops.

Much of Bangladesh's best farmland is on the river and coastal plains south of Dhaka. As a result, population is especially dense in this low-lying land at the head of the Bay of Bengal. Unfortunately, **cyclones**, as hurricanes or typhoons are called in this region, frequently sweep inland from the Indian Ocean across the Bay of Bengal, causing massive death and destruction.

Nepal and Bhutan

In Nepal and Bhutan, which lie in the towering Himalayas, most people live by herding or subsistence farming. About 95 percent of the people live in rural areas. Population is clustered in small mountain valleys. Most communities are isolated from transportation routes of any kind. The entire country of Nepal has only about 60 miles (97 kilometers) of railroad track. In Bhutan, only 1 person in 20 can read and write. In Nepal, 1 in 5 is literate. Per capita incomes are among the lowest in the world. Nepal's capital, Kathmandu (kat'man'dü'), is the only city of any size in either country.

Bangladesh is frequently ravaged by devastating tropical storms. Here, refugees huddle on the floodplain.

Sri Lanka

Sri Lanka is a tear-shaped island nation in the Indian Ocean located off the southeastern tip of India. Under British rule, the island was called Ceylon. After independence, the new nation changed its name to Sri Lanka, which translates as "resplendent island."

Nearly 80 percent of Sri Lanka's population is rural. Most of its people are subsistence farmers, but many work on large plantations. Coconuts are grown in the hot, wet lowlands. Higher up the slopes, rubber trees thrive. Still higher in the mountains, tea is the major crop. Tea accounts for nearly two thirds of Sri Lanka's annual exports. With government help, rice production has been increased during recent years. Yet the country still must import rice to feed its people.

391

REVIEWING THE FACTS

Define

1. caste
2. Green Revolution
3. cyclone

Answer

1. Describe the role of castes in India.

2. Why is farming in India unable to provide enough food to feed the people?

3. (a) How do most Afghans earn a living? (b) Where is Pakistan's major farming region?

4. How does weather cause suffering in Bangladesh?

5. (a) What are the major economic activities of Nepal? (b) Bhutan? (c) Sri Lanka?

Locate

Refer to the maps on pages 377 and 382.

1. Name the capitals of the following countries: (a) Afghanistan, (b) Pakistan, (c) India, (d) Bangladesh, (e) Sri Lanka, (f) Bhutan, (g) Nepal.

2. List the region's urban areas with over five million residents.

4 Southeast Asia

Southeast Asia has long been an area of great cultural mixing. Peoples from the Pacific islands, Africa, the Indian subcontinent, the Middle East, and China have helped shape the region's cultures. Today the region is in the midst of change and conflict. While countries like Singapore, Malaysia, and Brunei are rapidly modernizing, other countries — including Laos, Vietnam, and Kampuchea — are among the poorest in the world.

Burma

Burma is the largest country on the mainland of Southeast Asia. Most of Burma's people live in the fertile valley and delta region of the Irrawaddy River. They make their homes in small villages and farm tiny plots. The chief crop is rice. Farmers sell some of their rice to the government for export. In fact, over 40 percent of Burma's earnings from abroad come from rice exports. But most people earn little. They grow barely enough to feed their families.

Burma also produces some cotton, rubber, and minerals such as copper, lead, and tin. Teak, a hardwood that grows in upland rain forests, is a major export. Burma is one of the world's leading sources of this tropical hardwood.

The two largest cities are located along the Irrawaddy. Mandalay is the chief transportation and commercial center of northern Burma. Silk goods and gold and silver wares are major products made there. Rangoon, located near the mouth of the Irrawaddy, is Burma's capital. It is also the country's largest city, chief port,

Hand and animal labor are common throughout South Asia. Here, a buffalo pulls a cart in Burma.

Answers are in the Teacher's Guide.
The area including Southeast Asia, East Asia, and South Asia is often called the Rice Bowl. It is here that 95 percent of the world's rice is produced.

Thailand was called Siam until 1939.

Assign the Workbook activity for Chapter 15, Section 4, with pages 392–397.

and major manufacturing center. However, Burma has little manufacturing.

Burma is a closed country, sometimes called the Albania of Asia. Its present government was set up in 1962, when military leaders took power. Since then, they have made the Socialist party the only legal political party.

Thailand

In the Thai language, *Thailand* means "land of the free." The name is fitting. Thailand is the only country in Southeast Asia that was never ruled by a foreign power.

Rugged mountains cut Thailand off from Burma to the west and China to the north. The Mekong River forms a barrier separating it from Laos, its neighbor to the east. But most of the country lies on broad plains. The country's population is densest in the fertile valleys drained by the Chao Phraya River and its tributaries. Bangkok, located near the mouth of the Chao Phraya River, is the country's capital and largest urban center. The city of nearly five million is also the leading manufacturing and commercial area and a busy seaport.

The Thais are mainly farmers, and rice is the major crop. Most of Thailand's people live in small farming villages. The seeds and farming methods developed in the Green Revolution (page 389) have helped Thai farmers. Thailand has become the world's biggest exporter of rice. Plantation-grown rubber and teakwood are other important exports.

Thailand has a higher standard of living than most other countries of Southeast Asia. Nearly 85 percent of the people can read and write. Like other countries in the region, however, Thailand has had its share of unrest. Today the government is controlled by military leaders, who ended a short period of democracy in 1976. The government is faced with radical opposition at home, streams of refugees from Vietnam and war-torn Kampuchea, and recent economic hardships caused by the decline in prices for tin and rubber.

Kampuchea

Kampuchea, known as Cambodia until the 1970's, was a part of French Indochina. Once a mighty empire (page 385), Kampuchea is today a poor, agricultural country. It has been shaken by war since the late 1960's. In 1979, a Vietnamese-backed government ousted the Khmer Rouge government in a bloody invasion. Since then, the government has been fighting a coalition of rebel groups.

The years of unrest and fighting have severely hurt economic growth. There is little industry. Most Kampucheans live by farming the fertile plains bordering the Mekong River. Rice is the major crop. Like its neighbors, Kampuchea exports rice. However, production fell off during the 1970's. By the late 1970's, thousands of people were starving to death. The country still has few trained doctors, and many people die from diseases and war wounds. Thousands of Kampucheans have fled the country.

Laos

Laos is the least developed country in Southeast Asia. It is landlocked and has very poor transportation networks. The terrain is largely mountainous. Most people live in the Mekong River Valley, but isolated groups are found in the mountains. The chief economic activity is subsistence farming. Less than 5 percent of the land, however, is used for growing crops.

A civil war—fought almost without pause from the 1950's until 1975—

393

SPOTLIGHT ON KAMPUNG:

Tapping Rubber Trees in Malaysia

Feroz and Hamida are a brother and sister 15 and 16 years old. They live in Kampung, a village in the western part of the Malay Peninsula. Their family owns rubber trees in the nearby forest.

Each morning at dawn, Feroz and Hamida put on their long, bright-colored sarongs. Then they pedal their bicycles from their village to the forest. They carry special knives for cutting the trees so that the sap, called latex, can flow. Work starts early because the latex flows best in the morning.

By noon, the flow of latex stops. Feroz and Hamida return to the village for lunch. Afterward they return to the trees and collect the latex. Another villager combines formic acid with the latex in shallow pans. The mixture becomes crude rubber. The crude rubber is formed into sheets and squeezed dry between rollers.

Some of Kampung's rubber tappers sell sheet rubber to local Chinese merchants. But Feroz and Hamida save what they produce. When they have a large supply, Feroz takes it to Kuala Lumpur. There, he can sell it for a better price than he can get in the village.

To get to Kuala Lumpur, Feroz takes a bus over a paved road. The highway is an important linkage for everybody in Kampung. It allows rubber to reach world markets. It also enables food, clothing, and other articles to be brought to the village. Rice comes from Thailand. Transistor radios come from Japan and Korea. The highway gives tiny Kampung a link to the rest of the world.

After the long day's work, Feroz and Hamida can relax. Some days Feroz visits a coffee shop and chats with his friends. On other days, he goes to a Muslim shrine called a mosque. Hamida and her mother usually shop at the village market.

By early evening, all the members of the family have returned home. When they gather, the evening meal begins. It consists of rice, tapioca, vegetables, and perhaps — on special days — chicken. By the time it is dark, Feroz and Hamida are sound asleep.

brought economic development to a standstill. Today the Pathet Lao, or Laotian Communist party, rules. Per capita income remains among the lowest in the world.

Vietnam

Vietnam, like Kampuchea and Laos, has suffered from years of warfare. After two decades of separation, North and South Vietnam were reunited in 1975.

Before 1900, most rubber came from the Amazon Basin in Brazil. In 1876, Henry A. Wickham carried seeds for rubber plants back to England, where he successfully grew them in the Kew Botanical Gardens. The plants were then transported to Ceylon, the Malay Peninsula, Sumatra, and India, where they were grown on plantations.

Some students may wish to begin doing assignment number 3 under Exploring Further on page 399. In addition, a veteran of the war might be invited to share his or her experiences with the class.

Vietnam is still at war, backing the government of neighboring Kampuchea against rebel guerillas. Recently there has been fighting with China along the northern border. Hundreds of thousands of Vietnamese have left the country, seeking to escape the violence and to make better lives elsewhere.

In the past, South Vietnam was mainly a farming region, and North Vietnam had more industry. Now the government is helping farmers on the plains of the Red River in the north expand their output. Industries are being developed in the south. Progress is slow, however. The south remains the main farming area. The area is one of the world's major rice-producing regions. Rice is grown on collective farms in the Mekong Delta region. Rubber plantations are another important part of the south's economy.

Malaysia

Malaysia occupies the southern part of the Malay Peninsula and the northern quarter of the neighboring island of Borneo. Under British rule, Malaysia had large rubber plantations. Since independence, Malaysia has developed a good variety of economic activities. It exports such resources as rubber, tin, bauxite, palm oil, forest products, and petroleum. Malaysia is the world's leading producer of both natural rubber and tin. The government is using income from the export of these resources to help pay for manufacturing. Among Malaysia's manufactured goods are cement, rubber goods, chemicals, textiles, and processed foods.

Most of the country's people live on the coastal plain on the western side of the Malay Peninsula. Kuala Lumpur (kwäl'ə lùm'pùr'), the nation's capital and largest city, is also located there. About two thirds of the people of Malaysia live in cities.

Workers build an irrigation channel in Vietnam. Much of the country's labor is done by collective brigades.

Singapore and Brunei

Singapore and Brunei are the wealthiest countries of Southeast Asia. Singapore is a tiny island just off the southern tip of the Malay Peninsula. The former British colony became Southeast Asia's smallest independent nation in 1965. Since gaining its freedom, the country has thrived. Singapore is one of the world's leading trading centers and ports. But manufacturing is the most important part of the nation's economy. Singapore's industries include petroleum refining, shipbuilding and repair, and food processing. The country is also a major banking and business center.

Brunei is a **sultanate** (səlt'ə nāt'), or country ruled by a Muslim monarch. About twice the size of Rhode Island, Brunei lies on the north coast of Borneo. Its per capita GNP is one of the highest in the world. The source of Brunei's great wealth is oil. Yet only a small number of

395

WORLD DATA BANK

Country	Area in Square Miles	Population/Natural Increase		Per Capita GNP
Afghanistan	250,000	14,200,000	(2.6%)	$ 163
Bangladesh	55,598	107,100,000	(2.7%)	150
Bhutan	18,147	1,500,000	(2.0%)	160
Brunei	2,228	200,000	(2.6%)	17,580
Burma	261,216	38,800,000	(2.1%)	190
India	1,269,340	800,300,000	(2.1%)	250
Indonesia	735,355	174,900,000	(2.1%)	530
Kampuchea	69,900	6,500,000	(2.1%)	NA
Laos	91,429	3,800,000	(2.5%)	144
Malaysia	127,317	16,100,000	(2.4%)	2,050
Nepal	54,363	17,800,000	(2.5%)	160
Pakistan	310,402	104,600,000	(2.9%)	380
Philippines	115,830	61,500,000	(2.8%)	600
Singapore	224	2,600,000	(1.1%)	7,420
Sri Lanka	25,332	16,300,000	(1.8%)	370
Thailand	198,456	53,600,000	(2.1%)	830
Vietnam	127,243	62,200,000	(2.6%)	245

people share in the high standard of living. There are tens of thousands of subsistence farmers who live outside the major city, Bandar Seri Begawan (bun'dər ser'ē bə gä'wən).

Indonesia

Only four countries have more people than Indonesia. Indonesia's largest island, Java, has fertile lowlands that can support many farmers. This island is one of the most densely populated places in the world. It has more than 100 million people living in an area the size of New York State. Jakarta, the country's capital and the largest city of Southeast Asia, is located at the western end of Java.

Indonesia's motto is "Unity in Diversity." This motto reflects the fact that in Indonesia, there are more than 300 different ethnic groups. In addition to millions of Muslims, there are Hindus, Buddhists, and Christians. Unifying Indonesia's diverse peoples has been difficult. Conflicts between groups are common. A coup in 1965 resulted in the deaths of thousands. Today civil war smolders on the island of Timor.

Rubber, coffee, tea, sugar, oil palms, and tobacco are grown on Indonesia's large plantations. Rubber is the leading crop. Indonesia is one of the world's top rubber exporters.

There is also a great deal of subsistence farming in Indonesia. Farmers raise rice, maize, and other foods for their families on small plots of land. Some tobacco is also grown on family farms as a cash crop.

396

An Indonesian proofreader checks to see that Braille, raised type for blind readers, is typed correctly.

The country has some natural resources. Tropical hardwoods, bauxite, and tin are abundant. There are large reserves of oil and natural gas. The export of these fuels is now Indonesia's chief source of income, amounting to about 65 percent of its GNP.

The Philippines

Today nearly half the Philippine people work in agriculture. As in other countries once colonized by Spain, land has long been concentrated in the hands of a few very wealthy people. Most Filipinos are peasants who work land they do not own. The best farmland is on the island of Luzon, where fertile lowlands surround the city of Manila. Rice is the major crop. Many farmers raise high-yielding varieties of miracle rice. Commercial crops in-

clude sugar, pineapples, and coconuts, all of which are grown on plantations.

Since independence, the Philippines have developed some industries. Among these are food processing, textiles, and chemicals. There are also a number of minerals, but there is not enough iron, coal, or oil for heavy industry.

The Philippines were ruled by a dictator during the 1970's and 1980's. In 1986, an election was held. The dictator claimed victory. But most Filipinos believed government cheating had denied challenger Corazon Aquino the victory she had won. The people staged a largely peaceful rebellion. The dictator resigned, and Aquino became president.

Aquino's government had to deal with many problems. The years of dictatorship had damaged the economy and left bitter divisions among the people. The Philippines continued to have a rapidly growing population, urban slums, and great rural poverty.

REVIEWING THE FACTS

Define

sultanate

Answer

1. What crops are grown in large amounts in Southeast Asia?

2. Which three Southeast Asian countries have had the most success in industrializing their economies?

3. Describe the unrest that has held back economic development in the region.

Locate

Refer to the maps on page 377.

1. List the countries of Southeast Asia and their capitals.

2. Name the major mountain ranges of Southeast Asia.

397

Highlighting the Chapter

1. South Asia is divided into two sub-regions, India and its neighbors to the west and Southeast Asia to the east. The Indian subcontinent extends south from the highest mountains in the world. Large, fertile plains run east-west at the foot of the northern mountains. The mainland of Southeast Asia is mountainous. Several broad river valleys lie among the highlands. In the south, there are thousands of islands.

2. As a crossroads region, South Asia has great cultural diversity. Its peoples practice a variety of religions. Hinduism, Buddhism, and Islam all claim many followers. Population is dense in most of the region and is growing at very fast rates. Most countries of the region were European colonies until recently. Except in Singapore, Brunei, and parts of a few other countries, the chief means of earning a living is by farming. Methods remain traditional, and incomes are low.

3. India is the world's largest democracy. Its culture, shaped by Hinduism, is changing as the country becomes more urbanized and developed. Farming, however, remains the most important economic activity. Afghanistan, Pakistan, and Bangladesh depend on subsistence farming. The other nations of this subregion have little economic development.

4. The chief economic activity of mainland Southeast Asia is rice growing. The largest country, Burma, also produces hardwood, minerals, and rubber. Thailand has some manufacturing. Kampuchea, Laos, and Vietnam—torn by years of war—are poor, farming countries. Malaysia has begun to industrialize. Singapore has a great deal of trade and manufacturing, while Brunei has grown wealthy from oil exports. Indonesia also exports oil, but most of its people are farmers. The Philippines is another farming country; it exports tropical crops.

398

Speaking Geographically

Number a sheet of paper from 1 to 6. Then match the following words or terms with their definitions: subcontinent, Indochina, caste, Green Revolution, cyclone, sultanate.

1. A tropical hurricane or typhoon

2. Social group in India

3. Landmass separated from the rest of a continent by natural and cultural differences

4. Improved farming methods for developing countries, pioneered during the 1960's

5. Southeast Asian countries colonized by France

6. Country ruled by Muslim monarch

Testing Yourself

Number your paper from 1 to 10. Then write the word or short phrase that completes each of the following statements.

1. The major land region of the Indian peninsula is ____ .

2. Bhutan and ____ lie high in the Himalayan Mountains.

3. The ____ River drains India's vast northeastern plain.

4. ____ is the religion with the largest following in Indonesia.

5. Laos, Kampuchea, and Vietnam have ____ governments that are friendly with one another.

6. The ____ religion has helped shaped India's culture.

7. Wracked by civil war, landlocked ____ has little economic development.

8. In Burma, ____ is harvested in rain forests for export.

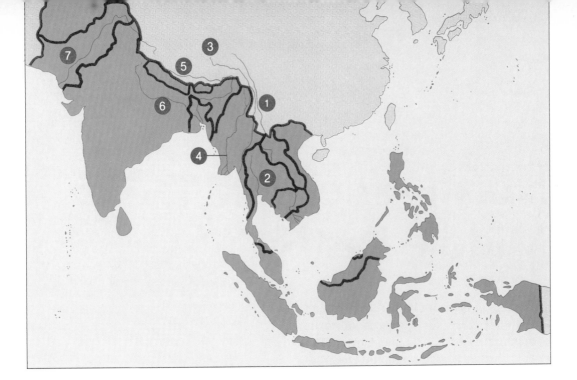

9. _____, a tiny island country, is highly industrialized and has a major port.

10. Tiny Brunei and the island nation of Indonesia earn money by exporting _____.

Building Map Skills

The map on this page shows the major rivers of South Asia. Number your paper from 1 to 7 and beside each number write the name of the river identified by that number on the map.

Applying Map Skills

Use the scale on the map on page 377 to calculate the following distances.

1. From Bombay, India, to Ho Chi Minh City, Vietnam

2. From Rangoon, Burma, to Jakarta, Indonesia

3. From Kabul, Afghanistan, to Colombo, Sri Lanka

4. From Karāchi, Pakistan, to Manila, Philippines

Exploring Further

1. The struggles for independence in South Asia were led by people with vastly differing goals and beliefs. Research and report on the beliefs and actions of one of the following independence leaders: Mohandas Gandhi (India), Prince Norodom Sihanouk (Kampuchea), Ho Chi Minh (Vietnam), Sukarno (Indonesia).

2. The Taj Mahal in northern India is thought to be one of the most beautiful buildings in the world. It was built at the orders of Shah Jahan, India's Mogul emperor, in the 1600's. Find out why Shah Jahan had the Taj Mahal built, what style the building's architecture is, and what the building looks like. Bring interior and exterior pictures of the Taj Mahal to class.

3. The participation of the United States in the war in Vietnam stirred strong emotions among Americans. To learn about people's feelings about the war, interview neighbors or family members who were young adults or adults during the years 1965 to 1973. Ask them what they thought of American involvement and how they felt about demonstrations against the war.

399

Ask students, "Why is *Middle East* a good way to describe this region?" (*It is in the middle of the Eastern Hemisphere.*) Why might the Middle East be called the crossroads of the world? (*It is the meeting place of three continents. Before the Age of Exploration, this description was, of course, more apt than it is today.*)

North Africa and the Middle East

The region made up of North Africa and the Middle East lies on parts of three continents — Africa, Asia, and Europe. The region reaches from the Atlantic Ocean as far east as the borders of Pakistan and Afghanistan in South Asia. It includes countries lying in the northern Sahara, a vast desert in Africa. It also includes the Middle East, or those countries extending from Egypt (which lies on the continent of Africa) to Iran in Southwest Asia. One Middle Eastern country — Turkey — lies on the northeastern shore of the Mediterranean. Its western tip is in Europe.

North Africa and the Middle East are united by physical and cultural features. Its people must cope with an extremely dry climate and constant shortages of water. Apart from oil — the region's black gold — there are few resources useful in modern industry. The Middle East was the starting place for three of the world's great religions — Judaism, Christianity, and Islam. Today over 90 percent of the people of North Africa and the Middle East are Muslims, or followers of Islam.

Such similarities, however, do not make North Africa and the Middle East a region of union and harmony. North Africa and the Middle East are areas of great diversity and complexity. Political unrest, armed conflicts between countries, and terrorism have been widespread for years.

400

The photograph shows a desert gas line in Abu Dhabi, United Arab Emirates.

1 The Physical Environment

Millions of years ago, much of North Africa and the Middle East was covered by a huge sea. The sea was rich in marine life. Through time, the waters receded. The fossil remains of the abundant sea life became buried beneath layers of sand and silt. Over a period of still more geologic ages, constant pressure from layers of rock changed the fossils into huge underground basins of petroleum.

Today platforms, pumps, pipelines, and other structures stand over those oil basins formed in the distant past. With this equipment, people draw oil from Earth. Except for these human-made features, the present landscape suggests few of its ancient secrets.

Landforms

Vast desert plains and plateaus cover most of North Africa and the Middle East. In North Africa, the sands, rocks, and gravels of the **Sahara** (sə har'ə) stretch across most of Morocco, Algeria, and Libya. The word *Sahara* is Arabic; it means "desert." In places, the Sahara is broken by steep-sided rocky plateaus cut by deep chasms.

The desert plain continues eastward across Egypt to the Red Sea. On the eastern side of the Red Sea, a desert plain also covers most of the Arabian Peninsula. There, as in parts of the Sahara, wind-blown sands ripple and shift, sometimes piling into large **dunes**, or ridges, resembling small mountains. The Rub Al Khali (rub' äl' käl'ē) is a sandy wasteland in the southern part of the Arabian Peninsula. Rub Al Khali means "empty quarter."

There are a number of mountainous areas in North Africa and the Middle East. The region's mountains are generally low and rugged. To the west, the Atlas Mountains dominate Morocco and northern Algeria. To the southeast are the Asir and Hadramawi ranges of the Arabian Peninsula. To the northeast is a highlands region, the **Armenian Knot**. It includes the mountains of both Iran and Turkey. Iran's Zagros Mountains, which lie along the border with Iraq, are just west of its dry central plateau.

The northernmost country of the region, Turkey, also has a central highlands area, the Anatolian Plateau. This plateau lies between the Taurus Mountains to the south and the Pontic Mountains to the north.

Narrow plains rim the coast throughout North Africa and the Middle East. The lowlands lie along the Mediterranean Sea, the Red Sea, and the Persian Gulf.

Climates and Ecosystems

The climate map on page 404 shows why some geographers call North Africa and the Middle East the dry world. Arid and semiarid conditions prevail in about 90 percent of the region.

The Desert Rainfall is scant throughout this dry world. Some desert areas go for several years with no rain at all. The deserts have little plant life. Vegetation grows, however, in a few places. There, rivers and underground springs support date palms and other large plants.

Despite the generally dry conditions, destructive rains sometimes strike the desert. Where there are few or no plants to slow runoff, water quickly fills up **wadis** (wäd'ēz), ancient stream beds that are normally dry and empty. Torrents of water run through wadis, overflowing the banks and creating **flash floods**. Though the water seeps into the earth and disappears quickly, the floodwaters can

401

Have students locate the countries and landforms of this region on the map on pages 402–403 as each is discussed.

Assign the Workbook activity for Chapter 16, Section 1, with pages 401–405.

North Africa and the Middle East: Physical

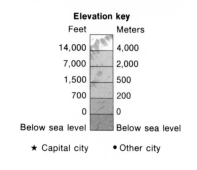

Elevation key

Feet		Meters
14,000		4,000
7,000		2,000
1,500		500
700		200
0		0
Below sea level		Below sea level

★ Capital city   • Other city

Highest point—Mt. Demavend
     Elevation: 18,602 ft/5,670 m

Lowest point—Dead Sea
     Depth: -1296 ft/-395 m

Longest river—Euphrates River
     Length: 1,715 mi/2,760 km

Largest lake—Lake Urmia
     Area: 2,239 sq. mi./5,800 sq. km

Area—4,710,665 sq. mi/12,200,568 sq. km

Population—306,650,000

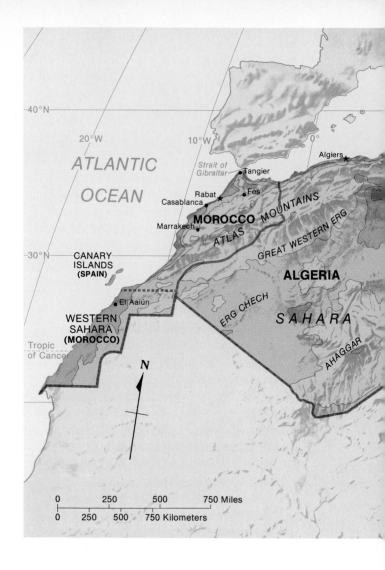

Map Study *What are the westernmost mountains in the region? The northernmost? Name the northernmost city in Africa. Which of the region's countries border the Red Sea? The Arabian Sea?*

sweep away villages and fields, killing people and livestock.

During the dry season, a wind blows northward from the interior of Africa. This wind, called the **sirocco** (sə räk'ō), whips up dust storms as it crosses the Sahara. The dust turns the sky dark as night. Desert dwellers take cover inside tents tightly secured to the ground. In cities to the north, people seal windows and shut doors for days at a time.

Temperatures under the cloudless desert skies are extreme. Months may pass with daytime temperatures staying above 100°F (38°C). When the sun goes down, however, the desert sands cool rapidly. Nighttime temperatures may dive to below freezing.

The Steppes Narrow fringes of steppe surround many of the region's desert areas. Steppe also covers the high plateaus of Turkey and Iran. Steppe areas receive enough rainfall to support some crops. They also have natural grasses on which sheep, goats, and other kinds of livestock graze.

The Sahara is the largest desert in the world; it is almost as big as the United States, covering more than three million square miles. Only 20 percent of it is dune.

Answers to Map Study questions: the Atlas Mountains; the Pontic Mountains; Tunis; Egypt; Saudi Arabia; Yemen; People's Democratic Republic of Yemen, Oman

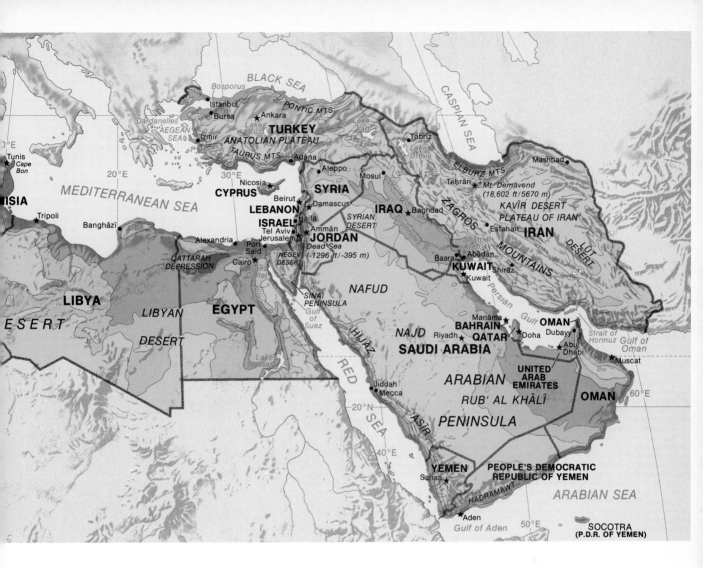

Since the 1960's, droughts have occurred regularly in the steppe areas of North Africa. Lack of rainfall and overgrazing in many areas have stripped the steppe of its grasses. In effect, the desert has spread to land that was previously steppe. North African countries are trying to restore steppe areas. They are planting trees and grasses that can withstand drought. They are also trying to encourage people to grow crops rather than to continue grazing animals.

The Moist Areas Several long strips of lowlands lie along the western and eastern Mediterranean and the southern shore of the Caspian Sea. Small as they are compared with the deserts, these coastal lowlands are of great importance to the people, especially in countries that face the Mediterranean Sea. The coastal areas are important because they receive enough rainfall during the winter wet season for farming. As in other Mediterranean climate areas, their summers are dry and sunny.

In the past, forests covered some of the moist coastal and highland areas of the Middle East. However, for several thousand years, people have been cutting the trees without replanting. Now many of the once-forested areas are barren except for a few low shrubs.

403

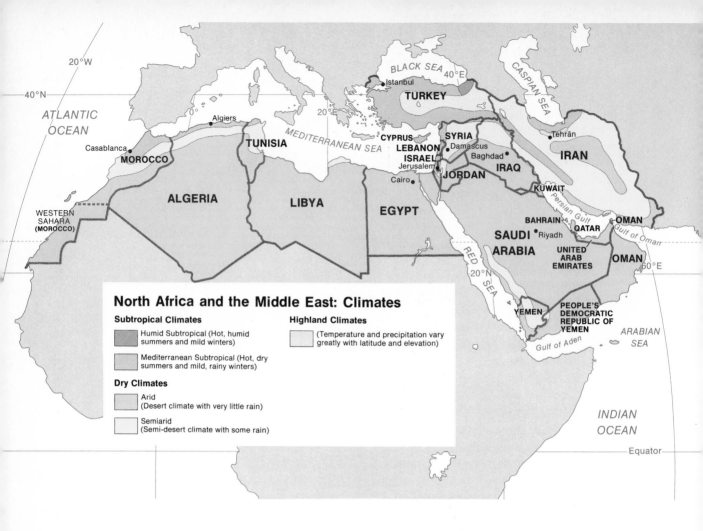

North Africa and the Middle East: Climates

Subtropical Climates

▨ Humid Subtropical (Hot, humid summers and mild winters)

▨ Mediterranean Subtropical (Hot, dry summers and mild, rainy winters)

Dry Climates

▨ Arid (Desert climate with very little rain)

☐ Semiarid (Semi-desert climate with some rain)

Highland Climates

☐ (Temperature and precipitation vary greatly with latitude and elevation)

Map Study *What is the major climate of the region? Areas bordering the Mediterranean Sea have what sorts of climates? In which country is there an area with a highland climate?*

Lifelines of Water Links to supplies of water are the region's lifelines. The desert is too dry to support many people. Population clusters around areas with supplies of water. In the desert, oases around springs and wells are islands of life in seas of sand.

Oases, some of them of vast size, also form around rivers. The major river oasis of North Africa lies along the Nile. Two

Dry plateaus and mountains surround one of the region's oases. Many crops—including dates, wheat, and millet—are grown in oases.

Answers to Map Study questions: arid; Mediterranean subtropical, semiarid, arid; Iran
The area extending from the Mediterranean Sea to the Persian Gulf, which encompasses the Tigris-Euphrates rivers, is called the Fertile Crescent. In this hospitable area, Sumer, the world's first civilization, arose.

great tributaries — the Blue Nile and the White Nile — flow from the rainy highlands in central Africa. They come together at the southern edge of the desert. From this point, the Nile flows northward into the Mediterranean.

The Jordan River begins in highlands in northern Israel. It flows south through the Sea of Galilee, emptying into the Dead Sea, an inland saltwater lake. The Dead Sea's surface lies nearly 1,300 feet (395 meters) below sea level, the lowest point of dry land on Earth.

Other important rivers of the region flow from the Armenian Knot. The Tigris and Euphrates in Iraq flow southeastward into the Persian Gulf. The land between the rivers is the fertile plain, where the earliest urban cultures arose.

REVIEWING THE FACTS

Define

1. Sahara
2. dune
3. Armenian Knot
4. wadi
5. flash flood
6. sirocco

Answer

1. What landforms dominate North Africa and the Middle East?

2. Why is this region sometimes called the dry world?

3. (a) Which parts of the region get the most rain? (b) During which season does most rain fall?

4. Why are coastal areas of special importance to North African and Middle Eastern countries?

Locate

Refer to the map on pages 402–403.

1. Which countries of the region lie almost entirely in mountains?

2. Name the region's island countries.

2 The Human Imprint

North Africa and the Middle East have about 20 percent more land and approximately 10 million more people than the United States. Turkey, with more than 52 million residents, has the largest population in the region. Some of the smaller countries — including Bahrain, Cyprus, and Qatar — have fewer than one million people apiece. In general, the population growth rates of the region's countries are among the highest in the world.

Population and Settlement

People in North Africa and the Middle East live near supplies of water. They inhabit the moist coasts, the semiarid steppes and uplands, and the green oases of the fertile river valleys. Some of these areas — the Nile Valley in particular — are densely populated. A few nomadic peoples still inhabit desert areas.

City Life People settled in cities in the Middle East and North Africa long ago. Some of Earth's earliest cities were established in the region. Such cities as Baghdad, Jerusalem, Damascus, Istanbul, Mecca, Cairo, Alexandria, Algiers, and Tunis are all many hundreds of years old. Traditional activities continue in these cities. Many ancient buildings of plaster and tile remain. They are homes, workshops, and places of worship.

The region's cities are also centers for trade, education, and government. In Teheran, Tel Aviv, Beirut, and other cities, tall buildings of steel and glass rise among the traditional dwellings and public buildings.

City populations throughout the region are growing rapidly. One important cause is migration from rural areas. Unable to house and employ all the new arrivals, many cities are ringed by slums.

405

Several cities are mentioned on this page. Make sure students know where each is located.

Answers are in the Teacher's Guide.

Assign the Workbook activity for Chapter 16, Section 2, with pages 405–412.

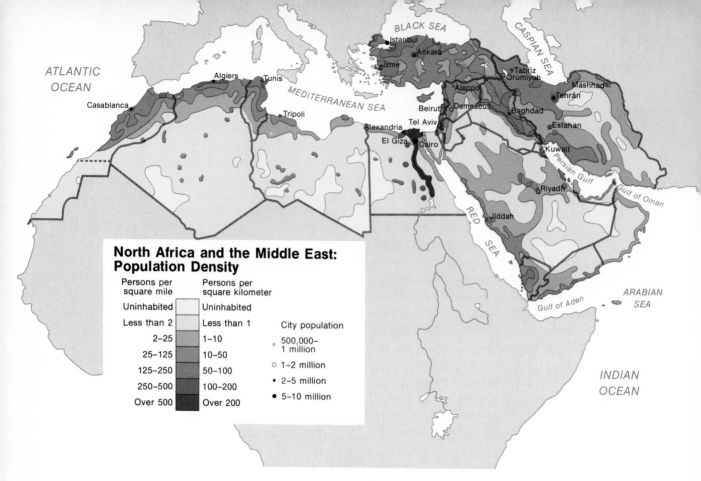

North Africa and the Middle East: Population Density

Persons per square mile	Persons per square kilometer
Uninhabited	Uninhabited
Less than 2	Less than 1
2–25	1–10
25–125	10–50
125–250	50–100
250–500	100–200
Over 500	Over 200

City population

○ 500,000–1 million

○ 1–2 million

● 2–5 million

● 5–10 million

Map Study   *Use the map on pages 402–403 to name the river along which the region's most densely populated area lies. Tell how most of the region's inland area differs from the coastal areas in population density. Which countries have large areas with virtually no people?*

● Only one wall remains of the ancient temple of Jerusalem. It is holy to Jews.

Three Great Religions   The Middle East was the birthplace of three modern religions. Judaism is the oldest of these. It dates back to the time of the early cities of the Tigris-Euphrates Valley. Judaism is a **monotheistic** (män′ə thē is′tic) religion. That is, its followers worship a single God. Jews, or followers of Judaism, believe that God spoke through prophets such as Moses to reveal the moral and spiritual laws that people should follow. These laws were later expressed in the Old Testament of the Bible.

The early Jews believed that these laws formed a covenant, or promise, between God and the Jewish people. The people promised to obey God's commandments and in return expected to receive God's

406

protection. Their homeland, Israel, would prosper only if they obeyed God.

Christianity is also a monotheistic religion that began in the Middle East. It grew out of Judaism about 2,000 years ago. Christianity is based on the teachings of Jesus, a Jew from **Palestine** (or the area occupied by present-day Israel and part of present-day Jordan). At the time of Jesus' birth, Palestine was part of the Roman empire.

Christians believe that Jesus was the son of God, whose coming was expected by many Jews. The New Testament — which along with the Old Testament makes up the Christian Bible — is a record of Jesus' teachings and actions.

In the first century A.D., many people in the eastern Mediterranean region, which was ruled by Rome, became Christians. Christianity also spread to Rome, and it eventually became the most widely practiced religion in Europe and the Americas.

Although Judaism and Christianity began in the Middle East, Christians and Jews are minorities in most of the region's countries. Only Lebanon has a sizable Christian population. Jews are the majority in Israel.

Most people living in North Africa and the Middle East today follow Islam, the third great monotheistic faith born in the region. Islam began with the teachings of Muhammad, who was born in Mecca, a city on the Arabian Peninsula, in A.D. 570. As a young adult, Muhammad was a wealthy merchant. He came to believe that God had chosen him as the prophet for the Arab people. Muhammad was strongly influenced by both Judaism and Christianity. Like Moses and Jesus, he urged his followers to obey God's laws. In fact, the word for followers of Islam is *Muslim*, which is Arabic for "one who submits."

Muslims pray at an Islamic mosque in Fez, Morocco.

Muhammad's teachings are collected in the holy book of Islam, called the Koran (kô ran'). Written in Arabic, the Koran describes the Islamic faith in Allah, or God. It also states rules for worship and conduct. Faithful Muslims pray five times every day, keep the fast of Ramadan, and try to visit the holy city of Mecca at least once. The Koran forbids Muslims to gamble, eat pork, or drink alcoholic beverages. It provides rules for business and family life as well. For example, according to the Koran, women may appear in public only with their faces veiled and in the company of an adult male family member.

Islam Today After the death of Muhammad in A.D. 632, his followers spread their new religion by conquering other peoples. Riding on horseback and armed with swords, Muslim warriors swept across North Africa and much of the Middle East. They captured lands as far west as Spain and as far east as India, establishing a vast empire. Most of the conquered people converted to Islam. Many learned Arabic, the language of their new rulers.

407

MAP WORKSHOP

Reading Maps and Tables of Oil Economics

Thirteen countries belong to the Organization of Petroleum Exporting Countries (OPEC). The map on this page shows the names and locations of these nations.

The United States has long been a leading buyer of OPEC oil. Today, however, the United States buys less OPEC oil than in the past. The table on this page shows recent trends in oil purchases by the United States from OPEC nations. It divides these purchases into purchases from Arab members of OPEC and purchases from all members of OPEC.

Use the map and the table to help in answering the following questions.

1. Which countries of North Africa and the Middle East belong to OPEC?

2. (a) List the OPEC countries of Southeast Asia. (b) Of Africa south of the Sahara. (c) Of South America.

3. (a) In which year did the United States buy the most oil from all OPEC nations combined? (b) In which year did it buy the most oil from Arab members of OPEC?

4. Look at oil purchases made by the United States from OPEC nations for the years 1978–1981. Compare the amounts purchased from the total OPEC community with the amounts purchased from only the Arab producers. Did the United States buy more or less than half its OPEC oil from Arab countries in this period?

5. What happened to the amount of oil bought by the United States from OPEC nations between 1978 and 1985?

U.S. IMPORTS OF OIL FROM OPEC COUNTRIES (thousands of barrels per day)

Year	Arab OPEC Members	All OPEC Members
1973	915	2,993
1978	2,963	5,751
1979	3,056	5,637
1980	2,551	4,300
1981	1,848	3,323
1982	854	2,146
1983	632	1,862
1985	472	1,830

Source: U.S. Department of Energy.

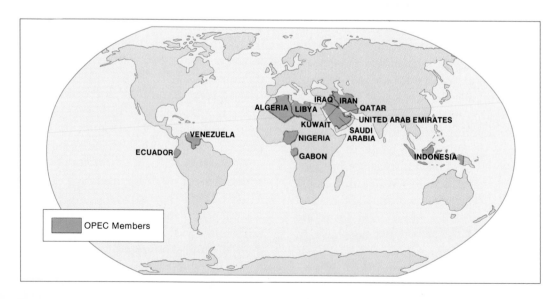

OPEC Members

As a result of these conquests, Muslims of North Africa and the Middle East are divided in important ways. For example, the region includes people of many different ethnic and national backgrounds. Turks, Egyptians, and Iranians are among the largest Islamic groups.

Muslims also are divided into a number of different branches. Each interprets the Koran in its own way. The **Sunni** (sŭn'ē') branch has the most followers. The far-smaller **Shiite** (shē'īt') branch is concentrated in Iran. Its followers generally seek to establish Islamic governments that strictly follow Shiite traditions. Shiites oppose efforts to alter Islam.

Some Muslims are willing to accept changes in their religious practices. For example, in the 1920's, the government of Turkey started a movement to modernize Islam in that country. It permitted the use of the Turkish language in place of Arabic in worship and outlawed such practices as the veiling of women.

Political Patterns

Today there are 21 countries in North Africa and the Middle East. Much of the area was ruled by the Ottoman Turks for several hundred years (page 314). During the 1800's and the early 1900's, the Ottoman empire's hold on the region weakened. France, Italy, Spain, and the United Kingdom took control of much of North Africa during these years.

The Ottomans sided with Germany in World War I. As a result of their defeat, they lost their remaining lands in the region. By 1918, all that was left of the former empire was the country of Turkey. France and the United Kingdom took over the administration of Syria, Iraq, Lebanon, and Palestine.

Nationalist feelings were strong during the years of foreign rule. In the 1900's,

these feelings exploded. In the years just before and just following World War II, wars for independence shook the region. Most countries of the region won their independence in those years.

As you will read, North Africa and the Middle East are still volatile areas. Several armed conflicts rage there today. A good example of the unrest in the region is the relationship between Israel and its neighbors (pages 419–421).

Most countries of the region have authoritarian governments. Although constitutions may provide for elected representatives, monarchs or other authoritarian leaders hold real power. In Saudi Arabia, for example, the royal Saud family rules. Its rule began in the early years of this century.

Monarchs also rule Bahrain, Jordan, Kuwait, Morocco, Oman, and the United Arab Emirates. In a number of these countries, the monarch is known as an **emir** (i mir'). Other countries — including Syria, Yemen, and Iraq — are socialist, one-party states. Iran is an Islamic republic. That is, Muslim religious leaders control the government.

Many of the region's governments are quite unstable. Coups occur frequently in the region. The most stable democracy in the area is Israel. Israel has a parliamentary form of government.

Economic Patterns

The Industrial Revolution did not spread to North Africa and the Middle East during the 1800's and early 1900's. For the most part, people in the region held to their old ways. Manufacturing and industry, therefore, are only in the beginning stages today.

Agriculture Many people of North Africa and the Middle East still live by agriculture. In coastal areas, there is

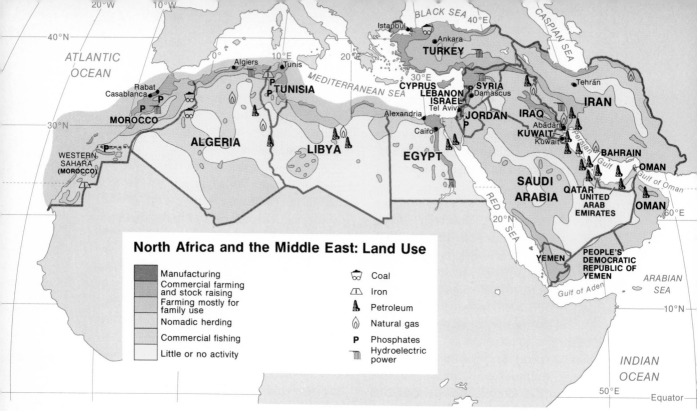

North Africa and the Middle East: Land Use

Manufacturing
Commercial farming
and stock raising
Farming mostly for
family use
Nomadic herding
Commercial fishing
Little or no activity

Coal
Iron
Petroleum
Natural gas
P Phosphates
Hydroelectric
power

Map Study   *Near what body of water are the region's greatest deposits of oil? Where does most of the region's commercial farming and stock raising take place?*

enough rainfall for farmers to grow fruits, olives, grapes, wheat, and tobacco. Farmers sell such crops for cash. Tunisia, for example, is the world's leading exporter of olive oil.

In inland areas, where there is enough water, farmers grow barley and millet. In drier areas, the major crops are corn, fruits, vegetables, and cotton. The dry lands, of course, must be irrigated. In some areas, underground tunnels called *qanats* bring ground water to fields. In other areas, pipelines or open canals bring water from rivers or wells. Raw cotton grown in the irrigated Nile Valley makes up about half of Egypt's total exports. Where the land is not irrigated, nomads herd animals.

Oil and Other Industries   The export of oil is a key to development in the region. Oil sales have brought a number of countries great wealth. Among them are the

countries of the Arabian Peninsula — including Saudi Arabia, Kuwait, the United Arab Emirates, Qatar, Bahrain, and Oman — as well as Libya, Iraq, and Iran. Countries bordering the Persian Gulf have about one third of the world's known reserves of natural gas.

The oil-rich countries have funds for modernization. Iran, Saudi Arabia, and a few others process petroleum products. In urban areas, they have refineries that make chemicals and fertilizers.

Although the region is not rich in other natural resources, North Africa has deposits of salt, potash, and phosphates (which are used in fertilizers, detergents, and baking soda). Morocco and Tunisia are two of the world's largest exporters of phosphates. Morocco has built fertilizer-making plants. Turkey has enough iron and coal to support steelmaking. The region also processes foods and makes tex-

Answers to Map Study questions: Persian Gulf; along the Mediterranean coast, in the Nile Valley, and in southern Iraq

Ask students to identify the most common land-use activity in North Africa and the Middle East. *(nomadic herding)*

WORLD DATA BANK

Country	Area in Square Miles	Population/Natural Increase		Per Capita GNP
Algeria	919,591	23,500,000	(3.2%)	$ 2,530
Bahrain	239	400,000	(2.8%)	9,560
Egypt	386,660	51,900,000	(2.6%)	680
Iran	636,293	50,400,000	(3.2%)	NA
Iraq	167,923	17,000,000	(3.3%)	NA
Israel	8,019	4,400,000	(1.7%)	4,920
Jordan	37,737	3,700,000	(3.7%)	1,560
Kuwait	6,880	1,900,000	(3.2%)	14,270
Lebanon	4,015	3,300,000	(2.2%)	NA
Libya	679,359	3,800,000	(3.0%)	7,500
Morocco	172,413	24,400,000	(2.5%)	610
Oman	82,031	1,300,000	(3.3%)	7,080
Qatar	4,247	300,000	(3.0%)	15,980
Saudi Arabia	829,996	14,800,000	(3.1%)	8,860
Syria	71,498	11,300,000	(3.8%)	1,630
Tunisia	63,170	7,600,000	(2.5%)	1,220
Turkey	301,382	51,400,000	(2.1%)	1,130
United Arab Emirates	32,278	1,400,000	(2.6%)	19,120
Yemen Arab Republic	75,290	6,500,000	(3.4%)	520
Yemen, People's Democratic Republic of	128,560	2,400,000	(3.0%)	540

tiles, cement, and some light industrial products.

Oil in the Future Some estimates suggest that oil may be gone from the Middle East in 25 years. Oil-exporting countries want to earn as much as they can from oil sales in the meantime. Many belong to the Organization of Petroleum Exporting Countries (OPEC) (page 408). OPEC members agreed to raise oil prices dramatically in the 1970's. Higher prices gave OPEC countries increased income.

Since the 1970's, however, industrial countries have cut back on their use of oil and found new sources of the precious fuel. As sales fell in the mid-1980's, some OPEC members lowered their prices. When oil prices dropped, the income of oil-exporting countries also tumbled.

Transportation Linkages Three continents — Europe, Asia, and Africa — meet in the Middle East. Since ancient times, the area has been a commercial crossroads and a cultural meeting ground. Merchants shipped goods through the region. Travelers bound for Europe or Asia brought new ideas and interests.

Transportation still plays a vital part in the region's economies. The Mediterranean Sea links the region with Europe.

In 1973, OPEC members agreed to raise oil prices and cut off shipments of oil to the United States in reaction to American support for Israel in the October War. The realization that dependence on Middle Eastern oil made the West vulnerable to such tactics led to concerted efforts to conserve oil and find new sources of energy.

There is a great deal of trade between the countries of Western Europe and those of North Africa and the Middle East. The Soviet Union also buys and sells goods in the region. Its ships reach the area by sailing through the Black Sea and the Bosporus and Dardanelles straits.

As in the past, goods bound for other parts of the world pass through the Middle East. For example, shippers can reach the Indian Ocean from the Mediterranean by sailing through the Suez Canal and the Red Sea. Opened in 1869, the Suez Canal cuts through 100 miles (160 kilometers) of the Isthmus of Suez, between the Mediterranean and the Red seas. The canal also provides a major shipping route for oil tankers leaving the Persian Gulf bound for Europe. Egypt controls the Suez Canal and gains income from the fees paid by ships passing through it.

REVIEWING THE FACTS

Define

1. monotheistic
2. Palestine
3. Sunni
4. Shiite
5. emir

Answer

1. What three major religions began in the Middle East?

2. What kind of government is most common in the region?

3. (a) In what areas of the region is there agriculture? (b) What economic activity has brought great wealth to some countries in the region?

Locate

Refer to the map on pages 402–403.

1. In what country are the Bosporus and the Dardanelles found?

2. Name the Persian Gulf port cities.

3 North Africa

The Sahara dominates the landscape of North Africa. During the Ice Age, the climate of North Africa and the Sahara was much wetter than it is today. There were woodlands and grasslands. Early peoples of the region lived by hunting and gathering. Perhaps some 10,000 years ago, the area grew arid. This caused important changes in the way people in the region lived. The population declined. People took up a variety of new ways of life.

Desert Dwellers

The first of the present-day peoples known to live in North Africa after the region became arid were the Berbers. The Berbers probably migrated from the Middle East around 2000 B.C. Their descendants are scattered throughout North Africa today, especially in the highlands of Morocco and Algeria. There, most are farmers. Some, especially the Tuaregs (twä'regz'), live as nomads.

Many Berber families follow traditional occupations. Children carry on the same jobs as their parents. In northern Morocco, Berber craftworkers make leather and wood into beautiful bags and elaborate boxes. In southwestern Morocco, some Berbers are expert well diggers. From the city of Mogador on the Atlantic coast come Berbers who are famous as tumblers and acrobats in circuses throughout the world.

Many other ethnic groups live in the Sahara and coastal areas of North Africa. Although some people of the area still speak ancient languages, most speak Arabic. This language was introduced during the days of the Islamic empire. Most of the region's peoples became Muslims in those years. Today, more than 98 percent of all North Africans are Muslims.

Have students note the location and importance of the Persian Gulf, the Gulf of Oman, the Gulf of Aden, the Red Sea, the Suez Canal, and the Bosporus and Dardanelles straits. *Answers are in the Teacher's Guide.* Assign the Workbook activity for Chapter 16, Section 3, with pages 412–414.

The Tuaregs are nomads of the Sahara. They ruled the area of Algeria until about 1900. Today they still herd sheep and goats.

The Rural Landscape

Despite the dry climate, farming is important to North Africa's people. There are croplands wherever enough water is available. In coastal areas, farmers grow wheat, barley, and millet in the fall, planting just before the winter rains come. They harvest their crops at the beginning of the hot, dry summer. They also produce olives, figs, and nuts, which can withstand heat and drought.

In some coastal areas, winter rains are not reliable. There, and in large desert oases, farmers irrigate their fields. In some places, they build reservoirs and dig canals through their fields. In other places, they use slanting wells, which tap groundwater from higher land and carry it downslope in tunnels. Farmers in the Moroccan mountains build terraces to catch rainwater as it runs downhill.

On irrigated lands, farmers grow citrus fruit, grapes, vegetables, cotton, and sugarcane. Groves of date palms grow near oases. These trees have long roots that tap moisture deep in the earth.

Desert nomads raise animals to produce meat and animal hides. They trade with people living in oasis villages for grain and other necessities. The nomads also depend on the oases for water for themselves and for their herds of goats, sheep, and camels.

There is not enough suitable farming and grazing land in North Africa for the region's swelling population. In the search for oil in North Africa, however, drillers have discovered water deep below the Sahara. Such supplies might ease the water shortages for a time. On the other

North Africa's Berbers have long used falcons for hunting game in the desert.

413

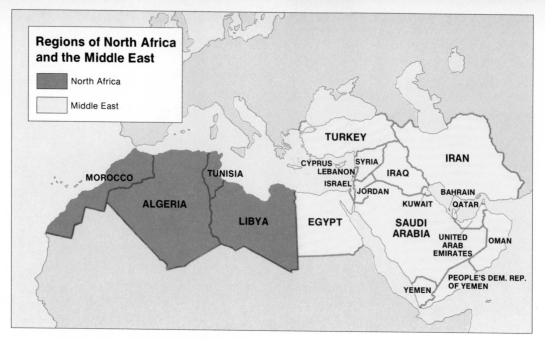

Map Study *Name the two regions shown on the map. Which country on the continent of Africa is in the same region as Iran?*

hand, such water resources are not renewable. In addition, experts believe that tapping them will upset the environmental balance of the area.

Oil wealth has helped Libya in particular to expand farming and develop new industries. However, in many countries the benefits of oil wealth have gone to ruling groups. Oil income has also been used to pay for military forces rather than economic development.

The Urban Landscape

Most of North Africa's cities lie along the Mediterranean coast. Many look much as they did centuries ago. A wall surrounds each city. Near the center of the city, there is a marketplace, called the *suq* (sŭk). Close by is a mosque and a public bathhouse. Large government buildings also lie near the city center.

Tangier is a good example of one of these ancient port cities. It is located on the Strait of Gibraltar, a narrow waterway that separates North Africa from the coast of Spain. The city has almost no manufacturing. Tourism, trade, and traditional activities are most important.

Tangier has given its name to the tangerine, a citrus fruit grown in the area. Like all major North African cities, Tangier has both very old sections and new parts. Next to its farmer's market, for example, are modern tourist hotels. Local people shopping at the market can leave their donkeys in a yard nearby.

REVIEWING THE FACTS

Answer

1. What people first lived in arid North Africa?

2. (a) What are the chief agricultural products of North Africa's coastal areas? (b) Inland arid areas?

3. In which part of the region are North Africa's cities located?

Locate

Refer to the map on pages 402–403.

1. Name the capital of each North African country.
2. Which country of North Africa lies closest to Europe?

414

Texas Essential Elements 3A. Interrelationships of people and their environments. 3B. Economic importance of water, energy sources, and other productive resources to regions. 3C. Agricultural base of regions. 3D. Uses, abuses, and preservation of natural resources and the physical environment. 4D. Major cultural, political, and economic activities within and among major world regions.

4 The Middle East

The Middle East has a complex mix of peoples and cultures. Egyptians, Turks, Iranians, Israelis, and people of the Arabian Peninsula each have their own ethnic, national, and historic backgrounds. There are larger numbers of Jews and Christians in the Middle East than in North Africa.

Still, at least 90 percent of the people of the Middle East are Muslims. The Arabic language is a major language in every country except Iran, Israel, and Turkey. In fact, the term *Arab countries* usually refers to the countries of the Middle East except Israel, Iran, and Turkey.

Farming: Achievements and Challenges

Egypt, Jordan, Israel, Syria, Lebanon, and Turkey all border the Mediterranean. Along the coast, farmers depend on the winter rains to water their crops. Outside these areas, on the Arabian Peninsula and in Iraq and Iran, farming can take place only with the help of irrigation. As in North Africa, there are many subsistence farmers. The methods of these subsistence farmers have changed very little since ancient times.

Some farmers plant vegetables and date palms near wadis. Even when the wadis are dry, there is at least some water a few feet underground for the roots of plants. Flash floods, however, can endanger fields and crops when heavy rains fall upstream.

Nomadic herders also live in parts of the Middle East. Members of one group, the **Bedouin** (bed'ə wən), still herd sheep and camels in parts of the Arabian Peninsula, Syria, and Jordan. The Bedouin are known for their hospitality and strong sense of personal honor.

In Dogubeyazit, Turkey, an Islamic wedding ceremony follows centuries-old customs (top). The bride and the groom display the dowry, money contributed by the family of the bride. ● *In Iran, hand-knotted carpets are spread in the sun to dry. Such carpets sell for high prices in foreign markets.*

415

SPOTLIGHT ON THE NEGEV:

Farming in the Desert

A desert known as the Negev covers about 60 percent of Israel. It is a forbidding land of rocky hills and sandy soil. The little rain that falls there each year evaporates quickly in the hot desert sun. It is not a place where one would expect to find flourishing farms. Yet people have been growing crops in the Negev since biblical times.

Ancient farmers invented a method that made the most of their limited water supply. They built low walls of stone at right angles across wadis—dry streambeds that slice down the hills of the Negev. In the rainy season, when the wadis briefly turn into raging rivers, the stone walls slowed the water. They also kept soil from eroding. Later, farmers built channels of loose rock to bring water from the wadis to huge basins they built nearby. There irrigation ditches channeled some of the water to fields that lay at the base of the hills. The rest of the water was stored underground to avoid rapid evaporation.

With such methods, farmers in biblical times were able to turn half-a-million acres of desert into farmland. Over the centuries, the methods they used were forgotten, and their fields abandoned. Yet the need to make the most of a limited water supply has increased. Therefore, in the 1950's, a team of Israeli scientists restored the old walls and channels so that modern farmers could take advantage of the old technology. Other scientists searched for new ways of conserving water in the desert. They found a solution in a water supply that farmers had never been able to use.

Beneath the Negev lies a huge aquifer —a layer of earth that contains water trapped in rock and clay. People have long known about aquifers, but until recently these aquifers could not be used successfully to grow crops. The water was too salty for most plants.

Although scientists can remove salt from water, it is a very costly process. The Israelis sought a more practical solution to the problem. The answer turned out to be the development of strains of grains, fruits, and vegetables that can grow in sand on a diet of liquid fertilizer and salty water. Israeli fields planted with these strains can produce as much as three or four harvests a year of such crops as wheat, peanuts, melons, tomatoes, eggplants, peppers, dates, zucchini, and even avocados.

To make sure their fields get exactly the right amount of water and fertilizer, the farmers depend on a solar-powered computer nicknamed Einstein. It releases water and fertilizer directly to the root system of each plant through thin plastic tubes. In this way no water is wasted.

The new technology saves water in another way too. The new strains produce very high yields. For example, the midget wheat grown in the Negev produces 35 percent more grain than fields planted with full-sized plants.

Many people are carefully watching the experiments in the Negev. The technology developed there could be used to expand the food supply of countries around the world. Indeed Israeli specialists are now training scientists and farmers in 54 nations. Their methods are being used in dry areas from Africa's Sahara to the Texas panhandle.

416

The Nile Valley Much of the Nile Valley lies in eastern Egypt. Farmers along the Nile successfully used basin flooding irrigation for thousands of years. Basin flooding worked like this. After spring rains, the Nile spilled over its banks. Farmers trapped floodwaters by building low, mud dikes around their soaked fields. The low walls captured rich silt as well as water. Farmers planted their crops in the wet, fertile soils.

In 1971, the completion of a huge dam changed irrigation methods along the Nile. Egypt built the Aswan Dam near its southern border. Behind the dam is Lake Nassar, one of the world's largest artificial lakes. The Aswan Dam and Lake Nassar enable Egyptians to control the seasonal flooding of the Nile. They can then provide the valley with a steady, year-round water supply. In addition, they have created over a million new acres of irrigated cropland.

Egypt benefited from the Aswan Dam in other ways. The dam nearly doubled Egypt's supply of electrical power. Many more Egyptian homes received electricity for the first time. The dam also provided energy for new factories making textiles, chemicals, and fertilizers.

However, the Aswan Dam has caused some environmental problems. For one thing, it traps the Nile's load of silt. As a result, fields downstream from the dam no longer get periodic deposits of fertile silt. Without these silt deposits, the river's shoreline is eroded. In addition, the reservoir behind the dam covers land that was once farms and villages as well as ancient historical sites.

Low Productivity Many farms in the Middle East are not very productive. This problem is growing worse. As population rises, farm plots get smaller and smaller. Families tending smaller plots grow less food than those with larger farms.

Traditional farming methods are still used in much of the Middle East. Here, a cow-powered pump is used to draw water.

In addition, many of the region's farmers are tenant farmers, who pay part of their crop as rent to the landowner. After paying rent, tenant farmers are often left with little money for tools, seed, and fertilizer.

Middle Eastern governments today have a number of land-reform programs. Some are giving tenant farmers land of their own. But as long as farms remain small, it is not economical to use large farm equipment. Therefore, some countries have started cooperative farms. Under this system, farmers own larger farms jointly and share farm machinery.

Farming in Israel is more successful than elsewhere in the region. Modern irrigation has made the desert into an oasis garden. Most of Israel's farms are privately owned. Yet there are cooperative farms called **kibbutzes.**

417

The United Nations decided, in 1947, that both the Jews and the Palestinians had legitimate claims to Palestine. It recommended that the land be partitioned, making homelands for both peoples. The Israelis accepted this offer and founded a state, but the Palestinians refused because they denied the Jewish claim to any part of Palestine.

Oil Wealth and Its Effects

The area surrounding the Persian Gulf has about half the world's known oil reserves. Saudi Arabia alone has more than a third of the world's reserves. Along with several nearby countries, Saudi Arabia is a leading oil exporter. Yet other Middle Eastern countries, such as South Yemen, have no oil.

In the oil-rich countries, most wealth is in the hands of a few government officials and leading families. People with great wealth and luxuries live near areas of deep poverty.

Still, oil income has brought dramatic changes. Standards of living have risen for many of the people. Governments have built schools, hospitals, and apartments. In Kuwait and Saudi Arabia, whole new cities are being built almost overnight. For example, Jubail will be the center of Saudi Arabia's chemical industry. Planners hope this ultra-modern city, begun in 1977, will have a population of 350,000 by the year 2000.

A Region of Conflicts

Wars and conflicts in the Middle East affect the daily lives of many of its people. The hostilities stem from various sources. The region's conflicts have roots in the distant past.

The Palestinians Under the supervision of the United Nations, Israel became a country in 1948. Since before 1900, Jews from many parts of the world had been moving to Palestine, the ancient homeland of the Jewish people. Immigration increased in the 1940's, when Jews fled Europe during the Holocaust (page 289).

Arabs who lived in Palestine began to fear that they would soon be outnumbered. After the establishment of Israel in 1948, thousands of Palestinian Muslims fled the area. They did not want to live in a land governed by the Israelis, even though the Israelis were willing to have them stay.

Most of the Palestinians had no place to go outside of Israel. Nearby countries did not want to admit them as new citizens.

Much of the Middle East's oil is shipped from Persian Gulf ports. In this photo, tankers are filled at dockside in Kuwait.

So the fleeing Palestinians were settled in makeshift camps. Since 1948, many former Palestinians and their descendants have spent their entire lives in such camps in Jordan and other Arab countries. A large number of Palestinians also live on the West Bank of the Jordan River on land controlled by Israel.

Many Palestinians wish to have a country of their own. A loosely knit group of fighters known as the Palestine Liberation Organization (PLO) claims to represent the Palestinians. The PLO's expressed aim is to establish a permanent homeland for the refugees. For years, the PLO has refused to recognize Israel's right to exist as an independent country.

Members of PLO groups have attacked Israeli towns and villages as well as military targets. The PLO has carried out a number of terrorist bombings and hijackings of airplanes in the Middle East. Israelis have responded by attacking PLO bases. Civilians have died in many of the raids and bombings.

In recent years, the PLO has splintered into rival factions. It has been driven out of its strongholds in a number of countries. For example, Israel launched a large-scale military action to clear the PLO out of Lebanon in 1982 (page 421). PLO leaders fled the country as Israel routed their fighters. Since then, however, PLO fighters have reappeared in Lebanon. Syria has sent aid both to the PLO and to some Christian groups to keep any group from winning a victory.

The Arab-Israeli Conflict Arab countries opposed the Jewish settlement of Palestine. Even so, the settlers eventually formed the country of Israel. Arab governments refused to recognize the new country. In fact, armies from Syria, Lebanon, Jordan, Iraq, and Egypt swept into Israel the very day Israel became a country. The Israelis were ready. After two

FROM ASIA TO EUROPE IN A SPLASH

The Bosporus Strait marks a boundary between the continents of Europe and Asia. The cities on both shores — Istanbul and Uskúdar (us′kə där′) — belong to Turkey. Each year a group of Americans living in Istanbul swims from Asia to Europe — about half a mile (nearly 1 kilometer). They top off the event with a pancake breakfast.

months of bitter fighting, they not only beat back the Arab armies but also increased their territory.

The peace established in 1948 was fragile. Fighting broke out again in 1956, when Israel — fearing another invasion — attacked Egypt's Sinai Peninsula. Israel had gained more land by the time the fighting ended. This land gave Israel access to the Red Sea.

Again fearing Arab attack, Israel struck at its neighbors in 1967. The Six Day War ended with Israel in control of still more Arab land. For several years, Egyptian and Israeli forces fought minor skirmishes. This uneasy peace lasted until 1973, when Egypt and Syria attacked Israel. After weeks of furious combat, the fighting stopped, with Israel still in control of the lands it had gained in 1967.

419

Texas Essential Elements 4D. Major cultural, political, and economic activities within and among major world regions. 4F. Geographic influences on various issues.

Distinguishing between Fact and Opinion

It is important to evaluate information you receive. One way to evaluate information is to consider whether it is fact or opinion.

A fact is a statement that can be verified. It is possible to prove that a statement is a fact by finding evidence that shows that the information is true. For example, the following statement is a fact: "More than a third of the Middle East and North Africa is desert." The accuracy of that statement can be checked in an encyclopedia or other reference work.

An opinion, on the other hand, cannot be verified. Opinions are beliefs, preferences, and judgments. When people express opinions, they sometimes use opinion words. These include *perhaps*, *maybe*, and *apparently*. "The Middle East is perhaps the most difficult part of the world in which to live," is an opinion. It is impossible to prove this statement. It reflects, not a fact, but what someone thinks or feels.

The statements below concern a war that broke out between Iran and Iraq in 1980 (page 421). The war has been fought with great bitterness. Air strikes against cities, the use of poisonous gases, and human-wave attacks by foot soldiers have marked the conflict. At great cost in life, the edge has see-sawed back and forth between the two neighbors.

Read each statement carefully and decide whether it is a fact or an opinion. Number your paper from 1 to 10 and write either fact or opinion next to each number.

1. After several months of skirmishing over a border river, Iran and Iraq began open warfare in September 1980.

2. Military pressure from within Iran may cause the country to fall like a house of cards.

3. Most Iranians are Shi'ite Moslems, while nearly half of Iraqi Moslems are of the Sunni sect.

4. By April 1986, there were 500,000 casualties in the Iran-Iraq war.

5. By July 1987, more than a million people had died in the Iran-Iraq war.

6. Iraq appears to have just reason for going to war with Iran, its neighbor in the Middle East.

7. On July 20, 1987, the United Nations Security Council called for a cease-fire in the Iran-Iraq war.

8. If Iran and Iraq do not honor the United Nations resolution, it could weaken the United Nations as a peace-making body.

9. Kuwaiti oil tankers have been reregistered to fly the American flag in order to qualify for American protection as they sail through the Persian Gulf.

10. In time, Iran may be forced to change its revolutionary policies and make peace with the West.

Answers are in the Teacher's Guide.

For their efforts to promote peace in the Middle East, Anwar Sadat and Menachem Begin were awarded the 1978 Nobel Peace Prize. Sadat was assassinated in 1981 by Egyptians who opposed his policies.
Assign the Workbook activity for this chapter's Skill Workshop with page 420.

Israel and Egypt signed a peace treaty in 1979. However, tension in the area remains high. Most Arab countries still recognize Israel's enemy, the PLO, as the representative of the Palestinians. Some governments—Syria and Libya among them—provide support for the PLO.

Civil War in Lebanon For a time, Lebanon—Israel's neighbor to the north —seemed to be a model for other countries in the Middle East to follow. Even though its population was religiously and culturally diverse, the country had what appeared to be a stable government supported by most Lebanese.

The situation fell apart in the 1970's. Palestinian refugees and some PLO members began moving their camps into Lebanon. The Lebanese people disagreed about how to deal with these newcomers. Muslims at first welcomed the Palestinians. Christians opposed their presence in the country. Rival armed groups began to fight one another in street battles.

By 1975, the country was in a state of civil war. The government could not control the fighting. As many as 20 different groups struggled to win control of Lebanon. Some were backed by foreign countries, including Israel, Syria, and Iran. Today much of Lebanon is in ruins. The capital of Beirut, once a beautiful resort, has been almost completely destroyed.

The Situation in Iran Until 1979, Iran was ruled by an authoritarian monarch known as the shah. With the help of the United States and Western European countries, the shah tried to modernize Iran. He did away with some Muslim traditions and developed the oil industry.

Many Iranians opposed the changes made by the shah. In addition, they felt that he kept too much oil wealth for his family. They disliked his brutal methods of ruling and his secret police.

In 1978, Iranians joined in a powerful movement to overthrow the shah. Eventually Shiite Muslims became the leading group in the movement. When the shah fled Iran late in 1979, Shiite religious leaders, called **ayatollahs** (ī'ə tȯl'əz), assumed control.

The Shiites set up an authoritarian religious government. The government has arrested, jailed, and put to death thousands of opponents of strict Islamic rule. Since the Islamic takeover, Iran has been largely closed to outsiders.

In 1980, Iran and Iraq went to war. Both sides claimed to be fighting over a boundary. The real conflict, however, was religious. Shi'ites control Iran, while Sunnis hold power in Iraq.

By 1987, other nations were drawn into the conflict. The United States became involved in protecting Persian Gulf oil shipping routes. In 1988, a tentative cease fire was achieved between Iran and Iraq.

REVIEWING THE FACTS

Define

1. Bedouin
2. kibbutz
3. ayatollah

Answer

1. Why is farming unproductive in much of the Middle East?

2. How has oil income affected Middle Eastern countries?

3. Describe four conflicts in the region.

Locate

Refer to the maps on pages 402–403 and 406.

1. List the countries of the Middle East and their capitals.

2. What part of the Middle East is most sparsely settled?

Tell students that groups of radical terrorists have further undermined political stability in the Middle East. For example, in 1983, nearly 300 people were killed by terrorist attacks in Beirut. In 1985, terrorists hijacked the *Achille Lauro*, a cruise ship, and several airplanes. *Answers are in the Teacher's Guide.*

421

GEOGRAPHY LABORATORY

Highlighting the Chapter

1. North Africa and the Middle East are known as the dry world. The chief land feature of the region is desert, broken in a few places by plateaus or mountains and ringed with coastal plains. The largest area of desert is the Sahara, which extends across the southern part of North Africa. Fertile lands, with available water, are found in oases and along river valleys.

2. Residents of the region cluster around supplies of water. Cities dot the coasts and river valleys. Most people in the region are Muslims. However, the Middle East was the starting place of Judaism and Christianity as well as Islam. The 21 countries of the region belonged to foreign powers before this century. Independent today, these nations are involved in a variety of conflicts. Most are ruled by authoritarian governments. Israel, a democracy founded in 1948, is an exception. Although many people of North Africa and the Middle East farm and few work in industry, some countries have earned great wealth by exporting the region's most important industrial resource — oil.

3. Farmers in North Africa grow wheat and other grains along the Mediterranean coast and citrus fruit, grapes, and cotton on irrigated inland fields. Nomads — producing meat and animal hides — still live in desert areas. Ancient cities lie along the Mediterranean.

4. Several Middle Eastern countries are among the leading exporters of oil. Despite projects like the Aswan Dam, farming is not productive. Israel's agriculture stands out in its use of modern methods. Israel and its Arab neighbors have been in conflict since the establishment of Israel in 1948. Most of the Arab governments do not recognize Israel as a nation. Other sources of instability in the region include the civil war in Lebanon and the war between Iran and Iraq.

Speaking Geographically

Number your paper from 1 to 8. Then write the word or term from the list below beside the number of the definition to which it corresponds.

Armenian Knot   Sahara
ayatollah   Sunni
kibbutz   sirocco
Palestine   wadi

1. Large desert in western part of North Africa

2. An ancient stream bed that is dry except during heavy rainfalls

3. Mountainous region from which major rivers of the Middle East drain

4. A branch of Islam

5. Early name for the area now occupied by Israel and part of Jordan

6. A Shiite religious leader

7. A cooperative farm in Israel

8. The hot, dry wind that blows over the Sahara from the interior of Africa

Testing Yourself

Number your paper from 1 to 7. For each of the following items, write a statement explaining how the listed words or terms are related to one another.

1. Mediterranean, Red, Caspian

2. Atlas, Zagros, Pontic

3. Nile, Tigris, Euphrates

4. Baghdad, Cairo, Damascus

5. The Koran, the Old Testament, the New Testament

6. OPEC, Arabian Peninsula, Persian Gulf

7. Suez Canal, Lake Nassar, Aswan Dam

422

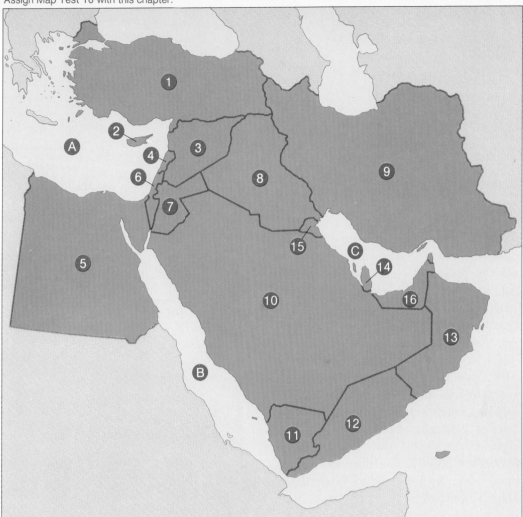

Building Map Skills

Sixteen Middle East countries are numbered on the map on this page. Write the numbers 1 to 16 on your paper, and name the country that goes with each. The three letters on the map identify important bodies of water in the Middle East. Name them.

Applying Map Skills

Write a short statement to describe the location of the Middle East. To help in preparing your statement, look at the maps in this chapter and the Atlas (pages 486–487).

Exploring Further

1. "There are three keys to understanding the Middle East — sand, water, and oil." Explain the meaning of this statement: Which factors will remain important in the region's future?

2. Judaism, Christianity, and Islam had their beginnings in the Middle East. Choose one of these religions for further research. Report on its teachings. What holidays do its followers celebrate? When and how do they worship? In what parts of the world is the religion practiced? Include a world map — colored to show the countries in which a majority of the population follows the religion — with your report.

423

Less than 100 years ago, so little was known about Africa that it was called the Dark Continent. By 1914, almost the whole of Africa had been colonized by European powers. Since World War II, Africa has become a continent of many independent nations, large and small. This chapter examines the problems confronting these new countries: political, economic, and environmental.

Africa South of the Sahara

Africa is a large continent, second in area only to Asia. Yet, despite its large size, Africa's coastline is short, measuring about 22,000 miles (35,000 kilometers). The coastline is short because it is smooth, with few peninsulas, capes, or bays. Europe, which is only about one third as large as Africa, has many more miles of coast.

The African continent is mostly a plateau. It has no mountains that compare with the Rockies, Andes, or Himalayas.

Africa also has the world's largest desert area — the Sahara, which covers an expanse about as large as the United States. Thinly populated, vast, and dry, the Sahara is a transition zone between people and cultures on the continent. North of the Sahara is a Muslim, Arabic-speaking world with many connections to other countries around the Mediterranean Sea. South of the Sahara, a rich variety of cultures developed separately. This chapter takes you to sub-Saharan Africa, the part of the continent that lies mostly south of the Sahara.

Sub-Saharan Africa is a region of rapid change. From the late 1800's until the 1960's and 1970's, most of Africa was under the rule of European colonialism. Most of the nations in sub-Saharan Africa were formed during the past 30 years. As African countries won independence, many changed their European names to African ones. These new names are a sign of the great changes in the region.

424

The photo shows the city of Abidjan, the capital of Cote d'Ivoire. Ask Students, "What did the photographer hope this picture would convey about life in Abidjan?" *(the side-by-side existence of modern and traditional ways of life)* Students will see, as they read Chapter 17, that this picture is emblematic of Africa as a whole.

1 The Physical Environment

If the theory of continental drift is correct, Africa may have been the core land from which South America, Australia, and the Indian subcontinent broke away. Some features of sub-Saharan Africa help scientists interested in learning about Earth's crust and tectonic plates.

Landforms

Most of Africa south of the Sahara is a huge, high plateau. It forms the whole center of the continent. Near the coasts, the land drops sharply in steep cliffs called **escarpments**. The only lowlands are narrow strips along the coasts.

The African plateau is cut by four great rivers—the Nile, the Zaire (zī'ər), the Niger (nī'jər), and the Zambezi (zam bē'zē). In their long, winding journeys to the sea, these rivers drop in a series of falls and rapids. When they reach the escarpment, they cut deep gorges. Spectacular Victoria Falls on the Zambezi drops 420 feet (126 meters) into a deep narrow gorge bordered by steep cliffs.

The Great Rift Valley runs through the eastern part of the African plateau. The valley is a 40-mile-wide (65-kilometer-wide) zone where two tectonic plates began pulling apart millions of years ago. On a map, the rift shows as a series of long, narrow lakes, seas, and valleys. It begins in the Middle East near the Dead Sea, forms the Red Sea trench, and enters the African plateau in Ethiopia. From there, it runs south through Kenya, Tanzania (tan'zə nē'ə), and northern Mozambique (mō'zəm bēk'). Lakes Tanganyika (tan'gən yē'kə) and Nyasa (nī as'ə) mark the path of the Great Rift Valley. Overall, the rift is about 4,000 miles (6,500 kilometers) long.

Volcanic activity, which often occurs near the edges of tectonic plates, is still taking place along the rift. Mount Elgon, Mount Kenya, and Mount Kilimanjaro (kil'ə mən jär'ō) are the three largest volcanic peaks along the Great Rift Valley. Kilimanjaro is Africa's highest mountain.

Climates and Ecosystems

In latitude, Africa is the most tropical of all the continents. Except for the southernmost tip, almost all of sub-Saharan Africa lies between the Tropic of Cancer and the Tropic of Capricorn.

Despite its tropical latitude, parts of Africa have a cool and comfortable climate because of high elevations. Most of the African plateau, for instance, lies at least 1,000 feet (300 meters) above sea level. Nairobi (nī rō'bē), the capital of Kenya, is close to the equator. Yet the city has never experienced a temperature above 87°F (30°C), and nighttime temperatures may drop as low as 50°F (10°C).

Rainfall varies widely from region to region in Africa. Some areas near the equator receive heavy, tropical rains, but parts of the Sahara are among the driest in the world. In most of Africa, rainfall is seasonal. Much rain falls during the wet season, but during the dry season, months may pass without a drop of rain.

The Equatorial Zone The areas of heaviest rainfall are close to the equator, within about five degrees north or south of it. Rain forests grow in the western equatorial zone, along the southern coast of the continent's bulge. Where original rain-forest growth remains, trees may grow more than 100 feet (30 meters) high, their leaves forming a thick canopy that blocks out sunlight. However, much of Africa's original rain forest has been cleared. Shorter, secondary growth has replaced many tall rain-forest trees.

Have students locate the four major rivers of sub-Saharan Africa on the map on page 426.
Through which of the region's countries do they flow? (Nile—Sudan; Zaire—Congo, Zaire;
Niger—Nigeria, Niger, Benin, Mali, Guinea; Zambezi—Mozambique, Zimbabwe, Zambia,
Botswana) Assign the Workbook activity for Chapter 17, Section 1, with pages 425–428.

425

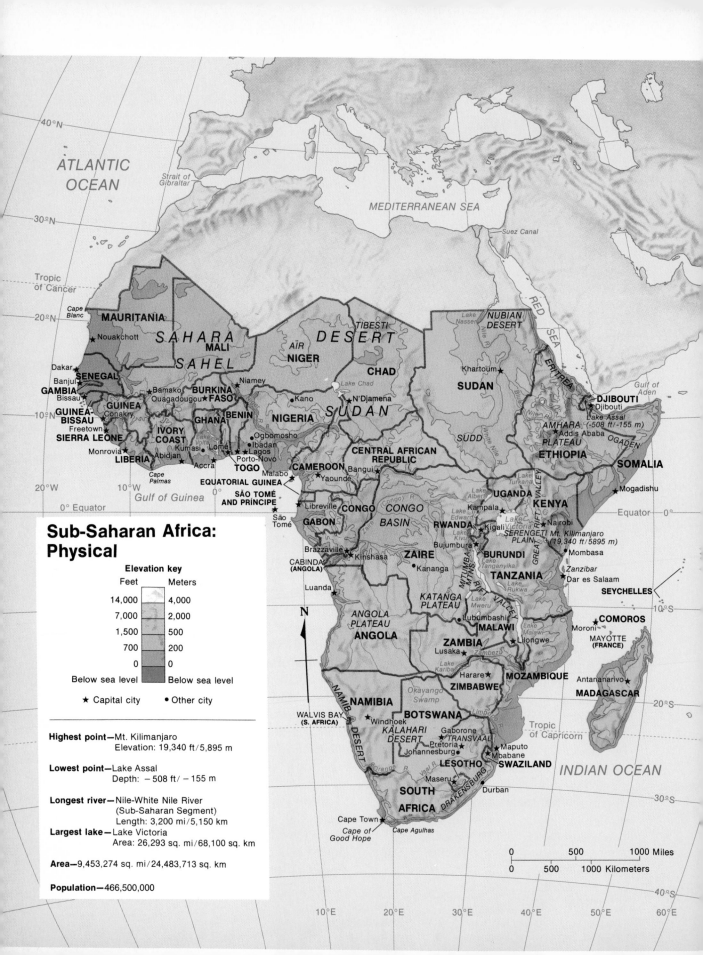

ATLANTIC
OCEAN

Strait of
Gibraltar

MEDITERRANEAN SEA

Suez Canal

Tropic
of Cancer

Cape
Blanc

MAURITANIA

NUBIAN
DESERT

Lake
Nasser

RED SEA

SAHARA

MALI

DESERT

TIBESTI

AÏR

Nouakchott

SAHEL

NIGER

Khartoum

CHAD

SUDAN

Dakar
Banjul
SENEGAL
GAMBIA
Bissau
GUINEA-
BISSAU
Freetown
SIERRA LEONE
Monrovia
LIBERIA

Niamey
Bamako
Ouagadougou
GUINEA
BURKINA
FASO
Conakry
GHANA
BENIN
IVORY
COAST
Kumasi
Lomé
Abidjan
Accra
Cape
Palmas

Kano
N'Djamena

NIGERIA

Ogbomosho
Ibadan
Lagos
Porto-Novo
TOGO

SUDAN

SUDD

Blue Nile
White Nile

ERITREA

Gulf of
Aden

DJIBOUTI
Djibouti
Lake Assal
(-508 ft/-155 m)
AMHARA
Addis Ababa
PLATEAU
ETHIOPIA
OGADEN
SOMALIA

Malabo
CAMEROON
EQUATORIAL GUINEA
SÃO TOMÉ
AND PRÍNCIPE
São
Tomé
Libreville
GABON
Yaounde
Bangui

CENTRAL AFRICAN
REPUBLIC

Lake
Turkana
UGANDA
Lake
Albert
Kampala
KENYA
Nairobi
Lake
Edward
Lake
Victoria
Mt. Kilimanjaro
(19,340 ft/5895 m)

Mogadishu

Sub-Saharan Africa:
Physical

Elevation key

Feet		Meters
14,000		4,000
7,000		2,000
1,500		500
700		200
0		0
Below sea level		Below sea level

★ Capital city   • Other city

CONGO

CONGO
BASIN

Congo R.

Zaire R.

RWANDA
Kigali
Brazzaville
Kinshasa
CABINDA
(ANGOLA)
ZAIRE
Kananga
Luanda

BURUNDI
Bujumbura
SERENGETI
PLAIN
MTUMBA MTNS.
Lake
Kivu
Lake
Tanganyika
TANZANIA
Lake
Rukwa
GREAT RIFT VALLEY

Mombasa

Zanzibar
Dar es Salaam

SEYCHELLES

Highest point—Mt. Kilimanjaro
    Elevation: 19,340 ft/5,895 m

Lowest point—Lake Assal
    Depth: −508 ft/−155 m

Longest river—Nile-White Nile River
    (Sub-Saharan Segment)
    Length: 3,200 mi/5,150 km

Largest lake—Lake Victoria
    Area: 26,293 sq. mi/68,100 sq. km

Area—9,453,274 sq. mi/24,483,713 sq. km

Population—466,500,000

N

KATANGA
PLATEAU
Lake
Mweru
RIFT VALLEY

Lubumbashi

COMOROS
Moroni
MAYOTTE
(FRANCE)

ANGOLA
PLATEAU
ANGOLA

MALAWI
Lake
Malawi
Lilongwe

ZAMBIA
Lusaka
Zambezi R.

Lake
Kariba
Harare

MOZAMBIQUE

Antananarivo
MADAGASCAR

NAMIB DESERT

WALVIS BAY
(S. AFRICA)

Okavango
Swamp
NAMIBIA
Windhoek

ZIMBABWE
BOTSWANA

Limpopo

Tropic
of Capricorn

KALAHARI
DESERT
Gaborone
TRANSVAAL
Pretoria
Johannesburg

Maputo
Mbabane
SWAZILAND

INDIAN OCEAN

Orange R.
Vaal R.

LESOTHO
Maseru

SOUTH
AFRICA

DRAKENSBURG

Durban

Cape Town
Cape of
Good Hope
Cape Agulhas

0		500		1000 Miles
0	500		1000 Kilometers	

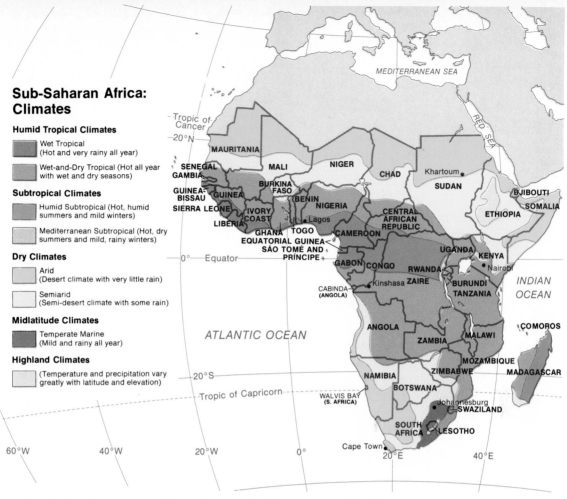

Sub-Saharan Africa: Climates

Humid Tropical Climates

Wet Tropical
(Hot and very rainy all year)

Wet-and-Dry Tropical (Hot all year
with wet and dry seasons)

Subtropical Climates

Humid Subtropical (Hot, humid
summers and mild winters)

Mediterranean Subtropical (Hot, dry
summers and mild, rainy winters)

Dry Climates

Arid
(Desert climate with very little rain)

Semiarid
(Semi-desert climate with some rain)

Midlatitude Climates

Temperate Marine
(Mild and rainy all year)

Highland Climates

(Temperature and precipitation vary
greatly with latitude and elevation)

Map Study *Where are the main highlands areas in sub-Saharan Africa? What are the region's island countries? In what countries is the Great Rift Valley?* • *Describe the climate in the central part of sub-Saharan Africa. How does the climate differ in the northern and southern parts? In what ways is it the same?*

The Savannas and Steppes Savannas cover the largest share of sub-Saharan Africa. Savannas mixed with woodlands lie both north and south of the equatorial rain forest. Tall grasses cover the plateau. Low-growing, flat-topped trees stand scattered over the grasslands. On the savannas are herds of giraffes, elephants, zebras, and other wildlife.

The savanna climate is tropical wet and dry. If you travel the savannas during the dry season, you will see barren, brown land covered with withered grasses. Then, when the rainy season arrives, the savanna turns lush and green.

Both the northern and the southern savannas meet zones of semiarid steppe, where the grass becomes shorter and the trees fewer. The narrow strip of steppe that lies across Africa between the northern savanna and the Sahara is called the Sahel (sə hel'). *Sahel* is an Arabic word meaning "shore." The Sahel is a kind of shore, bordering the sea of sand that makes up the Sahara.

Rainfall in the steppes occurs in long cycles spread over many years. During wet years, livestock herds and crops thrive and grow. Human population may increase also. Dry years, however, can

427

IN SEARCH OF THE NILE

The Nile is the longest river in the world—4,142 miles (6,627 kilometers). During the 1800's, several non-Africans searched for its source. Richard Burton, John H. Speke, and Samuel Baker—all from England—led major expeditions. They disagreed about where the Nile began. The expedition of an American journalist, Henry M. Stanley, helped to prove Speke's theory correct. The source of the Nile, he discovered, is Lake Victoria. The river plunges from the lake down Rippon Falls.

bring catastrophe. Since the late 1960's, the Sahel has been very dry. Livestock have died, and crops have failed. In Mali, Niger, Ethiopia (ē'thē ō'pē ə), and other parts of the Sahel, millions of people have died of starvation and diseases caused by malnutrition. Many survivors have been forced to leave their homes and move to already overcrowded cities. The desperate people depend on aid from foreign countries for food.

428

The Deserts Moving still farther from the equator to the north and south, conditions become very dry. To the north is the vast Sahara (which means simply "desert"). As you learned in Chapter 16, the Sahara spans the northern part of Africa from the Atlantic Ocean to the Red Sea. Southern Africa has two desert regions, the Namib (nə mib') and the Kalahari (kal'ə här'ē). Altogether, Africa has a third of the world's dry lands.

The Subtropical South At the southern tip of Africa, the tropics give way to subtropical climates. Parts of this area have a Mediterranean climate like that of southern California. The eastern part is humid subtropical, much like the southeastern United States.

REVIEWING THE FACTS

Define

escarpment

Answer

1. (a) Describe the major landforms of sub-Saharan Africa. (b) What effect does the overall landform have on climate?

2. (a) What is Africa's Great Rift Valley? (b) What evidence shows that this is a region of tectonic activity?

3. (a) What are the major ecosystems of sub-Saharan Africa? (b) Which one covers the largest share of the region?

Locate

Refer to the maps on pages 426–427.

1. Name the country where the mouth of each of these rivers is located: (a) Zambezi (b) Zaire (c) Niger (d) Limpopo

2. Mount Kilimanjaro stands on the border between what two countries?

3. Name the climate zone in which each of the following cities lies: (a) Cape Town (b) Nairobi (c) Johannesburg

Texas Essential Elements 3B. Economic importance of water, energy sources, and other productive resources to regions. 3C. Agricultural base of regions. 4C. Population distribution, growth, and movements. 4D. Major cultural, political, and economic activities within and among major world regions. 4E. Settlement patterns in terms of rural/urban location, structure, and function.

2 The Human Imprint

The cultural history of sub-Saharan Africa reaches far into the past. Archaeologists have found evidence that the earliest humans may have lived in eastern equatorial Africa well over a million years ago. Thus, Africa may have been the first home of human beings.

Population and Settlement

Today about 475 million people live in sub-Saharan Africa. In such a large area, this means an average population density of about 50 persons per square mile (20 per square kilometer), well below the world average. This figure is misleading, however. Few people live in the large areas of desert. Thus, densities are much higher in the lands that are well suited for settlement.

Most of sub-Saharan Africa's people live along the tropical coasts of western Africa. Other areas of heavy settlement occur near lakes, in river valleys, in the equatorial highlands of eastern Africa, and in the subtropical southern part of the continent. Many of these places do not have enough food or jobs to support such great populations. Hunger, malnutrition, and poverty are constant problems in the region.

Rural-Urban Distribution About 70 percent of Africa's people live in rural villages. As in most developing regions,

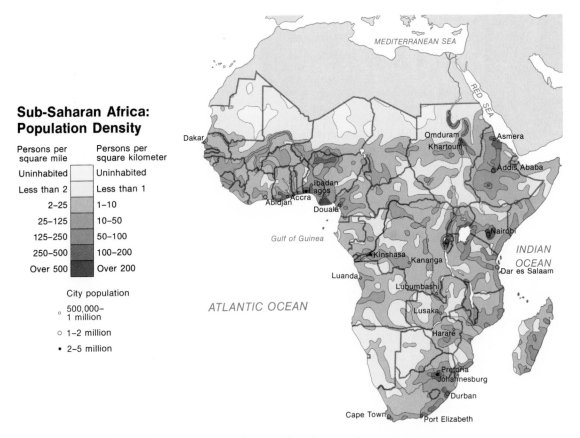

Sub-Saharan Africa: Population Density

Persons per square mile	Persons per square kilometer
Uninhabited	Uninhabited
Less than 2	Less than 1
2–25	1–10
25–125	10–50
125–250	50–100
250–500	100–200
Over 500	Over 200

City population
- ◦ 500,000–1 million
- ○ 1–2 million
- ● 2–5 million

Map Study *What is the most sparsely populated part of sub-Saharan Africa? Name the region's three largest cities.*

429

High population growth rates are closely linked to low per capita income. Of the world's 35 poorest nations, 23 are in Africa, where per capita incomes are often low. The region's high birth rate is accompanied by a high rate of infant mortality. In Africa as a whole, 127 out of every 1,000 children born alive die before their first birthday.

however, many rural Africans are moving to cities. City populations are growing rapidly. Johannesburg, South Africa; Kinshasa, Zaire; Lagos, Nigeria; Addis Ababa, Ethiopia; Abidjan, Ivory Coast (Cote d'Ivoire); and several other cities have all grown to more than 1 million during the past 30 years. Newcomers must often find makeshift housing in the slums that surround most African cities.

High Growth Rates Africa's population increases by nearly 3 percent each year — the highest rate of increase for any continent. The birth rate in Africa has been high for a long time. In the past, the death rate was also high, especially among children. Modern medicine and disease control, however, have helped lower the death rate. As a result, about 45 percent of the population today is under 15 years of age. This population pattern puts a heavy burden on working adults, who have to support the young people. It also strains the budget of governments to educate them.

If the present rate of population increase continues, sub-Saharan Africa's population will double by the year 2010. African governments face the twin problems of controlling population growth and improving the economic conditions of their countries.

A Complicated Region Sub-Saharan Africa has a great variety of cultures. There are hundreds of different African ethnic groups with long histories. Among these groups, there are more than 1,000 African languages. In addition to its language, each group has its own customs, beliefs, and rules for behavior.

Because of ties of kinship, history, and culture, people feel a deep loyalty to their own ethnic group. Many Africans have stronger loyalties to their ethnic group than they do to their country. Conflicts among some ethnic groups go back for centuries and have sometimes led to civil war in African countries.

Some African ethnic groups are very large. The Yoruba (yȯr′ə bə), Hausa (haủ′sə), and Ibo (ē′bō′) of western Africa all number several million. The Kikuyu (ki kü′yü), Luo, Luhya, and Kamba of eastern Africa also have more than a million members. Other ethnic groups may have only a few hundred members. One of the smallest groups, the Kung of the Kalahari, speak what may be the oldest of Africa's many languages. The largest family of languages in Africa is the Bantu group.

People of European or Asian descent live as minorities in a number of countries. The country of South Africa has the largest European and Asian minorities, but Zimbabwe (zim bäb′wē), Kenya, and other countries of eastern Africa also have sizable groups.

Eastern African countries also have minority groups whose ancestors came from the Arabian Peninsula. A major language spoken in eastern Africa is Swahili (swä hē′lē), a mixture of African and Arabic words. It developed several centuries ago from the trading contacts between Africans and Arab seafarers.

Political Patterns

Sub-Saharan Africa's cities and urban empires date back at least 4,000 years. The development of nations, however, has taken place only recently, since the end of European colonial rule in the 1960's and 1970's.

Early Kingdoms and Extensive Trade One of the earliest and best-known African empires was that of Kush, along the Nile River in the northern part of today's Sudan. The Kushite kingdom probably arose about 2000 B.C. and lasted until around A.D. 370. A number of Kushite cities stood along the Nile, including the capital city of Meroë (mer'ə wē).

The Kushites traded widely. Ships and caravans carried Kushite iron to India and possibly China. Gold, ivory, ebony, spices, animal skins, and other goods from southern and central Africa passed through Kush.

Kush was a great ironworking center of the ancient world. Rich iron deposits lay along its portion of the Nile. Kush may have been the source from which ironworking skills spread south and west to other parts of sub-Saharan Africa.

In Africa's western savanna region, many powerful and wealthy kingdoms succeeded one another. Between A.D. 700 and 1700, a number of empires waxed and waned in western Africa. Among these were Ghana, Mali, Songhai, and Benin (bə nin'). Like Kush, most of these kingdoms based their power on control of important trade routes, especially the north-south routes over which salt and gold were traded. People of the Sahara and the Sahel traded salt from the desert with groups of people living in the southern forest regions. In exchange, the southern peoples offered gold, ivory, spices, and forest resources.

The emirs, or Muslim princes, of Kano, Nigeria, date back to the 1400's.

The places on the savanna where the two groups of traders met grew into thriving cities. Kano, Gao, Walata, and Timbuktu were some of the cities of the trading kingdoms. Kano, in northern Nigeria, is still an important city. The other cities, including Ife (ē'fā) and Benin, were located south of the savanna kingdoms and were the centers of farming communities. Metalworkers in Ife and Benin crafted statues and other fine art from bronze.

Christianity has gained many followers in Africa in recent years. Here, Ugandans worship in one of their country's Christian churches.

431

MAP WORKSHOP

Interpreting a Map of Colonial Territories

Political maps show the boundaries people draw to divide the land into countries, states, or other areas served by a certain government. Color then often distinguishes one area from another.

The map of Africa shows how the continent was divided in the year 1914, just before World War I began. You can see that most parts of the continent were then colonies of one of several European countries. Today there are more than 50 independent nations of Africa. Discover the boundary changes for yourself by comparing the colonial map on this page with the political map of Africa on page 498 of the Atlas.

1. Which two European countries had the largest colonial areas in Africa?

2. Angola and Mozambique are two countries where colonial boundaries have not changed much. To which European nation did they belong?

3. What two independent nations were formed from Rhodesia?

4. Which two African nations were never European colonies?

5. What is the name of the present-day country completely surrounded by South Africa?

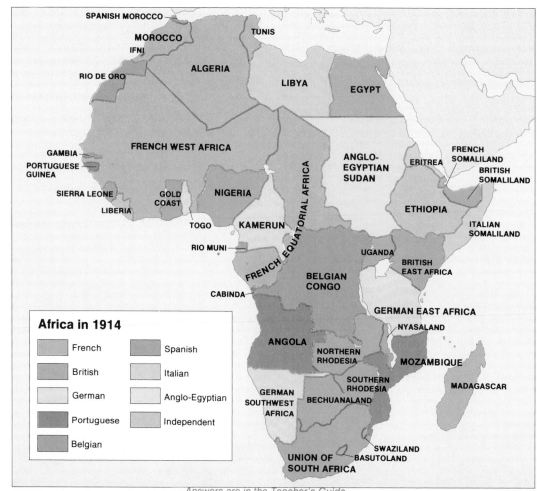

Africa in 1914

French
British
German
Portuguese
Belgian
Spanish
Italian
Anglo-Egyptian
Independent

SPANISH MOROCCO
MOROCCO
IFNI
RIO DE ORO
TUNIS
ALGERIA
LIBYA
EGYPT
FRENCH WEST AFRICA
GAMBIA
PORTUGUESE GUINEA
SIERRA LEONE
LIBERIA
GOLD COAST
NIGERIA
TOGO
KAMERUN
RIO MUNI
FRENCH EQUATORIAL AFRICA
ANGLO-EGYPTIAN SUDAN
ERITREA
FRENCH SOMALILAND
BRITISH SOMALILAND
ETHIOPIA
ITALIAN SOMALILAND
UGANDA
BELGIAN CONGO
CABINDA
BRITISH EAST AFRICA
GERMAN EAST AFRICA
NYASALAND
ANGOLA
NORTHERN RHODESIA
MOZAMBIQUE
SOUTHERN RHODESIA
MADAGASCAR
GERMAN SOUTHWEST AFRICA
BECHUANALAND
SWAZILAND
BASUTOLAND
UNION OF SOUTH AFRICA

Answers are in the Teacher's Guide.
432
Assign the Workbook activity for this chapter's Map Workshop with this page.

In equatorial western Africa, a kingdom known as Kongo controlled the region around the mouth of the Zaire River. Along the coast of eastern Africa, trade routes across the Indian Ocean brought ships to Mombasa, Mogadishu, and many other cities. These became wealthy transfer points after about A.D. 900.

European Contact and the Slave Trade
European voyagers first sailed to parts of sub-Saharan Africa in the late 1400's. The Portuguese, British, and Dutch stopped along the coasts to trade with Africans or take on any supplies for the remainder of the long voyage between Europe and Asia. Trade along the coasts replaced trade across the Sahara, and many of the great trading cities of the savanna withered away.

At first, the Europeans were most interested in gold and spices. During the 1600's, however, they turned more and more to the slave trade. Arab traders on Africa's east coast also bought slaves. All together, European and Arab slave ships may have carried as many as 20 million Africans away from their homelands and into lives of forced labor in the Americas, Persia, and India.

The slave trade lasted from the 1600's to the early 1800's. During those centuries, it took countless lives. Thousands of captives died during the long and terrible voyage across the Atlantic. Still more lives were lost in Africa itself, in the "slave wars"—wars waged to win captives by African groups who took part in the slave trade. Besides the suffering and the loss of life, the slave trade deeply disrupted many African cultures.

European Colonization Until well into the 1800's, African traders controlled the flow of gold, spices, and ivory that came from inland, keeping their sources secret. Europeans generally were limited to trading stations along the coast.

The relationship between Europe and Africa changed completely during the 1800's. Christian missionaries and adventurers from Europe journeyed into the interior of the continent. Then European governments claimed territories in Africa as colonies. Great Britain, France, Germany, Belgium, Spain, and Portugal all took parts of Africa. They agreed among themselves on boundaries, paying little attention to the people and cultures of Africa. The map on page 432 shows the division of Africa into colonies of European countries.

Only two countries in present-day Africa were never colonies. Free blacks from the United States established Liberia (lī bir′ē ə) in 1822 and made it a free republic in 1847. Ethiopia too remained independent under its own kings.

While European rulers wanted to increase their power and prestige by winning colonies in Africa, business leaders wanted raw materials for their factories and markets for their manufactured goods. Europeans developed mines and plantations to obtain natural resources from Africa. They built some railroads to carry raw materials to the coasts for shipment to Europe.

Africans did most of the labor in the mines and plantations. Some Africans attended schools founded by missionaries and learned a European language. A few young Africans went to study in European universities.

Independence After the end of World War II in 1945, strong feelings of nationalism spread over Africa. Africans wanted an end to colonial rule. They wanted African nations governed by African leaders.

The west African country of Ghana was the first to gain independence, taking its name from the ancient kingdom. The British, who had called the colony the

The slave trade damaged the African economy in two ways: (1) it depleted the population of its youngest and strongest men and women by kidnapping them and by causing constant warfare; (2) it discouraged economic development by satisfying local rulers' desires for luxury items without enriching most of the population.

433

Sub-Saharan Africa: Land Use

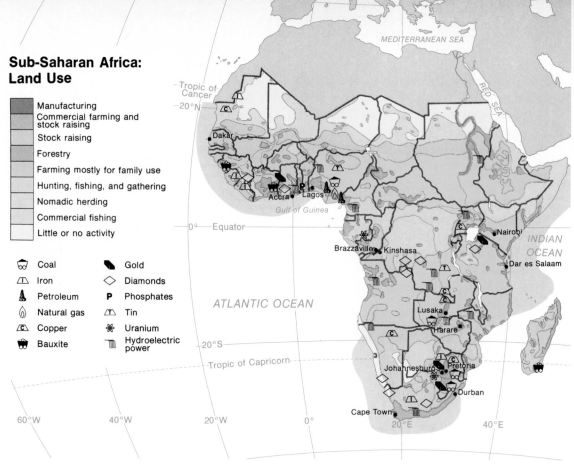

Manufacturing
Commercial farming and stock raising
Stock raising
Forestry
Farming mostly for family use
Hunting, fishing, and gathering
Nomadic herding
Commercial fishing
Little or no activity

Coal
Iron
Petroleum
Natural gas
Copper
Bauxite
Gold
Diamonds
Phosphates
Tin
Uranium
Hydroelectric power

Map Study *Which parts of sub-Saharan Africa have the most industrial resources? Use the map on page 426 to determine which countries have coal. Gold. Bauxite. Petroleum.*

Gold Coast, gave up their rule in 1957. Zimbabwe, Britain's former colony of Southern Rhodesia, was the last to become independent, in 1980. Namibia, although no longer a European colony, is still subject to the rule of the neighboring country of South Africa.

The new African nations set up governments modeled on European democracies. However, most of the new nations have had problems with unstable governments. Revolutions, coups, and civil wars have been common. Military leaders often have set up authoritarian governments. Many of these leaders have been charged with selfishness and corruption. A few have been cruel dictators who murdered their opponents and suppressed the rights of their citizens.

Conflict among ethnic groups has caused some of the troubles that plague governments in sub-Saharan Africa. The boundaries of the new nations tended to follow boundaries set during colonial rule. The Europeans established boundaries that suited their own purposes. These boundaries sometimes separated African groups that had traditional ties. In other instances, they brought together groups that had long been enemies. Some of these groups now find it difficult to work together as one people in a united nation.

Economic Activities

Developing strong and modern economies is a chief goal among almost all sub-Saharan Africa's nations.

434

The cacao tree, from which cocoa is produced, is found in the equatorial zone. About half of the world's supply of cocoa comes from Africa.

Agriculture Two thirds of sub-Saharan Africa is unsuitable for farming because of either too much or too little rainfall. In wet, tropical areas, heavy rains wash nutrients from the soil. On the other hand, about half of sub-Saharan Africa has too little rain to grow crops without the help of irrigation.

Despite these difficulties, 70 percent of Africa's people are farmers. Most are subsistence farmers, growing such crops as yams, millet, rice, sorghum, and bananas. Plantains, tropical fruit resembling bananas, and manioc, a root plant from which tapioca is made, are also staple food crops. Subsistence farmers trade their surpluses, if they have any, at local markets one or two days a week.

Many farmers also raise some cash crops, such as bananas, cocoa, coconuts, kola nuts, palm oil, coffee, sugar, and cotton. These are valuable export crops, and governments all over Africa are helping farmers to improve their yields. However, many people believe that Africa's limited farmland should be used for food crops to feed the region's people.

Mining Africans have mined iron and gold since ancient times. Today more than half the world's gold comes from Africa's mines. Copper, diamonds, and manganese became important during colonial times. Since independence, African nations have more than doubled their mining operations. Uranium and cobalt have joined the list of earlier mine products. Nigeria has discovered and developed important petroleum deposits.

African nations export some of their mineral wealth to gain much-needed capital. But they are also using much of it themselves to start their own industries.

Industry and Energy Until recently, there was little industry in Africa despite the continent's resources. During colonial times, Europeans had discouraged

Farmers on the savannas of northern Cameroon raise much cotton.

the development of local industries so that Africans would buy goods made in Europe. When African countries first became independent, they generally lacked the money to start factories. Few workers had the skills or training for industry. Another problem was the small local market for manufactured goods.

Among the first industries to develop have been food processing, textiles, and building materials such as cement. The pulp, paper, and wood-products industries are also fairly well developed in some countries. All these businesses provide goods that countries need to raise the standard of living for their people.

Other industrial development is under way. Zimbabwe produces steel. Ghana has an aluminum industry. Nigeria and Angola could develop chemical industries from their oil deposits.

The most industrially developed nation of sub-Saharan Africa is South Africa. South Africa's industries are based on its vast mineral wealth. It is the world's leading producer of diamonds and gold. It also has valuable deposits of coal, uranium, copper, iron ore, manganese, nickel, and cobalt. With these

435

Most land use in Africa is not intensive because the soil lacks humus, which means that it loses its fertility quickly. For this reason, the same plot cannot be used year after year as is done in Europe and North America.

Country	Area in Square Miles	Population/Natural Increase		Per Capita GNP
Angola	481,351	8,000,000	(2.5%)	$ 550
Benin	43,483	4,300,000	(3.0%)	270
Botswana	231,803	1,200,000	(3.4%)	840
Burkina Faso	105,869	7,300,000	(2.8%)	140
Burundi	10,745	5,000,000	(2.9%)	240
Cameroon	183,568	10,300,000	(2.7%)	810
Central African Republic	240,533	2,700,000	(2.5%)	270
Chad	495,753	4,600,000	(2.0%)	NA
Comoros	694	400,000	(3.3%)	280
Congo	132,046	2,100,000	(3.4%)	1,020
Djibouti	8,494	300,000	(2.5%)	1,168
Equatorial Guinea	10,830	300,000	(1.8%)	417
Ethiopia	471,776	46,000,000	(2.3%)	110
Gabon	103,347	1,200,000	(1.6%)	3,340
Gambia	4,363	800,000	(2.1%)	230
Ghana	92,100	13,900,000	(2.8%)	390
Guinea	94,927	6,400,000	(2.4%)	320
Guinea-Bissau	13,946	900,000	(2.0%)	170
Ivory Coast	124,503	10,800,000	(3.0%)	871
Kenya	224,961	22,400,000	(3.9%)	290
Lesotho	11,718	1,600,000	(2.6%)	480
Liberia	43,000	2,400,000	(3.3%)	470
Madagascar	226,656	10,600,000	(2.8%)	250

resources, South Africa has been able to develop many different industries. As a result, South Africa has the highest GNP and the highest per capita income in sub-Saharan Africa. Yet these figures are misleading. Most of the country's wealth is in the hands of people of European ancestry. Blacks do most of the work, yet they have little of the country's wealth.

As industry grows in sub-Saharan Africa, waterpower may become the major source of energy. Africa's rivers have nearly 30 percent of the world's hydroelectric potential. Some power plants, including two large ones on the Zambezi River and others on the Zaire River, are already operating. More are planned.

Linkages In sub-Saharan Africa, there is a great need for better transportation linkages. Almost everything about the physical environment makes these linkages difficult and expensive to build. The falls and rapids make river transportation impossible in places. The escarpments, heavy rainfalls, desert sand, and thick rain forests also make it hard to build roads and railroads.

Since independence, African nations have begun the work of building linkages both within countries and among nations. Air travel and transport have grown rapidly. Because of the costs of surface linkages, air linkages will remain vital.

A third of the nations of Africa are land-locked—they have no outlet to the sea.
Point out that the same conditions that make river travel impossible in many places give Africa its great potential for hydroelectric development.

Country	Area in Square Miles	Population/Natural Increase		Per Capita GNP
Malawi	44,745	7,400,000	(3.2%)	170
Mali	478,764	8,400,000	(2.9%)	140
Mauritania	397,954	2,000,000	(3.0%)	410
Mozambique	309,494	14,700,000	(2.6%)	NA
Namibia	318,259	1,300,000	(3.3%)	NA
Niger	489,189	7,000,000	(2.9%)	200
Nigeria	356,668	108,600,000	(2.8%)	NA
Rwanda	10,170	6,800,000	(3.7%)	290
São Tomé and Príncipe	371	100,000	(2.7%)	310
Senegal	75,749	7,100,000	(2.8%)	370
Seychelles	108	100,000	(1.9%)	NA
Sierra Leone	27,699	3,900,000	(1.8%)	370
Somalia	246,201	7,700,000	(2.5%)	270
South Africa	471,444	34,300,000	(2.3%)	2,010
Sudan	967,494	23,500,000	(2.8%)	330
Swaziland	6,703	700,000	(3.1%)	650
Tanzania	364,900	23,500,000	(3.5%)	270
Togo	21,927	3,200,000	(3.1%)	250
Uganda	91,135	15,900,000	(3.4%)	NA
Zaire	905,564	31,800,000	(3.1%)	170
Zambia	290,583	7,100,000	(3.5%)	400
Zimbabwe	150,803	9,400,000	(3.5%)	650

Sub-Saharan Africa in the World

After independence, many African countries continued to trade heavily with their former colonial rulers. France is still an important trading partner for its former West African colonies, as is West Germany for Tanzania, and Belgium for Zaire, and the United Kingdom for its former colonies. African trade patterns have become global, however, in recent years. Sub-Saharan countries are also growing markets for developed nations. Nigeria and Tanzania, for example, buy many Japanese imports.

Africans feel that much of their future growth depends on trade relations and economic cooperation within Africa itself. In 1963, 30 African countries

People living outside the city of Dakar, Senegal, depend on buses to get to and from urban marketplaces.

Shortly after independence, government programs in many African nations gave top priority to industrial development and export crops at the expense of agricultural production for domestic consumption. Because this drew millions of Africans from traditional work as farmers, agricultural output plummeted.

founded the Organization of African Unity (OAU). The OAU now has 50 members. Through this organization, African nations work toward common scientific, political, economic, and defense goals.

In their relations with other countries of the world, many sub-Saharan Africans consider themselves nonaligned nations. Being nonaligned means that they have not taken sides with either the Soviet Union and the Communist countries or with the United States and its democratic allies. Some African countries have experimented with socialist economies.

Many African leaders say they are not concerned with the difference between Communist and non-Communist countries. The difference between the rich and poor countries, they say, is more important. Both the United States and the Soviet Union are vastly wealthy countries by African standards. African leaders feel that the developed nations, non-Communist and Communist alike, should be sources of aid for all the world's poor and developing countries.

The United States, the Soviet Union, and other developed countries give direct aid in the form of money, machinery, food, and medicine to African nations. Some of this aid comes from governments and some from private organizations. For example, in 1985, many popular musicians from the United States and Europe joined to give a world television concert. Viewers on both sides of the Atlantic contributed money to buy food for famine victims in Ethiopia. The difficulties that volunteers met taking the supplies to the famine victims dramatically illustrated the need for better linkages in Africa. Some of the money had to be spent to buy trucks to deliver the food. Even then the rugged lands and lack of roads blocked the way to some areas.

International organizations such as the United Nations have also been valuable sources of aid for Africa. The World Bank, with funds contributed by many developed countries, loans money to African nations. UN organizations have built schools and provided teachers. The World Health Organization (WHO) has worked extensively in Africa. By going from village to village with vaccines, WHO workers wiped out smallpox completely. WHO medical teams still distribute vaccines and medicines for other diseases throughout Africa.

REVIEWING THE FACTS

Answer

1. Describe the population distribution of sub-Saharan Africa.

2. What was the main contributing factor that led to the rise of rich cities in the early kingdoms of sub-Saharan Africa?

3. What effects did the arrival of Europeans have in the region?

4. During what years did most of the countries in sub-Saharan Africa win their independence?

5. Describe the part that each of the following activities plays in West Africa's economy? (a) agriculture (b) mining (c) manufacturing

6. How do sub-Saharan countries view their relations with both Communist and non-Communist powers?

Locate

Refer to the map on page 426.

1. Name the body of water that lies (a) west of Senegal, (b) east of Sudan, (c) north of Somalia, (d) south of Ivory Coast, (e) east of Swaziland.

2. Name the lake on the border between (a) Zaire and Tanzania, (b) Tanzania and Mozambique.

438

SPOTLIGHT ON THE FUTURE:

The Importance of Education in Kenya

In a typical high school classroom in Kenya, forty or more students sit quietly at double desks, taking notes as their teacher lectures and copying down formulas and definitions. If students miss a key term, they cannot refer back to their textbooks. There are only a handful of books in the room, and few students can afford to buy their own.

When Kenya was a colony, the country did not have many schools. Since independence, education has become the nation's top priority. Although the government has built many schools in recent years, only elementary school is free. The nation cannot yet afford to provide free high school educations.

Convinced that education is their best hope for the future, many parents are willing to make great sacrifices to send their sons and daughters to high school. They quickly discover, however, that there are not enough schools for everyone. Even the high schools run by the government are too expensive for many families, especially if students must live away from home in order to attend.

Kenyans have found an answer to the problem in *harambee*, a word that means "to pull together" or "self-help." It is Kenya's motto, and a term that Jomo Kenyatta, the nation's first prime minister, used frequently in speeches in the early 1960's. He wanted to motivate the people of Kenya to help themselves rather than to expect the government to solve their problems.

As part of the harambee movement, many villages built secondary schools. Church groups donated some of the money. Villagers organized fund-raising campaigns to provide the rest. Those who had no money to give donated their labor.

Once the schools were built, villagers had to provide books, desks, chairs, and other equipment. They also had to find a way to pay teachers. Most of the money comes from tuition. Yet costs must be kept low as even a small fee is more than many families can afford.

As a result, many harambee schools barely survive from one year to the next. In years when the rains fail and crops wither in the fields, enrollments drop so sharply that some schools must close. Even in good times, most schools cannot provide enough textbooks or paper.

Teacher salaries are a problem too. Harambee schools pay too little to attract the most qualified or experienced teachers. As a result, most teachers have had little formal training. Yet each must teach in two or three subject areas. The curriculum includes Kiswahili, English, history, geography, science, mathematics, and religious education.

Students in harambee schools are aware that they are not getting as good an education as those who attend more expensive schools. Only two harambee students in 1000 will attend a university. Yet these students are just as bright as those who go to government schools. They are not, however, as well prepared for college.

Why then do so many students continue to flock to harambee schools? They point out that if they did not go, they would have no chance at all of going to college. They enthusiastically tell visitors, "Yes [the chances are slim], but I think that *I* can succeed" or "yes, but some *do* make it."

3 West and Central Africa

West Africa is made up of the countries in the bulge of western Africa. It includes Niger, Nigeria, Mali, Mauritania, and all the countries west or south of them. These 15 countries together are about five sixths the size of the United States.

Central Africa includes Chad, Cameroon, the Central African Republic, Zaire, Congo, and Gabon. Equatorial Guinea and the island nation of São Tomé and Príncipe (saù tə mā and prin'sə pə) are also part of Central Africa.

West Africa

The northern parts of West Africa — in Mauritania, Mali, and Niger — extend well into the Sahara. These lands are thinly settled. Thus, most of the region's 187 million people live farther south, along the coast of the Gulf of Guinea. Nigeria has more people than any other country in Africa — over 95 million.

West Africa's coast has many large and growing cities, such as Dakar, Abidjan, Accra, and Lagos. Most of the cities started long ago as small market towns. They then grew to foreign trade centers. Some were administrative centers during

Map Study *Which regions of sub-Saharan Africa border the Atlantic Ocean? The Indian Ocean? The Red Sea?*

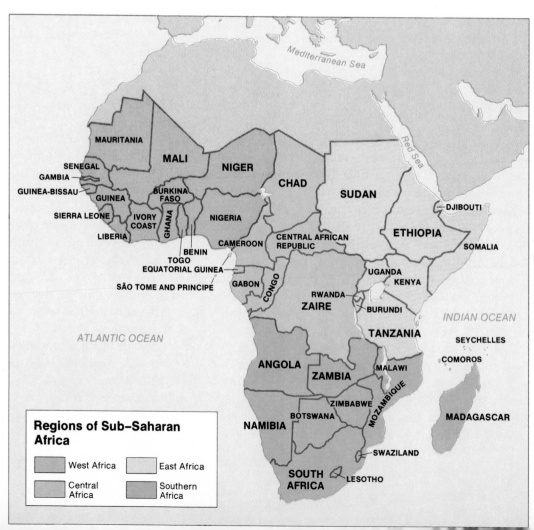

Lagos, Nigeria's capital, is one of the most modern cities in Africa.

Even a muddy pool of water is a precious resource in the dry Sahel.

the colonial period and later became capitals of independent nations.

The many cultures of the region come together in the cities. Most people speak English or French—the languages of the European countries that colonized the region—in addition to one or more African languages. For example, people in Nigeria, Gambia, Ghana, and Sierra Leone speak English.

Farming Along the heavily populated coast of West Africa, even rural areas may average 700 people per square mile. Most people are subsistence farmers, raising corn, yams, manioc, and sweet potatoes.

Commercial farming is growing rapidly. In the Sahel and savanna regions of Senegal and Gambia, there are peanut farms. The humid regions of Gambia have coffee plantations. Palm oil comes from plantations in Nigeria and Benin, and rubber from Liberia. Cocoa is a cash crop for small farmers in Ghana. All these crops are sold in the developed world.

In the dry northern Sahel region, bordering the Sahara, people long lived by herding. They raised camels, cattle, goats, and sheep. The drought that struck this region in the late 1960's killed hundreds of thousands of people. Since then, governments have tried to encourage herders to give up their traditional way of life to become farmers or villagers.

Mining and Manufacturing Mining is a rapidly growing part of the economy in some West African countries. Mining is now the chief source of income in Mauritania, Guinea, Sierra Leone, and Liberia. Oil exports amount to 90 percent of Nigeria's national income. Important mineral products in West Africa are iron ore, diamonds, and bauxite.

Manufacturing has also grown since independence. Nigeria is the most industrialized country in West Africa. Its first industries were food processing, textiles, lumber, and cement. As Nigeria developed its rich oil deposits, chemical and oil-refining industries also became important. However, Nigeria relied too heavily on its oil wealth. When world oil prices dropped suddenly in the early 1980's, Nigeria's income from trade was cut in half. Its economy suffered greatly.

441

Answers to Map Study questions: Atlantic—West Africa, Central Africa, Southern Africa;
Indian—East Africa, Southern Africa; Red Sea—East Africa
Assign the Workbook activity for Chapter 17, Section 3, with pages 439–443.

Plans for the Future West African governments are working to better the lives of their people. Cocoa farmers of Ghana, with government help, are diversifying their crops to avoid disaster when world demand is low. Economic planners are working to improve linkages and to develop energy from the Niger, Senegal, and Gambia rivers. The Economic Community of West African States (ECOWAS) is trying to encourage trade among the countries of the region.

Central Africa

The eight countries of Central Africa range in size from giant Zaire to tiny São Tomé and Príncipe. The middle of Central Africa, near the equator, is primarily rain forest. To the north and south, savannas cover the land. Most of Central Africa's people live in the savanna regions. As in West Africa, people of Central Africa use the languages of former colonizing nations in their governments, schools, and businesses. At the same time, they also keep their traditional customs and languages.

Agriculture The economies of Central African countries face great difficulties in developing. A large portion of the people lives by subsistence farming, giving the countries little cash income. Soils are poor almost everywhere.

In the forest areas, farmers practice **slash-and-burn agriculture**. They clear a patch of land by cutting down the trees and brush and then burning them on the spot. The ashes from the burned vegetation help to fertilize the soil. Farmers use such fields for a few years until the soil is worn out. Then they must clear new fields. The problem with slash-and-burn farming is that it requires a lot of land for each farmer.

The main tropical food crops are bananas, yams, sweet potatoes, cassava, and taro. Farmers in the forest region raise little livestock because of sleeping sickness, a disease that is carried by the tsetse fly. Sleeping sickness can wipe out livestock herds and may also affect people.

In the savanna areas, fields are more permanent. Savanna farmers also keep chickens and livestock, such as goats, pigs, and sheep.

Natural Resources and Linkages Central Africa has great mineral wealth. Most of the region's economic gains are based on its mineral resources. Diamonds are mined in the Central African Republic and Zaire. Industrial diamonds from Zaire account for a large part of the total world supply. Southern Zaire has a rich variety of other minerals as well. It is a major producer of cobalt, copper, and tin.

Timber is another abundant resource in Central Africa. From tropical rain forests come such hardwoods as mahogany and ebony. Another wood, called okoume (ō ke'mā), is used to make plywood.

Most of Central Africa has a great need for linkages. The Zaire River is a major

Oceangoing ships travel about 80 miles (130 kilometers) up the Zaire River to Matadi, Zaire's main port.

442

waterway, but boats cannot sail all the way down it to the ocean because of rapids. In some places, goods are transferred from boats to railroads to go around falls and rapids. These transfers make moving goods expensive and slow.

Improvement Efforts and Goals All countries of the region recognize the need to develop energy resources and industries and provide more food for their people. The country of Zaire alone has the potential to be the world's largest producer of hydroelectric power. Zaire also plans to increase agricultural production by giving farmers better seeds and tools. The Central African Republic plans to improve road networks so that goods can get from farms to markets. The government of Gabon is using money from oil exports to build processing industries for its mineral, petroleum, and forest wealth.

REVIEWING THE FACTS

Define

slash-and-burn agriculture

Answer

1. How do the ecosystems of these regions change from north to south?

2. Where are the most densely settled regions of West Africa?

3. (a) What resource is most important to the economy of Nigeria? (b) What problem did its dependence on this resource cause Nigeria?

4. Why is the Zaire River important to Central Africa?

Locate

Refer to the map on page 426.

1. Name the five countries of West and Central Africa that have no coast.

2. Name the four countries that border Lake Chad.

Addis Ababa is Ethiopia's capital and largest city. This photo shows its modern city hall.

4 East and Southern Africa

The nine nations of East Africa include Sudan and Ethiopia and all the countries east and south, through Kenya and Tanzania. On the west, the Great Rift Valley with its slender lakes marks the border of the region. Thus, Rwanda (rù än'də), Uganda, and Burundi (bù rün'dē) are part of the region. So are Djibouti (jə büt'ē) and Somalia (sō mäl'ē ə). Somalia lies on the easternmost part of the African mainland, sometimes called the Horn of Africa.

Southern Africa lies south of Zaire and Tanzania. Other countries of the region are Angola, Zambia, Malawi, Mozambique, Zimbabwe, Botswana, and Namibia. Swaziland and Lesotho are two small countries lying within South Africa. Madagascar, Seychelles, and Comoros are island nations off the eastern coast.

East Africa

East Africa is a place of beautiful landscapes and sharp contrasts. Mount Kilimajaro, Africa's highest mountain, is

Assign the Workbook activity for Chapter 17, Section 4, with pages 443–447.
Answers are in the Teacher's Guide.
Students should refer often to the four maps at the beginning of this chapter as they read about the countries in East and Southern Africa.

443

snow-covered all year, though it lies nearly on the equator. In Djibouti, Africa's lowest land area plunges to the shores of salty Lake Assal, more than 500 feet (155 meters) below sea level.

Grasslands, forests, and even marshes are scattered over the area. The Sudd, a treeless area of shallow standing water, lies along the upper Nile in southern Sudan. The Sudd is the world's largest marsh. However, much of East Africa is arid or semiarid and often sparsely populated. About 80 percent of the people, in fact, live on 10 percent of the land area.

Rural cultural traditions are very strong among East Africans. Only about 20 percent of the people live in cities, and many return to their rural homes after a time.

Agriculture As in other parts of Africa, East Africans grow both subsistence and cash crops. Important cash crops of East Africa are coffee, cotton, sisal, tea, cloves, sugar, and peanuts.

Kenya, Somalia, and Sudan have all opened up dry lands to farming through

Subsistence farmers in Sudan work their fields by hand labor.

irrigation. Africa's most successful irrigation system and one of its most important farming areas is the Gezira (jə zir′ə) in Sudan. The Gezira is the wedge of land where the White Nile and the Blue Nile meet. With its irrigation system that was built in 1900, the Gezira produces millet, sesame, peanuts, and cotton.

Herding is an important activity in some areas. Some ethnic groups count their wealth in cattle. People with large herds have the greatest wealth and status. Under this system, herders keep as many cattle as possible, rather than selling any for profit. The large herds sometimes overgraze the grasslands, leading to severe soil erosion.

Industry and Resources Kenya is the most industrialized country in East Africa, with the cities of Nairobi and Mombasa as its main centers. Kenya's industries produce building materials and processed foods such as frozen fish, meat, coffee, tea, and fruit. Mombasa has refineries that process oil from the Persian Gulf.

Tourism, which brings little money to other parts of sub-Saharan Africa, is an important business in several East African countries. In Kenya, it has become a chief source of foreign income. Most visitors come to see Kenya's famous wildlife preserves.

The search for resources has recently revealed some mineral deposits, including nickel in Burundi. Burundi's government, international organizations, and private companies are studying ways to mine the nickel. In the main, however, East Africa lacks the metals and fuels needed for industry. As a result, the region's economic growth has been slow. East Africa also needs money, skilled workers, modern linkages, and political stability in order to develop strong, modern economies.

444

Have students look at the Atlas map of the world (pages 486–487) and ask why East Africa is of strategic importance to the superpowers. What major sea route does it border? *(the passage between the Mediterranean Sea and the Indian Ocean)*

Nairobi is the capital of Kenya. It is a center of commerce, industry, and transportation in East Africa. The University of Kenya is located here.

Southern Africa

Southern Africa, like all of Africa, has many different African ethnic groups. This region also has more people of European ancestry than any other part of sub-Saharan Africa. Many people of European ancestry live in Zambia and Zimbabwe, but by far the largest group live in the country of South Africa.

South Africa   South Africa is the only country in Africa where people of European ancestry still control the government. Large groups of settlers from both the Netherlands and Great Britain came to South Africa from the 1600's to the early 1900's. The people whose ancestors came from the Netherlands are known as Afrikaaners. Ever since South Africa has been independent of Great Britain, Afrikaners have held political power.

Black South Africans outnumber whites by about five to one. However, the black population has few political rights. The South African government pursues a policy of apartheid (ə pär' tāt), which means apartness.

Under apartheid, the white minority holds the economic and political power of the nation. This has affected every part of life in South Africa. Blacks can live only in certain areas. They have separate — often very poorly maintained — schools, hospitals, parks, playgrounds, and beaches. There are also special laws that limit their actions and achievements.

In 1959, the government went even further in separating blacks and whites. It set aside certain areas for the ten major black ethnic groups within South Africa. These homelands included the poorest, driest, least valuable land. The government forced thousands of blacks to leave their homes and settle on these lands.

South African police have killed many blacks protesting apartheid. Here, mourners attend a funeral for 19 of the victims.

445

The homelands set aside for the black ethnic groups in South Africa were also called Bantustans. The South African government recognized some of the Bantustans as independent states, but no other country recognized them as such.

SKILL WORKSHOP

Using Graphs to Trace Literacy Rates

Developing nations are building many additional schools to improve the level of education among their people. They want their people to acquire the skills and knowledge needed to develop their economies and to raise standards of living.

A nation's adult literacy rate tells the percentage of people over the age of 15 who can read and write. In industrial countries, this percentage is very high, usually over 90 percent. Many of the developing countries have a much lower rate. In the early 1980's, Mali's literacy rate was 10 percent, Ethiopia's 8 percent, and Niger's only 5 percent.

Developing countries, however, are making important progress in raising their literacy rates. The graphs below show a definite rising trend for the years from 1960 to 1980.

1. In which world region did the percentage of literate adults almost double between 1960 and 1980?

2. In which world region are more than one half the adults still illiterate?

3. Which of the developing regions has the highest literacy rate?

4. By about how much did the rate of literacy in Asia and the Pacific increase between 1960 and 1980?

5. As of 1980, what percentage of adults in developing nations was still illiterate?

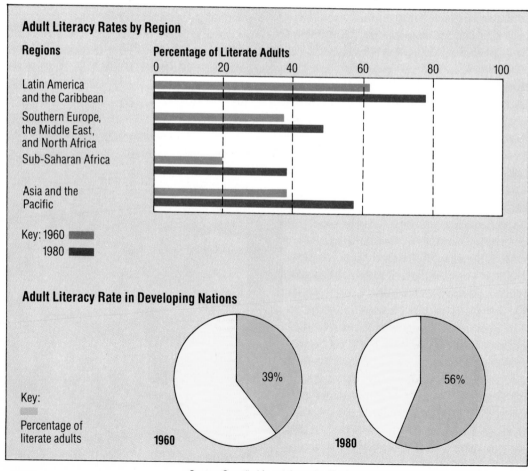

Adult Literacy Rates by Region

Regions — Percentage of Literate Adults

Key: 1960 / 1980

Adult Literacy Rate in Developing Nations

Key: Percentage of literate adults

1960 — 39%   1980 — 56%

Source: Compiled from Information Please Almanac and Population Reference Bureau

446

Mining is an important part of Zimbabwe's economy.

South Africa is now undergoing great social and political turmoil. Encourage students to watch the newspapers for articles about new developments there. *Answers are in the Teacher's Guide.*

Zimbabwe has many different economic activities. Its farmers grow both subsistence and commercial crops. It also has a great deal of mining, with good deposits of gold, chrome, copper, tin, iron, and coal. Zimbabwe, along with Zambia, also benefits from the hydroelectric power dams on the Zambezi River. With its many crops and minerals, Zimbabwe's potential for development is strong.

South Africa has great mineral wealth and is the most industrially developed country in Africa. Its economy contrasts greatly with that of Namibia, the least developed country in South Africa. For more than 60 years, Namibia has been ruled by the white-controlled government of South Africa. South Africa covets the rich deposits of copper and diamonds that lie beneath Namibia's surface. It also fears an independent black government so near its border. Namibians have been fighting for their freedom since the 1960's. In 1966, the United Nations declared that South Africa should grant Namibia independence. South Africa refused. Therefore, fighting continues.

Blacks and an increasing number of white South Africans are opposed to their government's policy of apartheid. During the 1980's, the efforts of black South Africans to obtain full citizenship and equal political and economic rights have increased. Both protestors and the government have resorted to violence. Many countries throughout the world have agreed with South African protestors and condemned apartheid.

Some changes are being made as a result of these pressures. For example, the government no longer pursues its hated policy of the homelands. It also no longer forces blacks to carry special passes. Many of these changes, however, are cosmetic. They do not address the real issues of apartheid.

Economic Development Economic activities in Southern Africa differ from one country to another. In Botswana, Mozambique, Malawi, and Madagascar, most people depend on some form of agriculture to make their living. Cash export crops are cashew nuts, tea, sugar, cotton, and tobacco. People in Madagascar also grow rice and raise cattle.

REVIEWING THE FACTS

Define
apartheid

Answer
1. What types of agriculture are important in East Africa?

2. How has the policy of apartheid affected black South Africans?

Locate
Refer to the map on page 426.

1. What countries border Lake Victoria.

2. Name the countries for which these are the capital cities: (a) Harare; (b) Windhoek; (c) Dar es Salaam; (d) Addis Ababa; (e) Nairobi; (f) Pretoria; (g) Kampala

447

Although Rhodesia (now Zimbabwe) declared its independence in 1965, it was not recognized by the British government until 1980.
Have students look back at the physical map on page 426 and identify the two deserts in Namibia.

GEOGRAPHY LABORATORY

Highlighting the Chapter

1. Sub-Saharan Africa is the part of the continent lying south of the Sahara. Most of this region lies in the tropics. High plateau elevations, however, greatly modify tropical temperatures. The equatorial zone of Central and West Africa has the heaviest rainfall and rain forest ecosystems. Savanna, steppe, and desert areas extend north and south from the equatorial zone, making much of the region too dry for cropping without irrigation. East Africa, even in the equatorial zone, is also mostly made up of arid or semiarid steppe and grassland.

2. Most people in sub-Saharan Africa live in rural villages, but cities are growing rapidly. Sub-Saharan Africans have developed more than 1,000 different languages, spoken among hundreds of different ethnic groups. At various times in the past, large empires arose, often based on wealth from trade. Europeans first arrived in the 1500's. After centuries of coastal trade, including the slave trade, Europeans colonized almost all of sub-Saharan Africa during the 1800's. After World War II, African nationalism swept the continent. Now sub-Saharan Africa is divided into independent nations.

The majority of Africans are subsistence farmers, but commercial crops are increasing in importance. Many African countries have mineral and some oil wealth, which they are rapidly developing. Africa's rivers provide great hydroelectric potential. African nations are also working to build internal transportation linkages. Politically, many African nations consider themselves nonaligned.

3. The countries of West and Central Africa include some of the most densely settled parts of Africa. To the north are the dry lands of the Sahel. In the southern part of the region are tropical rain forests. Oil income has helped Nigeria develop its industries. Central Africa too has considerable mineral wealth.

4. East and Southern Africa include several countries with large minorities of European ancestry. In South Africa, a white minority controls the country and has adopted a policy of apartheid, under which blacks have few rights. South Africa has great mineral wealth and is the most industrially developed country of Africa.

Speaking Geographically

Use the terms you learned in this chapter to complete the following sentences.

1. A steep cliff that marks the edge of a plateau is called a(n) _____.

2. The system of farming in which forest growth is cut down and burned to fertilize fields that will be used for only a few seasons is called _____.

3. The South African government's policy of strict separation between blacks and whites is called _____.

4. Those countries that do not wish to ally themselves with either the Communist or non-Communist nations are called _____.

Testing Yourself

Number your paper from 1 to 15. Select the best answer to complete each sentence and write it on your paper.

1. Most of sub-Saharan Africa is a (plateau, lowland, mountainous) region.

2. Sub-Saharan Africa is located mainly in the (high, middle, low) latitudes.

3. (Desert, Savanna, Rain forest) ecosystems cover most of sub-Saharan Africa.

4. The (Sudd, Sahel, Gezira) is a narrow strip of steppe located just south of the Sahara.

448

5. The population growth rate in sub-Saharan Africa is (low, average, high) compared to that of other continents.

6. The largest family of languages in Africa is (Kung, Bantu, Swahili).

7. The earliest of the great kingdoms that arose in sub-Saharan Africa was (Ife, Kongo, Kush).

8. During the (1600's, 1700's, 1800's), European governments divided nearly all of Africa into colonies.

9. One country that was never a colony is (Ghana, Ethiopia, Mozambique).

10. Most sub-Saharan African countries won their independence between (1957 and 1980, 1923 and 1945, 1980 and 1985).

11. The majority of the population in sub-Saharan Africa makes a living in (agriculture, mining, industry).

12. A major source of potential energy for sub-Saharan Africa is (coal, uranium, hydroelectric power).

13. The country with the most developed industry in sub-Saharan Africa is (Zaire, South Africa, Namibia).

14. An overall problem that holds back economic development in sub-Saharan Africa is the lack of (linkages, mineral resources, farmland).

15. One thing common to sub-Saharan countries is the (lack of rainfall, importance of tourism, ethnic diversity).

Building Map Skills

Number your paper from 1 to 10. Beside each number, write the name of the country it identifies on the map on this page. Now write the letters A to E on your paper. After each letter, write the name of the body of water identified by that letter on the map.

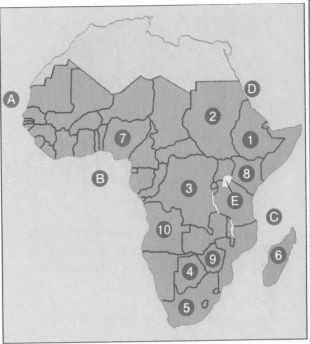

Applying Map Skills

Use the maps on pages 426, 427, 429, and 434 to compare Ethiopia and South Africa. Make a chart to compare the landforms, climate, land use, and population densities of the two countries.

Exploring Further

1. Archaeologists have found fossils at Olduvai Gorge in Tanzania, which scientists hope will give them information about early humans. *National Geographic*, November 1985 (Volume 168, Number 5), includes information on these and other interesting fossil finds in Africa. Write a summary of this article.

2. Look in the newspaper for articles on countries in sub-Saharan Africa. Choose an issue that a country there is facing today. Find out how this issue began and how it is being dealt with.

449

GEOGRAPHY LABORATORY

This chapter will take students on a journey to the land down under — Australia, Antarctica, and other islands of the South Pacific. To get started, ask students what Rick Springfield, the duckbill platypus, nineteenth-century convicts, and merino sheep have in common. *(Australia)* Then have them volunteer other information about Australia. Where is it located? What are its exports?

The South Pacific

The South Pacific is a region with much more water than land. In fact, another name for the region is Oceania. Oceania covers a huge area—more than one quarter of Earth's surface. Yet none of Earth's regions has as few people as the South Pacific.

There are two continents in the South Pacific region, Australia and Antarctica. Oceania also has thousands of islands. Some, like the Hawaiian Islands, are long archipelagos. Others, like Wake Island, are alone in the great ocean.

The islands were formed mainly in two different ways. Some are volcanoes that grew higher and higher each time they erupted. Eventually their tips rose above sea level. They then formed islands. These volcanic islands lie where the edges of tectonic plates push and slip against one another. Volcanic islands are generally steep and mountainous.

The second way the islands of the South Pacific formed was from coral. Coral is the skeletons of tiny sea animals. Millions of these tiny animals live in groups, settling on the rims of volcanoes beneath the sea. As the coral builds up, it makes a semicircular island called an atoll. The protected area of water within the atoll is called a lagoon. Coral islands are generally flat, rising only a few feet above sea level.

450

The photo shows Sydney, the capital of New South Wales. Sydney is the oldest and largest city in Australia, with a population of about 3.5 million. Its magnificent harbor and strategic position on the southeast coast of Australia make it one of the most important ports in the South Pacific.

1 The Physical Environment

The ocean separates the South Pacific region from other lands. For centuries, the lands of Oceania (ō shē an'ē ə) were isolated, cut off from the rest of the world. Hundreds and often thousands of miles separate small islands and island groups from one another.

The Ocean

As seen from a plane or ship, the vast Pacific Ocean may appear monotonously the same. However, its features vary greatly from place to place. In some areas, huge mountains rise from its floor, their peaks forming islands. Elsewhere, the ocean floor plunges to depths of 30,000 feet (9,000 meters) and more.

The Pacific's ecosystems change from place to place, just as ecosystems do on land. Near the equator, surface temperatures average 80°F (27°C). The cold waters surrounding Antarctica are near 32°F (0°C) all year. Besides these differences caused by latitude, currents of warm or cool water make a variety of local ecosystems in the ocean.

The ocean also has abundant marine life. Whales of many kinds are the largest form of sea life. Salmon, tuna, anchovies, and sardines are taken from Pacific waters. So are crabs, lobsters, shrimps, and oysters. Even seaweed is harvested from the sea, to be used as food and in making such products as ice cream and toothpaste.

Despite the ocean's vast size, however, its resources must still be used with care. The effects of overharvesting and pollution are already becoming evident in parts of the Pacific. Today scientists study the ocean to learn how to protect its marine life.

Landforms

The two largest landmasses of Oceania are the continents of Australia and Antarctica. The rest of the region's land consists of widely scattered islands.

Antarctica Antarctica centers on the South Pole. This continent is made up of a solid land mass and several large islands buried beneath a huge ice cap. Under the ice are mountains, valleys, and plains. Antarctica even has a smoking volcano — Mount Erebus (er'ə bəs).

Locked in Antarctica's ice cap is the largest amount of fresh water in the world. The frozen ground beneath the ice cap contains many minerals. Recently scientists have even found remains of plants, suggesting that Antarctica was once located in warmer latitudes before continental drift moved it to its present polar location.

Australia Australia lies between the Pacific and Indian oceans. With an area of about 2,968,000 square miles (7,700,000 square kilometers), the continent is a little smaller than the 48 adjoining states of the United States.

Australia is the flattest of the world's continents. Even the highest peak of its Great Dividing Range reaches only 7,316 feet (2,230 meters). This range is well named. It separates the narrow, well-watered plain on Australia's southeastern coast from the dry, desolate plains and low plateaus to the west. These western plains and plateaus are the lands Australians named the **outback.**

Off the northeastern coast of Australia lies a huge **reef** called the Great Barrier Reef. A reef is a strip or ridge that rises near the water's surface. Many reefs are made of rock, but this one is made of **coral,** the skeletons of millions of tiny sea animals. The Great Barrier Reef is the largest coral reef in the world. Early

Answers to Map Study questions on page 453: Indian and Pacific oceans, Timor, Coral, and
Tasman seas; largest land areas are Australia, Papua New Guinea, South Island, North Island,
and Tasmania (Antarctica not shown). Micronesia is 1,400 miles northeast of Australia;
Melanesia is just northeast of Australia; and Polynesia lies 2,800 miles east of Australia.
Assign the Workbook activity for Chapter 18, Section 1, with pages 451–456.

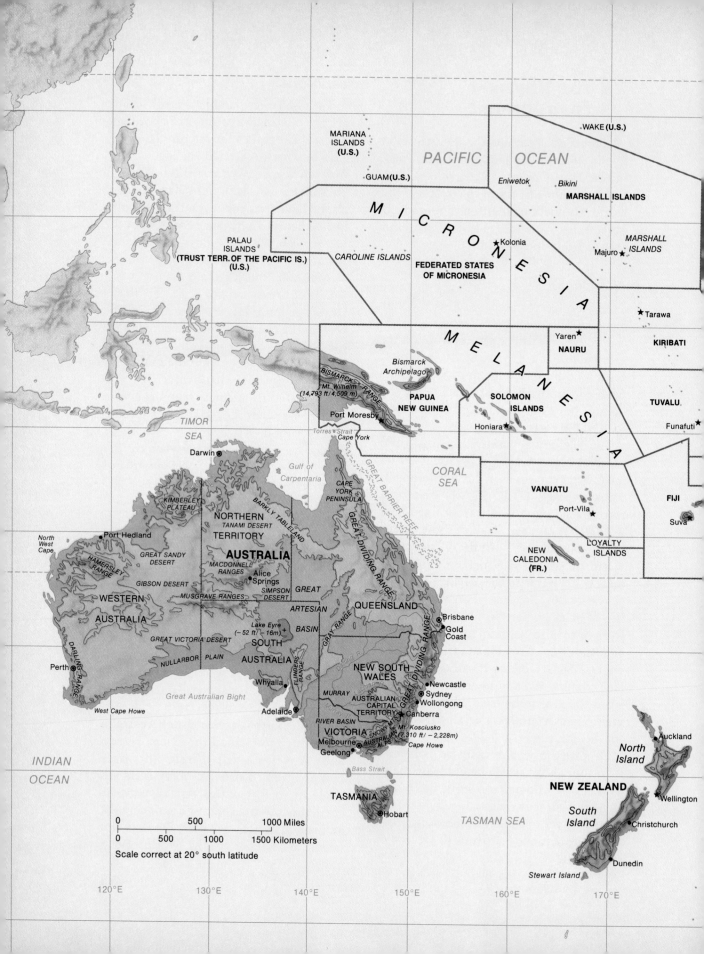

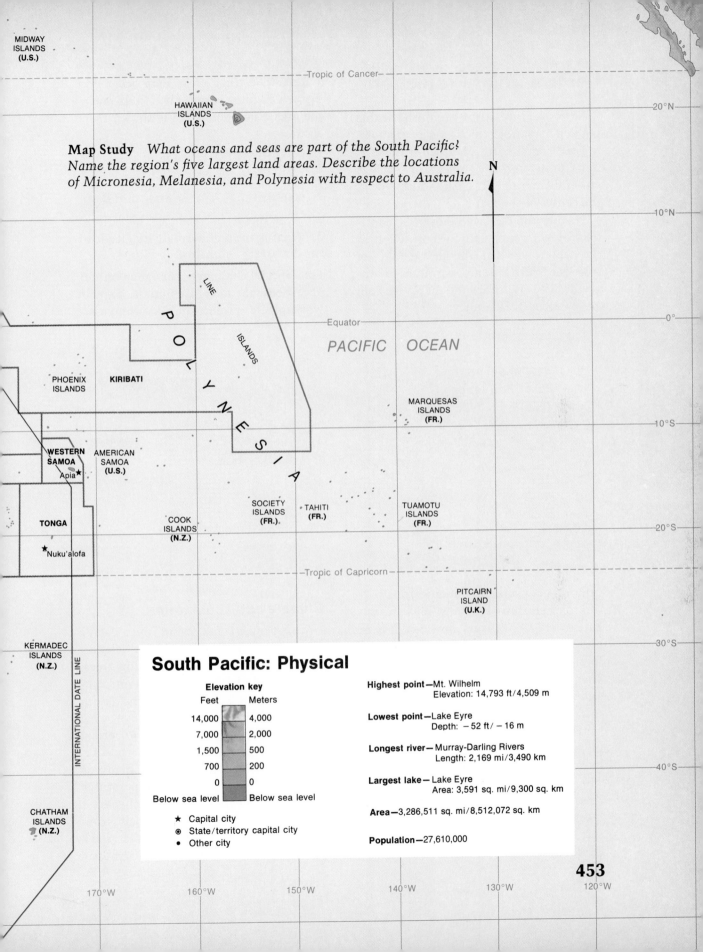

MIDWAY
ISLANDS
(U.S.)

Tropic of Cancer

20°N

HAWAIIAN
ISLANDS
(U.S.)

Map Study   *What oceans and seas are part of the South Pacific?*
Name the region's five largest land areas. Describe the locations
of Micronesia, Melanesia, and Polynesia with respect to Australia.

N

10°N

LINE

ISLANDS

P
O
L
Y
N
E
S
I
A

Equator

0°

PACIFIC   OCEAN

PHOENIX
ISLANDS

KIRIBATI

MARQUESAS
ISLANDS
(FR.)

10°S

**WESTERN
SAMOA**

Apia ★

AMERICAN
SAMOA
(U.S.)

SOCIETY
ISLANDS
(FR.)

TAHITI
(FR.)

TUAMOTU
ISLANDS
(FR.)

TONGA

★ Nuku'alofa

COOK
ISLANDS
(N.Z.)

20°S

Tropic of Capricorn

PITCAIRN
ISLAND
(U.K.)

KERMADEC
ISLANDS
(N.Z.)

INTERNATIONAL DATE LINE

30°S

South Pacific: Physical

Elevation key

Feet	Meters
14,000	4,000
7,000	2,000
1,500	500
700	200
0	0
Below sea level	Below sea level

★ Capital city
◉ State/territory capital city
• Other city

Highest point—Mt. Wilhelm
Elevation: 14,793 ft/4,509 m

Lowest point—Lake Eyre
Depth: − 52 ft/ − 16 m

Longest river—Murray-Darling Rivers
Length: 2,169 mi/3,490 km

Largest lake—Lake Eyre
Area: 3,591 sq. mi/9,300 sq. km

Area—3,286,511 sq. mi/8,512,072 sq. km

Population—27,610,000

CHATHAM
ISLANDS
(N.Z.)

40°S

170°W   160°W   150°W   140°W   130°W   120°W

Texas Essential Element 1C. Geographical tools and methodologies.

Using a Polar Projection

As you learned at the beginning of this book, a map projection is a way of showing the round Earth on a flat surface. A polar projection is a projection that has either the North Pole or the South Pole at the center of the map.

The map on this page shows the continent of Antarctica with the South Pole at the center. The straight lines extending from the South Pole are meridians of longitude. The circles around the South Pole are parallels of latitude.

Remember that every map projection distorts Earth in some way. On this map, the area near the center is shown most accurately.

1. (a) What is the latitude of the South Pole? (b) Of the Antarctic Circle?

2. (a) Is Antarctica in the high, middle, or low latitudes? (b) How do you know?

3. What is the approximate longitude of the Antarctic Peninsula?

For a special challenge The map on this page does not have a compass. Explain why no polar projection has a compass.

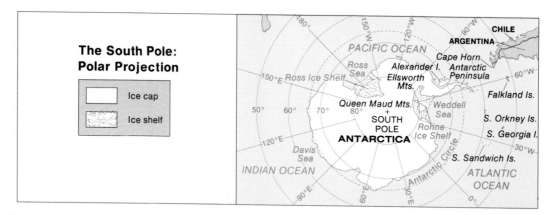

explorers considered it a dangerous barrier for their ships. For today's marine scientists and scuba divers, however, it is an underwater paradise of great beauty and interest.

The Islands Geographers divide Oceania's islands into three large groups: Micronesia (mī′krə nē′zhə), meaning "small islands"; Melanesia (mel′ə nē′zhə), meaning "black islands"; and Polynesia (päl′ə nē′zhə), meaning "many islands." The islands of Oceania are generally small. New Guinea, in Melanesia, and North and South islands, which lie in southern Polynesia and make up New Zealand, are exceptions.

Climate and Ecosystems

Most people think of the South Pacific as a land of sun-bathed tropical islands, gentle breezes, and swaying palm trees. Actually, all of Earth's climates and ecosystems occur someplace in the South Pacific region.

The lowest temperature ever recorded was taken on the Antarctic ice cap: −127°F (−88°C). In contrast, many of the tropical islands enjoy temperatures that average near 80°F (27°C) all year.

Oceania's rainfall varies widely from place to place too. In parts of Australia's outback, years may pass without a drop

454

Answers are in the Teacher's Guide.

Assign the Workbook activity for this chapter's Map Workshop with this page.

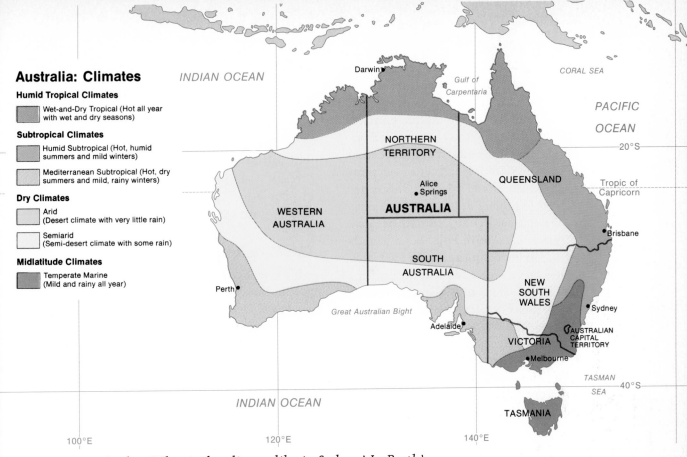

Australia: Climates

Humid Tropical Climates

Wet-and-Dry Tropical (Hot all year with wet and dry seasons)

Subtropical Climates

Humid Subtropical (Hot, humid summers and mild winters)

Mediterranean Subtropical (Hot, dry summers and mild, rainy winters)

Dry Climates

Arid (Desert climate with very little rain)

Semiarid (Semi-desert climate with some rain)

Midlatitude Climates

Temperate Marine (Mild and rainy all year)

INDIAN OCEAN

CORAL SEA

Darwin

Gulf of Carpentaria

PACIFIC OCEAN

NORTHERN TERRITORY

QUEENSLAND

20°S

Alice Springs

AUSTRALIA

Tropic of Capricorn

WESTERN AUSTRALIA

Brisbane

SOUTH AUSTRALIA

Perth

NEW SOUTH WALES

Great Australian Bight

Sydney

Adelaide

AUSTRALIAN CAPITAL TERRITORY

VICTORIA

Melbourne

INDIAN OCEAN

TASMAN SEA

40°S

TASMANIA

100°E   120°E   140°E

Map Study   *What is the climate like in Sydney? In Perth?*

of rain. However, the windward slope of Hawaii's Mount Waialeale (wī äl′ā äl′ā) is the world's wettest spot. It receives an average of 460 inches (1,170 centimeters) of precipitation a year.

Antarctica   Antarctica is a barren continent with a polar ecosystem. It is home only to coastal penguins and seals. Explorers, scientists, and photographers who visit Antarctica must live in special camps to protect themselves from the extreme cold.

Australia   In addition to being the flattest continent, Australia is also the driest. A third of its land is desert, and another third is semiarid. Only the northern and eastern edges of the continent have enough rain for forests.

Along the southeastern coast, rainfall is plentiful. Temperatures are mild. The southeast is Australia's most productive farming region. It is also the part of the country where the most people live.

Australia's northern coast and the Cape York Peninsula are the wettest parts of the continent. This area has a wet-and-dry tropical climate, getting 40 to 60 inches (100 to 150 centimeters) of rain each year. Savanna grasslands and forests of eucalyptus and acacia thrive there.

Most of Australia — the continent's interior and west coast — is a lonely desert or steppe ecosystem. The prevailing winds come across the ocean from the east, but the Great Dividing Range blocks these moisture-bearing winds from reaching inland Australia. The lands west of the mountains receive little rain. In the outback, only an occasional thunderstorm waters the thirsty land. Then plants grow and bloom quickly. Almost as quickly they wither as the moisture

Answers to Map Study questions: Sydney has a humid subtropical climate; Perth has a Mediterranean subtropical climate.

Ask students, "What season is it now in Australia?" *(the opposite of the season it is in the Northern Hemisphere)*

455

evaporates. Their seeds lie in the ground for months, waiting for the next rain.

The Islands In contrast to Australia, New Zealand has a true marine climate, similar to that of Western Europe. Even its interior is close enough to the ocean to enjoy its moderating influence on temperatures. On North Island, winters are mild and summers are warm and rainy. South Island has a cooler climate because it is nearer the South Pole. Both islands have enough precipitation for lush forests and grasslands and for farming.

The large islands of Melanesia lie near the equator. They have wet tropical climates and tropical rainforest ecosystems. In the rest of Oceania, temperatures vary with elevation on the large, mountainous islands. The smaller islands have tropical or subtropical climates with wet and dry seasons. Except where people have cleared the land, most smaller islands have dense stands of tropical vegetation.

REVIEWING THE FACTS

Define

1. outback
2. reef
3. coral

Answer

1. Why is Oceania a good name for this region?

2. Describe the major landforms of each of the following: (a) Antarctica, (b) Australia, (c) the islands.

3. Describe the various climate zones of Australia.

Locate

Refer to the map on pages 452–453 to name the capital city of each of the following countries: (a) Australia, (b) New Zealand, (c) Papua New Guinea, (d) Vanuatu, (e) Fiji.

456

2 The Human Imprint

The people of Oceania are few in number and widely scattered across the region. The groups who settled the region long ago developed a wide variety of cultures. In the past 250 years, these groups of people have increasingly felt the impact of European cultures.

The People of the South Pacific

No one is certain how or when the first people came to the South Pacific region. To reach Oceania from mainland Asia, early peoples had to travel over vast expanses of open sea. Archaeologists believe that the earliest human beings in Australia may have arrived about 40,000 years ago. Many of the smaller islands of the Pacific were discovered and settled only during the past 2,000 years.

Early Peoples Australia's original people are known as the Aborigines (ab'ə rij'ə nēz). (This term can refer to the people of any land who have lived there from the distant past.) The Australian Aborigines traditionally lived by hunting and gathering. Their tools were made of wood, hide, bone, or stone. One of their weapons was the boomerang, a curved wooden throwing stick that required considerable skill to make and use. Religious ceremonies and art were important parts of Aborigine culture.

New Zealand was settled about 1,000 years ago by a group of people known as Maoris (mou'rēz). They took over New Zealand from earlier groups about whom little is known. The Maoris gave their new country a beautiful name— Aotearoa, meaning "the long, white cloud." The people lived by farming, not by hunting and gathering. The Maoris were also great warriors and skilled wood-carvers.

Answers are in the Teacher's Guide.

Assign the Workbook activity for Chapter 18, Section 2, with pages 456–461.

The early islanders were skilled navigators and sailors. They island-hopped in large canoes with outriggers (long poles that extended from the sides of a canoe and kept it from tipping). Carried by winds and currents, people moved frequently among the many islands of Micronesia, Melanesia, and Polynesia. As a result, the languages and cultures of the islands are a complicated blend.

European Exploration No European had ever seen any of the South Pacific regions before the 1500's. Early European geographers believed there was a great unknown southern continent they called *Australis* ("southern land"). They mistakenly thought that such a landmass was needed to balance the northern continents. Otherwise, they said, Earth would be top-heavy and would turn upside down.

Bit by bit, facts replaced legends. In 1642, the Dutch explorer Abel Tasman charted the west coast of New Zealand and the island that bears his name—Tasmania (taz mā'nē ə). A British explorer, Captain James Cook, made three voyages to the South Pacific. He mapped the coasts of New Zealand and eastern Australia, discovered Hawaii, and even explored the edge of Antarctica.

Contact with Europe and later with the United States brought change to the people of Oceania. All over the South Pacific, traditional cultures have suffered great changes.

In some places, European conquest meant disaster. The last Tasmanian died in 1876. In Australia, European settlers drove the Aborigines from the best lands and killed many in fighting. Still more Aborigines died of diseases carried by the Europeans. New Zealand's Maoris fought fiercely to hold their homeland, and many died. For a while, it appeared that both the Aborigines and the Maoris would die out. Today, however, both

The Maoris have maintained their tradition of fine wood carving. Their works reflect their ancient culture.

groups are making a place for themselves in modern society. Yet they have done so at the cost of losing much of their traditional culture.

Settlement Patterns Today people of European descent make up 90 percent of the population in Australia and New Zealand. In other parts of Oceania, however, Europeans make up a smaller part of the population.

Some 24 million people live in Oceania. Of this number, about 16 million live in Australia. Recall that Australia is about the size of the 48 adjoining states of the United States. Its 16 million people are only 7 percent of the population of the United States. Thus, Australia is very thinly populated.

The overall population density of Oceania is about 7 persons per square mile of land. In the United States, only Alaska and Wyoming are more thinly settled. However, this figure can be misleading. Hawaii, for example, has more than 150 people per square mile, about the same as the state of California. Fiji has

457

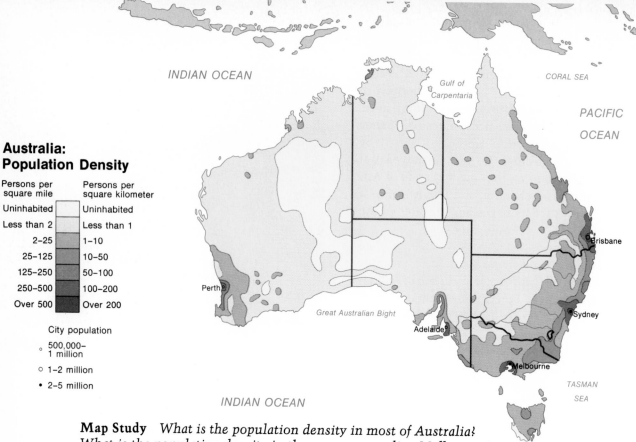

Australia: Population Density

Persons per square mile	Persons per square kilometer
Uninhabited	Uninhabited
Less than 2	Less than 1
2–25	1–10
25–125	10–50
125–250	50–100
250–500	100–200
Over 500	Over 200

City population

○ 500,000– 1 million

○ 1–2 million

● 2–5 million

Map Study *What is the population density in most of Australia? What is the population density in the area surrounding Melbourne? Which is larger, Brisbane or Adelaide?*

100 people per square mile—almost identical to South Carolina.

Nearly three of every four people of Oceania live in cities. This figure is comparable to the urban density of North America and Europe. Making a living by farming or herding in arid Australia, or in the mountains of Oceania's smaller islands, is very difficult. City living, with jobs, schools, social life, and medical centers, is much more attractive to many people in the region than is rural life.

In Australia, about 85 percent of the people live in cities, making Australia the most urbanized continent. Sydney has more than 3 million people. Melbourne has nearly 3 million people. Both Brisbane and Adelaide have populations of nearly 1 million. In the outback, however, the population averages less than 1 person per square mile.

On the mountainous islands of Melanesia, Micronesia, and Polynesia, nearly everyone lives on the narrow coastal plains. On the low-lying coral atolls, most people settle near the calm inner lagoon, away from the often stormy sea.

Political Patterns

Early European exploration and trade brought the Spanish, Portuguese, Dutch, English, and French to the South Pacific. By war, treaty, or purchase, European nations gradually won control of the lands of Oceania. In the European scramble for the Pacific islands, the region's political map became very complex.

Australia was a British colony until 1901, when it became a self-governing country within the British Empire. New Zealand too was a British colony during the 1800's. It became independent in

458

1907. Both Australia and New Zealand are now members of the British Commonwealth (page 222). Elsewhere in the South Pacific, the British also held much of Melanesia.

Spain held most of Micronesia until 1898, when the United States gained control of Guam in the Spanish-American War. Spain's other island territories were sold to Germany. After World War I, Germany's islands passed to Japan. Then, after World War II, Micronesia became a Trust Territory of the United States. Many Micronesian island groups remain under the control of the United States today.

In Polynesia, France controls Tahiti, the Marquesas, the Society Islands, and others. The United States took over the Hawaiian Islands in 1898. In 1959, Hawaii became a state. The United States also controls American Samoa. Tiny Pitcairn Island is a colony of the United Kingdom, and the Cook Islands are a self-governing territory of New Zealand.

Independence is spreading in Oceania's islands. During the 1960's, Western

Samoa and Nauru gained their independence. Fiji, Kiribati, the Solomon Islands, Tonga, and Tuvalu also won independence. Vanuatu became self-governing in 1980.

Economic Patterns

Economic development in Oceania differs according to landforms, climates, ecosystems, resources, and culture. The original peoples of the South Pacific lived by fishing, hunting, gathering wild foods, and raising such crops as taro (a starchy root) and yams. European settlers changed the region's economy. They paid cash for resources and crops. Thus, the islanders changed from a subsistence economy to a cash economy.

Farming In both Australia and New Zealand, the raising of livestock, especially sheep, is a major activity. Australia's semiarid ecosystem and flat land are well suited to livestock grazing. Australia is the world leader in wool production and a major producer of livestock.

New Zealand's mild, more humid climate makes it a good place for mixed

WORLD DATA BANK

Country	Area in Square Miles	Population/Natural Increase		Per Capita GNP
Australia	2,967,896	16,200,000	(0.8%)	$10,840
Fiji	7,054	700,000	(2.3%)	1,700
Kiribati	266	62,000	(1.6%)	NA
Nauru	8	8,000	(1.3%)	21,400
New Zealand	103,737	3,300,000	(0.8%)	7,310
Papua New Guinea	178,259	3,600,000	(2.4%)	710
Solomon Islands	10,985	300,000	(3.6%)	510
Tonga	270	107,000	(1.9%)	NA
Tuvalu	10	8,000	(1.7%)	570
Vanuatu	5,699	200,000	(3.3%)	NA
Western Samoa	1,104	200,000	(2.4%)	660

459

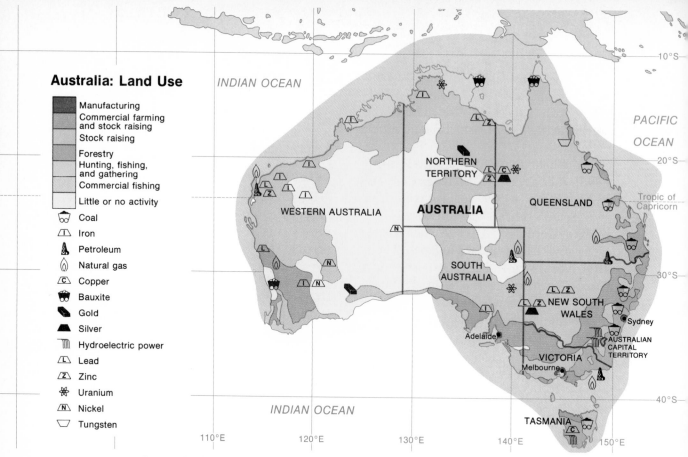

Australia: Land Use

- Manufacturing
- Commercial farming and stock raising
- Stock raising
- Forestry
- Hunting, fishing, and gathering
- Commercial fishing
- Little or no activity

- Coal
- Iron
- Petroleum
- Natural gas
- Copper
- Bauxite
- Gold
- Silver
- Hydroelectric power
- Lead
- Zinc
- Uranium
- Nickel
- Tungsten

INDIAN OCEAN

PACIFIC OCEAN

NORTHERN TERRITORY

QUEENSLAND

WESTERN AUSTRALIA

AUSTRALIA

SOUTH AUSTRALIA

NEW SOUTH WALES

Sydney

AUSTRALIAN CAPITAL TERRITORY

Adelaide

VICTORIA

Melbourne

INDIAN OCEAN

TASMANIA

Tropic of Capricorn

10°S
20°S
30°S
40°S

110°E 120°E 130°E 140°E 150°E

Map Study *Which Australian provinces include manufacturing centers? Along which coast have the most coal deposits been discovered? The most iron?*

farming. It too is a major producer of wool, meat, and dairy products.

Most people on the low coral islands still live by fishing and subsistence farming. Soils on these atolls are thin and poor. Fresh water is scarce. Yams, coconuts, rice, corn, bananas, and taros are typical food crops.

The high islands are better suited for farming because their volcanic soil is more fertile and they have more fresh water. On some high islands, you will find large plantations, usually run by Europeans. Coconuts are a big cash crop. Coconut meat is dried to make a product called copra, which is used in cooking oil, margarine, soap, and cosmetics. New Guinea also raises cash crops of coffee and cacao.

Resources Australia is the richest of Oceania's countries in resources. It has good supplies of many minerals and also energy resources. Much of Australia has not yet been fully explored for minerals, and Australians still hope for rich new finds.

Mining has become important on some islands. For example, Nauru in Micronesia has some of the richest phosphate deposits in the world. Wealth from this mineral fertilizer gives this tiny nation of fewer than 8,000 citizens one of the highest per capita gross national products in the world—nearly $21,500 in the mid-1980's! New Guinea and the Solomon Islands have copper deposits.

Industry Australia is the leading industrial country in Oceania. Much of the

Answers to Map Study questions: Manufacturing is done in New South Wales and Victoria; coal—east coast; iron—northwest coast

The discovery of gold in the mid-1800's led to gold rushes that brought many new immigrants to Australia and New Zealand.

land around Sydney and Melbourne is used for manufacturing. The kinds of industry range from clothing and food processing to steel, electronics, appliances, and precision instruments. Australia's rich deposits of minerals and fuels provide a good base for even greater industrial growth in the future.

Much of New Zealand's industry is based on the processing of agricultural goods. Isolation from world markets and a small population do not encourage the growth of heavy industries in this remote country. The other islands of Oceania also face these barriers to the development of industry.

REVIEWING THE FACTS

Answer

1. How did the arrival of Europeans affect the cultures and economies of the earlier people of Oceania?

2. Explain why this statement is true but misleading: Oceania has a low population density.

3. (a) Why is Oceania's political history a complicated one? (b) What political trend has affected much of the region since the 1960's?

4. Describe the major economic activities of each of the following: (a) Australia, (b) New Zealand, (c) an atoll, (d) a volcanic island.

Locate

Refer to the maps on pages 452–453 and 458.

1. (a) In what region of Australia do most of the people live? (b) What city is a population center on the western coast?

2. Find Australia's largest uninhabited region. What natural features occur there that explain its lack of population?

3 Australia

Australia is the only country that occupies an entire continent. Its low landforms and dry climate make it different from other continents. Distance also sets Australia apart. Being far away from other countries has affected many aspects of Australian life.

Australia's Regions

The economic and cultural heartland of Australia is the narrow region along the eastern and southeastern coasts. This region lies between the Pacific Ocean and the Great Dividing Range. It is the most densely populated and the most economically developed part of the country. The climate is mild, moist, and pleasant. The land is well suited to farming in the level areas and to grazing in the highlands. This coastal region is also where Australia's major cities are located.

West of the Great Dividing Range lies the Great Artesian (är tē′zhən) Basin. This region is named for its many **artesian wells** and springs. Artesian wells exist where a layer of groundwater is trapped between two hard layers of rock somewhere below the soil. When a person drills a well down to the layer of water, the water flows upward naturally, under its own pressure. In central Australia, such wells supply water for thousands of sheep and cattle on ranches.

The land west of the Great Artesian Basin is known to Australians as the outback. Little water and sparse vegetation make the outback a difficult place in which to eke out a living. It is sparsely populated and perhaps always will be. On the fringe of the interior desert, there are scattered ranches and small towns. There are a few mining towns, such as Alice Springs, in the interior. However, most of

461

Answers are in the Teacher's Guide.

Assign the Workbook activity for Chapter 18, Section 3, with pages 461–465.

Sydney is Australia's largest city.

the outback is nearly empty of people. Hundreds of miles may separate the few homes and ranches.

Today the automobile, the airplane, and the radio are changing life for people in the outback. Most homes and settlements are now connected by telephone and by roads. In an emergency, people can radio for a doctor or a flying ambulance. Many children attend school classes by listening to special School of the Air radio programs.

Despite the hardships of living in the outback, many Australians still think of it as a land of opportunity. The new transportation and communication linkages may help in finding and developing new resources in the outback. Recent finds of petroleum, natural gas, and nickel have added to the economic development of Australia's vast interior.

The People of Australia

As you have read, the first settlers of Australia were the Aborigines, who reached the continent about 40,000 years ago. The first European settlement in Australia was at Botany Bay in 1788. Later this settlement became the city of Sydney.

Settlers soon found that the best use of land was raising sheep. Wool was light in weight, high in value, and easy to ship to textile mills in England. Later, cattle ranching and wheat growing also became important activities.

Australia's population grew during the 1800's and early 1900's, but growth was usually slow. One reason was the government's rules about immigration. Until World War II, few immigrants were accepted from any countries except those of the British Isles. After World War II, the Australian government changed its laws to encourage immigration from other European countries. About half the new immigrants still came from the United Kingdom, but some also came from Germany, Austria, Poland, Italy, and Greece. Asians too are now settling in Australia.

In the past, the Aborigines shared little in Australia's growing prosperity. When the Europeans first arrived, about 300,000 Aborigines lived in Australia.

AUSTRALIAN SLANG
Bush — *Any rural area*
Back of beyond — *Most distant place*
The Big Smoke — *A city*
Hard yacker — *Tiring work*
Mob — *Flock (of sheep)*
Outback — *Inland region*
Jumbuck — *Sheep*
Digger — *Once a miner, now a soldier*
Willy-willy — *A cyclone*
Up a gumtree — *In a mess*
Station — *A sheep ranch*

462

Today there are only about 150,000. Some still live in the outback or in the remote Northern Territory. Others work on ranches or farms. Some are now moving to the cities to find work. Australia's Aborigines are seeking ways to take a more active part in Australian life.

Australia's British heritage shows in its government, which is much like that of Canada and other former British colonies. Australia has a parliament led by a prime minister and a cabinet. The head of state is the British king or queen, who is represented by a governor-general. Australia's capital is at Canberra, a planned city of 250,000 that was built to be the center of government.

Economic Development

Agriculture has always been Australia's most important economic activity. The country's greatest source of wealth is still sheep raising. Australia produces 30 percent of the world's total supply of wool. Some sheep ranches are larger than the smallest European countries or American states.

Cattle raising is another important activity in Australia. Cattle graze in the savannas of the north and along the eastern coast. They are also found in the southwest, near Perth.

Wheat is the major crop of Australia. Special varieties have been developed for growing in drier areas. In the tropical region near Brisbane, growers raise sugarcane and tropical fruits like pineapple. Cotton is also grown in this warm region.

Mining too is an important activity in Australia. The continent has almost all the major minerals. Australia is a leading producer of bauxite, mining about 30 percent of the world's total supply. Iron ore, copper, tin, silver, uranium, nickel, lead, zinc, and diamonds are also mined

Tourists climb Australia's Ayers Rock, the largest rock in the world.

in Australia. Large deposits of coal, petroleum, and natural gas mean there is plenty of fuel for Australia's industries.

Industry was slow to develop in Australia. Having few people, Australia needed comparatively few manufactured goods. For years, it was less expensive to import many manufactured goods than to produce them locally. Then, during World War II, Australia was cut off from Europe and the Americas. Australians had no markets for their raw materials and no way to get manufactured goods. To save their economy, Australians

In western Australia, many sheep ranches like this one lie within vast areas of flat, open land.

463

SPOTLIGHT ON THE WALLACE LINE:

Why Kookaburra Sits in the Old Gum Tree

Australia is the home of many unusual plants, birds, and animals. Many of them are found nowhere else.

One of Australia's special plants is the eucalyptus (yü′kə lip′təs) tree. The eucalyptus tree—called a gum tree in Australia—is native only to Australia. Because it travels well, however, a variety known as the ghost gum is being planted in many parts of the world. It is being used to stop the spread of deserts.

Up in the evergreen leaves of the gum tree, you may find a koala (kō äl′ə). This furry, friendly little animal is about two feet long and lives on a diet of eucalyptus leaves. Another creature you might find in a eucalyptus tree is a kookaburra (kùk′ə bėr′ə). The kookaburra sometimes surprises passersby with wild laughter.

Other unique Australian creatures are these:

- the kangaroo, an animal that raises its young in the mother's pouch.

- the duckbill platypus (plat′i pəs), half bird and half beast. It lays eggs, but it suckles its young and is covered with fur.

- the emu (ē′myü), a large, awkward bird that cannot fly. It can flatten a farmer's crops as it runs over them.

Why are such unusual birds, animals, and plants found only in the Australian region? A British naturalist, Alfred Russell Wallace, suggested a possible explanation about a hundred years ago.

Wallace thought that Australia's isolation might be one reason for its unusual plant and animal life. He suggested that

The kookaburra (upper left) and cassowary (lower right) are two of Australia's birds. Cassowaries grow to 4.9 feet (1.5 meters) in height. The kangaroo (upper right) lives on the grasslands. The koala (lower left) lives on the leaves of the gum tree.

an imaginary line in the southwestern Pacific separated Australia from Asia. Without contact, animal life on these two continents developed in widely different ways.

On the Asian side of the "Wallace line" were many of the better-known animals. Only on the Australian side did you find those kooky kookaburras, koalas, and kangaroos. These interesting creatures still give a special quality to life "down under"—south of the equator and far from other lands.

began to build their own industries. Since that time, Australia has become more and more industrialized. Manufactured goods now account for about 20 percent of all exports.

Australia depends heavily on trade. Each year it ranks between fifteenth and twentieth in foreign trade among the countries of the world. Today trade with the United Kingdom is less important than in the past. Instead, Japan buys the largest share of Australia's exports. Australia gets the major share of its imports from the United States.

REVIEWING THE FACTS

Define

artesian well

Answer

1. Describe the following regions of Australia: (a) the eastern and southeastern coast, (b) the Great Artesian Basin, (c) the outback.

2. How did immigration to Australia change after World War II?

3. Describe Australia's government.

4. What are Australia's main agricultural activities?

5. (a) What natural advantages does Australia have for industry? (b) Why did industry suddenly begin to develop in Australia?

Locate

Refer to the map on page 460.

1. For what economic activity is most of Australia's land used?

2. Name two manufacturing regions in Australia.

3. What type of economic activity might be a sign of Aborigines who still follow their traditional ways of life?

4 The Islands

After thousands of years of traditional life and a century or more of colonial rule, the islands of Oceania are changing rapidly today. Some islands have gained their independence. Others are pushing for more self-government.

Economic changes are coming to many of the islands too. New Zealand has become a modern, industrialized country. Some of the smaller islands are also looking for ways to industrialize or to improve agriculture. Faster air travel has brought a thriving tourist industry to some islands. Balmy tropical weather, white coral sand beaches, and beautiful scenery attract thousands of tourists each year.

One of the most promising activities for the future may be fishing. The Pacific is rich in marine life. In the past, islanders caught only enough to feed themselves. Now the development of commercial fishing could bring them another source of income.

Students in a New Zealand high school prepare for jobs in a modern economy by learning the basics of chemistry.

As each group of islands is discussed, have students locate it on the map on pages 452–453.
Assign the Workbook activity for Chapter 18, Section 4, with pages 465–469.
Answers are in the Teacher's Guide.

Using An Almanac

An almanac is a valuable source for learning about the countries of the world. Almanacs contain recent data, or information, on such topics as population, government policies, per capita income, and economic growth.

To begin your research on Australia, choose an almanac and turn to its index. The index may be in the front or the back of the almanac. Countries and topics are listed in alphabetical order in the index. Find the entry on Australia. You can then turn to the pages that cover the information you want.

Two sections from an almanac appear below. The first column is part of the index. The second column is part of an article on Australia. Use the index and the article to answer the following questions about Australia.

1. (a) On what page can you find information about Australia's area? (b) About Australia's cities?

2. (a) What is the largest city in Australia? (b) Which cities in Australia have over a million people?

3. (a) What is the estimated population of Australia? (b) What percentage of the population is between the ages of 15 and 44?

4. What type of government does Australia have?

5. Where is Australia located?

6. (a) Who is head of state? (b) Who is the governor-general?

GENERAL INDEX

Australia

Commonwealth of Australia

People: Population (1985 est): 15,345,000. **Age distrib. (%):** 0–14: 23.7; 15–44: 47.0; 45+: 29.3. **Pop. density:** 5.2 per sq. mi. **Urban** (1984): 85%. **Ethnic groups:** British 95%, other European 3%, aborigines (including mixed) 1.5%. **Languages:** English, aboriginal languages. **Religions:** Anglican 36%, other Protestant 25%, Roman Catholic 33%.

Geography: Area: 2,966,200 sq. mi., almost as large as the continental U.S. **Location:** SE of Asia, Indian Ocean is W and S, Pacific Ocean (Coral, Tasman seas) is E; they meet N of Australia in Timor and Arafura seas: Tasmania lies 150 mi. S of Victoria state, across Bass Strait. **Neighbors:** Nearest are Indonesia, Papua New Guinea on N, Solomons, Fiji, and New Zealand on E. **Topography:** An island continent. The Great Dividing Range along the E coast has Mt. Kosciusko, 7,310 ft. The W plateau rises to 2,000 ft. with arid areas in the Great Sandy and Great Victoria deserts. The NW part of Western Australia and Northern Territory are arid and hot. The NE has heavy rainfall and Cape York Peninsula has jungles. The Murray River rises in New South Wales. **Capital:** Canberra. **Cities** (1982 est): Sydney 3,310,500; Melbourne 2,836,800; Brisbane 1,124,200; Adelaide 960,000; Perth 948,900.

Government: Type: Democratic, federal state system. **Head of state:** Queen Elizabeth II, represented by Gov. Gen. Ninian Martin Stephen; in office: July 29, 1982. **Head of Government:** Prime Minister Robert James Lee Hawke; born Dec. 9, 1929; in office: Mar. 11, 1983. **Local divisions:** 6 states, 2 territories. **Defense:** 2.8% of GNP.

Answers are in the Teacher's Guide.
Assign the Workbook activity for this chapter's Skill Workshop with this page.

On some islands, economic development has caused major changes. Many people from rural areas are moving into the few small towns and cities. Often, however, there are not enough jobs for all the newcomers. As a result, some islanders have migrated to more industrialized countries.

NOT EXACTLY POCKET MONEY

In the Caroline Islands (Micronesia), people once used carved stone disks as money. The largest of these "coins" were more than two times wider than a person's height. Their owners—either individuals or villages—used them to buy land. Or they used them to pay priests, witch doctors, or victors in battle. There was no need for a bank, though. The disks were so heavy that they were rarely moved.

New Zealand

New Zealand is the most developed of the island countries in Oceania. Geographically it is part of the island group, Polynesia. New Zealand is about 1,200 miles (1,900 kilometers) from Australia, its nearest neighbor.

Regions   New Zealand's two largest islands are known simply as North Island and South Island. Like other locations along the Rim of Fire, New Zealand has a number of active volcanoes. Mount Ruapehu (rü′ə pä′hü) on North Island last erupted in 1975.

Jagged mountain peaks and steep-sided fjords are a sign that glaciers once covered New Zealand. You can still see mountain glaciers in the Southern Alps on South Island.

Mountains divide South Island into two regions. West of the mountains is a narrow strip of densely forested land that receives more than 200 inches of rainfall in some places. East of the mountains are fertile plains, where farmers grow grain and graze sheep.

North Island has three areas. The northern part is a narrow, sparsely settled peninsula. The southern part has fertile plains and several rivers. The center of North Island is a high, volcanic plateau. The region is much like Yellowstone Park in the United States, with geysers, boiling mud, and hot springs.

The People of New Zealand   Today about 90 percent of the population is of European descent. About 8 percent are Maoris. The Maoris take an active part in the country's society and economy. Their leaders have been elected to parliament. People from other Pacific islands make up the other 2 percent of the population.

Most of New Zealand's people live on North Island. As in Australia, about 85 percent of the whole population live in

467

Russell, North Island, is one of New Zealand's harbor towns (top). • *Sheep thrive on the rich grass of New Zealand's hillsides.*

towns and cities. The largest cities are Auckland, the main industrial center, and Wellington, the capital.

Economic Development Most of New Zealand's wealth comes from agriculture. In fact, mutton, beef, and wool provide nearly 75 percent of the country's export income.

Though agriculture is the most important economic activity in New Zealand, there are many other resources and activities. Forests are a source of wealth. New Zealand is a major exporter of wood products. Fishing has also been important since early times.

With its low population, New Zealand exports much of what it produces. When the country's major trading partner, the United Kingdom, joined the European Economic Community, New Zealand had to look to other countries such as Australia, Japan, and the United States for new partners in trade.

New Zealand has an abundance of energy. Its many rivers provide hydroelectric power. It also has deposits of coal, oil, and natural gas. These energy resources are helping New Zealand build new industries. A new steel mill opened recently near Auckland, and an aluminum smelter to process Australian bauxite has been built on South Island. Other industries are food processing, paper and wood products, textiles, metal products, chemicals, and transportation equipment. More than 40 percent of New Zealand's people work in industry. Trade, industry, and agriculture combine to give New Zealand one of the highest standards of living in the world.

Air travel encourages another source of income — tourism. On North Island, visitors are drawn to the bubbling mud pools, geysers, and smoking volcanoes. On South Island, tourists flock to mountain lakes, trout streams, fjords, ski slopes, and glaciers. There is even a tourist flight over Antarctica's ice cap.

Melanesia

The islands of Melanesia lie in the southwestern Pacific Ocean. New Guinea is the largest of them. The western half of the island is part of Indonesia. The eastern part is an independent country called Papua New Guinea.

New Guinea has many cultures. In the mountains and rain forests are groups of people who live by hunting and gathering. Others live in small, scattered villages and practice subsistence farming. Still others live in the few coastal cities. The country as a whole remains one of the world's least developed and least known.

Other islands of Melanesia include New Caledonia, Fiji, the Solomon Islands, and Bougainville. On Bougainville, copper deposits are mined and exported.

468

Micronesia

Micronesia is located to the north of Melanesia. Most of the islands of Micronesia are small, low-lying coral atolls.

The small size and population of the islands in Micronesia have made it difficult for them to become independent. However, Nauru, with its rich phosphate deposits, became independent in 1968. Wake Island, Guam, and some other islands in Micronesia are important stopping places for ships and planes traveling between Hawaii and the countries of Asia. The United States also uses some of the islands as military bases.

The people of Micronesia speak a variety of languages. Most people speak several Micronesian tongues. English is now widely used in school and business, especially by young adults. Japanese is spoken by many older people, who learned it when the Japanese held the area during World War II.

Polynesia

East of Melanesia and Micronesia in the central Pacific Ocean lie thousands of islands that make up Polynesia. Besides New Zealand, this triangular region includes Hawaii, Samoa, Tahiti, and Kiribati. These far-flung islands occupy an area greater than all of North America.

The people of Polynesia share a common culture, language, and history. Interestingly, in places as far apart as New Zealand and Hawaii, people tell similar stories about their past. They often mention an ancient homeland called Hawaiki.

Although ways of life differ from one island to another, there are many similarities among the people of these islands. One similarity is mastery of the sea. Long before the coming of the Europeans, the Polynesians used their seagoing outrigger canoes to sail to other places in their own

Bags of dried copra lie ready for export from Tahiti. Dried copra is used as a fertilizer or as fodder.

region and to other parts of the Pacific as well. In fact, the sea is important to almost every aspect of Polynesian life.

REVIEWING THE FACTS

Answer

1. Name two economic activities of increasing importance for the islands' future.

2. What are New Zealand's most important exports?

3. Name the three large groupings of islands in Oceania.

Locate

Refer to the map on pages 452–453.

1. (a) What are the approximate latitude and longitude of the Hawaiian Islands? (b) Of Dunedin, New Zealand?

2. Name five United States territories that lie in the area between the latitudes of 10°N and 20°N and between the longitudes of 140°E and 170°E.

469

GEOGRAPHY LABORATORY

Highlighting the Chapter

1. The South Pacific includes two continents — Antarctica and Australia — and many, many islands. The three large island groups are Melanesia, Micronesia, and Polynesia. Islands in the region have been formed by volcanic action or by the buildup of coral. Climates and ecosystems vary from the polar to the tropical.

2. Before the 1600's, the people of Oceania developed a wide variety of cultures. These groups included Australia's Aborigines and New Zealand's Maoris. In the 1600's, Europeans began to explore and trade with the area. Later, European settlers arrived. The cultures of Europe and the United States have strongly influenced the region, sometimes with tragic results for earlier groups. Oceania's average population density is low. However, the great majority of the people live in cities. Today there are many independent countries in the region, but some islands are still controlled by the United States, France, and the United Kingdom. Australia and New Zealand are members of the British Commonwealth and are Oceania's leading industrial countries.

3. Australia's economic, cultural, and urban heartland is its eastern and southeastern coasts. West of the Great Dividing Range lies the less populated Great Artesian Basin. Still farther west is the harsh desert landscape of the outback. Agriculture, especially sheep ranching, is Australia's main source of wealth. Industry has grown quickly since World War II, helped by the country's rich supply of minerals and fuels.

4. New Zealand is the most economically developed of the islands. New Zealand depends heavily on farming and sheep raising but also has forest resources, minerals, and a plentiful supply of energy. Both for New Zealand and for the many smaller islands, tourism is a growing business; and commercial fishing may grow in importance.

470

Speaking Geographically

Match each of the following words or terms with its correct meaning.

1. outback
2. reef
3. coral
4. artesian well

a. a kind of small sea animal whose skeletons may form islands

b. the dry, thinly populated interior of Australia

c. a place where water flows to the surface by natural pressure

d. a ridge that rises near the surface of the sea

Testing Yourself

Number your paper from 1 to 10. Write the name of the place or places in the South Pacific region to which each description applies.

1. An island group that became a state in 1959

2. Two former British colonies, now members of the British Commonwealth

3. A region with a name meaning "many islands"

4. The two largest cities in Australia

5. The continent where the world's lowest temperature was recorded

6. A large island country with a marine climate similar to that of much of Western Europe

7. The homeland of the Aborigines

8. The island group that includes Wake, Guam, and many tiny atolls

9. The capital of Australia

10. The largest island in Melanesia, split between Indonesia and an independent country

Building Map Skills

Number your paper from 1 to 5. After each number, write the number of the place identified by that number on the map on this page.

Applying Map Skills

1. (a) What type of climate does the Australian town of Alice Springs have? (b) The town of Darwin? (c) The province of Tasmania?

2. Name two provinces in Australia in which gold has been found.

3. What mineral resource is found on the Cape York Peninsula?

4. What is the population density over most of the outback?

5. (a) What island capital city lies closest to the international date line? (b) Name the two island capital cities that lie closest to the equator.

Exploring Further

1. Captain James Cook was one of the great explorers of all time. Prepare a report on his voyages and discoveries. Make a map to illustrate your report.

2. Many American soldiers served in the South Pacific during World War II, and the United States still has many military bases in the area. Interview someone in your community who has been stationed there. Ask the person to show you on a map the places where he or she was stationed and to describe the region.

3. From a travel agent or the library, get information on the different islands of Hawaii. Plan an itinerary for a trip through the islands. What places will you visit on each island? What different means of transportation can you use?

4. Do research to find out how coral is formed and what the different types of coral look like. Also find out what animals live near coral reefs.

471

GLOSSARY

acid rain. Rainwater that has been chemically changed into an acid by industrial air pollution or automobile exhaust. (p. 98)

adaptation. Cultural adjustment to the conditions of the environment. (p. 90)

agribusiness. Farming on a large scale to produce huge quantities of food. The farms are often owned by corporations and are heavily mechanized. (p. 200)

agriculture. The farming of land and the herding of animals. (p. 133)

alliance. An agreement among nations to assist one another if threatened or attacked. (p. 179)

alpine. Referring to mountains. (p. 217)

altiplano. A high plateau between mountains. (p. 274)

apartheid. The policy of the South African government to keep the races separate. It gives all economic and political power to white citizens. (p. 445)

archaeologist. Scientist who studies past cultures by examining artifacts left behind. (p. 128)

archipelago. A chain of islands. (p. 24)

arid. Very dry. (p. 67)

Armenian Knot. A region that includes the mountains of Iran and Turkey. (p. 401)

artesian well. A deep well in which water flows upward naturally, under its own pressure, from between two layers of hard rock. (p. 461)

artisan. A skilled worker who makes things by hand. (p. 137)

Atlantic provinces. The four provinces in the Appalachian Highlands of Canada: New Brunswick, Nova Scotia, Prince Edward Island, and Newfoundland. (p. 227)

authoritarian government. A system of government in which one person or small group of people has complete authority for making and carrying out the laws. (p. 167)

axis. An imaginary line through the center of Earth, from pole to pole, around which Earth rotates. (p. 48)

ayatollah. A Shiite Muslim religious leader. (p. 421)

balance of trade. The record of a nation's imports and exports. (p. 178)

basin. A low-lying area of land surrounded by land of higher elevation; an area drained by a river and its tributaries. (p. 189)

bay. A body of water partly enclosed by land but having a wide opening to the sea. (p. 23)

Bedouin. Nomadic herders in parts of the Arabian Peninsula, Syria, and Jordan. (p. 415)

Benelux. An abbreviation for the low countries: Belgium, the Netherlands, and Luxembourg. (p.300)

bicameral. Made up of two lawmaking chambers. Congress is a bicameral legislature. (p. 193)

bilingual. Using or able to use two languages. (p. 219)

biotic resource. A plant or animal resource. (p. 109)

birth rate. The number of live births per 1,000 people in a given year. (p. 155)

Bolsheviks. The group of revolutionaries that established a Communist government in Russia; later known as the Communist Party of the Soviet Union. (p. 336)

border. A dividing line between countries. (p. 165)

broadleaf. Having wide leaves. Most broadleaf trees lose their leaves every fall and grow new ones in the spring. (p. 81)

bronze. A metal made of copper and tin. (p. 137)

buffer state. A country that lies between rival countries. (p. 366)

cabinet. A group of advisers to a country's head of government. (p. 223)

Canadian Shield. A horseshoe-shaped area of hills and plateaus covering about half of Canada. (p. 219)

cape. A point of land reaching into the sea. (p. 25)

capital good. A product used mainly in industry or for transportation. (p. 317)

cardinal direction. One of the four main directions: north, south, east, or west. (p. 10)

caste. A group of people who are equal in religious purity, according to Hindu belief. Caste determines status, occupation, and whom a person may associate with in traditional Indian social system. (p. 388)

Central Plains. The wetter, eastern portion of the vast plain in the middle of the United States. (p. 188)

character. A series of pen or brush strokes representing a word or syllable in the Chinese language. Characters are used in place of an alphabet. (p. 354)

chemical weathering. The breaking down and wearing away of rock by means of chemical changes in the rock. (p. 107)

climate. The pattern of weather in a particular place over many years. (p. 47)

climax. The final stage of succession in an ecosystem's plant life. (p. 78)

climax vegetation. The final vegetation in the succession of an ecosystem's plant life. It will renew itself, becoming the permanent vegetation of that ecosystem. (p. 78)

coastal plain. A lowland along an ocean. (p. 185)

collective farm. A farm run by farmers under government direction. The farmers work together and earn a share in the farm's income. (p. 321)

colony. A territory, settlement, or country governed by another country. (p. 145)

COMECON. Council for Mutual

Economic Assistance. All Eastern European countries except Yugoslavia and Albania belong to COMECON, trading with few tariffs or other trade barriers. (p. 319)

commercial activity. The production of goods in order to sell them. (p. 172)

common market. An organization of countries whose purpose is economic cooperation and free trade without tariffs within the group. (p. 178)

Common Market. The European Economic Community, made up of twelve Western European countries. Its purpose is economic cooperation and free trade without tariffs within the group. (p. 291)

commune. A collective farm in China. The members of a commune jointly own and farm commune lands. (p. 364)

communism. The system of government ownership and control of nearly all resources and businesses. The Soviet Union, China, Cuba, and the countries of Eastern Europe all practice forms of communism. (p. 172)

compass rose. The part of a map that shows all four cardinal directions plus the intermediate directions. (p. 10)

condensation. The changing of water vapor into a liquid (water) or a solid (ice). (p. 55)

confederation. A loose association of states or provinces under a common government. (p. 222)

conservation. The wise use and protection of resources from loss or waste. (p. 112)

constitutional monarchy. A system of government in which the head of state is a king or queen who has little real power. The country is governed by a parliament and a prime minister. (p. 289)

consumer. Someone who buys goods and services. (p. 173)

consumer goods. Products that are used by individuals, such as food, clothing, refrigerators, etc. (p. 317)

continent. Any of the seven largest landmasses on Earth: Europe, Asia, Africa, North America, South America, Australia, and Antarctica. (p. 24)

continental. Referring to climate of inland areas. Continental climates are very cold in winter and very hot in summer. (p. 59)

continental drift. A theory that the continents have changed position over millions of years. (p. 27)

continental shelf. A plain that extends from continental coasts under the ocean. (p. 41)

contour farming. The plowing and planting of fields across the slope of the land so that the furrows prevent water runoff. (p. 114)

coral. The skeletons of millions of tiny sea animals. (p. 451)

core. The center part of the earth. It has two sections: an inner core of hot, solid metal and an outer core of liquid metal. (p. 28)

coup. A sudden overthrow of an existing government by a small group, usually of military officers. (p. 263)

Creole. A person of Spanish ancestry born in Middle America. (p. 240)

crop rotation. Growing different crops in different years to keep the soil fertile. (p. 114)

crust. The outer layer of the earth, made mostly of rock. (p. 28)

cultural borrowing. The adopting of practices or goods from other cultures. (p. 127)

Cultural Revolution. An effort by radical leaders to speed up change in China during the 1960's. Old ways of life and foreign ideas were attacked.(p. 359)

culture. The total way of life followed by a group of people, including what they do, make, believe, value, and teach their young. (p. 125)

culture region. A place where people's ways of living are similar. People within a culture region may have a common history, similar religious beliefs, or speak the same language. (p. 126)

current. Water in motion. (p. 58)

cyclones. A name for hurricanes or typhoons in the area of the Bay of Bengal. (p. 391)

dairy farming. Production of milk and cheese from cows. (p. 199)

death rate. The yearly number of deaths per 1,000 people. (p. 155)

degrees. Units of measurement for determining latitude and longitude. (p. 16)

delta. An often triangular-shaped deposit of sand and soil at the mouth of a river. (p. 36)

democratic government. A system of government in which power rests with the people. (p. 167)

desert. A very dry region. (p. 91)

developing country. A country that is just beginning to industrialize. (p. 163)

dialect. A form of a language that differs from other forms of the same language in vocabulary, pronunciation, and grammar. (p. 354)

dictator. Someone who has complete control of a government, including the making and carrying out of laws. (p. 167)

direction arrow. On a map, the arrow that always points north. (p. 10)

domesticated. Referring to animals that depend on humans for protection and care. (p. 132)

dune. A ridge of sand piled up by the wind. Dunes resemble mountains. (p. 401)

economic system. The organized way in which people decide what and how much will be produced and how the output will be distributed. (p. 126)

GLOSSARY

ecosystems. A particular environment, including its living and nonliving elements and the ways they work together. (p. 78)

ejido. A type of communal farm in Mexico, in which the land belongs to the whole community but each family works a plot of its own. (p. 247)

elevation. Height above sea level. (pp. 8, 25)

emir. The monarch of some Arab countries. (p. 409)

energy fuels. Minerals that are used to run furnaces, machinery, automobiles, etc. They include coal, petroleum, and natural gas. (p. 110)

equator. The latitude of 0°, from which parallel other parallels are measured in degrees. The equator is exactly halfway between the North and South Poles. (p. 2)

equinox. The time of year (March 20 or 21 and September 22 or 23) when day and night are of equal length all around the world. (p. 51)

erosion. The process by which rock and soil are worn away from Earth's surface and moved to another place. It is caused by water, wind, gravity, or ice. (p. 36)

eruption. The sudden volcanic explosion of Earth's molten inner core, caused by tectonic forces. (p. 32)

escarpment. A steep cliff. (p. 425)

estancia. A large sheep or cattle ranch in South America. (p. 277)

ethnic group. A group of people sharing customs and traditions that give them a feeling of identity. Often they have the same language, religion, and ancestry. (p. 311)

European Economic Community. Twelve countries of Western Europe that promote economic cooperation and free trade within the group. It is also called the Common Market. (p. 291)

evaporation. The change of water from a liquid to a gas. (p. 53)

executive branch. The branch of government that carries out the laws. (p. 193)

export. To sell goods to another country. (p. 177)

fall line. The point at which the Atlantic Coastal Plain and the Piedmont meet. Rivers flowing toward the ocean break into waterfalls and rapids at the fall line. (p. 205)

famine. A severe food shortage. (p. 155)

fault. A break in Earth's surface along which the crust moves. (p. 30)

faulting. Tectonic action resulting when one tectonic plate grinds against another, catches hold, and bends Earth's crust until a break opens in the surface. (p. 30)

federal government. A system under which the central government shares power with states or provinces. (p. 166)

fjord. A steep valley formed by a coastal glacier and filled with sea water. (p. 40)

flash flood. A sudden rush of water in a river or stream. (p. 401)

fold. A buckle in Earth's crust, with a wavelike pattern. Folding is the result of the pushing together of two sections of the crust. It produces mountains or valleys. (p. 29)

fossil fuel. A nonmetallic resource used for energy: coal, petroleum, or natural gas. Fossil fuels were formed from plants and animals that died millions of years ago. (p. 111)

free enterprise. An economic system under which private individuals own most of the resources, technology, and business and can run them as they see fit. Competition among businesses determines prices. (p. 171)

free trade. Low or no tariffs on goods traded between nations. (p. 178)

frontier. A stretch of unsettled territory. (p. 165)

gasohol. A mixture of gasoline and alcohol made from agricultural crops. (p. 270)

gaucho. An Argentine cowboy. (p. 277)

general secretary. The Soviet official who directs the work of the Secretariat of the Communist party. He is the most powerful official in the Soviet Union and is usually also the premier. (p. 338)

geographer. A scientist who studies the physical conditions of Earth's surface and how people and places influence one another. (p. 1)

glacier. A body of ice that moves slowly and irregularly. Glaciers occur in mountain and polar regions. (p. 38)

global grid. A network of lines made up of the parallels of latitude and the meridians of longitude. (p. 16)

governor general. The official who represents the British monarch in Canada. (p. 223)

Grand Banks. A large, shallow expanse of the North Atlantic just off the coast of Newfoundland. It is one of the world's best fishing grounds. (p. 227)

great circle route. The shortest distance between any two points on Earth. (p. 18)

Great Plains. The western portion of the vast interior plain of the United States. (p. 188)

Green Revolution. Better methods of growing rice and wheat, developed by scientific research in the 1960's. These promised to increase crops in many Third World countries. (p. 389)

grid. A system of parallel, crisscross lines, each line of which is identified by numbers or letters. (p. 14)

gross national product (GNP). The total value of all goods and services produced by a country in one year. (p. 175)

groundwater. Fresh water deep in the earth that supplies springs and wells. (p. 55)

Guianas. Guyana, Suriname, and French Guiana. They are located along the Atlantic, east of Venezuela. (p. 262)

gulf. Ocean partly surrounded by land, usually larger than a bay. (p. 23)

habitat. A particular physical environment in which certain plants and animals grow or live naturally. (p. 125)

head of government. The leading official of a government. (p.223)

head of state. The symbolic leader of a nation. (p. 222)

heavy industry. Manufacturing that uses large amounts of raw materials and large machines. It produces bulky goods that can be transported only by rail or ship. (p. 298)

hemisphere. Any half of the earth. (p. 2)

hibernate. To pass the winter in a sleepy, inactive condition, surviving on the stored-up fat within the body. (p. 95)

highlands. Areas that stand higher than surrounding areas, such as mountains and plateaus. (p. 8)

high relief. Land that has frequent, sizable drops and rises in its surface. (p. 8)

hill. A raised area of land lower than a mountain. (p. 25)

Hispanics. People of Spanish ancestry. (p. 190)

Holocaust. The Nazi program to wipe out all the Jews of Europe by rounding them up and sending them to death camps. By the end of World War II, about six million Jews had been killed. (p. 289)

humid. Referring to air containing a lot of moisture. (p. 62)

humus. Decayed animal or vegetable matter found in the soil. It

contains nutrients that make the soil fertile. (p. 107)

hunters and gatherers. People who live by killing wild animals and collecting wild plants. (p. 128)

hydroelectric power. Electricity created by water-driven turbines. (p. 215)

hydrologic cycle. The process of water's constant movement from the sea, to the atmosphere, to Earth, and back to the sea. The processes involved are evaporation, condensation, transpiration, precipitation, and runoff. (p. 53)

Ice Age. A time in geologic history when glaciers covered large areas of Earth. (p. 40)

immigrant. A person who leaves one country to settle in another. (p. 159)

import. To buy goods from another country. (p. 177)

Indian. An inhabitant of the Americas before the arrival of Europeans. (p. 145)

Indochina. Name for Vietnam, Laos, and Kampuchea when they were under French rule. (p. 385)

Indo-European. Refers to a language family containing the Romance, or Latin-based, languages and the Germanic languages. (p. 281)

infant death rate. In a given year, the number of infants per 1,000 live births who die before their first birthday. (p. 155)

interdependent. Refers to the reliance of nations on one another to meet their needs. (p. 177)

intermediate directions. The directions halfway between the cardinal directions: northeast, southeast, southwest, and northwest. (p. 10)

Inuit. Another name for the Eskimo people. (p. 218)

irrigation. The bringing of water to fields through ditches, canals, pipes, or overhead sprays. (p. 87)

island. A landmass smaller than a

continent and completely surrounded by water. (p. 24)

isthmus. A narrow strip of land joining two larger land areas. (p. 24)

judicial branch. The nation's courts. It is the branch of government that judges whether people's actions are in accord with the laws. (p. 193)

junta. A military council ruling a country. (p. 277)

key. The legend, or part of the map, that shows one meaning of colors and symbols used. (p. 6)

kibbutz. An Israeli cooperative farm. (p. 417)

kolkhoz. A collective farm in the Soviet Union. It is owned by the people who work on it. (p. 340)

landform. A natural feature of Earth's surface measured by elevation, such as mountains, hills, plateaus, and plains. (p. 25)

latitude. The distance north or south of the equator. (p. 51)

lava. Melted rock that escapes through Earth's crust to the surface during a volcanic eruption. (p. 31)

leached. Referring to soil drained of its nutrients. (p. 108)

leeward. Referring to the side of a mountain or other place that faces away from the prevailing winds. (p. 60)

legend. The key, or part of the map, that shows the meaning of the colors and symbols used. (p. 6)

legislative branch. The branch of government that makes the laws. (p. 193)

life expectancy. The number of years scientists expect an average person born in a given year to live. (p. 156)

light industry. Manufacturing that uses small quantities of raw materials and small tools to

GLOSSARY

produce goods that can be easily shipped by truck. (p. 298)

linkage. A network that moves people, things, or information from one place to another. (p. 171)

literate. Able to read and write. (p. 287)

loess. A thin layer of rich soil left behind by glaciers and carried by the wind to another place. (p. 40)

Low Countries. Belgium, the Netherlands, and Luxembourg. (p. 300)

lowlands. Areas that are lower than surrounding areas, such as valleys and plains. (p. 8)

low relief. Land that rises or falls only slightly over a considerable distance. (p. 8)

mantle. A layer of heavy rock and metal that lies under Earth's crust. It surrounds Earth's core. (p. 28)

marine. Refers to climates moderated by the ocean. (p. 59)

martial law. A condition under which the military has the authority to rule a country. (p. 315)

mechanical weathering. The breaking down and wearing away of rock by physical forces. (p. 107)

megalopolis. One huge city made up of smaller, neighboring metropolitan areas. (p. 164)

meridian of longitude. One of the imaginary lines on the global grid going halfway around the globe. Each meets another meridian at the poles. (p. 16)

mestizo. A person of mixed European and Indian ancestry. (p. 239)

metallic resource. A mineral that contains or yields metal. (p. 110)

metropolitan area. A city and its surrounding suburbs. (p. 164)

Middle Atlantic States. New York, New Jersey, Pennsylvania, Maryland, and Delaware. (p. 197)

migration. The movement of people from one country or region to another. (p. 157)

minority. Any small group within a country that differs — usually ethnically, religiously, or racially — from most of the population. (p. 313)

mobile. Able or prone to move often from one place to another. (p. 192)

monotheistic. Worshiping a single God. (p. 406)

monsoon. A kind of wind in Asia that brings a wet season when it blows from the sea and a dry season when it blows from the land. (p. 463)

moraine. A ridge of soil and rock deposited by a retreating glacier. (p. 40)

mountain. A high, rugged landform. (p. 25)

nation. Group of people who share a common territory and who believe they belong together because they share similar beliefs and values. (p. 168)

nationalism. The belief that people who consider themselves a nation ought to have their own land and government. (p. 169)

nationalize. To place under government control. (p. 264)

natural resource. Any material or element from the environment that is used by humans. (p. 103)

needleleaf. Having leaves shaped like a needle; referring to cone-bearing, mostly evergreen trees like pine, spruce, fir, and hemlock. (p. 81)

neutral. Not taking sides in international conflicts. (p. 290)

New England. Maine, New Hampshire, Vermont, Massachusetts, Rhode Island, and Connecticut. (p. 197)

nomad. A member of a group of people who wander from place to place and have no permanent dwellings. (p. 135)

nonaligned. Not linked to any superpower. (p. 343)

nonmetallic mineral. A mineral that does not contain metal. Nonmetallic minerals include stone, sand, and salt. (p. 110)

nonrenewable resource. Any resource that is limited and cannot be replaced. (p. 104)

Norden. The northernmost countries of Western Europe: Iceland, Finland, Sweden, Norway, and Denmark. (p. 293)

nuclear energy. The energy produced by splitting uranium atoms in a controlled environment such as a nuclear power plant. (p. 119)

nutrient. Any soil substance that provides food for plants. (p. 85)

oasis. A place in the desert that has a natural spring or surface water. (p. 93)

orbit. The elliptical path Earth follows around the sun. (p. 48)

ore. Rock that contains large amounts of metal. (p. 110)

outback. Dry, desolate plains and low plateaus in the western part of Australia. (p. 451)

Pacific Rim. Those countries that border or lie in the Pacific Ocean. (p. 363)

paddy. A flooded rice field. (p. 360)

Palestine. The area occupied by present-day Israel and part of present-day Jordan. (p. 407)

pampas. The large grassy plains in southern Latin America, particularly in Argentina. (p. 85)

parallel of latitude. One of the imaginary lines that circles the globe in an east-west direction; each is parallel to the equator. (p. 16)

parent material. Bits of bedrock that are broken down to form the soil. (p. 107)

parliament. A branch of government that both makes a nation's laws and sees that they are carried out. (p. 222)

parliamentary democracy. A

GLOSSARY

system of government with two branches. The parliament, or elected legislature, both makes the laws and sees that they are carried out; a national court system decides cases arising under the laws. (p. 222)

peninsula. A finger of land jutting out from a landmass and almost entirely surrounded by water. (p. 24)

peon. A poor, landless farmer. (p. 247)

per capita GNP. The average value of products and services produced for each person in a given year. (p. 175)

permafrost. Permanently frozen soil located below the surface of the ground. (p. 71)

petroleum. A fossil fuel and nonrenewable mineral resource. It is used to produce gasoline, heating oil, and chemicals used in the production of plastics, fertilizers, and many other things. (p. 111)

physical environment. The conditions on Earth; made up of the nonliving, life-sustaining elements — soil, air, water, and energy — and of living things — plants and animals. (p. 77)

physical map. A map showing features that nature has determined, such as lakes, rivers, or the condition of the land. (p. 8)

plain. A large area with either level or rolling land. (p. 25)

plantation. A large farm worked by people who live on it. In the Americas, plantations were worked by slave laborers into the 1800's. (p. 205)

plateau. A broad, flat landform that is higher in elevation than a plain and is bordered by an escarpment. (p. 25)

polar ice cap. A large sheet of glacial ice covering one of Earth's poles. Parts of the Arctic and Antarctic that are always covered with such ice. (p. 90)

polar regions. The high latitudes, lying between latitude 66½° and

90° (the Arctic and Antarctic Circles and the North and South Poles). (p. 51)

political map. A map showing the way people have divided the land. It shows political features such as cities and boundaries between countries. (p. 6)

population density. The average number of persons per unit of area. (p. 161)

prairie. A grassland with tall and medium-height grasses and few trees. (p. 86)

precipitation. Water that falls to the ground as rain, snow, sleet, or hail. (p. 55)

premier. The head of the Council of Ministers of the Soviet Union. *Premier* is also sometimes used interchangeably with *prime minister.* (p. 337)

prevailing wind. A wind that blows almost constantly from a certain direction. (p. 56)

primary economic activity. The first step that people take in developing their land and resources. Primary economic activities include hunting and gathering, farming and herding, forestry, mining, and fishing. (p. 170)

prime meridian. The meridian of 0° longitude, from which degrees of longitude are counted east or west. It runs through Greenwich, England. (p. 16)

prime minister. In parliamentary government, the leader chosen by the majority party, and the head of government. (p. 223)

projection. A drawing of all or part of round Earth on a flat surface in a systematic way, based on a grid system. (p. 4)

Protestant. Referring to a branch of Christianity. Protestant churches were formed in Northern Europe when reformers broke away from the Catholic Church in the 1500's. (p. 287)

province. A political unit within a country. (p. 222)

pulp. The soft fiber of wood products that is ground and mixed with water to make paper. (p. 225)

radiation. The sun's rays or the means by which the sun's energy reaches Earth. (p. 47)

rain forest. A forest of dense trees with wide leaves, located in the low latitudes, or tropics. The trees keep their leaves all year round and require heavy rainfall. (p. 84)

raw material. Any resource that can be made into a product. (p. 103)

recyclable resource. A resource, such as water or aluminum, that can be used over and over again. (p. 104)

reef. A strip or ridge that rises near the water's surface. A reef can be made of rock or coral. (p. 451)

relief. The difference between the highest and lowest points of land in a certain area. (p. 8)

representative democracy. A governmental system in which the people elect leaders to represent them or carry out their wishes. (p. 167)

revolution. The movement of Earth around the sun. (p. 48)

rift. A split or separation in Earth's crust caused by the pulling apart of tectonic plates. (p. 29)

river system. A river with all its streams or tributaries. (p. 24)

rotation. The spinning of Earth on its axis. (p. 48)

rural. Referring to the country (as opposed to the city). (p. 159)

Russ. Traders from Scandinavia who ruled the Slavs in the Ukraine during the 800's. (p. 333)

Sahara. A sand-and-gravel desert stretching across most of Morocco, Algeria, and Libya. (p. 401)

satellite. Referring to Eastern European countries because they

GLOSSARY

have little independence and are controlled by the Soviet Union. (p. 315)

savanna. A grassland in the tropics. (p. 85)

scale. The line on a map that tells how many miles or kilometers on Earth are represented by certain units of measurement. (p. 12)

scribe. Someone in ancient cities who made a living by writing letters and business contracts for merchants and others. (p. 137)

sea. An area of salt water or ocean partly surrounded by land. (p. 23)

sea level. The level of the ocean's surface, from which elevation and depth are measured. (p. 8)

secondary economic activity. The second step people take in developing resources and raw materials into products. Secondary economic activities include manufacturing, processing, etc. (p. 170)

semiarid. Referring to a climate with 10 to 20 inches of precipitation a year. Semiarid climates have definite seasonal changes, and the amount of rainfall in the short rainy season is not always reliable. (p. 67)

service. A tertiary economic activity involving the distribution of goods to people. (p. 170)

Shiite. A member of a branch of Islam concentrated primarily in Iran. Shiites generally seek to establish Islamic governments that strictly follow Shiite traditions and oppose efforts to alter Islam. (p. 409)

Siberia. The land of northern Asia, lying in the Soviet Union east of the Ural Mountains. (p. 330)

silt. Eroded material, such as soil and very small pieces of rock, carried and deposited by water. (p. 36)

sirocco. A wind that blows northward from the interior of Africa during the dry season. It whips up dust storms in the Sahara. (p. 402)

slash-and-burn agriculture. A method of farming used in the tropics, in which trees and undergrowth are cut and burned to produce nutrients for the soil. (p. 442)

socialism. A system under which the government owns most basic resources and large industries and has some control over smaller, privately owned businesses. (p. 171)

soil. A mixture of rock particles and decayed plant matter found on the surface of Earth. (p. 78)

solar energy. Energy that comes from the heat of the sun. (p. 119)

solstice. The time of year when the difference in the length of day and night is at a maximum. The summer solstice occurs about June 22, and the winter solstice about December 22. (p. 51)

Soviet Central Asia. A region stretching from the Caspian Sea to China. (p. 334)

sovkhoz. A large, government-owned state farm in the Soviet Union. (p. 340)

standard of living. A measure of how well off a person or population is. (p. 173)

state farm. A farm that is run as a government-owned business. The farmers are paid wages by the government. (p. 321)

steppe. Flat, treeless land with short grass and a semiarid climate (p. 87)

strait. A narrow channel of water connecting two larger areas of water. (p. 23)

strip-mining. The removal of a large area of the top layer of soil to get at mineral or fuel deposits near the surface. (p. 116)

subarctic. Referring to the climate found bordering the Arctic Circle. It is characterized by long, very cold winters; short, cool summers; and moderate precipitation. (p. 70)

subcontinent. A large landmass that is part of a whole continent but separated from it by natural barriers and differences in culture. (p. 377)

subsistence activity. The production of just enough crops, animals, and crafts for people's own use, with no surplus. (p. 174)

suburb. A community on the outskirts of a city. (p. 159)

succession. A very slow change in an area's vegetation from one variety of plants to other kinds. (p. 78)

sultanate. A country ruled by a Muslim monarch. (p. 395)

Sunni. The largest branch of Islam. (p. 409)

symbol. On a map, a color, line, dot, or small picture that represents something on Earth. (p. 6)

taiga. A subarctic needleleaf forest. (p. 217)

tariff. A tax on imports. (p. 178)

technology. All the tools and methods people use in developing their resources and producing goods and services. (p. 126)

tectonic activity. All the forces working within Earth that move or form landform features: folding, faulting, volcanoes, and plate movements. (p. 28)

tectonic plate. A moving section of Earth's crust. (p. 28)

temperate zone. The area of Earth lying in the middle latitudes and characterized by great changes in temperature from place to place and season to season. (p. 52)

terracing. The process of building flat, steplike platforms on hillsides and mountainsides for the purpose of growing crops. Terraces also prevent erosion of the soil. (p. 114)

tertiary economic activity. The distribution of products to people. Tertiary economic activities are also called services and include transportation and communication. (p. 170)

theory. An idea that seeks to

explain how something works or came to be. (p. 27)

topsoil. The thin upper layer of the soil that forms the surface of the land in most places. (p. 107)

totalitarian government. A system in which nearly every activity of citizens is subject to government control. (p. 167)

trade wind. A wind that blows steadily toward the equator — from the northeast in the tropics north of the equator, and from the southeast in the tropics south of the equator. (p. 238)

transpiration. The process by which plants give off water vapor. (p. 53)

tree line. An imaginary line on mountains, above which trees do not grow. (p. 73)

tributary. A stream or river that feeds into a larger stream or river. (p. 24)

Tropic of Cancer. The parallel of latitude $23\frac{1}{2}°$ north of the equator. (p. 51)

Tropic of Capricorn. The parallel of latitude $23\frac{1}{2}°$ south of the equator. (p. 51)

tropics. The low latitudes, lying between the Tropic of Cancer and the Tropic of Capricorn. The tropics have almost equal days and nights and a warm climate. (p. 51)

truck farming. The raising of poultry, fruits, and vegetables for sale. (p. 199)

tsar. The emperor and absolute ruler of Russia before the 1917 revolution. (p. 333)

tsunami. A giant wave in the ocean caused by an underwater earthquake. (p. 42)

tundra. A flat or rolling plain in the arctic regions, with a climax vegetation of short grasses, mosses, and lichens. Even during the short summer, there is a layer of permafrost. (p. 90)

unitary government. A system under which the central government makes basic decisions and governments of states, departments, or provinces see that they are carried out. (p. 166)

Ural-Altaic. Referring to a language family that includes Asian and Hungarian languages. (p. 313)

urban. Having to do with cities. (p. 137)

vegetation. Plant life. (p. 78)

wadi. A river in an arid land that dries up and disappears during certain times of the year. (p. 401)

water vapor. Water in a gaseous form. (p. 53)

weather. The condition of the atmosphere at any one time, including its temperature and humidity. (p. 47)

welfare state. A country whose government provides many free services, such as medical care and old-age insurance, to improve public welfare. (p. 289)

windward. Referring to the side of a mountain or other place that faces the prevailing wind. (p. 60)

WORLD REFERENCE SECTION

Facts about Earth

Circumference around the equator:
    24,902 miles (40,075 kilometers)

Circumference around the poles:
    24,859 miles (40,008 kilometers)

Distance to the center of Earth:
    about 3,963 miles (6,370 kilometers)

Weight:
    6,600,000,000,000,000,000,000,000
    (6.6 sextillion short tons or sextillion metric tons)

Surface area:
    197,000,000 square miles
    (510,360,000 square kilometers)

Land area: (about 30 percent of total)
    57,889,000 square miles
    (150,250,000 kilometers)

Water area: (about 70 percent of total)
    139,300,000 square miles
    (360,100,820 square kilometers)

Rotation:
    Rotates once every 23 hours, 56 minutes, 4.09 seconds

Revolution:
    Revolves once every 365 days, 6 hours, 9 minutes, 9.54 seconds

Earth Extremes

Highest point of land:
    Mount Everest (Nepal, Tibet)
    29,028 feet (8,848 meters) above sea level

Lowest point of land:
    Shore of the Dead Sea (Israel, Jordan)
    1,299 feet (396 meters) below sea level

Longest river:
    Nile (Egypt, Suday, Uganda) 4,160 miles
    (6,698 kilometers)

Largest lake:
    Caspian Sea (U.S.S.R., Iran) 143,240 square miles
    (371,100 square kilometers)

Deepest lake:
    Lake Baikal (U.S.S.R.), 5,315 feet (1,620 meters) deep

Largest desert:
    Sahara (North Africa), 3,500,000 square miles
    (9,100,000 square kilometers)

Largest island:
    Greenland (North Atlantic), 840,000 square miles
    (2,176,000 square kilometers)

Largest gorge:
    Grand Canyon (Arizona, U.S.A.), 277 miles (446 kilometers) long; 1 to 18 miles (1.6 to 29 kilometers) wide; 1 mile (1.6 kilometers) deep

Deepest gorge:
    Hells Canyon (Idaho, U.S.A.), 7,900 feet (2,408 meters) deep

Biggest cave:
    Mammoth-Flint Ridge cave system (Kentucky, U.S.A.), more than 180 miles (290 kilometers) of underground passageways

Largest iceberg:
    Seen 150 miles (240 kilometers) west of Scott Island (South Pacific) in 1956; at least 12,000 square miles (31,000 square kilometers), bigger than Belgium.

WORLD REFERENCE SECTION

Climate and Weather Records

Average surface temperature:
  75°F (14°C)

Hottest recorded temperature:
  136°F (58°C), at Al Aziziyah, Libya, in 1922

Coldest recorded temperature:
  −126.6°F (−88°C) at Vostok, Antarctica, in 1983

Strongest recorded wind:
  231 miles per hour (372 kilometers per hour), at Mount Washington, New Hampshire (U.S.A.), in 1934

Rainiest spot:
  Mount Waialeale, Hawaii (U.S.A.), average annual rainfall of 460 inches (1,168 centimeters)

Driest spot:
  Atacama Desert (Chile), less than .003 inch (.76 millimeter) rain per year

Facts about Oceans

Ocean	Area	Average depth	Greatest depth
Pacific	64,186,300 square miles (166,000,000 square kilometers)	12,925 feet (3,939 meters)	35,810 feet (10,915 meters) Mariana Trench
Atlantic	33,420,000 square miles (86,600,000 square kilometers)	11,730 feet (3,575 meters)	28,374 feet (8,648 meters) Puerto Rico Trough
Indian	28,350,000 square miles (73,400,000 square kilometers)	12,598 feet (3,840 meters)	23,376 feet (7,125 meters) Java Trench
Arctic	5,105,700 square miles (13,200,000 square kilometers)	3,407 feet (1,039 meters)	16,804 feet (5,122 meters) Eurasian Basin

Highest tides: Bay of Fundy (Nova Scotia, Canada), 53 feet (16.2 meters)

Largest seas: South China Sea (1,148,500 square miles)
  Caribbean Sea (971,400 square miles)
  Mediterranean Sea (969,100 square miles)

WORLD REFERENCE SECTION

Facts about Continents

Continent	Area	Population
Asia	17,120,642 square miles (44,340,000 square kilometers)	2,994,098,800
Africa	11,700,000 square miles (30,300,000 square kilometers)	577,861,000
North America	9,410,000 square miles (24,370,000 square kilometers)	410,809,000
South America	6,860,000 square miles (17,770,000 square kilometers)	280,210,000
Antarctica	5,905,000 square miles (14,000,000 square kilometers)	none permanent
Europe	3,840,000 square miles (9,940,000 square kilometers)	723,445,200
Australia	2,968,000 square miles (7,700,000 square kilometers)	16,200,000

Source: Donnelley Cartographics

The Longest River on Each Continent

Nile (Africa)
4,160 miles (6,690 kilometers)
Amazon (South America)
4,000 miles (6,440 kilometers)
Mississippi-Missouri-Red Rock (North America)
3,880 miles (6,240 kilometers)

Yangzi-Kiang (Asia)
3,964 miles (6,378 kilometers)
Volga (Europe)
2,194 miles (3,530 kilometers)
Darling (Australia)
2,310 miles (3,717 kilometers)

The Five Biggest Islands

Island	Location	Area
Greenland	Atlantic Ocean	840,000 square miles (2,176,000 square kilometers)
New Guinea	Pacific Ocean	306,000 square miles (791,000 square kilometers)
Borneo	Pacific Ocean	280,000 square miles (725,400 square kilometers)
Madagascar	Indian Ocean	226,658 square miles (587,042 square kilometers)
Baffin	Arctic Ocean	195,928 square miles (507,600 square kilometers)

WORLD REFERENCE SECTION

The Five Highest Waterfalls

Angel Falls (Venezuela)
3,212 feet (979 meters)
Southern Mardalsfossen (Norway)
2,149 feet (655 meters)
Tugela (South Africa)
2,014 feet (614 meters)
Cuquenán (Venezuela)
2,000 feet (610 meters)
Sutherland (New Zealand)
1,904 feet (580 meters)

The Five Largest Lakes

Caspian Sea (U.S.S.R., Iran)
143,240 square miles (370,992 square kilometers)
Lake Superior (U.S.A., Canada)
31,700 square miles (82,124 square kilometers)
Lake Victoria (Tanzania, Uganda)
26,293 square miles (68,100 square kilometers)
Aral Sea (U.S.S.R.)
24,904 square miles (64,518 square kilometers)
Lake Huron (U.S.A., Canada)
23,100 square miles (59,596 square kilometers)

Facts about the United States

Area: 3,622,285 square miles
(9,381,356 square kilometers)
Population:
238,800,000
Highest point: Mount McKinley, Alaska
20,320 feet (6,194 meters)
Lowest point: Death Valley, California
−282 feet (−86 meters)

Coldest spot: Barrow, Alaska
average annual temperature 9°F (−13°C)
Warmest spot: Death Valley, California
average annual temperature 78.2°F (25.7°C)
Highest recorded temperature: Death Valley, California
134°F (57°C), July 10, 1913
Lowest recorded temperature: Prospect Creek, Alaska
−79.8°F (−62.1°C), January 23, 1971

Largest Cities in the United States

City	Population	City	Population
New York, NY	7,262,700	Detroit, MI	1,086,220
Los Angeles, CA	3,259,300	San Diego, CA	1,015,190
Chicago, IL	3,009,530	Dallas, TX	1,003,520
Houston, TX	1,728,910	San Antonio, TX	914,350
Philadelphia, PA	1,642,900	Phoenix, AZ	894,070

Source: Statistical Abstract of the United States

WORLD REFERENCE SECTION

States Ranked by Area

Rank	Name	Area	Rank	Name	Area
1	Alaska	591,004 sq mi (1,530,700 sq km)	26	Wisconsin	56,153 sq mi (145,436 sq km)
2	Texas	266,807 sq mi (691,030 sq km)	27	Arkansas	53,187 sq mi (137,754 sq km)
3	California	158,706 sq mi (411,049 sq km)	28	North Carolina	52,669 sq mi (136,413 sq km)
4	Montana	147,046 sq mi (380,848 sq km)	29	Alabama	51,705 sq mi (133,915 sq km)
5	New Mexico	121,593 sq mi (314,925 sq km)	30	New York	49,108 sq mi (127,190 sq km)
6	Arizona	114,000 sq mi (295,260 sq km)	31	Louisiana	47,752 sq mi (123,677 sq km)
7	Nevada	110,561 sq mi (286,352 sq km)	32	Mississippi	47,689 sq mi (123,515 sq km)
8	Colorado	104,091 sq mi (269,596 sq km)	33	Pennsylvania	45,308 sq mi (117,348 sq km)
9	Wyoming	97,809 sq mi (253,326 sq km)	34	Tennessee	42,144 sq mi (109,152 sq km)
10	Oregon	97,073 sq mi (251,419 sq km)	35	Ohio	41,330 sq mi (107,044 sq km)
11	Utah	84,899 sq mi (219,889 sq km)	36	Virginia	40,767 sq mi (105,586 sq km)
12	Minnesota	84,402 sq mi (218,601 sq km)	37	Kentucky	40,410 sq mi (104,660 sq km)
13	Idaho	83,564 sq mi (216,432 sq km)	38	Indiana	36,185 sq mi (93,720 sq km)
14	Kansas	82,277 sq mi (213,098 sq km)	39	Maine	33,265 sq mi (86,156 sq km)
15	Nebraska	77,355 sq mi (200,350 sq km)	40	South Carolina	31,113 sq mi (80,582 sq km)
16	South Dakota	77,116 sq mi (199,730 sq km)	41	West Virginia	29,232 sq mi (62,760 sq km)
17	North Dakota	70,702 sq mi (183,119 sq km)	42	Maryland	10,460 sq mi (27,092 sq km)
18	Oklahoma	69,956 sq mi (181,186 sq km)	43	Vermont	9,614 sq mi (24,900 sq km)
19	Missouri	69,697 sq mi (180,516 sq km)	44	New Hampshire	9,279 sq mi (24,032 sq km)
20	Washington	68,139 sq mi (176,479 sq km)	45	Massachusetts	8,284 sq mi (21,456 sq km)
21	Georgia	58,910 sq mi (152,576 sq km)	46	New Jersey	7,787 sq mi (20,169 sq km)
22	Florida	58,664 sq mi (151,939 sq km)	47	Hawaii	6,471 sq mi (16,759 sq km)
23	Michigan	58,527 sq mi (151,586 sq km)	48	Connecticut	5,018 sq mi (12,997 sq km)
24	Illinois	56,345 sq mi (145,934 sq km)	49	Delaware	2,045 sq mi (5,295 sq km)
25	Iowa	56,275 sq mi (145,753 sq km)	50	Rhode Island	1,212 sq mi (3,140 sq km)

Total area of the United States:
In 1790 — 891,364 square miles
In 1860 — 3,021,295 square miles
In 1985 — 3,622,285 square miles

States Ranked by Population

Rank	Name	Population	Rank	Name	Population
1	California	26,365,000	26	Colorado	3,231,000
2	New York	17,783,000	27	Arizona	3,187,000
3	Texas	16,370,000	28	Connecticut	3,174,000
4	Pennsylvania	11,853,000	29	Iowa	2,884,000
5	Illinois	11,535,000	30	Oregon	2,687,000
6	Florida	11,366,000	31	Mississippi	2,613,000
7	Ohio	10,744,000	32	Kansas	2,450,000
8	Michigan	9,088,000	33	Arkansas	2,359,000
9	New Jersey	7,562,000	34	West Virginia	1,936,000
10	North Carolina	6,255,000	35	Utah	1,645,000
11	Georgia	5,976,000	36	Nebraska	1,606,000
12	Massachusetts	5,822,000	37	New Mexico	1,450,000
13	Virginia	5,706,000	38	Maine	1,164,000
14	Indiana	5,499,000	39	Hawaii	1,054,000
15	Missouri	5,029,000	40	Idaho	1,005,000
16	Wisconsin	4,775,000	41	New Hampshire	998,000
17	Tennessee	4,762,000	42	Rhode Island	968,000
18	Louisiana	4,481,000	43	Nevada	936,000
19	Washington	4,409,000	44	Montana	826,000
20	Maryland	4,392,000	45	South Dakota	708,000
21	Minnesota	4,193,000	46	North Dakota	685,000
22	Alabama	4,021,000	47	Delaware	622,000
23	Kentucky	3,726,000	48	Vermont	535,000
24	South Carolina	3,347,000	49	Alaska	521,000
25	Oklahoma	3,301,000	50	Wyoming	509,000

State with lowest density of population:
0.7/sq mi — Alaska

State with greatest density of population:
986/sq mi — New Jersey

Source: Statistical Abstract of the United States

ATLAS

World: Political

- - - - -   Disputed boundaries

Scale:
0 — 1000 — 2000 — 3000 Miles
0 — 1000 — 2000 — 3000 Kilometers

GREENLAND (DEN.)

ALASKA (U.S.)

60°

CANADA

40°

UNITED STATES

ATLANTIC OCEAN

Tropic of Cancer

20°

HAWAII (U.S.)

MEXICO

THE BAHAMAS
DOMINICAN REPUBLIC
PUERTO RICO (U.S. COMM.)
VIRGIN ISLANDS (U.S.)
ANTIGUA AND BARBUDA
DOMINICA
BARBADOS
ST. VINCENT AND THE GRENADINES
TRINIDAD AND TOBAGO

CUBA
JAMAICA HAITI
BELIZE
ST. CHRISTOPHER AND NEVIS
SAINT LUCIA
GRENADA

GUATEMALA
EL SALVADOR
HONDURAS
COSTA RICA
PANAMA
NICARAGUA

VENEZUELA
GUYANA
SURINAME
FRENCH GUIANA (FR.)

COLOMBIA

ECUADOR

PACIFIC OCEAN

0°   Equator

KIRIBATI

PERU

BRAZIL

WESTERN SAMOA

TONGA
20°

BOLIVIA

PARAGUAY

Tropic of Capricorn

40°

CHILE

URUGUAY

ARGENTINA

180°   160°   140°   120°   100°   80°   60°   40°
60°

SOVIET UNION

EUROPE

80°N

20°E

ATLANTIC

Arctic Circle

ICELAND

OCEAN

60°N

SWEDEN   FINLAND

NORWAY

DENMARK

UNITED KINGDOM

IRELAND

NETHERLANDS   EAST GERMANY   POLAND
BELGIUM   WEST
LUXEMBOURG   GERMANY   CZECHOSLOVAKIA
SWITZERLAND   AUSTRIA   HUNGARY
FRANCE   LIECHTENSTEIN
MONACO   ROMANIA
SAN MARINO   YUGOSLAVIA
ANDORRA   ITALY   ALBANIA   BULGARIA
40°N
SPAIN
PORTUGAL
GIBRALTAR (U.K.)   GREECE   TURKEY
MALTA
CYPRUS

Scale:
0 — 500 — 1000 — 1500 Miles
0 — 500 — 1000 — 1500 Kilometers

486

ARCTIC OCEAN

ICELAND

Arctic Circle

NORWAY   FINLAND

SWEDEN

UNITED DENMARK

KINGDOM

IRELAND   SOVIET UNION

NETH. E. POLAND

W. GER.

BEL. GER.

CZECH.

FRANCE SWIT. AUST. HUNG.   MONGOLIA

YUGO. ROMANIA

ITALY BUL.   NORTH

PORTUGAL SPAIN   ALB.   KOREA

GREECE TURKEY   PEOPLE'S REPUBLIC OF   JAPAN

MALTA   CHINA   SOUTH

TUNISIA CYPRUS SYRIA   KOREA

LEBANON IRAQ   TAIWAN

MOROCCO   ISRAEL IRAN AFGHANISTAN

JORDAN   PACIFIC OCEAN

WESTERN   ALGERIA LIBYA EGYPT KUWAIT PAKISTAN

SAHARA   BAHRAIN QATAR   BHUTAN

(MOR.)   SAUDI ARABIA   NEPAL

MAURITANIA   UNITED ARAB INDIA BURMA

CAPE   EMIRATES BANGLADESH LAOS

VERDE MALI NIGER CHAD   OMAN   VIETNAM

SENEGAL   SUDAN YEMEN PEOPLE'S DEMOCRATIC THAILAND   MARSHALL ISLANDS

GAMBIA BURKINA   REPUBLIC OF YEMEN   KAMPUCHEA

GUINEA FASO   DJIBOUTI   FEDERATED STATES

BISSAU GUINEA BENIN   SRI LANKA   OF MICRONESIA

SIERRA IVORY NIGERIA CENTRAL AFRICAN ETHIOPIA PHILIPPINES

LEONE COAST   REPUBLIC   BRUNEI   KIRIBATI

LIBERIA   CAMEROON   MALDIVES MALAYSIA

GHANA TOGO   SOMALIA   Equator NAURU

EQUATORIAL GUINEA UGANDA   SINGAPORE   TUVALU

SÃO TOMÉ AND PRÍNCIPE CONGO KENYA   INDONESIA PAPUA

GABON RWANDA   NEW SOLOMON

ZAIRE BURUNDI   SEYCHELLES   GUINEA ISLANDS

TANZANIA   VANUATU

ANGOLA   COMOROS   FIJI

MALAWI   INDIAN OCEAN

ZAMBIA

MOZAMBIQUE   AUSTRALIA

NAMIBIA ZIMBABWE

BOTSWANA MADAGASCAR MAURITIUS

SWAZILAND

SOUTH LESOTHO   NEW ZEALAND

AFRICA

20°   0°   20°   40°   60°   80°   100°   120°   140°   160°   180°

Antarctic Circle

487

World: Land Use

- ⬛ Manufacturing
- ⬛ Commercial farming and stock raising
- ⬛ Stock raising
- ⬛ Forestry
- ⬛ Farming mostly for family use
- ⬛ Hunting, fishing, and gathering
- ⬛ Nomadic herding
- ⬛ Commercial fishing
- ⬜ Little or no activity

NORTH AMERICA

SOUTH AMERICA

ATLANTIC OCEAN

PACIFIC OCEAN

Tropic of Cancer

Equator

Tropic of Capricorn

ARCTIC OCEAN

Arctic Circle

EUROPE

ASIA

AFRICA

PACIFIC OCEAN

Equator

INDIAN OCEAN

AUSTRALIA

20° 0° 20° 40° 60° 80° 100° 120° 140° 160° 180°

Antarctic Circle

ANTARCTICA

World: Population Density

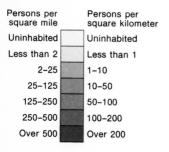

Persons per square mile	Persons per square kilometer
Uninhabited	Uninhabited
Less than 2	Less than 1
2–25	1–10
25–125	10–50
125–250	50–100
250–500	100–200
Over 500	Over 200

• Major cities

ARCTIC OCEAN

Arctic Circle

Leningrad
Moscow

London
EUROPE

Paris

ASIA

Beijing

Seoul

Tehran

Tokyo

Cairo

Chongqing

Shanghai

Delhi

Karachi

Calcutta

Bombay

Bangkok

Manila

PACIFIC OCEAN

AFRICA

Equator

INDIAN OCEAN

Jakarta

AUSTRALIA

20°   0°   20°   40°   60°   80°   100°   120°   140°   160°   180°

Antarctic Circle

ANTARCTICA

491

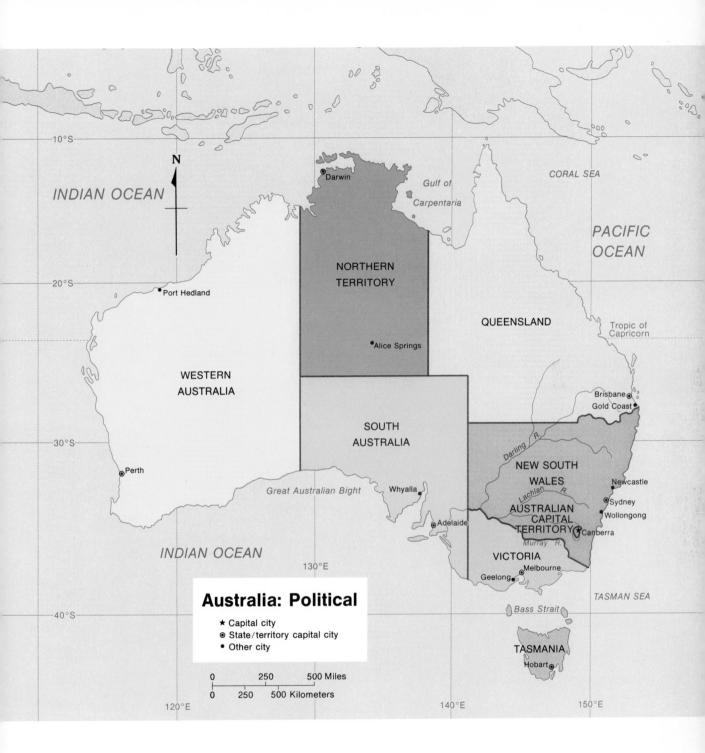

INDIAN OCEAN

N

CORAL SEA

PACIFIC OCEAN

Gulf of Carpentaria

Darwin

NORTHERN TERRITORY

QUEENSLAND

Tropic of Capricorn

Port Hedland

WESTERN AUSTRALIA

Alice Springs

SOUTH AUSTRALIA

Brisbane
Gold Coast

Darling R.

NEW SOUTH WALES

Newcastle

Lachlan R.

AUSTRALIAN CAPITAL TERRITORY

Sydney
Wollongong

Perth

Great Australian Bight

Whyalla

Adelaide

Canberra

Murray R.

VICTORIA

Melbourne

INDIAN OCEAN

130°E

Geelong

TASMAN SEA

Bass Strait

Australia: Political

★ Capital city
⊙ State/territory capital city
● Other city

TASMANIA

Hobart

| 0 | 250 | 500 Miles |
| 0 | 250 | 500 Kilometers |

120°E   140°E   150°E

10°S

20°S

30°S

40°S

499

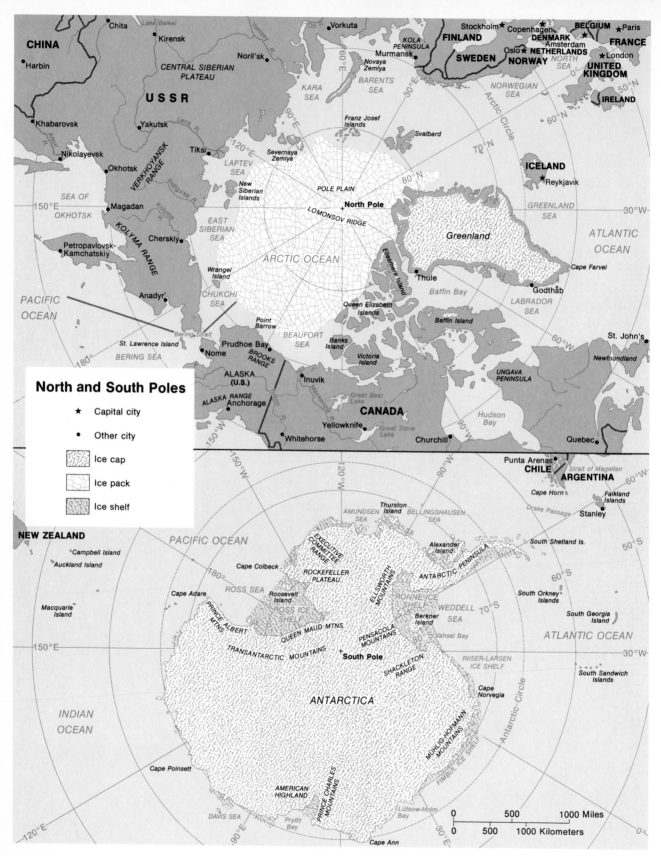

North and South Poles

★ Capital city

● Other city

Ice cap

Ice pack

Ice shelf

North Pole map labels:

CHINA • Chita • Kirensk • Lake Baikal • Noril'sk • Vorkuta • Stockholm ★ Copenhagen ★ BELGIUM ★ Paris • FINLAND • KOLA PENINSULA • Murmansk • DENMARK • Amsterdam • NETHERLANDS • FRANCE

CENTRAL SIBERIAN PLATEAU • Yenisey R. • Ob R. • Novaya Zemlya • SWEDEN • NORWAY • Oslo ★ • London • UNITED KINGDOM

• Harbin • NORTH SEA • IRELAND • 50°N

U S S R • 90°E • KARA SEA • BARENTS SEA • NORWEGIAN SEA • Arctic Circle • 60°N

• Khabarovsk • Yakutsk • Lena R. • Franz Josef Islands • Svalbard • 70°N

• Nikolayevsk • Tiksi • 120°E • Severnaya Zemlya • LAPTEV SEA • 80°N • ICELAND • Reykjavík ★

VERKHOYANSK RANGE • Indigirka R. • New Siberian Islands • POLE PLAIN • North Pole + • Greenland • GREENLAND SEA • 30°W

• Okhotsk • Magadan • Kolyma R. • 150°E • EAST SIBERIAN SEA • LOMONSOV RIDGE • ATLANTIC OCEAN

SEA OF OKHOTSK • KOLYMA RANGE • ARCTIC OCEAN • Ellesmere Island • Thule • Cape Farvel

• Cherskiy • Wrangel Island • Queen Elizabeth Islands • Baffin Bay • Godthåb

• Petropavlovsk-Kamchatskiy • CHUKCHI SEA • LABRADOR SEA

PACIFIC OCEAN • Anadyr' • Point Barrow • BEAUFORT SEA • Banks Island • Baffin Island • 60°W • St. John's

• Bering Strait • St. Lawrence Island • BERING SEA • 180° • Nome • Prudhoe Bay • BROOKS RANGE • Victoria Island • Newfoundland

ALASKA (U.S.) • Inuvik • UNGAVA PENINSULA

ALASKA RANGE • Anchorage • Mackenzie R. • Great Bear Lake • Hudson Bay

• Whitehorse • Yellowknife • CANADA • Great Slave Lake • Churchill • Quebec • 90°W • 150°W

South Pole map labels:

NEW ZEALAND • Campbell Island • Auckland Island • PACIFIC OCEAN • Thurston Island • AMUNDSEN SEA • BELLINGSHAUSEN SEA • Alexander Island • South Shetland Is. • 50°S

Punta Arenas • CHILE • Strait of Magellan • ARGENTINA • 60°W • Cape Horn • Falkland Islands • Stanley • Drake Passage

• Macquarie Island • 180° • Cape Colbeck • EXECUTIVE COMMITTEE RANGE • ROCKEFELLER PLATEAU • ANTARCTIC PENINSULA • ELLSWORTH MOUNTAINS • South Orkney Islands • 60°S

• Cape Adare • ROSS SEA • Roosevelt Island • RONNE ICE SHELF • WEDDELL SEA • 70°S • South Georgia Island

150°E • ROSS ICE SHELF • QUEEN MAUD MTNS. • PENSACOLA MOUNTAINS • Berkner Island • Vahsel Bay • ATLANTIC OCEAN

PRINCE ALBERT MTNS. • TRANSANTARCTIC MOUNTAINS • South Pole + • SHACKLETON RANGE • RIISER-LARSEN ICE SHELF • 30°W

INDIAN OCEAN • 150°E • ANTARCTICA • Cape Norvegia • South Sandwich Islands

• Cape Poinsett • MÜHLIG-HOFMANN MOUNTAINS • FIMBUL ICE SHELF

AMERICAN HIGHLAND • PRINCE CHARLES MOUNTAINS • Lützow-Holm Bay • 30°E

120°E • DAVIS SEA • Prydz Bay • Cape Ann • 90°E

0 500 1000 Miles
0 500 1000 Kilometers

500

Name	Latitude	Longitude	Page(s)
Abadan, city in Iran	30°15′ N	48°30′ E	497
Abidjan, city in Ivory Coast . . .	5°19′ N	4°2′ W	498
Abu Dhabi, capital of the United Arab Emirates	24°15′ N	54°28′ E	497
Accra, capital of Ghana	5°40′ N	0°15′ W	498
Adare, cape in Antarctica	71°17′ S	170°14′ E	500
Addis Ababa, capital of Ethiopia.	9° N	38°44′ E	498
Adelaide, city in Australia	34°46′ S	139°8′ E	499
Aden, capital of the People's Democratic Republic of Yemen	12°48′ N	45° E	497
Aden, Gulf of, Southwest Asia	11°45′ N	45°45′ E	497
Adriatic Sea, Southern Europe	43°30′ N	14°27′ E	496
Aegean Sea, Southern Europe and Southwest Asia	39°4′ N	24°56′ E	496
Afghanistan, country in South Asia	33° N	63° E	497
Alabama, state in the United States.	32°50′ N	87°30′ W	493, 494
Alabama River, Alabama	31°20′ N	87°39′ W	493
Alaska, state in the United States.	64° N	150° W	492, 494, 500
Alaska, Gulf of, Alaska	57°42′ N	147°40′ W	492, 494
Alaska Range, Alaska	62° N	152°18′ W	500
Albania, country in Europe . . .	41°45′ N	20° E	496
Albany, capital of New York . .	42°40′ N	73°50′ W	493
Albert, Lake, between Uganda and Zaire.	1°50′ N	30°40′ E	498
Alexander Island, Antarctica . .	71° S	71° W	500
Alexandria, city in Egypt	31°12′ N	29°58′ E	498
Algeria, country in Africa	28°45′ N	1° E	498
Algiers, capital of Algeria	36°51′ N	2°56′ E	498
Alice Springs, city in Australia	23°38′ S	133°56′ E	499
Al-Kuwait, capital of Kuwait . .	29°4′ N	47°59′ E	497
Allegheny River, Pennsylvania.	41°10′ N	79°20′ W	493
Alma-Ata, city in the U.S.S.R. . .	43°19′ N	77°8′ E	497
Altamaha River, Georgia	31°50′ N	82° W	493
Amazon River, Brazil	2°3′ S	53°18′ W	495
Amderma, city in the U.S.S.R.	69°45′ N	61°39′ E	496
American Highland, Antarctica	72° S	79° E	500
Amman, capital of Jordan. . . .	31°57′ N	35°57′ E	497
Amsterdam, capital of the Netherlands.	52°21′ N	4°52′ E	496
Amundsen Sea, part of the Pacific, off Antarctica	72° S	110° W	500
Amur River, Asia	49°38′ N	127°25′ E	497, 500
Anadyr, city in the U.S.S.R. . .	64°47′ N	177°1′ E	497, 500
Anadyr River, U.S.S.R.	65°30′ N	172°45′ E	500
Anchorage, city in Alaska. . . .	61°12′ N	149°48′ W	492, 494, 500
Andaman Islands, India	11°38′ N	92°17′ E	497
Andorra, country in Europe. . .	42°30′ N	2° E	496
Andorra la Vella, capital of Andorra.	42°38′ N	1°30′ E	496

Name	Latitude	Longitude	Page(s)
Angara River, U.S.S.R.	52°48′ N	104°15′ E	497
Angola, country in Africa	14°15′ S	16° E	497
Ankara, capital of Turkey	39°55′ N	32°50′ E	497
Ann, cape in Antarctica.	66°10′ S	51°22′ E	500
Annapolis, capital of Maryland	39° N	76°25′ W	493
Antananarivo, capital of Madagascar.	18°51′ S	47°40′ E	497
Antarctic Circle, parallel of latitude marking the South Frigid Zone	66°33′ S		500
Antarctic Peninsula, Antarctica	70° S	65° W	500
Antigua-Barbuda, country in the Caribbean Sea	17°15′ N	61°5′ W	494
Arabian Sea, Asia	16° N	65°15′ E	497
Aral Sea, U.S.S.R.	46°47′ N	62° E	497
Arctic Circle, parallel of latitude marking the North Frigid Zone	66°33′ N		494, 497, 500
Arequipa, city in Peru	16°27′ S	71°30′ W	495
Argentina, country in South America	35°30′ S	67° W	495
Arizona, state in the United States.	34° N	113° W	492
Arkansas, state in the United States.	34°50′ N	93°40′ W	492
Arkansas River, Oklahoma	35°20′ N	94°56′ W	493, 494
Arkhangelsk, city in the U.S.S.R.	64°30′ N	40°25′ E	496
Asunción, capital of Paraguay.	25°25′ S	57°30′ W	495
Athens, capital of Greece	38° N	23°38′ E	496
Atlanta, capital of Georgia . . .	33°45′ N	84°23′ W	493, 494
Auckland Island, New Zealand	50°30′ S	166°30′ E	500
Augusta, capital of Maine	44°19′ N	69°42′ W	493
Austin, capital of Texas	30°15′ N	97°42′ W	492
Australia, country in the South Pacific	30° S	140° E	494
Australian Capital Territory, New South Wales	35°30′ S	148°40′ E	499
Austria, country in Europe . . .	47°15′ N	11°53′ E	496

B

Name	Latitude	Longitude	Page(s)
Baffin Bay, Canada.	72° N	65° W	494, 500
Baffin Island, Canada.	67°20′ N	71° W	494, 500
Baghdad, capital of Iraq	33°14′ N	44°22′ E	497
Bahamas, country in the Caribbean Sea	26°15′ N	76° W	494
Bahia Blanca, city in Argentina	38°45′ S	62°7′ W	495
Bahrain, country in Southwest Asia	26°15′ N	51°17′ E	497
Baikal, Lake, U.S.S.R.	53° N	109°28′ E	497, 500
Baku, city in the U.S.S.R.	40°28′ N	49°45′ E	497
Balearic Islands, Spain	39°25′ N	1°28′ E	496
Balkhash, Lake, U.S.S.R.	45°58′ N	72°15′ E	497
Baltic Sea, Europe	55°20′ N	16°50′ E	496,497

GAZETTEER

Name	Latitude	Longitude	Page(s)
Baltimore, city in Maryland...	39°20′ N	76°38′ W	493, 494
Bamako, capital of Mali	12°39′ N	8° W	498
Bandar Seri Begawan, capital of Brunei................	4°52′ N	113°38′ E	497
Bangalore, city in India	13°3′ N	77°39′ E	497
Banghazi, city in Libya	32°8′ N	20°6′ E	498
Bangkok, capital of Thailand..	13°50′ N	100°29′ E	497
Bangladesh, country in South Asia	24°15′ N	90° E	497
Bangui, capital of the Central African Republic	4°28′ N	18°35′ E	498
Banjarmasin, city in Indonesia	3°18′ S	114°32′ E	497
Banjul, capital of Gambia	13°28′ N	16°39′ W	498
Banks Island, Canada	73° N	123° W	500
Barbados, country in the Caribbean Sea...........	13°30′ N	59° W	494
Barcelona, city in Spain	41°25′ N	2°8′ E	496
Barents Sea, U.S.S.R.	72°14′ N	37°28′ E	496, 500
Barranquilla, city in Colombia	10°57′ N	75° W	495
Basel, city in Switzerland	47°32′ N	7°35′ E	496
Basra, city in Iraq	30°35′ N	47°59′ E	497
Bassaterre, capital of St. Christopher and Nevis	17°20′ N	62°42′ W	494
Bass Strait, Australia.......	39°40′ S	145°40′ E	499
Baton Rouge, capital of Louisiana	30°28′ N	91°10′ W	492
Beaufort Sea, Alaska	70°30′ N	138°40′ W	494, 500
Beijing, capital of the People's Republic of China..........	39°55′ N	116°23′ E	497
Beirut, capital of Lebanon....	33°53′ N	35°30′ E	497
Belfast, city in Northern Ireland	54°36′ N	5°45′ W	496
Belgium, country in Europe...	51° N	2°52′ E	496, 500
Belgrade, capital of Yugoslavia	44°48′ N	20°32′ E	496
Belize, country in Central America	17° N	88°40′ W	494
Bellinghausen Sea, Antarctica	72° S	80°30′ W	500
Belmopan, capital of Belize ..	17°15′ N	88° 47′ W	494
Belo Horizonte, city in Brazil..	19°54′ S	43°56′ W	495
Bengal, Bay of, Asia	17°30′ N	87° E	497
Benin, country in Africa	8° N	2° E	498
Bergen, city in Norway	60°24′ N	5°20′ E	496
Berkner Island, Antarctica ...	79°30′ S	49°30′ W	500
Bering Sea, between Asia and North America...........	58° N	175° W	492, 494, 497, 500
Bering Strait, Alaska	64°50′ N	169°50′ W	492, 500
Berlin, city in East Germany ..	52°31′ N	13°28′ E	496
Bermuda, territory of the United Kingdom in the Caribbean Sea...........	32°20′ N	65°45′ W	495
Bern, capital of Switzerland ..	46°55′ N	7°25′ E	496
Bhutan, country in South Asia.	27°15′ N	90°30′ E	497
Bighorn River, Montana.....	45°50′ N	107°15′ W	492
Bilbao, city in Spain........	43°12′ N	2°48′ W	496
Birmingham, city in Alabama .	33°31′ N	86°49′ W	493, 494
Birmingham, city in the United Kingdom..........	52°29′ N	1°53′ W	496
Biscay, Bay of, Europe......	45°19′ N	3°51′ W	496
Bismarck, capital of North Dakota	46°48′ N	100°46′ W	492

Name	Latitude	Longitude	Page(s)
Bissau, capital of Guinea-Bissau	11°51′ N	15°35′ W	494
Black Sea, Europe and Asia ..	43°1′ N	32°16′ E	496, 497
Blanc, cape in Mauritania	20°39′ N	18°8′ W	498
Blue Nile River, Africa......	12°50′ N	34°10′ E	498
Bogotá, capital of Colombia ..	4°38′ N	74°6′ W	495
Boise, capital of Idaho	43°43′ N	116°30′ W	492
Bolivia, country in South America	17° S	64° W	495
Bologna, city in Italy	44°30′ N	11°18′ E	496
Bombay, city in India	18°58′ N	72°50′ E	497
Bon, cape in Tunisia........	37°4′ N	11°13′ E	498
Bonn, capital of West Germany	50°44′ N	7°6′ E	496
Bordeaux, city in France.....	44°50′ N	0°37′ W	496
Boston, capital of Massachusetts	42°15′ N	71°7′ W	493, 494
Bothnia, Gulf of, Europe.....	63°40′ N	21°30′ E	496
Botswana, country in Africa ..	22°10′ S	23°13′ E	498
Brahmaputra River, India....................	26°45′ N	92°45′ E	497
Brasília, capital of Brazil	15°49′ S	47°39′ W	495
Bratislava, city in Czechoslovakia	48°9′ N	17°7′ E	496
Brazil, country in South America	9° S	53° W	498
Brazos River, United States ..	33°10′ N	98°50′ W	492, 494
Brazzaville, capital of the Congo.................	4°16′ S	15°17′ E	498
Bridgetown, capital of Barbados	13°8′ N	59°37′ W	494
Brisbane, city in Australia....	27°30′ S	153°10′ E	499
Bristol, city in the United Kingdom................	51°29′ N	2°39′ W	496
Brooks Range, Alaska	68°20′ N	159° W	500
Brunei, country in Southeast Asia	4°52′ N	113°38′ E	497
Brussels, capital of Belgium ..	50°51′ N	4°21′ E	496
Bucharest, capital of Romania	44°23′ N	26°10′ E	496
Budapest, capital of Hungary .	47°30′ N	19°5′ E	496
Buenos Aires, capital of Argentina	34°20′ S	58°30′ W	495
Buffalo, city in New York	42°54′ N	78°51′ W	493, 494
Bujumbura, capital of Burundi.	3°23′ S	29°22′ E	498
Bulgaria, country in Europe ..	42°12′ N	24°13′ E	496
Burgas, city in Bulgaria	42°29′ N	27°30′ E	496
Burkina Faso, country in Africa	13° N	2° W	498
Burma, country in South Asia.	21° N	95°15′ E	497
Burundi, country in Africa....	3° S	29°30′ E	498

C

Name	Latitude	Longitude	Page(s)
Cabinda, territory, part of Angola	5°33′ S	12°12′ E	498
Cairo, capital of Egypt	30° N	31°17′ E	498
Calcutta, city in India.......	22°32′ N	88°22′ E	498
Calgary, city in Canada	51°3′ N	114°5′ W	494

Name	Latitude	Longitude	Page(s)
Cali, city in Colombia	3°26′ N	76°30′ W	495
California, state in the United States	38°10′ N	121°20′ W	492
Cameroon, country in Africa . .	5°48′ N	11° E	498
Campbell Island, New Zealand	52°30′ S	169° E	500
Canada, country in North America	50° N	100° W	494, 500
Canadian River, Oklahoma . . .	34°53′ N	97°6′ W	492
Canary Islands, Spain	29°15′ N	16°30′ W	496
Canberra, capital of Australia .	35°21′ S	149°10′ E	499
Cape Horn, Chile	56° S	67° W	495, 500
Cape May, New Jersey	38°55′ N	74°50′ W	494
Cape Town, capital of South Africa	33°48′ S	18°28′ E	498
Caracas, capital of Venezuela .	10°30′ N	66°58′ W	495
Cardiff, city in Wales	51°30′ N	3°18′ W	496
Caribbean Sea, between North and South America	14°30′ N	75°30′ W	494
Carpentaria, Gulf of, Australia	14°45′ S	138°50′ E	499
Carson City, capital of Nevada	39°10′ N	119°45′ W	492
Cartagena, city in Spain	37°46′ N	1° W	496
Cartanega, city in Colombia . .	10°30′ N	75°40′ E	495
Casablanca, city in Morocco .	33°32′ N	7°41′ W	498
Caspian Sea, Asia	40° N	52° E	497
Castries, capital of Saint Lucia	14°1′ N	61° W	494
Cayenne, capital of French Guiana	4°56′ N	52°18′ W	495
Cayman Islands, territory of the United Kingdom, in the Caribbean Sea	19°45′ N	79°50′ W	494
Celebes, island, part of Indonesia	21°15′ S	120°30′ E	497
Central African Republic, country in Africa	7°50′ N	21° E	498
Central Siberian Peninsula, U.S.S.R.	55° N	33°30′ E	500
Ceylon. *See* Sri Lanka.			
Chad, country in Africa	17°48′ N	19° E	498
Chad, Lake, Africa	13°55′ N	13°40′ E	498
Chambal River, India	26°5′ N	76°37′ E	497
Champlain, Lake, between New York and Vermont	44°45′ N	73°20′ W	493
Chang Jiang (Yangzi River), China	36°17′ N	114°31′ E	497
Channel Islands, Europe	49°15′ N	3°30′ W	496
Chao Phraya River, Thailand .	16°13′ N	99°33′ E	497
Charleston, capital of West Virginia	38°20′ N	81°35′ W	493
Chattahooche River, between Alabama and Georgia	31°17′ N	85°10′ W	493
Chattanooga, city in Tennessee	35°1′ N	85°15′ W	493
Chelyabinsk, city in the U.S.S.R.	55°10′ N	61°25′ E	497
Chengdu, city in China	30°39′ N	104°04′ E	497
Cherskiy, city in the U.S.S.R. . .	65°0′ N	143°0′ E	500
Chesapeake Bay, Maryland . .	38°20′ N	76°15′ W	493
Cheyenne, capital of Wyoming	41°10′ N	104°49′ W	492
Chicago, city in Illinois	41°49′ N	87°37′ W	493, 494
Chile, country in South America	35° S	72° W	495

Name	Latitude	Longitude	Page(s)
China, People's Republic of, country in Asia	36°45′ N	93° E	497
Chita, city in the U.S.S.R.	52°9′ N	113°39′ E	500
Chongqing, city in China	29°38′ N	107°30′ E	497
Chukchi Sea, between the Arctic Ocean, Asia, and Alaska	69° N	171° W	500
Churchill, city in Canada	59°7′ N	93°50′ W	500
Cincinnati, city in Ohio	39°8′ N	84°30′ W	493, 494
Clark Fork River, Montana . . .	47°50′ N	115°35′ W	492, 493
Cleveland, city in Ohio	41°30′ N	81°42′ W	493, 494
Colbeck, cape in Antarctica . . .	77°6′ S	157°48′ W	500
Cologne, city in West Germany	50°56′ N	6°57′ E	496
Colombia, country in South America	3°30′ N	72°30′ W	495
Colombo, capital of Sri Lanka .	6°58′ N	79°52′ W	497
Colorado, state in the United States	39°30′ N	106°55′ W	492
Colorado River, United States	36°25′ N	112° W	492, 494
Columbia, capital of South Carolina	34° N	81° W	493
Columbia River, United States and Canada	46°20′ N	123° W	492, 494
Columbus, capital of Ohio . . .	40° N	83° W	493
Comoros, country off the east coast of Africa	12°50′ S	42°45′ E	498
Conakry, capital of Guinea . . .	9°31′ N	13°43′ W	498
Concepción, city in Chile	36°51′ S	72°59′ W	495
Concord, capital of New Hampshire	43°10′ N	71°30′ W	493
Congo, country in Africa	3° S	13°48′ E	498
Connecticut, state in the United States	41°40′ N	73°10′ W	493
Connecticut River, United States	43°55′ N	72°15′ W	493
Constanta, city in Romania . . .	44°12′ N	28°36′ E	496
Copenhagen, capital of Denmark	55°43′ N	12°27′ E	496
Coral Sea, Oceania	13°30′ S	150° E	499
Cordoba, city in Argentina . . .	30°20′ S	64°3′ W	495
Corsica, island, part of France	42°10′ N	8°55′ E	496
Costa Rica, country in Central America	10°30′ N	84°30′ W	494
Crete, island, part of Greece . .	35°15′ N	24°30′ E	496
Cuba, country in the Caribbean Sea	22° N	79° W	494
Cumberland River, United States	36°45′ N	85°33′ W	493
Curitiba, city in Brazil	25°20′ S	49°15′ W	495
Cyprus, country in Asia	35° N	31° E	497
Czechoslovakia, country in Europe	49°28′ N	16° E	496

D

Name	Latitude	Longitude	Page(s)
Dacca. *See* Dhaka.			
Dakar, capital of Senegal	14°40′ N	17°6′ W	498
Dallas, city in Texas	32°45′ N	96°48′ W	492, 494

GAZETTEER

Name	Latitude	Longitude	Page(s)
Damascus, capital of Syria...	33°31' N	36°18' E	497
Danube River, Europe	48°35' N	10°38' E	496
Dar es Salaam, capital of Tanzania	6°58' S	39°17' E	498
Darling River, Australia	31°50' S	143°20' E	499
Darwin, city in Australia	12°25' S	131° E	499
Davis Sea, Antarctica.......	66° S	92° E	500
Davis Strait, Canada	66° N	60° W	494
Dayton, city in Ohio	39°45' N	84°15' W	493
Delaware, state in the United States...................	38°40' N	75°30' W	493
Delaware Bay, Delaware and New Jersey...............	39°5' N	75°10' W	493
Delaware River, United States	41°50' N	75°20' W	493
Denmark, country in Europe ..	56°14' N	8°30' E	496
Denmark Strait, between Greenland and Iceland	66°30' N	27° W	494
Denver, capital of Colorado ..	39°44' N	104°59' W	492
Des Moines, capital of Iowa..	41°35' N	93°37' W	492
Des Moines River, United States...................	43°45' N	94°20' W	492
Detroit, city in Michigan	42°22' N	83°10' W	493, 494
Dhaka, capital of Bangladesh.	26°41' N	85°10' E	497
Djibouti, capital of Djibouti ...	11°34' N	43° E	498
Djibouti, country in Africa....	11°35' N	48°8' E	498
Dnepropetrovsk, city in the U.S.S.R.	48°32' N	34°10 E	496
Dnepr River, U.S.S.R.	46°47' N	32°57' E	496
Dnestr River, U.S.S.R.	48°21' N	28°10' E	496
Doha, capital of Qatar	25°17' N	51°32' E	497
Dominica, country in the Caribbean Sea...........	15°30' N	61°45' W	494
Dominican Republic, country in the Caribbean Sea	19° N	70°45' W	494
Donestk, city in the U.S.S.R...	48° N	37°35' E	496
Don River, U.S.S.R.........	49°50' N	41°30' E	496
Dortmund, city in West Germany...............	51°31' N	7°28' E	496
Dover, capital of Delaware ...	39°10' N	75°30' W	493
Drake Passage, waterway between South America and Antarctica	57° S	65° W	500
Dresden, city in East Germany	51°5' N	13°45' E	496
Dublin, capital of Ireland	53°20' N	6°15' W	496
Duero River, Spain	41°30' N	5°10' W	496
Durban, city in South Africa ..	29°48' S	31° E	498
Dusseldorf, city in West Germany.................	51°14' N	6°47' E	496

E

Name	Latitude	Longitude	Page(s)
East China Sea, Asia.......	30°28' N	125°52' E	497
East Siberian Sea, U.S.S.R...	73° N	153°28' E	500
Ebro River, Spain	41°30' N	0°35' W	496
Ecuador, country in South America	0°	78°30' W	495

Name	Latitude	Longitude	Page(s)
Edinburgh, city in Scotland...	55°57' N	3°10' W	496
Edmonton, city in Canada....	53°33' N	113°28' W	494
Edward, Lake, Zaire........	0°25' S	29°40' E	498
Egypt, country in Africa	26°58' N	27°1' E	498
El Aqiun, capital of the Western Sahara...........	26°45' N	13°15' W	498
Elbe River, Europe.........	53°47' N	9°20' E	496
Ellesmere Island, part of Canada	81° N	80° W	500
Ellsworth Mountains, Antarctica	77° S	90° W	500
El Paso, city in Texas.......	31°47' N	106°27' W	492, 494
El Salvador, country in Central America...........	14° N	89°30' W	494
English Channel, between the United Kingdom and France ..	49°45' N	3°6' W	496
Equatorial Guinea, country in Africa	2° N	7°15' E	498
Erie, Lake, between the United States and Canada....	42°15' N	81°25' W	493, 494
Ethiopia, country in Africa ...	7°53' N	37°55' E	498
Eufaula, Lake, Oklahoma ...	35°16' N	95°35' W	492
Euphrates River, Asia	36° N	39°30' E	497
Everglades, swamp in Florida.	25°35' N	80°55' W	493
Executive Committee Range, Antarctica	76°50' S	126° W	500

F

Name	Latitude	Longitude	Page(s)
Falkland Islands, territory of the United Kingdom, near South America	50°45' S	61° W	495, 500
Faroe Islands, Denmark.....	62° N	7° W	496
Farvel Kap, cape in Greenland	60° N	44° W	500
Fes, city in Morocco	34°8' N	5° W	498
Fiji Islands, Melanesia......	18°40' S	175° E	497
Finger Lakes, New York State	42°40'	77°30' W	493
Finland, country in Europe ...	62°45' N	26°13' E	496
Flathead Lake, Montana.....	47°57' N	114°20' W	492
Flores, island, part of Indonesia	8°14' S	121°8' E	497
Florida, state in the United States...................	30°30' N	84°40' W	493
Florida Keys, islands, part of Florida	24°33' N	81°20' W	494
Florida, Straits of, North America	24°10' N	81° W	493
Fortaleza, city in Brazil	3°35' S	38°31' W	495
Fort Lauderdale, city in Florida	26°7' N	80°9' W	493
Fort Peck, lake in Montana...	47°52' N	106°59' W	492
Fort Worth, city in Texas	32°45' N	97°20' W	492
France, country in Europe ...	46°39' N	0°47' W	496
Frankfort, capital of Kentucky.	38°10' N	84°55' W	493

Name	Latitude	Longitude	Page(s)
Frankfurt, city in West Germany	52°42′ N	13°37′ E	496
Franz Josef Land, islands, part of the U.S.S.R.	81°32′ N	40° E	497, 500
Fraser River, Canada	52°40′ N	122°55′ W	494
Freetown, capital of Sierra Leone	8°30′ N	13°15′ W	498
French Guiana, French territory in South America	4°20′ N	53° W	495

G

Name	Latitude	Longitude	Page(s)
Gabon, country in Africa	0°30′ S	10°45′ E	498
Gaborone, capital of Botswana	24°28′ S	25°59′ E	498
Galápagos Islands, part of Ecuador	0°10′ S	87°45′ W	495
Galveston Bay, Texas	29°39′ N	94°45′ W	492
Gambia, country in Africa	13°38′ N	19°38′ W	498
Ganges River, India	34°32′ N	87°58′ E	497
Gdansk, city in Poland	54°20′ N	18°40′ E	496
Geelong, city in Australia	38°6′ S	144°13′ E	499
Geneva, Lake, Switzerland	46°28′ N	6°30′ E	496
Genoa, city in Italy	44°23′ N	9°52′ E	496
Georgetown, capital of Guyana	7°45′ N	58°4′ W	495
Georgia, state in the United States	32°40′ N	83°50′ W	493
Germany, East, country in Europe	53°30′ N	12°30′ E	496
Germany, West, country in Europe	51°45′ N	8°30′ E	496
Ghana, country in Africa	8° N	2° W	498
Gibraltar, territory of the United Kingdom in Southern Europe	36°8′ N	5°22′ W	496
Gibraltar, Strait of, between Africa and Europe	35°55′ N	5°45′ W	496
Gila River, Arizona	32°41′ N	113°50′ W	492
Glasgow, city in Scotland	55°54′ N	4°25′ W	496
Godthab, capital of Greenland	64°10′ N	51°32′ W	494, 500
Gold Coast, city in Australia	28°5′ S	153°25′ E	499
Goose Lake, California	41°56′ N	120°35′ W	492
Gor'kiy, city in the U.S.S.R.	56°15′ N	44°5′ E	496
Goteborg, city in Sweden	57°39′ N	11°56′ E	496
Gotland, island off Sweden	57°35′ N	17°35′ E	496
Great Australian Bight, bay in Australia	33°30′ S	127° E	499
Great Bear Lake, Canada	66°10′ N	119°53′ W	494, 500
Great Salt Lake, Utah	41°19′ N	112°48′ W	492, 494
Great Slave Lake, Canada	61°37′ N	114°58′ W	494, 500
Greece, country in Europe	39° N	21°30′ E	496
Green Bay, Wisconsin	44°55′ N	88°4′ W	493
Greenland, country in North America	74° N	40° W	494, 500
Green River, United States	38°30′ N	110°10′ W	492

Name	Latitude	Longitude	Page(s)
Greensboro, city in North Carolina	36°4′ N	79°45′ W	493
Greenville, city in South Carolina	34°50′ N	82°25′ W	493
Grenada, country in the Caribbean Sea	12°2′ N	61°27′ W	494
Guadalajara, city in Mexico	20°41′ N	103°21′ W	494
Guadeloupe, island of France, in the Caribbean Sea	16°7′ N	61°19′ W	494
Guangzhou, city in China	23°7′ N	113°15′ E	497
Guatemala, capital of Guatemala	15°45′ N	91°45′ W	494
Guatemala, country in Central America	15°45′ N	91°45′ W	494
Guayaquil, city in Ecuador	2°16′ S	79°53′ W	495
Guinea, country in Africa	10°48′ N	12°28′ W	498
Guinea-Bissau, country in Africa	12° N	20° W	498
Guinea, Gulf of, Africa	2° N	1° E	498
Guyana, country in South America	7°45′ N	59° W	495

H

Name	Latitude	Longitude	Page(s)
Hague, The, capital of the Netherlands	52°5′ N	4°16′ E	496
Hainan, island, part of China	19° N	111°10′ E	497
Haiti, country in the Caribbean	19° N	72°15′ W	494
Hamburg, city in West Germany	53°34′ N	10°2′ E	496
Hamilton, city in Canada	43°15′ N	79°51′ W	494
Hanoi, city in Vietnam	21°4′ N	105°50′ E	497
Hanover, city in West Germany	52°24′ N	9°44′ E	496
Harare, city in Zimbabwe	17°50′ S	29°30′ E	498
Harbin, city in China	45°40′ N	126°30′ E	497, 500
Harrisburg, capital of Pennsylvania	40°15′ N	76°50′ W	493
Hartford, capital of Connecticut	41°45′ N	72°40′ W	493, 494
Hartwell Lake, Georgia	34°30′ N	83° W	493
Havana, capital of Cuba	23°8′ N	82°23′ W	494
Hawaii, island, part of Hawaii	19°35′ N	155°30′ W	494
Hawaii, state in the United States	22° N	158° W	492, 494
Helena, capital of Montana	46°35′ N	112°1′ W	492
Helsinki, capital of Finland	60°10′ N	24°53′ E	496
Hilo, city in Hawaii	19°44′ N	155°1′ W	492, 494
Hobart, city in Australia	43° S	147°30′ E	499
Ho Chi Minh City, capital of Vietnam	10°46′ N	106°34′ E	497
Hokkaido, island in Japan	43°30′ N	142°45′ E	497
Honduras, country in North America	14°30′ N	88° W	494
Hong Kong, island in Asia	21°45′ N	115° E	497
Honolulu, capital of Hawaii	21°18′ N	157°50′ W	492, 494

GAZETTEER

Name	Latitude	Longitude	Page(s)
Honshu, island in Japan	36°50′ N	135°20′ E	497
Houston, city in Texas	29°46′ N	95°21′ W	492, 494
Howe, Cape, Australia	37°30′ S	150°40′ E	499
Huang He, river in China	34°28′ N	116°59′ E	497
Hudson Bay, Canada	60°15′ N	85°30′ W	494, 500
Hudson River, New York	41°55′ N	73°55′ W	493
Hungary, country in Europe . .	46°44′ N	17°55′ E	496
Huron, Lake, United States and Canada	45°15′ N	82°40′ W	493, 494
Hyderabad, city in India	17°29′ N	79°28′ E	497

Name	Latitude	Longitude	Page(s)
James River, South Dakota . .	46°25′ N	98°55′ W	492
Japan, country in Asia	36°30′ N	133°30′ E	497
Japan, Sea of, Asia	40°8′ N	132°55′ W	497
Java, island, part of Indonesia	8°35′ S	111°11′ E	497
Jefferson City, capital of Missouri	38°34′ N	92°10′ W	493
Jerusalem, capital of Israel . .	31°46′ N	35°14′ E	497
Jiddah, city in Saudi Arabia . .	21°30′ N	39°15′ E	497
Johannesburg, city in South Africa	26°8′ S	27°54′ E	498
Jordan, country in Southwest Asia	30°15′ N	38° E	497
Juan de Fuca, Strait of, between the United States and Canada	48°25′ N	124°37′ W	492
Juneau, capital of Alaska	58°25′ N	134°30′ W	492, 494

I

Name	Latitude	Longitude	Page(s)
Ibadan, city in Nigeria	7°17′ N	3°30′ E	498
Iceland, country in Europe . . .	65°12′ N	19°45′ W	496, 500
Idaho, state in the United States	44° N	115°10′ W	492
Illinois, state in the United States	40°25′ N	90°40′ W	493
Illinois River, Illinois	40°52′ N	89°31′ W	493
India, country in Asia	23° N	77°30′ E	497
Indiana, state in the United States	39°50′ N	86°45′ W	493
Indianapolis, capital of Indiana	39°45′ N	86°8′ W	493, 494
Indigirka River, U.S.S.R.	67°45′ N	145°45′ E	500
Indonesia, country in Asia . . .	4°38′ S	118°45′ E	497
Indus River, Pakistan	26°43′ N	67°41′ E	497
Inuvik, city in Canada	68°40′ N	134°10′ W	500
Ionian Sea, Europe	38°59′ N	18°48′ E	496
Iowa, state in the United States	39°45′ N	86°8′ W	492, 493
Iran, country in Asia	31°15′ N	53°30′ E	497
Iraq, country in Asia	32° N	42°30′ E	497
Ireland, country in Europe . . .	53°33′ N	13° W	496
Irrawaddy River, Burma	23°27′ N	96°25′ E	497
Islamābād, capital of Pakistan	33°55′ N	73°5′ E	497
Israel, country in Asia	32°40′ N	34° E	497
Istanbul, city in Turkey	41°2′ N	29° E	497
Italy, country in Europe	43°58′ N	11°14′ E	496
Ivory Coast (Cote d'Ivoire), country in Africa	7°43′ N	6°30′ W	498
Izmir, city in Turkey	38°25′ N	26°37′ E	497

K

Name	Latitude	Longitude	Page(s)
Kabul, capital of Afghanistan .	34°39′ N	69°14′ E	497
Kama River, U.S.S.R.	56°52′ N	54°35′ E	496
Kampala, capital of Uganda . .	0°19′ N	32°25′ E	498
Kampuchea, country in Asia . .	12°15′ N	104° E	497
Kananga, city in Zaire	6°14′ S	22°17′ E	498
Kanawha River, United States	37°55′ N	81°50′ W	493
Kano, city in Nigeria	12° N	8°30′ E	498
Kānpur, city in India	26° N	82°45′ E	497
Kansas, state in the United States	38°30′ N	99°40′ W	492
Kansas City, city in Missouri . .	39°5′ N	94°35′ W	492, 494
Karāchi, city in Pakistan	24°59′ N	68°56′ E	497
Kara Sea, U.S.S.R.	74° N	68° E	500
Kariba Lake, Africa	17°15′ S	27°55′ E	498
Katanga Plateau, Zaire	8°30′ S	23° E	498
Kathmandu, capital of Nepal . .	27°49′ N	85°21′ E	497
Katowice, city in Poland	50°15′ N	19° E	496
Kattegat Strait, between Denmark and Sweden	56°57′ N	11°25′ E	496
Kauai, island, part of Hawaii . .	22°9′ N	159°15′ W	494
Kazan, city in the U.S.S.R. . . .	55°50′ N	49°18′ E	496
Kentucky, state in the United States	37°30′ N	87°35′ W	493
Kentucky River, United States	36°20′ N	88°50′ W	493
Kenya, country in Africa	1° N	36°53′ E	498
Khabarovsk, city in the U.S.S.R.	48°35′ N	135°12′ E	497, 500
Khar'kov, city in the U.S.S.R. . .	50° N	36°10′ E	496
Khartoum, capital of the Sudan	15°34′ N	32°36′ E	498
Kiev, city in the U.S.S.R.	50°5′ N	30°40′ E	496
Kigali, capital of Rwanda	1°59′ S	30°5′ E	498
Kingston, capital of Jamaica . .	18° N	76°45′ W	494
Kingstown, capital of St. Vincent and the Grenadines . .	13°10′ N	61°14′ W	494

J

Name	Latitude	Longitude	Page(s)
Jackson, capital of Mississippi	32°17′ N	90°10′ W	493
Jacksonville, city in Florida . .	30°20′ N	81°40′ W	493, 494
Jakarta, capital of Indonesia . .	6°17′ S	106°45′ E	497
Jamaica, country in the Caribbean Sea	17°45′ N	78° W	494

Name	Latitude	Longitude	Page(s)
Kinshasa, capital of Zaire....	4°18′ S	15°18′ E	498
Kirensk, city in the U.S.S.R...	57°47′ N	108°22′ E	500
Kivu, Lake, Zaire..........	1°45′ S	28°25′ E	498
Klamath River, California and Oregon................	41°40′ N	122°25′ W	492
Knoxville, city in Tennessee ..	35°58′ N	83°55′ W	493
Kola Peninsula, U.S.S.R.....	67°15′ N	37°40′ E	497
Kolomna, city in the U.S.S.R..	55°6′ N	38°47′ E	496
Kolyma Range, U.S.S.R.	63°0′ N	157°0′ E	500
Kolyma River, U.S.S.R.	66°30′ N	151°45′ E	497, 500
Krakow, city in Poland......	50°5′ N	20° E	496
Kuala Lumpur, capital of Malayasia..............	3°8′ N	101°42′ E	497
Kumasi, city in Ghana	6°45′ N	1°35′ W	498
Kuril Islands, part of the U.S.S.R.	46°20′ N	149°30′ E	497
Kuwait, country in Southwest Asia	29° N	48°45′ E	497
Kuybyshev, city in the U.S.S.R.	53°10′ N	50°5′ E	496
Kyūshū, island in Japan	32°27′ N	131°3′ E	497

L

Name	Latitude	Longitude	Page(s)
Labrador Sea, between Canada and Greenland	57° N	53° W	494, 500
Lachlan River, Australia.....	33°54′ S	145°15′ E	499
Lagos, capital of Nigeria.....	6°27′ N	3°24′ E	498
Lahore, city in Pakistan	32° N	74°18′ E	497
Lanai, island, part of Hawaii ..	20°48′ N	157°6′ W	494
Lansing, capital of Michigan..	42°45′ N	84°35′ W	493
Laos, country in Southeast Asia	11°30′ N	102° E	497
La Paz, capital of Bolivia	16°31′ S	68°3′ W	495
Laptev Sea, U.S.S.R.	75°39′ N	120° E	500
Las Vegas, city in Nevada ...	36°12′ N	115°10′ W	492
Lebanon, country in Southwest Asia	34° N	34° E	497
Leeds, city in the United Kingdom...............	53°48′ N	1°33′ W	496
Le Havre, city in France.....	49°31′ N	0°7′ E	496
Leipzig, city in East Germany .	51°20′ N	12°24′ E	496
Lena River, U.S.S.R.	68°39′ N	124°15′ E	496, 497, 500
Leningrad, city in the U.S.S.R.	59°15′ N	30°30′ E	496
Lesotho, country in Africa....	29°45′ S	28°7′ E	498
Lhasa, city in China........	29°41′ N	91°12′ E	496
Liberia, country in Africa	6°30′ N	9°55′ W	498
Libreville, capital of Gabon...	0°23′ N	9°27′ E	498
Libya, country in Africa	27°38′ N	15° E	498
Liechtenstein, country in Europe	47°4′ N	10° E	496
Lilongwe, capital of Malawi ..	13°59′ S	33°44′ E	498
Lima, capital of Peru	12°6′ S	76°55′ W	495

Name	Latitude	Longitude	Page(s)
Limpopo River, Africa	23°15′ S	27°46′ E	498
Lincoln, capital of Nebraska ..	40°49′ N	96°43′ W	492
Lisbon, capital of Portugal ...	38°42′ N	9°5′ W	496
Little Rock, capital of Arkansas...............	34°42′ N	92°16′ W	493
Liverpool, city in the United Kingdom...............	53°25′ N	2°52′ W	496
Loire River, France	47°19′ N	1°11′ E	496
Lome, capital of Togo	6°8′ N	1°13′ E	494
London, capital of the United Kingdom...............	51°30′ N	0°7′ W	496
Long Island Sound, between Connecticut and New York ...	41°5′ N	72°45′ W	493
Los Angeles, city in California.	34° N	118°15′ W	492, 494
Louisiana, state in the United States................	30°50′ N	92°50′ W	493
Louisville, city in Kentucky...	38°15′ N	85°45′ W	493
Lower Red Lake, Minnesota..	47°58′ N	94°31′ W	492
Luanda, capital of Angola....	8°48′ S	13°14′ W	498
Lubumbashi, city in Zaire....	11°40′ S	27°28′ E	498
Lusaka, capital of Zambia ...	15°25′ S	28°17′ E	498
Luxembourg, capital of Luxembourg	49°38′ N	6°30′ E	496
Luxembourg, country in Europe	49°30′ N	6°22′ E	496
Luzon, island, part of the Philippines	17°10′ N	119°45′ E	497
L'vov, city in the U.S.S.R.....	49°51′ N	24°1′ E	496
Lyon, city in France	45°44′ N	4°52′ E	496

M

Name	Latitude	Longitude	Page(s)
Macau, territory of Portugal in South Asia	22° N	113° E	497
Mackenzie River, Canada....	63°38′ N	124°23′ W	494, 500
Mackinac, Strait of, Michigan.	45°50′ N	84°40′ W	493, 494
Macquarie Island, Australia ..	54°36′ S	158°45′ E	500
Madagascar, country in Africa	18°5′ S	43°12′ E	498
Madison, capital of Wisconsin	43°5′ N	89°23′ W	493
Madras, city in India	13°8′ N	80°15′ E	497
Madrid, capital of Spain.....	40°26′ N	3°42′ W	496
Magadan, city in the U.S.S.R..	63° N	170°30′ E	500
Magellan, Strait of, between South America and Tierra del Fuego..................	54° S	71° W	500
Maine, state in the United States................	45°25′ N	69°50′ W	493
Malabo, capital of Equatorial Guinea	3°45′ N	8°47′ E	498
Malawi, country in Africa	11°15′ S	33°45′ E	498
Malaysia, country in Southeast Asia	4°10′ N	101°22′ E	497
Maldives, country in South Asia	4°30′ N	71°30′ E	497

GAZETTEER

Name	Latitude	Longitude	Page(s)
Male, capital of the Maldives .	4°30′ N	73° E	497
Mali, country in Africa	15°45′ N	0°15′ W	498
Malmö, city in Sweden.	55°36′ N	12°58′ E	496
Malta, country in Europe	35°52′ N	13°30′ E	496
Managua, capital of Nicaragua	12°10′ N	86°16′ W	494
Manama, capital of Bahrain . .	26°1′ N	50°33′ E	497
Manchester, city in the United Kingdom.	53°28′ N	2°14′ W	496
Manila, capital of the Philippines	14°37′ N	121° E	497
Maputo, capital of Mozambique	26°50′ S	32°30′ E	498
Maracaibo, city in Venezuela .	10°38′ N	71°45′ W	495
Marrakech, city in Morocco . .	31°38′ N	8° W	498
Marseilles, city in France. . . .	43°18′ N	5°25′ E	496
Martinique, island of France, in the Caribbean Sea	14°30′ N	60°37′ W	494
Maryland, state in the United States.	39°10′ N	76°25′ W	493
Maseru, capital of Lesotho . . .	29°9′ S	27°11′ E	498
Mashhad, city in Iran	36°17′ N	59°30′ E	497
Massachusetts, state in the United States.	42°20′ N	72°30′ W	493
Maui, island, part of Hawaii . .	20°52′ N	156°2′ W	494
Mauritania, country in Africa .	19°38′ N	13°30′ W	498
Mayotte, island of France, near Africa	13°7′ S	45°32′ W	498
Mbabane, capital of Swaziland	26°18′ S	31°14′ E	498
Mead, Lake, Arizona and Nevada	36°20′ N	114°14′ W	492
Mecca, city in Saudi Arabia . .	21°27′ N	39°45′ E	497
Medan, city in Indonesia	3°35′ N	98°35′ E	497
Medellin, city in Colombia . . .	6°15′ N	75°34′ W	495
Mediterranean Sea, between Africa, Asia and Europe	36°22′ N	13°25′ E	496, 497, 498
Mekong River, China	24°45′ N	100°31′ E	497
Mekong River, Thailand and Laos.	17°53′ N	13°57′ E	497
Melbourne, city in Australia . .	37°52′ S	145°8′ E	499
Memphis, city in Tennessee . .	35°07′ N	90°03′ W	493
Mexico, country in North America	23°45′ N	104° W	494
Mexico City, capital of Mexico	19°28′ N	99°9′ W	494
Mexico, Gulf of, North America	25°15′ N	93°45′ W	494
Miami, city in Florida	25°45′ N	80°11′ W	493, 494
Michigan, state in the United States.	45°55′ N	87° W	493
Michigan, Lake, United States	43°20′ N	87°10′ W	493, 494
Milan, city in Italy	45°29′ N	9°12′ E	496
Milk River, Canada and the United States.	48°25′ N	108°45′ W	492
Milwaukee, city in Wisconsin .	43°3′ N	87°55′ W	493, 494
Mindanao, island, part of the Philippines	7°30′ N	125°10′ E	497
Minneapolis, city in Minnesota	44°58′ N	93°15′ W	493, 494
Minnesota, state in the United States.	46°10′ N	90°20′ W	493
Minnesota River, Minnesota . .	45°4′ N	96°3′ W	492
Minsk, city in the U.S.S.R. . . .	53°54′ N	27°35′ E	496

Name	Latitude	Longitude	Page(s)
Mississippi, state in the United States.	32°30′ N	89°45′ W	493
Mississippi River, United States.	31°50′ N	91°30′ W	493, 494
Missouri, state in the United States.	38° N	93°40′ W	492, 493
Missouri River, United States .	40°40′ N	96° W	492, 494
Mobile Bay, Alabama.	30°26′ N	87°56′ W	493
Mogadisho, capital of Somalia	2°8′ N	45°22′ E	498
Molokai, island in Hawaii	21°15′ N	157°5′ W	494
Moluccas, island in Indonesia .	2°40′ S	127°15′ E	497
Mombasa, city in Kenya	4°3′ N	39°40′ E	498
Monaco, capital of Monaco . . .	43°43′ N	7°4′ E	496
Monaco, country in Europe . . .	43°43′ N	7°4′ E	496
Mongolia, country in East Asia	46° N	100° E	497
Monrovia, capital of Liberia . .	6°18′ N	10°47′ W	498
Montana, state in the United States.	47°10′ N	111°50′ W	492
Monterrey, city in Mexico. . . .	25°43′ N	100°19′ W	494
Montevideo, capital of Uruguay	34°50′ S	56°10′ W	495
Montgomery, capital of Alabama.	32°23′ N	86°17′ W	493
Montpelier, capital of Vermont	44°20′ N	72°35′ W	493
Montreal, city in Canada	45°30′ N	73°35′ W	494
Montserrat, island of the United Kingdom, in the Caribbean Sea.	16°48′ N	62° N	494
Morocco, country in Africa . . .	32° N	7° W	498
Moroni, capital of Comoros . .	11°41′ S	43°16′ E	498
Moscow, capital of the U.S.S.R.	55°45′ N	37°37′ E	496
Mozambique, country in Africa	20°15′ S	33°53′ E	498
Muhlig-Hofmann Mountains, Antarctica	72° S	5°20′ E	500
Munich, city in West Germany	48°8′ N	11°35′ E	496
Murmansk, city in the U.S.S.R.	69° N	33°20′ E	496
Murray River, Australia	34°12′ S	141°20′ E	499
Muscat, capital of Oman	23°23′ N	58°30′ E	497
Mweru Lake, between Zaire and Zambia.	8°50′ S	28°50′ E	498

N

Name	Latitude	Longitude	Page(s)
Nagoya, city in Japan	35°9′ N	136°53′ E	497
Nairobi, capital of Kenya	1°17′ S	36°49′ E	498
Namibia, Africa	19°30′ S	16°13′ E	498
Nancy, city in France.	48°42′ N	6°11′ E	496
Nanjing, city in China.	32°4′ N	118°46′ E	497
Naples, city in Italy	40°37′ N	14°12′ E	496
Narvik, city in Norway	68°21′ N	17°18′ E	496
Nashville, capital of Tennessee	36°10′ N	86°48′ W	493
Nassau, capital of the Bahamas.	25°5′ N	77°20′ W	494
Nasser, Lake, Egypt.	23°50′ N	32°50′ E	498
Ndjamena, capital of Chad . . .	12°7′ N	15°3′ E	498

Name	Latitude	Longitude	Page(s)
Nebraska, state in the United States	41°45′ N	101°30′ W	492
Negro, river in Brazil	0°18′ S	63°21′ W	495
Nelson River, United States . .	56°20′ N	93°59′ W	494
Nepal, country in Asia	28°45′ N	83° E	497
Netherlands, country in Europe	53°1′ N	3°57′ E	496
Netherlands Antilles, islands in the Caribbean Sea	52°15′ N	5°30′ E	494
Nevada, state in the United States	39°30′ N	117° W	492
Newark, city in New Jersey . .	37°32′ N	122°02′ W	493
Newcastle, city in Australia . .	33° S	151°55′ E	499
New Delhi, capital of India . . .	28°43′ N	77°18′ E	497
Newfoundland, province in Canada	48°15′ N	56°53′ W	494
New Guinea, island near Asia .	5°45′ S	140° E	497
New Hampshire, state in the United States	43°55′ N	71°40′ W	493
New Jersey, state in the United States	40°30′ N	74°50′ W	493
New Mexico, state in the United States	34°30′ N	107°10′ W	492
New Orleans, city in Louisiana	30° N	90°5′ W	493, 494
New Siberian Islands, U.S.S.R.	76°45′ N	140°30′ E	497, 500
New South Wales, state in Australia	32°45′ S	146°14′ E	499
New York, city in New York State	40°40′ N	73°58′ W	493, 494
New York, state in the United States	42°45′ N	78°5′ W	493
New Zealand, country, part of Polynesia	42° S	175° E	497
Niamey, capital of Niger	13°31′ N	2°7′ E	498
Nicaragua, country in Central America	12°45′ N	86°15′ W	494
Nicobar Island, part of India . .	8°28′ N	94°4′ E	497
Nicosia, capital of Cyprus. . . .	35°10′ N	33°22′ E	497
Niger, country in Africa	18°2′ N	8°30′ E	498
Nigeria, country in Africa	8°57′ N	6°30′ E	498
Niger River, Africa.	5°33′ N	6°33′ E	498
Nikolayevsk, city in the U.S.S.R.	53°40′ N	140°50′ E	500
Nile River, Africa.	19°15′ N	32°30′ E	498
Nizhnyaya Tunguska, river in the U.S.S.R.	64°13′ N	110°30′ E	497
Nome, city in Alaska	64°30′ N	165°20′ W	492, 494, 500
Norfolk, city in Virginia.	36°55′ N	76°15′ W	493
Noril'sk, city in the U.S.S.R. . .	69° N	87°11′ E	500
North Carolina, state in the United States.	35°40′ N	81°30′ W	493
North Dakota, state in the United States.	47°20′ N	101°55′ W	492
Northern Divina River, U.S.S.R.	63° N	42°40′ E	496
Northern Territory, state in Australia	18°15′ S	133° E	499
North Korea, country in Asia. .	38°45′ N	130° E	497
North Platte River, United States.	41°20′ N	102°40′ W	492
North Sea, Europe	56°9′ N	3°16′ E	496, 500
Norvegia Cape, Antarctica . . .	71°25′ S	12°18′ E	500
Norway, country in Europe . . .	63°48′ N	11°17′ E	496, 500
Norwegian Sea, Europe	66°54′ N	1°43′ E	496, 500
Nouakchott, capital of Mauritania.	18°6′ N	15°57′ W	498
Novaya Zemlya, island in the U.S.S.R.	72° N	54°46′ E	497
Novokuznetsk, city in the U.S.S.R.	53°43′ N	85°59′ E	497
Novosibirsk, city in the U.S.S.R.	55°9′ N	82°58′ E	497
Nyasa (now called Malawi), Lake, Africa.	10°45′ S	34°30′ E	498

O

Name	Latitude	Longitude	Page(s)
Oahe, lake in South Dakota . .	44°28′ N	100°34′ W	492
Oahu, island, part of Hawaii . .	21°38′ N	157°48′ W	494
Ob River, U.S.S.R.	62°15′ N	67° E	496, 497, 500
Oder River, East Germany . . .	52°40′ N	14°19′ E	496
Odessa, city in the U.S.S.R. . .	46°28′ N	30°44′ E	496
Ogbomosho, city in Nigeria. . .	8°8′ N	4°15′ E	498
Ohio, state in the United States	40°30′ N	83°15′ W	493
Ohio River, United States. . . .	37°25′ N	88°5′ W	493, 494
Okavango Swamp, Botswana .	19°30′ S	23°2′ E	498
Okeechobee, Lake, Florida. . .	27° N	80°49′ W	493
Okhotsk, city in the U.S.S.R.. .	59°28′ N	143°32′ E	500
Okhotsk, Sea of, Asia	56°45′ N	146° E	497
Oklahoma, state in the United States.	36° N	98°20′ W	492
Oklahoma City, capital of Oklahoma	35°27′ N	97°32′ W	492, 494
Olympia, capital of Washington	47°2′ N	122°52′ W	492
Omaha, city in Nebraska	41°48′ N	95°57′ W	492, 494
Oman, country in Asia	20° N	57°45′ E	497
Oman, Gulf of, Asia.	24°24′ N	58°58′ E	497
Omsk, city in the U.S.S.R. . . .	55°12′ N	73°19′ E	497
Ontario, Lake, between the United States and Canada. . .	43°35′ N	79°5′ W	493, 494
Orange River, Namibia and South Africa.	29°15′ S	17°30′ E	498
Oregon, state in the United States.	43°40′ N	121°50′ W	492
Orinoco River, Venezuela	8°32′ N	63°13′ W	495
Orlando, city in Florida.	28°32′ N	81°22′ W	493
Osaka, city in Japan	34°40′ N	135°27′ E	497
Oslo, capital of Norway	59°56′ N	10°41′ E	496, 500
Ostrava, city in Czechoslovakia	49°51′ N	18°18′ E	496
Ottawa, capital of Canada. . . .	45°25′ N	75°43′ W	494
Ouagadougou, capital of Upper Volta.	12°22′ N	1°31′ W	498
Oulu, city in Finland	64°58′ N	25°43′ E	496

GAZETTEER

Name	Latitude	Longitude	Page(s)
P			
Pakistan, country in South Asia	28° N	67°30′ E	497
Palanca, city in the U.S.S.R...	59°7′ N	159°58′ E	497
Palermo, Italy	38°8′ N	13°24′ E	496
Palmas, Cape, Libya	4°22′ N	7°44′ W	497
Panama, country in Central America	8°35′ N	81°8′ W	494
Panama Canal, Central America	9° N	81° W	494
Panama City, capital of Panama	8°35′ N	81°8′ W	494
Paraguay, country in South America	24° S	57° W	495
Paramaribo, capital of Surinam	5°50′ N	55°15′ W	495
Parana River, Brazil	13°5′ S	47°11′ W	495
Paris, capital of France	48°51′ N	2°20′ E	496
Peace River, Canada	56°14′ N	117°17′ W	494
Pearl River, Louisiana and Mississippi	31°6′ N	89°44′ W	493
Pecos River, United States. . .	31°10′ N	103°10′ W	492
Pee Dee River, North Carolina and South Carolina	34°1′ N	79°26′ W	493
Pend Oreille Lake, Idaho	48°9′ N	116°38′ W	492
Pennsylvania, state in the United States.	41° N	78°10′ W	493
Penobscot Bay, Maine	44°20′ N	69° W	493, 494
Penobscot River, Maine.	45° N	68°36′ W	493, 494
Pensacola Bay, Florida	30°25′ N	87°6′ W	493
Pensacola Mountains, Antarctica	83°45′ S	55° W	500
Peoria, city in Illinois	40°45′ N	89°35′ W	493
Perm, city in the U.S.S.R.	58° N	56°15′ E	496
Persian Gulf, Asia	27°38′ N	50°30′ E	497
Perth, city in Australia	31°50′ S	116°10′ E	499
Peru, country in South America	10° S	75° W	495
Petropavlovsk-Kamchatskiy, city in the U.S.S.R.	53°13′ N	158°56′ E	500
Philadelphia, city in Pennsylvania.	40° N	75°13′ W	493, 494
Philippines, country in Asia . .	14°25′ N	125° E	497
Phoenix, capital of Arizona. . .	33°30′ N	112° W	492, 494
Phnom Penh, capital of Kampuchea.	11°39′ N	104°53′ E	497
Pierre, capital of South Dakota	44°22′ N	100°20′ W	492
Pit River, California	40°58′ N	121°42′ W	492
Pittsburgh, city in Pennsylvania.	40°26′ N	80°1′ W	493
Platte River, United States . . .	40°50′ N	100°40′ W	492, 494
Poinsett, cape in Antarctica . .	65°42′ S	113°18′ E	500
Point Barrow, Alaska.	71°23′ N	156°30′ W	500
Poland, country in Europe . . .	52°37′ N	17°1′ E	496
Pontchartrain, Lake, Louisiana	30°10′ N	90°10′ W	493
Po River, Italy	44°57′ N	12°38′ E	496
Port-au-Prince, capital of Haiti	18°35′ N	72°20′ W	494
Port Hedland, Australia	20°30′ S	118°30′ E	499
Portland, city in Oregon	45°31′ N	123°41′ W	492, 494
Porto, city in Portugal	41°10′ N	8°38′ W	496
Porto Alegre, city in Brazil . . .	29°58′ S	51°11′ S	495
Port-of-Spain, capital of Trinidad and Tobago	10°44′ N	61°24′ W	494
Porto-Novo, capital of Benin. .	6°29′ N	2°37′ E	498
Port Said, city in Egypt	31°15′ N	32°19′ E	498
Portugal, country in Europe . .	38°15′ N	8°8′ W	496
Powder River, Montana and Wyoming	45°18′ N	105°37′ W	492
Powell, Lake, Utah	37°26′ N	110°25′ W	492
Prague, capital of Czechoslovakia	59°5′ N	14°30′ E	496
Pretoria, administrative capital of South Africa	25°43′ S	28°16′ E	498
Prince Albert Mountains, Antarctica	76° S	161°30′ E	500
Prince Charles Mountains, Antarctica	72° S	67° E	500
Providence, capital of Rhode Island	41°50′ N	71°23′ W	493
Prudhoe Bay, Alaska	70°0′ N	148°35′ N	492, 494, 500
Prydz Bay, Antarctica.	69° S	76° E	500
Puerto Rico, commonwealth of the United States	18°16′ N	66°50′ W	494
Puget Sound, Washington . . .	47°49′ N	122°26′ W	492
Punta Arenas, city in Chile . . .	53°9′ S	70°48′ W	500
P'yongyang, capital of North Korea	39°3′ N	125°48′ E	497
Pyramid Lake, Nevada.	40°2′ N	119°50′ W	492
Q			
Qatar, country in Asia	25° N	52°45′ E	497
Quebec, city in Canada.	46°49′ N	71°13′ W	494
Quebec, province of Canada. .	51°7′ N	70°25′ E	494
Queen Elizabeth Islands, Canada	78°20′ N	110° W	500
Queen Maud Islands, Antarctica	85° S	179° W	500
Queensland, state in Australia	22°45′ S	141°1′ E	499
Quezon City, city in the Philippines	14°40′ N	121°2′ E	497
Quito, capital of Ecuador	0°17′ S	78°32′ W	495
R			
Rabat, capital of Morocco . . .	33°59′ N	6°47′ W	497
Raleigh, capital of North Carolina	35°45′ N	78°39′ W	493

Name	Latitude	Longitude	Page(s)
Rangoon, capital of Burma...	16°46′ N	96°9′ E	498
Rapid City, city in South Dakota................	44°6′ N	103°14′ W	492
Recife, city in Brazil........	8°9′ S	34°59′ W	495
Red River, United States....	31°40′ N	92°55′ W	492, 494
Red Sea, Africa and Asia....	23°15′ N	37° E	497, 498
Republican River, Kansas...	39°40′ N	97°40′ W	492
Reykjavik, capital of Iceland..	64°9′ N	21°39′ W	496, 500
Rhine River, Europe........	50°34′ N	7°21′ E	496
Rhode Island, state in the United States............	41°35′ N	71°40′ W	493
Rhodes, island, part of Greece	36°10′ N	28° E	496
Rhone River, France.......	45°14′ N	4°53′ E	496
Richmond, capital of Virginia.	37°35′ N	77°30′ W	493
Riga, city in the U.S.S.R.....	56°55′ N	24°5′ E	496
Riiser-Larson Ice Shelf, Antarctica..............	68°55′ S	34° E	500
Rio de Janeiro, city in Brazil.	22°50′ S	43°20′ W	495
Rio Grande, river in the United States............	37°44′ N	106°51′ W	492, 494
Riyadh, capital of Saudi Arabia	24°31′ N	46°47′ E	497
Roanoke River, United States.	36°17′ N	77°22′ W	493
Rochester, city in New York..	43°15′ N	77°35′ W	493
Rockefeller Plateau, Antarctica..............	80° S	135° W	500
Romania, country in Europe..	46°18′ N	22°53′ E	496
Rome, capital of Italy......	41°52′ N	12°37′ E	496
Ronne Ice Shelf, Antarctica..	78°30′ S	61° W	500
Roosevelt Island, Antarctica..	79°30′ S	168° W	500
Roosevelt Lake, Washington.	48°12′ N	118°43′ W	492
Rosario, city in Argentina....	32°58′ S	60°42′ W	495
Roseau, capital of Dominica..	15°17′ N	61°23′ W	494
Ross Ice Shelf, Antarctica...	81°30′ S	175° W	500
Ross Sea, Antarctica.......	76° S	178° W	500
Rostov, city in the U.S.S.R. ..	47°38′ N	39°15′ E	496
Rotterdam, city in the Netherlands..............	51°55′ N	4°27′ E	496
Rukwa, Lake, Tanzania.....	8° S	32°25′ E	498
Rwanda, country in Africa...	2°10′ S	29°37′ E	498
Rybinsk, city in the U.S.S.R...	58°2′ N	38°52′ E	496
Ryukyu Islands, Japan......	27°30′ N	127° E	497

S

Name	Latitude	Longitude	Page(s)
Sabine River, United States..	31°35′ N	94° W	492
Sacramento, capital of California..............	38°35′ N	121°30′ W	492
Sacramento River, California.	40°20′ N	122°7′ W	492
St. Christopher and Nevis, country in the Caribbean Sea.	17°5′ N	62°38′ W	494
St. Clair, Lake, between Canada and the United States.	42°25′ N	82°30′ W	493
St. Georges, capital of Grenada	12°2′ N	61°57′ W	494
St. Johns, capital of Antigua..	17°7′ N	61°50′ W	494

Name	Latitude	Longitude	Page(s)
St. Lawrence, island off the coast of Alaska..........	63°10′ N	172°12′ W	492
St. Lawrence River, Canada and the United States.......	48°24′ N	69°30′ W	492, 494
St. Louis, city in Missouri....	38°39′ N	90°15′ W	493, 494
St. Lucia, country in the Caribbean Sea............	13°54′ N	60°40′ W	494
St. Paul, city in Minnesota...	44°57′ N	93°5′ W	493
St. Petersburg, city in Florida.	27°47′ N	82°38′ W	493
St. Pierre and Miquelon, islands of France, in the Caribbean Sea............	46°49′ N	56°15′ W	494
St. Vincent and the Grenadines, country in the Caribbean Sea............	13°20′ N	60°50′ W	494
Sakakawea, Lake, North Dakota...............	47°49′ N	101°58′ W	492
Sakhalin, island in the U.S.S.R.	51°52′ N	144°15′ E	497
Salem, capital of Oregon....	44°55′ N	123°3′ W	492
Salt Lake City, capital of Utah	40°45′ N	111°52′ W	492, 494
Salton Sea, California......	33°28′ N	115°43′ W	492
Salvador, city in Brazil......	12°59′ S	38°27′ W	495
Salween River, Burma......	26°46′ N	98°19′ E	497
Samarkand, city in the U.S.S.R..............	39°42′ N	67° E	497
Sanaa, capital of Yemen....	15°17′ N	44°5′ E	497
San Antonio, city in Texas...	29°25′ N	98°30′ W	492, 494
San Bernardino, city in California..............	34°7′ N	117°19′ W	492
San Diego, city in California..	32°43′ N	117°10′ W	492, 494
San Francisco, city in California..............	37°45′ N	122°26′ W	492, 494
San Francisco Bay, California.	37°45′ N	122°21′ W	492
San Joaquin River, California.	37°10′ N	120°51′ W	492
San Jose, capital of Costa Rica	9°57′ N	84°5′ W	494
San Jose, city in California...	37°20′ N	121°54′ W	492, 494
San Juan, capital of Puerto Rico................	18°30′ N	60°10′ W	494
San Marino, capital of San Marino................	44°55′ N	12°26′ E	496
San Marino, country in Europe	43°40′ N	13° E	496
San Salvador, capital of El Salvador..............	13°45′ N	89°11′ W	494
Santa Fe, capital of New Mexico...............	35°10′ N	106° W	492
Santiago, capital of Chile....	33°26′ S	70°40′ W	495
Santo Domingo, capital of the Dominican Republic........	18°30′ N	69°55′ W	494
São Francisco River, Brazil..	8°56′ S	40°20′ W	495
São Paulo, city in Brazil....	23°34′ S	46°38′ W	495
São Tome, capital of Sao Tome and Principe.........	0°20′ N	6°44′ E	498
São Tomé and Príncipe, country in Africa..........	1° N	6° E	498
Sapporo, city in Japan......	43°2′ N	141°29′ E	497
Sardinia, island near Italy...	40°8′ N	9°5′ E	496
Saskatchewan River, Canada.	53°45′ N	103°20′ W	494
Saudi Arabia, country in Asia.	22°40′ N	46° E	497
Savannah River, Georgia and South Carolina..........	33°11′ N	81°51′ W	493

511

GAZETTEER

Name	Latitude	Longitude	Page(s)
Scioto River, Ohio	39°10′ N	82°55′ W	493
Seattle, city in Washington. . .	47°36′ N	122°20′ W	492, 494
Seine River, France	49°21′ N	1°17′ E	496
Semarang, city in Indonesia . .	7°3′ S	110°27′ E	497
Senegal, a country in Africa . .	14°53′ N	14°58′ W	498
Seoul, capital of South Korea .	37°35′ N	127°3′ E	497
Seram, island part of Indonesia	2°45′ S	129°30′ E	497
Severnaya Zemlya, island part of the U.S.S.R.	79°33′ N	101°15′ E	497, 500
Sevilla, capital of Spain	37°29′ N	5°58′ W	496
Shackleton Range, Antarctica.	78°30′ S	36°1′ W	500
Shanghai, city in China	31°14′ N	121°27′ E	497
Shetland Islands, part of the United Kingdom	60°35′ N	2°10′ W	500
Shikoku Island, Japan	33°43′ N	133°33′ E	497
Sicily, island, part of Italy . . .	37°38′ N	13°30′ E	496
Sierra Leone, country in Africa	8°48′ N	12°30′ W	498
Singapore, capital of Singapore	1°18′ N	103°52′ E	497
Singapore, country in Asia . . .	1°22′ N	103°45′ E	497
Skagerrak, strait in Europe. . .	57°43′ N	8°28′ E	496
Skopje, city in Yugoslavia. . . .	42°2′ N	21°26′ E	496
Smoky Hill River, Kansas. . . .	38°40′ N	97°32′ W	492
Snake River, United States. . .	46°35′ N	117°20′ W	492, 494
Sochi, city in the U.S.S.R. . . .	43°35′ N	39°50′ E	497
Socotra Island, part of the People's Democratic Republic of Yemen	13° N	52°30′ E	497
Sofia, capital of Bulgaria.	42°43′ N	23°20′ E	496
Somalia, country in Africa . . .	3°28′ N	44°47′ E	498
South Africa, country in Africa	28° S	24°50′ E	498
South Australia, state in Australia	29°45′ S	132° E	499
South Carolina, state in the United States.	34°15′ N	81°10′ W	493
South China Sea, Asia	15°23′ N	114°12′ E	497
South Dakota, state in the United States.	44°20′ N	101°55′ W	492
South Georgia Islands, territory of the United Kingdom in South America . . .	54° S	37° W	495, 500
South Korea, country in East Asia	38° N	130° E	497
South Orkney Islands, territory of the United Kingdom, near Antarctica	60°35′ S	45°30′ W	500
South Platte River, United States.	40°40′ N	102°40′ W	492
South Sandwich Islands, territory of the United Kingdom, near Antarctica	58° S	27° W	500
South Shetland Islands, Antarctica	62° S	60° W	500
Spain, country in Europe	40°15′ N	4°30′ W	496
Springfield, capital of Illinois .	39°46′ N	89°37′ W	493
Sri Lanka, country in Asia . . .	8°45′ N	82°30′ E	497
Stanley, city in the Falkland Islands	51°46′ S	57°59′ W	495, 500
Stockholm, capital of Sweden.	59°23′ N	18° E	496, 500
Stuttgart, city in West Germany	48°48′ N	9°15′ E	496

Name	Latitude	Longitude	Page(s)
Sucre, capital of Bolivia	19°6′ S	65°16′ W	495
Sudan, country in Africa	14° N	28° E	498
Suez Canal, Egypt	30°53′ N	32°21′ E	498
Sumatra, island, part of Indonesia	2°6′ N	99°40′ E	497
Superior, Lake, between Canada and the United States .	47°38′ N	89°20′ W	493, 494
Surabaya, city in Indonesia . .	7°23′ S	112°45′ E	497
Suriname, country in South America	4° N	56° W	495
Susquehanna River, Pennsylvania	39°50′ N	76°20′ W	493
Svalbard, islands of Norway. .	77° N	20° E	500
Sverdlovsk, city in the U.S.S.R.	56°15′ N	60°36′ E	497
Swaziland, country in Africa. .	26°45′ S	31°30′ E	498
Sweden, country in Europe. . .	60°10′ N	14°10′ E	496
Switzerland, country in Europe	46°30′ N	7°43′ E	496
Sydney, city in Australia.	33°55′ S	151°17′ E	499
Syria, country in Asia.	35° N	37°15′ E	497

T

Name	Latitude	Longitude	Page(s)
Tabriz, city in Iran	38° N	46°13′ E	497
Tagus River, Spain and Portugal	39°40′ N	5°7′ W	496
Tahoe, lake between California and Nevada	39°9′ N	120°18′ W	492
Taipei, capital of Taiwan.	25°2′ N	121°38′ E	497
Taiwan (Formosa), country in Asia	23°30′ N	122°20′ E	497
Tallahassee, capital of Florida	30°25′ N	84°17′ W	493
Tampa, city in Florida	27°57′ N	82°25′ W	493
Tampa Bay, Florida	27°35′ N	82°38′ W	493
Tanana River, Alaska.	64°26′ N	148°40′ W	492
Tanganyika, Lake, Africa	5°5′ S	29°40′ E	498
Tanzania, country in Africa. . .	6°48′ S	33°58′ E	498
Tashkent, U.S.S.R.	41°23′ N	69°4′ E	497
Tasmania, island off Australia.	41°28′ S	142°30′ E	499
Tasman Sea, Oceania	29°30′ S	155° E	499
Tbilisi, city in the U.S.S.R. . . .	41°41′ N	44°45′ E	497
Tegucigalpa, capital of Honduras	14°8′ N	87°15′ W	494
Tehran, capital of Iran	35°45′ N	51°30′ E	497
Tennessee, state in the United States.	35°50′ N	88° W	493
Tennessee River, United States.	35°10′ N	88°20′ W	493
Texas, state in the United States.	31° N	101° W	492
Texoma, Lake, Oklahoma. . . .	34°3′ N	96°28′ W	492
Thailand, country in Asia	16°30′ N	101° E	497
Thames River, United Kingdom	51°26′ N	0°54′ E	496
Thessaloniki, city in Greece . .	40°38′ N	22°59′ E	496

Name	Latitude	Longitude	Page(s)
Thimbu, capital of Bhutan. . . .	27°33′ N	89°42′ E	497
Thule, city in Greenland	76°34′ N	68°47′ W	494, 500
Thurston, island near Antarctica	71°20′ S	98° W	500
Tianjin, city in China	39°8′ N	117°14′ E	497
Tiber River, Italy	42°30′ N	12°14′ E	496
Tierra del Fuego, Chile and Argentina	53°50′ S	68°45′ W	495, 500
Tigris River, Southwest Asia .	34°45′ N	44°10′ E	497
Tiksi, city in the U.S.S.R.	71°42′ N	128°32′ E	497, 500
Timisoara, city in Poland	45°44′ N	21°21′ E	496
Timor, island, part of Indonesia	10°8′ S	125° E	497
Tirane, capital of Albania	41°48′ N	19°50′ E	496
Titicaca, Lake, between Peru and Bolivia	16°12′ S	70°33′ W	495
Togo, country in Africa.	8° N	0°52′ E	498
Tokyo, capital of Japan	35°41′ N	139°44′ E	497
Toledo, city in Ohio	41°40′ N	83°35′ W	493
Tombigbee River, Alabama . .	31°45′ N	88°2′ W	493
Topeka, capital of Kansas . . .	39°2′ N	95°41′ W	492
Toronto, city in Canada	43°40′ N	79°23′ W	494
Trenton, capital of New Jersey	40°13′ N	74°46′ W	493
Trinidad and Tobago, country in the Caribbean Sea	11° N	61° W	494
Tripoli, capital of Libya	32°50′ N	13°13′ E	498
Trondheim, city in Norway . . .	63°25′ N	11°35′ E	496
Tucuman, city in Argentina. . .	26°52′ S	65°8′ W	495
Tulsa, city in Oklahoma	36°8′ N	95°58′ W	492
Tunis, capital of Tunisia	36°59′ N	10°6′ E	498
Tunisia, country in Africa	35° N	10°11′ E	498
Turin, city in Italy.	45°5′ N	7°44′ E	496
Turkana, Lake, Kenya	3°0′ N	35°30′ E	500
Turkey, country in Europe and Asia	38°45′ N	32° E	497
Turks and Caicos, islands of the United Kingdom, in the Caribbean Sea	21°25′ N	71°10′ W	494
Turku, city in Finland	60°28′ N	22°12′ E	496
Tyrrhenian Sea, Italy	40°10′ N	12°15′ E	496

U

Name	Latitude	Longitude	Page(s)
Ufa, city in the U.S.S.R.	54°45′ N	55°57′ E	496
Uganda, country in Africa. . . .	2° N	32°28′ E	498
Ulaanbaatar, capital of Mongolia.	47°56′ N	107° E	497
Ungava Peninsula, Canada. . .	59°55′ N	74° W	500
Union of Soviet Socialist Republics (U.S.S.R.), country in Europe and Asia.	60°30′ N	64° E	496, 497, 500
United Arab Emirates, country in Southwest Asia . . .	24° N	54° E	497

Name	Latitude	Longitude	Page(s)
United Kingdom, country in Europe	56°30′ N	1°40′ W	496
United States, country in North America	38° N	110° W	492, 493, 494
Ural River, U.S.S.R.	49°50′ N	51°30′ E	496
Urmia, Lake, Iran	37°40′ N	45°30′ E	497
Uruguay, country in South America	32°45′ S	56° W	495
Urumqi, city in China	43°48′ N	87°35′ E	497
Utah, state in the United States	39°25′ N	112°40′ W	492

V

Name	Latitude	Longitude	Page(s)
Vaal River, South Africa.	28°15′ S	24°30′ E	498
Vaduz, capital of Liechtenstein	47°10′ N	9°32′ E	496
Vahsel Bay, Antarctica.	77°48′ S	34°39′ W	500
Valencia, a city in Spain	39°26′ N	0°23′ W	496
Valletta, capital of Malta	35°50′ N	14°29′ E	496
Valparaiso, city in Chile	32°58′ S	71°23′ W	495
Van, salt lake in Turkey	38°4′ N	43°10′ E	497
Vancouver, city in Canada . . .	49°16′ N	123°6′ W	494
Vänern Lake, Sweden	58°52′ N	13°17′ E	496
Vattern Lake, Sweden	58°15′ N	14°24′ E	496
Venezuela, country in South America	8° N	65° W	495
Venice, city in Italy	45°25′ N	12°18′ E	496
Verkhoyansk Range, U.S.S.R.	67°43′ N	133°33′ E	500
Vermont, state in the United States.	43°50′ N	72°50′ W	493
Victoria, state in Australia . . .	36°46′ S	143°15′ E	499
Victoria Island, Canada	70°13′ N	107°45′ W	494, 500
Victoria Lake, Africa	0°50′ S	32°50′ E	498
Vienna, capital of Austria	48°13′ N	16°22′ E	496
Vientiane, capital of Laos. . . .	18°7′ N	102°33′ E	497
Vietnam, country in Asia	18° N	107° E	497
Virginia, state in the United States.	37° N	80°45′ W	493
Virgin Islands, territory of the United States.	18°15′ N	64° W	494
Vistula River, Poland.	52°48′ N	19°2′ E	496
Vladivostok, city in the U.S.S.R.	43°6′ N	131°47′ E	497
Volga River, U.S.S.R.	47°30′ N	46°20′ E	496
Volgograd, city in the U.S.S.R.	48°40′ N	42°20′ E	496
Volta, Lake, Ghana	7°10′ N	0°30′ W	498
Vorkuta, city in the U.S.S.R. . .	67°28′ N	63°40′ E	500
Voroshilovgrad, city in the U.S.S.R.	48°34′ N	39°20′ E	496

GAZETTEER

Name	Latitude	Longitude	Page(s)
W			
Wabash River, Illinois and Indiana	38° N	88° W	493
Walvis Bay, South Africa	22°50′ S	14°30′ E	498
Warsaw, capital of Poland	52°15′ N	21°5′ E	496
Washington, state in the United States	47°30′ N	121°10′ W	492
Washington, D.C., capital of the United States	38°50′ N	77° W	493, 494
Weddell Sea, Antarctica	73° S	45° W	500
Western Australia, state in Australia	24°15′ S	121°30′ E	499
Western Sahara, part of Morocco	23°5′ N	15°33′ W	498
West Virginia, state in the United States	39° N	80°50′ W	493
Whitehorse, city in Canada	60°39′ N	135°1′ W	500
White Nile River, Sudan	14° N	32°35′ E	498
White River, river in South Dakota	43°48′ N	100°5′ W	492
Whyalla, city in Australia	33° S	137°32′ E	499
Willamette River, Oregon	44°15′ N	123°13′ W	492
Windhoek, capital of Namibia	22°5′ S	17°10′ E	498
Winnipeg, city in Canada	49°53′ N	97°9′ W	494
Winnipeg, Lake, Canada	52° N	97° W	494
Wisconsin, state in the United States	44°30′ N	91° W	493
Wisconsin River, Wisconsin	43°14′ N	90°34′ W	493
Wollongong, city in Australia	34°26′ S	151°5′ E	499
Woods, Lake of the, Canada and the United States	49°25′ N	93°25′ W	492
Wrangel, island of the U.S.S.R.	56°15′ N	132°10′ W	497, 500
Wuhan, city in China	30°30′ N	114°15′ E	497
Wyoming, state in the United States	42°50′ N	108°30′ W	492
X			
Xi River, China	22°25′ N	113°23′ E	497

Name	Latitude	Longitude	Page(s)
Y			
Yakutsk, city in the U.S.S.R.	62°13′ N	129°49′ E	497, 500
Yalta, city in the U.S.S.R.	44°29′ N	34°12′ E	496
Yangzi River (Chang Jiang), China	30°30′ N	117°25′ E	497
Yaounde, capital of Cameroon	3°52′ N	11°31′ E	498
Yellowknife, city in Canada	62°29′ N	114°38′ W	500
Yellow Sea, Asia	35°20′ N	122°15′ E	497
Yellowstone River, Montana	46°28′ N	105°35′ W	492
Yemen, country in Southwest Asia	15°45′ N	44°30′ E	497
Yemen, People's Democratic Republic of, country in Southwest Asia	14°45′ N	46°45′ E	497
Yenisey River, U.S.S.R.	67°48′ N	87°15′ E	497, 500
Yerevan, city in the U.S.S.R.	40°10′ N	44°30′ E	497
Yokohama, city in Japan	35°37′ N	139°40′ E	497
Yugoslavia, country in Europe	44°48′ N	17°29′ E	496
Yukon River, Alaska	62°10′ N	163°10′ W	494, 500
Yukon Territory, Canada	63°16′ N	135°30′ W	494
Yumen, city in China	40°14′ N	96°56′ E	497
Z			
Zagreb, city in Yugoslavia	45°50′ N	15°58′ E	496
Zaire, a country in Africa	1° S	22°15′ E	498
Zaire River, Africa	1°10′ N	18°25′ E	498
Zambezi River, Africa	15°45′ S	33°15′ E	498
Zambia, country in Africa	14°23′ S	24°15′ E	498
Zaporozh'ye, city in the U.S.S.R.	47°20′ N	35°5′ E	496
Zimbabwe, country in Africa	17°50′ S	29°30′ E	498

a ..... hat, match, carry	i ...... if, hit, native, mirror	u ..... up, love, but
ā ..... say, late, paid, ape	ī ...... ice, sight, buy, pirate	ü ..... rule, dew, youth, cool
ä ..... father, mop, rock, car		u̇ ..... put, foot
au̇ ..... shout, cow, proud	ō ..... hope, snow, soap	
	ȯ ..... raw, ball, bought, horn	ə ..... *a* in above
e ..... let, met, very		*e* in open
ē ..... meat, free, even, money	oi ..... oil, joy, coin	*i* in happily
		o in gallop
ėr .... term, learn, worm, fur		*u* in circus

METRIC CONVERSION CHART

Approximate Conversions from Metric Measures

When You Know	Multiply by	To Find
LENGTH		
millimeters	0.04	inches
centimeters	0.4	inches
meters	3.3	feet
meters	1.1	yards
kilometers	0.6	miles
AREA		
square centimeters	0.16	square inches
square meters	1.2	square yards
square kilometers	0.4	square miles
hectares (10,000 m²)	2.5	acres
MASS AND WEIGHT		
grams	0.035	ounces
kilograms	2.2	pounds
metric ton (1,000 kg)	1.1	short tons
VOLUME		
milliliters	0.03	fluid ounces
milliliters	0.06	cubic inches
liters	2.1	pints
liters	1.06	quarts
liters	0.26	gallons
cubic meters	35.0	cubic feet
cubic meters	1.3	cubic yards
TEMPERATURE (exact)		
degrees Celsius	9/5 (then add 32)	degrees Fahrenheit

Approximate Conversions to Metric Measures

When You Know	Multiply by	To Find
LENGTH		
inches	2.5	centimeters
feet	30.0	centimeters
yards	0.9	meters
miles	1.6	kilometers
AREA		
square inches	6.5	square centimeters
square feet	0.09	square meters
square yards	0.8	square meters
square miles	2.6	square kilometers
acres	0.4	hectares
MASS AND WEIGHT		
ounces	28.0	grams
pounds	0.45	kilograms
short tons (2,000 lb)	0.9	metric tons
VOLUME		
teaspoons	5.0	milliliters
tablespoons	15.0	milliliters
cubic inches	16.0	milliliters
fluid ounces	30.0	milliliters
cups	0.24	liters
pints	0.47	liters
quarts	0.95	liters
gallons	3.8	liters
cubic feet	0.03	cubic meters
cubic yards	0.76	cubic meters
TEMPERATURE (exact)		
degrees Fahrenheit	5/9 (after subtracting 32)	degrees Celsius

Source: U.S. DEPARTMENT OF COMMERCE, National Bureau of Standards, Washington, D.C. 20234

INDEX

516

INDEX

INDEX

INDEX

INDEX

INDEX

ACKNOWLEDGMENTS

We wish to express our thanks to the following for permissions:

Mr. Herbert Block for permission to reprint a cartoon from *The Herblock Gallery* (Simon and Schuster, 1968). Copyright © by Herbert Block.

The World Almanac & Book of Facts for permission to reprint excerpts. THE WORLD ALMANAC & BOOK OF FACTS 1985, copyright © Newspaper Enterprise Association, Inc., 1984, New York, NY 10166.

The World Book encyclopedia for permission to reprint an excerpt from the index. THE WORLD BOOK, copyright © 1983, World Book, Inc.

Every reasonable effort has been made to trace the owners of other copyright materials in the book, but in some instances this has proved impossible. The publishers will be glad to receive information leading to more complete acknowledgments in subsequent printings of the book and in the meantime extend their apologies for any omissions.

Cartoons **133, 225, 235, 323, 366:** Walter Fournier
Graphs and Diagrams **26, 42:** Jean Helmer (Publishers' Graphics, Inc.). **8, 47, 61, 63, 66, 67, 68, 69, 70, 71, 72, 118, 121, 134, 156, 157, 176, 193, 223, 266, 318, 337, 341, 358, 384, 466:** Omnigraphics, Inc.
Maps R. R. Donnelley Cartographic Services
Marsh Communications, Inc.

Cover Photo Jonathan T. Wright (Bruce Coleman Inc.)
Photo shows a chain link suspension bridge in Nepal.
Photo Credits **vii:** The Granger Collection.

Unit One: 20: National Aeronautics and Space Administration (NASA).

Chapter One: 22: NASA. **23:** Greg Mancuso (Stock, Boston). **24:** *l, r* NASA. **31:** Wide World Photos. **32:** James Mason (Black Star). **36:** United States Travel Services (USTS). **37:** M.W. Williams, National Park Service (NPS). **38:** *t* NASA; *b* NPS. **39:** Tom Bean (Tom Stack & Associates). **41:** *t* Soil Conservation Service (SCS); *b* USTS. **43:** *l* United States Geological Services (USGS); *r* NPS.

Chapter Two: 46: *t* NASA; *m* Jessica Anne Ehlers (Bruce Coleman Inc.); *b* NASA. **48:** NASA. **57:** N. Shah (Shostal Associates). **62:** *t* Otto Lang; *b* Lee B. Ewing. **63:** Florida Division of Tourism. **66:** Peter Menzel (Stock, Boston). **67:** Silvio Fiore (Shostal Associates). **68:** *t* Grant Heilman (Grant Heilman Photography); *b* Douglas Gilbert (CLICK/Chicago). **69:** Jack Kollman. **70:** Gary Milburn (Tom Stack & Associates). **71:** W.E. Ruth (Bruce Coleman Inc.). **72:** James N. Butler. **73:** Robert Harding (Robert Harding Associates).

Chapter Three: 76, 77: NASA. **78:** E.R. Degginger. **79:** NPS. **81:** SCS. **84:** *t* NPS; *b* Breck P. Kent. **85:** Agency for International Development (AID). **86:** Phil Degginger (Bruce Coleman Inc.). **87:** Fred J. Maroon (Maroon Photography Inc.). **88:** NASA. **89:** *t* NASA; *b* Fish and Wildlife Service (FWS). **90:** NASA. **91:** *l* SCS; *r* NPS. **92:** USTS. **93:** *t* NASA; *b* M. Koene (H. Armstrong Roberts). **94:** Bob and Clara Calhoun (Bruce Coleman Inc.). **95:** *l* NPS; *r* Jeff Rotman. **97:** NASA. **99:** *l* Roy Whitehead (Photo Researchers); *r* Martin Rogers (Woodfin Camp & Associates).

Chapter Four: 102: Geopic™(c) Earth Satellite Corporation. **103:** Midd Hunt (Corporate Image Productions). **105, 106:** NASA. **107:** SCS. **109:** *tr* United States Department of Agriculture (USDA); *mr* United States Forest Service; *bl* SCS; *br* USDA. **110:** American Iron and Steel Institute. **111:** C.C. Lockwood (Bruce Coleman Inc.). **113:** *t* USTS; *b* SCS. **114:** *tl, bl* USDA; *r* NASA. **115:** *t* SCS; *b* Arthur Levine. **116:** Christopher Harris (Shostal Associates). **119:** USDA.

Unit Two: 122: Dennis Hallinan (FPG).

Chapter Five: 124: Douglas Mazonowicz (Gallery of Prehistoric Art). **125:** *t* John Henebry, Jr.; *b* Shostal Associates. **127:** *l* Pablo Picasso, *Guitar.* Paris (1912, early). Sheet metal and wire, $30\frac{1}{2} \times 13\frac{1}{8} \times 7\frac{5}{8}''$. Collection, The Museum of Modern Art, New York. Gift of the artist; *r* Lee Boltin (Lee Boltin Picture Library). **128:** Giraudon (Art Resource, NY). **129:** Field Museum of Natural History. **131:** SCALA (Art Resource, NY). **137:** The University Museum, University of Pennsylvania. **138:** *l* Ashmolean Museum, Oxford; *r* Michael Holford, British Museum. **139:** Peabody Museum of Salem. **140:** Excavations of The Metropolitan Museum of Art, 1919–20; Rogers Fund and Edward S. Harkness Gift, 1920. **143:** *t* SCALA (Art Resource, NY); *b* Detail, *Ladies Preparing Newly Woven Silk.* Emperor Sung Hui-Tsung. China, Sing Period, early 12th century. Handscroll, ink and colors on silk. H: .37 cm L: 145.3 cm. Chinese and Japanese Special Fund. Courtesy, Museum of Fine Arts, Boston. **144:** Giraudon (Art Resource, NY). **145:** Michael Holford, National Maritime Museum. **147:** Milt & Joan Mann (Cameramann International). **149:** The Granger Collection. **151:** The Bettmann Archive.

Chapter Six: 154: Bill Stanton (International Stock Photo). **156:** Shaw McCutcheon (Shostal Associates). **158:** *l* Cameron Davidson (Bruce Coleman Inc.); *r* Finnish National Tourist Office. **161:** *t* Robert Frerck (Odyssey Productions, Chicago); *b* Dr. Georg Gerster (Photo Researchers). **163:** Charles Harbutt (Archive). **165:** Milt & Joan Mann (Cameramann International). **167:** *l* Tass from Sovfoto; *r* Hanson Carroll. **168:** *t* Historical Pictures Service, Chicago; *b* M. Renaudeau (Leo De Wys, Inc.). **169:** Mark Antman (The Image Works). **170:** *l* Norman Meyers (Bruce Coleman Inc.); *r* Dick Luria (FPG). **171:** G. Cloyd (Taurus Photos). **172:** Milt & Joan Mann (Cameramann International). **173:** *t* D. Corson (H. Armstrong Roberts); *b* Dan McCoy (Rainbow). **174:** Robert Frerck (Odyssey Productions, Chicago). **175:** Baldev Kapoor (Shostal Associates). **177:** Jill Brown (Robert Harding Associates). **178:** Don Smetzer (CLICK/Chicago).

ACKNOWLEDGMENTS

Unit Three: 182: Paul Chesley (Photographers Aspen).

Chapter Seven: 184: Jim Olive (Click/Chicago). **185:** Jeff Foott (Tom Stack & Associates). **190:** Roger Malloch (Magnum Photos). **191:** Culver Pictures. **194:** John E. Fogle (The Picture Cube). **197:** Scott Thode (International Stock Photo). **198:** Wendell Metzen (Bruce Coleman Inc.). **199:** K. Scholz (H. Armstrong Roberts). **201:** Craig Aurness (Woodfin Camp & Associates). **203:** Bill Strode (Woodfin Camp & Associates). **205:** W. Metzen (H. Armstrong Roberts). **206:** Paul Fusco (Magnum Photos). **207:** Roloc. **208:** Grant Heilman (Grant Heilman Photography). **210:** C. Foussat (H. Armstrong Roberts).

Chapter Eight: 214: David Falconer (Image Finders). **215:** Patrick Morrow (Image Finders). **219:** *t* Robert Glander (Shostal Associates); *b* George Kurfin (CLICK/Chicago). **222:** Eric Carle (Shostal Associates). **229:** *t* E. Otto (Miller Services); *b* David Falconer (Image Finders). **230:** Historic Parks and Sites, Newfoundland and Labrador. **231:** George Hall (Woodfin Camp & Associates).

Chapter Nine: 234: Peter Menzel. **237:** A Nogues (Sygma). **239:** Allan A. Philiba. **241:** Randy Taylor (Sygma). **246:** Craig Burleigh © 79 BFZ. **247:** *t* Paula Wright (Shostal Associates); *b* Victor Englebert (Black Star). **249:** Peter Menzel. **250:** John Metelsky. **251:** Peter Menzel. **253:** Fred Ward (Black Star).

Chapter Ten: 256: Chip Peterson/Rosa Maria de la Cueva Peterson. **261:** Eberhard E. Otto (FPG). **262:** Organization of American States. **263:** Robert Fried (D. Donne Bryant). **268:** Kurt Scholz (Shostal Associates). **269:** Ray Manley (Shostal Associates). **270:** *l* ZEFA (H. Armstrong Roberts); *r* Sebastiao Salgado (Magnum Photos). **272:** Bernard Pierre Wolff (FPG). **273:** Inter-American Development Bank (IADB). **274:** Art Resource, NY. **275:** E. Manewal (Shostal Associates). **277:** E. Comesana (Shostal Associates).

Chapter Eleven: 282: Elliott Erwitt (Magnum Photos). **283:** E. Eigstler (Shostal Associates). **187:** V. Phillips (Leo De Wys, Inc.). **291:** E. Streichan (Shostal Associates). **294:** Susan McCartney (Photo Researchers). **295:** Julius Fekete (FPG). **297:** British Airways. **298:** Will McIntyre (Photo Researchers). **299:** *l* Bernard Pierre Wolff (Photo Researchers); *r* Fritz Henle (Photo Researchers). **300:** Embassy of the Netherlands. **302:** D. Forbert (Shostal Associates). **303:** Milt & Joan Mann (Cameramann International). **304:** Peter Menzel. **305:** Kurt Scholz (Shostal Associates).

Chapter Twelve: 308: Tom McHugh (Photo Researchers). **311:** Milt & Joan Mann (Cameramann International). **312:** Kurt Scholz (Shostal Associates). **314, 315:** Wide World Photos. **317:** Bruno Barbey (Magnum Photos). **321:** Leonard Freed (Magnum Photos). **322:** Earl Young. **323:** Leonard Freed (Magnum Photos). **324:** W.H. Hodge (Peter Arnold, Inc.). **325:** H. Armstrong Roberts.

Chapter Thirteen: 328: Emil Schultess (Black Star). **334:** Tass from Sovfoto. **337:** *t* B. Manushin (Novosti Press Agency); *b* Kurt Scholz (Shostal Associates). **338, 342:** Tass from Sovfoto. **344:** J. Strohm (Shostal Associates). **346:** *t* Shostal Associates; *b* Novosti Press Agency. **347:** *l* Tass from Sovfoto; *r* Jacques Jangoux (Peter Arnold, Inc.). **348:** Shostal Associates. **349:** Tass from Sovfoto.

Chapter Fourteen: 352: K. Scholz (H. Armstrong Roberts). **359:** Roloc. **360:** P.J. Griffiths (Magnum Photos). **361:** Wu Jiguo (Xinhua News Agency). **365:** Karen Rubin (Photo Researchers). **367:** *l* John Henebry, Jr.; *r* Leslie Swartz. **368:** M. Koene (H. Armstrong Roberts). **369:** David Burnett (Contact Stock Images). **370:** ZEFA (H. Armstrong Roberts). **371:** *t* Kurt Scholz (Shostal Associates); *b* Embassy of Japan. **372:** Hiroji Kubotoa (Magnum Photos). **373:** Bruno J. Zehnder (Peter Arnold, Inc.).

Chapter Fifteen: 376: J. Messerschmidt (Bruce Coleman Inc.). **385:** Ray Manley (Shostal Associates). **389:** *t* Jehangir Gazdar (Woodfin Camp & Associates); *b* Robert Frerck (Odyssey Productions, Chicago). **390:** *l* ZEFA (H. Armstrong Roberts); *r* AID. **391:** Wide World Photos. **392:** Roland Birke (Peter Arnold, Inc.). **394:** Mary M. Hill, World Bank. **395:** Ivan Poluner (Bruce Coleman Inc.). **397:** Ian Steele (International Stock Photo).

Chapter Sixteen: 400: H. Armstrong Roberts. **404:** Earl Young. **406:** Marvin E. Newman (Woodfin Camp & Associates). **407:** Robert Frerck (Odyssey Productions, Chicago). **413:** *t* Fred Bavendam (Peter Arnold, Inc.); *b* Earl Young. **415:** *t* Robert Fried; *b* Carl Purcell. **416:** Dan Porges (Peter Arnold, Inc.). **417:** ZEFA (H. Armstrong Roberts). **418:** Bruno Barbey (Magnum Photos).

Chapter Seventeen: 424: Shostal Associates. **431:** *t* Bruno Barbey (Magnum Photos); *b* Chris Steel Perkins (Magnum Photos). **435:** Shostal Associates. **437:** D. Waugh (Peter Arnold, Inc.). **440:** Carl Purcell, AID. **441:** *l* Bruno Barbey (Magnum Photos); *r* Carl Purcell, AID. **442:** Tomas Friedmann (Photo Researchers). **443:** Shostal Associates. **444:** Michael Yamashita (Woodfin Camp & Associates). **445:** *t* Earl Young; *b* J. Chiasson (Gamma-Liaison). **447:** Eric Lessing (Magnum Photos).

Chapter Eighteen: 450: Shostal Associates. **457:** Betty Crowell. **462:** Robert Frerck (Odyssey Productions, Chicago). **463:** *t* Betty Crowell; *b* Australian Tourist Commission. **464:** *tl* Australian Tourist Commission; *bl* K. Richardson (Shostal Associates); *tr* Embassy of Australia; *br* Carl Purcell. **465:** G.R. Roberts. **468:** *t* New Zealand Consulate General; *b* H. Hughes (Shostal Associates). **469:** Milt & Joan Mann (Cameramann International).

528